Communications
in Computer and Information Science   19

Miltiadis D. Lytras   John M. Carroll
Ernesto Damiani   Robert D. Tennyson
David Avison   Gottfried Vossen
Patricia Ordonez De Pablos (Eds.)

The Open Knowledge Society

A Computer Science and
Information Systems Manifesto

First World Summit on the Knowledge Society, WSKS 2008
Athens, Greece, September 24-26, 2008
Proceedings

 Springer

Volume Editors

Miltiadis D. Lytras
Open Research Society, NGO, Gerakas Attikis, Greece
E-mail: lytras@open-knowledge-society.org

John M. Carroll
The Pennsylvania State University, University Park, PA, USA
E-mail: jcarroll@ist.psu.edu

Ernesto Damiani
University of Milan, Crema (CR), Italy
E-mail: damiani@dti.unimi.it

Robert D. Tennyson
University of Minnesota, Minneapolis, MN, USA
E-mail: rtenny@umn.edu

David Avison
ESSEC Business School, Cergy Pontoise Cedex, France
E-mail: avison@essec.fr

Gottfried Vossen
University of Muenster, Muenster, Germany
E-mail: vossen@uni-muenster.de

Patricia Ordonez De Pablos
University of Oviedo, Oviedo-Asturias, Spain
E-mail: patrio@uniovi.es

Library of Congress Control Number: 2008935396

CR Subject Classification (1998): K.4, J.1, I.2, K.3, K.6

ISSN   1865-0929
ISBN-10   3-540-87782-7 Springer Berlin Heidelberg New York
ISBN-13   978-3-540-87782-0 Springer Berlin Heidelberg New York

Springer is a part of Springer Science+Business Media

springer.com

© Springer-Verlag Berlin Heidelberg 2008
Printed in Germany

Typesetting: Camera-ready by author, data conversion by Scientific Publishing Services, Chennai, India
Printed on acid-free paper   SPIN: 12529865   06/3180   5 4 3 2 1 0

Preface

It is a great pleasure to share with you the Springer CCIS proceedings of the First World Summit on the Knowledge Society - WSKS 2008 that was organized by the Open Research Society, NGO, http://www.open-knowledge-society.org, and hosted by the American College of Greece, http://www.acg.gr, during September 24–27, 2008, in Athens, Greece.

The World Summit on the Knowledge Society Series is an international attempt to promote a dialogue on the main aspects of a knowledge society toward a better world for all based on knowledge and learning.

The WSKS Series brings together academics, people from industry, policy makers, politicians, government officers and active citizens to look at the impact of information technology, and the knowledge-based era it is creating, on key facets of today's world: the state, business, society and culture.

Six general pillars provide the constitutional elements of the WSKS series:

- Social and Humanistic Computing for the Knowledge Society—Emerging Technologies and Systems for the Society and Humanity
- Knowledge, Learning, Education, Learning Technologies and E-learning for the Knowledge Society
- Information Technologies—Knowledge Management Systems—E-business and Enterprise Information Systems for the Knowledge Society
- Culture and Cultural Heritage—Technology for Culture Management—Management of Tourism and Entertainment—Tourism Networks in the Knowledge Society
- Government and Democracy for the Knowledge Society
- Research and Sustainable Development in the Knowledge Society

The summit provides a distinct, unique forum for cross-disciplinary fertilization of research, favoring the dissemination of research that is relevant to international research agendas such as the EU FP7.

In the first event of the series, the Athens 2008 First World Summit on the Knowledge Society, five main tracks and four workshops were organized. Volume 19 of the Springer *Communications on Computer and Information Sciences* Series, summarizes 95 articles that were selected after a double-blind review process from 286 submissions, contributed by 530 co-authors.

In this volume of CCIS you will find excellent quality research that summarizes sound propositions for advanced systems toward a knowledge society.

Figure 1 summarizes the context of the research presented at WSKS 2008.

I would like to thank the authors from 65 countries for their submissions; the Program Committee members and their subreviewers for the thoroughness of their reviews; and the colleagues at the American College of Greece for the great support they offered in the organization of the event on the Aghia Paraskevi Campus.

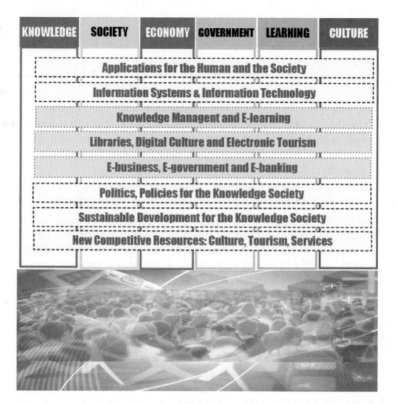

Fig. 1.

We are honored for the support and encouragement of the Editors-in-Chief of the ten ISI SCI/SSCI listed journals that agreed to publish special issues from extended versions of papers presented in the summit:

- Robert Tennyson, Editor-in-Chief of *Computers in Human Behaviour*
- Amit Sheth, Editor-in-Chief of *International Journal of Semantic Web and Information Systems*
- Witold Pedrycz, Editor-in-Chief of *IEEE Transactions on Systems, Man, and Cybernetics - Part A: Systems and Humans*
- Charles Crook, Editor-in-Chief, and Deputy Editor R. Joiner of the *Journal of Computer-Assisted Learning*
- Joseph Psotka and Bernard Scott, Editors-in-Chief of *Interactive Learning Environment*
- Keng Siau, Editor-in-Chief of the *Journal of Database Management (JDM)*
- Mohammed Dorgham, Editor-in-Chief of the *International Journal of Technology Management*
- Patricia Ordonez De Pablos, Editor-in-Chief of the *International Journal of Learning and Intellectual Capital.*

I am also honored that John Carroll, Robert Tennyson and my good friend Ambjorn Naeve supported the event with their keynotes. You can find more information at: http://www.open-knowledge-society.org/keynotes.htm

A great thank you also to Alfred Hofmann, Springer, and his staff for the excellent support in all the development phases of the proceedings of LNCS/LNAI 5288 and CCIS 19.

Our warmest appreciation, respect and thank you to the President of the American College of Greece, David G. Horner, and Lila Mordochae, Associate Dean, School of Business Administration, The American College of Greece, for their support and critical contribution to the success of WSKS 2008. A great thank you also to the Head of the CIS department at The American College of Greece, Jenny Vagianou and to all the members of the CIS Society for their efforts in making this event an unforgetable experience for all the participants.

Last but not least, a big thank you to the staff and members of the Open Research Society, for their great efforts during the summit organization and the joint vision to promote a better world for all based on knowledge and learning.

We need a better world. We can contribute with our sound voices to the various agendas, policies and actions. We invite you to join your voice with ours and all together to shape a new deal for our world: education, sustainable development, health, opportunities for well-being, culture, collaboration, peace, democracy, technology for all.

Looking forward to seeing you at the second event of the series, for which you can find more information at: http://www.open-knowledge-society.org/summit09.htm.

With 55 special issues already agreed for WSKS 2009, and 8 main tracks, we want to ask for your involvement and we would be happy to see you joining us. Give a hand!

On behalf of the Program and Organizing Committee, thank you – Efharisto Poli!

July 2008   Miltiadis D. Lytras

Organization

WSKS 2008 was organized by the Open Research Society, NGO, http://www.open-knowledge-society.org, and in cooperation with The American College of Greece, http://www.acg.gr

Executive Committee

General Chair of WSKS 2008

Miltiadis D. Lytras

President, Open Research Society, NGO

Miltiadis D. Lytras is the President and Founder of the Open Research Society, NGO. His research focuses on the Semantic Web, knowledge management and e-learning, with more than 100 publications in these areas. He has co-edited / co-edits, 25 special issues in international journals (e.g., *IEEE Transaction on Knowledge and Data Engineering, IEEE Internet Computing, IEEE Transactions on Education, Computers in Human Behaviour, Interactive Learning Environments, Journal of Knowledge Management, Journal of Computer-Assisted Learning*, etc.) and has authored/ ((co-)edited) 22 books (e.g., *Open Source for Knowledge and Learning Management, Ubiquitous and Pervasive Knowledge Management, Intelligent Learning Infrastructures for Knowledge-Intensive Organizations, Semantic Web-Based Information Systems, China Information Technology Handbook, Real-World Applications of Semantic Web and Ontologies, Web 2.0: The Business Model*, etc.) . He is the founder and officer of the Semantic Web and Information Systems Special Interest Group in the Association for Information Systems (http://www.sigsemis.org). He serves as the (Co) Editor-in-Chief of 12 international journals (e.g., *International Journal of Knowledge and Learning, International Journal of Technology-Enhanced Learning, International Journal on Social and Humanistic Computing, International Journal on Semantic Web and Information Systems, International Journal on Digital Culture and Electronic Tourism, International Journal of Electronic Democracy, International Journal of Electronic Banking, International Journal of Electronic Trade* etc.) while he is associate editor or editorial board member in seven more.

WSKS 2008 Co-chairs

David Avison

Distinguished Professor in Information Systems
President-Elect of the Association for Information Systems

David Avison is Distinguished Professor of Information Systems at ESSEC Business School, near Paris, France, after being Professor at the School of Management at

Southampton University for nine years. He has also held posts at Brunel and Aston Universities in the UK, and the University of Technology Sydney and University of New South Wales in Australia, and elsewhere. He is President-Elect of the Association of Information Systems (AIS). He is joint editor of Blackwell Science's *Information Systems Journal* now in its 18th volume, rated as a 'core' international journal. So far, 25 books are to his credit including the fourth edition of the well-used text *Information Systems Development: Methodologies, Techniques and Tools* (jointly authored with Guy Fitzgerald). He has published a large number of research papers in learned journals, edited texts and conference papers. He was Chair of the International Federation of Information Processing (IFIP) 8.2 group on the impact of IS/IT on organizations and society and is now Vice Chair of IFIP Technical Committee 8. He was past President of the UK Academy for Information Systems and also Chair of the UK Heads and Professors of IS and is presently a member of the IS Senior Scholars Forum. He was joint Program Chair of the International Conference in Information Systems (ICIS) in Las Vegas (previously also Research Program Stream Chair at ICIS Atlanta), joint Program Chair of the IFIP TC8 conference at Santiago Chile, Program Chair of the IFIPWG8.2 conference in Amsterdam, Panels Chair for the European Conference in Information Systems at Copenhagen and Publicity Chair for the entity-relationship conference in Paris and Chair of several other UK and European conferences. He was joint Program Chair of the IFIP TC8 conference in Milan, Italy in 2008. He also acts as consultant and has most recently worked with a leading manufacturer developing their IT/IS strategy. He researches in the area of information systems development and more generally on information systems in their natural organizational setting, in particular using action research, although he has also used a number of other qualitative research approaches.

Ernesto Damiani

University of Milan, Italy

Ernesto Damiani is a professor at the Department of Information Technology, University of Milan, where he leads the Software Architectures Lab. Professor Damiani holds/has held visiting positions at several international institutions, including George Mason University (Fairfax, VA, USA) and LaTrobe University (Melbourne, Australia). He is an Adjunct Professor at the Sydney University of Technology (Australia). He has written several books and filed international patents; also, he has co-authored more than 200 research papers on advanced secure service-oriented architectures, open source software and business process design, software reuse and Web data semantics. Professor Damiani is the Vice Chair of IFIP WG 2.12 on Web Data Semantics and the secretary of IFIP WG 2.13 on Open Source Software Development. He coordinates several research projects funded by the Italian Ministry of Research and by private companies including Siemens Mobile, Cisco Systems, ST Microelectronics, BT Exact, Engineering, Telecom Italy and others.

Thomas Davenport

President's Chair in Information Technology and Management at Babson College

Voted the third-leading business-strategy analyst in *Optimize* magazine's October 2005 issue, Tom Davenport is a world-renowned thought leader who has helped hundreds of companies revitalize their management practices. An agile and prolific thinker, Davenport has written or co-authored 12 best-selling business books and has been a creator and early proponent of several key business ideas including: knowledge management, human approaches to information management, business process reengineering, and realizing the value of enterprise systems.With his vast storehouse of industry stories, research and data, and cutting-edge ideas, Davenport balances research-based business acumen with practical application. His areas of expertise include improving the productivity of knowledge workers, information and knowledge management, attention management, idea generation, innovation, competing on analytics, managing enterprise applications for business value, and business process reengineering.

John Davies

BT Exact, UK

Dr. John Davies leads the Next Generation Web research group at BT. Current interests center around the application of Semantic Web technology to knowledge management, information retrieval and service-oriented architectures. He is Industrial Chair of the Semantic Web Services Initiative, co-organizer of the European Semantic Web Conference series and Project Director of the SEKT EU integrated project. He has written and edited many papers and books in the areas of Web-based information management, knowledge management and the Semantic Web and has served on the Program Committee of many conferences in related areas. He is a Fellow of the British Computer Society and a Chartered Engineer. Earlier research at BT led to the development of a set of knowledge management tools which are the subject of a number of patents. These tools are now marketed through Exago Ltd. (www.exago.com), of which Dr. Davies is Chief Technology Officer.

Gottfried Vossen

University of Münster, Germany

Gottfried Vossen is Professor of Computer Science in the Department of Information Systems at the University of Münster in Germany. He is the European Editor-in-Chief of Elsevier's *Information Systems—An International Journal*, and a Director of the European Research Center for Information Systems (ERCIS) in Münster. His research interests include conceptual as well as application-oriented problems concerning databases, information systems, electronic learning, and the Web.

Program Chair

Patricia Ordonez De Pablos   University of Oviedo, Spain

Organizing Committee

Hosting Organization – The American College of Greece

David G. Horner   President, The American College of Greece
Lila Mordochae   Associate Dean, School of Business
                                   Administration, The American College of Greece
Jenny Vagianou   Head, CIS Department, The American College of
                                       Greece

Workshops and Tutorials Chairs

Ambjorn Naeve   Royal Institute of Technology, Sweden
Miguel Angel Sicilia   University of Alcala, Spain

Publicity Chair

Ekaterini Pitsa   Open Research Society, Greece

PhD Symposium Chair

John M. Carroll   The Pennsylvania State University, USA

Exhibition Chair

Efstathia Pitsa   University of Cambridge, UK

Sponsoring Organizations

Gold

Inderscience Publishers, http://www.inderscience.com

Program and Scientific Committee Members (Serving also as Reviewers)

Adrian Paschke   Technical University Dresden, Germany
Adriana Schiopoiu Burlea   University of Craiova, Romania
Agnes Kukulska-Hulme   The Open University, UK
Ahmad Syamil   Arkansas State University, USA
Aime' Lay-Ekuakille   University of Salento, Italy
Alan Chamberlain   University of Nottingham, UK

Chunzhao Liu	Chinese Academy of Sciences, China
Claire Dormann	Carleton University, Canada
Claus Pahl	Dublin City University, Ireland
Constantinos T. Artikis	University of Bradford, UK
Cui Tao	Brigham Young University, USA
Damaris Fuentes-Lorenzo	IMDEA Networks, Spain
Daniel R. Fesenmaier	Temple University, USA
Daniel Tse	City University of Hong Kong, Hong Kong (China)
Daniela Leal Musa	Federal University of Sao Paulo, Brazil
Daniela Tsaneva	Cardiff School of Computer Science, UK
Darijus Strasunskas	Norwegian University of Science and Technology (NTNU), Norway
David O'Donnell	Intellectual Capital Research Institute of Ireland, Ireland
David R. Harding	Jr. Arkansas State University, USA
Dawn Jutla	Saint Mary's University, Canada
Denis Gillet	Swiss Federal Institute of Technology in Lausanne (EPFL), Switzerland
Diane H. Sonnenwald	Director, Göteborg University and University College of Borås, Sweden
Dimitri Konstantas	University of Geneva, Switzerland
Dimitris N. Chryssochoou	University of Crete, Greece
Douglas L. Micklich	Illinois State University, USA
Duncan Shaw	Aston University, UK
Dusica Novakovic	London Metropolitan University, USA
Edward Dieterle	Harvard Graduate School of Education, USA
Ejub Kajan	High School of Applied Studies, Serbia
Elena García-Barriocanal	University of Alcalá, Spain
Elena Verdú Pérez	University of Valladolid, Spain
Emma O'Brien	University of Limerick, Ireland
Eric Tsui	The Hong Kong Polytechnic University, Hong Kong (China)
Eva Rimbau-Gilabert	Open University of Catalonia, Spain
Evanegelia Karagiannopoulou	University of Ioannina, Greece
Evangelos Sakkopoulos	University of Patras, Greece
Evripidis Korres	OPEN RESEARCH SOCIETY, Greece
F.F. Cai	London Metropolitan University, UK
Fernanda Lima	Universidade Catolica de Brasilia, Brazil
Filippo Sciarrone	Università "Roma Tre", Italy
Francesc Burrull	Polytechnic University of Cartagena, Spain
Francesca Lonetti	ISTI - Area della Ricerca CNR, Italy
Francisco Palomo Lozano	University of Cádiz, Spain
Gang Wu	Tsinghua University, China
Gary D. Robinson	Chair, Capella University, USA
Gavin McArdle	University College Dublin, Ireland
George A. Jacinto	Arkansas State University, USA

Georgios Skoulas	University of Macedonia, Greece
Gianluca Elia	University of Salento, Italy
Gianluigi Viscusi	University of Milano-Bicocca, Italy
Giovanni Vincenti	D.Sc. Gruppo Vincenti, S.r.l. Rome, Italy
Giuseppe Pirrò	University of Calabria, Italy
Giuseppe Vendramin	University of Salento, Italy
Vincenza Pelillo	University of Salento, Italy
Gregg, Janie	University of West Alabama, USA
Grigorios N. Beligiannis	University of Ioannina, Greece
Guillermo Ibañez	Universidad de Alcalá, Spain
Hai Jiang	Arkansas State University, USA
Haim Kilov	Stevens Institute of Technology, USA
Hajah Gy Hashim	University Technology Mara (UiTM), Malaysia
Hamidah Ibrahim	Department of Computer Science, Universiti Putra Malaysia, Malaysia
Hanh H. Hoang	Hue University, Vietnam
Hanne Erdman Thomsen	Copenhagen Business School, Denmark
Hanno Schauer	Universität Duisburg-Essen, Germany
Heinz V. Dreher	Curtin University of Technology, Australia
Helena Corrales Herrero	University of Valladolid, Spain
Helena Villarejo	University of Valladolid, Spain
Hui Yang	San Francisco State University, USA
Hyggo Almeida	University of Campina Grande, Brazil
Ian Taylor	LSU, USA
Inma Rodríguez-Ardura	Open University of Catalonia, Spain
Ino Martínez León	Universidad Politécnica de Cartagena, Spain
Ioan Marius Bilasco	Laboratoire Informatique de Grenoble (LIG), France
Ioanna Constantiou	Copenhagen Business School, Denmark
Ioannis Papadakis	Ionian University, Greece
Ioannis Stamelos	AUTH, Greece
Irene Daskalopoulou	University of the Peloponnese, Greece
Isabel Ramos	University of Minho, Portugal
James Braman	Towson University, USA
Jan-Willem Strijbos	Leiden University, The Netherlands
Javier De Andrés	University of Oviedo, Spain
Javier Fabra	University of Zaragoza, Spain
Jeanne D. Maes	University of South Alabama, USA
Jeannette K. Jones	American InterContinental University (AIU), USA
Jens O. Meissner	Lucerne School of Business, Switzerland
Jerome Darmont	University of Lyon (ERIC Lyon 2), France
Jesus Contreras	ISOCO, Spain
Jesús Ibáñez	University Pompeu Fabra, Spain
Jianhan Zhu	The Open University, UK
Johann Gamper	Free University of Bozen-Bolzano, Italy
Jon A. Preston	Clayton State University
Jorge Gracia	University of Zaragoza, Spain
Jose Jesus García Rueda	Carlos III University of Madrid, Spain

José Luis García-Lapresta	Universidad de Valladolid, Spain
Jose Luis Isla Montes	University of Cadiz, Spain
Jose M. Hernandez-Munoz	Universidad Carlos III de Madrid, and TELEFONICA I+D, Spain
Josemaria Maalgosa Sanahuja	Polytechnic University of Cartagena, Spain
Joseph C. Paradi	University of Toronto, Canada
Joseph Feller	University College Cork, Ireland
Joseph Hardin	University of Michigan, USA
Joze Gricar	University of Maribor, Slovenia
Juan Gabriel Cegarra Navarro	Universidad Politécnica de Cartagena, Spain
Juan Manuel Dodero	University of Cádiz, Spain
Juan Miguel Gómez Berbís	Univesidad Carlos III de Madrid, Spain
Juan Pablo de Castro Fernández	University of Valladolid, Spain
Juan Vicente Perdiz	University of Valladolid, Spain
Juan Ye	University College Dublin, Ireland
Julià Minguillón	Universitat Oberta de Catalunya (UOC), Spain
Jyotishman Pathak	Mayo Clinic College of Medicine, USA
Karim Mohammed Rezaul	University of Wales, UK
Karl-Heinz Pognmer	Copenhagen Business School, Denmark
Katerina Pastra	Institute for Language and Speech Processing, Greece
Ken Fisher	London Metropolitan University, UK
Kleanthis Thramboulidis	University of Patras, Greece
Konstantinos Kotis	University of the Aegean, Greece
Konstantinos Tarabanis	University of Macedonia, Greece
Kylie Hsu	California State University at Los Angeles, USA
Lambros Skarlas	University of Patras, Greece
Laura Papaleo	DISI, Italy
Laura Sanchez Garcia	Universidade Federal do Parana, Brazil
Laurel D. Riek	Cambridge University, UK
Lazar Rusu	Royal Institute of Technology (KTH), Sweden
Leonel Morgado	University of Trás-os-Montes e Alto Douro, Portugal
Leyla Zhuhadar	Western Kentucky University, USA
Lily Diaz-Kommonen	University of Art and Design Helsinki, Finland
Linda A. Jackson	Michigan State University, USA
Liqiong Deng	University of West Georgia, USA
Lori L. Scarlatos	Stony Brook University, USA
Lubomir Stanchev	Indiana University - Purdue University Fort Wayne, USA
Luis Angel Galindo Sanchez	Universidad Carlos III de Madrid, Spain
Luis Iribarne	Departamento de Lenguajes y Computacion, Universidad de Almeria, Spain
Luke Tredinnick	London Metropolitan University, UK
Lynne Nikolychuk	King's College London, UK
M. Carmen de Castro	Universidad de Cádiz, Spain
M. Latif	Manchester Metropolitan University, UK

Mahmoud Youssef	Arab Academy for Science and Technology, Egypt
Maiga Chang	Athabasca University , Canada
Manolis Vavalis	University of Thessaly, Greece
Manuel Rubio-Sanchez	Rey Juan Carlos University, Spain
Marco Temperini	Universita La Sapienza, Italy
Marcos Castilho	Departamento de Informática da Universidade Federal Paraná, Brazil
Marcos Martin-Fernandez	Associate Valladolid University, Spain
Maria Chiara Caschera	IRPPS-CNR, Rome, Italy
Maria Grazia Gnoni	University of Salento, Lecce, Italy
Maria de Lourdes Machado-Taylor	CIPES- Center for Research in Higher Education Policies, Portugal
Maria Helena Braz	Technical University of Lisbon, Portugal
Maria Jesús Martinez-Argüelles	Open University of Catalonia, Spain
María Jesús Segovia Vargas	Universidad Complutense de Madrid, Spain
María Jesús Verdú Pérez	University of Valladolid, Spain
Maria Joao Ferreira	Universidade Portucalense, Portugal
Maria Papadaki	University of Ioannina, Greece
Maria Pavli-Korres	University of Alcala de Henares, Spain
Marianna Sigala	University of Aegean, Greece
Marie-Hélène Abel	Université de Technologie de Compiègne, France
Mariel Alejandra Ale	Universidad Tecnológica Nacional (UTN), Argentina
Markus Rohde	University of Siegen, Germany
Martijn Kagie	Erasmus University Rotterdam, The Netherlands
Martin Beer	Sheffield Hallam University, UK
Martin Dzbor	The Open University, UK
Martin J. Eppler	University of Lugano, Switzerland
Martin Wolpers,	Fraunhofer FIT.ICON, Germany
Mary Meldrum	Manchester Metropolitan University Business School, UK
Maurizio Vincini	Università di Modena e Reggio Emilia, Italy
Meir Russ	University of Wisconsin, Green Bay, USA
Mercedes Ruiz	University of Cádiz, Spain
Mey (Ongech) Brenda	Ludwig Maximilian University of Munich, Germany
Michael Derntl	University of Vienna, Austria
Michael O'Grady	University College Dublin, Ireland
Michael Veith	University of Siegen, Germany
Miguel L. Bote-Lorenzo	University of Valladolid, Spain
Miguel-Angel Sicilia	University of Alcalá, Spain
Miha Škerlavaj	Univerza v Ljubljani, Slovenia
Mikael Collan	Institute for Advanced Management Systems Research, Finland
Mike Cushman	London School of Economics and Political Science, UK
Mohamed Amine Chatti	RWTH Aachen University, Germany
Monika Lanzenberger	Technische Universitaet Wien, Austria
Muhammad Shafique	International Islamic University, Pakistan

Nadia Pisanti	University of Pisa, Italy
Nancy Alonistioti	University of Piraeus, Greece
Nancy Hauserman Williams	University of Iowa, USA
Nancy Linwood	DuPont, USA
Luis Álvarez Sabucedo	University of Vigo, Spain
Nelson K.Y. Leung	University of Wollongong, Australia
Nick Higgett	De Montfort University, UK
Nicola Capuano	University of Salerno, Italy
Nilay Yajnik	NMIMS University, Mumbai, India
Nineta Polemi	University of Piraeus, Greece
Noah Kasraie	Arkansas State University, USA
Nuran Fraser	The Manchester Metropolitan University, UK
Nuria Hurtado Rodríguez	University of Cádiz, Spain
O.J. Ebohon	De Montfort University, UK
Omar Farooq	Loughborough University, UK
Paige Wimberley	Arkansas State University, USA
Panagiotis T. Artikis	University of Warwick, UK
Pancham Shukla	London Metropolitan University, UK
Pankaj Kamthan	Concordia University, Canada
Paola Di Maio	Content Wire, UK
Paola Mello	University of Bologna, Italy
Paolo Toth	University of Bologna, Italy
Patricia A. Walls	Arkansas State University, USA
Paul A. Kirschner	Open University of the Netherlands, The Netherlands
Paul G. Mezey	Memorial University, Canada
Pedro J. Muñoz Merino	Universidad Carlos III de Madrid, Spain
Pedro Soto-Acosta	University of Murcia, Spain
Peisheng Zhao	George Mason University, USA
Pekka Muukkonen	University of Turku, Finland
Per Anker Jensen	Copenhagen Business School, Denmark
Peter Gomber	Johann Wolfgang Goethe-Universität Frankfurt, Germany
Phil Fitzsimmons	University of Wollongong, Australia
Pierre Deransart	INRIA-Rocquencourt, France
Pilar Manzanares-Lopez	Technical University of Cartagena, Spain
Pirkko Walden	Abo Akademi University, Finland
Ralf Klamma	RWTH Aachen University, Germany
Ramon J. Duran Barroso	University of Valladolid, Spain
Raquel Hijón Neira	Universidad Rey Juan Carlos, Spain
Raymond Y.K. Lau	City University of Hong Kong, Hong Kong SAR
Razaq Raj	Leeds Metropolitan University, UK
Razvan Daniel Zota	Academy of Economic Studies Bucharest, Romania
Ricardo Colomo Palacios	Universidad Carlos III de Madrid, Spain
Ricardo Lopez-Ruiz	University of Zaragoza, Spain
Rob Potharst	Erasmus University, The Netherlands
Robert Fullér	Åbo Akademi University, Finland

Roberto García   Universitat de Lleida, Spain
Roberto Paiano   University of Salento, Italy
Roman Povalej   Institute AIFB University of Karlsruhe, Germany
Rushed Kanawati   LIPN – CNRS, France
Russel Pears   Auckland University of Technology, New Zealand
Ryan Robeson   Arkansas State University, USA
Sabine H. Hoffmann   Macquarie University, Australia
Sadat Shami   Cornell University, USA
Salam Abdallah   Abu Dhabi University, United Arab Emirates
Samiaji Sarosa   Atma Jaya Yogyakarta University, Indonesia
Sean Mehan   University of the Highlands and Islands, Scotland, UK
Sean Wolfgand M. Siqueira   Federal University of the State of Rio de Janeiro (UNIRIO), Brazil
Sebastian Matyas   Otto-Friedrich-Universität Bamberg, Germany
Seppo Virtanen   University of Turku, Finland
Sergio Ilarri   University of Zaragoza, Spain
Shantha Liyanage   Macquarie University, Australia
Shaoyi He   California State University, USA
She-I Chang   National Chung Cheng University, Taiwan (China)
Sherif Sakr   University of New South Wales, Australia
Sijung Hu   Loughborough University, UK
Silvia Rita Viola   Università Politecnica delle Marche - Ancona, Italy
Silvia Schiaffino   Univ. Nac. del Centro de la Pcia, Argentina
Sima Yazdani   Cisco Systems, USA
Sinuhe Arroyo   University of Alcalá de Henares, Spain
Sonia Berman   University of Cape Town, South Africa
Soror Sahri   Université Paris-Dauphine, France
Sotirios Goudos   Aristotle University of Thessaloniki, Greece
Sotiris Kotsiantis   University of the Peloponnese, Greece
Spyros D. Arsenis   University of Thessaly, Greece
Staffan Elgelid   Arizona State University, USA
Stefan Hrastinski   Uppsala University, Sweden
Stephan Lukosch   FernUniversität in Hagen, Germany
Steve Barker   King's College London, UK
Steve Creason   Metropolitan State University, USA
Stone Schmidt   Arkansas State University, USA
Suneeti Rekhari   University of Wollongong, Australia
Taha Osman   Nottingham Trent University, UK
Takaharu Kameoka   Mie Univeristy, Japan
Tarun Abhichandani   Claremont Graduate University, USA
Teck Yong Eng   University of London, UK
Terrill L. Frantz   Carnegie Mellon University, USA
Thanos C. Papadopoulos   The University of Warwick, UK
Tobias Ley   Know-Center, Austria
Toyohide Watanabe   Nagoya University, Japan
Universitat Libre de Bruxelles   Belgium

Upasana Singh	University of KwaZulu, South Africa
Vaclav Snasel	VSB-Technical University of Ostrava, Czech Republic
Vagan Terziyan	University of Jyvaskyla, Finland
Val Clulow	Monash University, Australia
Véronique Heiwy	IUT de Paris, France
Vincenzo Ciancia	University of Pisa, Italy
Violeta Damjanovic	Salzburg Research Forschungsgesellschaft, Austria
Virginie Sans	Université de Cergy-Pontoise, France
Vlasios Voudouris	London Metropolitan University, UK
Walt Scacchi	University of California, USA
Weili Wu	University of Texas at Dallas, USA
Xavier Calbet	EUMETSAT, Germany
Luisa M. Regueras	University of Valladolid, Spain
Xiaohua (Tony) Hu	Drexel University, Philadelphia, USA
Xihui (Paul) Zhang	University of Memphis, USA
Yang Li	British Telecom, UK
Yannis Charalabidis	National Technical University of Athens, Greece
Yihong Ding	Brigham Young University, USA
Ying Liu	Lecturer, The Hong Kong Polytechnic University, Hong Kong (China)
Yolaine Bourda	SUPELEC, France
Yuan An	Drexel University, USA
Yujian Fu	Alabama A&M University, USA
Yun Shen	University of Bristol, UK
Yvon Kermarrec	Institut Télécom / Télécom Bretagne, France
Zaiyong Tang	Salem State College, USA
Ziqi Liao	Hong Kong Baptist University, Hong Kong (China)
Zuleyka Diaz Martinez	Universidad Complutense de Madrid, Spain

Table of Contents

Significant Learning Communities –
A Humanistic Approach to Knowledge and Human
Resource Development in the Age of the Internet

Renate Motschnig-Pitrik

University of Vienna, Research Lab for Educational Technologies
renate.motschnig@univie.ac.at

Abstract. This paper aims to bring together the potentials inherent in humanistic, person-centered encounter groups with collaborative learning supported by interactive web spaces. The resulting socio-technical systems are referred to as Significant Learning Communities. They are based on the notion of significant learning, subsuming processes of personal and knowledge development based on constructive relationships between individuals and their environment. The paper characterizes Significant Learning Communities, compares them with similar relationship systems, reflects on the role of web-based tools, and identifies both the challenges and benefits of the new socio-technical construct.

1 Introduction

While learning communities, web-based communities [1], and person-centered encounter groups are appreciated for their respective benefits, their integration has – to the best of the author's knowledge – not been investigated so far. This does not come as a surprise since encounter groups, typically, are based on full interpersonal presence of their participants and could not -- with equal quality and effect – be simulated online. However, often people participating in person-centered encounter groups or workshops – i.e. unstructured or just loosely structured, facilitated talking and listening circles in an atmosphere of realness, acceptance, and empathic understanding – develop a sense of community and connection [2] [3] and want to continue their contact. Some wish to learn – in the sense of grow – personally, others want to share interests and create new knowledge even long after the end of the workshop.

Similarly, in an academic educational setting, students who had participated in encounter groups mentioned positive effects on various kinds of interpersonal relationships [4]. Some of the participating students wrote masters theses that were among the best in terms of creativity, originality, and relevance, and grew out of a highly engaged and self-organized working style. Some of these students stay in e-mail contact, appreciate meeting person to person and have sincere interest in repeating the encounter experience. This appears to be a decent basis for mutual, informal, yet deep and significant learning from one another as well as from the group processes.

These were just two of several settings exemplifying some features of a particular kind of socio-technical system referred to as a Significant Learning Community (SILC). In its core it consists of a sequence of encounter meetings combined with an

M.D. Lytras et al. (Eds.): WSKS 2008, CCIS 19, pp. 1–10, 2008.

interactive web-space providing a virtual meeting and sharing space for preparatory and follow-up exchanges and resources.

In order to characterize significant learning, I quote Carl Rogers' [5] original specification: "Significant learning combines the logical and the intuitive, the intellect and the feelings, the concept and the experience, the idea and the meaning. When we learn in that way, we are whole."

Research on encounter groups has confirmed that participants move in the direction of higher (inter-)personal competence, such as becoming more expressive, better understanding of self and others, and improving their interpersonal relationships [2] [3] [4] [6] [7] [8] [9]. In the virtual world knowledge communities, special interest groups, and, for example, the open source movement has provided numerous benefits for several people. Hence, it appears only natural to put the respective ideas and settings together into a combined framework.

My initial experience as a participant and facilitator in SILCs leads me to look for evidence of experiencing mutually enriching relationships and vast opportunities for creating new knowledge and learning. In this context several questions arise such as: How can SILCs best be built and cultivated? How can the arising patterns of connecting and creating new knowledge and insight best be captured, supported, and researched? What are the success factors for following constructive real *and* virtual processes? Indeed, the media-choice theories, e.g. [10] allow one to derive several benefits from combining web-based and face-to-face interactions. This is mainly because each medium (including immediacy) comes with advantages and disadvantages such that a thoughtful mix may contribute to bringing about the best of each medium in a particular setting.

We may ask: Why, at present, is there a need for SILCs, what can they achieve for us? The present appears to be characterized by a tendency towards increasing competition in the workplace, a rise in the amount of work done in potentially distributed teams, a need for almost instantaneous communication and knowledge development, and a decrease in the size of families and the time children stay with their parents before attending kinder garden or other daycare facilities. Under these circumstances, how can we meet the demands our society is imposing on us and, at the same time, show responsibility in our personal and professional lives? The technology push often dominates human behavior, leaving little time and space for the individual to reflect on where we are and to make any sustainable change in the direction of increasing satisfaction in our own functioning – not to speak about improving a whole system. Thus, SILCs can be conceived of as settings for life-long development of humans as whole persons, including cognitive, affective, social, and technological facets.

In a nutshell, this proposal builds on the ideas of the Person-Centered Approach [5] [11] [12] as originally developed by Carl Rogers (USA: 1902 – 1987) and suggests a way that may support humans of the knowledge society in developing as whole persons with feelings as well as meanings, personal and professional interests, demands on sharing as well as silence, in settings of presence and distance, both real and virtual.

In a society in which there is less time for social family life and yet the demands on social competences at the workplace are rising [13], this contribution introduces Significant Learning Communities (SILCs). The concept is meant to be characterized and evolved at the same time as SILCs are lived, reflected, and researched. While the next

Section characterizes SILCs and compares them with similar settings, the third Section focuses on the technology-supported aspects, such as the functionality of web-based tools to support SILCs. The forth Section discusses settings for introducing/implementing SILCs. Finally, conclusions are drawn and issues for further research are discussed.

2 Characteristics of a Significant Learning Community

The idea of a *Significant Learning Community* (SILC) is to further long lasting, constructive relationships of persons who want to "learn" from each other in some way they consider significant. The members of a SILC may follow some shared mission (in the minimal case to significantly learn from one another) or some subject matter of common interest to them. Each might have their specific goals, yet learn from the personal experience as well as knowledge or wisdom of the other.

SILCs derive their value-base from the Person-Centered Approach. They orient themselves on the humanistic conception of human beings as basically constructive persons striving to maintain and to enhance their organisms, if provided with the proper atmosphere. The latter is governed by person-centered core attitudes, or in other words, each person's (inter)personal dispositions of congruence, acceptance, and empathic understanding. In a SILC, these dispositions are assumed to be complemented by the participants' openness, resourcefulness and sharing with respect to some common purpose, mission, or – typically transdisciplinary – field of interest.

One central component of SILCs are person-centered encounter groups for allowing community building and personal growth. Yet, SILC have a longer life period than typically short or time-limited encounter groups. Participants in SILCs typically are virtually connected on a regular basis and thus can share meanings, ideas, feelings, experiences, reflections, any time and anywhere. Persistence and virtual connectedness are the main distinguishing criteria with respect to "pure" person-centered encounter groups. The central focus on person-centered attitudes, relationships, and interpersonal sharing at all levels are the main distinguishing criteria regarding other kinds of groups and communities.

More concisely, a SILC is characterized by tending to manifest, in a fluent and flexible way, the following features:

- Members or participants are first of all whole persons rather than playing roles;
- Congruent, acceptant, and empathically understanding exchange of meaning, feeling, ideas, thoughts, leads to significant learning;
- Members feel free to combine the personal with the professional, the intellectual with the intuitive, cognitions with feeling, meanings and skills;
- Openness, resourcefulness and sharing with respect to some common purpose, or – typically transdisciplinary – field of interest pervades the community as it develops as an open relationship system communicating with its environment [2], in particular with other relationship systems.
- A central component are regular person-centered encounter groups or workshops allowing for personal growth;
- SILCs typically are long lived. They have a longer life period than individual encounter groups

- Virtual interconnectedness allows for sharing and interaction any time and any-where;
- Members actualize their potentials in interdependent relationship with others in a self-organized way.
- SILCs are dynamic, open systems. In particular, they are open to members of any nation or culture.

Thus, in a SILC the actualization or forward movement of individuals proceeds in interaction with each other and their environment. It is supported by the formative tendency, directed towards greater order and interconnectedness [12] [14] without the control by external forces or imposed rigid constructs.

In order to further characterize SILCs let us differentiate them against similar notions.

Encounter group. In an encounter group time is constrained to the particular meeting or pre-scheduled series of meetings. A common goal or "field of interest" typically is personal development and/or community building. As a difference, a SICL is long lived, encompasses virtual contact between meetings, and typically has, in addition to personal development, other common purposes or goals.

T-group. In a T-group reflection is central, roles are explicit and time is typically constrained.

Self managed team. Typically, self-managed teams tend to be purely work-based. Their members need to be able to perform one other's job, at least temporarily, and to effectively work on common proceeds. Members share responsibility for work related tasks [13].

Family. Families are, technically speaking, "constrained" by the necessity to be rela-tives by blood relationship or other formal rules. Many family relationships (parent-child) are complementary by nature. A SILC is in many respects similar to a family, the bonds, however, are more loose, relationships tend to be symmetric, and member-ship is by sharing the goal or purpose and common value rather than by some social rule.

Professional Community. SICLs differ from professional communities [15] mainly in its core orientation and purpose. While a SILCs encourages the exchange of personal issues and integrates personal expression with professional issues, the Pro-fessional Community is primarily aimed at the professionalization in some field. Fur-thermore, the Professional Community has self-reflection as an explicit means while a SILC focuses on significant learning in a constructive atmosphere.

Learning community. A learning community (Wikipedia) is "a group of people who share common values and beliefs, are actively engaged in learning together from each other" [16]. Such communities form templates for a collaborative, interdisciplinary approach to higher education [17] [18]. According to [19], community psychologists state that there are four key factors that define a sense of community: (1) *membership*, (2) *influence*, (3) *fulfillment of individuals needs* and (4) *shared events and emotional connections*. According to this characterization, all four key factors also apply to

SILCs such that the latter indeed can be viewed as "subspecies" of learning communities, given a broad interpretation of "learning".

Community of Practice. Lave and Wenger [20] described a Community of Practice (CoP) as "a set of relations among persons, activity and world, over time and in relation with other tangential and overlapping CoPs." Typically, members of CoPs have a shared set of interests and are motivated to do something about them and are self-generating. Thus, while CoPs and SILCs share many characteristics, there exist differences in focus and main purpose: Whereas the CoP is organized around a *common practice*, a SILC is formed around *human resource and knowledge development*, or, in other words, a self-organized, interdependent "way of becoming" leading to a "way of becoming knowledgeable".

3   Role of the Virtual Spaces and Interconnection in SILCs

A notable characteristic of a SILC is its blend of face-to-face and web-based communication. In the following we focus on the web support of a SILC and investigate, in how far online tools contribute to collaborative construction of knowledge, and to building, or "growing" relationships and community. For this reason we take a look at the functions that can be supported by interactive web-based tools in the context of SILCs. These include:

- Sharing of resources such as materials, facts, circumstances, situations, processes is supported. The shared "materialized" resources can be attended to and edited, complemented, improved cooperatively. This process can lead to a cooperative construction of a shared knowledge base consisting of material resources such as documents, links, slide-shows, videos, etc.
- Distant cooperation between members is supported such that intercultural communication and connectedness can be achieved much faster than without online contact [21].
- Shared virtual spaces for process reflection allow for locating where we are and what was going on in meetings. This may improve understanding and form a basis or landscape for coming tasks and/or meetings. In particular, subsequent encounters need not start from scratch but can draw upon shared experience. In this way, continuity between encounters is provided. In other words, the forming of a shared meaning can well continue online.
- Virtual spaces allow one to come back to group situations as experienced in the group and enrich them with current meaning, consider them in their relevance and transfer to situations outside of meetings.
- Web-based communication encourages the expression of persons who tend to be more reserved in spontaneous expression or who have missed a meeting.
- Frameworks for the organization of meetings and conferences can be applied.
- In general there is a better and faster information flow.
- The technology support for SILCs typically can be provided by web services such as:
- Mailing list

- Structured spaces with document uploads and discussion
- Wikis, forum, chat
- Blogs

In my educational endeavors with SILC-like settings, in this case advanced academic courses including encounter groups and web support, the alteration between face-to-face and online phases showed, amongst others, the following features or regularities [4] [8] [22] [23] :

- Face-to-face phases are more effective, if students can loosely prepare themselves in advance, in terms of studying the goals, raising expectations, acquiring a gross idea on what they can expect and what is expected from them.
- Face-to-face phases are more effective, if they can be continued online. "Effective" in this context is understood as leading to further thought or sharing and offering meaningful perspectives that can be followed on.
- Writing makes issues explicit and persistent, you can return to them as often as you like, thus *iterating* towards more meaning and insight.
- Reflective writing after intriguing face-to-face sharing seems a natural and fruitful source for self-organizing new knowledge.
- With web technology, contact can continue between meetings. Some issues, in particular between two persons, may be clarified by virtual communication and face-to-face time can be used to move on in the group process.
- Blending ways of expression seems to be more acceptant of the individual preferred ways of expression: Many quiet students write insightful reactions.
- Those who miss a session can catch up more easily.
- Structured, interactive spaces tend to be helpful; in particular, if more than 2-3 people cooperate, for example to edit a shared document.
- Intentions, observations, feelings tend to become more explicit and conscious. Sharing them tends to lead to more trust within the community.
- Blended ways of expression appear to accelerate the group process [4].

In particular, the author has repeatedly experienced that person-centered attitudes like congruence, acceptance, and deep understanding are critically helpful in effective communication, in face-to-face and also in online settings [9]. For example, with experiencing and communicating person-centered attitudes, misunderstandings and/or difference can be tackled openly but constructively such that they tend not to end up with over-annoyed participants or just "quasi"-solutions. It needs to be said, however, that person-centered attitudes need time to develop. They can neither be "turned on" by pure will nor be learned by pure receptive learning. They rather need to be perceived and lived in relationship with others.

4   Candidate Situations for Initiating SILCs

To make the concept of a SILC more concrete I sketch some real world situations that appear to be particularly well suited to be realized as SILCs. Note, however, that further research as well as practice is required to allow for the transfer of initial experience in a few settings to a broader range of situations.

One candidate scenario for building a SILC is a research community at a faculty [24] or a transdisciplinary research group that finds meaning and progress in sharing. Such a group typically exists at a university or at the interface between university and industry. In this type of setting, the author has personal-relational experience [25]: For example, we live a SILC with the colleagues and some (intercultural) PhD students of the Research Lab for Educational Technologies at the University of Vienna. There are, amongst others, regular meetings (about once a month) that are only loosely structured such that participants can share whatever is most important for them in the given situation and context. Participants are virtually connected by a web-service-based environment called CEWebS [26]. It offers introductory information, contacts, shared resources, Wikis, forum, and open reaction sheets to be submitted after each block such that they can be read by the whole community. As an example of students' reflections consider the following note from a student after the second meeting in a PhD seminar:

"To me it seems very interesting to see that I am not the only one who has difficulties in finding a suitable topic for my PhD. It brings me peace to find out that others meet quite the same challenges and are also passing through levels of development. Personally, I was surprised to see how many PhD students share the same broad field of interest and which connections arise from this acquaintance. I do like the idea of forming a community and I find it particularly meaningful since we can share with colleagues and thus mutually inspire us to think about our theses."

Another student wrote: "I got a good overview on what others are doing. Being left on my own, I sometimes think that I am stuck, but as I see that others have similar problems I gain confidence. My hope for finishing the thesis rises. Thereby I acknowledge that it is up to me. I must take my time and research, write and read. NO colleague or supervisor can and SHOULD do this for me. In the end there should be a result that I can be proud of."

A further setting for a SILC is a group of educators or facilitators who want to promote significant learning with the help of using new media. They would typically share their resources as well as their experiences, provide each other supervision as colleagues and collaboratively explore new tools and practices. Another structurally similar but typically international "application" of SILCs are international (research) project teams that invite creative solutions and need to share resources and ideas face-to-face as well as online [27].

In a similar vein, a further setting for a SILC is a group/team of facilitators who offer encounter groups. They coordinate their efforts in organizing the workshops with the help of online tools and regularly meet for encountering, either as a whole group or in subgroups depending on the co-facilitation team constellations. Before, after, and between workshops, facilitators can share experiences and build knowledge for personal and professional development as well as for (participatory action) research. This setting appears to be particularly appealing in an international context. It is hypothesized here and needs to be confirmed by further research that the encounter meetings lead to increase quality of work activities due to a higher sensitivity and congruence of participants resulting from well-functioning encounter group meetings [3] [6] [7].

In general, SILCs can be proposed to any group of life-long "learners" sharing interest in some area along with willingness to invest time and effort in advancing "their area" while growing as human beings in relationship with others.

5 Conclusion and Further Research

This paper introduced Significant Learning Communities (SILCs) as socio-technical settings by characterizing their features from a psychological, social, and technical viewpoint. While the author could draw on initial, clearly positive experiences with SILCs in academic settings, practice and research evidence in a broader field is sought in order to be able to promote SILC as effective socio-technical inventions of the internet age. Particular research questions in the technological realm are which Web 2.0 services and tools are well suited to support SILCs and how participants can effectively establish appropriate "usage cultures" regarding the tools offered by interactive web applications. In the area of human relationship an interesting question is: "Which (inter)personal qualities or dispositions would be particularly promotive in building and 'growing' a SILC that is considered effective by its participants." Or, "Are there (inter)personal qualities or dispositions that slow down the processes in a SILC or even stand against the building or growth of a SILC? If yes, which are they?" These and several other questions arise when trying to find out about the success factors for initiating and "growing" SILCs as well as the challenges arising in the process. In any case, the author currently thinks that besides theoretical considerations the lived, engaged experience in SILCs is essential in further shaping the initial concept as presented in this paper. This must not be expected to be a smooth and fast process. When considering the laws of dynamic, open systems [28] and self-organized actualization of the human potential, we must appreciate that SILCs cannot be expected to provide "quick fixes" to problem situation but will require time and effort to develop and to sustain.

References

1. Sowe, S.K., Karoulis, A., Stamelos, I., Bleris, G.L.: Free Open-Source Learning Community and Web-Based Technologies. IEEE Learning Technology 6, 27–29 (2004)
2. Barrett-Lennard, G.T.: Relationship at the Centre - Healing in a Troubled World. Whurr Publishers, Philadelphia (2005)
3. Rogers, C.R.: Carl Rogers on Encounter Groups. Harper Row, New York (1970)
4. Motschnig-Pitrik, R.: Can Person Centered Encounter Groups Contribute to Improve Relationships and Learning in Academic Environments? In: Behr, M., Cornelius-White, J.H.D. (eds.) Development and Interpersonal Relation - Person-Centered Work, PCCS Books (2008)
5. Rogers, C.R.: Freedom to Learn for the 80's. Charles E. Merrill Publishing Company, Columbus (1983)
6. Barrett-Lennard, G.T.: Steps on a Mindful Journey: Person-centred expressions. PCCS Books (2003)

7. Lago, C., MacMillan, M.: Experiences in Relatedness: Group Work and the Person Centred Approach. PCCS Books, Ross (1999)
8. Motschnig-Pitrik, R.: Person-Centered e-Learning in Action: Can Technology help to manifest Person-centered Values in Academic Environments? Journal of Humanistic Psychology 45, 503–530 (2005)
9. Motschnig-Pitrik, R., Nykl, L.: The Application of Technology Enhanced Learning in Person Centered Education Including Encounter groups. In: Proc. International Conference on Information and Communication Technology in Education, Rožnov, CZ (2007)
10. Dennis, A.R., Valacich, J.S.: Rethinking Media Richness: Towards a Theory of Media Synchronicity. In: Proc. 32nd Hawaii International Conference on System Sciences, Maui, Hawaii, USA (1999)
11. Rogers, C.R.: On Becoming a Person - A Psychotherapists View of Psychotherapy. Constable, London (1961)
12. Rogers, C.R.: A Way of Being. Houghton Mifflin Company, Boston (1980)
13. Ryback, D.: Putting Emotional Intelligence to Work - Successful Leadership is More Than IQ. Butterworth-Heinemann, Boston (1998)
14. Cornelius-White, J.H.D.: The actualizing and formative tendencies: Prioritizing the motivational constructs of the person-centered approach. Person-Centered and Experiential Psychotherapies 6, 129–140 (2007)
15. Schrittesser, I., Logar, S., Wenninger, B.: Professional Communities - Potentials and Limits of Blended Learning Scenarios. In: Proc. Networked Learning Conference 2006, Lancaster, England (2006)
16. Smith, B.L., McCann, J.: Reinventing Ourselves: Interdiciplinary Education, Collaborative Learning, and Experimentation in Higher Education. Anker Publishing, Boston (2001)
17. Gabelnick, F., MacGregor, J., Matthews, R.S., Smith, B.L.: Learning Communities: Creating Connections Among Students, Faculty, and Disciplines. New Directions for Teaching and Learning 41 (1990)
18. Palloff, R.M., Pratt, K.: Collaborating Online. Learning Together in Community. Jossey-Bass, San Francisco (2005)
19. Bonk, C.J., Wisher, R.A., Nigrelli, M.: Learning Communities, Communities of practices: principles, technologies and examples. In: Littleton, K., Miell, D., Faulkner, D. (eds.) Learning to Collaborate: Collaborating to Learn. Nova Science Publishers, New York (2004)
20. Lave, J., Wenger, E.: Situated Learning: Legitimate Peripheral Participation. Cambridge University Press, Cambridge (1991)
21. Goodyear, P., De Laat, M., Lally, V.: Using Pattern Languages to Mediate Theory-Praxis Conversations in Designs for Networked Learning. ALT-J Research in Learning Technology 14, 211–223 (2006)
22. Motschnig-Pitrik, R.: Two Technology-Enhanced Courses Aimed at Developing Interpersonal Attitudes and Soft Skills in Project Management. In: Proc. First European Conference on Technology Enhanced Learning, EC-TEL 2006, Crete, Greece (2006)
23. Motschnig-Pitrik, R.: The Effects of a Blended Course Including Person Centered Encounter Groups on Students' Learning, Relationships, and Teamwork. In: Proc. Networked Learning Conference 2006, Lancaster, UK (2006)
24. Neville, B.: Creating a Research Community. Qualitative Research Journal (2008)
25. Motschnig-Pitrik, R., Figl, K.: The Effects of Person Centered Education on Communication and Community Building. In: Proc. ED-MEDIA 2008, Vienna, Austria (2008)

26. Mangler, J., Derntl, M.: CEWebS - Cooperative Environment Web Services. In: Proc. 4th International Conference on Knowledge Management (I-KNOW 2004), Graz, Austria (2004)
27. Motschnig-Pitrik, R.: Preparing Students for Project Communication and Cooperation based on Person Centered Technology Enhanced Learning. In: Hochgerner, J., Čornejová, I. (eds.) Communication in International R&D Projects, A Perspective from Social Sciences and Humanities. Barrister & Principal, Brno (2008)
28. Kriz, J.: Self-actualization: Person-Centred Approach and Systems Theory. PCCS Books (2008)

Wisdom Networks: Towards a Wisdom-Based Society

Nikunj Dalal

Department of Management Science and Information Systems
Spears School of Business
Oklahoma State University
Stillwater, OK 74078
nik.dalal@okstate.edu

Abstract. In a world inundated by information, knowledge, and entertainment, there is a dire need for wisdom. We propose a vision for wisdom networks – communities that aim to actualize and inculcate wisdom in specific domains – towards creating a wisdom-based society. Wisdom networks are enabled and empowered by information technologies. We draw upon multiple theoretical perspectives to view wisdom as a holistic quality that transcends and includes elements of information, knowledge, understanding, values, and many other dimensions. Wisdom networks are involved in the creation and dissemination of wisdom-based learning, wisdom-based counseling, participation in community initiatives, and building linkages with other wisdom networks. The hallmark of a wisdom network is an honest and deep inquiry into key issues in a domain, keeping the common universal good in mind. We propose key characteristics of wisdom networks and provide examples. We recognize that this vision is evolving and we explore research issues that arise in the design and implementation of wisdom networks. We underscore the need for wisdom computing research. Supporting wisdom is a critical challenge for social and humanistic computing and knowledge management.

Keywords: Wisdom Networks, Wisdom, Knowledge, Society, Information Systems, Information and Communication Technologies.

1 Introduction

Of all whose discourses I have heard, there is not one who attains to the understanding that wisdom is apart from all.

Heraclitus, fragment 108

The world is inundated with data, information, knowledge, and entertainment. Human needs and wants fueled by money and power are drivers of this movement. As societies become increasingly dependent on the production, dissemination and use of knowledge [1], the focus is increasingly on developing software and hardware technologies to capture, store, process, manage, and deliver *information* and *knowledge*. But there is hardly any attention given to *wisdom*. This is very surprising. "If there is anything the world needs, it is wisdom. Without it, I exaggerate not at all in saying

M.D. Lytras et al. (Eds.): WSKS 2008, CCIS 19, pp. 11–18, 2008.

that very soon, there may be no world. . ." said Robert J. Sternberg, 2003 President of the American Psychological Association [2]. Ackoff among others has fervently observed, there is a real need to progress from data, information, knowledge, and understanding to wisdom [3].

In this paper, we propose a vision for wisdom networks – communities that aim to actualize and inculcate wisdom in their domains – towards creating a wisdom-based society working for the common good. To articulate this vision, we first clarify what we mean by wisdom in this context because the term has been used in many different ways. Next, we introduce the concept of wisdom networks and propose its characteristics. Then, we explore research issues in design and implementation. We conclude by underscoring the importance of wisdom support with the help of information and communication technologies.

2 What Is Wisdom?

Wisdom has been a focus of philosophical and religious traditions since antiquity. Over the past few decades, it has attracted some interdisciplinary interest (though not enough) from academic fields besides philosophy. Not surprisingly, there is little agreement on a general definition of wisdom, though most people seem to have an intuitive notion of its characteristics. As many wisdom researchers have recognized, "…wisdom is difficult to conceptualize and operationalize, and also is expensive and time-consuming to study [4]." Table 1 summarizes a few of many perspectives on wisdom.

Table 1. Some perspectives on wisdom

Work	Definition
Dictionary [5]	• accumulated knowledge or erudition or enlightenment • the trait of utilizing knowledge and experience with common sense and insight • ability to apply knowledge or experience or understanding or common sense and insight • the quality of being prudent and sensible
Balance Theory of Wisdom	"Wisdom is the application of intelligence, creativity, and knowledge to the common good by balancing intrapersonal (one's own), interpersonal, (others'), and extrapersonal (institutional or other larger) interests over the long and short terms, through the mediation of values, so as to adapt to, shape, and select environments." [4, p. 287] Wisdom arises in a person-context interaction.
Berlin Wisdom Paradigm	Conceptually, wisdom is excellence in mind and virtue and, on a more psychological level, it is excellence in the conduct and meaning of life. It is expert knowledge in "the fundamental pragmatics of life". The fundamental pragmatics of life refer to questions about life planning, life management, and life review – basically, issues relating to the conduct and meaning of life [6]

Table 1. (*continued*)

Ardelt	Wisdom is an integration of cognitive, reflective, and affective personality characteristics in an individual. Cognitive characteristics include an understanding of life and a desire to know the truth. Reflective characteristics include the perception of phenomena and events from multiple perspectives, which requires self-examination, self-awareness, and self-insight. Affective characteristics include sympathetic and compassionate love for others [7].
Maxwell	Wisdom is the capacity to realize what is of value in life, for oneself and others [8],
Western philosophies	Wisdom includes inquiry and examination of one's life, truth, dialectics, multiple perspectives, goodness, happiness, values, morals, love, and others.
Eastern philosophies	Wisdom includes inquiry, truth, non-duality, consciousness, emptiness, meditation, enlightenment, absolute understanding of reality, empathy, and others.

In this paper, we draw upon the strengths of all major perspectives, and take the view that wisdom includes elements of information, knowledge, inquiry, understanding, insights, common-sense, values, judgments, ethics, life pragmatics, empathy, self-knowing and other such attributes and dimensions but is "apart from all" and transcends all boundaries and dimensions. This general wisdom may act differently in domain-specific ways. Wisdom is often taken to be a higher form of knowledge. We take the view that wisdom is not knowledge *per se* but may be partly represented by knowledge (that we call wisdom-based knowledge). However, this knowledge has to be actualized and manifested in an individual for it to be seen as wisdom.

3 Wisdom Networks

The raison d'être of wisdom networks is to actualize deep holistic wisdom in individuals and their communities as well as in the overall populace at large, towards the creation of a wisdom-based society for the common good. It should be clarified that our conception of a wisdom network is qualitatively and fundamentally different from that of a knowledge network though there is some similarity in functionality and structure.

The core of a wisdom network is made up of select concerned individuals enabled by information technologies acting in the spirit of true inquiry and guided by wisdom in their domain of interest. A wisdom network has a focal domain though it draws from and contributes to related domains. Some examples of the types of questions wisdom networks may address in different domains are explored in Table 2. Given its primary intent of actualizing wisdom, we conceive of wisdom networks as performing several different functions.

Table 2. Examples of wisdom network domains and sample questions

Type of domain	Domain	Inquiry question	Counseling question
Medical	Bio-ethics	Should people be allowed to sell their organs?	Do I really need surgery?
Self	Self-knowing	What does it mean to know oneself?	How do I deal with my anger?
Organizational	A specific organization	What is the right relationship between management and labor?	Help: I think I will be fired. What should I do?
Society	Preservation of culture	Why do we want to preserve cultures?	Our children do not speak our mother tongue. What should we do?
Religion	A specific religion	What does this religion teach us about wisdom?	How do I truly follow my faith?
Government	A specific governing body	What is the right role of government?	How can my complaint be redressed?

3.1 Inquiry

Inquiry implies the raising of key issues in the domain and serious well-intentioned attempts to find the truth in an objective way unbiased by commercial, professional, and personal interests. The relentless, passionate, and objective inquiry into the truth of an issue is the hallmark of a wisdom network. All its other functions, though important, are in the service of its primary imperative of carrying out an honest and deep inquiry. The inquiry is primarily seen as an activity carried out by an individual but enabled by access to other individuals and inquiring mechanisms. Inquiring mechanisms, among other things, include inquiring systems [9] that can be operationalized to provide access to stored data, information, models, contrasting and multiple perspectives, and pertinent knowledge. The inquiry process may include reflective dialogues "in which self-awareness, intuition, reflection, and listening are key elements; where participants are observing their own thinking processes, biases, self-image, motivation, beliefs, and conditioning while having a dialogue about the issues at hand [10]." The inquiry process is critical and should not be reduced to a mere exchange of opinions and ideas. Furthermore, the results of the inquiry process should be subject to ongoing validation.

3.2 Creation of Wisdom-Based Learning

During the course of an inquiry, considerable wisdom-based knowledge is generated. This includes transcripts of inquiry sessions, recorded insights and experiences, as well as other types of interactive multimedia content created specifically for participants. Relevant discussion about the content such as responses, feedback, and comments may be further added to the main content. Scholarly research guided by wisdom has a place here.

3.3 Community Initiatives

A wisdom network, as we conceive it, is not simply an online repository of wisdom-based knowledge. Interaction with the community is very important in understanding and furthering wisdom. Participants in the network collectively in groups and individually would be encouraged to volunteer in wisdom education and dissemination projects, both online and in the physical world. Such initiatives may include courses, educational projects, and societal experiments. The learning gained from such projects would become part of the "wisdom-base".

3.4 Wisdom-Based Counseling

We recognize that there will be people accessing a wisdom network who are not primarily interested in the type of inquiry described earlier but instead are looking for authoritative answers to their personal questions or to solve a problem they are facing. A wisdom network provides resources in the form of people and knowledge to facilitate such counseling needs. In this sense, a wisdom network performs a function similar to that of an expert discussion forum in which a user may post a question and get replies from experts in the domain. Moreover, a wisdom network will not just provide objective and empathetic responses to questions; it could be instrumental in taking the questioner beyond their original question to a deeper and broader inquiry.

3.5 Linkages with Other Wisdom Networks

Unlike knowledge, wisdom cannot be confined to the boundaries of a discipline. Because wisdom transcends domains, a wisdom network cannot exist in isolation of other networks. It is important that a wisdom network be designed to be living, dynamic, and connected to other wisdom networks. A wisdom network must regularly interact with other wisdom networks (and not just from similar domains), in order to form networks of networks – larger wisdom networks from which smaller, more focused networks can draw upon as needed. So for example, a network in the medical ethics domain may regularly interact with networks in the philosophy domain. The "smallness" of the network permits greater focus and cohesion and its "largeness" allows it to be challenged from becoming a comfort zone of homogeneous thinking.

4 Design and Implementation Issues

In this section, we pose some preliminary design, implementation, and wider academic research issues, mindful that no attempt is being made to be comprehensive.

Our search of existing communities on the Internet indicates the active presence of social networks (such as facebook.com), entertainment and gaming networks (such as secondlife.com), and knowledge networks (e.g., The climate change knowledge network at www.cckn.net, whose focus "is to bring together expertise, experience and perspectives from research institutes in developing and developed countries active in the area of climate change") but it is difficult to find wisdom networks in the deep sense of the term. One example of what is largely a knowledge network in the knowledge domain but shares some features of a wisdom network is the Open Research Society. The Open Research Society [11] is a non-governmental nonprofit organization with goals that include providing free access to knowledge to all people, promoting volunteering and learning, and providing training. Another example of a knowledge network that may be seen as an emerging wisdom network in the self-knowing domain is the Knowsys project [12]. Still in its prototype phase, it is described as a "collaboratively authored living knowledge resource providing interactive access to the frontiers of human self knowledge and the wisdom of the ages [12]". The site is conceived as a self-organizing gathering place to: compare notes, cross-fertilize ideas, obtain help, and seek personal empowerment. Likewise, a few other such sites can be found but virtually all of these are largely knowledge networks providing access to a variety of resources but perhaps, lack the type of inquiry mechanism, the focus on wisdom, the community initiatives, and the linkages – all acting in concert – that are central to our conception of a wisdom network.

How can such a wisdom network as we have proposed be designed and implemented? It is critical that the wisdom network preserves its primary wisdom intent and its focus on true inquiry and is not reduced to yet another forum where there is just a proliferation of information, opinions, and knowledge or to a specialized knowledge network whose major unspoken intent is to protect its turf. Hence, we see the wisdom network as constituted of a small core group of "wise" volunteer leaders at the forefront of the inquiry and involved in the co-creation of wisdom content in a specific domain, around which there is a chosen larger group of volunteers participating in inquiry, counseling, linkages, and other initiatives of the wisdom network. A proposal for such a structure raises many issues. Foremost is the issue of the constitution of the core group of inquirers. How is such a group to be constituted? Who decides who should join? It, perhaps, make sense for a single committed inquirer to start a wisdom network and over time, invite very few carefully selected individuals to join as co-inquirers and co-creators of wisdom content. How is the selection to be done? As with any organization, there will be a need for clear governance mechanisms and policies but unlike other organizations, we believe a wisdom network will benefit from a decentralized benevolent structure, free of authoritarianism, where inputs are sought from all core inquirers. Further, we believe a wisdom network needs to be a non-profit organization beholden to no one. What makes for an effective organization in this context is clearly an issue for further research.

Another important design issue is the choice of technologies. The technologies selected for a wisdom network should enable the following functionality at a minimum:

- Ability to create inquiry mechanisms of various kinds including online dialogues focused on self-understanding and issue-understanding
- Ability to jointly create joint documents
- Ability to classify, categorize, annotate, and search the wisdom-based knowledge
- Ability to easily navigate from one unit of content to another related unit

- A validation engine to continually validate content in light of new content
- Sharing of opinions, experiences, perspectives
- Ability to recommend content based on user's needs

How is this support to be achieved and what technologies could provide this support? Because a wisdom network must support an inquiring mechanism, besides blogs, wikis, discussion forums, chats and other common communication platforms, newer hardware and software technologies and markup languages that help capture communication aspects such as gestures, thoughts, emotions, insights and attitudes will be useful. One can imagine, for example, how self-understanding can be aided if there is an automatic way to track each instance of anger during an inquiry session, and then to observe the correlations between the incidences of anger and specific topics under discussion. Also useful would be decision support systems containing personality-analysis tools; systems that challenge common assumptions, patterns, and ways of thinking; systems that permit unobtrusive recording of faces, conversations, and moods; and tools that track physical changes linked to emotional changes such as biofeedback devices [10].

Wisdom networks as conceived aim to actualize wisdom in individuals and communities. What does it mean to actualize wisdom? In the first place, it is difficult to even agree on a definition of wisdom, so how can this very amorphous and unstructured quality be actualized and measured? These gaps point to the burning need for research in wisdom. Surprisingly, wisdom has received little attention in the information systems and knowledge management areas. There is a need to develop ontologies for wisdom-based knowledge. Information systems researchers can especially contribute in uncovering and examining the links between data, information, knowledge, understanding, and wisdom. Moreover, there is a wide variety of knowledge, information, and data readily available in various formats on the Internet. Can we create mechanisms to extract and imbibe wisdom from extant knowledge, information, and data? Can we find ways to address T.S. Eliot's lament: "Where is the wisdom we have lost in knowledge?"

Another set of issues relate to the management of wisdom and wisdom-based knowledge. How is wisdom to be created, modeled, represented, shared, and managed? Knowledge management issues, in this context, now can be seen as wisdom management issues.

Ultimately, wisdom research also needs to transcend disciplinary boundaries. Nicholas Maxwell, philosopher asserts: "We need a revolution in the aims and methods of academic inquiry. Instead of giving priority to the search for knowledge, academia needs to devote itself to seeking and promoting wisdom by rational means, wisdom being the capacity to realize what is of value in life, for oneself and others, wisdom thus including knowledge but much else besides…. Acquiring scientific knowledge dissociated from a more basic concern for wisdom, as we do at present, is dangerously and damagingly irrational [8]."

5 Concluding Remarks

There is a dire need for wisdom in today's world. From our perspective, wisdom transcends all boundaries and divisions but it also includes domain-specific wisdom that draws from unbounded wisdom. There is a place for data, information, knowledge, goodness, values, morality, and ethics but unless these dimensions are rooted in wisdom, even the most well-intentioned projects may end as catastrophic failures. Hence, supporting wisdom is a critical challenge for social and humanistic computing and knowledge management.

In this relatively unexplored but vital space, we have proposed a vision for wisdom networks and have explored its potential characteristics. We have raised what we see are some key research issues. It must be emphasized that this vision is but a start and that by its very nature, the vision will evolve as it becomes a focal point of inquiry of intelligent minds. Clearly, this is just a beginning and a lot more work is needed. The development and effective use of information technologies to create and share wisdom, what we call "Wisdom Computing", is a new frontier having implications for individuals, societies and governments. In the final analysis, it is the responsibility of every individual to help ensure that a wisdom-based world does not remain merely a utopian ideal.

References

1. Stehr, N.: Societal Transformations, Globalization and the Knowledge Society. International Journal of Knowledge and Learning 3, 139–153 (2007)
2. Sternberg, R.J.: Wisdom, Intelligence, and Creativity Synthesized. Cambridge University Press, New York (2003)
3. Ackoff, R.L.: From Data to Wisdom. Journal of Applied Systems Analysis 16, 3–9 (1989)
4. Sternberg, R.J.: Words to the Wise About Wisdom? Human Development 47, 286–289 (2004)
5. Word net, http://wordnet.princeton.edu
6. Baltes, P.B., Kunzmann, U.: The Two Faces of Wisdom: Wisdom as a General Theory of Knowledge and Judgment about Excellence in Mind and Virtue vs. Wisdom as Everyday Realization in People and Products. Human Development 47, 290–299 (2004)
7. Ardelt, M.: Wisdom as expert knowledge system: A critical review of a contemporary operationalization of an ancient concept. Human Development 47, 257–285 (2004)
8. Maxwell, N.: http://www.knowledgetowisdom.org/
9. Churchman, C.: West: The Design of Inquiring Systems: Basic Concepts of Systems and Organization. Basic Books, New York (1971)
10. Dalal, N.: Toward Reflective Dialogue based Inquiring Systems. In: The 12th Americas Conference on Information Systems, Acapulco, Mexico, August 4-6, 2006 (2006)
11. Open Research Society, http://www.open-knowledge-society.org
12. Knowsys project, http://www.wisdombase.org

Step by Step Framework for Evaluation of In-Formation Technology Benefit in Social Scenarios

Esteban Vaquerizo[1], Yolanda Garrido[1], Jorge Falcó[1], Theresa Skehan[2],
Alba Jiménez[1], and Roberto Casas[1]

[1] Tecnodiscap Group, University of Zaragoza
María de Luna 1, Ed. Ada Byron, 50018 Zaragoza Spain
{evaqueri,ygarrido,jfalco,alba.jimenez,rcasas}@unizar.es
[2] Swedish Institute of Assistive Technology
Sorterargatan 23, Vinsta, Vällingby Sweden
terry.skehan@hi.se

Abstract. Evaluation of IT with end users is necessary to create systems that provide real benefit to society. Usually, evaluation is considered only as a trial of technology with users simply responding to questionnaires. Nevertheless, the process implies many aspects that should not be overlooked. In this paper we present a detailed framework that attempts to present all the mandatory and advisable issues that should be addressed in an evaluation of IT with users. This framework is valid for laboratory tests, and is also specifically recommended for social scenarios; for example day centers, user's dwellings, etc. This framework is being used in a European project where hundreds of users test technology in different scenarios.

1 Introduction

Information and communication technologies play an increasing role in our lives, offering new opportunities and choices, improving public services and facilitating communication between people. The main objective of the MonAMI project is to demonstrate that accessible, useful services for elderly and disabled persons living at home can be delivered in mainstream systems and platforms.

It is clear that when IT usefulness is evaluated in social scenarios of this size many considerations must be taken into account. There are various stakeholders involved: social, industrial, technological, governmental, and of course the end users. Thus, evaluation should consider a variety of aspects that correspond to the different actors'perspectives [1]. There are many approaches for the evaluation of IT within the field of the elderly and people with disabilities. For example, there are questionnaires that evaluateuser satisfaction [2]; psychosocial impact [3]; milieu, person, technology and training impact [4]; functional independence [5]; or the quality of life change [6]. These questionnaires are commonly used and are useful tools. But they address only the tip of the iceberg; it is necessary to take into account many more aspects to perform an integral and useful evaluation of IT inside social scenarios.

In this paper we propose a detailed framework for IT evaluation in social scenarios. We raise many isssues that have been raised through the large scale field trails (with

M.D. Lytras et al. (Eds.): WSKS 2008, CCIS 19, pp. 19–23, 2008.
© Springer-Verlag Berlin Heidelberg 2008

many users in many countries) proposed in MonAMI project. The framework includes legal and ethical considerations that are needed when working with end users (disabled or not); how to define a complete and useful evaluation protocol that includes more than just questionnaires; important considerations needed to be addresses to run tests not only in laboratories, but also in the end users' social context (homes, residences, work places, etc.); and some guidelines about the issues to be considered when terminating testing to ensure that the user does not experience a reduction of his/her quality of life

2   Framework Description

2.1   Ethical and Legal Issues Previous to Evaluation with Users

Technology frequently has a large impact on ethical and social issues. Designers usually concentrate on technological aspects and tend to ignore the impact of their designs. It is claimed that social and ethical issues are not the responsability of scientific staff and should be taken into account by policy makers, caretakers, social workers, etc. Nevertheless, it is recognisedthat the technical design of many devices and services include characteristics that affect the rights of the users and that can not be removed because they are substantially rooted in the conception of the application.

It is necessary to take into account legal issues before starting to test technolgy with persons. There are four steps in the procedure and which culminates with approval by the Local Ethical Committee.

Project Frame: It is essential to givethe Local Committee a *document explaining the project* giving details about main goals, tools to be used, technology involved and expected benefits.

Civil Responsibility Insurance: Before any action is started, a *liability insurance policy* to cover any possible inconveniences /damages /injuries related to the testing or experienced within the test facilities.

Protection of User Personal Data: Each country has its own laws that protect personal privacy. It is mandatory to follow National, Local and European legal requirements as well as the internal norms of the Institution to which the group belongs concerning protection of user personal data. Contemplating the above mentioned norms and legislation, the *Personal Data Protection Protocol document* on security procedure is created.

Redaction of Informed Consent: This document, besides the regulation already described, should be based on Helsinki Declaration [7]. Furthermore, external and internal advice will be required to design a draft of the document. Once the draft is approved and validated by the Research Team and the Project Coordination, the final *informed consent* is ready to be presented to the Local Ethical Committee.

With all the collected documentation, the research group should apply for *project approval by the Local Ethical Committee.*

2.2   Evaluation Protocol Definition and User Selection

Following the aim of achieving the evaluation protocol definition and user selection it is necessary to take into account several actors: local and regional administrations, administrative and legal stakeholders, eser entities, service providers and technology developers such as universities and companies.

Local and regional administrations such as state and city governments and, ethical committee, contribute with official support to the project

It is essential that user entities take part in the project as they are specialists in assisting and working with people to whom the technology will be addressed. User entities, in conjunction with technology developers, will therefore contribute with local support to the project and advise on the selection and description of user profile scenarios and technology. In addition, they have to validate the evaluation tools to get user profiles, to measure the user's quality of life and the evaluation procedure in general.

Technology developers have the responsibility of explaining the project goals and the technology itself.

The result of this collaborative work between the university administration, local and regional administration, user entities and technology developers is compiled in the document *Protocol of Evaluation with Users*.

Another outcome is the *Collaboration Agreements* signed with user entities and local administrations and companies to guarantee the fulfillment of the promises made by the different parts. From these agreements, scenarios and volunteer users are identified and nominated to take part in the project.

2.3 Test with Users: Technical Evaluation

Once the scenarios are defined and volunteers are identified, two tasks are carried out simultaneously: management of scenarios and technology and management of users.

The **management of scenarios** mainly involves the technology installation process. Before installation, it is necessary to ensure that the scenarios are adapted for technological and the user's needs. Sometimes it is essential make a proposal for adaptation of the construction. The next step is to make a pre-study to guarantee general coherence and integration of the services and to ensure accessibility and security for all users. This study must identify the control points to ensure a good quality of service during and after the experiment, that gives the user a 'help line' to contact in case of possible technical failures.

The first action in the **management of users** is to make a presentation of the project to a group of users explaining clearly main goals and giving a detailed description of the testing which will be carried out. Once the group of users is informed and the decision to take part in the project is made, the informed consent form must be signed by each of the volunteers. Subsequently, volunteers will fill out a questionnaire prior to evaluating the technology. This questionnaire is essential to evaluate changes in the user's quality of life and the service's utility. It is necessary to receive the informed consent of the user previous to the start any action (e.g. collection of information, testing, etc). Once the voluntaries understand the evaluation process, the technology and the scenario testing can begin. Finally, post-test questionnaires must be filling out to gain final results of the experiment.

2.4 Finishing the Evaluation Process and Dissemination

When the project ends, it should be taken into account that several devises might need to be uninstalled. If so, there are four main tasks to be carried out:

Devices management: users who have been testing the devices during the development of the project may keep them, only if an external company takes responsibility for maintenance. If there is no company for that can maintain the service, the entire infrastructure must be uninstalled.

Users' management: users who have been relocated for the testing should be relocated (e.g to a senior dwellings or a senior citizen's home).

Licences and permissions: The termination of the activities and use of the FU centre should be communicated to the owner of the facility/facilities in order to revert the rights acquired previously.

Unregister services: All services contracted, such as water and electrical energy supply or insurances should be cancelled when finishing the testing.

Data obtained from the investigation must be disseminated by specialized and not specialized media such as TV, radio, press, Websites in Internet, etc. The spreading of the information should be carried on from the very beginning of the investigation for people who might be concerned with the topic to be informed while the investigation is been developed.

3   Framework Summary

In this section we summarize the framework. All the neccesary steps are detailed within a common temporal line from the previous legal steps, the definition of the protocol considering ethical guidelines, the technology and users management needed to perform the tests, the dissemination needed all along the project and the final de-installation of technology. All these steps are detailed in figure 1.

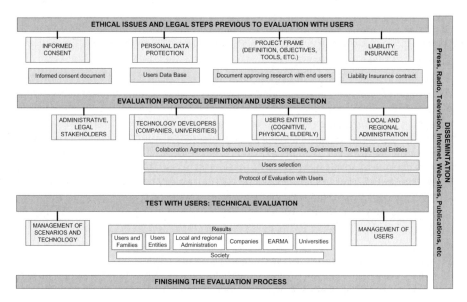

Fig. 1. Resumed scheme of the framework

Figure 1 also shows the stakeholders involved in the whole evaluation and the partial documents and results produced during the process: informed consent document, users database, document approving ethical issues, liability insurance, collaboration agreements, protocol of evaluation and final results.

4 Conclusions

In this paper we have presented a multidisciplinary framework for IT evaluation in social scenarios. Traditionally, technology evaluation only focuses on questionnaires and results. This framework expands the concept many other issues important to the end users, e.g legal, ethical and social issues. We include the legal and ethical steps that are necessary to carry out when working with end users: liability insurance, informend consent, users' database with adequate protection, and ethical commitee approval. We also provide guidelines for a multidisciplinary design of the evaluation protocol and user's selection. The participation of all the stakeholders implicated in the scenarios is of key importance. In this aspect would be interesting to sign collaboration agreements between institutions, user associations, universities, companies, etc. The framework also includes important matters concerning user and technology management to ensure correct testing of the technology.

Acknowledgments

This work was supported in part by the by the European Union, under the projects MonAMI and EasyLine+.

References

1. Ballantine, J.A., Galliers, R.D., Stray, S.J.: Information systems/technology evaluation practices: evidence from UK organizations. Journal of Information Technology 11, 129–141
2. Demers, L., Monette, M., Lapierre, Y., Arnold, D.L., Wolfson, C.: Reliability, validity, and applicability of the Quebec User Evaluation of Satisfaction with Assistive Technology (QUEST 2.0) for adults with multiple sclerosis. Disability and Rehabilitation 24, 21–30 (2002)
3. Day, H., Jutai, J., Campbell, K.: Development of a scale to measure the psychosocial impact of assistive devices: lessons learned and the road ahead. Disability and Rehabilitation 24, 31–37 (2002)
4. Goodman, G., Tiene, D., Luft, P.: Adoption of assistive technology for computer access among college students with disabilities. Disability and Rehabilitation 24, 80–92 (2002)
5. Shone, S.M., Ryan, S., Rigby, P.J., Jutai, J.W.: Toward a comprehensive evaluation of the impact of electronic aids to daily living: evaluation of consumer satisfaction. Disability and Rehabilitation 24, 115–125 (2002)
6. Scherer, J., Cushman, L.A.: Measuring subjective quality of life following spinal cord injury: a validation study of the assistive technology device predisposition assessment. Disability and Rehabilitation 23, 387–393 (2001)
7. World Medical Association, Declaration Of Helsinki about Ethical Principles for Medical Research Involving Human Subjects. Last revision (2004)

The Knowledge Society Agenda in Romania: From Experts' Vision to Public Perception

Horatiu Dragomirescu[1] and Florin Gheorghe Filip[2,3]

[1] Bucharest University of Economics - ASE, 6 Piata Romana, Bucharest 010374, Romania
[2] Romanian Academy, 125 Calea Victoriei, Bucharest 010071, Romania
[3] National Institute of Economic Research, 13 Calea 13 Septembrie,
Bucharest 050711, Romania

Abstract. The paper pertains to operationalising the Knowledge Society concept in Romania, following two lines of inquiry: a) drawing insights from a foresight exercise undertaken by domestic experts for vision-building purposes, and b) assessing the current public perception on the respective issue and proposing a desirable alternative to it. At experts' vision level, the experience with a Romanian Academy's project, with a Delphi survey as its core, is described. At the public perception level, a set of cliché-type implicit assumptions, assumed to be shared country-wide, is specified, against which a set of descriptors corresponding to an informed awareness stage is proposed. The main conclusion consists in recognising that gradually reaching the convergence between experts' vision and public informed awareness on the Knowledge Society agenda appears to be a pre-requisite for the advance of this new society type in Romania.

Keywords: concept operationalisation, knowledge society, public perception, vision.

1 Introduction

According to Lytras and Sicilia, the Knowledge Society can be defined in terms of a comprehensive set of entities and relationships that underlie knowledge performance: *"Knowledge Society is a new strategic position of our society where the Social and the Economic perspective is concentrated on the exploitation of emerging technologies, and well-defined knowledge and learning infrastructures are the main vehicles for the implementation of knowledge and learning strategies. The final milestone is a society with access to knowledge and learning for everyone"* [1].

Romania's integration in the Europe of Knowledge involves the operationalisation of the Knowledge Society concept at a national level, based upon rendering the respective concept intelligible in a pragmatic sense, well beyond the status of a metaphor [2] that could, at most, just suggest the modality and path of the societal evolution in the post-industrial era.

In the recent scholarly literature, most of the operationalisation attempts concerning the Knowledge Society take a predominantly quantitative perspective, related to metrics - such as scores and composite indexes - of the various aspects of this society's

M.D. Lytras et al. (Eds.): WSKS 2008, CCIS 19, pp. 24–31, 2008.

development at either country level or cross-countries, e.g. member states of the European Union, of the OECD etc.

For instance, Spangenberg [3] designed a comprehensive set of indicators oriented towards both knowledge and Information & Communications Technology (ICT), that enable quantifying the sustainability of the Knowledge Society in a multi-dimensional framework that include economic, social, environmental and institutional aspects, further interlinked along three main axes: socio-economic, economic-institutional and socio-institutional.

As to the composite indexes, Barzilai-Nahon [4] reviewed the Digital Access Index, devised by the International Telecommunication Union, the Network Readiness Index (NRI), proposed by the World Economic Forum, INSEAD, and InfoDev, and the Digital Divide Index (DIDIX); the latter is aimed at measuring the digital divide - thought of as an expression of knowledge gaps - on an aggregate level, with a focus on disadvantaged social groups, facing exposure to diverse risk factors [5].

More recently, the Digital Opportunity Index (DOI) was devised, which is based on 11 ICT indicators, grouped in three categories - opportunity, infrastructure and utilization, - that renders it a useful benchmarking tool [6]. According to the World Information Society Report [7], Romania ranked the 50th among the 181 countries surveyed, its DOI level of 0,52 (similar to Turkey's and Russian Federation's) placing it at the bottom of the high-level DOI country group; the top three positions on this scale are held by South Korea (0,8), Japan (0,77), and Denmark (0.76).

Operationalisation attempts of a qualitative nature are also reported in the recent literature. For instance, the sustainable Knowledge Society concept was proposed in this line of inquiry; it is stated to represent a desirable alternative against extrapolating the New Economy model, that would lead, in the long run, to unsustainability, *"not so much in economic competitiveness, as in relation to social problems (loss of cohesion, growing disparities) and to environmental problems"*[8].

2   Case Study: Experts' Vision-Building on the Knowledge Society Advance in Romania through a Foresight Exercise

In accordance with the growing interest worldwide in foresight studies on Knowledge Society topics, the Romanian Academy unfolded, in 2001-2002, a priority project of a futures research type, aimed at contributing to the vision-building process pertaining to the advance of this new type of society in Romania [9].

2.1 Background of the Project

The IS - KS project was carried out entirely autonomously from the institutional point of view, due to the particular status of the Romanian Academy as the country's main scientific and cultural institution, politically neutral.

Before the respective project being launched, the distinction between the Information Society and the Knowledge Society was rather vague in domestic perception, both to the public and decision-makers; moreover, the importance of the IS - KS issue for Romania was officially recognised in declarative, rather than strategic commitment terms. Therefore, one of the main endeavours of the early

2000's consisted of facilitating the shift from reflection to action in the field of IS - KS, so that this issue held a top position not only on the research agenda, but also on the policy and decision-making one.

2.2 Account of Main Facts and Insights Drawn

The core part of the project consisted of a Delphi survey [10], devoted to (1) conceptually structuring the IS - KS issue, (2) evaluating the existing state of IS - KS in Romania and pointing out the trends, (3) formulating strategic options at national level, and (4) defining landmarks and options relevant to major stakeholders (policy and administrative decision-makers, academic and professional communities, business sector, mass-media etc.).

The Delphi technique was applied through an Internet-based survey, panelists were experts specializing in fields directly related to the main aspects of the IS – KS subject (ICT, economics, social sciences, cognitive sciences, law etc.) and got proactively involved on a voluntary (no fee) basis. Under these circumstances, the costs incurred were rather negligible, However, this proved to be the right choice versus the alternative of having a foresight study contracted with a consultancy.

The Delphi survey contributed to confirming the hypothesis proposed by Drăgănescu [11], that progressing towards the Knowledge Society appears to be a priority for Romania's near future, that could be achieved through a leapfrog-type evolution; moreover, the explicit link between the IS - KS issue and Romania's accession to the European Union was evidenced.

The IS - KS project became a reference for other subsequent national foresight works, also stimulating research interest and further participation of domestic experts in international future-oriented studies.

3   Public Perceptions on the Knowledge Society Issue in Romania: from Implicit Pre-suppositions to Informed Awareness

Clarifying public perception regarding the Knowledge Society issues draws its major importance from the fact that Romania, as a member state of the European Union, has to be an integral part not only of the internal market and of the communitary institutional system, but also of the European Research and Higher Education Area.

Relying upon implicit presuppositions, that is understanding the Knowledge Society syntagm intuitively only, has led to cliché-type public perceptions, which can distort understanding and action of the social actors involved in the respective process, the persistence of which could affect Romania's positioning within the Europe of Knowledge. Should one agree that we are "witnessing a change from a social world in which 'things' simply 'happened' to a world in which things are more and more 'made' to happen" [12], an alternative set of explicit representations regarding the fulfillment of the Knowledge Society objectives in Romania is hereby formulated in terms of the desideratum of a public informed awareness, which can be articulated into a paramount strategic vision.

A parallel between the two sets of perceptions is given in table 1.

Table 1. Sets of public perceptions concerning Knowledge Society in Romania

Cliché-type perceptions in place, based upon implicit presuppositions	Perceptions corresponding to the desideratum of informed awareness
- Developing the Knowledge Society in Romania represents an alignment to a global trend	- Developing the Knowledge Society in Romania is fostered by the existence of a publicly shared aspiration towards this type of society
- Knowledge Society in Romania is a medium term future issue	- The Knowledge Society in Romania is a priority of the near future and requires immediate action
- The Knowledge Society endeavour is relevant for economically developed countries in the first place	- The Knowledge Society advance (filling the knowledge gaps) can and should be synchronised with the process of fulfilling the economic convergence (filling the development gaps)
- Promoting Knowledge Society relies mainly upon intellectual elites	- Promoting the Knowledge Society involves concurrent contributions from a wide range of individual and collective actors
- The main factor of the evolution by the Knowledge Society is represented by e-readiness	- The evolution towards the Knowledge Society depends upon the widespread presence of its typical mentalities, patterns and practices

Source: our elaboration.

The corresponding perceptions belonging to the two sets are comparatively analysed below, in terms of their specific content and implications.

a). Perceptions regarding the essence of the society evolution process: from just an alignment to a global trend towards the assertion of a Romanian vocation regarding the Knowledge Society

At the level of the common understanding presently in place, the advance of the Knowledge Society is perceived as an expression of a global trend, supposed to become manifest, sooner or later, in different fields of activity and various regions of the world; the processes aimed at aligning with the respective trend would, therefore, implicitly accompany the unfolding of the phenomenon of globalization.

By contrast, an integrated vision concerning promoting Knowledge Society in Romania should take into consideration, besides the above global trend, the actual existence of vocation towards this type of society, as confirmed by the Romanian contribution to the European and world scientific and cultural thesaurus, the important national innovative potential, the higher education system quality and youth openness to the new technologies.

b). Perceptions regarding the time horizon: from the medium-term future towards promoting the Knowledge Society as a near future top priority for Romania.

According to the current public perception, the Knowledge Society progress in Romania appears to be targeted towards the medium or even long-term future; due to current digital divide and information illiteracy affecting less favoured regions of the country, mainly rural communities, it might appear to some that it would perhaps be too early for engaging on the path towards the Knowledge Society.

Within an alternative approach, the existing knowledge and digital infrastructure gaps could actually be outrun through the agency of short-run triggering out leap-type development rendered possible mainly by ICT implementation within matured organizational and societal systems.

c). Perceptions regarding the process relevance: from an advanced countries privilege towards synchronising the knowledge-based development with fulfilling economic convergence Europe-wide.

Considering the Knowledge Society as an objective to be approached by advanced states originates from the assumption that, with them, the knowledge-based economy is already functional, while in the rest of countries it either lies at incipient stages or is still a desideratum only.

The development gaps occurred along the industrial era seem to inhibit the Knowledge Society advance in the affected countries, thus limiting both the resources designed towards such an evolution and the knowledge generation, absorption and use. The development gaps can be correlated with the knowledge-related ones and vicious circles appear between them, thus leading to amplifying problematic effects on both sides.

As a alternative to the above delineated cliché, an systemic representation might be adopted, consisting in concurrently unfolding the catching-up process and promoting the Knowledge Society objectives in Romania; this would, in turn, entail an adequate management of both the economic development gaps and the knowledge-related ones.

d). Perceptions regarding promoters: from an intellectual elite's concern towards active participation of a wide range of social actors.

A possible explanation of the social actors' relatively neutral, contemplative position as against the Knowledge Society issues resides in the existing implicit presupposition that this undertaking should be reserved to intellectual elites, which act from inside the research, educational and cultural system to the other activity sectors' benefit.

An alternative to this perception consists in promoting the Knowledge Society as a multi-actor undertaking, entailing active contributions of a wide range of participants [13]: business companies, education, research and cultural institutions, the public administration and citizens, all these fields of application apt to evolve towards a knowledge-based operation, systematically use knowledge work practices, and explicitly act as producers and users of new ideas and insights.

As pointed out by Mongardini, *"the phenomenology of the social as complex fact should be tackled not from ideal images, those of synthesis, and valuatively open to discussion, of society, class, elite, etc., but at its source: as a relation of configuration which continually reproduces itself, between sociality as a constitutive form of collective life, and the dimension of individuality directed towards the social, which internally reproduces sociality and on the basis of that structures individual life"* [14].

e). Perceptions regarding the systemic change sources: from the digital technologies revolution towards the Knowledge Society technological and functional vectors.

The digital technologies revolution can be synthetically defined through the *e* factor's exponential dynamics, resulting in a rapid succession of the generations of ICT solutions, as well as the Internet expansion as an infrastructure hosting a wide range of activities typical to the contemporary economy and society: e-business, e-government, e-learning etc. The *e* factor has decisively contributed to the evolution from the industrial society to the information society, as illustrated by the growth of the information sector of the advanced economies and the development of the ICT networked infrastructure at national and global scale.

All these elements, although required as pre-conditions, are not sufficient for evolving from the Information Society to the Knowledge one, as the sources of this change cannot be limited to the sophistication of the technological infrastructure and the ICT wider application. As Jaarl Bengtsson emphasised, referring to the globalizing contemporary socio-economic system, *"the amount, nature and purpose of the processes aimed at producing, disseminating and using knowledge are the brain, while the ICT are its heart"* [15].

A particular attention should be paid to ensuring the necessary match between the vanguard generations of advanced ICTs, such as, for instance, the semantic web [16] and, respectively, the generations of organizational patterns and practices adopted for implementing them; knowledge work can be catalysed by enacting community-type frameworks and collaborative configurations of project-based action as opposed to rigid, mechanistic organizational patterns and obsolete, "myopic" management conducts.

Innovation, collaborative design and learning as paramount provinces of the transition towards the Knowledge Society presuppose, on their promoters' behalf, not only a proactive behaviour and an inquiring spirit in search of novelty, but also the assumption of a responsible legitimacy ethics, aimed at harmonising the creative commitment with morality in managing both knowing as a process and the resulting individual, organizational and social knowledge.

4   Implications and Prospects

Getting to both an experts' vision and an informed public awareness appear to be pre-requisites for the advance of the Knowledge Society in Romania. However, these would be still insufficient, as the expected progress could not emerge bottom-up only; it also involves, as a top-down complement, adequate policy support and government sustained endorsement, based upon relevant foresight studies. In addition, according to Tsipouri [17], in the European Union member and candidate states, certain supranational interventions, of the kind of the Regional Information Society Initiative (RISI), should also be conducted.

In Romania's case, the "Knowledge-Based Economy" project [18], launched by the Government in 2005, with financial support from the World Bank, is aimed at setting up about 200 telecentres meant to provide citizens, mainly in rural areas and small towns, with access to information and online services; the respective undertaking is actually of a catching-up type, as it consists of accomplishing still unfulfilled, but stringently urgent tasks pertaining to the preceding, Information Society stage.

Being a multi-purpose, multi-stakeholder process, Knowledge Society development at a national scale is best supported by a co-operative framework, based upon a referential such as the Triple Helix of university – industry – government; to this end, the respective model, already institutionalised in several countries as a partnership for innovation, should be extended through including a fourth helix, that is the public (citizens), as suggested by its own initiators, Etzkowitz and Leydesdorff [19]. This could be a path towards promoting the Knowledge Society as an *"expert society for democratizing knowledge"*, as proposed by Scardamalia [20]. In Šlaus's words, *"Each country has to find its own way to build knowledge-based society, but the best model is that patterned after the development of science. Not only that humankind has achieved its greatest successes in science, but scientific activity is also an example of a free, open society"* [21].

5 Conclusions

In the early 21st century, the Knowledge Society is recognised and tackled as a major theme for futures research at both national and international level.

Fulfilling the Knowledge Society objectives in Romania requires from the relevant social actors - business companies, educational, scientific and cultural institutions, public administration, citizens - an immediate, convergent and integrated vision-oriented action; the IS - KS project carried out in the early 2000's under the aegis of the Romanian Academy represented a pioneering national foresight exercise, that substantially contributed to the crystallisation of such a vision on the prospects and stakes of this new society's advance over a 10 years horizon.

Consequently, a must is getting at an adequate, informed awareness at the public level, on the Knowledge Society issues, by replacing some clichés which distort understanding of the relevance, priority, feasibility and determinism of the advance towards this new societal development stage. As milestones in creating an articulated public perception in this respect, one should consider tackling Romania's aspiration and commitment towards the Knowledge Society, synchronising the own knowledge-based development with the catching-up process of economic convergence Europe-wide, as well as promoting the Knowledge Society objectives with means peculiar to the very essence of this type of society.

References

1. Lytras, M.D., Sicilia, M.A.: The Knowledge Society: a Manifesto for Knowledge and Learning. Int. J. Knowledge and Learning 1, 1–11 (2005)
2. Ungar, S.: Misplaced Metaphor: A Critical Analysis of the Knowledge Society. Canadian Rev. Sociology & Anthropology 40, 331–347 (2003)
3. Spangenberg, J.: Will the Information Society be Sustainable? Towards Criteria and Indicators for a Sustainable Knowledge Society. Int. J. Innovation and Sustainable Development 1, 83–102 (2005)

4. Barzilai-Nahon, K.: Gaps and Bits: Conceptualizing Measurements for Digital Divide/s. The Information Society 22, 269–278 (2006)
5. Hüsing, T., Selhofer, H.: DIDIX: A Digital Divide Index for Measuring Inequality in IT Diffusion. IT & Society 1, 21–38 (2004)
6. Sciada, G. (ed.): From the Digital Divide to Digital Opportunities. Measuring Infostates for Development. ORBICOM in association with NRC Press, Canada Institute for Scientific and Technical Information, Montreal (2005)
7. ITU/UNCTAD: World Information Society Report: Beyond WSIS. International Telecommunication Union, Geneva, 164–168 (2007)
8. Fontela, E.: Toward a Sustainable Knowledge Society. Reports of Expert Group in Key Technologies for Europe, Brussels (2005)
9. Filip, F.G., Dragomirescu, H., Predescu, R., Ilie, R.: IT Tools for Foresight Studies. Stud. Informatics and Control 13, 161–168 (2004)
10. Filip, F.G., Dragomirescu, H.: Report on the Outcome of the Delphi Survey on the Information Society - Knowledge Society in Romania. J. Ec. Forecasting 4, 99–104 (2001)
11. Drăgănescu, M.: Information and Knowledge Society. Vectors of the Knowledge Society. In: Filip, F.G. (ed.) Information Society - Knowledge Society. Concepts, Solutions and Strategies for Romania, pp. 43–112. Expert Publishing House, Bucharest (2001) (in Romanian)
12. Stehr, N.: Societal Transformations, Globalisation and the Knowledge Society. Int. J. of Knowledge and Learning 3, 139–153 (2007)
13. Kalfoglou, Y.: Knowledge Society Arguments Revisited in the Semantic Technologies Era. Int. J. of Knowledge and Learning 3, 225–244 (2007)
14. Mongardini, C.: From Society to the Social Actor: A Reconsideration of Agency and its Determinants in Sociological Analysis. Int. Sociology 2, 403–417 (1987)
15. Bengtsson, J.: Higher Education: Trends and Challenges. In: 15th International Conference on Higher Education. The Impact of Higher Education on the Development of Community and Society, Irbid, 30 August - 2 September (2001)
16. Naeve, A.: The Human Semantic Web. Shifting from Knowledge Push to Knowledge Pull, Int. J. of Semantic Web and Information Systems 1, 1–30 (2005)
17. Tsipouri, L.: Europe and the Information Society: Problems and Challenges for Supranational Intervention. J. of Comparative Policy Analysis 2, 301–319 (2000)
18. European Commission, http://www.epractice.eu/document/580
19. Leydesdorff, L., Etzkowitz, H.: Can The Public be Considered as a Fourth Helix in University–Industry–Government Relations? In: Report on the Fourth Triple Helix Conference, 2002, Science and Public Policy, vol. 30, pp. 55–61 (2003)
20. Scardamalia, M.: Knowledge Society Network (KSN): Toward an expert society for democratizing knowledge. J. of Distance Education (Suppl. 3, Learning Technology Innovation in Canada) 17, 63–66 (2003)
21. Šlaus, I.: Political Significance of Knowledge in Southeast Europe. Croat. Med. J. 44, 3–19 (2003)

A Framework for the Knowledge Society Ecosystem:
A Tool for Development

Saad Haj Bakry and Ali Al-Ghamdi

King Saud University, P.O Box 800, 11421, Riyadh, Saudi Arabia
shb@ksu.edu.sa, asghamdi@ksu.edu.sa

Abstract. With the increasing worldwide need for the development of the knowledge society, multi-disciplinary research concerned with the subject is becoming of increasing importance. This paper introduces a framework that provides a comprehensive scope of the knowledge society ecosystem that organizes and integrates its various issues. The framework gives a tool for identifying, structuring, and inter-relating, knowledge society problems that need to be investigated. At the core of the framework is the "knowledge circle", with its activities of knowledge generation, diffusion, and utilization that can lead to sustainable development. The framework considers the basic domains, interacting with these activities, to be based on the STOPE view of "strategy, technology, organization, people, and the environment". The paper addresses the use of the framework as a generic common base for future investigations on the development of the knowledge society.

Keywords: Knowledge society; Knowledge economy; Ecosystem; ICT: information and communication technology; Technology readiness; Third millennium universities.

1 Introduction

Throughout history, knowledge has always been the driving force behind development. Knowledge generation in the past two centuries was unprecedented, and this was reflected by the extend of development that has taken place, which exceeded all past development throughout history. The turn to this 21st century has seen worldwide emphasis on providing further support to knowledge for further development; and there are many examples of this.

At the world level, the United Nations (UN) member states adopted, in September 2000, the Millennium Development Goals (MDG), which included directions toward supporting science and technology innovation and the generation of knowledge [1]. In addition, two world summits, organized by the International Telecommunications Union (ITU), on the development of the information society, were held in Geneva in December 2003, and in Tunis in November 2005 [2].

The World Bank Institute established the Knowledge for Development Program (K4D) for the purpose of promoting knowledge and learning for better world. The

M.D. Lytras et al. (Eds.): WSKS 2008, CCIS 19, pp. 32–44, 2008.

program introduced the Knowledge Assessment Method (KAM) to enable the investigation of knowledge for development issues in countries, so that opportunities and challenges can be identified. The method has "83 variables", "14" of which are considered to be key variables; and these are based on seven main dimensions: overall performance of the economy, economic regime, governance, the innovation system, education, gender, and the information and communications technology (ICT) [3].

In Europe, the European Union (EU) summit, held in Lisbon in March 2000, emphasized the need for transformation to the knowledge society [4]. At the Arab world level, the United Nations Development Program (UNDP) has published a series of reports on Arab human development; the second of these report was specifically on building the knowledge society [5].

Individually, various countries, including Arab countries, have been planning for transformation to the knowledge society. For example, the Saudi government, through its Ministry of Economy and Planning (MOEP), and King Abdulaziz City for Science and Technology (KACST), issued in 2002, the Saudi "National Policy for Science and Technology" . The policy provided directions toward building the knowledge society. At present, national plans are initiating projects for the achievement of this target [6, 7].

Examples in support of the transformation to the knowledge society are not only associated with international organizations or countries, but they are also related to independent organizations, universities, and individuals. The Open Research Society based in Athens, Greece is actively involved in Knowledge Society issues and is the sponsor of the "1st World Summit on the Knowledge Society" to be held in September 2008 [8].

Al-Aghar think tank group in Saudi Arabia is actively involved in promoting ideas and supporting efforts associated with building the knowledge society in the country. In January 2008, it organized a conference in Jeddah, Saudi Arabia, under the logo "Toward a Knowledge Economy" [9]. In addition, the group held several workshops concerned with exchanging views and developing recommendations on future directions toward the knowledge society; the last of which was held in Riyadh, in May 2008, in collaboration with KACST [10].

The largest and oldest university in Saudi Arabia, King Saud University (KSU), is directing its efforts toward contributing to the transformation of the country to the knowledge society; and it is, in some circumstances, giving itself an additional "KSU" name: Knowledge Society University. The university has established many knowledge activities support programs, including a special program on the knowledge society. In October 2008, it is holding its first conference on the "Knowledge Based Economy" [11].

Many individual authors have contributed ideas to the development of the knowledge society. An important example of a book, on the subject, published in English in 2007, is entitled "revolutionary wealth", by Alvin Toffler [12]. Another example of a book, published in Arabic in 2008, is entitled "knowledge society eco-system" by Saad Haj Bakry, one of the authors of this paper [13]. He also had another Arabic book on the subject, published in 2005, and entitled "transformation to the knowledge society [14].

The above review of activities on the development of the knowledge society is of course not exhaustive; it is driven by key examples. From looking at these examples, it is apparent, that no eco-system comprehensive framework for the knowledge society that can organize investigations and support plans is available. Although KAM of the World Bank provides a wide range of indicators, concerned with the knowledge society, these indicators can be improved and re-organized to better represent the full-scope of issues associated with the knowledge society.

This paper attempts to produce the target comprehensive framework that provides a structured based for the issues of the knowledge society eco-system. The framework hopefully gives a common and organized ground for discussing these issues, investigating problems associated with them, and deriving plans for future development. In addition, the paper addresses the use of the framework, and presents examples of problems that need to investigated for better understanding of the current state of the knowledge society, and consequently for better insight into the requirements of its future development plans.

2 The Proposed Framework

Talking about an eco-system opens the ground to trying to identify what is meant by such a system. According to encyclopaedias [15, 16], "ecology" is of Greek origin, and means the "study of". It has been widely used to refer to the "scientific study of relationships of animals, plants and the environment". Based on this an "eco-system" is defined as "any situation where there is relationships between organisms and their environment". From this argument, the proposed framework derives its conceptual principles.

The principles upon which the proposed framework is based are the following:

- identifying knowledge activities upon which the "knowledge society" is based, and establishing the interactions among these activities;
- defining and structuring the "entities" associated with the knowledge activities, according to well-recognized domains; and
- emphasizing the "environment" within which the eco-system behaves, including development "strategy" and directions.

In the following, the proposed framework is described, considering these basic principles.

2.1 Knowledge Activities

There are three main types of knowledge activities that feed the knowledge society with its fresh blood "knowledge". These activities are:

- knowledge generation;
- knowledge diffusion; and
- knowledge utilization.

Knowledge generation is achieved through research and innovation. Research institutions, including advanced universities, are concerned with knowledge generation;

and various organizations, including schools and the other dedicated institutions, encourage innovation, and support the innovation culture. Knowledge diffusion among human resources is the role of all education institutions, in addition to the media. Knowledge utilization is the function of business organizations, including those of the private sector, and those of the public sector, whether delivering products or providing services.

Knowledge utilization organizations, receive their required business knowledge, in the form of ideas and human skills, from knowledge generation and knowledge diffusion institutions. However, these three main types of knowledge activities are, to a large extend, disconnected, and generally working in isolation, as illustrated in Figure 1.

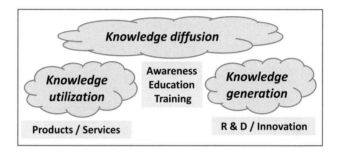

Fig. 1. Knowledge activities disconnected

The proposed framework emphasizes that knowledge activities should be closely connected, so that knowledge is generated and diffused toward effective utilization, and support to development. Figure 2 shows how the knowledge activities can be structured as a circle, with each main type of activity supporting the others, and all together reaching out to contributing to sustainable development. This circle can be called the knowledge circle, or the "knowledge and development circuit", which is the core of the knowledge society.

The "knowledge and development circle (KDC)" is driven by various living entities; and these entities are introduced in the following.

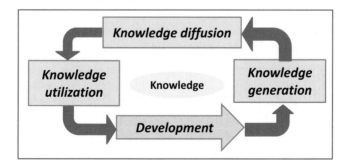

Fig. 2. Knowledge & development circle: KDC

2.2 Knowledge Entities

Entities concerned with the knowledge and development circle can be structured according to three main domains: "technology, organization and people (TOP)". These domains have been used, in the past, in various studies concerned with national development [17]. In his related work, Bakry has added two other domains: strategy and the development environment (SE). He used the five domains STOPE in different studies, and example of these is given in [18].

Although SE domains may not include living entities like TOP domains, they include development procedures, interaction rules, current state features, and future development directions. Considering STOPE, the general structure of the proposed framework is illustrated in Figure 3. In the following, the TOP domains are addressed; and this followed by considering the SE domains.

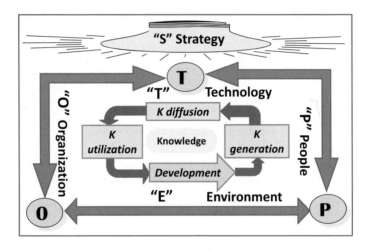

Fig. 3. A view of the knowledge society ecosystem

"Technology" is, of course, a major player in the knowledge society. It can be viewed as associated with two dimensions:

- knowledge society, or knowledge sensitive technologies; and
- ICT: information and communication technology.

Knowledge society technologies are the knowledge sensitive technologies that can lead to products and services from which wealth can be generated, and jobs can be created. Ambitious countries give priorities to reaching an edge in such technologies, so that they can enhance their development. Ireland, for example, has done so by giving priority to information technology and to bio-technology; and being successful in doing so, it has achieved remarkable development [19].

ICT is not only among the above knowledge society technologies, but it also has another important function. It supports doing things: faster, cheaper, better, more secure, and with a difference that lead to new opportunities (FCBSD). By doing so, the use of this technology leads to efficient management, in practically all fields of business, at the personal level, organization level, national level, and the international level [18].

"Organizations" concerned with knowledge include those associated with knowledge generation, knowledge diffusion, and knowledge utilization, as discussed above. These organizations may be competing with one another, or they may be working together in partnerships. Both competitions and partnerships may be national or international; and they are viewed as useful for the advancement of the knowledge society. Competitions usually support creativity, and partnerships usually provide synergy.

There are also other organizations concerned with the knowledge society. These include government organizations directing and supporting national development. They may also include private and civil society organizations, in addition to international organizations, concerned with national and world development.

"People" are, of course, the core of the knowledge society. They are there along the path of KDC: the knowledge and development circle. They are the originators of knowledge, and they are the target of knowledge diffusion. In addition, they work toward knowledge utilization, and they enjoy its development outcome.

It is important to the knowledge society to have active people along the path of the knowledge development circle. For this purpose, what may be called the "knowledge sense" should be developed in people, so that the circle is activated, and enhanced development is achieved. This sense is not only associated with educational qualifications, but it is also related to interest and enthusiasm; and this is affected by the knowledge environment, and by future development plans, which are addressed in the following.

2.3 Knowledge Environment and Strategy

The knowledge environment can promote, and can also demote, the activities of KDC; and can consequently contribute positively, or may be negatively, to the knowledge society. It can be viewed as associated with four main dimensions: social, cultural, economical, and organizational.

For identifying the knowledge environment, the issues considered by the world bank KAM, can be taken into account. These issues are given in Table 1, together with the total number knowledge indicators and the number of key knowledge indicators associated with each of these issue [3]. The Table also includes examples of the indicators related to the various issues.

The presentation given in [10] address the innovation environment and includes six elements, starting with the letter "i", and called the "6 (I)". These elements can also be partly considered in identifying the knowledge environment. These elements are given in Table 2; which shows that they are not far from the issues considered by KAM. Both can be combined, with new ideas and other related experiences, so that better understanding, and enhanced assessment indicators of the knowledge environment can be produced.

Table 1. World Bank Knowledge Assessment Method (KAM) indicators [3]

Issue	Key indicators	Total indicators	Examples
Innovation system	3	24	Number of journal articles per million people.
Education	3	14	Adult literacy (15 and above: %)
Gender	0	5	Females in labour force (%)
ICT	3	12	Computers per thousand people.
Economic performance	2	9	Annual GDP growth (%)
Economic regime	1	12	Tariff and non-tariff barriers.
Governance	2	7	Rule of law: security.
(Total)	14	83	(An integrated view).

Table 2. The "6 (I)" view of the innovation environment [10]

(I) issue	Identification
Intellectual capital	Education and training / Entrepreneurship
Interaction	Interaction with the general public
Incentives	Financial support: funds & future markets.
Infrastructure	Physical & digital
Integrity systems	Processes, governance, practices, benchmarks, & security
Institutions policy	Directions and cooperations.

Supporting the environment would enhance the contribution of the entities of the knowledge society eco-system, given in Figure 3, to the activation of KDC. This should be considered in the development of strategies, plans and projects for the development of the knowledge society.

Figure 4 gives a view of the levels of planning for the development of the knowledge society. On top comes the national strategy, with its wide scope vision, and mission, and other strategic directions. Based on this national strategy comes the individual plans of the organizations; and their potential joint plans. The plans would require projects for practical implementation, and evaluation measures for monitoring and adjusting the required development.

Continuous development would be needed for achieving proactive response to change and to competition. In this respect, the six-sigma circular phases of "define, measure, analyze, improve, control: DMAIC" can be used [20].

As an example of initiating a strategy, proposed vision and mission for a targeted knowledge society, are given in [13], and are presented in Table 3 for review.. The procedural development of these vision and mission are based on the principles in [20], where the vision is considered to be looking at the target "benefits", while the mission is considered to be concerned with the target "functions".

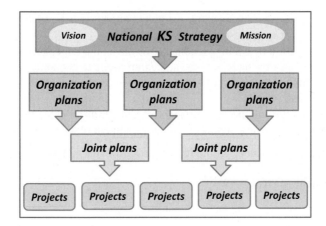

Fig. 4. Levels of planning

Table 3. An example of a vision and a mission for the knowledge society [13]

"S" issue	Proposed text
Vision	*Reaching and maintaining a state of knowledge excellence, associated with profound capabilities for the country and the people, and enhanced by distinguished development, with remarkable contributions to the human civilization.*
Mission	*Building an integrated knowledge eco-system that: supports the knowledge circle of knowledge generation, diffusion and utilization; enhances its activation through national and international cooperation; and making maximum use of its human, social and economic benefits, while using best tools for the achievement of this purpose.*

3   Using the Framework

The framework described above illustrates the scope of the knowledge society eco-system, and represents it in a generic, structured, and consequently flexible form. It reflects the multi-disciplinary nature of the problems associated with the knowledge society, and helps inter-relating them. Considering these features, the framework enables the refinement of the issues concerned with the knowledge society, and its associated problems, in an organized and integrated manner. This would help reaching deep into the problems and sub-problems of the knowledge society, while maintaining full comprehension of the various issues related to them.

The framework can therefore be used as a tool for well-organized investigations of knowledge society problems, and for devising plans for future development. The world bank KAM can help such studies [3], but not in the comprehensive manner illustrated by the framework, and not with the needed depth in understanding the problems considered, as will be discussed below.

In the following, four potential knowledge society problems are addressed, as examples of the problems that should be considered by researchers interested in the field. These problems include the following:

- Development of meaningful, credible and well-structured knowledge society assessment measures;
- Investigation of country readiness for developing specific knowledge intensive or sensitive technologies, and contributing to economic growth;
- Investigation of ICT utilization, and their support to the activation of the KDC; and
- Investigation of the requirements of the third-millennium universities that would provide new support to the development of the knowledge society.

Each of these examples of problems is addressed in the following.

3.1 Assessment Measures

Lord "Kelvin", the well-known 19th century scientist, once said: "when you can measure what you are speaking about, and express it in numbers, you know something about it; but when you cannot measure it, when you cannot express it in numbers, your knowledge is of a meager and unsatisfactory kind [13]". This explains why assessment measures are needed to complement the proposed framework of the knowledge society eco-system.

According to the nature of the proposed KDC and STOPE domains framework, multi-disciplinary, comprehensive, and well structured measures for the assessment of the knowledge society state, and the derivation of sound future development plans, need to be devised. Such measures would be of two main types:

- Generic measures that can be applied in practically all case-studies with different circumstances; and
- Specific measures that are associated with certain problems and case-studies.

The World Bank KAM indicators can be associated with the generic measures. However, these indicators suffer from a "substantial problem", when applied to different countries. The indicators are, in many cases, associated with the population, providing "measures per certain population volume" [3]. This is obviously misleading, since the age distribution differs among different countries.

It is of course unrealistic to apply such measures to countries with "50 %", or more, of its population being "20 years or under"; and also equally apply the same measures to countries with "20 %", or less, of its population being "20 years or under". Therefore, in the future, before considering KAM indicators among the generic measures, they need to be adjusted; and this would require a well-guided study, supported with global discussion.

The specific measures will be addressed below.

3.2 Readiness for New Technologies and Economic Development

One of the general definitions of the "knowledge economy" is that it is "the economy in which the generation and exploitation of knowledge has come to play a predominant part in the creation of wealth [21]". It has also been defined, in more specific terms as "the economy where knowledge is at the heart of value added, from high-tech manufacturing and ICT, through knowledge intensive services, to the overtly creative industries such as media and architecture [21]".

According to the above, countries wishing to explore knowledge-based economic development may choose to emphasize manufacturing, or providing services, based on knowledge sensitive technologies. This would require activating the knowledge circle, with regards to these technologies, for achieving the target development. This would require "looking before leaping", and here comes the need for investigating the readiness of the country for the attractive technologies concerned.

With its generic and elaborate features, the proposed framework of the knowledge society eco-system can be used as a base for the development of readiness assessment models, for different knowledge sensitive technologies, with regards to their association with various countries. Such models would consider KDC and its interaction with the various STOPE domains, together with the potential benefits. Generic and specific assessment measures may be developed and included in these models.

3.3 The ICT Role

ICT, with its FCBSD benefits, given above, provides an important dimension to the knowledge economy [18]. It represents one of the key features of the knowledge economy, as "it allows firms to exploit scientific and technical knowledge bases to give them an unprecedented competitive edge [21]". It is therefore important to investigate the ICT role in the knowledge society, for the purpose of enhancing its positive impact.

The proposed framework helps identifying the issues associated with the target investigation. The investigation would be mainly concerned with two important:

- ICT scientific and technical development and its impact on activating the knowledge circle, and the development of the knowledge society; and
- ICT governance and how to achieve its required objectives of maximizing both the efficiency and the effectiveness of ICT utilization.

An example of new development in ICT that can support the knowledge society is grid computing, which allows easy establishment of virtual computing environments, for virtual organizations, and for joint projects around the world [22]. With regards to ICT governance, while there are various ICT governance standards, their application seems to be facing difficulties. In addition, no single standard document, that accommodate the various governance requirements, is available as a reference for IT governance practices [23]. Therefore, work on the subject, to support ICT contribution to KDC and to the knowledge society, is needed.

3.4 Third Millennium Universities

Universities, as we know them, are the product of the second millennium; and over centuries they have had a successful role in promoting knowledge and supporting development [24]. However, the changing knowledge environment, and the need for transformation to the knowledge society, are leading to calls for opening new dimensions to what universities can do, and should do in the future [25]. The European Union (EU), in its Lisbon strategy, has recognized this, and identified universities as "important moving forces for achieving the EU goal of establishing the knowledge society" [26].

By presenting a comprehensive view of the knowledge society ecosystem, the proposed framework would provide a common ground for investigating and planning the role of universities in the new third millennium. The framework considers universities in its "organization" dimension, as knowledge organizations. Important examples and issues that should be promoted by the third millennium universities include: knowledge culture; research driven education; multi-disciplinary studies; technology incubators; science parks; "research, demonstration and development (RD&D) not only R&D [27]".

4 Remarks and Conclusions

Recognizing the increasing importance of transformation to the knowledge society, this paper has presented a tool for the development of the knowledge society ecosystem. The tool provides a generic base that gives a comprehensive view of the knowledge society, in a structured and well-organized manner. This generic base organizes the knowledge activities in an "integrated knowledge circle" that can lead to development (KDC); views the entities concerned through the domains of "technology, organizations and people (TOP)", and considers the development conditions associated with "environment and strategy (ES)"

The paper advocated the use of its tool in future investigations. It presented examples of fields that can be taken into account for enhancing the development of the knowledge society. They include: the development of knowledge society assessment measures; investigations of readiness for new technologies; studying the ICT role in the development of the knowledge society; and investigating the future of universities, by exploring their role in the emerging third millennium.

In conclusion, the paper calls for further discussions on the framework, and on its future improvement and refinement. It welcomes views on using the framework for future investigations on the development of the knowledge society. It also hopes to see researchers and planners developing models and empirical investigations based on the framework, or perhaps its modified versions. Having a common ground agreed on such studies would support the integration of the studies and ease the use of their benefits.

Finally, it should be noted that we all need to work together toward a society that: create ideas and innovate useful knowledge; diffuse knowledge and make it available to all; and apply knowledge and utilize it, not only for the benefit of some, but also for the benefit of all mankind. A world based on ethical competition and genuine cooperation in knowledge development and utilization, with positive attitude, is a world of peace and prosperity for all.

References

1. UN Millennium Development Goals (MDG) (accessed May 2008), `http://ddp-ext.worldbank.org/ext/GMIS/home.do?siteId=2`
2. ITU World Summit of the Information Society (accessed May 2008), `http://www.itu.int/net/search/searchframe.aspx`
3. World Bank, Knowledge for Development Program, Knowledge Assessment Method (KAM) (accessed May 2008), `http://www.worldbank.org/kam`
4. European Information Society (accessed May 2008), `http://ec.europa.eu/information_society/index_en.htm`
5. UNDP Arab Human Development Reports, 2nd Report: Building the Knowledge Society (2003) (accessed May 2008), `http://www.undp.org/arabstates/PDF2005/AHDR4_04.pdf`
6. National Science and Technology Policy for the Kingdom of Saudi Arabia, Saudi Ministry of Planning and King Abdulaziz City for Science and Technology, Riyadh, Saudi Arabia (2003)
7. King Abdulaziz City for Science and Technology (accessed May 2008), `http://www.kacst.edu.sa`
8. Open Research Society (accessed May 2008), http://www.open-knowledge-society.org
9. News on Al-Aghar think tank group in Saudi Arabia (accessed May 2008), `http://www.arabnews.com/?page=7esection=0rarticle=105446=d=9=m=1=y=2008`
10. Shariffadeen, M.A.: National innovation eco-system (NIE): Introductory remarks. In: Al-Aghar and KACST workshop on NIE, Riyadh, May 1-2 (2008) (2008)
11. King Saud University (accessed May 2008), `http://www.ksu.edu.sa`
12. Toffler, A., Toffler, T.: Revolutionary Wealth: How it will be created and how it will change our lives. Doubleday Business publication, USA (2007)
13. Bakry, S.H.: Knowledge Society Eco-System: In the watching eyes and hopeful minds. King Saud University publication, Saudi Arabia (2008)
14. Bakry, S.H.: Transformation to the Knowledge Society. King Abdulaziz Public Library publication, Saudi Arabia (2005)
15. Academic American Encyclopaedia, vol. 7. Arête Publishing Company, New Jersey (1981)
16. Wikipedia (accessed May 2008), `http://en.wikipedia.org/wiki/Ecology`
17. Linstone, H.A.: New era-new challenge, Technological Forecasting and Social Change: An International Journal (North-Holland). Special Silver Anniversary Issue (1969-1994) 47(1), 1–21 (1994)
18. Bakry, S.H.: Development of e-government: A STOPE view. International Journal of Network Management (Wiley Inter-Science) 14(6), 339–350 (2004)
19. Glass, A.: The culture of innovation. In: The First Saudi Innovation Exhibition, Riyadh, Saudi Arabia, King Abdulaziz and his Companions Foundation for Giftedness and Creativity, 9-12 (March 2008)
20. De Feo, J.A., Barnard, W.W.: Juran Institute Six Sigma: Breakthrough and Beyond: Quality Performance Breakthrough Methods. McGraw-Hill, New York (2004)
21. Brinkly, I.: Defining the knowledge economy, Knowledge economy program report, the Work Foundation, London, UK (July 2006), `http://www.theworkfoundation.com`
22. Arafah, M.A., Al-Harbi, H., Bakry, S.H.: Grid computing: a STOPE view. International Journal of Network Management (Wiley Inter-Science) 17(4), 295–305 (2007)
23. Weill, P., And Ross, J.W.: IT Governance: How Top Performers Manage IT Decision Rights for Superior Results. Harvard Business School Press, Boston (2004)

24. Rhodes, F.H.T.: The Role of the American University: The Creation of the Future. Cornell University Press, USA (2001), http://www.cornellpress.cornell.edu
25. Brodhead, R.H.: What are the universities good for, A speech by Duke President, Duke University, Apple iTunesU
26. Katsikas, S.K.: The university in the third millennium: which reforms are needed, Organization of Economic Cooperation and Development (accessed March 2008), http://www.oecd.org/dataoecd/
27. Tanaka, N.: The Japanese economy, A presentation at King Faisal Center for Research and Islamic Studies (KFCRIS), Riyadh, Saudi Arabia (April 2007)

The Green and Gold Road: Journal Management and Publishing Workflow Extensions for the DSpace Repository Platform

Andreas Geyrecker and Fridolin Wild

Vienna University of Economics and Business Administration
andreas.geyrecker@wu-wien.ac.at,
fridolin.wild@wu-wien.ac.at

Abstract. Today a major part of scientific publishing means distribution of articles through journals both in print and online. Articles are still the predominant publishing format, even in the web-based publishing era. In this paper we present an integrated journal management and publishing workflow based on the DSpace repository software. It is meant to suggest an approach which simplifies the authoring and submission process, including automated metadata extraction directly from the author's document. Delivering content in flexible ways helps to improve reading experience and enables better handling of archived scholarly material. Therefore, the system offers the publishing of repository content in different output formats, namely XHTML and PDF with the help of XSL stylesheets. Furthermore, it should make the set up and maintenance of journal issues easier. The new journal workflow allows flexible packaging of repository content and even automated production of print editions of journal issues.

Keywords: open access, journal management, institutional repository.

1 Introduction

Scientific publishing has been in a technological transformation process in recent years. Web-based publishing technologies are challenging the established publishing model by enabling scientific communication in a faster way. These new technologies allow unrestricted and open access to scholarly information. Methods offering free access are commonly referred to as open access. Open access is defined – among others – in the Budapest Open Access Initiative [1] as the free, immediate, permanent access to research results for anyone to use, download, copy and distribute.

There are two concepts of open access [2]:

- Self archiving of either published, peer-reviewed articles (postprints) or draft versions of articles (preprints) on an institutional repository – known as the *green road* to open access
- Open access journals – the *gold road* to open access.

M.D. Lytras et al. (Eds.): WSKS 2008, CCIS 19, pp. 45–52, 2008.

Institutional repositories – like *DSpace* (www.dspace.org) – provide web-based submission and the creation of metadata of scholarly material. DSpace uses a qualified version of Dublin Core metadata across all content. The metadata is indexed for searching and browsing, and the content is preserved in the repository for the long term. Institutional repositories also support the export of metadata via the OAI-PMH protocol (Protocol for Metadata Harvesting of the Open Archives Initiative) to make repository content available for harvesting.

Bailey [3] suggests the optimisation of repository platform software to more fully support electronic document publishing functions, such as e-journal management. Existing open source journal management systems (for example Open Journal Systems, http://pkp.sfu.ca/ojs) already assist and improve all stages of the journal publishing process. These stages include submission, peer review, copy editing and the publishing of journal articles. But such software still does not interoperate with repository software. In addition, it does not provide any improvements in simplifying the process of authoring and submission of articles, nor does it seek to reduce the effort of creating the final publication layout.

It is intended to follow Bailey's suggestion and propose the integration of *gold road* features into the *green road* DSpace repository platform. Our approach focuses on simplifying the authoring and submission process, archiving the content in a suitable preservation format and enabling flexible publishing in various formats. Furthermore, the solution provides simple setup and management of journal issues in DSpace.

2   The Journal and Publishing Workflows

2.1   DSpace

DSpace is a digital repository platform jointly developed by the MIT Libraries and Hewlett-Packard (HP). In March 2008, DSpace 1.5 was released. This new version has introduced many new features including a completely customizable *Manakin* user interface [4]. Manakin introduces an interface layer that allows customization of the repository interface according to specific needs. Manakin is based on *Apache Cocoon* (http://cocoon.apache.org), which uses the concept of pipelines: A *generator* produces SAX events that represent the input XML, *transformers* can alter the stream of SAX events and a *serializer* finally creates an output stream which is sent to the requesting client. This architecture means that a final page is generated through the sequential arrangement of components along a pipeline [4].

Manakin utilizes this pipeline concept to create its major architectural components: the *DRI schema*, *aspects*, and *themes*.

The Digital Repository Interface (*DRI*) is an XML representation of a DSpace repository page.

Manakin allows the creation of modular extensions. These extensions are called *aspects*. They allow existing features to be modified or new features to be created. In this way either minor changes regarding the display or even new workflow functionality can be added. An aspect expects a DRI XML document as input, modifies or adds content to this DRI page and generates an output DRI document. This allows aspects being connected together.

Themes allow the customization of the look-and-feel of a repository. This is achieved by applying XSL and CSS stylesheets to the final DRI page (see [4] for detailed information on the Manakin concepts).

Our proposal is to build a journal management and publishing extension utilizing the new Manakin aspects and themes concept.

2.2 DSpace Customizations

Introducing flexible publishing features requires some customization of the DSpace platform.

To allow on-the-fly generation of PDF we attached *Apache FOP* (http://xmlgraphics.apache.org/fop) to DSpace, a print formatter driven by XSL formatting objects (XSL-FO). This has been accomplished by adding a new serializer to Manakin's main Cocoon sitemap.

We have altered the default XSLT processor used by Manakin to the XSLT 2.0 compliant *Saxon* processor (http://saxon.sourceforge.net/). This allows us to use features introduced by XSLT 2.0 like regular expression handling in the conversion and publishing process.

The Manakin aspects and themes concept allows to package modifications in a clean way, without the need of changing existing functionalities. A Manakin theme, providing a distinct view of the repository and enabling the multi channel publishing pipelines, has been developed. We have also developed a new Manakin aspect providing journal management functionalities.

The solution is completely modular and can easily be adapted to handle different input formats (for example MS Office Open XML), different preservation or output format needs, by changing the underlying XSL stylesheets.

2.3 Article Authoring and Submission

We are proposing an authoring process using *OpenDocument Format (ODF)*. An author following simple authoring guidelines has to apply only four custom styles – provided by a template – to achieve a painless authoring and submission experience.

Sefton [5] reports that word-processing templates are used properly, "if you provide a feedback loop so people can see their document converted to HTML, then they do use and even like templates." We have established extended feedback options available immediately after uploading an article to the system, which is discussed in more detail below.

Evaluation work has been carried out to identify the most suitable *authoring* and *preservation format*.

For authoring, we have chosen the OpenDocument Format (ODF) because it allows the upload of a complete article and all embedded images at a single blow. OpenDocument is an open OASIS standard. OpenDocument files use an XML-based format and are stored in JAR (Java Archive) format. A JAR file is a compressed ZIP file that has an additional 'manifest' file that lists the contents of the archive. [6] The

OpenDocument format also preserves embedded formulae in MathML (Mathematical Markup Language), which is another advantage.

In his detailed analysis on preservation of word processing documents, Barnes [7] defines a "preservation format as one suitable for storing a document in an electronic archive for a long period. An access format is one suitable for viewing a document or doing something with it." Using an XML-based preservation format helps to achieve long-term preservation. XML formats are text-based and therefore accessible in the future. Having identified *DocBook* (www.docbook.org) and *XHTML* (http://www. w3.org/ TR/xhtml1) as viable options, we have finally chosen XHTML as preservation format. XHTML is also an excellent access format which can easily be viewed in a web browser. It offers sufficient possibilities to represent the document structure of scientific articles. Furthermore, XHTML supports the embedding of additional markup which reside in a separate namespace, for example MathML or SVG.

Another crucial factor to increase the scholars' acceptance of open access repositories is a simple submission process. Although Carr and Harnad [8] have found the amount of time spent on submitting papers is just about 40 minutes per year for a highly active researcher, the extra task to provide a camera-ready paper and to enter the metadata required by repositories puts an unnecessary burden on the submitter.

DSpace 1.5 introduces a new item submission system [9] which is now more configurable. The new submission system allows to rearrange submission steps, to remove steps and new steps to be added. It also allows the definition of different submission processes on a per collection basis.

The proposed article submission system includes an enhanced upload step, which post-processes the uploaded OpenDocument file. The file is unpacked and the content is being transformed into XHTML using an XSL stylesheet. A new DSpace item is generated and the article metadata – title, author names, affiliation, abstract, keywords – is being assigned to this new item. The metadata is also embedded in the output XHTML following the recommendation of the *Dublin Core Metadata Initiative* (http://dublincore.org/documents/dcq-html/).

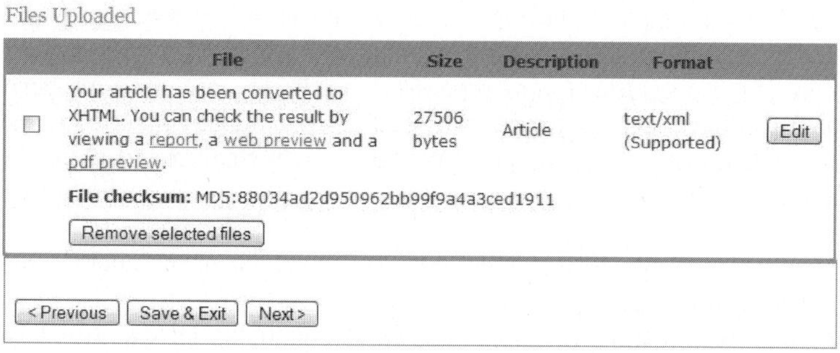

Fig. 1. Article upload - the author has immediate access to different output formats (XHTML web preview, PDF and a report view) to ensure that the article renders as expected

At the end of the upload and conversion step the submitter has different feedback options to check how good the converted article meets the repository requirements (Fig. 1):

- a report for quality control automatically detects the article metadata and provides an overview of the document structure by outlining the section headers
- a web preview (XHTML) renders the full text of the article according to the repository look-and-feel
- a PDF preview generates a high quality PDF, marked with a 'DRAFT' watermark on each page

The automated metadata extraction during the upload and conversion step allows to prepopulate the DSpace metadata form in the next submission step. The submitter only needs to double-check the already available data.

After completing the submission process, the item can be reviewed by an editor in a limited workflow system. In the current DSpace implementation, content can be reviewed by simply accepting the submitted item, changing some metadata or rejecting the item.

This simple workflow is insufficient in a journal management workflow. However, there is an upcoming Google Summer of Code 2008 project, which will seek for improvements to provide modular, configurable workflow steps (http://code.Google. com/soc/2008/dspace/appinfo.html?csaid=8FA09FBFA7C867B0). Our system currently utilizes the existing workflow features.

If a submitted article is approved by the collection editor, the item will be archived in the main *Articles* collection and mapped to the *Preprints* collection. Item mapping in DSpace means linking items to other collections. Moving items from one collection to another is not supported in DSpace.

2.4 Publishing into Various Formats

"The beauty of open access is that it allows endless possibilities in the ways in which information is packaged and presented to the reader. But these possibilities may not be so open if poorly chosen file formats introduce unwanted constraints or limitations." [10]

"The sooner we have HTML editions of scientific articles, next to or instead of PDF editions, the better. HTML and PDF files can both be open access, but HTML facilitates re-use of the content and PDF retards it." [11]

There is evidence of increasing demand to support multiple publishing formats for scientific content. Offering various viewing options means increasing and improving access to scholarly material.

Default item representation in DSpace means document delivery as it is preserved in the repository, mostly as PDF. Using an XML-based preservation format offers the flexibility of publishing content in various output formats. XML can easily be transformed into other XML languages like XHTML, WML, SVG and PDF.

The idea is to utilize the Manakin integrated Cocoon component to enable additional publishing features and viewing options of archived articles.

In order to enable content to be delivered to different output formats, we have built a new Cocoon generator (*BitstreamGenerator.class*) which queries DSpace for a particular repository item and passes it to the next step in a Cocoon pipeline. This allows us to offer different representations of DSpace items by setting up different pipelines in the theme's Cocoon sitemap. Each repository item can be displayed in XHTML and PDF format.

The PDF representation (Fig. 2) is being generated using XSL-FO and Apache FOP. The new FOP version (0.94) offers improved conformance to the W3C XSL-FO 1.0 standard. The page layout can be customized by changing the XSL stylesheet. This allows journal specific layout definitions.

http://hdl.handle.net/123456789/7 | pp. 1–5

Distributed Feed Networks for Learning

Fridolin Wild, Steinn E. Sigurdarson

Abstract

Recent studies indicate that blogs are the breakthrough user application of this decade. Yet, the blogosphere in its current form is suffering from various problems. The fuzziness of the audience, disconnectedness, fragmentation, and lack of conversational coherence may have their roots not only in sociological factors but technological shortcomings of the current infrastructure. These problems hinder an effective deployment of blogs in collaborative learning activities. Within this contribution, an interface specification for user-centred distribution of feed aggregation activities is proposed which is both a prerequisite and basic infrastructure for blog-based collaboration. By presenting an overview on the current state of the art in feed and interaction standards, a clear lack of support for active network management will be elaborated. The design requirements for a solution to fill this gap will be sketched and complemented by a step by step description of the communication process of the proposed 'FeedBack' specification. Preliminary results from a trial with a reference implementation for WordPress provide a proof of concept.

Index Terms — Technology-Enhanced Learning, TEL, ICT, Feeds

Fridolin Wild M.A., is researching within ProLearn, the EU Network of Excellence (NoE) for technology enhanced professional learning, and additionally within EU IST funded iCamp project, there being the technical manager and leading a work package on interoperability of social software tools for learning. Fridolin is the treasurer of the European Association of Technology-Enhanced Learning (EATEL). He works as a scientist at the Institute of Information Systems of the Vienna University of Economics and Business Administration.

Steinn E. Sigurdarson is a technology-enhanced learning researcher at the Vienna University of Economics and Business Administration, working on interoperability and social software tools for learning within the iCamp project. Steinn has a background in data integration projects in the corporate sector with a focus on open-source developments. Since 2006 he has been concentrating on social software development, among others as phase leader in the software development of the Cocell Minerva-funded project.

1 Learning with Blogs

The conglomerate of all blogs available online, the so-called 'blogosphere', has been certified to show a bursty evolution at least since 2001, where an eruptive rise can be identified not only regarding metrics of scale but also with respect to deepening community structures and higher degrees of connectedness [1,4]. As of December 2007, for example, the blog index and search site Technorati is indexing over 112 million blogs [2]. Blogging is obviously an increasingly popular phenomenon, although meta-studies reveal that

between one half and two thirds of all blogs are abandoned within only two months after their creation [3].

One of the reasons that blogs became so attractive is their ease of use, removing barriers of technoliteracy from web self-publishing [5]. There is a plethora of web-publishing tools, allowing the user to choose from a large variety of (non-)commercial hosting services (often available free of charge). Moreover, users can set up their own web-applications choosing from a rich portfolio of open- and closed-source products. Learning Light's eLearning Centre, for example, lists already back in 2006 more than 56 different products and online services in a vendor directory for blogging tools [6]. Publishing rich content with weblogs does not require any profound technical knowledge – knowledge such as language skills in the hypertext mark-up language required to create pages with a desktop html-editor or skills such as those necessary to set up a fully-fledged content management system.

Other than virtual classrooms, wikis, or forums, blogs inherently offer the option to build open networks for collaboration, without the need to establish a dedicated community engaging in communication first. A single blog may be considered to be individual publishing, the blogosphere as a whole, however, is participatory by nature [20].

It is not surprising then, that blogs became vehicles for knowledge management to already often form an integral part of teaching and learning processes. Blogs can be used to organize lectures, seminars, and discussions both between teachers and students. Herring et al. (2004) found in their study on blog genres that 57.5% of the blogs' authors investigated in a random sample of 203 blogs are students on a secondary and tertiary level [7]. However, at the same time, the major share of 70.4 % of the blogs are **person-**

1

Fig. 2. PDF article full text

The XHTML representation is being generated according to the repository look-and-feel. Displaying content online in XHTML can improve reading experience in the following ways [12]:

- references (cited work) can be linked to the appropriate full text (at least to the abstract, if the full text is not freely available)
- figures and images can be more comprehensive in size and colors
- outline the article structure for easier navigation
- in contrast to a print edition there are no space limitations

XHTML enables the use of semantic markup within articles, such as embedding Dublin Core metadata in *<meta>* elements or embedding microformats. This machine readable information increases interoperability with reference management tools like Zotero (http://www.zotero.org) or Connotea (http://www.connotea.org). As mentioned above, we include Dublin Core metadata in the XHTML preservation format during the upload and conversion submission step and then expose the metadata in the XHTML representation of the article.

2.5 Journal Issue Management

To encourage new possibilities in how repository content is presented to the reader and how content can be chunked into content packages like journals, we have developed a new Manakin aspect providing journal management functionalities. Therefore, we introduced a new parameter (*journal.community.handle*) in the DSpace configuration file, representing the main journal community. Descendant communities of the main journal community can be of arbitrary structure. Descendant collections of this community always represent journal issues.

The journal administrator is entitled to create new journal volumes and issues. She then can map items from the main *Articles* collection to the journal issue collection. This causes a new metadata entry being assigned to a mapped item (*DC.Relation.isPartOf*), indicating the handle identifier of the journal issue, which the article is now part of. Having done so, the journal administrator can reorder articles in a *table of contents* view.

After saving the final order a new DSpace *journal definition item* will be created. This item is an automatically generated RDF file, containing a list of all articles and metadata (journal name, volume, issue number) of the particular journal issue.

After final approval and publication all items are automatically unmapped from the *Preprints* collection and permissions are being changed, so that the journal issue is available for all DSpace users.

The journal definition file is also used to create a complete journal issue in PDF format, containing all articles and an automatically generated table of contents.

3 Conclusion – Further Work

Information systems bear the potential to facilitate, scaffold, and even automate parts of the processes in the value chain of journal publishing. Advanced open access publishing support systems make publishing workflows more efficient and encourage the dissemination of knowledge.

Today self archiving of scientific material is often limited to making the PDF version of an article available on an institutional repository. Scientific content is valued by its visibility and usability, therefore offering the content in multiple formats would make the content more open.

We have demonstrated that the concept of multi channel publishing and journal management can be incorporated in the DSpace repository platform. Our approach represents the attempt to achieve a combination of *green road* open access repository and *gold road* open access journal functionalities.

The new DSpace architecture offers comprehensive methods to build workflow extensions. Such extensions can provide a mechanism to ease the submission process and to reuse repository content as part of new publishing processes. Articles can be packaged into journals which adds a more structured view on repository content.

Automated typesetting using XSL-FO does have unavoidable limitations. But it is considered to be a robust system which offers sufficient features for high-quality PDF production.

Further developments of the proposed system can include the workflow integration of missing stages in the journal management process, like peer review. The system could also be extended to support additional input word-processing formats and to develop an automated citation lookup tool for better reference handling.

References

1. Budapest Open Access Initiative, Budapest Open Access Initiative (2002),
   http://www.soros.org/openaccess/read.shtml
2. Harnad, S.: Fast-Forward on the Green Road to Open Access: The Case Against Mixing Up Green and Gold, Ariadne (January 2005),
   http://www.ariadne.ac.uk/issue42/harnad/
3. Bailey Jr., C.W.: What is open access? In: Jacobs, N. (ed.) Open Access: Key Strategic, Technical and Economic Aspects. Chandos Publishing (2006)
4. Phillips, S., et al.: Manakin: A New Face for DSpace, D-Lib Magazine 13, no. 11/12 (December 2007),
   http://www.dlib.org/dlib/november07/phillips/11phillips.html
5. Sefton, P.: Why ICE works, PT's Blog (August 2007),
   http://ptsefton.com/blog/2007/08/10/09-25-10.681066/
6. Eisenberg, J.D.: OpenOffice.org XML Essentials. O'Reilly & Associates, Inc. (2006),
   http://books.evc-cit.info/oobook/book.html
7. Barnes, I.: Preservation of word processing documents (2006),
   http://www.apsr.edu.au/publications/preservation_of_word_pro
   cessing_documents.html
8. Carr, L., Harnad, S.: Keystroke Economy: A Study of the Time and Effort Involved in Self-Archiving (2005), http://eprints.ecs.soton.ac.uk/10688/
9. Donohue, T.G.: Configurable Submission System for DSpace (January 2007),
   https://www.ideals.uiuc.edu/handle/2142/207
10. Guédon, J.: Open access: a symptom and a promise. In: Jacobs, N. (ed.) Open Access: Key Strategic, Technical and Economic Aspects. Chandos Publishing (2006)
11. Sefton, P.: Why not HTML for online journals? People need the right tools, PT's Blog (August 2007), http://ptsefton.com/blog/2007/08/09/09-23-19.208941/
12. Willinsky, J.: The Access Principle: The Case for Open Access to Research and Scholarship. MIT Press, Cambridge (2006)

The Biggest Human GRID-s of the Future: Hybridization of Science and Public Education

László Z. Karvalics

Department of Library and Information Science, Faculty of Arts, University of Szeged,
Hungary 1037 Budapest, Remetehegyi u.106/A
zkl@hung.u-szeged.hu

Abstract. The information technology background systems of modern sciences produce an *incredible quantity of output signals*. For many of the sciences (primarily genetics, oceanography, meteorology/climatology, environmental sciences, nuclear physics, pharmacology, archeology, and, first of all, astronomy) it is more and more problematic to manage the content of their permanently swelling background stores Beside financial resources the "human agent", human infrastructure, is becoming one of the bottlenecks. If we need brains in a "pre-digestive" process, it can easily find them where the task is exactly to make these brains able to do (even) scientific work: in the school benches. With the pupils socialized in the adequate community scope, involving resources and learning basic knowledge to satisfy their sateless desire to know and with their teachers an alliance may be created, and the biggest human GRID will be composed from these hybrid online clusters – the new type of knowledge producing and learning communities.

Keywords: Science, Public Education, Megamachines, Brains, Human GRIDs.

1 Introduction: From (e-)learning to Knowledge Production

When speaking about (e-)learning, we prefer to deal with organizational and software problems rather than the expectable new qualities of the community and learning environment deriving for the age group of 10-18 from e-learning.

I introduce my arguments to show that **the future of (on-line) learning is connected to knowledge production.** I claim that, stepping far over the present objectives of the European Union, the advance of Education and Science towards each other is not merely an attribute, one possible characteristic of the several but the *only and essential factor of the future of e-learning at school.* Let us have a look at science first.

The information technology background systems of modern sciences produce an incredible quantity of output signals. For many of the sciences (primarily genetics, oceanography, meteorology/climatology, environmental sciences, nuclear physics, pharmacology and, first of all, astronomy) it is more and more problematic to manage the content of their permanently swelling background stores. Their clever and more and more intelligent agents, artificial intelligence systems and monitoring tools harrow so great fields that there is little energy and attention left for sowing.

M.D. Lytras et al. (Eds.): WSKS 2008, CCIS 19, pp. 53–56, 2008.

Meanwhile, the successes attained in the automatization of the elaboration of the elementary data mass reproduce the notion of unworkability at a higher level of elaboration. Earlier, scholars had to face this feeling only when surveying the professional literature, when coming across the limits of library services and referring/abstracting/checking systems. By now, however, even „own" sign production represents a quantitative limit. The recognition of the fact that the human brains being able to construe and place into context are missing from the process is getting stronger. Beside financial resources the "human agent", human infrastructure, is becoming one of the bottlenecks.

There is only one way out which has always been in front of the eyes of the scientific community but has never been taken seriously. If it needs brains in a "pre-digestive" process, it can easily find them where the task is exactly to make these brains able to do (even) scientific work: in the school benches. In case we take the initial demand (adequate mass of human interface necessary for elementary transformations at disposal) seriously, the schools are perfectly ready to fulfill the task. Financial limits do not appear because putting the building blocks of knowledge on top of each other is a "job duty" for them. If there is a problem, it is only organizational: how is it possible to involve hundreds of thousand and million children and teachers into living scientific programs so that they are not illustrations but real, interdepending work relations? Is the current problem world of science parcellable so that the solving, searching, collecting and systemizing of certain part questions can be left for the children?

I think that the answer is a multiple YES. With the pupils socialized in the adequate community scope, involving resources and learning basic knowledge to satisfy their sateless desire to know and with their teachers an alliance may be created, and – with Lewis Mumford's words – (online) megamachines can be built behind certain scientific problems [1].

So in case the involvement of fresh brains possible to be made work is an exciting chance and possibility form the respect of Science, how does it look from the other side, from the respect of School?

2   School and New Science

Let us collect the normative demands that have been articulated in relation to the school, the teaching and learning processes and the children of the information era in the previous years.

1. The teacher should not be a lesson-introducing machine but an animator. He/she should smartly conduct the pupils' independent knowledge operations which also use library and Internet resources, should only intervene at the critical points.

2. Education should move from desk-orthodoxy towards the horizontal forms of communication and the world of cooperating and problem solving communities of students.

3. Each child should be taught to think at an early age so that an apparatus also usable in the scientific survey of problems can evolve.

4. Education should build on the fact that children are self-confident and easy users of the world of information technological tools, and practically suck skills and knowledge up with their mother tongue.

5. Where possible, the principle of "learning by doing" and "exploration" must replace "cramming" learning.

If we wanted to build a pedagogical programme on the basic statements, we could not find a better solution **than involving millions of students and teachers into the well prepared and organized problem solving processes**, primarily based on network communication and group work, of some scientific fields [2].

Of course, most of the teachers having become tired of the reforms will instinctively protest since the acceptance of all these would generate the biggest series of change of ever times, and would change the teachers' role and the traditional curriculums of teacher training within one generation time. The teacher would not only be the master of a "subject" but an information broker between the scientific community, the top of the pyramid and the bottom. His primary function would be exposition (creation of certain "basic skills", the ability to join scientific group work in parallel with the arousing of interest). He would not think in school books but in knowledge packages which are fed adequately in the perfect point of time and are necessary to overcome certain heights and to acquire the common meanings.

We will be told that children are not able to do scientific work, they are small and immature, order should done in their heads first, they must learn to read perfectly, then we can think of making them components in a giant scientific machine. In fact, today there is no definite pedagogical trend searching what children aged 14-18 cannot do, the explorations aim at what and how they can do. If, on one hand, we believe Douglas Rushkoff [3], that the children are the great winners and skills machines of the 21st century, why do we doubt that they would do well as partakers of a real intellectual adventure opening a new horizon in the history of schools and sciences? Of course, the first to be done is to step over the myths and anti-utopian perspectives determining today's public speech.

In my opinion, the question to be asked is less and less whether it is a viable and rational programme to connect Science to Education, and is more and more what the typical methods of operation, sciences and problems of the new era will be, and how the transition leading there can be programmed.

The discourse must be begun as soon as possible, even if some solutions and demands "naturally" result from the programme itself.

The arousing of interest in sciences, the "magic", is dated back to the lower school years, but the first instructions can already be given here. The objective to make the child able to participate in scientific group work can organize the whole pedagogical process even in these years.

After the age of ten the building of the project organizations can be started in concentric circles. It seems obvious that in the "first circle" a system level including all the pupils and the adjusted and customized (to persons or elementary researcher communities) unique mini problems must exist. It is not necessary for everyone to follow a path to the solution of higher level problems, but everyone will be part of this elementary level problem community where they can do their part tasks as long as going to school, or even afterwards, as long as they live.

It is likely that in the second circle a kind of clustering will start, the certain scientific problems are possible to be distributed along typical attributes. And since the well chosen "topics" are of several dimensions and complex nature, a student, as the owner of a dedicated problem object, can be the member of even 3 or 4 problem communities organized around certain attributes.

It is important to highlight the fact that the existence as a component of a scientific mega-machine is only one side, one form of manifestation of school life; no total reorganization is done as compared to the former training-subject solutions, but only an internal reorganization of ratios.

The on-line work interfaces become clue participants. It is an interesting question whether the open platform of the Internet is suitable to manage the group work interfaces of never-ever-been sizes, of several ten thousands. But the really big question is whether the representatives of any science possess enough want and strength to enter this strange "new alliance" and whether there are disciplines seeming suitable to play this role.

3 Theses for Future Research

I draw up five theses as a kind of summary, but also as the framework of the surveys moving this way in the near future.

1. The programme of the "knowledge producing student" does not stand alone but is something that each of the important factors of the pedagogical reform process can be connected to.

2. The challenge is even deeper and more comprehensive: the quashing of the more and more definite capacity limits of Science.

3. The fusion will be seamless and multitudinous.

4. The base of the new learning and knowledge model is the to-be-solved problem divided into elementary pieces, and the "mediums" are the (hybrid) groups of teachers, researchers and students organized into various topic clusters.

5. The educational systems most rapidly adapting to the new model will attain competition advance.

References

1. Mumford, L.: The Myth of the Machine. Technics and Human Development, vol. 1. Harcourt Brace Jovanovich, New York (1967)
2. Rushkoff, D.: Playing the Future. What We Can Learn from Digital Kids. Riverhead Books, New York (1996)
3. Karvalics, Z., László – Vietorisz, T.: Information age education in a sustainable world Practice and Theory in Systems of Education, vol. 2(3-4), pp. 65–78 (2007), http://www.eduscience.hu/

The Grid for Learning

Nicola Capuano, Matteo Gaeta, Sergio Miranda, Francesco Orciuoli,
and Pierluigi Ritrovato

University of Salerno, Department of Information Engineering and Applied Mathematics,
via Ponte don Melillo, 84084 Fisciano (SA), Italy
ncapuano@unisa.it, {gaeta,smiranda,orciuoli,
ritrovato}@diima.unisa.it.

Abstract. Grid technologies are rising as the next generation of Internet by defining a powerful computing paradigm by analogy with the electric Power Grid. A Grid user is able to use his private workplace to invoke any application from a remote system, use the system best suited for executing that application, access data securely and consistently from remote sites, exploit multiple systems to complete economically complex tasks or to solve large problems that exceed the capacity of a single system. Grid could be used as a technology "glue" providing users with a uniform way to access resources by means of several devices. These technologies can provide, in a natural way, a support for Technology Enhanced Learning (TEL) by enabling new learning environments based on collaboration, social interaction, experience, realism, personalisation, ubiquity, accessibility and contextualisation. Nevertheless, to be effectively used in TEL, Grid must be complemented with other elements like semantics and educational modelling so bringing to the concept of "Grid for Learning" whose description is the object of this paper.

Keywords: distributed computing, grid, learning design, ontologies, semantics.

1 Introduction

Over the last few years, Technology Enhanced Learning (TEL) needs have been changing in accordance with ever more complex pedagogical models as well as with technological evolution, resulting in environments with very dynamic teaching and learning requirements. Such important requirements include, according to [5]:

– wide geographical distribution of learners and tutors who can potentially belong to many different educational institutions;
– access from anywhere, on any learners' computer platform and any software;
– support for a growing load of learning resources and users who access these resources;
– transparent share of an huge variety of both software and hardware learning resources;
– transparent access to shared, heterogeneous learning resources in very dynamic environments;

M.D. Lytras et al. (Eds.): WSKS 2008, CCIS 19, pp. 57–66, 2008.
© Springer-Verlag Berlin Heidelberg 2008

- multiple administrations from different organisations with specific educational policies;
- inherent dynamism of learners and tutors needs and changing learning resources;
- constant provision of user awareness and feedback so as to keep learners and tutors informed about what is happening in the learning environment resulting in an enhancement of cognitive, social and emotional support to on-line learning groups;
- flexibility to reuse pieces of learning resources of different granularity according to specific needs (e.g. customise a curriculum by reusing specific learning activities with different input data);
- facility to personalise, update, and meet learning resources by instructors and learners without technology skills.

These requirements represent a great challenge for traditional software platforms and tools but may be solved by relying on distributed paradigms like Service Orientation or Grid.

Grid technologies have started to be very popular in education due to the advantages that they offer being based on a secure, flexible and coordinated way of sharing resources in the Internet as well as on its enormous capability of information processing. In addition to the mentioned set of requirements, the Grid approach represents an ideal context for supporting and producing further benefits for TEL including [20]:

- adaptability at runtime to highly dynamic conditions in learning settings;
- interoperability by providing support to the great variety of learners' and tutors' computer platforms and software;
- scalability to a large number of single/group learners and tutors who can be distributed in very different locations;
- availability of an increasing number of heterogeneous and changing learning resources;
- integration of new and existing learning resources and tools as well as other legacy systems from their own or other educational organisations;
- support for notifications to learning participants about what is happening in their environment;
- high level of abstraction that allows all the actors involved in the learning process to easily perform their ideas by services.

In addition, within the TEL domain, Grid promotes collaborative development among all community participants, enhances coordination in the research community, enables sharing of best practices, improves the understanding of the virtual educational needs, etc. As a result Grid appears to be a good choice to support the development of the most pervasive and challenging TEL environments but must be complemented with other technologies in order to be fully effective.

Following this trend, a Special Interest Group of the European-wide Network of Excellence "Kaleidoscope" [17] have been dedicated to the establishment of an observatory on Grid applications to TEL in order to survey the field and to foster discussion among research groups spread in Europe. One of the results of this discussion is the definition of the "Grid for Learning" concept here presented.

After having introduced some research work related to the Grid and TEL in par. 2, the concept of Grid for Learning is presented in par. 3. Then some challenging scenario exploiting the defined concept is described in par. 4 while par. 5 presents concluding remarks.

2 Related Work

Before starting to introduce the concept of "Grid for Learning" it is useful to outline, according to [7], the most recent and significant works that contributed to the definition of the concept and to the development of technologies that make it possible.

The Grid Service Based Portal for Virtual Learning Campus [26] developed an environment which makes use of the Grid capabilities so that to make possible the dynamic sharing and coordination of heterogeneous resources which are found dispersed in the network. The project focuses on the development of a video digital library based on Grid for a Virtual Campus that allows an easy access and implementation of several services. In spite of being a project that aimed to take advantage of the capabilities that Grid technology provides, it is limited on a unique type of educative resources, like video, which a structure of services is developed for.

In [19] it is described a TEL platform based on Grid service technologies. In this platform the supply of virtual learning services designated for students, instructors and course suppliers is based on the resource administration for group collaboration based on Grid, allowing ubiquitous access to information and taking advantage of the potentiality of the computer systems. On the one hand, the advantage of this proposal is that it is the first one that elaborates on the use of Grid resources and their description through Grid technologies, in particular WSDL. On the other hand, it dictates the need for the development of a semantic model description that enables a more complete description of learning resources.

ULabGrid, an Infrastructure to Develop Distant Laboratories for Undergrad Students over a Grid, [2] proposes a new architecture that allows the educators to design remote collaborative laboratories for university students using the Grid infrastructure. This project is one of the first in its type in trying to combine the facilities that Grid provides in a practical scenario in order to achieve resource sharing and motivate collaborative work. In this sense the design of Grid-based collaborative learning scenarios should be supported by semantic descriptions that allow the best tracking of resources available in the network.

A further work proposes an Agent-Based Robust Collaborative Virtual Environment for TEL in the Service Grid [15]. In this virtual environment, all Web resources and services are accessed via service encapsulation, which may result in a more scalable and robust collaborative learning architecture. A very remarkable aspect of this work is the way it uses to implement complex services from more basic ones, though no use of semantic description is made to allow the automatic composition of complex services from lower level ones.

KGTutor, a Knowledge Grid Based Intelligent Tutoring System [29], proposes a model for the construction of intelligent tutoring in a more pleasant and effective way. The KGTutor is designed to provide better support to student centred distributed learning. Students' characteristics, such as previous knowledge and learning styles, are used to choose, organize, and deliver the learning materials to individual students. During learning progress, the system can also provide objective evaluations and customized suggestions for each student according to their learning performance. This system provides a very important work as far as student centred learning concerns, though it could be further strengthened through the use of aspects of semantic description of learning services.

In [25], a Grid Service Framework for Metadata Management in Self-e-Learning Networks focuses on how the use of metadata can be critical for Grid systems. More specifically, the semantic description constitutes a very beneficial extension of Grid environments. The Self e-Learning Network (SeLeNe) is used as a test application while a set of services is proposed which are implemented with OGSA. The project focuses on providing services that use learning objects metadata, based on a sufficiently generic approach so that they can be used by other Grid-based systems which need to make use of semantic descriptions.

ELeGI (European Learning Grid Infrastructure) [23] was aimed at providing an advance in the current practices of learning through the definition and implementation of a software architecture that achieves to unify the semantic Grid and information technologies in order to promote and give support to the definition and adoption of learning paradigms for the construction of knowledge that combines customized and ubiquitous techniques based on experiential, collaborative and contextualized learning. In this line, [13] presents a work about ontology based user modelling for personalization of Grid learning services. This work describes how the learning services of the Grid should support a user-centred, customized, contextualized, experiential and ubiquitous based learning approach.

The SELF project [1] proposes a learning environment that results from the integration of several technologies, specially the semantic Web, Grid technology, collaborative tools as well as customized tools and knowledge management techniques. SELF provides a mechanism for the intelligent search of services making use of semantic description tools. This project presents an important reference of the use of different technologies for the development of Grid-based learning scenarios, even though it is not based on semantic description models for the definition of its tools.

OntoEdu [14] is a flexible platform for online learning which is based on diverse technologies like ubiquitous computing, ontology engineering, Web semantics and computational Grid. It is compound of five parts: user adaptation, automatic composition, educative ontologies, a module of services and a module of contents; among these parts the educative ontology is the main one. The main objectives of OntoEdu are to obtain reusability of concepts, adaptability for users and devices, automatic composition, as well as scalability in functionality and performance.

The work developed in [18] presents a workflow framework for pervasive learning objects composition by employing a Grid services flow language. Learning objects are distributed in heterogeneous environments which have been used in order to allow effective collaboration and the reuse of learning objects; this fact can help users to learn with no limitations of time and space. This work shows the great opportunities that exist in those research groups which make use of Grid technology to develop innovative, pervasive and ubiquitous learning scenarios.

Finally, in the work referenced as "Semantic Search of Learning Services in a Grid-Based Collaborative System" [27], the authors have constructed an ontological description for collaborative work tools that allow one to make a manual search of the diverse resources that these tools provide within a Grid environment with the minimum of technical knowledge. This work proposes a Grid-based tool called Gridcole, which can serve as a basis to implement different conceptual approaches of Grid-based semantic description of learning services, thus extending and endowing it with an innovative, pervasive and ubiquitous projection.

3   The Grid for Learning Concept

In the beginning, **Grid** was synonym of meta-computing and according to this first vision, Kesselman and Foster attempted a first definition of the Grid as "… a hardware and software infrastructure that provides dependable, consistent, pervasive, and inexpensive access to high-end computational capabilities" [10]. Research has brought to a new vision of Grid that became synonym of infrastructure to manage "coordinate resource sharing and problem solving in dynamic, multi-institutional virtual organizations" [10] where the focus is on the concept of Virtual Organization (VO).

Currently, the evolution of Grid is marked by the adoption of a service oriented approach in designing Grid architectures. The Open Grid Services Architecture (OGSA) integrates key Grid technologies with Web Services mechanisms to create a distributed system framework for integrating, virtualizing and managing resources and services within distributed, heterogeneous and dynamic VO [11]. In addition, by adopting the Web Services Resource Framework (WSRF) [9] it is possible to define a Grid resource as a "stateless service acting upon a stateful resource" so applying a service model of an intermediate complexity between pure stateless services and pure conversational ones, thus allowing a simple way to compose services without loosing the advantages of state management.

Upon the OGSA model, different kinds of Grids have been raised like Computation, Data or Information Grid. Apart from the specific term, the key features of all these Grids are virtualization in term of services and dynamic policy-based provision of what is virtualized. Some of them deal with well known issues, like Computational Grid that provides the access to a large virtual computer and Information Grid permitting the access to a large virtual information source.

Among them a key role for TEL is played by the **Semantic Grid** that was defined by De Roure and other researchers as: "an extension of the current Grid in which information and services are given well-defined meaning, better enabling computers and people to work in cooperation" [8]. In other words a Semantic Grid is a Grid improved through standards and technologies of the Semantic Web [3] community, to make explicit and machine understandable the knowledge about resources and services as well as communities and individuals of communities.

A Semantic Grid relies on specifications like OWL-S [22] and WSMO [28] in order to semantically enriches resources virtualised through a service to let software agents compare the requirements of a service against its description to find the service that best satisfy the requirements. In this way it supports the automatic negotiation, discovery and composition of services.

For this reason the Semantic Grid is a good enabling infrastructure for TEL, able to fulfil many of the requirements listed in the first paragraph. It also supports personalization and knowledge creation, acquisition and evolution and can provide a wide and heterogeneous set of services and didactical resources for active experiences. It also supports the autonomous and dynamic creation of communities through the VO paradigm.

Nevertheless, in order to be fully exploited in the TEL domain the Semantic Grid should be enriched with **Educational Modelling** capabilities through the integration of feasible Education Modelling Languages (EMLs) and the provisioning of services discovery and composition capabilities driven by such languages. An EML can be defined as a semantic notation for units of learning to be used in TEL to support the reuse of pedagogical entities like learning designs, objectives, activities, etc. EMLs involves the description of learning processes and methods from a pedagogical and instructional rather then content-driven perspective.

IMS Learning Design (IMS-LD) [16] is currently the widest diffused EML and, according to [4], the one more feasible to be used as the basis in a Learning Grid environment. Through IMS-LD it is possible to describe a wide variety of pedagogical models, including group work and collaborative learning. It does not define individual pedagogical models but provides an high-level language that can describe many different models. The language describes how people perform activities using resources and services, and how to coordinate them into a learning flow.

Nevertheless IMS-LD is currently hardly exploitable in Semantic Grid environments due to several limitations coming from design-time resource binding. This imply a lacks of dynamicity i.e. services must be bind at design time rather that at execution time so hindering to fully exploit dynamic discovery and composition of learning services. To solve this problem [6] proposes semantic extensions to IMS-LD.

The integration of the above mentioned technologies bring us to the following definition of the **Grid for Learning**:

A Grid for Learning is an enabling architecture based on three pillars: Grid, Semantics and Educational Modelling allowing the definition and the execution of learning experiences obtained as cooperation and composition of distributed heterogeneous actors, resources and services.

This definition, coming from the Learning Grid Special Interest Group of Kaleidoscope can be seen as a generalisation of the "Semantic Grid for Human Learning" defined by Gaeta et al. in [12] where the focus was on complex learning experiences based on experiential-based conversational processes.

As shown in figure 1, if we refer to the well known two axis diagram that places the Semantic Grid in a two dimensional spaces (the scale of interoperability and the scale of data/computation), the Grid for Learning can be seen as a projection of the Semantic Grid on a third axis measuring the supported scale of pedagogies.

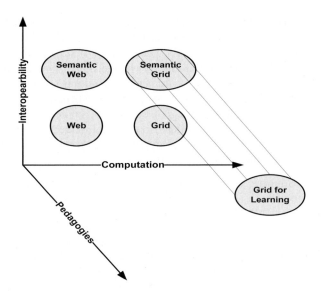

Fig. 1. The Grid for Learning with respect to Grid and Semantic Grid

4   Scenarios for a Grid for Learning

Several challenging scenarios related to the concept of Grid for Learning, as defined in the previous paragraph, and able to exploit available innovative features have been proposed in [21]. A selection of such scenarios is described below.

Enhanced Virtual laboratory. Students can access a virtual remote chemistry laboratory using different terminals (PDA, laptop, PC etc.). Students are identified by the system and a status of their work is stored at their user profile. Such information makes it possible to break and resume experiments that may require distributed simulation or aggregation of distributed information. Supercomputer facilities allow specifying and testing complex analysis, typically performed by groups of three students. Output of experiments may be numerical or graphical and adapted dynamically to the devices used by students. From time to time a synchronization period allows for comparing results between groups and getting partial marks.

Distance Programming Course based on Practice. This scenario is based on an existing TEL programming course where students are learning by doing more than by reading learning material. They are provided with programming exercises that are automatically corrected. Moreover, all attempts are stored so that students can consult their history. Compilation and program execution are implemented as services, students do not need to worry about downloading any programming environment. Grid technology, allows distributed code compilation and execution as well as a distributed storage of students' answers. Semantics allows for better personalization and flexible course composition.

Immersive Virtual Reality. A student is learning water and aquifer behaviour by using a TEL system. She can access introductory books to gain initial knowledge on the topic. She can also use a dynamically generated set of services that, according to her user profile and current PC capabilities create an immersive virtual reality. The service also informs the student about immersion requiring special equipment like gloves and glasses and about the nearest locations where such immersions are possible. Such immersions allow her to go deeper on the aquifer behaviour and on the characteristics of water. In these virtual sites, she also meets other students and interact with them. Learning occurs naturally as a result of experiments and interactions with other students.

The Field Trip. Students, equipped with PDAs, go on a field trip. While performing their activities, they store information under the form of photos, videos, text notes, audio comments, etc. Students can also access digital libraries and documents necessary for their work. The PDA, using user profile and context dependent information, automatically indexes these contents using appropriate metadata. All the contents stored by all students are sent, via an appropriate network to the Field Trip (FT) service created beforehand by the teacher. The FT service uses external services like high performance computing services to provide 3D reconstructions of photos, or to orchestrate speech to text and for text interpretation. Using an ontology based knowledge representation, the FT service can compare students' work with learning objectives and prepare a summary for the teacher in terms of progress and weakness. Using semantic based service searching and location capabilities, the FT service makes also possible for students to contact other students with similar interests or other students who are geographically near (Figure 2).

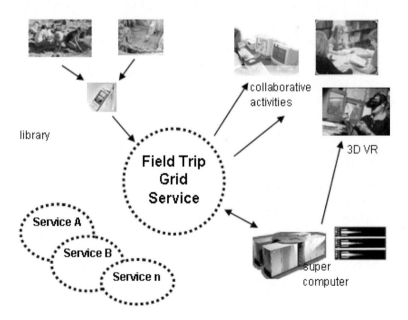

Fig. 2. The Field Trip Scenario

5 Conclusions

This paper described the concept of Grid for Learning as defined in the Learning Grid Special Interest Group of Kaleidoscope and contextualised it with respect to the relevant literature on the field. Some challenging scenario that may be implemented by relying on a Grid for Learning were also outlined. Further examples of systems based on the Grid for Learning concept as well as more details on enabling technologies and pedagogical implications of such concept can be found in [24].

It is important to note that the vision here proposed is strongly connected with the **Knowledge Society** perspective providing an effective mean for lifelong learning and knowledge spreading, leveraging on cooperation among distributed peers and capable of overcoming time and place barriers.

References

1. Abbas, Z., Umer, M., Odeh, M., McClatchey, R., Ali, A., Ahmad, F.: A Semantic Grid-based E-Learning Framework (SELF). In: Collaborative and Learning Applications on Grid Technology (CLAG), 5th International Symposium on Cluster Computing and Grid Cardiff, Wales, UK (May 2005)
2. Ardaiz, O., Artigas, P., Diaz de Cerio, L., Freitag, F., Gallardo, A., Messeguer, R., Navarro, L., Royo, D., Sanjeevan, K.: ULabGrid, an Infrastructure to Develop Distant Laboratories for Undergrad Students over a Grid. In: Fernández Rivera, F., Bubak, M., Gómez Tato, A., Doallo, R. (eds.) Across Grids 2003. LNCS, vol. 2970, pp. 265–272. Springer, Heidelberg (2004)
3. Berners-Lee, T., Hendler, J., Lassila, O.: The Semantic Web. Scientific American (May 2001)
4. Capuano, N., De Pascale, A.: Education Modelling Languages and Learning Grid. In: Capuano, N. (ed.) Learning Grid: a newsletter from the Kaleidoscope Learning Grid SIG, April 2007, vol. 11, pp. 4–8 (2007)
5. Capuano, N., Gaeta, M., Ritrovato, P.: The Anatomy of the Learning Grid. In: Salerno, S., Gaeta, M., Ritrovato, P., Capuano, N., Orciuoli, F., Miranda, S., Pierri, A. (eds.) The Learning Grid Handbook, Concepts, Technologies and Applications. The future of Learning, vol. 2, pp. 3–19. IOS Press, Amsterdam (2008)
6. Capuano, N., Gaeta, M., Iannone, R., Orciuoli, F.: Learning Design and run-time resource binding in a distributed e-learning environment. In: Capuano, N., Ritrovato, P., Murtag, F. (eds.) Proceedings of the 1st International Kaleidoscope Learning GRID SIG Workshop on Distributed e-Learning Environments, Vico Equense (NA), Italy, March 14 2005, Electronic Workshops in Computing, British Computer Society,
7. Daradoumis, A.: State of the Art on Learning Grid: Technological Perspective. In: Capuano, N. (ed.) Learning Grid: a newsletter from the Kaleidoscope Learning Grid SIG, December 2006, vol. 10, pp. 4–6 (2006)
8. De Roure, D., Jennings, N.R., Shadbolt, N.R.: The Semantic Grid: Past, Present, and Future. Proceedings of the IEEE 93(3), 669–681 (2005)
9. Foster, I., Frey, J., Tuecke, S., et al.: The WS-Resource Framework (2004)
10. Foster, I., Kesselman, C.: The Grid: Blueprint for a New Computing Infrastructure. Morgan Kaufmann, San Francisco (1999)
11. Foster, I., Kesselman, C., Nick, J., Tuecke, S.: The Physiology of the Grid: An Open Grid Service Architecture for Distributed System Integration (2002)

12. Gaeta, A., Gaeta, M., Orciuoli, F., Ritrovato, P.: Enabling Technologies for future learning scenarios: The Semantic Grid for Human Learning. In: Proceeding of the IEEE International Symposium on Cluster Computing and the Grid (CCGrid 2005), Cardiff, UK, May 9-12 (2005)
13. Gouardères, G., Conté, E., Mansour, S., Razmerita, L.: Ontology based user modelling for personalization of Grid learning services. In: Electronic Workshops in Computing (eWiC) series, British Computer Society
14. Guangzuo, C., Fei, C., Hu, C., Shufang, L.: OntoEdu: A Case Study of Ontology-based Education Grid System for E-Learning. In: GCCCE 2004 International Conference, Hong Kong (2004)
15. Huang, C., Xu, F., Xu, X., Zheng, X.: Towards an Agent-Based Robust Collaborative Virtual Environment for E-Learning in the Service Grid. In: Shi, Z.-Z., Sadananda, R. (eds.) PRIMA 2006. LNCS (LNAI), vol. 4088, pp. 702–707. Springer, Heidelberg (2006)
16. IMS Learning Design home,
    http://www.imsglobal.org/learningdesign/index.cfm
17. Kaleidoscope Learning Grid SIG Web site,
    http://grid.noe-kaleidoscope.org
18. Liao, C., Ou Yang, F.: A Workflow Framework for Pervasive Learning Objects Composition by Employing Grid Services Flow Language. In: Proceedings of the IEEE International Conference on Advanced Learning Technologies (ICALT 2004), pp. 840–841 (2004)
19. Luo, Z., Fei, Y., Liang, J.: On Demand E-Learning with Service Grid Technologies. In: Edutainment 2006, pp. 60–69 (2006)
20. Mac Randal, D., Dimitrakos, T.: A Vision about the Learning Grid. In: Capuano, N. (ed.) Learning Grid: a newsletter from the Kaleidoscope Learning Grid SIG, October 2004, vol. 2, pp. 2–8 (2004)
21. Merceron, A., Capuano, N., Orciuoli, F., Ritrovato, P.: Scenarios for a Learning GRID. In: Proceedings of SWEL 2007: Ontologies and Semantic Web Services for Intelligent Distributed Educational Systems held in conjunction with AIED 2007, Marina del Rey, USA, July 9 2007, pp. 74–79 (2007)
22. OWL Service Coalition OWL-S: Semantic Markup for Web Services (2004),
    http://www.w3.org/Submission/OWL-S/
23. Ritrovato, P., Gaeta, M.: Towards a Semantic Grid for Human Learning. IOS Press, Amsterdam (2005) ISBN: 1586035347
24. Salerno, S., Gaeta, M., Ritrovato, P., Capuano, N., Orciouli, F., Miranda, S., Pierri, A. (eds.): The Learning Grid Handbook, Concepts, Technologies and Applications. The future of Learning, vol. 2(3-19). IOS Press, Amsterdam (2008)
25. Samaras, G., Karenos, K., Christodoulou, E.: A Grid Service Framework for Metadata Management in Self-e-Learning Networks. In: Proc. Of the 2nd European Across Grids Conference (AxGrid), Nicosia, Cyprus (January 2004)
26. Sherly, E., Bindya, G., Deepa, L., Resmy, K.S.: A Grid Service Based Portal for Virtual Learning Campus. In: Liew, K., Shen, H., See, S., Cai, W., Fan, P., Horiguchi, S. (eds.) PDCAT 2004. LNCS, vol. 3320, pp. 86–89. Springer, Heidelberg (2004)
27. Vega-Gorgojo, G., Bote-Lorenzo, M.L., Gómez-Sánchez, E., Dimitriadis, Y.A., Asensio-Pérez, J.I.: Semantic Search of Learning Services in a Grid-Based Collaborative System. In: Proceedings of the 5th IEEE/ACM Int. Symposium on Cluster Computing and the Grid (CCGrid 2005), Workshop on Collaborative and Learning Applications of Grid Technology and Grid Education (CLAG) 2005, Cardiff, UK, pp. 19–26 (May 2005)
28. Web Services Modelling Ontology Working Group, http://www.wsmo.org/
29. Zhuge, H., Li, Y.: KGTutor: A Knowledge Grid Based Intelligent Tutoring System. In: Yu, J.X., Lin, X., Lu, H., Zhang, Y. (eds.) APWeb 2004. LNCS, vol. 3007. Springer, Heidelberg (2004)

Online Social Networks: Why Do "We" Use Facebook?

Pui-Yee Chiu[1], Christy M.K. Cheung[2], and Matthew K.O. Lee[3]

[1] Department of Finance and Decision Sciences, Hong Kong Baptist University
`05018781@hkbu.edu.hk`
[2] Department of Finance and Decision Sciences, Hong Kong Baptist University
`ccheung@hkbu.edu.hk`
[3] Department of Information Systems, City University of Hong Kong
`ismatlee@cityu.edu.hk`

Abstract. With the proliferation of online social networks, there has been a growing interest in understanding why people come and use this new type of communication platform. In this paper, we explore the factors that drive people to use online social networks (e.g., Facebook). We conceptualize the use of online social networks as intentional social action and examine the relative impact of social influence and social presence on We-Intention to use online social networks. An empirical study of Facebook users (n=182) find that We-Intention to use online social networks is strongly determined by social presence. Implications for research and practice are discussed.

1 Introduction

Social networking website is a kind of virtual communities that allows people to connect and interact with each other (Murray & Waller, 2007). Participation in online social networks becomes a new communication and interaction phenomenon. For example, the market share of the top 20 social networking websites grew by 11.5 percent from January 2007 to February 2007, accounted for 6.5 percent of all Internet visits in February 2007 (Hitwise, 2007). The popularity of social networking sites is highly depended on the number of people using it. It is also depended on the amount of interactions with other users in a personal network. Since social interactions and connection is the objective in online social networks, it is more appropriate to consider the use of online social networks as collective social action. Because of the newness of this phenomenon, there exists little research on intentional social actions in online social networks. In this paper, we aim at exploring the factors affecting the formation of intentional social action (e.g., We-Intention to use Facebook).

2 Theoretical Background

2.1 We-Intention

We-intention is defined as a "commitment of an individual to engage in joint action and involves an implicit or explicit agreement between the participants to engage in

M.D. Lytras et al. (Eds.): WSKS 2008, CCIS 19, pp. 67–74, 2008.
© Springer-Verlag Berlin Heidelberg 2008

that joint action" (Tuomela, 1995, p.9). The concept was initialized by a number of philosophers (e.g., Bratman, 1997, Tumolea, 1995), and was expressed in terms of "We together will perform X (X represents a joint action)". While I-intention is explained by individual-level reasons for performing the personal act, We-intention is explained by a person view the self as part of a social representation in performing a group act (Bagozzi & Lee, 2002). We-intention exists when a person believes not only that he can perform his part of their joint action, but also that he together with his fellow participants can perform the action jointly at least with some nonzero probability (Tuomela, 2006, p37).

2.2 Social Influence Theory

Kelman's social influence theory argues that psychological attachment (to specific behaviors) is the construct of interest that will motivate people to system use (Malhotra & Galletta, 2005). Social influence determines the changes in attitudes and actions produced by social influence which may occur at different "levels" (Kelman, 1958). Different level of changes corresponds to differences in the process whereby the individual accepts influence (Kelman, 1958). The three different processes of influence are: compliance, internalization and identification.

Compliance occurs when an individual perceives that a social actor wants him or her to perform a specific behavior, and the social actor has the ability to reward the behavior or punish non-behavior (Venkatesh & Davis, 2000). Internalization, operationalized by group norms, refers to the adoption of common self-guides for meeting idealized goals shared with others, because they are viewed as coinciding with one's own goal (Dholakia et al., 2004). Identification occurs when an individual accepts influence because he wants to establish or maintain a satisfying self-defining relationship to another person or a group (Kelman, 1958). The content of the behavior is irrelevant to the user who is motivated simply by the salience of the relationship (Bergami & Bagozzi, 2000).

2.3 Social Presence Theory

According to Short, Williams and Christie (1976), social presence is "the degree of salience of the other person in the interaction and the consequent salience of interpersonal relationships". Social presence is a subjective quality of the communication medium. Individual of any communications medium are in some sense aware of the degree of social presence of the medium and tend to avoid using medium that they think it requires higher degree of social presence than they perceive the medium to have (Short et al.,1976). The presence of others in virtual environment is important because it implies direct or indirect human contact (Gefen & Straub, 2004). Individual participates in the virtual social networking site can perform communication style that similar to face-to-face communication. Research has found that richer media (media with high social presence) tend to be preferred in communications settings where the task is ambiguous and uncertain (Straub & Karahanna, 1998).

3 Research Model and Hypotheses

As shown in Figure 1, We-intention is determined by social influence factors (i.e., subjective norm, group norms, and social identity) and social presence. Definitions and interrelationships of the constructs in the research model are addressed in the following section.

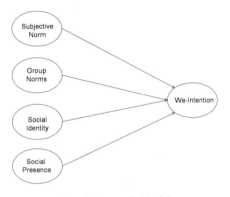

Fig. 1. Research Model

3.1 We-Intention to Use Social Networking Site

Intentions are assumed to capture the motivational factors that influence a behavior (Azjen, 1991). We-intention focuses on the presence of "we" together in making an intention that we will continue to use an online social networking site in the future. This is a joint intention made by a group of people that everyone will perform his/her own part (individual intention of joining and using online social networks continually) to perform a joint action together with others (continue to use online social networks together).

3.2 Social Influence and We-Intention to Use Social Networking Site

The social influence underlying subjective norm reflects the influence of expectations from significant others and represents what Kelman terms "Compliance". In IS adoption research, the compliance process appeared to be paramount. Before users have any actual usage experience with a new system, second-hand information, particularly from the primary reference groups (family or friends), are important for their usage decisions. However, it remains to be seen whether this is true for users of highly interactive online social network systems since, in contrast with standalone systems, these users are more exposed to other people's influences as they interact in the social network.

H1: A stronger subjective norm leads to a higher level of We-Intention to participate in an online social networking site.

The second mode of social influence characterized by group norms is similar to the term "Internalization" as suggested by Kelman (1958). Internalization is the adoption of a decision based on the similarity of one's values with the values of other group members. Thus, if a user realizes that he/she shares similar values or goals with other users in an online social networking site, we expect his/her We-Intention will increase.

H2: Stronger group norms lead to a higher level of We-Intention to participate in an online social networking site.

The third mode of social influence, identification, refers to the self-awareness of one's membership in a group, as well as the emotional and evaluative significance of this membership (Tajfel, 1978). Social identity can create a sense of belonging to an online social networking site when users view themselves as the members of the community. The psychological state of being part of the community in an online social network can be derived from either one of the following situation: (1) Affective social identity: A sense of emotional involvement with the community (2) Evaluative social identity: A sense of viewing themselves as self-worth to the community or (3) Cognitive social identity: A sense of self-awareness of being part of the community.

Together, the three components of social identity expected to have main effects on We-Intention of using the online social networking site. Thus, if a user holds strong social identity toward an online social networking site, we expect his/her We-Intention will increase.

H3: A stronger social identity leads to a higher level of We-Intention to participate in an online social networking site.

3.3 Social Presence and We-Intention to Use Social Networking Site

Social Presence Theory (Short et al.,1976) reveals that the higher degree of social presence in the medium, the higher the sociability of a medium. Thus, social presence is viewed as a quality of a communications medium. Some social networking sites emphasis on the presence of people involvement in order to facilitate communication through the net. For example, presence of others can be seen by the News Feed function, as it keeps tracks of friends' actions once they log in the online social network. Furthermore, non-user can also know the presence of their friends in an online social network through the Join Invitation function. Positive social presence would have a greater impact on individual to join and to continue using an online social networking site, since individuals tend to select the medium that they perceive to have the highest social presence (Flanagin & Metzger, 2001). Therefore:

H4: A higher level of social presence leads to a higher level of We-Intention to participate in an online social networking site

4   Research Design

Facebook (http://www.facebook.com), an online social networking site, was used in this study to examine intentional social actions in online social networks. An invitation message with the URL to the online questionnaire was posted on a number of online social groups of Facebook (mostly student groups). To increase the response rate, an incentive of supermarket vouchers was offered as lucky draw prizes. A screening question was used to ensure that the respondents were current active users of Facebook. In addition, they were told to follow an instruction before filling the questionnaire:

"Imagine that you are logging on to the Internet to engage in the group interaction and communication that you described above. You have a number of friends within Facebook that you regularly interact with. Please picture briefly in your mind the name and image of each online friend. Then, write your nickname and their nicknames in the table below".

These instructions were designed to capture the respondents' collectivity of using Facebook. To ensure that there was no duplicated respondents, IP addresses were recorded and checked.

The measures of the constructs in this study were borrowed from previous literature. All constructs were measured using multi-item perceptual scales. That means each construct was measured by a few items for construct validity and reliability. A seven-point Likert scale with 1=strongly disagree to 7=strongly agree was used.

5   Data Analysis and Results

Partial Least Square (PLS) was used to test the hypotheses in the research model and to ensure that the conclusion on structural relationship is drawn form a set of measurement instruments with psychometric properties. In this paper, we first report the result of the measurement model, and then the structural model.

Convergent validity is shown when each measurement item correlates strongly with its assumed theoretical construct. It can be examined by using the composite reliability (CR) and the average variance extracted (AVE). The critical values for CR and AVE are 0.7 and 0.5 respectively (Fornell & Larcker,1981). As shown in Table 1, except the measures for Subjective Norm, all the CR and AVE values meet the recommended thresholds.

Table 1. Psychometric Properties of Measures

Constructs	CR	AVE
We-Intention (INT)	0.97	0.95
Subjective Norm (SN)	0.59	0.50
Group Norms (GN)	0.89	0.80
Social Identity (SI)	0.90	0.60
Social Presence (SP)	0.90	0.70

Discriminant validity is shown when each measurement item correlates weakly with all other constructs except for the one to which it is theoretically associated. The square root of the AVE of each construct should be much larger than the correlation of the specific construct with any of the other constructs in the model (Chin, 1998). Table 2 shows that the squared root of AVE extracted for each construct, all AVE values are greater than the off-diagonal elements in the corresponding rows and column, demonstrating discriminant validity.

Table 2. Correlation Matrix and Psychometric Properties of Key Constructs

	INT	SN	GN	SI	SP
INT	**0.97**				
SN	0.15	**0.71**			
GN	0.40	0.08	**0.89**		
SI	0.37	0.09	0.57	**0.77**	
SP	0.42	0.12	0.47	0.53	**0.84**
Notes: Shaded diagonal elements are the square root of AVE for each construct					

Figure 2 show the results of the PLS structural model with the overall explanatory power, the estimated path coefficients and the associated t-values of the paths. All the significant paths are indicated with an asterisk. The model accounts for 24 percent of the variation in We-Intention to use online social networking sites. Social presence is the most significant exogenous variables of We-Intention with a path coefficient of 0.25. The result also shows that group norms is an important determinant of We-Intention with a path coefficient of 0.20.

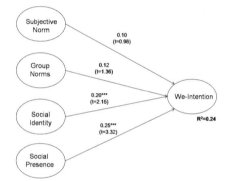

Fig. 2. PLS Results of the Research Model (Note: * $p<0.10$, ** $p<0.05$, ***$p <0.01$)

6   Discussion and Conclusion

Social networking website becomes very popular among internet users. Understanding "Why we use Facebook" becomes an interesting topic. In particular, we postulate the usage of online social networking sites as intentional social action. Social influence theory and social presence theory are adopted to explain the phenomenon. The results show that social presence has the strongest impact on we-intention to use Facebook. As Facebook is a kind of social networking sites, the presence of others is the most important feature that attracts users to use Facebook, especially for those who use Facebook as the platform for communication. The special feature "News Feed" in Facebook allows users to "see" the "social presence" in Facebook. The new function "Facebook Chat" also allows user to know the presence of friends in Facebook by giving them to chat online when they are using Facebook. Group norm also has a significant influence on We-Intention to use Facebook. When users realize the similarity of their values with their groups, they will have higher tendency on we-intention to use Facebook. However, social identity does not have any significant relationships with We-Intention. This may due to the numbers of communities the users have joined. If a user join too many communities, it is hard for him/her to create a sense of belonging to a specific group.

This study is one of the very first studies attempts to explain the collective behavior in Web 2.0 applications using intentional social action. Over the past two decades, IS researchers have demonstrated considerable interest in measuring personal intentions in traditional information systems adoption where the usage experience does not depend on other users (Davis et al., 1992). In online social networking sites in contrast, social interaction and connection is the objective. These social networking sites give everyone a place to share their personal stories, in words, pictures, and videos with their friends. They also connect people with friends and others who work, study, and live around them. They help people learn more about events, parties, and other social functions. We believe that We-Intention encapsulates social behaviors by the collective is a more appropriate approach to study user decision to use online social networks.

The result of this study is also important to practitioners. The popularity of a social networking website is highly depended on the number of people using it. Online social networks not only provide a place for people who have similar interests to join together and communicate, but also provide a lot of business opportunities to the online advertising and promotion industry. As social networking site is a place where people are grouped into different segments, businesses can easily target their products or services to their desired target groups. This would facilitate the sales of products or services. Viral marketing, which has a more influential power than other forms of marketing, can also be successfully used through the social networking activities within the site.

References

Azjen, I.: The theory of planned behavior. Organizational Behavior and Human Decision Processes 50, 179–211 (1991)

Bagozzi, R.P., Lee, K.H.: Multiple routes for social influence: The role of compliance, internalization and social identity. Social Psychology Quarterly 65(3), 226–247 (2002)

Bratman, M.E. (1997). I intend that We J. In Holmstrom-Hintikka, G., & Tuomela, R. (Eds). Contemporary Action Theory (pp. 49-63). Kluwer, Dordrecht: the Netherlands.

Bergami, M., Bagozzi, R.P.: Self-categorization, affective commitment, and group self-esteem as distinct aspects of social identity in an organization. British Journal of Social Psychology 39(4), 555–577 (2000)

Chin, W.W.: Issues and Opinion on Structural Equation Modeling. MIS Quarterly 22(1), vii-xvi (1998)

Davis, F.D., Bagozzi, R., Warshaw, P.R.: User acceptance of computer technology: A comparison of two theoretical models. Management Science 35(8), 982–1003 (1989)

Dholakia, U.M., Bagozzi, R.P., Pearo, L.K.: A social influence model of consumer participation in network- and small- group-based virtual communities. International Journal of Research in Marketing 21, 241–263 (2004)

Flangagin, A.J., Metzger, M.J.: Internet Use in the Contemporary Media Environment. Human Communication Research 27(1), 153–181 (2001)

Fornell, C., Larcker, D.F.: Evaluating structural equation models with unobservable variables and measurement error. Journal of Marketing Research 18(1), 39–50 (1981)

Gefen, D., Straub, D.W.: Consumer trust in B2C e-commerce and the importance of social presence: Experiments in e-products and e-services. OMEGA 32(6), 407–424 (2004)

Hitwise. Social networking visits increase 11.5 percent from january to february (March 14, 2007), Retrieved December 23, from Hitwise (2007)

Kelman, H.C.: Compliance, identification, and internalization three processes of attitude change. The Journal of Conflict Resolution 2(1), 51–60 (1958)

Malhotra, Y., Galletta, D.: A multidimensional commitment model of volitional systems adoption and usage behavior. Journal of Management Information Systems 22(1), 117–151 (2005)

Murray, K.E., Waller, R.: Social networking goes abroad. International Educator 16(3), 56–59 (2007)

Short, J., Williams, E., Christie, B.: Theoretical approaches to differences between media. In: The social psychology of telecommunication, pp. 61–76. Wiley, London (1976)

Straub, D.W., Karahanna, E.: Knowledge worker communications and recipient availability: Toward a task closure explanation of media choice. OSC 8(2), 160–175 (1998)

Tajfel, H.: Social Categorization, Social Identity, and Social Comparison. In: Tajfel, H. (ed.) Differentiation between social groups: Studies in the social psychology of intergroup relations. Academic Press, London (1978)

Tuomela, R.: The importance of us: A philosophy study of basic social notions. Stanford University Press, Stanford (1995)

Tuomela, R.: Joint Intention, We-mode and I-Mode. Stanford University Press, Stanford (2006)

Venkatesh, V., Davis, F.D.: A theoretical extension of the technology acceptance model: Four longitudinal field studies. Management Science 46(2), 186–204 (2000)

Localization of Educational Software for Deaf Children: Suggestions and Perspectives

Ioanna Antoniou-Kritikou and Constandina Economou

Institute for Language and Speech Processing/ 'Athena' Research Center, Artemidos 6,
151 25 Athens, Greece
agianna@ilsp.gr, enadia@ilsp.gr

Abstract. Nowadays it is widely accepted that the implementation of computer applications could establish better possibilities for equal participation in education for those groups of the population that previously felt excluded. The aim of this paper is to propose the localization of existing educational software as an alternative way to facilitate integration of deaf children attending the same classes with hearing ones. We suggest the adaptation of software to the needs of this target group with the incorporation of video in Greek Sign Language (GSL), in order to cover the lack of special instructional material, to strengthen the reading ability of deaf children and, finally, provide equal opportunities for all pupils.

Keywords: localization, educational software, GSL, deaf children.

1 Integration of Deaf Children into General Education

It has been widely accepted all over the world that pupils, irrespective of their disabilities or features that differentiate their national, cultural or social identity, have equal opportunities in their access to education with the rest of the school population. The provision of equal opportunities exceeds equality of access to education, and encompasses adaptation of the overall educational system [1].

The current Hellenic National Analytic Curricula for primary and secondary education have acknowledged the necessity to satisfy the special educational needs of certain categories of pupils and their right for integration and equal instructional opportunities in a school open to everyone. For the first time these curricula make various references to children with special needs and for the first time the Hellenic Pedagogical Institute of the Ministry of Education has formally prepared an Analytic Curriculum for Special Education. Despite these favorable conditions in the general school, children with special needs still have to overcome substantial obstacles in their education [1], [2].

As far as deaf and hard of hearing children are concerned and following international educational practices, there is a tendency in Greece for them to attend general school in classes of hearing children so as to receive the same instruction [3]. However, the attempt to offer equal quantity and quality of instruction fails unless a number of appropriate adaptations take place concerning accessibility of educational content, interactivity of resources and adequacy of instructional material for supporting self-learning.

M.D. Lytras et al. (Eds.): WSKS 2008, CCIS 19, pp. 75–82, 2008.

Nowadays the implementation of computer applications could establish better possibilities for equal integration in education for those groups of the population that previously felt excluded.

The aim of this paper is to suggest alternative ways to facilitate integration of children with disabilities -deaf among them- attending general classes; therefore, we propose further exploitation of already existing educational software, designed and developed for general education by its localization so as to cover the needs of various types of special education.

2   Greek Sign Language and Information Technology

Greek Sign Language (GSL) has been recognized as the official language of the Greek Deaf Community by Act of the Greek Parliament (Legislative Act 2817/2000, article 4) and it is one of the various visual languages of the world.

The fundamental semantic unit of all sign languages, including GSL, is the sign. The linguistic sign is transferred visually and expressed through: a) manual components (the shape of the palm and the place of the fingers, palm orientation, movement of the hand, repetition of movement, location of signing) and b) other, non-manual components (body position, facial expression, mouth patterns, head and body movement).

Until recently, there has been considerable lack of educational material for the support of GSL in schools; nowadays this gap is being filled through maturation of multimedia technologies and development of extremely user-friendly interfaces that facilitate accessibility of educational software by teachers and pupils alike without the need of considerable expertise in Information Technology [4].

Deaf or hard of hearing pupils need easily accessible educational material so as to overcome difficulties in processing acoustic stimuli (Legislative Act 304: 4195). Information Technology products and services can provide alternative ways for presentation and comprehension of any type of educational content. Since GSL is a language articulated in space and is based on iconicity to convey a meaning, video is the ideal means to express any linguistic message and should be incorporated in any educational software addressed to the deaf population; "the place for the production of the sign is ergonomically defined and includes the rectangle covering the top of the head up to the body and on average 20-30 centimetres beside the arms, always at the front of the body" [5].

3   Suggestions for Localization of Educational Software

'Localization' of a product is adaptation to the needs of a new market, different to the one for which it has already been designed and developed for, including transformation of the original product into a form acceptable, both linguistically and culturally, by the country, audience and generally the market for which it is targeted. The process of localization of educational software refers to adaptation of all the various elements that are included in it: software (program, tools), multimedia material (e.g. texts, pictures, sounds, videos, graphics), printed manuals, electronic manuals (e.g. on-line help), web documents, etc. [6].

Focal points of localization efforts [7] include, among others:

- language translation
- national varieties of languages
- local customs
- local content
- symbols
- aesthetics
- cultural values and social context

Localization of educational software for deaf children, who are bilinguals (in Modern Greek and GSL) involves much less effort. As the educational software that is adapted to the needs of the deaf is addressed to the same academic audience (attending the same classes), with common cultural patterns and rules[1], in the same geographical area, the process is limited to the need for translation of texts into another language which is, in this case, GSL.

It is important for the GSL specialist to be an expert in the subject(s) dealt with by the educational software in order to successfully translate both content and terminology. For instance, the sign specialist involved in the localization of software for mathematics or physics should be an expert in sciences, whereas the specialist involved in software for history or ancient Greek should be a philologist.

The incorporation of GSL presupposes adding video with the translation of all the texts (written and oral) included in the software. The different types of texts in educational software that need to be translated in GSL encompass the following:

- texts as part of the screen: this is easily adaptable with the incorporation of a video viewer with the GSL translation on the screen.
- texts appearing on screen after selection by the user (e.g. texts in menus, navigation buttons, help) or following an action (e.g. texts of the installation procedure, various software messages including messages for evaluation): since these texts appear in a viewer, the video viewer in GSL is incorporated in it.
- texts in graphics and pictures (e.g. captions in pictures and photographs, balloons in cartoons): functionally, the video viewer in GSL starts when the user clicks within the texts.
- oral narratives and video: depending on the case, they can be tackled in different ways. Narrations or videos accompanied by written text on screen need the incorporation of a video viewer in GSL. The written version is very useful for bilingual users since it can be dynamically linked to the video; the user can choose an extract of the text and watch the corresponding part of the video either in Greek or in GSL.

---

[1] According to the cultural approach to deafness, deaf children learning both Modern Greek and GSL become bilingual and bicultural. Since they attend general school, it is assumed that they are already familiar with the culture of the hearing ones [8].

- installation and user manuals: the manuals of the source software need to include all the fundamental functional changes resulting from the incorporation of the video in GSL. A video edition of these manuals in GSL could also be of great help to this special category of users since it could facilitate their navigation considerably.

4 Phases of Localization of Educational Software

The localization procedure of educational software for the deaf comprises two basic phases: a) the re-designing phase during which all necessary changes are selected and b) the developmental phase during which the video is produced and all the changes are incorporated in the source software.

Fig. 1. Localization of educational software

A. Re-design

Re-design refers to the selection of material to by translated in GSL as well as to the adaptation of screens. More explicitly, the re-designing phase can be analysed as follows:

- *Selection of all texts to be translated in GSL*

In general, localization of educational software in another language comprises translation of all types of texts (both oral and written) from the source to the target language. As far as GSL is concerned, taking into consideration that translation involves video production, this procedure can prove to be extremely time consuming and subject to different kinds of technical or financial restrictions. For instance, if the software comprises very long texts, then the duration of the produced videos will be very long; as a result, CD-ROMs run out of space and internet runs at a very low speed.

To address these problems, it is suggested to follow a phase of pre-selection of the texts to be translated. Each educational software imposes its own requirements and rules for its adaptation. However, in an attempt to minimize the changes during the localization procedure, it is recommended to convey in GSL the most important written resources, more particularly:

– texts considered as basic and essential for the comprehension of the subject matter in question, as well as the introductory texts (texts that introduce the users to the time and place and to what follows). When hypertext techniques are used, then the basic text is supported by video and the hotword links -if they lead to complementary information- remain untranslated (Figure 1).

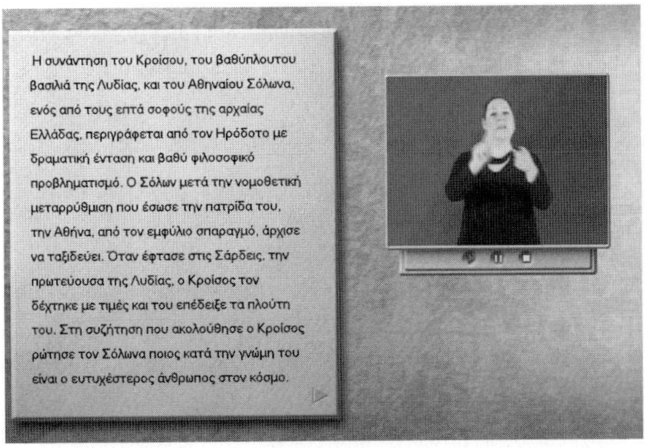

Fig. 1. Introductory text with hotwords (extracted from *Ancient Greek with* GSL[2])

Fig. 2. Written help supported by video in GSL (extracted from "Ancient Greek with GSL")

– help texts for the exercises (Figure 2), so that the users can understand in GSL what they have to do.
– help texts for all screens, so that users can navigate the software.
– evaluation texts of exercises, so that users know if they have answered correctly or not.

• *Re-designing of screens*

The introduction of the video viewer in the software involves the re-design of all relevant screens. This procedure can be more or less problematic depending on the complexity of the functionality of each screen.

In software designed and developed from scratch for the deaf, the video viewer in GSL would be a functional part of the screen. However, in cases of localization, the addition of video viewer may involve considerable amendments of the screen. In the

---

[2] *Ancient Greek with GSL*: Educational software for the teaching of Ancient Greek to Lower Secondary Education designed and developed by ILSP.

Fig. 3. Adaptation of a screen with the incorporation of video viewer (extracted from *Language travels with GSL*[3])

following screen (Figure 3), the incorporation of the video viewer is not very success-ful since it is 'squeezed' into the bottom margin of the screen. If the original graphic had been adapted, the result would have been better.

It goes without saying that, since the video is so important for the deaf, the video viewer should appear on screen on entering so as the users need not activate it by clicking a button.

B) Development

The developmental phase involves, initially, video recording and, then, its technical elaboration. The adaptation is completed by incorporating the video into the educa-tional software.

After the developmental phase and before the delivery of the final product, a test-ing phase takes place and the certification by the Hellenic Pedagogical Institute in order for the software to be deemed suitable for school use.

5   Conclusions and Perspectives

The Knowledge Society is the new context of our living and working. It aims to gen-erate knowledge, create a culture of sharing, fill societal needs and enhance quality of life in a sustainable manner. In this context, actions should be undertaken towards a better world based on knowledge and learning for all [9, 10], including people with disabilities.

In this perspective and regarding deaf children and their problem of integration in classes with hearing ones, there are still a number of issues to be taken into considera-tion and dealt with in the framework of the National Curriculum and the existing material and resources.

---

[3] *Language travels with GSL*: Educational software for the teaching of Modern Greek to Pri-mary Education designed and developed by ILSP.

An attempt to provide equal opportunities for all could be the design and development of educational software addressed exclusively to GSL users; in its simplest form, this software does not need written text on screen and can be limited to the presentation of information exclusively through video or other digital means.

On the other hand, the suggestion for localization of educational software to the needs of deaf or hard of hearing children is based on the idea of re-using already available software, saving time and financial resources; the ultimate goals are to cover the lack of special instructional material and other resources, to provide equal opportunities for all pupils and allow this particular target group to follow the National Curriculum, as far as possible. For this purpose, a committee of specialists from the Ministry of Education should examine the existing educational software and choose those that, with the incorporation of video in GSL, will help these pupils in their learning of various subject matters. This is a very important implication for government and policymakers.

Obviously, the adapted educational software is addressed to bilingual deaf children who have serious difficulties in reading. International data prove that only 3-5% of the deaf population can achieve equal reading abilities with hearing children attending the same classroom [11]. However, the reading ability of this target group can be strengthened by Computer Technologies. The technique of dynamic link of the text and the video allows users to choose any extract of the text and watch the corresponding part of the video in GSL (Figure 4).

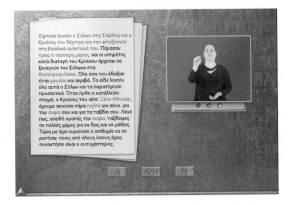

Fig. 4. Text and video dynamically linked (extracted from "Ancient Greek with GSL")

In conclusion, localization of existing software permits further exploitation of software developed to address the needs of another audience, strengthens the reading ability of deaf children and, finally, encourages a positive view towards the subject matter 'taught' through the software.

References

1. Pedagogical Institute: Analytic Curricula for the Deaf Children's Primary Education. Athens (2004a), http://www.pi-schools.gr/special_education/kofosi-a/kofosi-a-part-01.pdf

2. Pedagogical Institute: Analytic Curricula for the Deaf Children's Secondary Education. Athens (2004b), http://www.pi-schools.gr/special_education/kofosi-b/kofosi-b-part-00.pdf

3. Lambropoulou, V.: The vocational distribution of deaf people in Greece. In: Erting, C.J., et al. (eds.) The Deaf Way: Perspectives from the International Conference on Deaf Culture, pp. 791–793. Gallaudet University Press, Washington (1994)

4. Efthimiou, E., Fotinea, S.-E.: An adaptation-based technique on current educational tools to support universal access: the case of a GSL e-Learning platform. In: Courtiat, J.-P., Davarakis, C., Villemur, T. (eds.) Proc. of the TeL 2004 Workshop on Technology Enhanced Learning, Workshop to WCC-2004 (World Computer Congress), Toulouse, France, 22 August, pp. 177–186 (2004)

5. Efthimiou, E., Fotinea, S.-E.: I am Learning the Signs, Teaching Environment for Basic Vocabulary of Greek Sign Language (Teacher's Book), Athens, Institute for Language and Speech Processing /"Athena" R.C (2006)

6. E24 – KIRKI: Localization of International Educational Software in the Greek Educational System, Patras, Computer Technology Institute (1998)

7. Wikipedia, http://en.wikipedia.org/wiki/Internationalization_and_localization

8. Spinthouraki, I.: Bilingual-Bicultural Education Culturally Sensitive for Linguistic Minority Children: The Case of Deaf Children. In: Lambropoulou, V. (ed.) Cultural and educational Needs of the Deaf Child, pp. 181–192. University of Patras (2001)

9. Lytras, M., Sicilia, M.A.: The Knowledge Society: a manifesto for knowledge and learning. International Journal of Knowledge and Learning 1(1/2), 1–11 (2005)

10. Open Research Society, http://www.open-knowledge-society.org/society.htm

11. Di Perri, K.: ASL Phonemic Awareness in Deaf Children: Implications for Instruction. Doctoral Dissertation. Boston University, Ann Arbor (2004)

Bottleneck of Knowledge Society

Jaroslav Král[1,2] and Michal Žemlička[1]

[1] Charles University, Faculty of Mathematics and Physics,
Department of Software Engineering, Malostranské nám. 25, 118 00 Praha 1, CZ
jaroslav.kral@mff.cni.cz, michal.zemlicka@mff.cuni.cz
[2] Masaryk University, Faculty of Informatics,
Botanická 6a, 602 00 Brno, Czech Republic
kral@fi.muni.cz

Abstract. Knowledge is a precondition of prosperity and sustainability of human society. The pre condition of acquiring, development, and use of knowledge is a proper education. But what education in what extent? According to observations of current society there is a lack of people interested in the study of and willing to work in science [1,2], engineering [3], and manual jobs. There is a great demand for jobs in these areas [4] and current situation is considered to be a crucial threat for economic development and prosperity [5]. This paper discusses the possible reasons of it – low rewards, expensive and difficult study, prejudices [6], etc. A metareason can be the missing ability (and skill) to work hard and the fact that it is often forgotten that knowledge can be useful only if appropriate skills are trained. This situation is the consequence of the failure of social and educational processes, especially missing feedbacks in education systems. It is also the consequence of an improper use of IT emphasizing the use of IT in pedagogical (micro) process whereas the possibility to use IT as a tool enabling citizens and government to measure success and effectivity of education systems and their transformations is not used. It is caused by improper legislative and wrong practices of the collection and the use of data on education processes. A solution of this issue is proposed.

1 Introduction

It is generally accepted that knowledge societies only can succeed in long terms. Knowledge is the precondition sustainable success and prosperity. The fact that it is a necessary condition only (and not sufficient one) is often overlooked.

Let us repeat that a piece of knowledge k can contribute to the success of the society only if there are people able to understand, learn, and use it properly. For example a piece of knowledge can be understood as a part of some knowledge environment, e.g. civil engineering.

But it is does not suffice. There must be people able to apply and willing to apply k in real world processes, e.g. in design and construction of buildings. There must be properly trained people of various professions possessing appropriate talents and skills. The professionals should know not only how to do something

M.D. Lytras et al. (Eds.): WSKS 2008, CCIS 19, pp. 83–91, 2008.

but they must be able to do it and willing to do it – they must have appropriate skills. It is possible only if a properly tuned education system is used. It is a trivial fact but it has very nontrivial consequences as it is overlooked.

People should have a chance to make a well-founded decision what profession and therefore what education to choose for themselves or for their children. It is the issue of availability of data and information on education possibilities and prospects of job/labor market and the existence of tools for the development of the knowledge allowing a proper evaluation of education by citizens, government, and employers. We will see that IT can help a lot here but IT fails to help in this case now. It is probably one of crucial challenges for governments. The education systems are dynamic systems with a very slow feedback – many years are needed to find out whether the graduates of a new study program are successful or not. Such systems are difficult to control. Any solution strengthening and speeding up the feedback is very important.

At first we will discuss the facts indicating that the current information and knowledge on education systems is not satisfactory. We will describe the education issues in two different countries the education systems of which seem to have in spite of their differences similar basic problems. The issues are very likely typical for many (if not all) countries.

2   Are Engineers and Scientists of Any Use?

It is common all over the world that technical, scientific, and engineering (TSE) professionals are strongly needed but they are not available – compare e.g. the extensive survey research by Manpower in the last several years [7,4].

Similar complains can be heart form other sources. In the appeal "To Everyone Whose Voice Is Heart" more than 100 Czech scientists pointed out the falling quality of TSE education and languages education in Czech Republic. There has been almost no response.

The importance of science, technology, engineering, and mathematics (STEM) education was distinguished in the U.S.A. in fifties and even expressed in legislative.

```
The Congress hereby finds and declares that the security of
the Nation requires the fullest development of the mental
resources and technical skills of its young men and women.
```
                                    - National Defense Education Act of 1958

Now, after fifty years US government as well as professional bodies and academia complains that the situation in the education is not satisfactory. It is clearly visible from the following statements:

```
In the 21st century, economic power will be derived from skills
and innovation. Nations that don't invest in skills will weaken;
it is that straightforward.
```
                              - Louis Gerstner Jr., former chairman and CEO, IBM

High schools are failing to prepare too many of our students
for work and higher education.

- Achieve, Inc. and National Governors Association,
An Action Agenda for Improving America's High Schools, 2005

Many sources like [3,2] complain that the deficiencies in STEM education can threaten the position of the U.S.A. in the global world.

The above mentioned appeal from Czech Republic indicates the falling interests in STEM education and TSE professions and falling quality of graduates in STEM as well as in languages. We can find similar situation in the U.S.A.:

To prepare young Americans to understand the people
who will help to define the 21st century, nothing is more
important than our ability to converse in their native tongues.

- U.S. Secretary of State Condoleezza Rice

We can conclude that the situation in education in the countries like Czech Republic and the U.S.A. are similar. The similarity is to high degree supported by the above mentioned Manpower survey researches. We therefore discuss Czech Republic as a typical case.

It is a pity that the reasons for the STEM education deficiencies have not been in both countries analyzed enough. To detect reasons the following questions are to be answered:

– Are TSE professions and crafts poorly paid?
– What are the reasons for the prejudices like the negative sentiments against technology and general feeling of the public that TSE has no good perspectives and that TSE is not only difficult but also boring?
– What from the feelings is well founded?

Answers to the questions are not known yet. In any case the career data and information on graduates of particular schools, studies, etc. and on their professional success are in fact not available – not to speak about tools accessible by public providing information and analyzes of educational system. In other words the feedback in education systems is weak if any. We show the reasons for it using detailed facts from Czech Republic[1]. It appeared that:

1. Data on current incomes, jobs, and positions on people exists at tax offices, at bureau of statistics, at enterprises, and the office of social services.
2. Data on unemployment are in many countries collected at employment (labor) offices and partly at bureau of statistics.
3. Data on the schools' graduates exist at individual schools and in some offices and at enterprises.

To summarize: current education system is something like a business without responsibilities.

---

[1] Note that also the facts mentioned in [3] indicate once more that the situation in Czech Republic is not exceptional.

3   Looking through Blind Glasses

There can be many reasons for the above described situation. One reason can be something like the "fashion" that the technical and scientific knowledge and jobs are not simply "in". Note that many people argue against technologies although they intensively use them. It can be a consequence of the fact that STEM education is difficult, long, and needs besides knowledge also talents, many skills, and a hard work. Celebrities are proud that they were poor in mathematics. Inability to work (learn) hard can be besides deficiencies in STEM education yet another crucial issue – probably not only for STEM. It can also be so that STEM education offers little career, hard work, and low wages. What is the truth? We do not know it.

How to find the solution?

The solution can be in a proper application of information technologies. It appears that the described situation can be the greatest challenge for information technology. Suppose that we know the current or passed career positions and incomes of people having a specific education. It will give a possibility of a clear answer to one of the above questions and it is likely that it will significantly influence and simplify answers for the other questions in the future.

It is not too difficult technical problem to design an information system having an intelligent interface allowing gettting information useful for making the proper choice of profession(s) and school(s). The system can be also used to evaluate education processes designed by educationists. The main problem is not the existence of the data nor their precision or completeness but their accessibility caused by legislative barriers preventing to collect and use the data.

The system should be able to answer questions of the following types:

– What is career position and average wages of the graduates from given school and having given variant of education?
– What is the mean salary of the graduates/alumni of a given school n years after graduation and how many percent of unemployed are within them? The salaries can be also represented by a frequency diagram.
– What is the probability that a person with a given type of education would be n years after graduation unemployed?
– What is the probability for a graduate/alumni from a (given) high school that he/she successfully finishes a (given) university?

Further examples of the queries can be found in [8].

The issue is that almost all the needed data are private (sensitive) and that data and data links must be kept for a long time. It implies some data security threats. It is especially true for the data links. It is a technical problem that can be technically solved. But it is a problem from the legislative point of view. At present instead of controlling outputs of systems using sensitive data the inputs of the systems are banned. They are banned even in the case when the data are properly anonymized and data security procedures are effective enough. The technical solution will be discussed below. According our experience the greatest opposition against such information system is from influential lobby related to education bodies of educationists. The educationists especially the education theoretics prefer in fact if their products (graduates) are not to be evaluated/tested.

There is also many people having ideologically based arguments preferring so called free market without any limitations – quality control inclusive. Typical ideological opponents are researchers in pedagogy (educationists) permanently changing study plans and education methods but not providing any double blind experiments to test quality of their proposals. Other group of proponents is formed by parents that do not want to cooperate with schools – they just want to put their children into school and have no troubles with them looking after quality of their education quality inclusive. In Czech Republic high schools have economic autonomy. It, together with above discussed problems with educational feedback, implies that there is almost no responsibility for and control of the quality of educational processes.

4   Possible Implementation of the Information System

Our task can be shortly described as getting information that should be made available to the public from sensitive personal data that should be kept classified.

Currently there are places where pieces of the personal data are hold. We need to collect the data from the places, combine them, create the required information, and make the information available to the public.

The system should have two distinguished parts: one working with sensitive data and one working with the publishable information (Fig. 1).

The secure part contains offices collecting and having the data (as it is today), secure channels to special office collecting and combining the data (such behavior

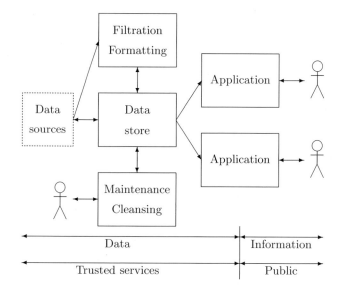

Fig. 1. Separation of sensitive data and publishable information

is similar to data collection and processing by bureau of statistics), accredited applications computing the required information from the (anonymized) data.

The open (public) part responds to user requests. It can collect requests statistics or even some requests – to get information on possible new questions and to be able to optimize the system.

It is possible to check responses of the system whether it contains only permitted information. All application processing the data must be certified that they really do what is expected and nothing more. It is reasonable to restrict the functionality as it ensures that no sensitive data are revealed.

There are two key technical issues: secure transfer of the data and secure processing. The data can be transferred using private networks and some high-security encryption. The problem is that the data will be available in the data processing center. It is possible to store them encrypted.

The processing itself requires access to decrypted data as it uses their semantic. As the processing can be composed from quite simple steps and performed in batches, batch processing with all its advantages can be used. Very simple applications allow analysis and easy certification of their code. The same holds for the scripts controlling the entire processing. It is, all the code can be analyzed and checked by multiple certification authorities that they do just the activities that they should and claim to do – that they do not send the sensitive data anywhere else.

We can conclude that the problem can be technically solved.

The problem is in legislative: the practice is that no one is allowed to use personal data to any other purpose than they have been collected. It is, if the data were collected for tax purposes they cannot be used for research or statistics[2]. It implies that the first what we should do is to say that we want such system and the second is to change the law so that it will allow the use of the data collected by state institutions to get useful information if the access to the data would stay as secure as it is now.

5   Education and Research

The top engineering professionals – especially software experts, e.g. programmers – are educated at universities. The problem is that main stream of software development must be based on multidomain knowledge – it is by people being (according to [9], compare also [3] and surveys by Manpower) versatilists. Versatilists are people able to acquire and combine knowledge from different domains. It is a known that professors at universities are in fact induced to do research in a quite narrow domains. The quality of research is evaluated by accreditation bodies during the evaluation of the university qualities. The evaluation is mainly based on metrics like the number of scientific publications, impact factors, and citations. It in practice implies that people are induced to pay extreme effort on very narrow research domain.

---

[2] It is a pity that in fact many laws admit to collect any anonymized data, other legislative rules in fact forget it.

It contradicts the principles and needs in the education of engineering experts, IT experts inclusive. It has some adverse effects on the education of teachers for primary and secondary schools the knowledge of who should not be too narrow and should be open. Such problem should be, we hope, solved but it needs research and looking for specific research methods.

An example of a profession where the combined skills and knowledge is needed is sales representative: they should understand their business processes as well as the knowledge domain needed to understand the products they sale.

6   Future Research

The above analysis indicates that the main issues of the proposed information system are:

- acceptance of the idea that the information system with the above given purpose should be developed;
- resistance of politicians and school lobbies;
- collection and accessibility of data on graduates and their jobs;
- missing collaboration of various offices of state administration.

The authors have together with their graduate students collected a lot of information on data collected/existing in Czech Republic needed to measure quality of education and success of school graduates.

It appeared that almost all needed data exists in an electronic form but they are scattered among various offices and there is no desire to integrate them. It requires the information system able to cooperate with the individual information systems of the offices. The principles of SOA (service-oriented architecture, [10,11]) can be applied here. Some bodies published data analyses. The quality of the documents was substantially reduced due the fact that related data available from other institutions were not used. It appeared that it was almost impossible to change it as it would have implied that a substantial part of e-government system would have to be updated. Surprisingly many people say that the evaluation of schools is a hopeless task in principle.

We will further analyze the issues and the related risks and ways to convict the public that the education control based on above discussed principles is a reasonable idea. We will analyze the technical and statistical issues of integration of sample research into the system and organizational issues how to build the institutes supervising the information system output so that privacy will not be threaten. The research could benefit from the results of the development of Czech e-government system.

7   Conclusions

The basic condition of the enhancement of the knowledge system in modern (knowledge) society and even the condition for its mere existence is that there are enough well educated and trained people in various knowledge domains – especially in STEM. Current situation implies that there must be well working and therefore well managed/controlled education system. It appears that it need not be the case.

A good management and a good use of an education system (e.g. good choice of a study type and a concrete school) should be based on proper knowledge that in turn can be based on school evaluation, personal contacts, and other information and knowledge sources. The issue is that the sources in dynamic global economy must be based on modern IT tools enabling creation, dissipation, and accessibility of the knowledge on the success of the graduates. Such tools must use an intelligent information system as an evaluation metatool.

We have seen that there are no substantial technical obstacles to build an information system supporting the evaluation. We have discussed the possible outputs of such a system and the principles of education success measurement. The used metrics can vary according the aims and needs of users (i.e. of public).

The problem is that there is no such system. It, together with social prejudices and political and legislative barriers, implies that needed information and knowledge are not available. It has in current dynamic economy crucial consequences for sustainable prosperity. The system can moreover support the analysis of labor market needs to optimize the lengths of education processes that are now sometimes (e.g. in education of craftsmen) unnecessarily long.

The research survey of Manpower [4] and also responses from the business circles indicate that in the majority of countries craftsmen, qualified workers, and technicians are badly needed. These professions were in Middle Europe educated in so called industrial and crafts schools. These schools were in Czech Republic closed in 1990-ies. The last students from these schools graduated at least three years earlier than the bachelors that should replace them. Many current bachelors must, however, be retrained to be good technicians. The effects of the retraining is moderate. It in fact implies that one or two ears of additional education must be provided. It is, some people are ready for their profession about five years later than before without possitive effects. Moreover, the bachelors are expected to have more general (abstract) knowledge whereas the former graduates have been expected to have better practical training (skills). It also substantially reduces the number of people in productive age. It is not only expensive but it shortens the period of productive work.

The main effect of the proposed information system can be the reduction of prejudices leading to bad profession selections, objectification of the evaluation of the changes of education systems and new education methods, various variants of e-learning inclusive. A proper information system can speed up the education feedback.

The development of the proposed system could be expensive as many data are not available in electronic form and there must be institutions guarantying data/information privacy. The main barriers are the politicians not realizing the importance of the problem and lobby of educators not willing to be under a stronger control. Last but not least issue is that academia is not active enough to change the situation in education systems and to develop corresponding knowledge.

It is likely that the proposed system could be used also for other purposes than the ones discussed in this paper. An example is the tools supporting analysis how to optimize investments into perspective knowledge and educational domains.

Acknowledgement. This research was partially supported by the Program "Information Society" under project 1ET100300517.

All verbatim citings are taken from [5].

References

1. Bhattacharjee, Y.: New questions push for more degrees. Science 318, 1052 (2007)
2. Mervis, J.: Congress pases massive measure to support reearch and education. Science 317, 736–737 (2007)
3. Jamieson, L.: Engineering education in a changing world. The Bridge (Spring 2007)
4. Manpower: 2007 talent shortage survey (2007),
   `www.manpower.com/research/research.cfm`
5. Spellings, M.: Answering the challenge of a changing world (2006)
6. Král, J., Žemlička, M.: Engineering education promotion and e-government. In: Pudlowski, Z.J. (ed.) Proceedings of 5th Global Congress on Engineering Education, Melbourne, Australia, pp. 155–158. UNESCO International Centre for Engineering Education (2006)
7. Manpower: Confronting the coming talent crunch: What's next? (2005)
   `http://www.manpower.com/mpcom/`
   `files?name=Talent_Shortage_Whitepaper_Global_Final.pdf`.
8. Král, J., Žemlička, M.: Engineering education – a great challenge to software engineering. In: Lee, R. (ed.) 7th IEEE/ACIS International Conference on Computer and Information Science, pp. 488–495. IEEE Computer Society, Los Alamitos (2008)
9. Morello, D.: The IT professional outlook: Where will we go from here (2005)
10. Erl, T.: Service-Oriented Architecture: Concepts, Technology, and Design. Prentice Hall PTR, Englewood Cliffs (2005)
11. Král, J., Žemlička, M.: Autonomous components. In: Jeffery, K.G., Hlaváč, V., Wiedermann, J. (eds.) SOFSEM 2000. LNCS, vol. 1963, pp. 375–383. Springer, Heidelberg (2000)

Emerging Approach to E2.0: The Case of Social Enterprise – First Results from a 1-Year Field Research

Mariano Corso[1], Antonella Martini[2], Luisa Pellegrini[2], and Andrea Pesoli[1]

[1] Polytechnic of Milano, P.zza Leonardo da Vinci 32,
20133Milano, Italy
{Mariano.Corso,Andrea.Pesoli}@polimi.it
[2] University of Pisa, Via Diotisalvi 2,
56100Pisa, Italy
{Antonella.Martini,Luisa.Pellegrini}@dsea.unipi.it

Abstract. Enterprise 2.0 refers to a set of organizational and technological approaches steered to enable new organization models, based on open involvement, emergent collaboration, knowledge sharing, internal/external social network development and exploitation. It aims to respond to the new features and needs of people and boosts flexibility, adaptability and innovation. Technologically, Enterprise 2.0 covers the application of social computing tools relating to Web 2.0, as well as the adoption of new technological and infrastructural approaches such as SOA, BPM, RIA and new service models such as Software-as-a-Service. The challenge for management theory is to provide empirically grounded and actionable knowledge for companies to design and implement new ICT-enabled (virtual) working environments able to extend the boundaries of their knowledge creation to their mobile workers, customers and suppliers. Based on evidence from 70 case studies and a collaboration approach, the chapter reports the E2.0 emerging model and focuses on collaboration and knowledge sharing aspects.

Keywords: Enterprise 2.0, organization model, collaboration, knowledge sharing, social network.

1 Introduction

The availability of new ICT-enabled services and particularly of web and mobile communication services makes it possible to overcome geographical (the work-place is everywhere the worker is), time (the worker creates value whenever it is required) and organizational barriers (the concepts of colleague, competitor and supplier have to be rethought and become more worker- and relationship-focused). In addition, the Information System (IS) evolution in terms of interoperability and integration is speeding up the convergence towards the web application usage, while making the borders of the different IS more and more fuzzy. Intranet, ERP and CRM, which were once distinct ICT application systems, are merging and overlapping, while developing increasingly into communication and collaboration tools.

M.D. Lytras et al. (Eds.): WSKS 2008, CCIS 19, pp. 92–100, 2008.

As a result of this continuous evolution, the emerging IS is not just a sum of its components, but it can be a working 'space' which gives complete support to workers' multidimensional needs. The above vision is what we have called *virtual Workspace* [5]: a creative, open working space focused on workers, their needs, specific working conditions and interaction with others.

Since 2006 a new emerging stage of the abovementioned process emerged: a sort of discontinuity in the Workspace scope evolution, pushed by further emerging worker needs and enabled by social computing tools, Service-Oriented Architecture (SOA), Business Process Management (BPM), mash-up and new supply model (i.e. Software-as-a-Service - SaaS). The borders of the virtual Workspace are breaking down as those needs cannot be satisfied inside a 'closed' organizational space anymore: that means not only to open to external actors, but also to rethink the traditional collaboration and knowledge management schemes. We refer to this trend as the Enterprise 2.0.

All this means that (new) ICT can become a key factor to design the near future organization.

However, to exploit the potential of the technology, we need to look at people and the 'way' they construct the environment in which they work and interact. The role – and the challenge – of ICT is, therefore, to reproduce a social reality made up of interpersonal relationships, collaboration and communication flows, and possibly enhance this reality by emphasizing openness and collaboration.

Basing on evidence from 70 case studies, this chapter intends to explore one of the Enterprise 2.0 models – the Social Enterprise, with the goal to provide an actionable interpretative framework.

2   The Emergence of Enterprise 2.0

The term "Enterprise 2.0" derives from Web 2.0 and is often used to indicate the introduction and implementation of social software inside a company, and the social and organizational changes associated with it. We think that E2.0 calls for a broader vision of either organizational and technological model evolution, which includes the design of an adaptive architecture (SOA and BMP), Web 2.0 collaboration tools and the virtual Workspace as enabling platform for connections and processes.

> *E2.0 is a set of organizational and technological approaches steered to enable new organization models, based on open involvement, emergent collaboration, knowledge sharing, internal/external social network development and exploitation.*

The emerging needs [1][7][13] that E2.0 tries to respond to can be divided into six key dimensions (Fig. 1):
- *open belonging*: people increasingly feel, and actually are, as "members" of extended dynamic networks rather than single organisations: through E2.0 technologies (content management systems shared by the Intranet, Extranet and Internet, KM tools and collaboration tools open to external players, Intranet integrated operating applications such as the supply chain management systems) it is possible to supply secure and selective access to information, tools and

connections that go beyond the company's boundaries, interacting in an increasingly rich and effective manner with suppliers, consultants, partners, customers and other networked players;

- *social networking*: people increasingly need to develop and maintain that network of relations that is becoming a more and more important asset for their professional efficiency [5][12]. E2.0 tools and approaches that track down people from basic information (such as the traditional telephone book or online presence) or by associating advanced profiles (such as competence mapping, expert search, social networks) support the development and management of relations to track and contact co-workers and experts inside and outside the organisation, keeping their interest, skill and role profiles updated at all times;

- *knowledge networks*: to prevent their knowledge and skills being "surpassed" soon, workers must be able to build their own network to have access to knowledge and information from different sources, both explicit (document management systems, Business Intelligence, video-sharing, pod-casting, RSS) and implicit (systems that ease interaction between experts, such as forums, mailing lists, surveys, blogs, folksonomies, wiki)[8];

- *emergent collaboration*: in an increasingly fast and unpredictable competitive scenario, people need to create cooperative settings in a fast, flexible way, even outside the formal organisational patterns. E2.0 technology enables people to do this, through faster and richer opportunities for interaction, both synchronous (chat, instant messaging, video-conference) and asynchronous (diary sharing, project management, exchange and co-editing of work documents, texting) which enable them to overcome geographical and time barriers in extended organisations;

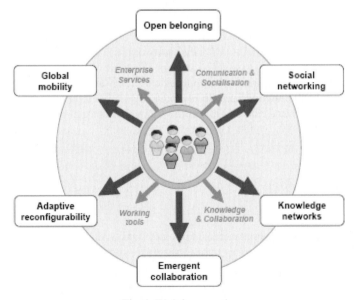

Fig. 1. E2.0 framework

- *adaptive reconfigurability*: in response to the endless changes taking place in corporate policies and strategies, people need to quickly reconfigure their own processes and activities. Such technologies as SOA, BPM, mash-up, SaaS, RIA can give the companies, and sometimes the users themselves, the tools they need to redefine and adapt their processes in a dynamic, flexible and personal way that can hardly be given by any traditional technology;
- *global mobility*: people spend an increasingly large share of their time far from the workplace and often in a state of mobility. New ICT enables them to be connected in any place and at any time of day through their own network of tools, thus making the workspace and working time more flexible, using systems for supplying staff services (authorisation workflows), internal communication, mobile office services (from simple emails to mobile access to the Intranet) and operational services, such as sales force automation and field force automation.

3   Methodological Notes

This article is based on evidence from the empirical research conducted by the E2.0 Observatory in Italy during 2007 and 2008. Considering the emergent nature of the phenomenon and a substantial lack of empirical researches, the proposed research methodology combines compared case studies, surveys and a sort of co-laboratory. Specifically:

- 70 case studies were carried out through a questionnaire and direct interviews to the management of medium/large-sized Italian companies (manufacturing, banking, PA, assurance, pharmaceutical, services);
- a survey was administered to 65 Chief Information Officers in order to understand their view of the E2.0 phenomenon
- an online community – Enterprise20.it (see http://www.enterprise20.it) – was developed in order to promptly receive cues and suggestions to refine the research.

In addition, direct interviews to main ICT players were performed in order to understand trends and scenarios on the vendor side.

Preliminary results have been discussed and validated through the Enterprise20.it, the online community (see http://www.enterprise20.it) created for the participating firms, vendors and experts to act as a laboratory and a landmark for the E2.0 phenomenon.

4   Emerging Models for Enterprise 2.0: The Social Enterprise Case

Three E2.0 models are emerging in the companies (Fig. 3):

- *Social Enterprise*(SE), aiming to create new collaboration, knowledge sharing and relation management models (24% of the cases);
- *Open Enterprise*(OE), tending to a great extension and opening of the Virtual Workspace boundaries in terms of access methods and external players (14% of the cases);

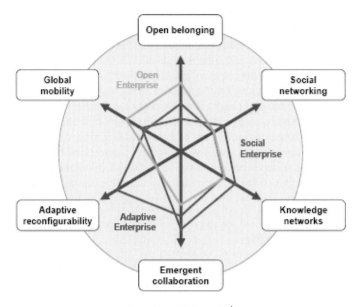

Fig. 2. The E2.0 model[1]

-   *Adaptive Enterprise* (AE), focused on flexibility and reconfigurability in corporate process management (14% of the cases).

Not all the analysed companies are following one of the above paths:48% of the cases are at their initial stage, with a limited support to all the dimensions.

Social Enterprise seems to be the most popular. As shown in red in Figure 3, it is the need for emergent collaboration, shared knowledge and development of internal and external social networks which drives the evolution of the organisational model. Although unable to start from technology, this is a process which can be enabled by it. The technology used includes both tools that have been available for some time in the ISs – such as document management, instant messaging, diary sharing, etc. – and innovative social computing tools borrowed from Web 2.0.

To understand the real impact of these tools on the organisation, a detailed analysis of the *SE* approaches was performed. It emerged a high level of maturity in terms of:

-   *commitment* the organisation gives to the community in terms of allocated resources (tools, people, etc) and level of legitimisation;
-   *level of users' involvement and participation.*

These Social Enterprises often create environments that are not targeted to the corporate population at large but to specific groups or communities. The level of users' participation and proactive involvement is high when they see the community as an important element to increase their wealth of knowledge, create new relations and

---

[1] The three models stand for the average support to the six dimensions in the organisations that adopted it (not the average in the overall sample).

increase their "organisational" effectiveness and visibility. In addition, a number of users, as well as using them, proactively participate in the creation of contents, take part in discussions and create interpersonal relations of trust and *mutual engagement*. At the same time, the top management's commitment is also high, and the organisation recognises the community as an important means to achieve its business purposes, by proactively supporting it and allocating it substantial resources.

Basing on the specific groups or community characteristics they are targeted to - the *focus* level (specificity of the involved members and therefore of the subjects addressed), *cohesion* (intensity of bonds between members), *stability* of involvement (time the community members remain in the community) and *interactivity* (frequency of relations between members) - four types of SE virtual environment con be selected (Fig.3):

- *Professional Families.* Environments targeted to communities of "cohesive" people which the members permanently belong to, with the members sharing the same interests and problems, usually relating to the same job (for instance, Information System, Research & Development communities, etc). Their purpose is to ease the exchange of knowledge, share *best practices* and network the "experts" to tackle common problems. In professional families, interaction is key, value is given by the creation of contents by the members, and participation is boosted by the quality of the resources and the availability of experts. In such cases, the "interactive" means are of primary importance but they must be combined so as to promote relations, exchanges, and let the members create and disseminate contents.

- *Teams.* Environments targeted to focused communities, which are often short lived because they are "instrumental" to achieving a shared but "transient" goal. A typical example are the communities that are created to manage projects the purpose of which is to support the operational process and encode implicit knowledge and documents that have not been formalised yet so that they can be reused in other projects. The means used in these cases usually boost synchronous and asynchronous cooperation between people.

- *Clubs.* Communities of people who have shared interests but are poorly cohesive (for instance, sales networks, promoters, etc.). They often stand out for a limited interaction between the members for whom contents are much more important than relations. The key ingredient to make it a community is therefore the involvement of the members in the creation of valuable contents. If the members do not participate in the creation of such contents, the benefits of a participatory system are thwarted, with the risk the community may disappear once the members have seen all they were interested in ("low stability"). Since at first the members are not prone to interacting with each other, "discussion" systems need not be used from the very start. However, with time, the most loyal members wish to be more involved in the contents and with other people with whom they share the same interests, so interactive tools need be introduced for such communities to turn into "stable families".

- *Agorae.* "Open" communities with limited members' focus and cohesion, which often result in transient involvement and variable levels of interactivity. The subjects addressed may vary, and the members do not establish permanent relations.

It is a temporary condition that risks disappearing unless it is ruled by the organisation (by setting up a focus, by pushing the members to be involved, etc.).

A classification of the aforesaid communities helps recognise how the members interact (with the others and with the content) and determine organisational and individual impacts. To do this, each SE case has been mapped in terms of impacts on three major dimensions:

- *Impact on processes:* we checked whether the community led to a change in the processes in terms of improving performance (efficiency and effectiveness) and in terms of innovation and change (redesign of the process);
- *Impact on knowledge:* it has been valuated the impact of the community on the creation and dissemination of implicit and explicit knowledge through systems that enhance people's skills and turn them into the organisation's shared assets;
- *Impact on connections:* we considered the effects in terms of support to the creation of vertical and horizontal relations, overcoming the barriers of traditional organisational structures and promoting cross-cooperation.

As to the impact on processes, it results that *families* and sometimes *clubs* usually have an impact in terms of improvement of performance and innovation. *Teams* help improve efficiency and effectiveness in the achievement of a specific goal, but because of their short life they hardly ever result in process innovation. Finally, *agorae* usually have limited impact on processes because of their members' poor focus and short-lived involvement.

Looking at the impact on knowledge, *families* support both the creation of new knowledge and the dissemination of encoded knowledge to all the members involved. Because they have few relational tools, *clubs* have more impact on the dissemination of encoded knowledge but hardly result in the members' creating new knowledge. *Agorae* usually help the members collect some information, which however is not often encoded and disseminated. Finally, *teams* help disseminate and create knowledge between few members.

Finally, looking at the impact on relations, *families* support both the creation of new connections, especially when the members are geographically distant and therefore could hardly come into contact with each other, and the management and enrichment of such relations by providing several tools for mutual help and exchange, *Teams* are very effective in managing connections through several interactive systems but, since they are closed and temporary, they hardly ever result in the creation of new, permanent relations. Usually, *agorae* are very open and help create new connections, which however are then managed in different spheres. At first, *clubs* do not support horizontal connections as much as they support instead vertical ones and interactions with contents, and therefore these communities have the lowest impact on horizontal connections.

The analysis of the cases shows that, regardless of the implemented model, the SE is a great opportunity and at the same time a fundamental challenge for the organisations: as times and costs decrease all the time, tools become newer and newer and more and more effective, people can be connected with each other and large amounts of information can be shared, overcoming geographical and time barriers and organisational barriers that hinder communication and knowledge transfer, creating new spaces of effectiveness and strategic and organisational flexibility.

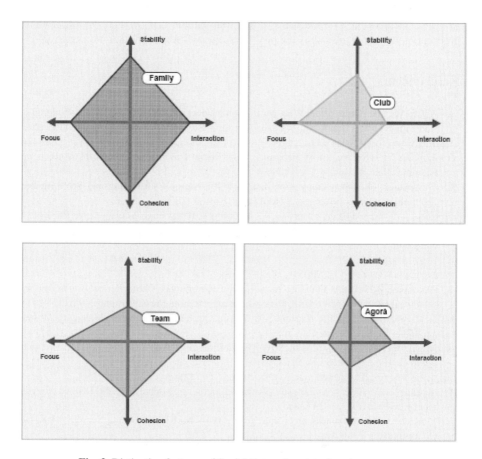

Fig. 3. Distinctive features of Social Enterprise virtual environments

5   The Need for a Governance of Enterprise 2.0

Main difficulties in E2.0 implementation are not from tech side but from a knowledge lack of opportunities, a difficulty in economic benefit identification and valuation, together with the need of organizational change. In other terms, the barriers are not technological but cultural ones: most of the companies manage the implementation project in a purely technical perspective without systematically facing the organizational and the change management aspects.

Particularly critical is the definition of *governance* - the organizational choices that determine the division of the responsibilities and the key criteria to be followed in the planning and management of an initiative. Inadequate decisions regarding governance are often difficult to be modified and can jeopardize the development possibilities and the project effectiveness.

E2.0 governance will be emergent, open and collaborative. The traditional governance systems are put in crisis: all the roles tend to move, at least in part, to final user, who will decide what to do, achieve it and then handle it by himself. Without an appropriate governance the risk is the proliferation of different and not integrated IS.

References

1. A.A.V.V.: The Future of the Web. MIT Sloan Management Review 48(3), 49–49 (2007)
2. Anderson, C.: The Long Tail: Why the Future of Business Is Selling Less of More. Hyperion, New York (2006)
3. Benkler, Y.: The Wealth of Networks: How Social Production Transforms Markets and Freedom. Yale University Press (2006)
4. Chesbrough, H.: Open Innovation: The New Imperative for Creating and Profiting from Technology. Harvard Business School Press, Boston (2003)
5. Corso, M., Giacobbe, A., Martini, A.: Rethinking Knowledge Management: the Role of ICT and the Rise of the Virtual Workspace. International Journal of Learning and Intellectual Capital 5(4) (2008)
6. Cross, R., Liedtka, J., Weiss, L.: A Practical Guide to Social Networks. Harvard Business Review 83(3), 124–132 (2005)
7. Davenport, T.H. (ed.): Thinking for a Living: How to Get Better Performances And Results from Knowledge Workers. Harvard Business School Press, Boston (2005)
8. Dearstyne, B.W.: Blogs, Mashups, & Wikis. Oh, My! Information Management Journal 41(4), 24–33 (2007)
9. Hinchcliffe, D.: Web 2.0 for the Enterprise? Enterprise Web 2.0 Blog Entry, 8 (February 2006) (Retrieved March 27, 2007),
   `http://blogs.zdnet.com/Hinchcliffe/?p=3`
10. McAfee, A.P.: Enterprise 2.0: The Dawn of Emergent Collaboration. MIT Sloan Management Review 47(3), 21–28 (2006)
11. McKinsey: How Business are using Web 2.0: A McKinsey Global Survey. McKinsey Quarterly (Retrieved April 29, 2008),
   `http://www.mckinseyquarterly.com/How_businesses_are_using_`
   `Web_20_A_McKinsey_`
12. Surowiecki, J.: The Wisdom of Crowds: Why the Many are Smarter Than the Few and How Collective Wisdom Shapes Business. Economics, Societies and Nations (2004)
13. Tapscott, D., Williams, A.D.: Wikinomics: How Mass Collaboration Changes Everything. Portfolio, New York (2006)

Emergent Innovation and Sustainable Knowledge Co-creation
A Socio-epistemological Approach to "Innovation from within"

Markus F. Peschl[1] and Thomas Fundneider[2]

[1] University of Vienna, Dept. of Philosophy, Cultures and Technologies of Knowledge
[Research Group], Vienna, Austria
[2] tfc consulting, Vienna, Austria
Franz-Markus.Peschl@univie.ac.at, tf@tfc.at

Abstract. Innovation has become one of the most important issues in modern knowledge society. As opposed to radical innovation this paper introduces the concept of *Emergent Innovation*: this approach tries to balance and integrate the demand both for *radically new knowledge* and at the same time for an *organic development from within* the organization. From a more general perspective one can boil down this problem to the question of how to cope with the new and with profound change (in knowledge). This question will be dealt with in the first part of the paper. As an implication the alternative approach of *Emergent Innovation* will be presented in the second part: this approach looks at innovation as a socio-epistemological process of "learning from the future" in order to create (radically) new knowledge in a sustainable and "organic" manner. Implications for knowledge society will be discussed.

Keywords: Knowledge society, (radical vs. incremental) innovation, emergent innovation, knowledge creation, change.

1 Innovation as a Key in a Knowledge Driven Society

Innovation has become one of the most important issues in modern knowledge society—not only in the context of business and technology, but also in many fields of science and (higher) education. What makes successful radical innovations so fascinating? What does creating "radically new knowledge" mean in the context of the so-called knowledge society? What would be the implications, if a whole society would understand itself as a *society of knowledge creators and innovators*? How can a *culture of radical innovation* be introduced into an organization or in a society, in its processes, educational systems, services, and business models which—despite their radical nature—fit into the existing structures of the organization/society?

Innovation is among the most challenging processes in the context of knowledge work. Nevertheless the creation of (radically) new knowledge is the key for almost every domain in a society, business or organization—even more so, if the main product or service is focused on knowledge. What makes innovation processes so difficult

M.D. Lytras et al. (Eds.): WSKS 2008, CCIS 19, pp. 101–108, 2008.

and challenging? Primarily, because they have something to do with the future and how to "behave" in the future; more specifically, with constructing knowledge which has to fit both into external future changes (including the resulting new requirements) and to what and where the organization will be at this point in time (e.g., concerning its technology, knowledge, human resources, etc.). In most cases these future states are almost impossible to predict accurately, because the underlying social, economic, technological as well as knowledge dynamics is too complex. In a way we are in a similar situation as science and technology always is: one is trying to predict an aspect of reality in order to increase the level of control over this aspect—the only way one can achieve this is to create new knowledge and apply it in various contexts. Hence, *innovation* and *knowledge* are intrinsically coupled in a complex knowledge process of: (i) acquiring knowledge (via observation, etc.), (ii) abstracting and constructing knowledge (understanding), (iii) creating new knowledge, and (iv) realizing this knowledge in concrete prototypes; (v) after fast cycle learning processes on these prototypes (vi) this newly generated knowledge gets embodied in the organization.

Hence, if a society understands itself as a knowledge society and if it puts innovation as a core issue on its agenda (e.g., European Commission [7]), we will have to find ways of integrating the processes of creating (radically) new knowledge into all levels of society—most importantly in the educational system, in the fields of ecological and climate issues, in the way how we do science, as well as business.

2 Innovation as a Process of Knowledge Creation

2.1 Classical Perspectives on Innovation

In the field of classical innovation management one differentiates between processes of *incremental* and *radical* innovation (e.g. [6] and many others). Incremental innovation is characterized by minor changes and optimizations which do not touch the underlying concepts; "...incremental innovation refines and extends an established design. Improvement occurs in individual components, but the underlying core design concepts, and the links between them, remain the same." (Henderson [8], p 11).

"Radical innovation, in contrast, is based on a different set of engineering and scientific principles and often opens up whole new markets and potential applications... Radical innovation often creates great difficulties for established firms and can be the basis for the successful entry of new firms or even the redefinition of an industry". ([8], p 9). While incremental innovation goes for optimization (see also level 2 of Figure 1) the focus of radical innovation is on changes in the more profound domain of core concepts or base principles. In most cases, making changes in these fundamental domains implies radical changes in the whole structure, society, product, or service (plus its context; e.g., by opening up completely new markets). In other words, radical innovation starts off with changes in the assumptions (see also level 3 and 4 of Figure 1). „A change in principle, then, fits with our intuition of what constitutes a novel technology. I will therefore define a new (radically novel) technology as one that achieves a purpose by using a new or different base principle than used before." ([2], p 278).

2.2 Strategies of Creating New Knowledge in a Changing Environment

Taking the radically knowledge oriented perspective on innovation having been laid out above seriously one can boil it down to the question of *how to cope with the new and with change by creating (radically) new knowledge*. After taking a look at possible strategies of knowledge creation in this section an alternative approach to innovation will be presented in the second part: *emergent innovation*. This approach looks at innovation as a socio-epistemological process of "learning from the future as it emerges" instead of imposing some external and artificial solution to a problem.

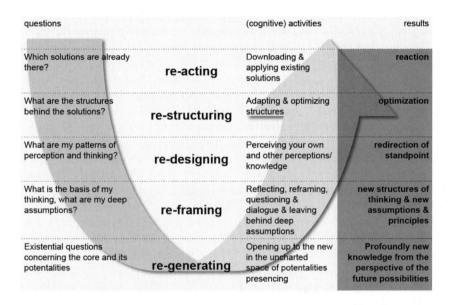

questions	(cognitive) activities		results
Which solutions are already there?	**re-acting**	Downloading & applying existing solutions	reaction
What are the structures behind the solutions?	**re-structuring**	Adapting & optimizing structures	optimization
What are my patterns of perception and thinking?	**re-designing**	Perceiving your own and other perceptions/ knowledge	redirection of standpoint
What is the basis of my thinking, what are my deep assumptions?	**re-framing**	Reflecting, reframing, questioning & dialogue & leaving behind deep assumptions	new structures of thinking & new assumptions & principles
Existential questions concerning the core and its potentalities	**re-generating**	Opening up to the new in the uncharted space of potentalities presencing	Profoundly new knowledge from the perspective of the future possibilities

Fig. 1. Strategies of how to cope with change (adapted from Scharmer [14])

Coping with change (see Fig. 1) is at the heart of any innovation process. In most cases the challenge is how to react to this change with a strategy which is based on new knowledge or—even better—to *anticipate* this change and proactively *shape the future* by developing and applying new knowledge. From a knowledge perspective this is a triple challenge: one has not only to react to a change which has occurred already; rather, (a) one has to *anticipate* this change and (b) to *relate* it to a possible future state of one's own knowledge (be it in one's own society, business, human resources, technology, etc.). (c) Above that, one has to *shape* a whole future scenario which integrates these domains in a (radical) innovation (radically new knowledge, business model, service, product, etc.). Of course, this is the most sophisticated form of dealing with the challenge of knowledge creation and change. In the following paragraphs we are going to discuss different levels and strategies of how to deal with change (see Figure 1; see also [14, 15]):

1. *Reacting and downloading* is the simplest way of responding to change. Already existing and well established behavioral, organizational, perceptual, or cognitive

patterns are applied to solve the problem or the learning/adaptation task. This is the most convenient and most economic way of reacting to change, because it requires only downloading of already prefabricated solutions, knowledge, patterns, etc. The price of this simple response is quite high: (i) the reactions are highly rigid and (ii) the resulting solutions or changes do not go very deep and in most cases do not even scratch the underlying issues of the problem. However, this mode of dealing with change is what most cognitive systems and organizations do most of their time.

2. *Restructuring and adaptation* goes one step further by not only applying already existing knowledge patterns, but to use these patterns as a blueprint which is *adapted* slightly to the current situation. From a cognitive perspective this is a highly efficient learning strategy, because it is not as rigid as downloading, but it can be done with minimal cognitive effort; namely, to make use of already existing knowledge, patterns, change them slightly and apply them to the new situation, task, etc. From the field of cognitive (neuro-)science these processes are well understood—these are the classical learning and adaptation processes well known from the domains of connectionism or computational neuroscience (e.g., [3, 10, 13] and many others). From this perspective it becomes clear that these processes are mathematically equivalent with processes of *optimization*. I.e., we are searching for an optimum in an already pre-structured space (of solutions). These processes of optimization normally lead to *incremental innovations* [6].

3. *Redesign and redirection*: The focus of this strategy to cope with change is to primarily explore one's own patterns of perception and thinking in order to be able to assume *new perspectives*. In that process the focus of attention shifts from the external object to the source of one's cognitive and perceptual activities—this shift is referred to as *redirection* (e.g., Depraz, Varela; [5, 16]). This can be done individually, however, it is much more effectively in a collective setting. The goal is to arrive at a position from which it is possible to take different standpoints and to understand what one's own patterns of perception and thinking are—these insights act as a starting point for creating new knowledge and for the following level of reframing.

4. *Reframing*: The process of redirection does not touch the domain of assumptions in most cases; downloading, adaptation, and optimization are sufficient for mastering everyday problems and challenges. In a way these solutions are not very interesting from the perspective of radical change, because they do not bring forth fundamentally new knowledge, insights, or understanding. Fundamental change is always connected with reflection of *deep assumptions* and stepping out of the—more or less consciously—chosen framework of reference. I.e., going beyond the boundaries of the pre-structured space of knowledge and "reframe" it in the sense of constructing and establishing new dimensions and new semantic categories. This process concerns the level of mental models, premises, deep assumptions and their change. In dialogue-like settings (e,g., Bohm; Isaacs [4, 9]) these assumptions are explored in a double-loop learning manner [1]. Going one step further, this process of reflection leads to the construction of completely new conceptual frameworks enabling the reframing of already well established cognitive structures. These are the basis for *radical innovations*.

5. *Re-generating, profound existential change, and "presencing"*: On a more fundamental level, change goes beyond reframing; it is not only concerned with intellectual or cognitive matters and modifying assumptions any more. In that more
   fundamental context, questions of *finality, purpose, heart, will*, etc. come to the
   fore—what they have in common is that they concern an *existential* level rather
   than a cognitive level. From a learning perspective these processes are realized in
   the *triple-loop learning strategy* (Peschl [11]). In this mode of learning change is
   not solely based on cognitive reflection any more, but more importantly on *existential reflection* and learning. In a way the goal is to bring the existential level of the
   person and the organization/society (i.e., its acting as well as its core) into a status
   of inner unity/alignment with itself and with its future potentials as well as with future requirements. What might sound esoteric is in fact a very old theme and philosophical issue going back at least to Aristotle's philosophy. Very often these
   questions concern the domain of the core/substance of the innovation object and of
   wisdom. Due to its existential character [11, 14, 15] refer to this mode of
   change/learning as *"presencing"*. It represents an approach to innovation which
   does not primarily learn from the past, but which shifts its focus towards *"learning
   from the future as it emerges"*. I.e., the goal is to be very close to the innovation
   object and at—the same time—completely open to "what wants to emerge" (out of
   the surrounding, out of the organization, its humans and its knowledge)—the difficult part in this approach is (i) to profoundly understand the situation (i.e., the core
   of the innovation object) plus its context, (ii) to match these insights with the potentials which want to emerge, and (iii) to bring them into a consistent and
   integrated picture. In short the process of presencing is about a fundamental examination of the *core* of the innovation object leading to a profound, holistic, and
   integrated understanding of this object including its context— only a highly nurtur-
   ing environment for generating profound new knowledge may give rise to *radical
   innovations* which are not only radically and fundamentally new and completely
   "out of the blue", but which are also *fitting well* into what emerges in society, in
   the organization, and in culture in general.

These strategies of coping with change and innovation do not exclude each other;
in most cases aspects of almost every level are present in one or the other way in
innovation processes—the interesting question for an organization or society is where
it shifts its focus to.

It is clear that levels 3–5 are *intellectually challenging* and demands for an explicit
culture of openness, knowledge creation, and real commitment to (radical) innovation
both on an individual and a collective level. From an innovation perspective, these
levels are most interesting—hence, the question: how can these innovation processes
of levels 4 and 5 be realized in organizational settings or in a whole society? Besides
their manifestations as entirely new, surprising, and convincingly coherent innovations, services, products, or business models the fascinating aspect of "real" fundamental innovations are the "mental innovations" and the "mental change processes"
of knowledge (creation) having led to these manifestations. How can they be brought
about?

3 Emergent Innovation

We are suggesting a newly developed concept as one possible answer to these questions: *Emergent Innovation*. this approach has been empirically tested in several educational and business settings. It follows a fundamentally different approach: it is a *socio-epistemological technology* focusing on the cognitive, epistemological, and social processes leading to a *"radical yet organic innovation from within"*.

Profoundly Understanding the Core as Prerequisite for Emergent Innovation
This kind of *innovation emerges* out of a process of (i) a profound understanding of the innovation-object and (ii) reflecting and letting-go of predefined patterns of perception and thinking (compare also U-Theory [14]). This leads to *radical, yet "organic innovations" in the sense of both respecting and developing/changing the core/essence of the innovation-object* (be it an aspect of society, business, service, product, idea, etc.). This socio-epistemological technology of emergent innovation is a highly fragile and intellectually challenging process which has to be held in a container which we are referring to as *enabling space* [12]; it is a multi-dimensional space enabling and facilitating these processes of knowledge creation. This enabling space comprises of a physical, social (trust, etc.), mental/cognitive, epistemological, as well as technological dimension.

"Innovation from within" and Thinking from the Future
Seeing, profoundly understanding, reflecting, and respecting what is (already) is at the focus in the first phases of the process of Emergent Innovation; it regards what is already there as a chance rather than an obstacle. Instead of imposing external and/or inadequate patterns or "wild ideas" to the object of innovation Emergent Innovation tries to respect and at the same time explore and develop the most radical and unforeseen potentialities of the (profound understanding of the) core/essence of what is already there. In other words, it explorers the space of *what is present in a latent manner* and what wants to emerge. In this sense emergent innovation is a kind of *"radical innovation from within"*.

Exploring this space of potentialities implies that Emergent Innovation looks at innovation as thinking from the perspective of future potentialities rather than of repeating, adapting, and extrapolating patterns from the past. The question *"what wants to emerge?"* is a clear pointer into the future and implicitly instructs the whole process of Emergent Innovation/knowledge creation. As an implication of the points above the knowledge being created in such a process of Emergent Innovation is not some kind of superficial innovation artificially grafted onto an organization by some external forces (or consultants); rather, it is an organically grown, yet radically new knowledge both fitting into the existing structures and bringing forth something radically new.

Emergent Innovation as a Collective Socio-epistemological Process of High Quality Knowledge Creation
In most cases, innovations do not just happen by chance. A culture of openness, learning, creativity, readiness for error, etc. must be fostered and rewarded in order to make innovation happen in an organization or even in a whole society.

Regardless of the many techniques available to stimulate innovations, most innovation processes are based on the classical process steps of: idea generation, idea selection, idea management and realization of plans. In many cases the techniques being used in this process are massive brainstorming sessions (quantity first), market research, user testing, external studies etc. Most outcomes of such an approach are *incremental* innovations, as the basic thinking behind these processes does not go beyond level 2 (see Figure 1). They are implicitly based on the assumption that radical innovation is based on "far out", "creative", and completely orthogonal ideas (grafted onto the business from the outside), on a high quantity of—in most cases low quality—ideas going through a rigorous selection/evaluation process, etc. which makes the whole process even more erratic and unpredictable.

The core idea is that *emergent innovation* is not primarily dependent on exceptional individuals who are supposed to create radical innovations, but that a larger number of members of an organization acquire the understanding and skills in the basic thinking that underpins the processes of levels 4 and 5 in Figure 1.

Emergent Innovation—Aspects for Knowledge Society
If innovation is a top priority in a knowledge society, it will have to find ways of integrating these issues into its most basic systems, such as the educational system, the way we do business, science, the way we deal with ecological issues, etc. Taking the approach of Emergent Innovation into account the following selection of points has turned out to be crucial with respect to questions of knowledge society:

- There has to be a clear focus on the processes of cognition, perception, and reflection as well as on training and changing them profoundly (via techniques of radical reflection, questioning, dialogue, deep observation, etc.).
- As Emergent Innovation primarily looks at and values what is already there society has to "relearn" to be more attentive, to listen and observe more deeply, to understand profoundly, etc. instead of hoping to find its fortune in only generating completely shrill and "far out" ideas which do not really fit their needs and desires.
- We have to learn to be silent and to wait: i.e., sometimes it is necessary to take some time of doing—superficially seen—"nothing" and listen to what wants to come forth instead of forcing some pseudo innovative activity. In other words, the focus is shifted towards the process of *emergence* of innovation (from within) and towards *enabling* this process (instead of imposing or forcing it; see "enabling space" [12]).
- If something new comes up in this process, we have to be prepared to act quickly and in a determined manner, however.

Acknowledgments. This project is funded by the ZIT (Center for Innovation and Technology, Vienna, Austria).

References

1. Argyris, C., Schön, D.A.: Organizational learning II. Theory, method, and practice. Addison-Wesley, Redwood City (1996)
2. Arthur, W.B.: The structure of invention. Research Policy 36, 274–287 (2007)

3. Bechtel, W., Abrahamsen, A.: Connectionism and the mind. Parallel processing, dynamics, and evolution in networks, 2nd edn. Blackwell Publishers, Malden (2002)
4. Bohm, D.: On dialogue. Routledge, London (1996)
5. Depraz, N., Varela, F.J., Vermersch, P.: On becoming aware. A pragmatics of experiencing. John Benjamins Publishing Company, Amsterdam (2003)
6. Ettlie, J.E., Bridges, W.P., O´Keefe, R.D.: Organisational strategic and structural differences for radical vs. incremental innovation. Management Science 30 (1984)
7. European Commission. Innovation management and the knowledge-driven economy. Brussels: European Commission, Directorate-general for Enterprise (2004)
8. Henderson, R.M., Clark, K.B.: Architectural Innovation: the reconfiguration of existing product technologies and the failure of established firms. Administrative Science Quarterly 35(1), 9–30 (1990)
9. Isaacs, W.N.: Dialogue and the art of thinking together: A pioneering approach to communicating in business and life. Doubleday Currency, New York (1999)
10. Peschl, M.F.: Constructivism, cognition, and science. An Investigation of its links and possible shortcomings. Foundations of Science 6(1), 125–161 (1999)
11. Peschl, M.F.: Triple-loop learning as foundation for profound change, individual cultivation, and radical innovation. Construction processes beyond scientific and rational knowledge. Constructivist Foundations 2(2-3), 136–145 (2007)
12. Peschl, M.F.: Enabling Spaces—epistemologische Grundlagen der Ermöglichung von Innovation und knowledge creation. In: Gronau, N. (ed.) Professionelles Wissensmanagement. Erfahrungen und Visionen, pp. 362–372. GITO, Berlin (2007)
13. Rumelhart, D.E., McClelland, J.L. (eds.): Parallel Distributed Processing: explorations in the microstructure of cognition. Foundations. MIT Press, Cambridge (1986)
14. Scharmer, C.O.: Theory U. Leading from the future as it emerges. The social technology of presencing. Society for Organizational Learning, Cambridge (2007)
15. Senge, P.M.: The fifth discipline. The art and practice of the learning organization. Doubleday, New York (1990)
16. Varela, F.: Three gestures of becoming aware (Interview with F.Varela; Paris, January 12, 2000) [27.04.2005] (2000), http://www.dialogonleadership.org/Varela-2000.pdf

Contribution to the Analysis of Motion Behaviour of People in a Region Using Video Frames

Ioannis Tzouvadakis[1] and Athanassios Stamos[2]

[1] School of Civil Engineering, NTUA, Greece, Iroon Polytechniou 9, 15780 Zografos
itzouvad@central.ntua.gr
[2] School of Civil Engineering, NTUA, Greece, Iroon Polytechniou 9, 15780 Zografos
stamthan@central.ntua.gr

Abstract. This paper aims to present the evolution of technical software which decodes the behavior of people who walk in the urban environment. It uses and analyzes video frames of a region which are recorded by a stationary, run of the mill, video camera. The software is able to track semi-automatically the motion of targets in a region of interest, and produce the route of the targets in a drawing environment and in a world coordinate system. The photogrammetric Direct Linear Transform (DLT) method with known terrain is used to extract the information from single video frames, simultaneously correcting the non-metric cameras' systematic errors. The Least Square Method is employed to achieve increased accuracy.

1 Introduction

This paper aims to present the evolution of technical software which decodes the behavior of people who walk in the urban environment. It uses and analyzes video frames of a region which are recorded by a stationary, run of the mill, video camera. The software was written by researchers and students of the National Technical University of Athens (NTUA). It has been tested with success to experimentally decode the motion behavior of people in disorderly queues (Tzouvadakis and Rentzos, 1999), the behavior of children in staircases (Theofanopouloy, 2001), the behavior of pedestrians on a walk (Tzouvadakis and Ioannidis, 2008), and generally any other study which focuses on the observation of the motion of a target (person, animal, vehicle) within a defined region, which is under the surveylance of a stationary video camera.

The idea of the software originated some years ago when the motion behavior of a large crowd of people in an out-of-doors disorderly queue had to be analyzed (Tzouvadakis and Rentzos, 1999), during a religious event. The people had to cross 2 narrow doors to enter a region of religious interest. The conclusions of the analysis would be used to redesign the region and the entries, in order to improve the motion velocity and the security of the participants. It must be noted that the crowd was generally quiet and patient due to the nature of the event. The awareness of the time and the place drove the participants to a special behavior, which aimed to minimize the delay of the queue, adopting mild manoeuvres in their motion, without being rude to their neighbors. Different behavior may be observed in soccer field entries, where similar disorderly queues are formed, when the participants are fans of soccer teams.

M.D. Lytras et al. (Eds.): WSKS 2008, CCIS 19, pp. 109–116, 2008.

The usefulness of the software was made obvious right from the beginning, when the first analysis of the crowd was tried. The perspective images had to be printed in film positives, and each one had to correlated with the geometry of region. The positions of individuals had to be manually marked on every positive they were visible, using a bright screen. The initial research aimed to determine the relationship between the real width of the entry and active width, the width that the people actually used. However, it also led to the realization of the principles for the construction of special software to automate the related procedures.

It was also evident that the extraction of information from the video frames of a given situation, without using computer and special software, led to somewhat amateur and very time consuming work, which would not easily give sufficient data to statistically document the behavior of the motion of the crowd in a given situation.

The construction of the software was eventually useful in other research as well. As an example, we report the observation of the children of elementary school as they exit the classroom towards the play ground (Theofanopouloy, 2001). The research aimed to design a safer staircase, adapted to the unpredictable behavior of small children, the spunkiest of which ran fast to the staircase, jumping the stairs and teasing continuously each other. As the architectural engineer acquires more information of their possible behavior, they can propose better design for the staircase (relationship between riser and trend, banister type, more frequent half landings etc), so that the danger of fall and injury of small children is minimized.

The software, until now, supported a plane observation region, horizontal or not, defined by 4 points, which were determined with topographic methods. The same 4 points were found on the video frames, and using them, the software correlated the perspective region on the video frames with the geometry of the real space. Thus, each person entering the region, could be a target for the analysis of his or her motion (fig. 1).

The observer and user of the software, can define a motion color of each target, as well as enter various information of the target in a database, such as description, gender, approximate age, clothing, cargo that the target possibly carries, information if the target accompanies children or others, humidity and temperature conditions, noise level of the region, and any other data about comfort or security which may affect the

Fig. 1. Region of interest and motion tracking

motion of a person in a region. Then the observer may follow with the mouse the motion of the target on a predefined sequence of video frames, until the target is out of the region. The software analyzes the relative position of the target to the region, and translates it to the real space, drawing every position of the route of the target in a drawing environment. It also computes the velocity of the motion, the total length of the route, and the time it took the target to cross the region. Then the observer may choose another target for the video frames and repeat the procedure. The data collected is entered in a database and can be statistically analyzed by appropriate software (Excel, SPSS etc).

2 Proposed Improvements

In this paper the following improvements to the software are proposed:

1. The observation region is not confined by 4 points, but may be the whole video frame.
2. The program can handle video frames more accurately taking into account differential scale and rotation errors.
3. More control points may be defined.
4. Exploitation of the elevation contour lines.

This leads to:

1. Better utilization of the video frames, since the whole frames may be used.
2. Ordinary, run of the mill video cameras may be used. This lowers the cost dramatically and increases flexibility since local to the site video cameras may be used.
3. Many control points can improve the accuracy, should an application need it.
4. The region of interest in is not confined in flat surfaces, but irregular terrain such as mountainous terrain can be analyzed.

The improvements require full photogrammetric analysis of each image frame. In particular the photogrammetric Direct Linear Transform (DLT) is used as described in the following sections. The DLT is complimented by the Least Square Method (LSM) for improved accuracy.

DLT has been used before for analysis of video frames in order to track arbitrary 3dimensional motion of objects or human beings (see for example (Page, Candelas and Belmar, 2006) and (Sorapong, 2006)), using frames from 2 or more different cameras simultaneously. However the motion of human beings is not arbitrary in the z-dimension, as they are confined to walk on the surface of the road, pavement, earth etc. Thus, the DLT in this method needs only 1 camera with obvious benefits in simplicity. One to one correspondence between the frame and the 3dimensional terrain may be established. The terrain may be determined once by conventional topographic methods.

3 Governing Photogrammetric Equations

Tracking moving targets like human beings in a video is a task that needs full photogrammetric approach. The video is decomposed to a series of frames or images. The image taken by a camera is a central projection, which means that the scale of the image is continuously different according to the distance of the various objects and the focal point.

The relationship between the image coordinates x, y (pixels) and the world coordinates X, Y, Z such as HGRS87 is given by (Dermanis, 1991):

$$x = x_0 - f \frac{R_{11}(X - X_0) + R_{12}(Y - Y_0) + R_{13}(Z - Z_0)}{R_{31}(X - X_0) + R_{32}(Y - Y_0) + R_{33}(Z - Z_0)} \tag{1}$$

$$y = y_0 - f \frac{R_{21}(X - X_0) + R_{22}(Y - Y_0) + R_{23}(Z - Z_0)}{R_{31}(X - X_0) + R_{32}(Y - Y_0) + R_{33}(Z - Z_0)}$$

where $x_0,$ y_0 are the coordinates of the projection of the focal point on the image, f is the focal length of the lens, and R_{ij} is the rotation matrix between the two system of coordinates, which are functions of the rotations ω, φ, κ between the systems. Note that the equations contain 7 independent parameters x_0, y_0, f, ω, φ, κ X_0, Y_0, Z_0.

The equations are extremely complex and usually the calculations are done in 3 or more steps. However they may be simplified to:

$$x = \frac{L_1 X + L_2 Y + L_3 Z + L_4}{L_9 X + L_{10} Y + L_{11} Z + 1} \tag{2}$$

$$y = \frac{L_5 X + L_6 Y + L_7 Z + L_8}{L_9 X + L_{10} Y + L_{11} Z + 1}$$

This form of the equations is called the Direct Linear Transform (DLT) since it is linear to the image coordinates, to the world coordinates and to the L_i coefficients (but not to any pair of them). The 11 coefficients L_i are functions of the parameters x_0, y_0, f, ω, φ, κ X_0, Y_0, Z_0 and thus only 9 of them are independent. Thus 2 extra conditions must be employed in order for the DLT equations to be equivalent to the Central Projections equations. This breaks the linearity of the DLT which is its big advantage.

The central projection equations are derived for a metric camera, which is camera which contains no or little error of differential scale (different scale in the x and y directions) and of differential rotation (different rotation with respect to the distance from the projection of the focal point). However a video camera is hardly metric, which means that it has to be corrected for these errors. It can be shown (Dermanis, 1991) that the 2 extra parameters of the DLT equations (2) stand for the correction of these errors.

4   Calculation of the DLT Coefficients

Equation (2) may be written as:

$$x = L_1 X + L_2 Y + L_3 Z + L_4 - L_9 X x - L_{10} Y x - L_{11} Z x \tag{3}$$

$$y = L_5 X + L_6 Y + L_7 Z + L_8 - L_9 X y - L_{10} Y y - L_{11} Z y$$

which is linear to the coefficients L_i. If the image and the world coordinates are known for 6 or more points (control points), then equation (3) can be written for all the control points, which leads to matrix equations:

$$[A] [L] = [B] \qquad (4)$$

which contain more equations than unknowns. The Least Square Method (Press et all, 1992) must be employed to solve for the optimized values of the coefficients L_i:

$$[A^T] [A] [L] = [A^T][B] \qquad (5)$$

Equation (5) is a system of 11 linear equations which are solved for the L_i.

5   Calculation of the DLT Coefficients in Multiple Images

The method of obtaining the DLT coefficients, must be employed for every single frame of the video. Clearly such a method is not practical as a video contains thousands of frames. However, if the video camera is fixed (for example on a tripod), then every frame will show the same region minus the moving objects. In a man made environment there are enough structures (for example buildings) to provide for control points which are identical in every frame. If the video camera is also digital, then the control points are projected to the same image position (pixel coordinates) and thus the coefficients calculated by (5) are the valid for every frame.

6   Calculation of World Coordinates of Image Object

Equation (3) calculates the image coordinates of an object, if the world coordinates of the same object are known. The reverse is needed in this paper. An object is being tracked on one or more frames, and its position in world coordinates are needed. However equation (3) can not be inverted since the position of an object is determined by 3 parameters X, Y, Z and (3) provides only 2 equations.

The third equation can be provided by the geometry of the region that is being tracked. Usually the tracked targets are human beings which walk on a flat surface. The Z coordinate on a flat surface is a linear, or for more accuracy, a bilinear function of the X, Y coordinates:

$$Z = f(X, Y) \qquad (6)$$

The parameters or coefficients of function f, can be computed with Least Square Method, if the X,Y,Z coordinates are known for 3 or more control points on the flat surface. Equation (6) compliments equation (3) and the X, Y, Z coordinates of the tracked object may be obtained.

In order to use equation (6) in conjunction with equation (3), the x, y image coordinate of the tracked target must refer to the point the target contacts that flat surface, which for a human being is his or her shoes. However the shoes may not be visible in a crowd, which leaves no other choice than the head. This modifies equation (6) to:

$$Z = f(X, Y)+H \qquad (7)$$

where H is the height of the human being. The height H must me estimated by the operator of the tracking procedure. Typically the video frames are shown on a graphics terminal and the operator clicks on the head of a selected human being on every frame. At the end of the job the operator must estimate the height of the human being, perhaps comparing to known heights on the scene such as the height of a door. The fact that the height is input only once for a large number of frames means that it is a minor issue. In fact, it is advantageous for statistical reasons to also estimate and input the gender, the age, the weight of the human being, as well as if he or she carries cargo heavy or light, etc. Note that this information is very difficult to obtain by automatic tracking software, at least in the present state of the art in computer vision.

7 Multiple Surfaces

The procedure may be repeated for many different flat surfaces that may exist in the region, so that effectively the whole image is utilized. For each flat surface a different relationship of the form (6) or (7) is computed. The surface that the tracked target moves on can efficiently be determined using Binary Spatial Partitioning Trees (Stamos, 2008), and the relationship of that surface is used for the determination of world coordinates of the target (fig. 2).

The determination of flat surfaces may be automated if the elevation contour lines of the scene are known. The contour lines are projected to the image using (2). Then the area of the image is split to triangles (Shewchuck, 1999) whose nodes are points of the contour lines. Each triangle is by a definition a flat surface which can be used as it was previously described. Note that the triangulation using the contour lines can also be used in the case that the region has no flat surfaces, as in mountainous terrain. Alternatively, Digital Terrain Model (DTM) or Digital Elevation Model (DEM) (Wilson and Gallant, 2001) may be used for the triangulation.

8 Conclusions

The software was fused into an open source CAD (Stamos, 2007) in order to take advantage of its input, presentation and manipulation capabilities as well as its user-friendly Graphical User Interface. The software was tested using simulated data. The results and the use of the software indicate that it is an accurate, user friendly, practical and comparatively fast tool for the analysis of human motion. The software is general enough to exploit the whole video frames and the topographic information available such as contour lines, DTM or DEM.

For further study and improvement the following are proposed:

1. Integration of common statistical analysis.
2. The ability to track, simultaneously and automatically, more than one target chosen by the observer.
3. Automatic and massive identification of moving targets, and automatic tracking of the targets as they enter, move through and exit the region of the interest. The authors are skeptical about this, because although the ability to track a moving object may be within the limits of photogrammetry today, the ability to describe a human being (age, cargo, gender etc) is so far, beyond the state of the art in computer vision.

Fig. 2. Triangulation of the region of interest (Athens subway)

References

Tzouvadakis, I., Rentzos, K.: Pedestrian motion in disorderly queues with respect to the evacuation of a region, TEXNIKA XRONIKA, vol. 1-2, 1999, Category II (Architecture, Urban and Region design) (1999)

Theofanopouloy, A.: Contribution to the computation and design of stair-cases, Diploma Thesis, School of Civil Engineering, NTUA, Athens (2001)

Tzouvadakis, I., Ioannidis, I.: Recording the tracks of pedestrians' motion using computer and video archives. Greek technical magazine (submitted, 2008)

Page, A., Candelas, P., Belmar, F.: Application of video photogrammetry to analyse mechanical systems in the undergraduate physics laboratory. European Journal of Physics, IOP electronic journals 27, 647–655 (2006)

Aootaphao, S., Sangworasil, M., Pintavirooj, C.: A 3d motion capture system using Direct Linear Transform and Quad-Tree searching scheme. In: 2nd International Symposium on Biomedical Engineering, Bangkok, Thailand, November 8-10 (2006)

Dermanis, A.: Analytical Photogrammetry, Editions Ziti, Thessaloniki Greece (1991) ISBN 960-431-004-6

Press, H.W., Teukolski, A.S., Vetterling, T.W., Flannery, P.B.: Numerical Recipes in Fortran. Cambridge University Press, Cambridge (1992)

Stamos, A.A.: Application of Binary Spatial Partitioning to Computer Aided Design. In: Athens, M.P., Topping, B.H.V. (eds.) Proceedings of the Sixth International Conference on Engineering Computational Technology. Civil-Comp Press, Stirlingshire (2008)

Shewchuk, J.R.: Applied Computational Geometry: Towards Geometric Engineering. In: Lin, M.C., Manocha, D. (eds.) FCRC-WS 1996 and WACG 1996. LNCS, vol. 1148, pp. 203–222. Springer, Heidelberg (1996) (From the First ACM Workshop on Applied Computational Geometry)

Wilson, J.P., Gallant, J.C.: Terrain Analysis: Principles and Applications. John Wiley and Sons, Chichester (2000)

Stamos, A.A.: ThanCad, a 2dimensional CAD. In: EuroPython 2007, Vilnious (2007)

The Human Web and the Domestication of the Networked Computer

Ellen Christiaanse

Amsterdam Business School, Universiteit van Amsterdam, Roeterstraat 11, Amsterdam,
The Netherlands
Esade Business School, Av. Pedralbes 62, Barcelona, Spain

Abstract. While information and communication is crucial for the survival of species, little is known about the way that humans have used (and abused) information and communication systems throughout human existence. It is our firm belief that the rise of the network society, the information society, the information age has firm roots in previous ages. However most of these accounts go back to, at most the industrial revolution. We adopt an information and communications systems lens to look at the history of mankind from a big history perspective using Spier's [10]) regime transformations to analyse how information and communication systems interacted with human development historically. The main questions we address are: What was the role of Information and Communication Systems in past regime transformations and what can we learn from that for the present and fourth regime transformation (of the domestication of the networked computer) we are going through? How have these communication infrastructures and information ecologies evolved and what can the past show us about the role of these developments in the near future?

Keywords: Human web, domestication of the networked computer, regimes, history of information systems, knowledge society.

1 Introduction

This paper develops the argument that information systems have not only existed for the last 50 years (as most accounts of ICT argue) or since the 17th century (as some more accurate readings would propose), but they are as old as mankind. This paper provides a historical account of how information and communication systems have greatly interacted with some major transformations in human society. In addition it theorizes on the impact of the internet as a communication system. It builds on literature which distinguishes 3 major phases in the history of mankind and provides accounts of the role of information and communication systems in each of these phases. The main argument is that the "domestication of information systems" is better understood when previous regime transformations and their dynamics are taken into account and investigated. Implications of these developments in relation to innovation and learning are provided.

Information and Communication systems, their design and use and the role of information have been studied by biologists, economists, ecologists, linguistics and

M.D. Lytras et al. (Eds.): WSKS 2008, CCIS 19, pp. 117–124, 2008.

historians to explain human and animal behavior. Nothing would work in the absence of information ([6] 1996). Hauser argues that basically 3 reasons underlie all communication among animals: 1) mating, 2) socialization and 3) survival. The last decade researchers often claimed that we humans are going through a communication revolution or we are entering an Information age [2,11] However, we argue that our information age is definitely not the first information age in history. Humans have always needed and communicated information and the field of information systems did not start in 1976 as a recent IFIP call for papers did suggest. We argue with Headrick [7] that the information age has no beginning, for it is as old as mankind. We live in such an age but it is certainly not the first information age nor is the PC the first information system we have built. This paper intends to deliberately take a broad multidisciplinary perspective and investigate the role of information and communication systems and their impact on humans and the societies they live in. In the subsequent sections we will first discuss the role of information systems in regime transformations. We argue that a fourth regime transformation can be distinguished, the *"domestication of information systems"* which is better understood when previous regime transformations and their dynamics are considered and investigated. We argue that each of the previous regime transformations have had information and communication systems implications. The final section links the fact that we now have a human web with networked domesticated PC's, to innovation and learning at the human species level.

2   Information and Communication Systems in History

We believe no profound understanding of the impact of information and communication systems can be obtained when limiting our study to the last 20-30 years, the years of the "invention" and proliferation of the computer and the Internet. It is our firm belief that the rise of the network society [2] , the information society [8,11] , the information age [3] has firm roots in previous ages. Sociologists and historians as well as information systems researchers have traced the roots of our present information age. However most of these accounts go back to, at most the industrial revolution [1,7,11]), claims that in the age of reason (1700-1850) information systems of all kinds were flourishing. He makes the important distinction between the use of the specific technology and the information systems applying that technology. Around 300 hundred years ago increasing interest in information of all sorts, led to information systems, which are the basis for today's information age. Systems of nomenclature, classification (plants and chemicals) measurement and the visual display of information (graphs, maps) are examples. He argues that *"Most historians attributed great significance to certain machines: the printing press, telegraph, the computer, but between the printing revolution and the 19th century lies a period that was less significant for its information handling machines but just as fertile in new information systems"*[1].

---

[1] We follow Headrick´s views of information systems as being much broader than communication systems. Communication systems in his view are systems like telegraphic and postal systems while information systems are systems that organize, transform, display, store or communicate information. In his view communication systems are a subset of information systems (Headrick p. 181).

We argue that the way societies and groups of people have organized themselves and have innovated has always been closely related to the way they communicated and transmitted and gathered information. Why people have organized themselves in specific communication network configurations? How have these communication infrastructures and information ecologies evolved and what can the past show us about the role of these developments in the near future?

3   Structuration Using the Notion of Regimes

To provide an historical account of how information and communication systems have greatly interacted with some major transformations in human society we base our arguments on the concept of "regime transformations" developed by Spier [10] When introducing the term regime, an important issue to address first is that Spier's timescale is slightly larger than we as information system scientists are used to, in our very young field of barely 30 years or 2-3 generations of researchers[2]. As is common among world historians [5,9,10,4] phenomena are viewed from the origins of human-kind or often even on cosmic scales. In their view even the inhabitants of modern societies by and large have the physiological make-up of gatherers and hunters. I will use the term regime in line with Spier's definition as "a more or less regular but ulti-mately unstable pattern that has a certain temporal permanence" (p.14). Spier's main argument is that the history of humanity can be structured referring to the three great ecological regime transformations which have taken place so far:

1) the domestication of fire (1.5 million years ago),
2) the domestication of plants and animals (8000-10000 years ago) and
3) the industrialization on the basis of engines driven by inanimate energy (late 1700 s).

While information systems researchers hardly ever go back more than 40 years and communication science as a field often starts with the invention of technologies like the telegraph, radio and TV, not much truly multidisciplinary research has been done on the topic. The domestication of fire, animals and plants has interacted with and affected the way the human web has organized itself but has never influenced man-kind as profoundly as the impact that new forms of ubiquitous computing and the domestication of information and communication systems have had. We argue that the roots of the domestication of information and communication systems are in the previous regime transformations and that a profound understanding of their impact can only be achieved by analyzing what these changes were and why some of these changes took place in certain societies but not in others. We argue that there has been an information and communication regime playing a role in mankind in each of these periods.

---

[2] On February 13th 2005 the question: "How old is the field of Information Systems? " was published on ISWorld asking whether the field started with the first course in IS, its first PhD student graduated or its first significant journal publication.

3.1   Information and Communication Systems during the First Regime Transformation: The Domestication of Fire

Spier bases his description of his first regime transformation on the argument that the possession of fire control may have been of decisive importance in an elimination contest that as a result of which only the fire-possessing victors survived [10, p. 46], [9] In the Paleolithic era, the existence of small groups that had limited contact with each other meant that exchanges of ecological information worked sluggishly. In a single lifetime, each individual was unlikely to encounter more than a few hundred individuals and most of that lifetime would have been spent in the company of no more then ten to thirty individuals who belonged to the same family. The amount of information that could have been exchanged in these networks was clearly limited [4, p. 184]. Consequently, inventions could very slowly spread everywhere before any group developed a decisive cultural advantage [10 p.50]. The human fire regime had further consequences on an ecological, social and communicative level. During the gatherer –hunter social regime, technical skills and social organization appear to have developed slowly.

3.2   Information and Communication Systems during the Second Regime Transformation: The Transformation to an Agrarian Regime

The domestication[3] of plants and animals around 8000-10.000 years ago had significant implications on the ways in which humans organized themselves and communicated. Why did the same crop have to be domesticated in several different parts of the world and why are there such huge differences in the spread of crops between continents? Diamond's "tilted axis theory" [5] links the spread of food production techniques to the diffusion of other technologies and inventions. He argues that through indirect links of food production systems and their consequences with other innovations like wheels and writing which were used to facilitate the transportation of food and its administration (goods inventories, record keeping) [5] certain innovations were communicated and spread around the world in distinct patterns related to the efficiency of the communication systems used.

The evolving agrarian social regime was very different from the hunters and gatherers [9]: "Since the early plant cultivators became tied to the land they had come to depend on, they also became more tightly bound to one another, processes of social differentiation accelerated. This had consequences for the social structures of these people. In addition the way they gathered information and communicated changed significantly. The first human webs of our distant ancestors were formed through the rise of speech, migration, and primitive agricultural groupings. The development of settled farming injected new kinds of information into the human web. Apprentice farmers exchanged and communicated skills, knowledge and breeding stock with their neighboring communities" as a result   sedentary agriculture lead to more complex societies and more advanced communication and information systems. Human webs became denser resulting in an additional need for more advanced communication and information systems.

---

[3] Spier defines domestication as "human efforts to actively influence the reproductive chances of other species" In   English it refers to both home and country.

3.3   Information and Communication Systems during the Third Regime Transformation: The Transition towards an Industrial Regime

The Industrial Revolution may be defined as the application of power-driven machinery to manufacturing. "The third large ecological regime transformation, industrialization on the basis of the large-scale use of engines driven by fossil fuels, lay at the root of this remarkable discontinuity" [10]). Improvements in infrastructure (transportation, communication technologies) in the late 1800s led to massive vertical integration because allocation of resources within the firm became cheaper than the cost of using the market. The way the telegraph and telephone contributed as communication systems to support the industrialization of societies has been very significant[4] [11]. The rapidly growing and intensifying means of long-distance communication would not have been possible either without an economy increasingly based on inanimate fuels: "The coupling of ever refined techniques of information processing to machines driven by inanimate fuels can be related to the rapidly growing and intensifying communication networks of various kinds [10], p. 78). The development of communication systems and information systems in all periods discussed above is heavily related to the way humans organized themselves. An important tool humans have to alter their environment has always been innovations in technology and so to coordinate their actions collectively they have always used communication and information systems. In summary, the industrialization of society could not have taken place without a long history of specific political, economic, socio-cultural, technical and scientific developments, most notably the first and second great ecological regime transformations as well as some of the social regime transformations associated with them, such as the formation of a regime of competing states and the associated drive for economic and military inventions.

3.4   The Fourth Regime Transformation: The Domestication of the Computer

Humans had designed increasingly complex production, transportation and other systems in the industrial revolution that required increasingly more computation and calculation. As a result various attempts to build calculating machines had been done mechanically (Babbage's Engines) and later electrically (punch card machines and the Mark1). However, we start our 4th regime transformation from the moment that these calculating machines became available to individuals with microprocessors that contained memory, logic, and control circuits, an entire CPU on a single chip and allowed for home-use personal computers or PCs. We refer to this as the "domestication of the computer": PC´s started to enter the home and workplaces of ordinary citizens. Once these PC´s were networked a real communication transformation began. Kelly [12] writing about 10 years of the Internet marvels: " *In the years roughly coincidental with the Netscape IPO, humans began animating inert objects with tiny slivers of*

---

[4] Interesting in this regard is the argument by Beniger (1986) that we have faced several control crises in periods were communication systems could not keep up with the speed of for example transportation or complex energy generating systems. He provides examples of train collusions due to the fact that the scheduling and location information was exchanged slower than the speed by which the trains traveled leading to significant numbers of accidents in the late 1800s.

intelligence, connecting them into a global field, and linking their own minds into a single thing. This will be recognized as the largest, most complex, and most surprising event on the planet. Weaving nerves out of glass and radio waves, our species began wiring up all regions, all processes, all facts and notions into a grand network. From this embryonic neural net was born a collaborative interface for our civilization, a sensing, cognitive device with power that exceeded any previous invention. The Machine provided a new way of thinking (perfect search, total recall) and a new mind for an old species."

The new networked information and communication we humans have had access to over the last 10-15 years obviously surpasses any communication system we have had before: *"With a significant number of people connected, the scope of the Web today is hard to fathom. The total number of Web pages exceeds 600 billion. That's 100 pages per person alive. How could we create so much, so fast, so well? In fewer than 4,000 days, we have encoded half a trillion versions of our collective story and put them in front of 1 billion people, or one-sixth of the world's population. That remarkable achievement was not in anyone's 10-year plan."* [12]. This information and communication system brought great changes in the organization, transmission, display, storage and communication of information. Making instant sharing with unlimited numbers of people possible, this technology provides us with the opportunity to have access to anything that has ever been written, designed, sung, drawn or painted and instantly share it and build upon it. The World Wide Web has only been around for 15 years but has allowed the human web to expand, interact and communicate more intensively and with more impact on societies then any period before. The domestication of the networked PC as our latest transformation has changed our collective information processing forever.

4 Conclusions

"Up to 500 years ago three different world zones were moving through similar trajectories at different speeds governed by different synergies of informational exchange" [4] (Christian 2004). We argue that only during the last 500 years have we slowly moved to a single global system of information exchange with collective learning at the human species level. The exact implications of collective learning through the ever more dense global communication since the internet, will remain unknown for a while, but other periods of intense communication (e.g. 18th century) led to quick transmission of innovations across cultures than before.

The Role of Density, Size and Variety as Characteristics of Networks
With Christian we argue that the size, diversity, and efficiency of information networks are an important large-scale determinant of rates of ecological innovation. Examining the size and variety of information networks in different parts in the world, together with the varying efficiency with which information is pooled within those networks, are of key importance to the understanding of communication systems for the spread of innovation. In earlier days the physical size of a region where the information was exchanged to a large extent defined the spread of certain innovations. Nowadays with ubiquitous mobile domesticated computers everywhere, size,

diversity and efficiency of information networks will be an even more important large scale determinant of rates of ecological innovation. Tracking the changing synergy of processes of collective learning, by examining the size and variety of information networks in different parts of the world, as well as the varying efficiency with which information was pooled within those networks, might be an important indicator for innovation. [4], p.184.

Efficiency and Speed of Transmission of Information for the Spread of Innovations

As we have seen above in all periods, the transmission and exchange of information about technological innovations and thus for the survival of groups was crucial. Innovations like fire control, hunting techniques, food production systems but also of guns, germs and steel spread around the world in distinctive patterns interacting with the social structures of their societies. Some innovations were slow (the wheel), some fast (the steam engine) depending on the communication systems in place at the time and in the society of the invention. The spread of innovations was always tightly linked to the communication and information systems available to distribute and share the new knowledge obtained ([5] 1997, [4].

Impact on Innovation: Collective Memory and Learning at the Network Level

Together the significantly increased volume and variety of the information being pooled and increased efficiency and speed at which information is shared (e.g hypertext) in networks will have implications for collective learning and collective knowledge exchange. Information and communication systems in our history have been key to the survival of the human species and to the supremacy of one group over another. We argue that the impact of our new information and communication system on speed and quality of innovation will be significant. Information systems facilitate processes of collective learning and associated changes accelerated by the accumulation of ecologically significant knowledge and will stimulate ecologically significant learning and innovation at the human species level. While hunter-gatherers used information systems to gain control over fire, we use information systems to gain control over each other. As McNeill and McNeill note, agriculture and the wheel were invented in a number of places, but the steam engine only had to be invented once. Collective learning at the human species level will significantly increase with more than half the store of human knowledge has been produced over the past 50 years [13]. The spread of innovations in the years to come will be much faster and more efficient than in previous times. Only by understanding these changes in a larger historic perspective and understanding how humans have communicated in the past and how this affected their social structures and lives, can we begin to understand the changes that information and communication technologies will bring. The domestication of the personal, networked and increasingly mobile computer will have a greater impact than any other type of domestication has ever had before.

The fact that we are no longer living in isolated communities without information exchange but are functioning in "an online global human web" where discoveries, innovations, patents, scientific publications and paradigms shifts can be shared instantly with all online, humans on our planet will reduce the "re-inventing of the

124   E. Christiaanse

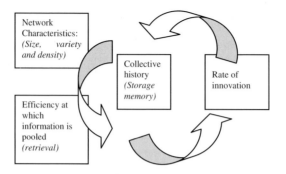

Fig. 1. Characteristics of the network, Efficiency of Pooled information and Rate of Innovation

wheel phenomenon" and provide us with the ability to build upon each others innovations. History though seems to have come full circle: many of us roam around cyberspace as gatherers and hunters, picking up whatever information item we encounter on our way. Even though we know what we came for and started off purposeful searches, the web in its present shape keeps distracting us and providing us with information items that we are not really looking for. We end up again as nomads, surfing endlessly to find relevant information for our mating, socialization and survival.

References

1. Beniger, J.R.: The Control Revolution: Technological and Economic Origins of the Information Society. Harvard University Press, Cambridge (1986)
2. Castells, M.: The Rise of the Network Society. Blackwell Publishing, Malden (2000)
3. Chandler, A.D., Cortada, J.W. (eds.): A Nation Transformed by Information: How Information Has Shaped the United States from Colonial Times to the Present. Oxford University Press, Oxford (2000)
4. Christian, D.: Maps of Time. University of California Press, Berkeley (2004)
5. Diamond, J.: Guns, Germs and Steel: The Fates of Human Societies. Norton & Company, New York (1997)
6. Hauser, M.D.: The Evolution of Communication. MIT Press, Cambridge (1996)
7. Headrick, D.R.: When information Came of Age: Technologies of Knowledge in the Age of Reason and Revolution, pp. 1700–1850. Oxford University Press, New York (2000)
8. Mansell, R., Steinmueller, W.E.: Mobilizing the Information Society: Strategies for Growth and Opportunity. Oxford University Press, Oxford (2000)
9. McNeill, J.R., McNeill, W.: The Human Web: A Bird's Eye View of World History. Norton & Company, New York (2003)
10. Spier, F.: The Structure of Big History. Amsterdam University Press, Amsterdam (1996)
11. Webster, F.: Theories of the Information Society, London, Routledge (2002)
12. Kelly (2005), http://www.wired.com/wired/archive/13.08/tech.html?pg=2&topic=tech&topic_set=
13. http://www.ncpa.org/bg/bg147/bg147a.html

Evaluation of the Energy Efficiency of Renewable Biomass Fuels: An Environmental and Financial Approach

Grigorios Kyriakopoulos

MS, Dr. Chemical Engineer and Public Researcher at National Technical University of Athens, School of Electrical and Computer Engineering, Electric Power Division, Photometry Laboratory, 9 Heroon Polytechniou street, GR 15780, Athens, Greece
Tel.: +30210-7723506
gregkyr@gmail.com, gregkyr@chemeng.ntua.gr

Abstract. European countries have recently been required to conform with the European legislation relating to the introduction of biofuels at local and national levels. In order to permit wider implementation of biofuels, the present study explored the use of life cycle analysis (LCA) as a potential tool for analyzing the use of biomass resources for domestic fuel. The LCA performed in this study used the RETScreen International software developed by Natural Resources Canada. This tool embodies a simplified form of the LCA methodology for simulating space heating of houses and domestic water heating. The financial feasibility and environmental sustainability of each proposed project was investigated.

Keywords: Biofuels, Environmental Sustainability, Financial Feasibility, Life Cycle Analysis, Renewable Energy Sources.

1   Introduction

Life cycle analysis (LCA) is an important and efficient tool for environmentally responsible management of various methods, particularly those related to the production, trading, utilization and reutilization, and disposal of products. This tool thus represents a powerful method to confront current energy-related and technological problems if the framework for LCA can be expanded to encompass these particular problems. Such a framework comprises the following elements:

1. Definition of the purposes and goals
2. Analysis of available data
3. Assessment of the method's effectiveness and
4. Interpretation of the results

Especially in the transportation sector, there has been widespread research on responses to the environmental impacts caused by the use of conventional fossil fuels (i.e., the large quantities of carbon dioxide (CO_2) released through the production and consumption of these fuels) and on the integration of biomass and biofuels within this energy sector. This literature has been presented at the research level or at the level of implementation and program actions [1-9].

M.D. Lytras et al. (Eds.): WSKS 2008, CCIS 19, pp. 125–136, 2008.

There has also been research to assess fuel choices with respect to the strict standards that have been proposed for CO_2 emissions. This research has raised three main questions [6]:

1. When is the most economically efficient time to begin the transition from gasoline and diesel to other fuels?
2. What kind of fuel would make this change most economically convenient?
3. In which sectors will it be most economically convenient to use biomass fuels?

Attempts to answer to these questions have been made using transportation models of global energy systems using parameters such as the cost of vehicles (e.g., fuel cells, transformers, and storage tanks), the production and distribution infrastructure structure, and the initial energy availability. Some key findings include:

1. Despite the strict restrictions on CO_2 emissions, diesel-based fuels will remain the main source of energy in the transportation sector for the next 50 years.
2. When the transition to alternative fuels is complete, the preferred form of fuel will be hydrogen, even though vehicles powered by hydrogen fuel cells are assumed to remain substantially more expensive than those powered by methanol fuel cells. Under certain specific circumstances, it is possible that there will be a transition period of some decades with an important contribution from methanol to the transportation sector.
3. Biomass is efficient in heating applications. Specifically, biomass can be used for heating because it is considered to be carbon-neutral, since each CO_2 molecule absorbed by biomass is released during burning, resulting in no net change.

Current analyses suggest that it will be difficult to replace diesel fuel in the transportation sector, thus the only possibility for reducing CO_2 emissions in the short term may involve domestic use of renewable fuels. Fuels that exist in large quantities in Greece and that have been proposed for use in domestic heating include straw, switchgrass, and peat. In the present research study, several aspects of the growth, harvesting, transportation, transformation, and use of these fuels were investigated, since this approach has the potential to cause significant positive environmental and socioeconomic impacts. The investigation of the proposed implementation of this approach was performed using certain tools of LCA analysis in which the impact of all the factors involved in a project are scrutinized and evaluated [10].

2   Knowledge, Resources and Databases

Nowadays, the importance of firms' innovation performance has received as the determining factor for economic sustainability from economists and managers. Recent studies have focused their investigation from the control of static, firm-specific resources to the acquisition, assimilation and exploitation of firm-specific knowledge. Furthermore, the correlation of innovation performance, social capital, firms' reputation and culture as well as knowledge acquisition and transfer has been reported in the relevant literature [11-12].

Among the above examined parameters, knowledge is considered utmost importance factor in sustainable microeconomic and macroeconomic growth. Indeed, Knowledge and Knowledge Management are not regarded as separate production factors, but as the output of economic interactions that can be stored and reused. Additionally, organizational performance could be enhanced through additional levels of knowledge processing, such as teams and communities of practice as well as knowledge portals which support the knowledge flows facilitation [13-15].

It is obvious that finding the appropriate knowledge material for economic growth is highly supported through web data mining, Resource-Based View (RBV), Capability LifeCycle (CLC) and Information Communication Technology (ICT) techniques. In order to combine data from various heterogeneous sources, software agents have to understand the semantics of the sources, since the source modeling is manual. Nevertheless, as the large number of sources comes online, it is impractical to expect users to continue modeling them my hand. Other difficulties facing the web users (individuals, managers, SME representatives) are the language and cultural differences as well as the adaptation to heterogeneous web sources [16-20].

Typical indicative examples of Knowledge Management utilization for specific educational and social frameworks have been reported in the literature. Specially, Knowledge Management was evaluated in the Australia Public Service [21], in strengthening African universities strategic role [22], in Intellectual Capital statements to Asia and Europe [23] as well as in the cost-effective University – Industry interactions [24].

The present study aims at revealing the importance of access and use of technical knowledge in the contemporary scientific sector of Renewable Sources utilization in a sustainable present and future Environment. The purpose of this paper is to combine an "inferior" and "underestimated" material, such as agricultural biomass raw byproducts to a prominent, vital and added-value material, useful for both the physical environment and the social cohesion of local agricultural communities. The bridging between the terms: "inferior" and "superior", "underestimated" and "valuable" is the accumulating knowledge of agricultural byproducts properties, depicting in the RETScreen software construction and framework. Finally, the social cohesion is the total balance by offsetting on the one hand the opening new jobs and support of the local agricultural economies following by diminishing the energy dependence from fossil fuels and on the other hand the substantial restriction of vital agricultures – initially aiming at humans feeding – for biofuels production.

3   Experimental

3.1   Application of the RETScreen International Software to LCA

For the analysis in this paper, I chose the RETScreen International software [25] developed by the Renewable Energy Deployment Initiative (REDI) sponsored by Natural Resources Canada (NRCan), since a literature review and Web search revealed no other readily available models that were well adapted to the modeling of domestic energy consumption. The projects that can be modeled by this software range from an initial exploratory investigation to a full study of the technical feasibility of constructing a heating system. The software allows an initial assessment of the energy capability and the economic effectiveness of a given renewable energy program. In performing this analysis, the software allows the investor to avoid incurring the large cost that would be required by a more formal study of the proposed project.

RETScreen was designed to overcome certain obstacles to the rapid evaluation of renewable sources of energy. These include limited consumer knowledge of and experience with renewable energy, the unreliability of previous renewable energy systems compared with highly evolved conventional heating technologies, the high cost of these novel technologies, the low cost of heating and cooling compared with the initial cost of constructing a new building, the unwillingness of homeowners to consider non-monetary values such as environmental impacts, and the inertia that has resulted from a prolonged period of low oil prices.

Another advantage of using the RETScreen software is that it encapsulates certain key tools of life cycle analysis in its design. For example, the fuel costs used by the model include a realistic assessment of all costs incurred in the production and transportation of the fuel and in the disposal of the wastes. In a full life cycle analysis, each of these phases of a fuel's life cycle would have to be modeled independently, and reliable data would have to be collected for each phase, and this process can be prohibitively expensive and time-consuming. Even a "streamlined" version of this analysis can be prohibitive, particularly for citizens who lack experience in this form of analysis.

3.2 Parameters of a Typical Project

The model examined in the present paper focused on the effectiveness of three biomass sources (straw, switchgrass, and peat) to determine whether they represented viable sources of heating energy in the Greek context. As study parameters, the analysis compared the results for three ambient temperatures (-4, 5, and 15°C) and for two percentages used to define the proportion of total energy consumption used to heat domestic water (20 and 40%).

3.3 Use of the RETScreen Software

The RETScreen software includes illustrations of the heating load, the power supply infrastructure, the energy model (here, using renewable biomass fuels to replace diesel fuel), and the cost analysis. The program's outputs include an illustration of the emissions of greenhouse-effect gases (GHG), and financial results including the after-tax Internal Rate of Return and Return on Investment (IRR and ROI) and the net present value (NPV) of the application based on data supplied by the user. Figure 1 illustrates this methodology. Tables 1 through 6 present the data [25] that was used in the present analysis.

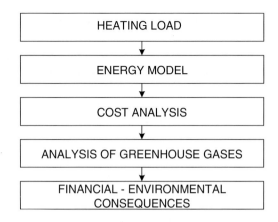

Fig. 1. An illustration of the process followed by the RETScreen software

Table 1. Heating load and application network

Parameter	Input value
Building clusters	7
Area heated per building cluster (m^2)	4650
Heating fuel type	#2 diesel
Design supply temperature (°C)	95
Design return temperature (°C)	65
Temperature differential (°C)	30
Oversizing of the main pipe network (%)	20
Total length of pipe in the main distribution line (m)	163
Total length of pipe in the secondary distribution line (m)	145

Table 2. Energy model for the proposed application

	Type of biomass fuel		
	Straw	Switchgrass	Peat
Building clusters	7	7	7
Total length of pipe (m)	308	308	308
Boiler capacity (kW)	384	384	384
Moisture content of fresh biomass (%)	30	15	8
"As fired" heating value of the biomass (MJ/t)	11 656	14 875	18 339
Capacity of backup heating system (kW)	250	250	250
Seasonal efficiency of boiler (%)	65	65	65

Table 3. Analysis of the application costs. Values in the table represent the cost in euros, followed by the % of the total cost in parentheses.

	Type of biomass fuel		
	Straw	**Switchgrass**	**Peat**
Initial cost			
Feasibility study (€)	5540 (2.1)	5540 (2.1)	5540 (2.1)
Development (€)	17825 (6.7)	17825 (6.7)	17825 (6.7)
Engineering (€)	10360 (3.9)	10360 (3.9)	10360 (3.9)
Energy equipment (€)	54500 (20.6)	54500 (20.6)	54500 (20.6)
Non-energy components of the physical plant (€)	147997 (56.0)	147997 (56.0)	147997 (56.0)
Miscellaneous (€)	28242 (10.7)	28242 (10.7)	28242 (10.7)
Annual cost			
Operating cost (€)	15400 (36.6 – 75.2)	15400 (37.1 – 80.0)	15400 (37.5 – 73.6)
Fuel / electricity (€)	5072– 26626 (24.8 – 63.4)	3860 – 26068 (20.0 – 62.9)	5527 – 25687 (26.4 – 62.5)
Periodic costs			
Replacement of boiler insulation after 7 years (€)	1000	1000	1000
Biomass heating system (1 boiler; €/kW)	140	140	140
Peak-load heating system (€/kW)	95	95	95
Biomass value (€/t)	8	5	15

Table 4. Analysis of greenhouse-effect gases

	Conventional (diesel) fuel		
Fuel type	#2 diesel	#2 diesel	#2 diesel
CO_2 emission factor (kg/GJ)	94.6	94.6	94.6
CH_4 emission factor (kg/GJ)	0.0020	0.0020	0.0020
N_2O emission factor (kg/GJ)	0.0030	0.0030	0.0030
GHG emission factor (t_{CO2}/MWh)	1.0690	1.0690	1.0690
	Biomass fuel [25]		
	Straw	**Switchgrass**	**Peat**
CO_2 emission factor (kg/GJ)	0	0	0
CH_4 emission factor (kg/GJ)	0.0320	0.0320	0.0320
N_2O emission factor (kg/GJ)	0.0040	0.0040	0.0040
GHG emission factor (t_{CO2}/MWh)	0.0110	0.0110	0.0110
Reduction in annual GHG emission (t_{CO2})	193.1	309.3	337.4

Table 5. Financial and environmental feasibility of the use of biomass fuels (assuming that the heating of domestic water account for 20% of total energy consumption)

Biomass fuel	Straw			Switchgrass			Peat		
	20% of energy used to heat domestic water								
$T_{environ.}$ (°C)	-4	5	15	-4	5	15	-4	5	15
Cost of reduction in GHG emission after income tax analysis ($€/t_{CO2}$)	65	-23	-176	59	-28	-182	68	-20	-174
Simple payback (years)	20.5	8.1	3.0	18.8	7.7	2.9	21.2	8.3	3.0
Period before positive cash flow (years)	14.8	7.3	3.2	13.9	7.0	3.2	15.0	7.4	3.3
IRR and ROI (%)	4.5	12.8	30.4	5.1	13.5	31.0	4.3	12.6	30.2
NPV (€)	-88015	49619	408176	-79196	61946	420634	-91344	44989	403496
Retail price of electricity (€/kWh)	0.15								
Annual increase in cost of electrici ty (%)	3								
Inflation rate (%)	2								
Discount rate (%)	10								
Project life (years)	25								

4   Results and Discussion

4.1   Environmental Assessment of the Project

According to the environmental specifications of the project, it is assumed that space heating is done with diesel and 100% of that would be displaced with biofuels, while water heating is done with coal and 100% of that would be displaced with biofuels. GHG emissions decreased dramatically (Table 4) when using renewable biomass fuels instead of coal. The annual reduction in GHG emission was greatest for peat, followed by switchgrass and straw. If the proportion of biomass fuel consumed for heating domestic water increases from 20% to 40% of total energy consumption, the additional reduction in annual GHG emission ranged from 30 to 32% for all three renewable fuels (Table 7).

Table 6. Financial and environmental feasibility of the use of biomass fuels (assuming that the heating of domestic water account for 40% of total energy consumption)

Biomass fuel	Straw			Switchgrass			Peat		
	40% of energy used to heat domestic water								
$T_{environ.}$ (°C)	-4	5	15	-4	5	15	-4	5	15
Cost of reduction in GHG emission after income tax analysis (€/t$_{CO2}$)	11	-50	-210	5	-56	-211	14	-48	-212
Simple payback (years)	11.9	5.7	2.1	11.1	5.4	2.1	12.2	5.8	2.1
Period before positive cash flow (years)	9.9	5.5	2.4	9.4	5.3	2.4	10.0	5.6	2.4
IRR and ROI (%)	8.8	17.7	40.8	9.4	18.5	41	8.6	17.4	41.1
NPV (€)	-19943	141165	642670	-9553	156185	646976	-23860	135472	649921
Retail price of electricity (€/kWh)	0.15								
Annual increase in cost of electrici ty (%)	3								
Inflation rate (%)	2								
Discount rate (%)	10								
Project life (years)	25								

Table 7. Environmental assessment of the project

	Type of biomass fuel		
	Straw	**Switchgrass**	**Peat**
Reduction in GHG emission (% compared with coal)		96	
Reduction (%) in annual GHG emission if heating of domestic water increases from 20% to 40% of the total energy	30	30	32

4.2   Socioeconomic Assessment of the Project

4.2.1   Economic Factors

The cost of the reduction of GHG emissions after income tax analysis (€/t_{CO2}) is only positive for an ambient temperature of -4°C at both levels of energy consumption for heating domestic water (Tables 5, 6), and the NPV for all uses of the biomass fuels was negative at this temperature. In our analysis, we assumed that no tax credit was provided to compensate the users of biomass fuels, as this is currently the situation in Greece; clearly, the provision of such a tax credit would greatly improve the economics of a transition to biomass fuels, and would thus provide an incentive for consumers to make this transition. The simple payback and the period until positive cash flow parameters decreased as the ambient temperature increased at both levels of energy consumption for heating domestic water (Fig. 2, 3). Furthermore, the "IRR and ROI" index values increased with increasing ambient temperature (Fig. 4).

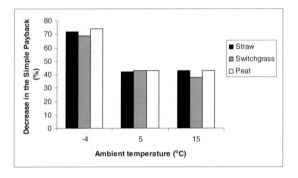

Fig. 2. Decrease in the simple payback period when the proportion of energy used to heat domestic water is increased from 20% to 40%

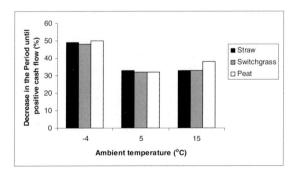

Fig. 3. Decrease in the period until positive cash flow when the proportion of energy used to heat domestic water is increased from 20% to 40%

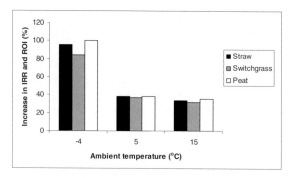

Fig. 4. Increase in the IRR and ROI index when the proportion of energy used to heat domestic water is increased from 20% to 40%

4.2.2 Political Factors

The transition to using renewable biomass fuels would involve a range of political factors, including support from local authorities, environmental groups, and farmers, as well as marketing activities to promote the use of the new fuels. The biggest challenges faced by efforts to obtain the necessary support for this transition include the fact that conventional fuels currently appear to be more advantageous and a lack of environmental regulations and subsidies to promote the use of these renewable fuels.

4.3 Evaluation of the Software Used in This Study

The software used in this study permits a simplified form of LCA that hides the complexity from the user. Specifically:

- It includes a database that contains reliable data on the three biomass resources (straw, switchgrass, and peat) that are most likely to be available to Greek citizens.
- It is easy to use and automatically generates a range of useful data based on relatively few inputs of data by the user.
- Simultaneous evaluation of the financial and environmental feasibility of the project provides a clear indication of the technical and environmental feasibility of the project and of the likelihood of its acceptance.
- The input process for technical and environmental data is simple and easy to understand.

The software had the following disadvantages:

- The data has various limitations, such as the difficulty of providing wide coverage of the potential geographical field (i.e., the software was developed for use in Canada, not Greece, thus some of the underlying parameters are not applicable to Greek conditions). This difficulty applies for both the worldwide diversity of natural resources and the specified restrictions defined by the software for the particular project and the materials selection. These parameters must be taken into consideration along with local technical and financial conditions. In addition, the software does not allow customization of the technical specifications of the pipe system defined by the model and of local environmental restrictions.

- Some of the input data may not be accurate for Greece, since the data depends on both the local economic and environmental conditions, and the effects of both on the input data will also change over time. As a result, the value of the data is likely to vary among countries and over time, thereby affecting the validity of the model results.

5 Conclusions

The aim of this study was to use the RETScreen software to investigate the potential of three renewable biomass fuels (straw, switchgrass, and peat) to reduce the environmental impacts of energy consumption for domestic heating in the Greek context. The results suggest that this software, if modified so that its underlying assumptions reflect the Greek context and if provided with suitable input data for that context, provides a quick and easy way to determine whether the transition to these biofuels appears sufficiently promising to merit a more detailed examination using tools such as a formal life cycle analysis. In the Greek context, the results are sufficiently promising that future research should investigate this transition in considerably more detail.

References

1. Kaj, J.: Renewable energy and efficiency improvements in the transport sector. Transport Sector Fuels Based on Renewable Energy project funded from: National Energy Agency of Denmark (1998)
2. Patyk, A., Reinhardt, G.: Life cycle analysis of biofuels for the transportation used in fuel cells and conventional technologies under European conditions, Institut for Energie und Umweltforschung (IFEU) Heidelberg GmbH (Institute for Energy and Environmental Research) (2001)
3. NBPBCO: The Biobased Products and Bioenergy Vision, Draft 18/7/2001. National Biobased Products and Bioenergy Coordination Office, Edition (2001)
4. NREL.: Alternative Fuels and Vehicles Offer Solutions to Imported oil, Air Pollution, Climate Change, U.S. Department of Energy, NREL (April 2002)
5. DTC.: Memorandum from the British Association for Biofuels and Oils (BABFO), Department for Transport consultation on ultra low carbon transport – hydrogen and biofuels (September 2003.)
6. Azar, C., Lindgren, K., Anderson, B.: Global energy scenarios meeting stringent CO^2 constraints—cost-effective fuel choices in the transportation sector. Energy Policy 31, 961–976 (2003)
7. Hund, G., Laverty, K.: 200 Proof Transportation: The potential for Ethanol as an Alternative Fuel. University of Washington, Global Commercialization of Environmental Technologies (2003)
8. Scotland, R.: The Recycling of Waste Wood by Thermal Conversion – A Report to Identify the Feasibility of Utilizing Waste Wood as a Feedstock for Use in Bioenergy Technologies, p. 37. Caledonian Shanks Centre for Waste Management, Glasgow Caledonian University (2003)

9. Maniatis, K.: Towards a Wider Use of Biofuels in Transportation. In: Directorate General for Energy and Transport (European Commission), 2CEN/TC 19 Symposium: Automotive Fuels 2003, Amsterdam, p. 30 (2003)
10. Svensson, G.: Annex XII: Assessment of Life Cycle Wide Energy – Related Environmental Impacts in the Pulp and Paper Industry. In: Final Report, IEA Programme on Advanced Energy – Efficient Technologies for the Pulp and Paper Industry, Institute for Energy Technology, Norway – Norwegian Water Resources and Energy Administration – Swedish National Energy Administration, p. 30. IEA Pulp and Paper Executive Committee (presented, 1999)
11. Pirolo, L., Presutti, M.: Towards a dynamic knowledge-based approach to the innovation process: an empirical investigation on social capital inside and industrial cluster. International Journal of Learning and Intellectual Capital 4(1/2), 147–173 (2007)
12. Lucas, L.M.: The role of teams, reputations and culture in effecting knowledge transfer. International Journal of Learning and Intellectual Capital 3(3), 323–338 (2006)
13. Zegveld, M.A.: The productivity and governance of company-specific knowledge. International Journal of Learning and Intellectual Capital 1(3), 317–333 (2004)
14. Dzbor, M., Motta, E., Stutt, A.: Achieving higher-level learning through adaptable Semantic Web applications. International Journal of Knowledge and Learning 1(1/2), 25–43 (2005)
15. Gupta, S., Bostrom, R.P.: Theoretical model for investigating the impact of knowledge portals on different levels of knowledge processing. International Journal of knowledge and Learning 1(4), 287–304 (2005)
16. Lerman, K., Plangprasopchock, A., Knoblock, C.A.: Semantic labeling of online information sources. International Journal on Semantic Web and Information Systems 3(3), 36–56 (2007)
17. Chung, H., Lieberman, H.: GlobalMind: Automated analysis of cultural contexts with multicultural. International Journal on Semantic Web and Information Systems 3(1), 65–95 (2007)
18. Kaykova, O., Khriyenko, O., Kovtun, D., Naumenko, A., Terziyan, V., Zharko, A.: General adaption framework: Enabling interoperability fro industrial web resources. International Journal on Semantic Web and Information Systems 1(3), 31–63 (2005)
19. Markellou, P., Rigou, M., Tsakalidis, A., Sirmakessis, S.: Shaping online learning communities and the way adaptiveness adds to the picture. International Journal of knowledge and Learning 1(1/2), 80–95 (2005)
20. Hodgkinson-Williams, C., Sieborger, I., Terzoli, A.: Enabling and constraining ICT practice in secondary schools: case studies in South Africa. International Journal of knowledge and Learning 3(2/3), 171–190 (2005)
21. Martin, B.: Knowledge management and the Australian Public Service: some lessons learned. International Journal of knowledge and Learning 1(1/2), 146–158 (2005)
22. Ahmed, A., Newton, D.J.: Strenghtening African universities' strategic role in knowledge and technology development: policies and practice from Sudan. International Journal of Learning and Intellectual Capital 2(1), 66–80 (2005)
23. Ordonez de Pablos, P.: Intellectual capital statements: what pioneering firms from Asia and Europe are doing now. International Journal of knowledge and Learning 1(3), 249–268 (2005)
24. Chakrabarti, A.K., Santoro, M.D.: Building social capital and learning environment in university-industry relationships. International Journal of Learning and Intellectual Capital 1(1), 19–36 (2004)
25. NRCan, RETScreen International calculating tool: 'BIOH3' supplied with the latest information of August 2005. Natural Resources Canada, CANMET Energy Diversification Research Laboratory (CEDRL) (2005),
http://www.retscreen.net/ang/d_o_view.php

Strategic Use of Information Technology in Profit and Non-profit Organizations from Tanzania and Sweden

Johnny Flores[1,2], Anayanci Lopez[1,2], Norman Vargas[1,2], and Lazar Rusu[1]

[1] Department of Computer and Systems Sciences, Stockholm University/Royal Institute of Technology, Sweden
[2] National University of Engineering, Nicaragua
johnnyfl@dsv.su.se, anayanci@dsv.su.se, normanv@dsv.su.se, lrusu@dsv.su.se

Abstract. Organizations have to deal with a dynamic environment such as new technologies, entrepreneurial ideas, strategic alliances, mergers and acquisitions, and regulatory change. A key for a well-functioning company is an efficient and effective strategic use of Information Technology (IT) supporting the business strategies, goals, and needs. It is also referred as Strategic Business and IT Alignment which is interpreted as a continuous process of conscious and coherent interrelation of all components and personnel of the business and the IT in order to contribute to the organization's performance over time. This paper reports an analysis of the Business and Information Technology Alignment by using Luftman's Strategic Maturity Assessment Model in case of a Tanzanian Profit Company and a Swedish Non-profit Company where both organizations have an intensive use of Information Technology.

1 Introduction

Organizations have to deal with a dynamic environment such as new technologies, entrepreneurial ideas, strategic alliances, mergers and acquisitions, and regulatory changes. A key for a well-functioning company is a efficient and effective strategic use of Information Technology (IT) supporting the business strategies, goals, and needs. The strategic benefit of deploying IT to support business functions is moreover seen as the basis for sustainable competitive advantage [1], and it has been reported to be positively associated with business performance indicators such as market growth, financial performance, and product-service innovation [2]. It also is referred as strategic business and IT alignment which is interpreted as a continuous process of conscious and coherent interrelation of all components and personnel of the business and the IT in order to contribute to the organization's performance over time [1]. Academics and practitioners have developed frameworks such as Information Systems Triangle [3] and theories such as the Strategy Alignment Maturity Assessment Model (SAMAM) [4][5][6]. Therefore in our research we have used SAMAM for analyzing the strategic use of IT in two organizations (a Tanzanian Profit Company and a Swedish Non-Profit Company) and for this purpose interviews were conducted with IT and business decisions makers for gathering essential information through a systematic and coherent case study approach.

M.D. Lytras et al. (Eds.): WSKS 2008, CCIS 19, pp. 137–146, 2008.
© Springer-Verlag Berlin Heidelberg 2008

2 Strategic Alignment Maturity Assessment Model (SAMAM)

The Strategic Alignment Maturity Assessment Model (SAMAM) [4][5][6] is oriented to assess the current state of alignment among the business and IT function. This model is depicted in figure 1 and its six criteria are used to determine how well the business and IT functions are aligned, and how this alignment might be improved. The SAMAM criteria are partnership, technology, skills/human resources, governance, communications, and competency/value.

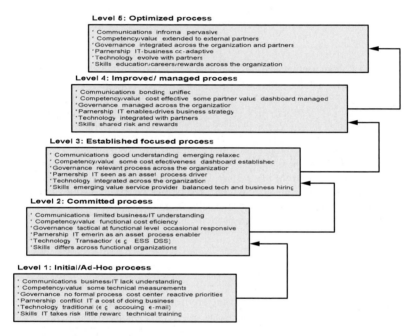

Fig. 1. Strategic Alignment Maturity Model [6]

The six IT-business alignment criteria are illustrated in Figure 3c and are defined at following: (1) *Communication Maturity*: Knowledge sharing across organizations; (2) *Measurement Maturity*: Value of IT in terms of contribution to the business; (3) *Governance Maturity*: Appropriate business and IT participants formally discuss and review the priorities and allocation of IT resources; (4) *Partnership Maturity*; how each organization perceives the contribution of the other; the sharing of risks and rewards; (5) *Technology Maturity*: the extent to which IT is able to: (a) Evaluate and apply emerging technologies effectively, (b) Enable or drive business processes and strategies as a true standard, (c) Solutions customizable to customer needs; (6) *Skills Maturity*: Career opportunities are factors that enhance the organization's cultural and social environment

The level of maturity indicates an organization's capability to align IT to business needs as it is shown in figure 1.

The criterion maturity level is determined through the evidences collected and the company maturity level is calculated as an average of the six IT – Business Maturity Criteria.

3   Strategic Use of IT in an Organization

Information technology [7][8] can provide the data needed for determining: (1) the effectiveness of a strategic-initiative; (2) the need to reengineer a business process; (3) changes in customer needs and expectations; and (4) new opportunities to improve customer satisfaction. If the company's IT fails to support its organizational systems, the result is a misalignment of the resources needed to achieve its goals.

The Information Systems Triangle [3] is a framework for understanding the impact of IS on organizations; it is presented in figure 2a, and composed by: (1) *Business strategy* which is the well-articulated vision of where a business seeks to go and how it expect to get there; (2) *Organizational strategy* which is the organization's design, as well as the choices it makes to define, set up coordinate, and control its work processes; (3) *Information Strategy* [9] which is the plant the organization uses in providing information systems and service.

The Strategic Alignment [10][4][11] promotes cross-functional and inter-organizational communication and allows for decentralized decision making and autonomous process teams. Therefore SAMAM (figure 2c) has been adopted for analyzing the strategic use of IT in an organization and this model includes the strategic systems triangle's components as it is shown in figure 2b.

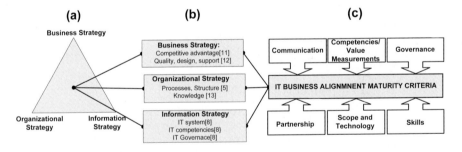

Fig. 2. (a) Information Systems Triangle, (b) Business, Organizational and IT Components, (c) IT-Business Alignment Maturity Criteria

4   Case Study Design

The case study design[1] (figure 3), has been developed for analyzing the strategic use of IT in a specific organization and attaining the established objectives. Using this

---

[1] Case studies should not be confused with "qualitative research"... "Some qualitative research follows to satisfy two conditions: (a) the use of close-up, detailed observation of the natural world by the investigator and (b) the attempt to avoid prior commitment to any theoretical model" [12].

approach we have investigated a contemporary phenomenon within its real-life context based on any mix of quantitative and qualitative evidences [12] as a useful technique to apply theories to the real life [13]. The case study has been designed and executed as a *descriptive pilot case study* as it is depicted in figure 3.

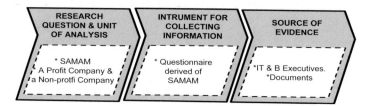

Fig. 3. Case Study Design

4.1   Research Question and Unit of Analysis

The research question used in our case studies is the following: What is the alignment level in a profit company and in a non-profit company? The *unit of analysis* [12] *is* looking to two organizations: A Tanzanian Profit Company and a Swedish Non-Profit Company which represents *maximum variation cases*[2] [13]. In the context of these two organizations the research question has looked mainly to analyze the strategic use of IT using the approach proposed in section 3.

4.2   The Instrument for Collecting the Information

A questionnaire has been developed based on SAMAM and its purpose was to collect the essential information about the current status of the IT/Business alignment in an organization. The questions[3] of SAMAM's Partnership criterion used in our case study are presented below as an example:

- Who is the main sponsor of IT projects?
- How is the business and IT relationship coordinated?
- Does the company have business strategy plan? How is it elaborated? What kind of input does it receive? Which are the roles of IT personnel in the business strategy planning?
- Does IT represent an enabler of activities, costs, an asset or a driver of future activities? Why?

4.3   Sources of Evidence

The case study's quality is determined by using *multiple sources of evidence* to collect information about the same phenomenon for the *construct of validity* [12]. The

---

[2] Maximum variation cases: the purpose of this type of case study is "to obtain information about the significance of various circumstances for case process and outcome (e.g. three to four cases that are very different on one dimension: size, form of organization, location, budget) [13].

[3] Its evidences are marked by (*) in table 1 and table 2.

sources of evidences are in our case the *semi-structured interviews*[4] and additional documents. Regarding the interview this is defined as "a flexible and adaptable way of finding things out" [14]. The advantages related to the interview could be mentioned as "focusing directly on case study topic" and also by "providing perceived causal inferences" but it can be easily biased [12]. On the other hand, documentation is a stable source which offers exactness and broad coverage but it may be deliberately blocked or selectively biased [12].

5   The Case Study Conduction

Two companies have been selected: a Tanzanian Profit Company and a Swedish Non-Profit Company, as case studies of *maximum variation*. The research approach in both case studies was done through interviews with IT and business decision makers for collecting the information necessary for assessing the IT/Business alignment.

5.1   The Case Study of a Tanzanian Profit (TP) Company

TP Company has a limited liability and is providing ICT Products and Services to the general public such as: Internet access, consultancy, web design and hosting, ICT training and it is having 148 employees and seven departments. The case study has been developed based on 3 interviews with IT/Business executives, which roles are Network Services Manager, Head Service Control Manager, and Deputy Managing Director. The evidences collected in this case study are presented in table 1.

Table 1. TP Company's Strategic Alignment Maturity Assessment

Communication Level: 3:(Good Understanding, Emerging Relaxed)
Evidence
– IT staff is informed about the business strategy plan through workshops, seminars.
– The Director's requests are received by the Service Control Organizational Unit, which sends to the manager of the department who is adequate to do this consultancy"
– Director – Manager and leaders (executives) are the IT project's sponsors
– TP company doesn't have a IT- Business liaison staff.
Measurements Level: 3 (Functional Cost Efficiency)
Evidences
– TP company has metrics by department: "You need to compare your expected output with your achievements"
– Related to Business, the focus is the assessment and measurements related to IT profit and costs.
– Improvements in their internal process are oriented to their measurements focus (investments or costs)
– TP Company has SLA's with external customers, but not into the company.

---

[4] Semi-structured interview: has predetermined questions, but the order can be modified based upon the interviewer's perception of what seems most appropriate. Question wording can be changed and explanations given; particular questions which seem inappropriate with a particular interviewee can be omitted, or additional ones included [14].

Table 1. (*continued*)

Governance Level: 2 (Tactical at functional level, Occasional Responsive)
Evidences
– The leaders of each department participate in the elaboration of the business strategy plan. The IT personnel participate in the workshop and give their opinions.
– TP Company does not have a document about the IT strategy plan. Every department has its goals. Every department cooperate within the Business Strategy Plan"
– TP Company's structure is decentralized and has several managers for different IT functions but doesn't have a CIO or someone in a similar function.
– The IT project prioritization is variable. In general, they said: "we decide looking to the profit and the time to be spent in the project. Service Control section is in charge to do the prioritization"
(*)Partnership Level: 3 (IT is seen as an asset; Process Driver)
Evidences
– IT enables business activities: "… because we are an IT company and almost all the consultancy are in the area of IT"
– "The Manager Director and the leadership of each department is the main sponsor of IT projects"
– Business and IT relationship is not managed: "…they have to coordinate according to the business strategy plan"
Technology Level: 3 (Integrated across the organization)
Evidences
– Their IT systems are transaction oriented; they have "…the system for registration of the students and the system for checking when somebody is no paying for the service"
– About technology standards the company has adopted the standard ISO 2000.
– IT Infrastructure is important to their strategies: "We have been working on creating the IT infrastructure to support the business organization"
Skills Level: 3 (Emerging Value Service Provider; Balanced Tech and Business Hiring)
Evidences
– Change Readiness: "Of course, we give a value if you bring and participate in the project. In this way we motivate the people"
– "Our interaction between IT Personnel and Business Personnel is through the intranet. The IT Personnel, Business Personnel and customers have social interaction in annual party.
– About attraction and retaining of the top talent personnel: "It is a big challenge, TP company is a limited one but is trying to do"
– "Some business personnel are trained for developing their IT skills competencies. They are trained by some IT staff"

5.2 The Case Study of a Swedish Non-profit (SN) Company

The SN Company is a school who carries out the education activities like: formal, non-formal and vocational adult education. The organization purpose is to align the education to the needs of the labor market and make people skilled in order to get better jobs. By using e-learning (a platform "edulink") this organization is providing end to end e-learning globally, with the vision: "Education for All". The case study has been developed based on the interviews with business executives, which roles are President CEO, Project Manager, and Teacher. The evidences collected are presented in table 2.

Table 2. SN Company Strategic Alignment Maturity Assessment

Communication Level: 4 (Bonding, Unified)
Evidences
– All the work of the staff depends of IT, they have IT skills and, even, they assess IT services. – Organizational Learning: The president emphasizes that: - They want to build-in possibilities of employees to develop themselves. – They have established time for learning–They are interested in "learning for the companies and employees" – Organizational culture can be observed a constructivist approach, President said: "…ride a bicycle is not something that someone can teach you, it should be learned by yourself" – According to the President, IT and Business are "development partners", they work together to improve the service of each other and they do it in an informal way – The communication at top level with their IT service providers, generally, is realized in an informal way.
Measurements Level: 3 (Some Cost Effectiveness; Dashboard Established.)
Evidences
– Their IT services are outsourced to a Finland company (F company). This company provides them IT services for their projects in Sweden and for projects with their partners in other countries (Africa, Pakistan, etc.) – They have agreements which establish the "minimal quality of service" and they consider that the IT service provided is very good (they have long term relationship, 10 years) – The F Company and SN company work together to improve their respective services. SN company is an "evaluator" of the IT provider (President said "…we use a product and we say what they have to change… they have improved a lot of things with our suggestions"); in this evaluations they are focused in "customer satisfaction" and find technologies which help them to reach their goals (effectiveness).
Governance Level: 3 (Relevant process across the organization.)
Evidences
– SN Company has a management document ("Styrdokument") which is elaborated considering suggestions from "students, teachers, partners and so on". – IT projects are prioritized considering their partners in other countries and the "Millennium goals" (it is a guide toward SN company mission and vision) – The top level relationship between SN Company and their IT service provider is, in general, in an informal way and the president is the main contact. – Organizational structure is Federal. They have a President and several "Principals" for projects.

Table 2. (*continued*)

– IT is completely integrated to their processes all their projects are supported by IT. Therefore, IT as a process driver and strategy enabler.
– Technologies are part of their vision.
– "We believe that information and communication technology (ICT) in education and working life empowers people to create and participate in knowledge sharing and net communities".

(*)Partnership Level: 5 (IT-Business Co-adaptive.)
Evidences
– TP Company perceives IT as a partner in creating value. The President said "we are testing application partners", but this relation "is not something official", they work together to improve their services. IT helps TP Company to do a better work and we tells to IT provider in the real life this technology is suitable and give suggestions about "what they have to change"
– IT enables or drives business strategy: the implementation of their strategies and processes depend of IT. They said, "... if the vision is 'to work in the refugee camps' and then the ICT solutions is for us 'how to do it'"
– IT service provider and TP Company have 10 years working together in a trust relationship.

Technology level:5 (Evolve with partners)
Evidences
– The main business process (end-to-end eLearning) completely depends of IT systems; therefore it is an enabler/driver of the business strategy.
– SN company has databases and a learning management system, eConferences, net communities, digital services, access to satellites
– SN Company has standards related eLearning.

Skills Level: 2 (differs across functional organization)
Evidences
– SN company gives bonus for innovation
– SN company has a trust relationship with the IT service provider and internally.
– "There is no resistance to change because the new IT projects are proposed by the employees themselves"
– Most of the IT Human resources are outsourced to a company located in Finland.

6 Case Studies' Implications

The maturity alignment in both case studies is presented in figure 4 and its implications are described below.

According to the evidences collected and presented in table 1: TP Company has the level of alignment 3, which corresponds to established process. This company is oriented to investments and costs, and has a common language of communication amongst its organizational units, but its communication is not flexible. On the other hand TP Company doesn't have an IT strategy but it has a business strategy plan. Moreover the TP Company has a Transactional IT systems and the attraction and retaining of top talent personnel is a big challenge for this organization.

According to the evidences collected and presented in table 2: SN Company has the level of alignment 4, which is corresponding to improved/managed processes. This Company has a flexible communication amongst its personnel and has created a learning organization based on constructivism approach. Moreover the SN Company has had a long term relationship with its IT provider and an effective IT system. Therefore the SN Company has adopted a management document for strengthening its cooperative works and is looking to promote innovation through bonus.

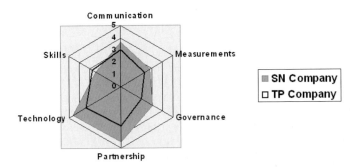

Fig. 4. Spider Diagram: Maturity Level of Alignment in TP Company and SN Company

7 Conclusions

As we have noticed Luftman's Strategic Alignment Maturity Assessment Model (SAMAM) is a well funded theory which is a good alternative for analyzing the strategic use of information technology. Moreover its main contribution is to provide a big picture of the current strategic IT/Business alignment level in an organization and its criteria are providing a clear image about what is happening from this perspective within an organization. From the analysis of the TP Company we have seen that this organization has an intensive use of IT, because it is an IT Service Provider and its business processes are running around IT services, its organizational structures are encompassed; its business planning process have a higher participation employees, but it doesn't have an IT Strategy. On the other hand the SN Company has an intensive use of IT and it is focused on global learning (based on using an e-learning platform that is outsourced). Moreover SN Company's projects are running around e-learning and the organization is addressed by Millennium Goals, but it does not have a business strategy, neither an IT strategy. In conclusion, by using the Luftman's SAMAN in the case of the organizations from Tanzania and Sweden we have drawn relevant information for IT and business decisions makers too about how these organizations are using IT today as a strategic resource and in which way they should act to improve this important issue in the near future.

References

1. Papp, R.: Strategic Information Technology: Opportunities for Competitive Advantage. Idea Group Publishing (2001)
2. Chan, Y., Huff, S.: Strategic Information Systems Alignment. Business Quarterly 58(1), 51–56 (1993)
3. Pearson, E., Saunders, C.: Managing & Using Information Systems- A Strategic Approach, 3rd edn. John Wiley & Sons, Chichester (2006)
4. Luftman, N.J.: Competing in the Information Age – Align in the Sand. Oxford Press (2003) ISBN 0-19-515953-5
5. Luftman, N.J.: Measure Your Business-IT Alignment. Optimize: Business execution for CIOs Magazine 26 (December 2003)
6. Luftman, N.J.: Assessing Business-IT Alignment Maturity. Communications of AIS 4(art 14), 1–50 (2000)
7. Lockamy, A., Smith, W.: A strategic alignment approach for effective business process re-engineering: linking strategy, processes and customers for competitive advantage. International Journal of Production Economics 50, 141–153 (1997)
8. Luftman, J.N., Lewis, P.R., Oldach, S.H.: Transforming the enterprise: the alignment of business and information technology strategies. IBM Systems J. 32(1), 198–221 (1993)
9. Chan, Y., Huff, S., Copeland, D.: Assessing realized information systems strategy. Journal of Strategic Information Systems, Elsevier Science B.V. 6, 273–298 (1998)
10. Henderson, J.C., Venkatraman, N.: Strategic alignment: a model for organizational transformation through information technology. In: Kochan, T.A., Useem, M. (eds.) Transforming Organizations, pp. 97–117. Oxford University Press, Oxford (1992)
11. Plazaola, L., Silva, E., Vargas, N., Flores, J., Ekstedt, M.: A Metamodel for Strategic Business and IT Alignment Assessment. In: Proceedings of the Conference on Systems Engineering Research (CSER 2006), Los Angeles, USA (April 2006)
12. Yin, R.: Case Study Research: design and methods, 2nd edn. Sage Publications Inc., Thousand Oaks (2002)
13. Flyvbjerg, B.: Five Misunderstandings About Case-Study Research. Qualitative Inquiry 12(2), 219–245 (2006)
14. Robson, C.: Real World Research: a resource for social scientists and practitioner - researchers, 2nd edn. (2002) ISBN 0-631-21305-8

Views on Globalization of Higher Education

Abdulkader Alfantookh and Saad Haj Bakry

King Saud University, P.O Box 800, 11421, Riyadh, Saudi Arabia
a@fantookh.com, shb@ksu.edu.sa

Abstract. This article is an elaboration on Stanford University panel discussion entitled "looking ahead: governance and democracy". The main speaker of the panel was Professor Paul Collier of Oxford University, with other contributors from Stanford. In exploring the topic, the panel discussed ways, and previous experience, concerned with driving less developed countries toward better future. Professor Collier suggested "four instruments" for influencing development in these countries. In this respect, "knowledge", which represents an important instrument for both human and economic development was overlooked. This article emphasizes "knowledge", and addresses the issue of "globalization of higher education (HE)" as an important "instrument" for better future, not only for the less developed countries, but also for the whole world. The scope of the article is limited to this instrument, and does not consider debating the views on the other "instruments" addressed by the panel.

Keywords: Higher education, Globalization of higher education, Mobility in higher education, Knowledge for development, Knowledge for world peace.

1 Introduction

In the Stanford panel [1], Paul Collier explored better future use of four western instruments for initiating and supporting suitable domestic democratic processes in less developed countries, for the purpose of improving their economic governance, and achieving higher growth. These western instruments were: the power of the western "media"; the western companies, that is the western "business community; western "public money for aid"; and the western "military". Collier elaborated on the use of each of these instruments in various circumstances, with examples associated with different countries. He also used results of statistical analysis to derive conclusions and recommendations.

In the same panel, the late John McMillan (passed away in March 2007) presented his research experience on the subject; and Larry Diamond gave, with enthusiasm, useful and insightful comments. However, non of the two, elaborated on the possibilities of the existence and deployment of development "instruments", other than those considered by Paul Collier.

This article considers the use of "knowledge", through "higher education: HE", as an "instrument" for influencing world development. The knowledge circle of knowledge "generation, diffusion and utilization" has been considered as a mean for both human and economic development [2]. In this article, the role of HE knowledge

M.D. Lytras et al. (Eds.): WSKS 2008, CCIS 19, pp. 147–152, 2008.

in forming the future of the world, from a "global viewpoint", is addressed. The article starts by a general background; and following this, it explains its views on the subject. Finally, it gives some comments and conclusions.

2 Background

This section provides a brief overview of HE, and its current development, as a background for both: addressing its "globalization", and explaining how this globalization can be used as an "effective instrument" for the creation of better future for the whole world. The presented background is concerned with highlighting the emergence of HE, in the west, and its international expansion during the second millennium. It is also concerned with exploring the current state and the future development plans for HE, both at the national level and at the international level.

2.1 Emergence of HE in the West

HE, as we know it, appeared in the second millennium; and Paris is known to have been one its early centres, where students from different parts of Europe use to study [3]. When English students were forbidden from studying in Paris, Oxford, in the UK, started to emerge as a new center, around the second century of the second millennium [3, 4]. The first college of Cambridge University, UK, started in 1284 [5], that is long before America was discovered in 1492 [6]. The foundation of Harvard University, as another Cambridge in the USA, goes back to 1636 [7].

HE has played, and is still playing, an important role in the life of people. Frank Rhodes of Cornell University, USA, considers the university to be "quiet, but decisive catalyst in modern society" [8]. He emphasizes that although the university does not do, or produce, what the society needs, it generates the knowledge and prepare the human skills necessary for its development and well-being.

During the last centuries of the second millennium, western countries encouraged spreading their higher education system beyond their national borders. For example, the American University of Beirut (AUB) started in 1862, with financial support raised both in the USA and England; and it was granted a charter by the State of New York in 1863 [9]. In addition, the American University of Cairo was founded later in 1919 [10].

2.2 Current State and Development Plans

At present, some western universities are opening new campuses in other countries. An example of this is Stanford University campus in China, which was opened in 2003 [11]. In addition, other western universities are establishing partnership with other national universities in different parts of the world. An example of this is the partnerships in which the German Technology University of Darmstad is engaged. The university has partnerships with other universities in: Africa, Australia and the Pacific, Asia, and America, including countries in North, Central and South America [12].

At the national level, western governments are concerned with planning for HE. For example the government of the Canadian province of Ontario initiated, in 2005, a plan for HE, under the name "reaching higher"; the plan increases investment in HE by "40 %" over the years "2005-2010". The plan emphasizes the following issues: providing "improved access" to HE; working toward "higher quality"; holding the HE institutions "accountable" for achieving "improved access and higher quality"; and supporting "better facilities". In addition, the plan considers supporting relationships between Ontario HE institutions, and promoting "mobility of students" among these institutions [13].

Western countries also supports "mobility of students" at the regional level. Examples of this include: "North America Mobility Project", which considers HE cooperation between Canada and Mexico [14]; "North America Mobility Grant Program" which considers cooperation in HE among USA, Canada and Mexico [15]; and the "International Mobility in HE Program", which currently considers cooperation between HE institutions in both Canada and Europe; in addition to cooperation among the three countries of North America [16].

At the international level, John Daniel of UNESCO (the United Nations Educational, Scientific and Cultural Organization) considers higher education to be international by nature, and to be compatible with globalization [3]. He emphasizes that, for a long time, both "students and ideas have been mobile" across national borders. Students have been able to study in foreign countries, and research ideas and knowledge have been flowing across countries through higher education institutions. In addition, he considers that another form of mobility is emerging, that is the "mobility of teaching", through distance learning.

The world conference on higher education, held in UNESCO headquarters in Paris, during the period "5-9 October 1998", issued a declaration on higher education for the 21st century. The declaration stated its purpose as "to preserve and reinforce the core mission of higher education – to educate, to train, to undertake research – and, particularly to contribute to the sustainable development and improvement of society as a whole" [17]. The declaration considers HE to be "a public service". It emphasizes its "academic autonomy and freedom"; and it stresses that it should be "accessible to all", and that this "should be based on merit", with "no discrimination" of any kind.

3   The Proposed Globalization of HE

HE, as a "provider of the public commodity of knowledge", is a strong candidate to be an "effective instrument" for better future for the whole world, leading to "peace, stability, and development". This would be subject to supporting it toward "creating a new global HE knowledge community of multi-cultural structure, based on equality and understanding". Achieving this mission is discussed in this section. The section explains the principles upon which the proposed HE globalization should be based; and it also gives suggestions on how this globalization can be achieved, emphasizing the main players involved.

3.1   HE Globalization

Starting with a brief statement, it can be said that the target principles of HE globalization are no more than "refinement, activation and extension of the current ideas and objectives concerned with HE", introduced in the "background section" above. This is explained, in more details, in the following.

There are two "initial principles", upon which globalization of HE should be based; they consider that: HE should be viewed as a "public commodity", and that this public commodity should become an "international right" to all those who enjoy credible school records. Associated with these principles, there are another two, that can be called the "core principles", because they drive HE globalization and the achievement of its goals and benefits. These core principles are: "global access to HE", and "global mobility in HE".

"Access" to HE should be expanded, on a large scale, especially in less developed countries, so that those, wherever they are, with credible access records, can receive the public commodity of HE. "Mobility" of students, researchers, teachers and knowledge, among HE institutions, at the world level, should be enabled. Of course the mobility of those, for world development, is a more civilized phenomena than the mobility of troops and weapons.

Global mobility of students, researchers, teachers and knowledge, would enhance inter-cultural understanding; and would also lead to international friendship among different people. The mobility of students would be particularly important for long term friendly relationships among nations; and the mobility of researchers and teachers, would be useful to future development of HE. Of course friendly personal relationships among a large volume of well-educated people, from different countries, is deeper and more beneficial, on the long run, than relationships among the political leaders of these countries.

Globalized "access" and globalized "mobility" require two "enabling principles" to be added to the above HE globalization principles. These principles are concerned with "enabling HE facilities", and with "enabling HE quality".

Facilities for new, or expanding HE institutions, including: buildings, lecture rooms, labs, equipment, information technology (IT), and residence halls, will be needed to support access expansion. In addition, the quality of HE courses and research will need to be controlled, in all HE institutions, at the world level, according to satisfactory quality levels, so that "mobility" is easily enabled. This will be useful for the promotion of the quality state of many universities all over the world, especially those of the less developed countries.

The above principles would create a "global multi-cultural knowledge community" of well-educated and highly skilled people, based on equality and understanding. This community would enjoy national and international influence, and it would enhance world peace and stability. It can act as a promoter and guardian of good governance, and as a driver of sustainable development.

The requirements associated with the above principles do not come without high cost, but this cost is actually an "investment" that would be beneficial to the whole world. The requirements also need "experience and management" capabilities. These support issues, for the achievement of the target HE globalization, are addressed in the following.

3.2 Achievement of HE Globalization

The achievement of the target "HE globalization" can take three basic forms. "Distinguished universities" of the west, and of other developed countries, can create "new campuses", all over the world, in a similar manner to Stanford foundation of its campus in China. This would support "global accessibility" and promote "global mobility", but only within the campuses of the distinguished university concrned. It would also satisfy the enabling principles by providing HE "facilities" in the international campuses, and by transferring "quality" to the countries of these campuses.

Another form of HE globalization is for distinguished universities to establish "partnerships", not only with other universities of the developed world, but also with the universities of the less developed counties, in a similar manner to what TU-Darmstad is doing. This would support HE "quality" in these countries, and it would also enhance "global mobility".

The third, and perhaps the most important, form would be associated with the responsibility of the "international community". An "international academic club" of professors and public figures from different parts of he world, who are enthusiastic about the "globalization of HE", should be established. The role of the club would be to generate international "discussions" on the issue; bring up new "ideas"; develop "plans"; initiate "projects", provide "follow-up", and accumulate "experience" toward the implementation of the target globalization. The club would also investigate how this globalization can contribute to the development of better world.

In order to perform its tasks, the proposed "international academic club" would need to raise financial support. International organizations such as UNESO, the United Nations Development Program (UNDP), the World Bank, and others would be potential supporters. Western, and other governments, may also provide support; this would be "investment" in world peace and stability. Of courses there are also other sources of support, such as independent donors, but this would depend on how well the issue is publicly presented. In this regard, the media can help by initiating a public forum on the issue.

4 Conclusions

Thanks to Stanford for "globalizing" its panel on "governance and democracy", through iTunes. This globalization has promoted international discussion across the world, like what the proposed "HE globalization" would also do; and of course this article is an example of this globalization. The article emphasizes that future discussions should not only consider the four western "instruments", concerned with world development, suggested by Paul Collier, but they should also take into account the international "HE globalization instrument" proposed here.

It is hoped that the article would initiate discussions on the three basic, laid out, dimensions of globalization of HE: the suggested "principles", the proposed "forms of implementation", and the required "support", including the potential sources of support. It is also hoped that the media would contribute to putting the issue in the "public domain". As a final comment, it should be noted that the image of "globalization" has not been very popular, creating opposition and riots in different parts of the world, when addressed within the context of the economy; if "knowledge and HE" is the context, the picture is likely to change.

References

1. Collier, P., McMillan, J., Diamond, L.: Looking ahead: governance and democracy, Center for Democracy Development and the Rule of Law. Freeman Spogli Institute for International Studies. Stanford Univesity, Apple iTunes (2006),
   `http://itunes.stanford.edu/`
2. Bakry, S.H.: Transformation to the Knowledge Society. King Abdulaziz Public Library, Riyadh, Saudi Arabia (2005) (in Arabic)
3. Daniel, J.: UNESCO Assistant Director General for Education (2001-2004), Views on Higher Education, UNESCO Website,
   `http://portal.unesco.org/education/en/ev.php-`
   `URL_ID=18906&URL_DO=DO_TOPIC&URL_SECTION=201.html`
4. History, University of Oxford Website,
   `http://www.ox.ac.uk/aboutoxford/history.shtml`
5. History, University of Cambridge Website,
   `http://www.cam.ac.uk/cambuniv/pubs/history/setting.html`
6. Discovering America,
   `http://www.welshdragon.net/resources/myths/madoc1.shtml`
7. Academic American Encyclopedia. Arete Publishing Company, USA (1981)
8. Rhodes, F.H.T.: The Role of the American University: The Creation of the Future. Cornell University Press, USA (2001), `http://www.cornellpress.cornell.edu`
9. History, The American University of Beirut (AUB) Website,
   `http://www.aub.edu.lb/about/history.html`
10. History, The American University of Cairo (AUC) Website,
    `http://www.aucegypt.edu/about/history.htm`
11. Reunion Homecoming, President's Address, Stanford University, Apple i-Tunes (2004),
    `http://itunes.stanford.edu/`
12. International Partners Universities, TU-Darmstadt,
    `http://en.wikipedia.org/wiki/Darmstadt`
    `_University_of_Technology`
13. Ontario Government plan for postsecondary education: Reaching higher (May 13, 2005),
    `http://www.gov.on.ca/`
14. North America Mobility Project,
    `http://www.arts.ualberta.ca/~nastudi/index1.php`
15. North America Student Exchange Program,
    `http://www.umanitoba.ca/outreach/intercultural/`
16. International Mobility Higher Education Program,
    `http://www.hrsdc.gc.ca/en/cs/comm/grants/programs/learning_l`
    `iteracy/international_mobility.shtml`
17. World conference on higher education, Paris, UNESCO Website (1998),
    `http://portal.unesco.org/education/en/ev.php-`
    `URL_ID=10699&URL_DO=DO_TOPIC&URL_SECTION=201.html`

Learning Objects for eLearning Systems

Erla M. Morales Morgado[1], Francisco J. García Peñalvo[2], Ángela Barrón Ruiz[1],
Hugo Rego[2], and Tiago Moreira[2]

[1] Department of Theory and History of Education,
University of Salamanca, Pº de Canalejas, 169, 37008, Salamanca, Spain
erlamorales@usal.es, ansa@usal.es
[2] Department of Computer Science, University of Salamanca, Plaza de los Caídos, S/N,
37008, Salamanca, Spain
fgarcia@usal.es, hugo_rego05@yahoo.com, thm@mail.pt

Abstract. Although LO management is an interesting subject to study due to
the current interoperability potential, it is not promoted very much because a
number of issues remain to be resolved. LOs need to be designed to achieve
educational goals, and the metadata schema must have the kind of information
to make them reusable in other contexts. This paper promotes the design,
implementation and evaluation of learning objects in the field of university
education, with a specific focus on the development of a metadata Typology
and quality evaluate tool.

Keywords: Learning Objects, Management, Quality, E-learning, Metadata,
Evaluation.

1 Introduction

Many studies have been done on the concept of learning objects (LOs) but no
consensus has been reached on a standard definition or on the technical and
pedagogical requirements. Specifications are being developed but have yet to be
normalized, and the use of metadata schemas is still under discussion. This has
prevented LO creation and management from becoming common practice.

This paper presents a proposal on the design, implementation and evaluation LOs
management tool for e-learning systems, containing quality criteria designed to enable
LOs to be standardized and attuned to educational needs. This proposal take into
account our own knowledge model, and comprises specific metadata value spaces for
classifying LOs into the LOM "5. Educational" metadata category.

The paper begins by outlining the development of learning objects and determines
what type of metadata should be applied (section 2). It goes on to describe how we
suggest to implement and evaluate LOs using our evaluation tool HEODAR
(*Herramienta de Evaluación de Objetos Didácticos de Aprendizaje Reutilizables*)
(section 3); Finally it presents our conclusions and plans for the next stages of our
work (section 5).

M.D. Lytras et al. (Eds.): WSKS 2008, CCIS 19, pp. 153–162, 2008.

2　Learning Objects Design

The first task to create a learning object is to choose a context where define a set of specific learning objectives with which built a knowledge model that served to produce a basic unit of learning which, in turn, served as the basis for designing. According to this, we suggest the following knowledge model [5] (fig.1).

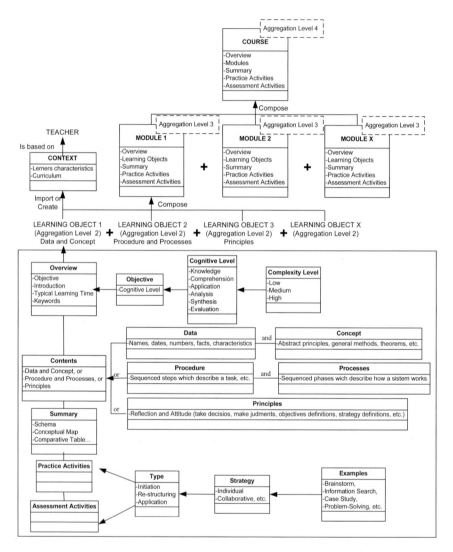

Fig. 1. Knowledge Model

On this basis it is possible to design specific learning objects taking into account pedagogical and technical issues.

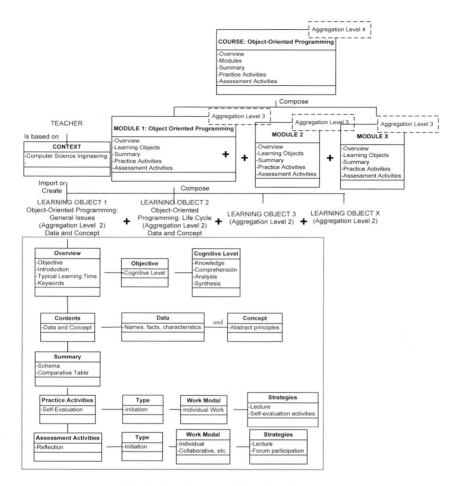

Fig. 2. Knowledge Model Application (LO1)

Figure 2, shows an example of a LO directed to the Object-Oriented Programming (OOP) option of the Computer Science course at Salamanca University [2]. We defined a set of specific learning objectives with which we built a knowledge model that served to produce a basic unit of learning which, in turn, served as the basis for designing LO1, entitled "Object-Oriented Programming: General Issues" [4] [6].

One of the key goals here is to enable a knowledge model to be used to standardize LOs, which is crucial for them to be tailored to educational needs, taking into account key elements for learning [7]. Following our knowledge model (Fig. 2) the LO1 was designed, created by Dreamweaver, and implemented by Moodle and finally was evaluated for learners according to HEODAR [10]. Here we have some comments they give us to consider improving LOs design:

- Add a glossary of key concepts and list of acronyms.
- Add examples to illustrate/clarify abstract concepts.

- Avoid table cells in web page design (as it impeded accessibility for sightless users).
- Highlight main points (e.g. in bold).
- Avoid too many references in short texts.
- Adjust window resolution to avoid too many scroll bars.

All the user comments are very useful in order to evaluate the LOs quality, for this reason, we suggest adding qualitative and quantitative LOs information into their metadata information as we are going to explain in section 4.

3   LOs Metadata Typology and Implementation

Sound LO management requires the incorporation of reliable metadata, but the viability of the only metadata schema currently regarded as a standard [2] has been called into question because it uses vast quantities of ill-defined types of data, and some of its metadata categories do not make it clear what kind of information has to be added, thus further complicating the task of LO management [8].

Although the lack of clarity in the IEEE LOM standard [2] makes its value spaces hard to interpret, most metadata editors today continue to use that standard without seeking to explain the meaning of each space.

We set out to address this issue – and, hence, to enable suitable LO management data to be introduced into learning environments – by devising a set of definitions to clarify the content of each value space in the LOM "5. Educational" metadata category as shows Table 1 (shady zone):

Table 1. Metadata Typology

5.1. Interactivity type	Predominant mode of learning supported by this learning object.
Active	LOs which have a high interactivity level (learners interact with many activities which promotes high cognitive levels, like taking decisions, design projects, etc.
Expositive	LOs featuring a very low interactivity level, with students receiving information yet remaining unable to interact with the content.
Mixed	LOs which have combined interactivity. Learners have the possibility to interact with sophisticated documents with multiple links.
5.2. Learning Resource Type	Specific kind of learning object. The most dominant kind shall be first.
5.3 Interactivity Level	The degree of interactivity characterizing this learning object. Interactivity in this context refers to the degree to which the learner can influence the aspect or behavior of the learning object .
Very Low	LOs which have an expositive interactivity level. Learners receive information and don't have interactivity possibilities.

Table 1. (*continued*)

Low	LOs with an expositive interactivity level – minimal student participation (web pages with few links)
Medium	LO content designed to promote smooth learning and application of knowledge
High	LOs related with high interactivity type of activities.
Very High	LOs related with very high interactivity type of activities which promotes users' productive activities e.g. take decisions, open answers, etc.
5.3 Semantic Density	The degree of conciseness of a learning object. The semantic density of a learning object may be estimated in terms of its size, span, or --in the case of self-timed resources such as audio or video-- duration.
Very Low	The LO contents information are not concise and are highly irrelevant.
Low	The LO contents information is low concise and low relevant
Medium	The LO contents information is medium concise and not very relevant.
High	The LO contents information is high concise e.g. an image together with a brief text.
Very High	The LOs contents are extremely concise, and very relevant e.g. a symbolic representation.
5.5 Intended End User Role	Principal user(s) for which this learning object was designed, most dominant first.
5.6 Context	The principal environment within which the learning and use of this learning object is intended to take place.
5.7 Typical Age Range	Age of the typical intended user.
5.8 Difficulty	How hard it is to work with or through this learning object for the typical intended target audience.
Very Easy	Basic, concrete, LO is easily recognized by users.
Easy	Information is easily associated with previous knowledge
Medium	It is possible to apply and understand the LO contents without difficulties.
Difficult	Complex. The LO is directed to high cognitive levels.
Very Difficult	The LO contains very complex information which requires applying high cognitive levels.

The metadata typology presented above promote to standardize the type of information added into metadata elements, in this way it is possible to know more exactly educational information about LOs and manage them in a suitable way according to specific goals.

There are different kinds of metadata editors and applications which consider the possibility to create LOs, add them metadata information and export them as a content package (CP) [3] e.g. eXelearning. However they don't consider the possibility to define some metadata typology. Is means, they don't aim the possibility to define what's the meaning of "low", "medium", "difficult", etc.

4   Learning Objects Evaluation

Current proposals for learning resource evaluation tools include web sites [11] [12] and multimedia tools, [13], and other proposals have been made for assessing the quality of LOs taking into account their instructional use-oriented design [14] and sequencing [15]. We drew on these to design an instrument that would enable learners to assess the value/quality of their LOs (see figure 3).

PEDAGOGICAL CRITERIA FOR LEARNING OBJECTS EVALUATION	D/N= Don't know, 1=Very Disagree, 2=Disagree, 3=Agree 4=Very Agree
PSYCHOPEDAGOGICAL	
Motivation and Attention	3,7
Presentation: Capture learners attention mantaning their motivation	3,6
Add important information: Information need to be relevant according to the LO subject	3,7
Learners participation: LO explains very clear how learners can to participate in the lesson	3,8
Professional competence	3,9
Learning objectives help users to achieve their professional competences	3,9
Difficulty level	3,6
Contents difficulty level: It needs to be suitable for user cognitive domain	3,6
Language: It needs to be suitable for previous users knowledge	3,5
Interactivity	3,5
Interactivity Level: It promotes opportunities to interact with LO in different ways	3,6
Interactivity type: LO interaction aims to achieve learning objectives	3,4
Creativity	3,8
It promotes self-learning	3,8
It promotes cognitive domain development	3,7
GENERAL COMMENTS (Describe some examples where this LO can be reused)	3,7

Fig. 3. Psychopedagogical item into Pedagogical criteria for LO evaluation

As seen in Figure 3, the evaluation tool (HEODAR) [10] was designed to gather qualitative and quantitative data about LOs.

Figure 3 shows a set of quality criteria for evaluating pedagogical aspects of LOs, and then divided those criteria into categories and sub-categories containing more detailed criteria.

The feedback gained from the space provided in LO evaluation tool for students to make comments provide very useful pointers to see what needed to be improved when developing other LOs.

To input the quantitative and qualitative data on the quality of LO1 into our metadata typology, we used the LOM "9. Classification" metatada category in combination with our own LO quality rating classification scheme. First we developed the LO quality rating scale shown in Table 2 (below).

Table 1 sets out the various LO ratings on the evaluation scale and explains their corresponding quality levels. We believe that quality measurement using a scale like this should be introduced into the "9. Classification" metadata category. Table 3 (below) shows our LOs quality rating scale into 9.Classification metadata category. Table 4 shows our prototype adaptation using the final quality score taken from the LO1 evaluation results (see Fig. 3).

Table 2. LO Quality Rating Scale

Ratings	Quality Meaning
1.0 – 1.5	**very poor**: too low. LO to be eliminated
1.6 – 2.5	**poor**: low, with much room for improvement
2.6 – 3.5	**satisfactory**: could be better
3.6 – 4.5	**high**: good but could be better still
4.6 – 5.0	**very high**: good, with no need for further improvement

Table 3. LOs Quality Rating Scale into 9. Classification metadata.

Nº	Name	Example
9	Classification	
9.1	Purpose	**Quality**
9.2	Taxon path	
9.2.1	Source	("is", "Rating")
9.2.2	Taxon	[**"Rating"**, ("is", "quality meaning")]
9.2.2.1	ID	**"Rating"**
9.2.2.2	Enter	"quality meaning"
9.3	Description	"LO has a "quality meaning" because...
9.4	Keywords	"high", "quality", "Alphanumeric values", etc.

Our proposed adaptation of the LOM "9. Classification" metadata category comprises the key quantitative and qualitative data collected with our LO quality evaluation tool.

In presenting a summary of learners' comments on LO quality, item "9.3. Description" provides a useful means of further improving that quality.

Finally, the "9.4. Keyword" item gives users the search words for finding and retrieving the best possible LOs to suit their needs [8].

Our thinking was as follows:

- Adding a quality value to the LO metadata category would help locate and retrieve an LO through a search based on keywords (e.g. quality, value, high, etc.) and alphanumeric values (e.g. CA_3.64). An alphanumeric value makes it possible to define a specific vocabulary for running an LO search.
- Using specific kinds of values would provide a means of developing more sophisticated search methods, e.g. using an intelligent agent to find and compare LOs according to quality criteria. This would require a multi-agent architecture enabling personal retrievals from multiple sources.
- LO management would be facilitated by incorporating LO quality ratings into semantic profiles [11],[12].

- IEEE LOM metadata categories at present do not consider classifying LOs according to quality ratings and, hence, most metadata editors do not offer the possibility of adding other types of classification criteria.
- The sample students' comments provided useful pointers for producing an enhanced and more user-friendly design for other prototypes.

Table 4. LO1 Quality Rating incorporated into LOM

Nº		Name	
9		Classification	Quality
9.1		Purpose	
9.2		Taxon path	
9.2.1		Source	LO Quality Rating Scale
9.2.2		Taxon	*CA_3.64 is quality 3.64
	9.2.2.1	ID	CA_3.64
	9.2.2.2	Enter	High
9.3		Description	LO considered high quality by sample students. Lowest scoring quantitative items were 'motivation', 'activities' and 'interactivity'. Qualitative feedback suggested adding a glossary and examples; avoiding use of table cells in LO design; using fewer references in text; and improving screen resolution
9.4		Keywords	quality, value, high, CA_3.64**

*CA = calidad (quality).
**"CA_3.64" (alphanumeric value).

5 Conclusion

The research outlined in this paper set out to test a model for enhancing LO management through evaluation of LO quality. Our knowledge model demonstrate how LOs can be established as a basic unit of learning, taking into account key educational needs. It can be used to adapt an LO to a specific type of course at university level.

The LO quality evaluation tool enable us to collect a wide range of information useful for improving LOs. In attributing a numerical value to LO quality, the rating scale helped specify exactly which data to incorporate into the metadata schema.

It is important to remember that metadata editors today only classify LOs according to specific established purposes. We used the LOM "9. Classification" metadata category because we believe it useful for defining and adapting new LO classification schemes that would allow users to acquire and manage LOs suited to their own individual needs.

Sorting evaluation criteria into different categories made it possible to evaluate the LOs from both pedagogical and technical points of view.

Our future work will focus on developing an LO creation tool based on our knowledge model. We will also seek to improve the quality of LOs by taking into account the accessibility issues that are crucial to LO management. Finally, we are aiming to promote intelligent agent-based automated working methods by developing a prototype multi-agent architecture for quality-based LO management.

Acknowledgements

This work was co-financed by the Spanish Ministry of Education and Science, the FEDER-KEOPS project (TSI2005-00960) and the Junta de Castilla y León local government project (SA056A07).

References

[1] Gil, A.B., Morales, E., García, F.J.: E-Learning Multi-agent Recommender for Learning Objects. In: IX Simposio Internacional de Informática Educativa, pp. 163–169 (2007) ISBN:978-972-8969-04-2

[2] IEEE LOM, IEEE 1484.12.1.: Standard for Learning Object Metadata (2002) (Retrieved June, 2007), http://ltsc.ieee.org/wg12

[3] IMS CP Content Packaging specification v1.1.3 (2003), http://www.imsglobal.org/content/packaging

[4] Morales, E.M., García, F.J., Barrón, Á., Gil, A.B.: Gestión de Objetos de Aprendizaje de calidad: Caso de estudio. In: SPDECE 2007. IV Simposio Pluridisciplinar sobre Objetos y Diseños de Aprendizaje Apoyados en la Tecnología (2007) ISBN 978-84-8373-992-1

[5] Morales, E.M., García, A.B., Barrón, Á.: Improving LO Quality through Instructional Design Based on an Ontological Model and Metadata. J.UCS. Journal of Universal Computer Science 13(7), 970–979 (2007)

[6] Morales, E.M., García, F.J., Barrón, A., Morales, E.M., Barrón, A., García, F.J.: Research on Learning Object Management. In: Cardoso, J., Cordeiro, J., Filipe, J. (eds.) Proceedings of the 10h International Conference on Enterprise Information Systems (ICEIS 2008), Barcelona, España, June 12-16, 2008, pp. 149–154. INSTICC Press (2008), http://www.iceis.org ISBN obra completa 978-972-8865-91-7

[7] Morales, E.M., García, F.J., Barrón, Á.: Key Issues for Learning Objects Evaluation. In: Ninth International Conference on Enterprise Information Systems. ICEIS 2007, vol. 4, pp. 149–154. INSTICC Press (2007)

[8] Morales, E.M., García, F.J., Barrón, Á.: Quality Learning Objects Management: A proposal for e-learning Systems. In: 8th International Conference on Enterprise Information Systems Artificial Intelligence and Decision Support Systems ICEIS 2006, pp. 312–315. INSTICC Press (2006) ISBN 972-8865-42-2 (B3)

[9] Morales, E.M., Gil, A.B., García, F.J.: Arquitectura para la recuperación de Objetos de Aprendizaje de Calidad en Repositorios Distribuidos. In: SCHA: Sistemas Hipermedia Colaborativos y Adaptativos. II Congreso Español de Informática CEDI 2007. 5ª Edición, vol. 1(1), pp. 31–38 (2007) ISSN 1988-3455

[10] Morales, E., García, F.J., Alonso, D.: HEODAR. Herramienta de Evaluación de Objetos Didácticos de Aprendizaje Reutilizables mediante Ránking en Moodle. In: 10th Simposio Internacional de Informática Educativa SIIE. En prensa (2008), `http://siie08.usal.es/`

[11] Marquèz, P.: Criterios de calidad para los espacios Web de interés educativo. Disponible en (2003), `http://dewey.uab.es/pmarques/caliWeb.htm`

[12] Torres, L.: Elementos que deben contener las páginas web educativas. Pixel-Bit: Revista de medios y educación 25, 75–83 (2005)

[13] Marquèz, P.: Elaboración de materiales formativos multimedia. Criterios de calidad. Disponible en (2000), `http://dewey.uab.es/pmarques`

[14] Williams, D.D.: Evaluation of learning objects and instruction using learning objects. In: Wiley, D.A. (ed.) The instructional use of LOs (2000), `http://reusability.org/read/chapters/williams.doc`

[15] Zapata, R.M.: Calidad en entornos virtuales de aprendizaje y secuenciación de Learning objects (LO). Virtual Campus 2006. V Encuentro de Universidades & eLearning, 111–119 (2006) ISBN 84-689-6289-92

Personalized Video Browsing and Retrieval in a Semantic-Based Learning Environment

Antonella Carbonaro

Department of Computer Science
University of Bologna
Mura Anteo Zamboni 7, I-40127 Bologna, Italy
Tel.: +39 0547 338830; Fax: +39 0547 338990
carbonar@csr.unibo.it

Abstract. The paper presents an ontological approach for enabling semantic-aware information retrieval and browsing framework facilitating the user access to its preferred contents. Through the ontologies the system will express key entities and relationships describing learning material in a formal machine-processable representation. An ontology-based knowledge representation could be used for content analysis and concept recognition, for reasoning processes and for enabling user-friendly and intelligent multimedia content search and retrieval.

Keywords: ontologies, image retrieval, learning system personalization, semantic techniques.

1 Introduction

Vast amounts of multimedia information including video are becoming ubiquitous as a result of advances in multimedia computing technologies and high-speed networks. Video is rapidly becoming the most popular media, due to its high information and entertainment power.

The main challenge is to index information retained in video in order to make them searchable and thus (re-) usable. This requires the multimedia content to be annotated, which can either be done manually or automatically. In the first case, the process is extremely work- and thus cost-intensive; in the second case, it is necessary to apply content-analysis algorithms that automatically extract descriptions from the multimedia data. The aim is to create a concise description of the multimedia content features, that is, its metadata. Metadata descriptions may vary considerably in terms of comprehensiveness, granularity, abstraction level, etc. depending on the application domain, the tools used and the effort made for creating the descriptions.

Multimedia annotation systems need standard output, which must be compliant with other tools for browsing or indexing. MPEG-7 [ISO/IEC] standard was defined for this purpose. It represents an elaborate standard in which a number of fields, ranging from low level encoding scheme descriptors to high level content descriptors, are merged to be useful for describing a video or part of it.

In text-based applications, it is often sufficient to annotate only the generic properties of the document (such as title and creator) and to perform keyword search,

M.D. Lytras et al. (Eds.): WSKS 2008, CCIS 19, pp. 163–171, 2008.

based on full-text information retrieval approaches. For non-textual resources, however, full text search is only an option if there are sufficient associated textual information (for example, Google's image search based on surrounding text in HTML or video retrieval based on subtitles, closed captions or audio transcripts). In many other cases content descriptions are inevitable. Since content descriptions are not often about the entire document (e.g. a specific shot in a film or a specific region in a picture), it is necessary to implement shot detection and keyframe extraction procedures to deal with video files.

An important step towards efficient manipulation and retrieval of visual media is semantic information representation [Calic et al. 2005], [Bloehdorn et al., 2004]. In the digital library community a flat list of attribute/value pairs is often assumed to be available. In the Semantic Web community, annotations are often assumed to be an instance of an ontology. Through the ontologies the system will express key entities and relationships describing video in a formal machine-processable representation. An ontology-based knowledge representation could be used for content analysis and object recognition, for reasoning processes and for enabling user-friendly and intelligent multimedia content search and retrieval.

In [Web search engine multimedia functionality Dian Tjondronegoro *, Amanda Spink 2008] they report findings from a study examining the state of multimedia search functionality on major general and specialized Web search engines. They investigated 102 Web search engines to examine the degree of multimedia searching functionality offered by major Web search engines and to compare the functionalities of each Web search engine which is significant for the development of more effective multimedia IR systems. Their findings show that despite the growing level of interest in multimedia Web search, most major Web search engines currently offer limited multimedia search functionality. Keywords are still used as the only mean of multimedia retrieval. For search formulation, ontology-based classification can help users in redesigning their query if it is too specific. For example, instead of looking for "aloe vera", users can be suggested to search on "green plants". Moreover, a unified indexing on keywords and semantic summaries will enable search engines to support users in finding related topics.

The aim of this paper is to present our video retrieval and browsing framework based on both collaborative and semantic approaches. The collaborative approach is exploited both in retrieving task (to cover recommendation and resource sharing tasks) and in semantic coverage of the involved domain. The semantic approach is exploited introducing an ontology space covering domain knowledge and resource models based on word sense representation. Also the ontology level exploits system collaborative aspect. We show how the semantic technologies can enhance the traditional e-learning keyword approaches facilitating the user retrieval and browsing by adding semantic information in the resource and user profiles.

We propose how to introduce a semantic-based representation of the information embedded in the video media both by user interaction and by ontology exploiting. The paper introduces Scout-V (Semantic-based Content management Tools - Video), our semantic video content annotation and retrieval system. Scout-V provides following web-based tools to help consumers to manage their video collection:

- a browsing application to enable users efficiently access their video collections,

- a shot detection application to automatically identify shot in the video measuring the similarity among frames,
- an annotation application to enable users easily annotate video sequences,
- an ontology editor application to enable users to modify the ontology tree creating all the necessary classes and instances,
- a video annotation recommendation application enable user to speed up annotation task proposing similar frames which have been annotated also by other users,
- an MPEG-7 file producer application to maintain the obtained video content description,
- a video retrieval application to offer semantic multimedia search functionality.

Applications that could benefit from semantic video representation are manifold, from education and training to medical, from entertainment to system analysis and evaluation, etc. For example, home entertainment systems (management of personal multimedia collections, including manipulation of content, home video editing, searching, etc.) need a mechanism to interpret human's queries, and retrieve the closest match. However, this search outcome may result very unsatisfactory due to the blurred link between the low-level measured features and the human semantic queries. This discrepancy between the way video data is coded digitally and the way it is experienced by a human user is called the semantic gap, [Smeulders et al., 2000]. Differently, in education, semantic annotations of video recording of lectures distributed over the Internet can be used to augment the material by providing explanations, references or examples, that can be used for efficiently access, find and review material in a student personal manner [Carbonaro and Ferrini, 2005], [Carbonaro, 2005]. Moreover, in television, semantic annotation of programmes, for example news, could produce electronic programme guides, which would allow the user to view details of forthcoming programmes in terms of entities referred to in particular broadcasts [Dowman et al., 2005].

2   Personalized Video Retrieval Framework

Traditional approaches to personalization include both content-based and user-based techniques [Dai and Mobasher, 2004]. If, on one hand, a content-based approach allows to define and maintain an accurate user profile (for example, the user may provides the system with a list of keywords reflecting hir/her initial interests and the profiles could be stored in form of weighted keyword vectors and updated on the basis of explicit relevance feedback), which is particularly valuable whenever a user encounters new content, on the other hand it has the limitation of concerning only the significant features describing the content of an item. Differently, in a user-based approach, resources are processed according to the rating of other users of the system with similar interests. Since there is no analysis of the item content, these information management techniques can deal with any kind of item, being not just limited to textual content. In such a way, users can receive items with content that is different from that one received in the past. On the other hand, since a user-based technique works well if several users evaluate each one of them, new items cannot be handled until some users have taken the time to evaluate them and new users cannot receive references until the system has acquired some information about the new user in order to make personalized predictions. These limitations often refer to as the sparsity and start-up problems [Melville et al., 2002]. By adopting a hybrid approach, a personalization system is able to effectively filter relevant resources from a wide heterogeneous environment like the Web, taking advantage of common interests of the users and also maintaining the benefits provided by content analysis.

A hybrid approach maintains another drawback: the difficulty to capture semantic knowledge of the application domain, i.e. concepts, relationships among different concepts, inherent properties associated with the concepts, axioms or other rules, etc. Semantic-based approach to retrieving relevant material can be useful to address issues like trying to determine the type or the quality of the information suggested from a personalized learning environment. In this context, standard keyword search has a very limited effectiveness. For example, it cannot filter for the type of information (tutorial, applet or demo, review questions, etc.), the level of information (aimed to secondary school students, graduate students, etc.), the prerequisites for understanding information, or the quality of information. Some examples of semantic-based e-learning systems can be found in Mendes and Sacks [Mendes and Sacks, 2004] and in Lytras and Naeve [Lytras and Naeve, 2005].

The aim of this paper is to present our personalized learning retrieval framework based on both collaborative and semantic approaches. The collaborative approach is exploited both in retrieving task (to cover recommendation and resource sharing tasks) and in semantic coverage of the involved domain. The semantic approach is exploited introducing an ontology space covering domain knowledge and resource models based on word sense representation. Also the ontology level exploits system collaborative aspect.

The Scout-V module assists authors in annotating video sequences. Each shot belonging to the video sequence can be annotated on the base of underlying ontologies. These descriptions are labelled for each shot and are stored as MPEG-7 descriptions in the output XML file. Scout-V can also save, open, and retrieve MPEG-7 files in order to display the annotations for corresponding video sequences. The Scout-V main page shows all the videos that should be elaborated performing shot detection, editing or removing. Given the segmentation of video content into video shots, the second step is to define the semantic lexicon to label the shots. A video shot can fundamentally be described by using five basic classes: agents, objects, places, times and events. These five types of lexicon define the initial vocabulary for our video content; they correspond to the SemanticBase MPEG-7 tags. We have also defined attributes to describe class characteristics. Each attribute corresponds to a specified MPEG-7 tag used in storing phase. By using the defined vocabulary for static agents, key objects, places, times and events, the lexicon is imported into Scout-V for describing and labelling each video shot. The shots are labelled for their content with respect to the selected lexicon. Note that the lexicon definitions are database and application specific, and can be easily modified and imported into the annotation tool.

Scout-V annotation tool is divided into three graphical sections: the Scene Matching frame in which are shown the algorithms that can be used to obtain video annotation recommendations (Block Truncation Coding, edge histogram, colour histogram), the Ontology Visualization frame, providing interactivity to assist authors of the annotation tool and the Video Presentation frame with the key frame image display and the frame characteristics. The Ontology Editor module allows to modify the ontology tree creating and populating all the necessary classes and instances. The aim of the instance creation phase is to effectively represent the domain knowledge, so as to achieve a better precision in the annotation task. Annotations are then stored and used by recommendation procedure to help users finding similar frames which have been annotated also by other users.

Once the scene as a whole has been annotated, the system produces a MPEG-7 file. The system comprises automatic shot detection and scene matching modules to obtain video annotation recommendations in a collaborative framework. By the shot detection method the video can be automatically segmented into shots. A shot is a contiguous sequence of video frames which have been recorded from a single camera operation [Grana et al.,]. The method is based on the detection of shot transitions (hart cuts, dissolves, and fades). One or more keyframes are extracted from the obtained shots set in dependence on the visual content dynamics. Several experiments tested the effectiveness of both the shot detection module and the frame matching module on the annotation process. More detailed description can be found in [Carbonaro and Ferrini, 2007].

The video retrieving framework is shown in Figure 1. We introduce an example ontology from the travel domain; it could be published on fixed URI's as OWL files. The ontology would define concepts such as ActivityProvider to link an Activity with a ContactAddress. There could be a set of subtypes of activities such as BungeeJumping or IceClambing, and these could be categorized into types like AdventureActivity. Based on the rich expressiveness of OWL, it is furthermore possible to define classes by their logical characteristics. For example, a class BackpackersDestination could be defined as a destination that offers budget accommodation and some adventure activities. These defined classes allow reasoners to automatically classify existing domain objects into matching categories.

Figure 2 shows the implemented ontology. The retrieving process starts with a keyword-based search. We use database textual fields to retrieve video that correspond to user query; these fields are concerning to both general video features like title, keywords and description and shot elements (see Figure 3). On the left-hand side of the screen we show the set of concepts extracted from the ontology that the user can use to perform a semantic-based video search. These concepts are ontology instances related both to performed query and to retrieved video. We can consider the retrieving function as an interactive transformation of the starting query. The user can iteratively performs concept-based search choosing a concept from the set of relevant extracted from the ontology using ontology properties that link individuals. Since visualized concepts are OWL individuals they are showed using their name in the ontology. Figure 4 shows the ontology-based search results using the keyword "snow": The related concepts are relative to winter sports, to those corresponding to the unique retrieved video and to the concepts child of returned class in the ontology.

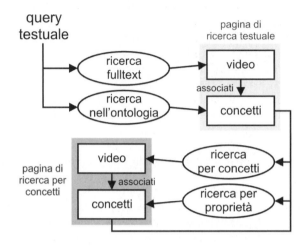

Fig. 1. Video retrieval functioning scheme

Fig. 2. Developed ontology

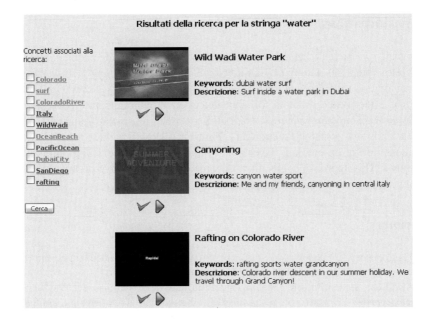

Fig. 3. Simple query results

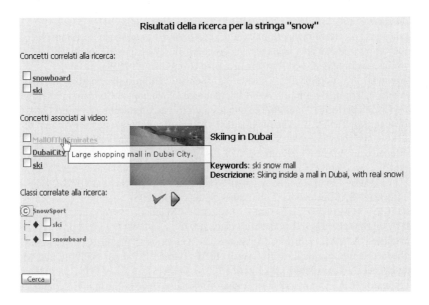

Fig. 4. Ontology-based search mode

3 Considerations

In this paper we have presented a methodology for semantic video content retrieving. The system comprises automatic shot detection and scene matching modules to obtain video annotation recommendations in a collaborative framework. Several experiments tested the effectiveness of both the shot detection module and the frame matching module on the annotation process. The ontology-based retrieving framework offers a valuable multimedia search functionality. Future works will include the study and the implementation of an ontology layer able to maintain several existing ontologies the user knows. This approach could allow to compare the knowledge of any user without having a single consensual ontology.

References

1. Tjondronegoro, D., Spink, A.: Web search engine multimedia functionality. Information Processing and Management 44, 340–357 (2008)
2. Bloehdorn, S., Petridis, K., Simou, N., Tzouvaras, V., Avrithis, Y., Handschuh, S., Kompatsiaris, Y., Staab, S., Strintzis, M.G.: Knowledge Representation for Semantic Multimedia Content Analysis and Reasoning. In: Proceedings of the European Workshop on the Integration of Knowledge, Semantics and Digital Media Technology (2004)
3. Calic, J., Campbell, N., Dasiopoulou, S., Kompatsiaris, Y.: A Survey on Multimodal Video Representation for Semantic Retrieval. In: The Third International Conference on Computer as a tool (Eurocon 2005). IEEE, Los Alamitos (2005)
4. Carbonaro, A.: Defining personalized learning views of relevant learning objects in a collaborative bookmark management system. In: Web-Based Intelligent e-Learning Systems: Technologies and Applications. Idea Group Inc. (2005)
5. Carbonaro, A., Ferrini, R.: Considering semantic abilities to improve a Web-Based Distance Learning System. In: ACM International Workshop on Combining Intelligent and Adaptive Hypermedia Methods/Techniques in Web-based Education Systems (2005)
6. Dowman, M., Tablan, V., Cunningham, H., Popov, B.: Web-assisted annotation, semantic indexing and search of television and radio news. In: Proceedings of the 14th international conference on World Wide Web, pp. 225–234 (2005)
7. Grana, C., Tardini, G., Cucchiara, R.: MPEG-7 Compliant Shot Detection in Sport Videos. In: Proceedings of IEEE International Symposium on Multimedia (ISM 2005), Irvine, California, USA, December 12-14, 2005, pp. 395–402 (2005)
8. ISO/IEC. Overview of the MPEG-7 Standard (version 8). ISO/IEC JTC1/SC29/WG11/N4980, Klagenfurt (July 2002)
9. Smeulders, A.W.M., Worring, M., Santini, S., Gupta, A., Jain, R.: Content based image retrievals at the end of the early years. IEEE Trans. on Pattern Analysis and Machine Intelligence 22(12), 1349–1380 (2000)
10. Carbonaro, R.F.: Ontology-based Video Annotation in Multimedia Entertainment. In: Proc. 3rd IEEE International Workshop on Networking Issues in Multimedia Entertainment (NIME 2007) - 2007 4th IEEE Communications and Networking Conference (CCNC 2007), Las Vegas, USA. IEEE Communications Society, Los Alamitos (2007)

11. Lytras, M.D., Naeve, A. (eds.): Intelligent Learning Infrastructure for Knowledge Intensive Organizations. Information Science Publishing, London (2005)
12. Mendes, M.E.S., Sacks, L.: Dynamic Knowledge Representation for e-Learning Applications. In: Nikravesh, M., Zadeh, L.A., Azvin, B., Yager, R. (eds.) Enhancing the Power of the Internet - Studies in Fuzziness and Soft Computing, vol. 139, pp. 255–278. Springer, Heidelberg (2004)
13. Dai, H., Mobasher, B.: Integrating semantic knowledge with web usage mining for personalization. In: Scime, A. (ed.) Web Mining: Applications and Techniques. Idea Group, Hershey

Intelligent Tutoring in the Semantic Web and Web 2.0 Environments

Vlado Glavinić[1], Slavomir Stankov[2], Marija Zelić[2], and Marko Rosić[2]

[1] Faculty of Electrical Engineering and Computing, University of Zagreb, Unska 3,
10000 Zagreb, Croatia
[2] Faculty of Science, University of Split, Teslina 12,
21000 Split, Croatia
vlado.glavinic@fer.hr,
{slavomir.stankov,marija.zelic,marko.rosic}@pmfst.hr

Abstract. The paper presents an approach to solving problems pertinent to intelligent tutoring in the Semantic Web/Web 2.0 environments within the TExSys (Tutor Expert System) model, an evolving series of ITSs our group has been developing for the last 15 years, following all Web technology generations being used in this period. We describe the way in which assigning intelligent tutoring tasks to personal agents enables solving the problems, additionally extending intelligent tutoring through the mobile, collaborative and social dimensions in the Semantic Web and Web 2.0 environments.

Keywords: Intelligent tutoring systems, Semantic Web, Web 2.0, Mobile learning, Agents.

1 Introduction

E-learning is one of the important services that the Web is to offer to its users. In fact, the development of the Web has paved the way to the development of Web-based e-learning systems. In the Web early stages it was possible to provide only the static teaching-related Web pages, supporting a very low level of interactivity between a student and the teaching matter. Representative technologies characterizing these beginnings encompass HTML and the Common Gateway Interface (CGI), themselves showing limitations which resulted in e-learning systems where only a few people developed the teaching contents due to limited interactivity possibilities. This further resulted in a sporadic renewal of the contents and thereby in the reduction of teaching potentials. The interactivity level of e-learning systems has increased since with the development of new technologies supporting dynamic generation of the Web documents, such as e.g. the Active Server Pages (ASP), the Java Server Pages (JSP) or the Hypertext Preprocessor (PHP). An additional increase of Web-based e-learning system capabilities was achieved by technologies enabling development of Web applications based on Service Oriented Architectures (SOA), such as e.g. Microsoft .NET technology. Besides, technologies based on the Extensible Markup Language (XML), which enable sharing of data among different systems, have been introduced in the Web environment, too.

M.D. Lytras et al. (Eds.): WSKS 2008, CCIS 19, pp. 172–177, 2008.

Two new Web concepts arise in the context of the above mentioned technologies: (i) the Semantic Web and (ii) Web 2.0. The Semantic Web is an extension of the present Web where information gets a well-defined meaning thus enabling cooperative work among software agents and users for the purpose of satisfying users' demands. The Semantic Web requires mechanisms which enable software agents to understand contents of the Web documents not only on the syntax but also on the semantic level. It was therefore necessary to define methods of displaying relations among knowledge elements within a document, as well as storing inference rules on data in the document. This was solved by means of ontology languages in the Web environment, such as e.g. the Web Ontology Language (OWL) and the DARPA Agent Markup Language (DAML). Within such an environment the typical process of accomplishing a task becomes a specific chain of adding new values where information is passed from one agent to another.

Conceptually the Semantic Web can be regarded as an environment for agent interaction, whereas Web 2.0 can be regarded as an environment for user interaction since its basic principles include: (i) cooperation, (ii) sharing and (iii) creativity. Web 2.0 does not require new technological specifications but conversely conceptualizes the way of developing and using Web Services through linked services which uphold the above principles. This is achieved by developing such Web tools as those for multimedia documents sharing (e.g. YouTube, Flickr and GoogleVideo), for communication (e.g. MySpace), ones transferring the standard desktop applications functionality to the Web (e.g. Google Docs) as well as social bookmarking ones which enable users to store, classify and search notes inside Web documents (e.g. Ma.gnolia).

2 Intelligent Tutoring Systems

The development of both Semantic Web and Web 2.0 affects conceptualization of any Web-oriented knowledge-based system and consequently of intelligent tutoring systems (ITSs). Intelligent tutoring systems are the generation of systems intended for support and improvement of the learning and teaching process. Their work is based on simulation of a human teacher in the learning and teaching process. The teaching paradigm of intelligent tutoring systems is based on the following features of a human teacher [1], [2]: (i) possession of domain knowledge, (ii) possession of knowledge on teaching methods, (iii) capability of diagnosing student's knowledge, (iv) capability of comparing the level of student's knowledge with the domain knowledge, i.e. determining the level of student's domain knowledge acquisition and (v) capability of adjusting teaching methods to students.

According to Major, the intelligent tutoring systems are adjusting to individual student's needs in the following ways [3]: (i) by varying the difficulty level of teaching contents presented to a student, (ii) by adjusting the presentation manner, (iii) by providing help to a student depending on his behavior during the system use and (iv) by adjusting the processing order of individual teaching units.

ITSs base their work on an iterative comparison of student's knowledge with a referent model and act after getting information on differences, if there are any.

Based on these principles we have developed an intelligent hypermedia authoring shell, the Tutor-Expert system (TEx-Sys). TEx-Sys has been developed within three technological generations [4]: (i) the on-site version (1992-2001, on-site TEx-Sys), (ii) the Web-oriented version based on the technology of dynamic generation of the Web documents (1999-2003, Distributed Tutor-Expert System (DTEx-Sys)) and (iii) the version based on Web Services (2003- , eXtended Tutor-Expert System (xTEx-Sys)). Figure 1 shows an illustration of the concept "Atom" in the course "Physics 1" in the latest TEx-Sys version.

3 Adaptation of Intelligent Tutoring Systems to the New Web Generation

By moving to the Semantic Web and Web 2.0 environments, ITSs as well as other knowledge-based systems inherit problems which have been met before: heterogeneity of users, information overload and interoperability, respectively. Heterogeneity of access devices, which is the result of increased usage of various mobile devices for accessing Web resources, arises as a new additional problem. Finally, as with the introduction of any new technology, let us note that it is often not enough to simply "copy" the pedagogical paradigm from the previous generation of systems but it is necessary to adequately adjust it to the new tutoring environment.

Due to nature of the Semantic Web, agents are provided with greater opportunities in performing complex tasks such as: (i) advanced Web search, (ii) using services provided by Web information systems and (iii) navigating various Web information systems thus ensuring their interoperability. Furthermore, agents' characteristics such as autonomy, learning capabilities, proactiveness and social skills enable development of high-quality systems. This has been our motivation for contemplating the TEx-Sys system as a multi-agent system when moving it to the new environment. The following ideas can be used in adaptation of any intelligent tutoring system.

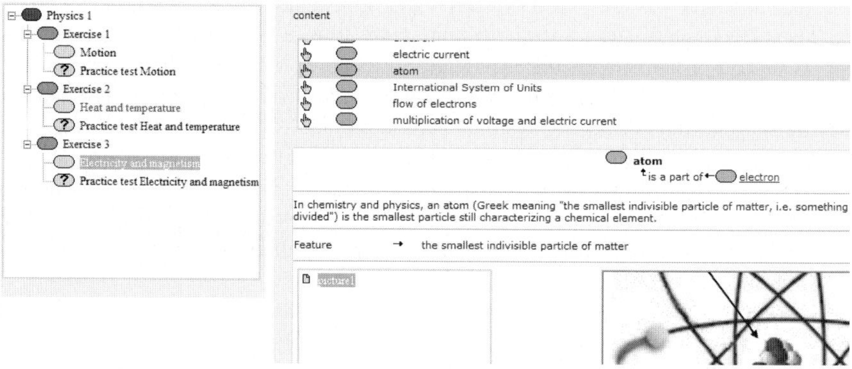

Fig. 1. Presentation of a concept in TEx-Sys

Our model enumerates and describes the TEx-Sys tasks to be taken over by agents in the new Web generation (Figure 2). They are the following:

- teaching,
- testing,

– enabling communication among the system's users,
– enabling authoring work,
– searching the common information space, and
– enabling access to the system by means of various mobile devices.

Teaching and testing are tasks requiring adaptation of the system to the student. Agents performing the teaching and testing should be equipped with the student's profile containing information on her/his learning background, previous test results, capabilities, preferences, learning goals, etc. Depending on this information the agents can suggest to the student a revision of previous lessons or some additional material, an exercise, a related test and so on. The agents' knowledge on the domain, teaching methods and students should be reusable. This can be achieved by publishing that knowledge structured with some ontology language like OWL, as well as by using standardized means like Web Services for accessing that knowledge.

Agent enabling communication among the system's users should have insight into their personal profiles in order to connect users with similar interests, thus enhancing the learning and teaching process [5]. The agent should also enable cooperative learning foreseen as a student-student interaction aimed at solving a mutual problem. Once again the students' personal profiles should be formatted in accordance with the Semantic Web standards so to enable usage as well as exchange of the profiles among interested agents.

Enabling authoring work is another important task assigned to an agent which should be carefully considered within the Semantic Web/Web 2.0 environments. A teacher can enrich the teaching contents with her/his teaching resources via the system's Web interface. A student can publish her/his notes or seminar papers which can then be accessed by other students with appropriate rights. All author contributions should be described by using ontologies in order to enable agents in searching and sharing of the contents.

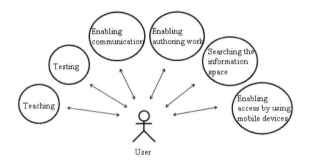

Fig. 2. TEx-Sys agent diagram

Searching the information space is a task given to an agent in order to avoid the state of information overload. It is evident that the application of a personal agent for searching the information space would enable easier performing of complex actions which the user carries out to obtain the desired results. Having insight into the user's personal profile, the personal agent can search the information space instead of the user, selecting data it finds to be of interest to the user.

Our model additionally extends intelligent tutoring through the mobile dimension. Mobile intelligent tutoring systems aim to improve the quality of learning by providing students with an easy, contextualized and ubiquitous access to knowledge [6]. The system should blend into the student's daily routine, by being at the reach of a hand, hence enabling the student to brush up on her/his knowledge, review some referent material, take a short quiz and the like; all this while waiting for a friend at an airport, waiting in a queue at a bank, traveling by train, etc. Agents enabling access to the system by means of mobile devices should be able to perform adaptation of the system to the mobile computing environment, namely different wireless networks (bandwidth, delay, error rate, interference and the like) as well as different mobile devices (screen size, memory, processing power). Some techniques include dynamic content adaptation, client-side navigation methods, various content delivery methods, etc [7].

4 Conclusion

The new Web generation enables sharing and reuse of data across applications, giving it a well defined meaning and making it possible for people as well as agents to understand and reason about that data. This presents authors of intelligent tutoring systems with great opportunities as well as a remarkable challenge of restructuring their systems for the new environment. The paper presents our approach to adaptation of intelligent tutoring systems to the Semantic Web/Web 2.0 environments, within the TEx-Sys model we have been developing for the last 15 years. We have discussed a potential multi-agent architecture of the system, where agents operating in the new environment are finally able to exchange data and communicate in order to better the system's functionality. Data on students, teaching methods, environment characteristics and such are described by using ontologies. The discussion is quite general and it can be used as an overall analysis of the new ITS structure. The following step includes performing a detailed analysis of the agents, their behavior and communication methods, as well as other issues such as privacy, performance and scalability.

Acknowledgments. This paper describes the results of research being carried out within the project 036-0361994-1995 *Universal Middleware Platform for e-Learning Systems*, as well as within the program *Intelligent Support for Ubiquity of e-Learning Systems*, both funded by the Ministry of Science, Education and Sports of the Republic of Croatia.

References

1. Stankov, S.: Isomorphic Model of the System as the Basis of Teaching Control Principles in the Intelligent Tutoring System. PhD Dissertation. Faculty of Electrical Engineering, Mechanical Engineering and Naval Architecture University of Split, Split (in Croatian) (1997)
2. Patel, A., Kinshuk, R.D., Oppermann, R.: Intelligent Tutoring Systems: Confluence of Information Science and Cognitive Science. In: Proc. 2001 Informing Science Conference, Krakow, pp. 392–397 (2001)

3. Major, N.: How Generic can Authoring Shells Become? In: Proc. AIED 1995 Workshop on Authoring Shells for Intelligent Tutoring Systems, Washington, pp. 75–82 (1995)
4. Stankov, S., Rosić, M., Žitko, B., Grubišić, A.: TEx-Sys model for building intelligent tutoring systems. Computers & Education (in press, 2007), doi:10.1016/j.compedu.2007.10.002
5. Glavinić, V., Rosić, M., Zelić, M.: Agents in m-Learning Systems Based on Intelligent Tutoring. In: Stephanidis, C. (ed.) HCI 2007. LNCS, vol. 4556, pp. 578–587. Springer, Heidelberg (2007)
6. Glavinić, V., Rosić, M., Zelić, M.: Extending Intelligent Tutoring Systems to Mobile Devices. In: Proc. 12th Int'l Conf. on Knowledge-Based and Intelligent Information & Engineering Systems, Zagreb. CD-ROM Proc., pp. 1–8 (2008)
7. Zhang, D.: Web Content Adaptation for Mobile Handheld Devices. Communications of the ACM 50, 75–79 (2007)

Knowledge Management and eLearning in Professional Development

George Sammour[1], Jeanne Schreurs[1], Abdullah Y. Zoubi[2], and Koen Vanhoof[1]

[1] Hasselt University, Diepenbeek, Belgium
George.sammour@uhasselt.be, Jeanne.Schreurs@uhasselt.be,
Koen.vanhoof@uhasselt.be
[2] Princess Sumaya University for Technology, Amman, Jordan
zoubi@psut.edu.jo

Abstract. The rapidly growing use of technology in education is changing the way in which knowledge is produced, stored and distributed. Online education has already been accepted as the way of the future, knowledge may be distributed across both time and space. Knowledge management techniques can be used to capture, organize and deliver this knowledge and management systems can be used to quickly identify the most relevant information and distribute it to meet specific needs. Light is shed, in this paper, on the basic concepts of knowledge management and eLearning. A discussion on and how knowledge management and eLearning can be integrated and leveraged for effective online education and training is presented.

1 Introduction

In recent years the rapid and continuing evolution of technology has converted our world into a knowledge society. A knowledge society strategy will ensure that all business operators and the public sector have sufficient skills needed in a rapidly developing information society. The Government will invest heavily in innovation environment, research and product development, anticipate and safeguard the supply of a trained workforce and ensure high-quality education. Moreover, the Government will promote open and lifelong learning and on-the-job training by means of information and communications technology.

Recent research reveals great interest to introduce Knowledge Management (KM) ideas to eLearning systems. It is argued that KM can facilitate an eLearning system [15]. The joint studies of KM and eLearning point out the same fundamental goal: facilitating organizational learning. Researchers try to analyze the similarity of the goals, methods of assessment, and some knowledge sharing processes both in KM and eLearning. An eLearning system within KM is traditionally analyzed as a knowledge resource repository, where the KM methods can be implemented to increase the effectiveness of knowledge dissemination [4].

The main features of eLearning are discussed which benefit of the knowledge management approach. At the end an integrated approach between KM and eLearning is introduced.

M.D. Lytras et al. (Eds.): WSKS 2008, CCIS 19, pp. 178–183, 2008.

2   Knowledge Management and e-Learning

2.1   Knowledge Management

Knowledge management is concerned with the identification, acquisition, distribution and maintenance of essential and relevant knowledge. Rowley describes the term Knowledge Management as follows: "Knowledge management is concerned with the exploitation and development of the knowledge assets of an organization with a view to furthering the organization's objectives [7]. Management has to cultivate and facilitate the sharing of knowledge and organizational learning. In brief, Knowledge Management is the management of processes that govern the creation, dissemination, and utilization of knowledge by merging technologies, organizational structures and people to create the most effective learning, problem solving, and decision-making in an organization.

place, knowledge needs should be clearly determined in the context of the.

2.2   ICT Enhanced Learning and eLearning Systems

With the increasing availability of Information and Communication Technology (ICT), the breadth and scope of distance teaching and learning process has changed dramatically. In the scope of this paper eLearning and online education will be defined as "the formally and systematically organized teaching and learning activities in which the instructor and the learner(s) use ICT to facilitate their interaction and collaboration".

In eLearning systems, the complete cycle of the teaching and learning process should be fulfilled. Important functional aspects within this coverage must be followed. Many of them have been exclusively developed alongside with research in eLearning while others have been adapted for eLearning requirements [12].

3   Integration of KM and Learning and Professional Development in a Company

3.1   Knowledge Delivery and Exchange

Knowledge management has evolved, and it becomes more integrated into the fabric of the organization. Knowledge management is becoming everyone's job. Main goal is to drive performance improvement of teams and individuals enterprisewide. Knowledge delivery/ exchange efforts focus on helping individuals make connections with subject matter experts. Knowledge exchange projects are designed to bring together knowledge seekers and knowledge sources in a way that they can interact with one another and more effectively share tacit knowledge. Individuals can discuss experiences, engage in complex problem solving and, in some cases, observe actual work activities. Knowledge exchange techniques include orientation, training, communities of practice, expertise location, mentoring/peer assist, alternative work arrangements.

3.2 Communities of Practice

A common knowledge exchange technique, *communities of practice,* brings together individuals who are likely to have the common context to effectively preserve organizational memory. This technique provides group validation of knowledge through the vetting and evaluation of materials. Participation in communities is closely aligned with the actual work of community members, so the knowledge is likely to be timely and highly relevant to their immediate knowledge needs. Community portals such as, newsletters, discussion forums, search engines..etc. plays important role in KM delivery.

3.3 The Evolution of KM and eLearning Integration

Learning can be seen as integrated in knowledge acquisition as part of the job of the employees. Education has to be a process of sharing and acquirement of knowledge, skills and competencies. Advantages of KM are very useful for that process. Knowledge management is a core part of teams training so capturing of knowledge process is very similar to the processes related to selection of most appropriate learning content in eLearning.

Outcome of effective learning process should be not only knowing facts for a separate subject but having practical skills and developing competency in the given domain so acquiring knowledge is more precise definition of the learning outcomes instead of learning facts for different related to domain topics. Therefore KM processes should be more deeply and successfully integrated in learning content delivery and learning activities support.

4 Similarity between KM and e-Learning Process

Knowledge management is a core part of teams training so capturing of knowledge process is very similar to the processes related to selection of most appropriate learning content in eLearning. Outcome of effective learning process should be not only knowing facts for a separate subject but having practical skills and developing competency in the given domain so acquiring knowledge is more precise definition of the learning outcomes instead of learning facts for different related to domain topics.

The desired outcome of learning should be knowledge acquisition and in combination with some practical skills gained in the process of education they have to present some type of competence. On this way communication and collaboration will be improved and free exchange of competencies will be provided.

4.1 Common Requirements / Characteristics of Knowledge Management and eLearning Systems

There are many common features shared between eLearning systems and knowledge management systems. Some of these are [13]:

System Architecture: knowledge management systems and eLearning environments share the same system architecture.

Collaboration and Communication: both systems enable and support rather rich communication and cooperation features. Different kinds of synchronous and asynchronous communication are possible, group scheduling, application sharing, instant messaging and other forms of cooperation are supported. Those tools guarantee successful education and team work. Both systems also include different tools related to work in groups or different types of virtual communities, or communities of practice.

Content as Learning Objects: Learning Objects are discrete chunks of reusable online learning materials. A learning object or knowledge element as it is sometimes called can be a text document, an element of animation, a streaming audio/video or other form of online content. Creating central repositories of reusable learning objects using object oeriented design and metadata and following the international standards for it, is serving the needs of both e-learning and knowledge management.

Personalization of delivered information: flexible eLearning systems and high quality KM-systems offer the possibility of personalization. The working environment can be adapted to the user needs and characteristics. Both systems are not closed or isolated. Information is most often shared among several resources and can be changed, extended, modified, removed on demand.

Learning objects are the appropriate technology for development and exchange of different types of information.

Access rules: in both worlds, users need to be identified by the system. Users have to register, they are attached to a defined profile and they are given access to relevant information only. Most often different layers of access rights enable the control of information access.

5   e-Learning Built upon Knowledge Management Methods, Models and Systems

Knowledge management tools and technologies can be applied to eLearning in several ways.

Via a portal customized information can be aggregated and integrated within a particular working environment, application or service, or use a single interface to target an individual user needs and interests. The following areas of eLearning in which knowledge management can be most effectively used have been identified [14].

5.1   Dynamic Delivery and Presentation of the Content

The portal can contain a repository of content that is modularized and arranged to facilitate access to it by the content developers.

We set forward a dynamic generation of LO's or course modules customised to the learner group on point of content and customised on point of presentation, fitting the preferences or characteristics of the individual learner and the used appliances by them.

5.2 Collaborative Learning and Communities of Practice

Collaborative learning involves students working together in some way to support the learning activity. They can do this by accessing a common set of learning material or by posting their own queries, observations or comments on the site. The collaboration can be between two individuals or between larger groups of learners. It can be built on the experience of knowledge management with communities of practice.

6 Conclusion

Emphasizes were made on the basic characteristics of eLearning and knowledge management and the main task of the research is to find common features of both domains. A combination of the advantages of both domains facilitates delivery of high quality education for satisfying specific educational needs of team members. An attempt has been made to identify the areas in which knowledge management concepts can be utilized in Learning within organizations and eLearning systems. The potential and limitations are briefly outlined. The use of Knowledge Management in eLearning will definitely impact the quality of the education that is delivered and deliverability of information in a manner of knowledge and information sharing.

References

1. Frappaolo, C., Toms, W.: Knowledge Management: From Terra Incognito to Terra Firma. The Delphi Group (1997)
2. Sherwood, C.: Knowledge Management for eLearning. In: International Conference on Engineering Education (2001)
3. Davidson, T.H., Prusak, L.: Working Knowledge–How Organizations Manage What They Know. Harvard Business School Press (1998)
4. Ponce, D.: What Can eLearning Learn from Knowledge Management? In: Proceedings of the 3rd European Knowledge Management School, San Sebastian (2003)
5. Woelk, D., Agarwal, S.: Integration of eLearning and Knowledge Management, http://www.elasticknowledge.com/ElearnandKM.pdf
6. Nonaka, I., Takeuchi, H.: The Knowledge-Creating Company: How Japanese Companies Create the Dynamics of Innovation. Oxford university press, New York (1995)
7. Rowley, J.: From Learning Organization to Knowledge Entrepreneur. Journal of Knowledge Management 4(1), 7–14 (2000)
8. Kidwell, J., Jilinda, M.: Vander Linde Karen and Sandra L Johnson, Applying Corporate Knowledge Management Practices in Higher Education, Educause Quarterly, No. 4 (2000)
9. Yordanova, K.: Integration of Knowledge Management and eLearning, Common Features. In: International Conference on Computer Systems and Technologies, CompSysTech 2007 (2007)
10. Mertins, K., Heisig, P., Vorbek, J.: Knowledge Management: Concepts and Best Practices, 2nd edn. Springer, Heidelberg (2006)
11. Rodney Mcadam Sandra McCreedy - Critical review of knowledge management models

12. Paranjpe, R.: Knowledge Management and Online Education. In: International Conference on Open and Online Learning (2003)
13. Denning, S.: The Springboard: How Storytelling Ignites Actio. In: Knowledge-Era Organizations. Butterworth Heinemann, Boston (2000)
14. Spector, M.J., Edmonds, G.S.: Knowledge Management in Instructional Design, ERIC Digest (September 2002)
15. Ravet, S.: eLearning and Knowledge Management. The Newsletter of the PROMETEUS Network 20, 2–6 (2002),
    http://prometeus.org/news/PROMETEUS_Newsletter20.pdf

MILCA – A Mobile and Interactive Learning Environment on Campus

Kin Choong Yow and Sintiani Dewi Teddy

School of Computer Engineering, Nanyang Technological University,
Nanyang Avenue, Singapore 639798
kcyow@ntu.edu.sg, sdt@pmail.ntu.edu.sg

Abstract. This paper aims at introducing a new platform for mobile and inter-active learning targeted as an effective communication medium between the professor and students during lectures. In this system, students and professors will be equipped with a Multimedia Messaging Service (MMS) capable device (which may be PDAs, Laptops, or Tablet PCs) that is connected on the campus-wide 802.11b Wireless LAN. During lectures, students can ask questions, re-sponse to questions or give immediate feedback on the lecture simply by com-posing an MMS message and sending it to the professor. The professor himself can choose to immediately respond to the comments or to delay his response so as not to disrupt the flow of the lecture. Interactive quizzes can also be carried out during lecture simply by having the professor sending out the question to students in MMS format, receiving their responses, and reviewing the results on the spot. The main advantage of this learning system is that MMS messaging is easily extensible to the mobile GSM networks, so students are not restricted to use it only on campus. This system is particularly beneficial in engineering edu-cation, since engineering students are generally tech-savvy, and therefore can easily adapt to this medium. This learning system will also encourage students to be more participative in the learning process, as students tend to be shy to speak up in front of large groups.

Keywords: Interactive Learning, Large Class Learning, Immediate Lecture Feedback, Multimedia Messaging Service.

1 Introduction

This is an era of global mobile communication, in which instant communication and information transfer are the major driving forces of the society. Keeping up with the advancement of technology, the learning process and system has gone through rapid changes too. The introduction of internet, online learning, and e-education has changed the way knowledge and education is being transferred to students all over the world. In this paper, a new learning platform developed in Nanyang Technological University (NTU) which utilizes the latest technologies to bring a mobile interactive learning environment into the classes in the Computer Engineering course will be described. This learning platform is targeted as an effective communication medium between the professor and the students, in attempt to enhance the quality of the learning process.

M.D. Lytras et al. (Eds.): WSKS 2008, CCIS 19, pp. 184–191, 2008.
© Springer-Verlag Berlin Heidelberg 2008

2 Pedagogical Issues

There are two key problems identified with the current learning system in Nanyang Technological University, Singapore. They are (1) the lack of interaction, and (2) the need to be physically present in the classroom.

Lack of Interaction
The education community has long discussed the challenges of facilitating student-instructor interaction in large classes [1], [2]). Several primary factors that inhibit student initiated interaction in large classes are feedback lag, student apprehension, and single-speaker paradigm [3]. The current learning systems are mostly of one-way communication, in which the professor is giving lectures to hundreds of students in a class [4]. Even in a tutorial or laboratory session, there are seldom feedbacks, comments or questions arise in classes. As a consequence to the one-to-many relationship between the professor and the students, there is lack of interaction between the students and the professor ([5],[6]).

The Need to be Physically Present
Distance learning is the main model where the need to be physically present can be eliminated ([7], [8]). In this model, there is the opportunity for student-to-student interactions and student-to-instructor interaction and the faculty do not change their role significantly from the traditional classroom, although presentations will have to adapt to the technology used [9]. However, in the ordinary classroom learning model, a student may be, say, 10 minutes late for a class, and that might cause the student to have difficulty following the rest of the lecture. So it will be desirable to apply the distance learning model to this scenario so that the student will still be able to follow the lessons and participate in student-to-instructor interaction.

In the vision of the 21st century classroom, students are equipped with portable wireless devices connected to an infrastructure, which enables polling, question queue, slide synchronization, and remote access ([10], [11]). However, such interactivity restricts the students to be connected to the same infrastructure. Students connected to other infrastructures may still be able to access information in the server but will lose the interactivity in the class.

Several Wireless classroom projects have been implemented ([12],[13],[14]) and tested with encouraging results. However, the implementation is restricted to a Local Area Network (LAN) coverage, making it impossible to carry out such interactive learning when a student is outside the LAN.

3 NTU's Mobile and Interactive Learning System

To overcome the above mentioned problems, a wireless mobile interactive learning solution is proposed with the following objectives in mind:

1) to provide interactive learning capabilities in classroom environment by allowing instant communication between the professor and the student through messaging services.

2) to extend the mobile learning opportunities in NTU to include the Wide Area Network (WAN) coverage provided by telephone companies.
3) to make wireless mobile interactive learning available to all students both on and off campus without having to incur costly hardware.

The new solution is based on two new wireless technologies, namely (1) Multimedia Messaging Service (MMS), and (2) Internet Naming Service (iName). Multimedia Messaging Service (MMS) is a new way of mobile communication and is believed to be one of the key driving forces of mobile data service business for 2.5G and 3G. Major advances in technology of instant messaging and the rapid evolution of the capabilities of mobile devices has made it possible to provide multimedia rich messaging application to mobile users. The project described in this paper made use of the MMS technology and wireless LAN infrastructure, to build a mobile learning platform.

The key idea is to make use of MMS service as the interactive communication medium during a class. Professors can check the understanding of students by posting a question during a class and the students will reply by MMS over the University's WLAN network. An application on the professor's console will then receive and be able to parse these responses and summarize them for the professor. When satisfied with the response, the professor can then proceed to the next part of his/her lecture.

Students can also post feedback messages to the professor during the class (e.g. to inform the professor that he/she needs to slow down on his explanation). These messages will appear on the professor's console and the professor can decide whether or not to respond to them. One of the advantages of using MMS is that this interaction can easily be extended to students who are not physically present in the classroom. The same data format can be used over WLAN or GPRS.

Live audio streaming of the lectures can be performed which allows the student to participate in a class even though he/she is not physically present in the classroom. The student can be on-campus and connected via WLAN, or be off-campus and connected via GSM/GPRS. The wireless devices used can even be a mobile phone, thus reducing the need to depend on expensive laptop or tablet PCs.

The iName technology serves to provide address abstraction for the whole service. With the iName service, the student only need to enter an intuitive text-based name such as "CE101Lecture" and the iName server will map it to a valid IP address. Similarly, the professor can instantly communicate with all his students no matter whether they are physically present in the classroom. The iName server will host the current dynamic IP address for connected laptops or PDAs, or phone numbers for mobile phone connections.

3.1 Overall Architecture

The overall architecture of the NTU Wireless Mobile Interactive Learning framework is shown in Fig. 1. Client devices such as PDAs, Tablet PCs, will be connected to the NTU LAN via wireless access points. The MMS sent by the students (e.g. lecture feedback) during a lecture will go through the iName server to determine the forwarding address of the professor. An application residing on the lecture console can then pick up the MMS and display it to the professor.

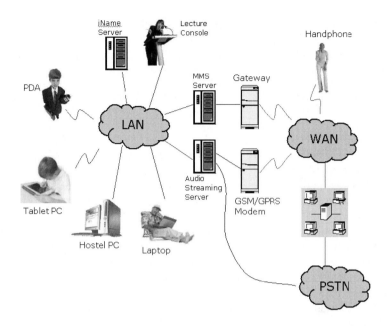

Fig. 1. The Overall Architecture of the Mobile Interactive Learning Framework

The professor may send out a pop quiz to its students via MMS. The MMS sent by the Lecture console will go through the iName server to determine the forwarding address of the students' client devices for all the students registered for his/her class. If the clients are on the WLAN, the iName server will return the client's dynamic IP address. If the clients are outside the WLAN, it will return a handphone number and the MMS server will send it out to the student's handphone on the GSM/GPRS telephone network (WAN).

3.2 Key Components

Multimedia Messaging Service

MMS [15], as its name suggests, is the ability to send and receive messages comprising of a combination of text, sound images and video to MMS capable handsets. The WAP-forum [16] and the the 3GPP[17] are the groups responsible for standardizing MMS. MMS employs the Wireless Application Protocol (WAP) and therefore it is bearer independent – supporting either Circuit Switched Data or General Packet Radio Service (GPRS). MMS should also eventually supports bearer such as Enhanced Data rates for GSM Evolution (EDGE) and 3G too.

MMS presentations are different from email presentations. MMS provides advanced layout and timing for multimedia contents in the message., which is not provided by email message. And also, neither IMAP3 not POP3 provide a standard technology to notify a non-connected client of an incoming mail.

The MMS-enabled device (e.g. PDAs) must be able to compose, send, receive and play an MMS message over the 802.11b WLAN. The MMS server sitting in the infrastructure network will serve two purposes: (1) MMS Centre (MMSC) that stores and forward the MMS messages, and (2) MMS Proxy/Relay that will send/receive MMS messages to the Wide-Area network through the gateway.

Internet Naming Service

iName is an internet naming service which translates a name query into network addresses such as IP address or mobile phone numbers. iName is designed to be a physically independent way of referencing any user in the system. All the components in the project address a particular user in the system with their respective iName. This frees the system from the need of knowing where and how the user is logged on to the system. To consolidate information regarding connectivity, each student's connection is passed through an iName server to identify current network connection type. The iName server then serves as a host to store the current dynamic IP address for connected laptops or phone numbers. Hence, if the established connection is through a handphone, the e-slides/video or audio transmission will be modified to MMS format and transmitted through the telecommunication network; while for LAN devices, the relevant information would be transmitted through the net.

4   System Evaluation

The first version of the system has been rolled out and tested on students in real classes. The test groups consist of two groups of the size 150 students, comprising of first year Computer Engineering students, in the subject of Engineering Mathematics. The system ran during the one-hour lectures in Engineering Mathematics, 3 times a week, for a duration of 2 months. All received messages were logged and displayed anonymously on the lecture console. Fig. 2 shows a screenshot of the integrated lecture console.

On average, in a typical one-hour lecture, 57 messages were received. These messages can be categorized into the following group headings with a mean distribution as follows:

Test Messages	6
Questions about subject	10
Requests for additional information / actions	10
Supportive messages	13
Feedback on Lectures	11
Error messages	2
Irrelevant Messages	5
Message Received	57

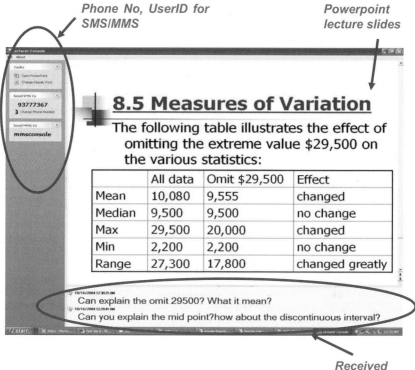

Phone No, UserID for SMS/MMS

Powerpoint lecture slides

Received messages

Fig. 2. Screenshot of the Integrated Lecture Console

From the messages received, a lot can be understood about the students' understanding and their needs. Because the system is anonymous, the students were not intimidated to speak freely. Also, the students lend support to one another to reinforce a request that many of them wants but is too shy to ask. This is something that could not have being possible without this interactive system.

In summary, some of the direct advantages observable from the test results are:

- Students are more active in giving feedbacks. From the test conducted, the increment in the level of participation of the students in class can be easily seen. Students who are shy to feedback are also able to participate interactively.
- The professor can get a feel of students' needs and the their understanding level. The comments posted indirectly reflect the understanding level of the student, and therefore based on the comments, the professor can adjust the pace of learning.
- Whenever the professor receives multiple and different responses, he/she can query the class to get a consensus.

However, there are also some disadvantageous noticeable from the testing:

- Overwhelming replies which makes it difficult for the professor to address all of the student's needs.

- The professor will have to be able to split his concentration between the subject and the reponses coming from students.
- Irresponsible remarks can be quite disruptive.

The overall responses shown favorable results. Messages from the student includes *"Nice system , well done !"* and *"Agree..! Asik2.. This program is cool.."*. Students in general finds this beneficial and are eager to make use of the system. The main advantage of this learning system is that MMS messaging is easily extensible to the mobile GSM networks, so students are not restricted to use it only on campus. Sending MMS messages on the Wireless LAN will be free to students on campus, and only at a low cost outside. This system is particularly beneficial in engineering education, since engineering students are generally tech-savvy, and therefore can easily adapt to this medium. This learning system will also encourage students to be more participative in the learning process, since usually students tend to be shy to speak up in large groups.

5   Conclusion

In this paper, a new mobile interactive learning system developed at Nanyang Technological University is presented. A system that allows instant feedback on teaching has been developed using MMS on the campus-wide Wireless LAN. The system made use of two new wireless technologies, namely MMS and iName. The proposed system enables instant lecture feedback to be delivered and direct student assessment to be conducted in classes. This learning system is intended to encourage students to be more participative in the learning process. Sending MMS is free on campus, and it is easily extensible to GSM networks.

Acknowledgements

The work in this paper is supported by the Hewlett-Packard Philanthropy Grant 2003 for Applying Mobile Technologies in a Learning Environment.

References

1. Geske, J.: Overcoming the drawbacks of the large lecture class. College Teaching 40(4), 151–154 (1992)
2. Gleason, M.: Better communication in large courses. College Teaching 34(1), 20–24 (1986)
3. Anderson, R.J., Anderson, R., Vandergrift, T., Wolfman, S., Yasuhara, K.: Promoting Interaction in Large Classes with Computer Mediated Feedback. In: Proceedings Computer Support for Collaborative Learning 2003 (CSCL 2003), Norway (2003)
4. Barajas, M., et al.: Virtual Classrooms in Traditional Universities: Changing Teaching Cultures Through Telematics. In: Proceedings World Conference on Educational Multimedia and Hypermedia, Freiburg, Germany (1998)
5. Miner, R.: Reflections on teaching a large class. Journal of Management Education 16(3), 290–302 (1992)

6. Mortera-Gutiérrez, F.: Instructor Interactions in Distance Education Environments. Journal of Interactive Learning Research 13(3), 191–209 (2002)
7. Brown, R.E.: The Process of Community-Building in Distance Learning Classes. Journal of Asynchronous Learning Networks 5(2), 18–35 (2001)
8. Bullen, M.: Participation and Critical Thinking in Online University Distance Education. Journal of Distance Education 13(2), 1–32 (1998)
9. Andronico, A., Carbonaro, A., Colazzo, L., Molinari, A.: Personalisation services for learning management systems in mobile settings. International Journal of Continuing Engineering Education and Life Long Learning 14(4-5), 353–369 (2004)
10. Dominick, J.: Ready or Not – PDAs in the Classroom., Syllabus Magazine (September 2002), http://www.syllabus.com/article.asp?id=6705
11. Handheld Learning, Using Handheld Technologies for Leading, Teaching, and Learning, http://educatorspalm.org/hhl/teachlearn/teachlearn.html
12. Evan, E., Morgan, M., Berger, M., Bilkey, B., Wood, K.: Wireless Classroom, October 2002. Information Technology at Purdue, Purdue University (2002), http://ics.purdue.edu/rss/wireless.ppt
13. Shotsberger, P.G., Vetter, R.: Teaching and learning in the wireless classroom., Internet Watch (March 2001), http://aa.uncwil.edu/numina/documents/internet%20watch%20final.pdf
14. University of Kentucky, Wireless Classroom Project, http://www.dcs.uky.edu/~wc/
15. Ericsson, Multimedia Messaging Service, http://www.ericsson.com/technology/tech_articles/MMS.shtml
16. Open Mobile Alliance, "WAP Forum", http://www.wapforum.org
17. 3GPP, 3GPP TS 23.140: MMS Functional Description, http://www.3gpp.org/

An Evolutionary Approach for Domain Independent Learning Object Sequencing

Luis de-Marcos, José-Javier Martínez, José-Antonio Gutiérrez, Roberto Barchino, and José-María Gutiérrez

Computer Science Department. University of Alcalá.
Ctra. Barcelona km 33.6. Alcalá de Henares, Spain
{luis.demarcos,josej.martinez,jantonio.gutierrez,
roberto.barchino,josem.gutierrez}@uah.es

Abstract. The process of creating e-learning contents using reusable learning objects (LOs) can be broken down in two sub-processes: LOs finding and LO sequencing. Although semiautomatic tools that aid in the finding process exits, sequencing is usually performed by instructors, who create courses targeting generic profiles rather than personalized materials. This paper proposes an evolutionary approach to automate this latter problem while, simultaneously, encourages reusability and interoperability by promoting standards employment. A model that enables automated curriculum sequencing is proposed. By means of interoperable competency records and LO metadata, the sequencing problem is turn into a constraint satisfaction problem. Particle Swarm Optimization (PSO) and Genetic Algorithm (GA) agents are designed, built and tested in real and simulated scenarios. Results show both approaches succeed in all test cases, and that they handle reasonably computational complexity inherent to this problem, but PSO approach outperforms GA.

Keywords: e-Learning, Learning Object Sequencing, Evolutionary Computation, Genetic Algorithm, Particle Swarm Optimization (PSO).

1 Introduction

Web-based adaptive courses and systems are supposed to be able to achieve some important features including the ability to substitute teachers and other students support, and the ability to adapt to (and so be used in) different environments by different users (learners) [1]. These systems may use a wide variety of techniques and methods. Among them, curriculum sequencing technology is "to provide the student with the most suitable individually planned sequence of knowledge units to learn and sequence of learning tasks [...] to work with". These methods are derived from adaptive hypermedia field and rely on complex conceptual models, usually driven by sequencing rules [2]. E-learning traditional approaches and paradigms, that promote reusability and interoperability, are generally ignored, thus resulting in (adaptive) proprietary systems (such as AHA! [3]) and non-portable courseware. But e-learning approaches also expose their own problems. They lack flexibility, which is in increasing demand. "In offering flexible [e-learning] programmes, providers essentially rule out the possibility of having instructional designers set fixed paths through the curriculum" [4].

M.D. Lytras et al. (Eds.): WSKS 2008, CCIS 19, pp. 192–197, 2008.

But offering personalized paths to each learner will impose prohibitive costs to these providers, because the sequencing process is usually performed by instructors. So, "it is critical to automate the instructor's role in online training, in order to reduce the cost of high quality learning" [5] and, among these roles, sequencing seems to be a priority.

In this paper, an innovative sequencing technique that automates teacher´s role is proposed. E-Learning standards and the learning object paradigm are used in order to promote and ensure interoperability. Learning units' sequences are defined in terms of competencies in such a way that sequencing problem can be modeled like a classical Constraint Satisfaction Problem (CSP) and Artificial Intelligence (AI) approaches could be used to solve it. Genetic Algorithms (GAs) and Particle Swarm Optimization (PSO) are AI techniques that have proven a good performance for solving a wide variety of problems. So, GAs and PSO are used to find a suitable sequence within the solution space respecting the constraints. In section 2, the conceptual model for competency-based learning object sequencing is presented. Section 3 describes both evolutionary approaches (PSO and GA) for solving the problem. Section 4 presents the results obtained when agents are tested in simulated scenarios as well as in a real world situation (course sequencing in an online Master in Engineering program). And finally, in Section 5 conclusions are summarized and future research lines are presented.

2   Competency-Based Sequencing

Competencies can be formally described as "multidimensional, comprised of knowl-edge, skills and psychological factors that are brought together in complex behavioral responses to environmental cues" [6]. Some e-learning trends are trying to standardize competency definitions so that they could be interchanged and processed by ma-chines. According to RDCEO [7] and IEEE [8] nomenclature, a competency record is called 'Reusable Competency Definition' (or RCD). RCDs can be attached to LOs in order to define its prerequisites and its learning outcomes. We have used this ap-proach to model LO sequences. By defining a competency (or a set of competencies) as a LO outcome, and by identifying the same competency as the prerequisite for another LO (figure 1), a constraint between the two LOs is established so that the first LO must precede the second one in a valid sequence.

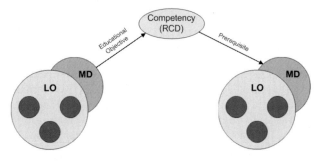

Fig. 1. LO sequencing through competencies

Meta-Data (MD) definitions are attached to LOs, and within those definitions references to competencies (prerequisites and learning outcomes) are included. LOM [9] records have been used for specifying LO Meta-Data. LOM element 9, 'Classification', is used to include competency references.

3 Competency-Based Intelligent Sequencing

Given a random LOs' sequence modeled as described above (with competencies representing LOs prerequisites and learning outcomes), the question of finding a correct sequence can be envisaged as a classical Constraint Satisfaction Problem (CSP). In this way, the solution space comprises all possible sequences (n! will be its size, total number of states, for n LOs), and a (feasible) solution is a sequence that satisfies all established constraints. LO permutations inside the sequence are the operations that define transitions among states.

Genetic algorithms are an evolutionary computation technique that mimics gene's evolution to solve problems. A random initialized population of individuals is created. Each individual contains a coded state or solution (gene) to the problem; and an iterative process of recombination, mutation and selection is used to evolve population and, simultaneously, the solution. GAs that use specific representation and operators for handling permutations are called permutation GAs or permut-GAs and can be employed to solve constraint satisfaction problems [10]. Permut GA with order recombination, swap mutation and generational replacement with elitism was implemented in order to test its performance for solving the LO sequencing problem.

On the other hand, particle swarm optimization is an evolutionary computing optimization algorithm that mimics the behaviour of social insects like bees. A random initialized particles population (states) flies through the solution space sharing the information they gather. Particles use this information to adjust dynamically their velocity and cooperate towards finding a solution. Goodness of each solution is calculated using a function called fitness function. Original PSO [11, 12] is intended to work on continuous spaces. A version that deals with permutation problems was introduced in [13]. This discrete approach was employed and a full-informed version of the PSO was implemented in order to test its performance for solving the LO sequencing problem. Several ways to tune the PSO agent were tested [14], but only a velocity check policy improved performance. Finally, the fitness function for both agents was a standard penalty function.

4 Experimental Results

Both algorithms for LOs sequencing described above were designed and implemented using the object oriented paradigm. We wanted to test their performance in real and simulated scenarios. As a real-world problem, we chose a problem concerning course sequencing for a Master in Engineering (M.Eng.) program in our institution. The (web engineering) M.Eng, program comprises 23 courses (subjects) grouped in:

- Basic courses (7) that must be taken before any other (kind of course). There may be restrictions between two basic courses, for example the 'HTML' course must precede the Javascript course,
- Itinerary' courses (5) that must be taken in a fixed ordered sequence.
- Compulsory courses (5). There may be restrictions between two compulsory courses.
- Elective courses (6). Additional constraints with respect to any other course may be set.

All courses have an expected learning time that ranges from 30 to 50 hours. They are delivered online using a LMS, namely EDVI LMS [15], and every course has its metadata record. Competency records were created to specify LOs' restrictions, and LOM metadata records were updated to reflect prerequisite and learning outcome competencies as detailed in section 2. A feasible sequence must have 23 LOs satisfying all constraints. The graph showing all LOs and constraints is too large to be shown in this paper, and so it is also difficult to calculate the exact number of feasible solutions. Some estimation have been used, we have estimated that the relation among feasible solutions and total solutions order is $8,9 \times 10^{12}$. This number reflects the number of states (non-feasible solutions) for each feasible solution.

One hundred tests were run computing mean fitness values evolution using the best configuration found for each agent (figure 2). Both agents converge, but PSO approach outperforms GA.

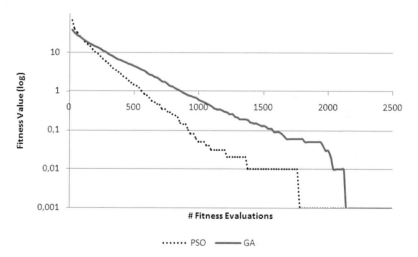

Fig. 2. Agents' performance in a real world problem

The tested scenario may seem to have many feasible solutions so that it is questionable whether PSO would still achieve a good performance in 'challenging' scenarios. So, additional test sequences of 5, 10, 20, 30, 40, 50, 60, 75 and 100 LOs with only one feasible solution were designed. Each test suite was run 100 times for each agent and mean values were computed. Figure 3 shows the results and it also supports the argument that PSO outperforms GA. It could also be inferred that both agents handle reasonably combinatorial explosion for this particular problem. It should be noted that while the number of learning objects grows linearly the size of the solution space grows exponentially.

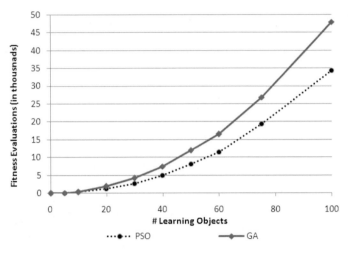

Fig. 3. Agents' scalability in simulated scenarios

5   Conclusions and Future Work

Automated LO sequencing is a recurring problem in the e-learning field that could be approached employing models that ensure interoperability along with artificial intelligence techniques. The purpose of the study was to design, develop and test two agents that perform automatic LO sequencing through competencies in order to study the completeness and performance of both approaches. A model that employs competencies as a mean for defining constraints between learning object has been presented, so that a sequence of LOs is represented by relations among LOs and competencies. New sequences can be derived if permutation operations are allowed between LOs in the sequence. Hence the sequencing problem is turn into a permutation problem, and the aim is to find a sequence that satisfies all restrictions expressed in the original model. A GA that handles permutation problems has been developed and the PSO for permutation problems has been adapted to the LO sequencing problem. Results show that both agents succeed in solving the problem and that PSO implementation outperforms GA agent.

Further implications arise from the model proposal (section 2): (1) E-learning standards are promoted. XML records and bindings are used, so elements will be easily interchanged and processed by compliant systems. (2) Instructor's role is automated reducing costs. Sequencing process works even in complex scenarios were humans face difficulties. Instructors could spend saved time performing other activities within the learning action. And (3), the model can be extended to an automated intelligent system for building personalized e-learning experiences. But this third implication is linked to future work. Sequencing process can be complemented with gap analysis process and competency learner modeling techniques to build personalized courses.

Acknowledgements. This research is funded by the University of Alcalá FPI research staff education program and by the Spanish Ministry of Industry, Tourism and Commerce Plan Avanza program (grant PAV-070000-2007-103).

References

1. Brusilovsky, P.: Adaptive and Intelligent Technologies for Web-based Education. Künstliche Intelligenz, Special Issue on Intelligent Systems and Teleteaching 4, 19–25 (1999)
2. Karampiperis, P.: Automatic Learning Object Selection and Sequencing in Web-Based Intelligent Learning Systems. In: Zongmin, M. (ed.) Web-Based Intelligent E-Learning Systems: Technologies and Applications. Idea Group, London (2006)
3. De Bra, P., Aerts, A., Berden, B., Lange, B.d., Rousseau, B., Santic, T., Smits, D., Stash, N.: AHA! The adaptive hypermedia architecture. In: Proceedings of the fourteenth ACM conference on Hypertext and hypermedia. ACM Press, Nottingham (2003)
4. van den Berg, B., van Es, R., Tattersall, C., Janssen, J., Manderveld, J., Brouns, F., Kurvers, H., Koper, R.: Swarm-based sequencing recommendations in e-learning. In: Proceedings 5th International Conference on Intelligent Systems Design and Applications, 2005. ISDA 2005, Wroclaw, Poland, pp. 488–493 (2005)
5. Barr, A.: Revisiting the -ilities: Adjusting the Distributed Learning Marketplace, Again? Learning Technology Newsletter 8, 3–4 (2006)
6. Wilkinson, J.: A matter of life or death: re-engineering competency-based education through the use of a multimedia CD-ROM. In: Proceedings of IEEE International Conference on Advanced Learning Technologies, 2001, pp. 205–208 (2001)
7. IMS: Reusable Definition of Competency or Educational Objective - Information Model. IMS Global Learning Consortium (2002)
8. IEEE: Learning Technology Standards Committee (LTSC). Standard for LearningTechnology - Data Model for Reusable Competency Definitions. IEEE (2008)
9. IEEE: Learning Technology Standards Committee (LTSC). Learning Object Metadata (LOM). 1484.12.1. IEEE (2002)
10. Eiben, A.E., Smith, J.E.: Introduction to Evolutionary Computing. Springer, Berlin (2003)
11. Eberhart, R., Kennedy, J.: A new optimizer using particle swarm theory. In: Proceedings of the Sixth International Symposium on Micro Machine and Human Science. MHS 1995, Nagoya, Japan, pp. 39–43 (1995)
12. Kennedy, J., Eberhart, R.: Particle swarm optimization. In: Proceedings, IEEE International Conference on Neural Networks, Perth, WA, Australia, vol. 4, pp. 1942–1948 (1995)
13. Shi, X.H., Zhou, Y., Wang, L.M., Wang, Q.X., Liang, Y.C.: A Discrete Particle Swarm Optimization Algorithm for Travelling Salesman Problem. Computational Methods, 1063–1068 (2006)
14. de-Marcos, L., Pages, C., Martinez, J.J., Gutierrez, J.A.: Competency-Based Learning Object Sequencing Using Particle Swarms. In: 19th IEEE International Conference on Tools with Artificial Intelligence. ICTAI, vol. 2, pp. 111–116. IEEE Press, Patras (2007)
15. Barchino, R., Gutiérrez, J.M., Otón, S.: An Example of Learning Management System. In: Isaías, P., Baptista, M., Palma, A. (eds.) IADIS Virtual Multi Conference on Computer Science and Information Systems (MCCSIS 2005), vol. 1, pp. 140–141. IADIS Press, Virtual (2005)

Semantic Reasoning in
Advanced E-Learning Brokerage Systems

Juan M. Santos, Rubén Míguez, Luis Anido, and Martín Llamas

Department of Telematics Engineering, University of Vigo
ETSET, Campus Universitario s/n, 36310, Vigo (Pontevedra), Spain
{Juan.Santos,rmiguez,Luis.Anido,Martin.Llamas}@det.uvigo.es

Abstract. This paper focuses on the problematic of the intermediation among a user who looks for an appropriate online course and those suppliers which could offer it. More specifically, it briefly describes a proposal of a development framework that allow the construction of advanced brokerage systems in the e-learning domain. This framework makes use of semantic technologies in order to improve the traditional search systems and to make it easier the management of the involved information.

Keywords: Brokerage, Course Search, Personalized Search, Semantic Technologies, Knowledge Engineering.

1 Introduction

Offer of online courses is high and it is still growing. This fact, positive by itself, raises the need of appropriate searching mechanisms allowing users and organizations to locate the educational services that best fit their requirements.

A critical factor for the development of course oriented searching systems in the e-learning domain is the right description of those courses offered by academic institutions. Transfer of this information from educational content providers to platforms supporting searching functionalities is not solved today due to the lack of standardized data models. What we have so far is data models for the description of Learning Objects. These data models aim at providing further reusability capabilities but they were not designed for describing particular courses deployed and being used and offered by particular educational institutions. This is the reason why some standardization bodies (e.g. CEN/ISSS WS-LT) are devoting efforts to the development of Course Description models.

During the last several years we have been developing a semantic-based model that covers both the description of courses being offered at particular online educational institutions and the learner profile of those students that could be potentially interested in those courses.

The ontological and heuristic sub-models of the developed semantic framework are used as the background for the definition of a system-architecture for the implementation of brokerage systems in the educational domain. This would allow the development of a Knowledge Based System that will provided personalized searches

M.D. Lytras et al. (Eds.): WSKS 2008, CCIS 19, pp. 198–203, 2008.

by semantic inference taken into account the learner's profile to people looking for appropriate on-line courses. That proposal is briefly discussed throughout this paper.

2 Building the Knowledge Society

The Knowledge Society is a society where knowledge is made accessible to a broad segment of the society, which in turn should be able to assimilate and use it. ICT is an important pillar for the construction of knowledge societies because of its role in knowledge dissemination, diffusion and exchange [1]. Advantages of ICT based learning (e-learning) have been extensively discussed in literature. Despite its remaining drawbacks, many institutions in different countries have invested in ICTs for providing flexible, open, distance and virtual education in order to broaden access and provide lifelong opportunities.

In a knowledge society, where a high and growing number of heterogeneous educational service providers are present, raises the need of appropriate searching mechanisms that allows particular users and organizations to locate the most suitable educational offers for their requirements.

Currently there exists several high-quality popular search engines (like Google or Yahoo!) that provide users with results based on Information Retrieval theories; however they do not offer the appropriate support for particular contexts like e-learning. Thus, the institutions that deliver on-line courses usually promote their educational services mainly by means of the publication of electronic catalogues that are accessible through the institution's own web pages. A potential student makes use of these catalogues in order to obtain detailed information on the different courses offered and, in the case of finding some suitable, to carry out the corresponding enrolment request. To locate alternative courses to the one found is usually a complex task since the user has to manually repeat the search operation in all the institutions that he/she knows.

The educational services intermediation systems (or educational brokers) are entities that makes it easier, on the one hand, to the different academic institutions, the publication and dissemination of electronic catalogues of offered courses and other educational resources in a common repository, and, on the other hand, to the users and potential students, the searching, comparison and location of educational resources suitable to their needs and preferences. The existence of advanced and specialized e-learning brokers can contribute to the building of a global Knowledge Society.

3 Brokerage Framework

In order to facilitate the development of final e-learning brokerage systems, we have identified and defined a set of reference models (c.f. Fig. 1). The construction of these models has been guided by the following principles:

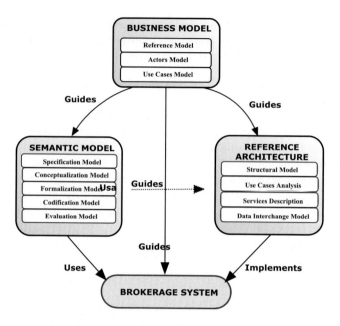

Fig. 1. E-learning Brokerage Framework

- The use of the latest standardized models from the learning technologies standardization process to improve interoperability and to facilitate the integration of external systems in the proposed brokerage framework.
- The improvement of the traditional search mechanisms with the incorporation of knowledge representation techniques.
- The use of context-specific information (like enrolment dates, description of the institution, description of the delivering tools, etc.) to improve search results. Not only the descriptions of the online course are used, but also those added services offered by the institution delivering the course. Thus, students can use broader information to make their choice.
- The performing of queries taking into account the user profile, i.e. the needs of the user and its preferences regarding time availability, difficulty level, obtained degree, etc. Thus, personalization is improved over the current situation.
- The conformance with common protocols, practices and interoperability.

3.1 Business Model

The first stage in the construction of an e-learning broker is the definition of a suitable Business Model. This model must conveniently characterize the stakeholders, actors and generic data flows involved in the intermediation processes.

We have identified 4 basis actors in our Business Model: the *Administrator* (the user responsible of the maintenance of the brokerage system), the *ESP Manager* (the user that acts on behalf of a particular Educational Services Provider –ESP-), the *Student* (a registered user that access to the brokerage system in order to search appropriate courses) and the *Guest* (a sporadic and non registered user that uses the system to locate courses without personalized services). For each of these actors, a set of use cases has been defined in order to guide the design and development of the subsequent models.

3.2 Semantic Model

For the construction of a semantic based e-learning broker, it is necessary to define a supporting semantic model to make explicit the knowledge in the domain. The developed semantic model includes a particular ontology to embody the existential knowledge, and a specific inference rule set to embody the heuristic knowledge.

- *Ontology.* We have developed ELEARNING-ONT, an OWL [2] ontology that facilitates the automatic management of the data collected and the development of advanced brokerage services in the e-learning domain. ELEARNING-ONT [3] includes the definition of the concepts, and their inter-relations, needed to characterize users/students, courses, academic institutions and educational platforms. The construction of this ontology was guided by the recommendations from Noy and McGuinness [4] and the development activities proposed in METHONTOLOGY [5], a mature methodological process in the Knowledge Engineering area. One key point has been to keep the knowledge already defined and agreed upon in the domain. During the last years, several organizations and institutions have been working towards the development of standards, specifications and recommendations aimed at solving the interoperability problems currently found in the e-learning domain [6]. Several of these standards are the basis for the definition of ELEARNING-ONT: metadata models for describing learning resources, formats for defining competencies, schemas for represent learner information, data models for describing accessibility issues, etc.
- *Heuristic rule set.* Data collected by the broker must be transformed into OWL statements (or facts) that use the terms and properties defined in ELEARNING-ONT. Logic rules can be used by an inference engine for processing and enriching the stored information and for drawing semantic conclusions. We define two basic groups of rules [7]: i) rules that allow making explicit knowledge that is hidden or implicit in the knowledge base and ii) rules that allow inferring new knowledge by matching the preferences and characteristics of a particular user with the properties of the registered courses and their particular context. This set of Horn-like rules, established in order to facilitate and enhance the searching processes, has been modelled through the SWRL [8] semantic language.

3.3 Reference Architecture

The design of our semantic-based e-learning brokerage system is organized in a set of layers (c.f. Fig. 2), with a clear separation of responsibilities among them, in order to support a high extendibility and maintainability. The design approach is based on two architectural patterns: SOA (Service-Oriented Architecture) and MVC (Model-View-Controller).

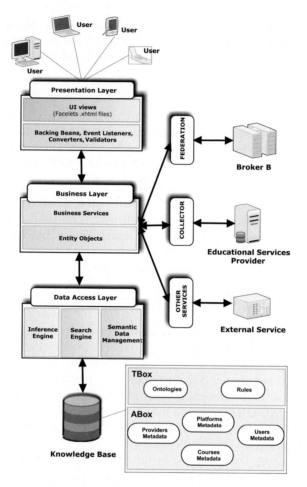

Fig. 2. E-learning Brokerage Reference Architecture

- *Knowledge Base (KB) Layer.* Here, it is available all the information collected and inferred by the broker. It is a repository where the semantic knowledge and the factual knowledge are stored. Factual knowledge is stored as OWL statements that make use of the terms identified in ELEARNING-ONT.
- *Data Access Layer.* It encapsulates the services to access and interact with the particular data stored by the broker, allowing different and exchangeable COTS databases and reasoners to be used.
- *Business Layer.* It includes generic transaction services that can be used by the components in the top layer of the architecture, allowing a clear and scalable separation of responsibilities. This tier relies on SOA specific architectural principles. Interfaces of the public services are available at a registry component.

- *Presentation Layer.* It is a wrapper tier where user interfaces are embedded and additional application specific value-added services may be included.

4   Conclusions

This paper briefly describes some of the main results of our research group in the e-learning brokerage area. Currently, there exists a working prototype that has already proved the proposed concepts. Authors are involved in different projects both at national and European level where the deploying and further testing is taking place.

Acknowledgments. We want to thank "Ministerio de Educación y Ciencia" and "Consellería de Innovación e Industria" for their partial support to this work under grants TIN2007-68125-C02-02 and PGIDIT06PXIB322270PR.

References

1. Bubtana, A.: The Role of Higher Education in the Construction of Knowledge Societies. In: Proc. of UNESCO World Summit on Information Society (2005)
2. McGuinness, D.L., van Harmelen, F.: OWL Web Ontology Language Overview. W3C Recommendation (2004)
3. Santos, J.M., Anido, L., Llamas, M.: Design of a Semantic Web-based Brokerage Architecture for the E-learning Domain. A Proposal for a Suitable Ontology. In: 35th IEEE/ASEE Frontiers in Education, Indianapolis (2005)
4. Noy, N.F., McGuinness, D.L.: Ontology Development 101: A Guide to Creating Your First Ontology. Standford-Protégé Project Report (2000)
5. Fernández, M., Gómez, A., Sierra, A.S.: Building a chemical ontology using Methontology and the Ontology Design Environment. Intelligent Systems 14, 37–45 (1999)
6. Anido, L., Rodríguez, J., Caeiro, M., Santos, J.M.: Observing Standards for Web-Based Learning from the Web. In: Laganá, A., Gavrilova, M.L., Kumar, V., Mun, Y., Tan, C.J.K., Gervasi, O. (eds.) ICCSA 2004. LNCS, vol. 3044. Springer, Heidelberg (2004)
7. Santos, J.M., Llamas, M., Anido, L.: Work in Progress: Identification of Inference Rules for a Semantic E-learning Brokerage Architecture. In: 36th Annual Frontiers in Education Conference, San Diego, California (2006)
8. Horrocks, I., Patel-Schneider, P.F., Boley, H., Tabet, S., Grosof, B., Dean, M.: SWRL: A Semantic Web Rule Language Combining OWL and RuleML. W3C Member Submission (2004)

The Use of Wireless Network in Education

Spiros Panetsos

Associate Professor
Department of Electronic Engineering Educators
School of Pedagogical and Technological Education
s.panetsos@aegean.gr

Abstract. Wireless networks will play an important role in education. New educational models and wireless architectures have been proposed to enhance collaborative training. Wireless networks can provide a dynamic educational environment. However, the lack of fixed infrastructure in wireless networks generates new research problems. This paper examines the ways wireless technology work and the required prerequisites to integrate it into the educational area. It also describes educational opportunities and challenges of teaching in a real time wireless classroom environment. Additionally, this paper refers to the constraints and barriers, which prevent wireless networks from being accepted. It provides educational models and techniques in order to easier the transition from traditional computerized training systems to wireless training systems. Lastly, the paper compares models and architectures in educational wireless networks, taking into consideration the shortages of the educational systems, and predicts future trends and perspectives of integrated educational environments.

Keywords: Wireless networks, multicast services, wireless educational environment, models.

1   Introduction

Nowadays the new technology of information and communication provides a number of affordable wireless network solutions independent of place restrictions, time, and installations of wires. Wireless networking refers to the utilization of industry standards, where nodes (computers) communicate without needing to be wired. The infrastructure of this network predefines the existence of standard protocols that must be adaptable or oriented according to the demands such as the components that affects the network capacity and quality of services (QoS). The continuous growth of wireless technology has supplement the area of business and education, where the exchange of data was unattainable or unadvisable with wiring networks, as well as sophisticated applications where network wiring is impossible. The infrastructure models of wireless technology especially in educational systems can be focused on a model that uses an access point or base station to communicate with a wired network.

The advantages by communicating wirelessly are obvious in education. Students, faculty and staff increasingly want boundlessly network access from general-purpose classrooms, meeting rooms, auditoriums, labs and even the hallways of campus buildings. There is interest in creating mobile computing labs utilizing laptop computers

M.D. Lytras et al. (Eds.): WSKS 2008, CCIS 19, pp. 204–212, 2008.

equipped with wireless Ethernet cards. Recently, industry has made significant progress in resolving some constraints that have affected the widespread adoption of wireless technologies. Some of the constraints have included disparate standards, low bandwidth, and high infrastructure and service cost.

The wireless technology can support the institutional mission and provide cost-effective solutions. Wireless is being adopted for many new applications: to connect computers, to allow remote monitoring and data acquisition, to provide access control and security, and to supply a solution for environments where wires may not be the best implementation. New technologies rapidly find acceptance in the university environment. To determine the appropriate application of wireless communication, the campus community will be fully engaged to ensure that this developing technology will be used to enhance the teaching, learning, and research environment. Moreover, these networks can function efficiently in multicasting transmissions where the participants are dispread in a specific area.

This paper presents an overview of existing wireless technologies in educational system and recommendations for future deployment of wireless technologies.

2 Wireless Ad-Hoc Networks

Our researches are concentrated on the advantages of wireless networks that seem to be more valuable considering the time and place restrictions, in an educational system. A wireless network is a collection of nodes participating in a covered area of transmission and cooperating to exchange data wirelessly. The topology depends on the movement of the nodes and the gain of bandwidth of the routing protocol and the type of communication [1]. A major component that predefined the type of transmission concerns whether the transfer of data is designate unicast, multicast or broadcast communication. In each case the routing protocol defers according to rules and objectives of a successful communication and minimum allocation of bandwidth and power restrictions of wireless nodes [2]. Wireless networks facilitate a dynamic educational system where participants enter or leave a training session without notifying a centralized manager of the network. The lack of infrastructure gives a model of communication nodes that are adaptive in continuous changes. Factors such as power expended, variable wireless link quality, and topological changes, become relevant issues during the survey of the shortest path from source to destination.

Models and implementation of a wireless network can solve different necessities in an educational environment where the challenges are increasing. These networks provide flexibility, collaborative training, dynamic interaction, and adaptive architecture for group communication. In a wireless network each computer is equipped with a wireless networking interface card covering a transmission area where each computer (node) which interferes in this area can constitute the bridge to the rest of the network operating either as a destination or a relay. Another model concerns the interaction of a group of nodes with a wireless access point using one node as the bridge which is determined to communicate through this point with the wired network of the campus or the educational institute. In this case the topology and the range of the wireless network are dependent also on the range and the transmission rate of the access point.

Wireless networks do not have a specific infrastructure and predefined locations where they can exchange information with stable rates. Each node in network is functioning simultaneously as server and as source – destination of the message that is transmitted through the network. Wireless networks could be defined as a subcategory of a cellular system as the behaviour of the nodes and the range of transmission simulate a cellular form. Of course it is risky to say that they will work at the same way when decentralized. Differences are increased when there is mobility and entering or leaving of a node from the range of transmission or there isn't any node to behave as a relay for the destination node. Additionally, the behaviour of the routing protocol is changing dynamically and according to factors that do not exist in a cellular system. The key difference between wireless networks and cellular networks is the absence of base stations, which results in every node in the network getting an equal share of the network management functions. For example, every node is a router and every node must be capable of locating other nodes and tracking them as they move. The main interest in wireless networks is focused on the self-configuration of the network especially during movements or dynamic changes in nodes.

2.1 Requirements for Wireless Communication

The mobile wireless communication network must be a seamless and flexible part of the infrastructure. To achieve this, we assume that it should meet the following objectives [3].

- The node in a wireless network must be able to communicate with other nodes, and with any host in the Internet through an access point.
- There should be means to uniquely identify a node both in fixed and in mobile network.
- In any effort of communication nodes should be able to exchange data at different ways and according to network topology.
- Wireless network must support congestion controls, different architectures, hardware technologies, network or transport protocols and multiple mobility management protocols.
- The existing hosts in the fixed network should be capable of using the mobile access with no requirements for change.
- Network architecture should facilitate the transportation of a message where the nodes' resources are limited.
- Protocols should be able to realize the condition of the network such as transactions failure, increase or decrease of mobile nodes and shortest paths from source to destination with minimum consumption of resources.
- The architecture of a group communication should be reasonably secure.

2.2 Routing Protocols and Services

The wireless communication can be categorized [4], [5] according to:
1. The applications, which include

- Voice
- access in the Internet
- web browsing
- paging and short messaging
- subscriber information services
- transport of files and video - conferences.

2. The systems, which include

- cellular systems
- wireless phones
- wireless local networks
- wide region wireless systems of data
- paging systems
- satellite systems

3. The region that it can cover

- very small area (in a working place, a room)
- small area (in a building, one building square)
- large area (a city or in world scope)

The problems that are incurred in the growth of wireless ad-hoc networks are:

- The determination of requirements in:
  o Speed.
  o Reliability.
  o Guarantee of requirements in quality of services (QoS). Because of the limited and shareware bandwidth of network, and the lack of central controller of these resources, the nodes are compelled to negotiate with regard to the management of resources that is required for the benefit of quality of services at length of path.
- The bandwidth of transmission via the wireless connections. The management of transmission bandwidth is another component that should be recorded at the behaviour of a protocol as it is known that the bandwidth is consumed not only for the parcels of "clean information" that we want to transmit but also for the transmission of parcels of routing.
- The study of various forms of wireless networks and infrastructures and the search of hybrid form of network that it will serve individually.
- The consumption of energy as the participating nodes spend their energy in signals among them and installation of paths of most optimal way in a dynamic wireless network.
- The need of implementation of such networks or hybrid forms.
- The consumption of energy caused by the supply of one node which is related more with the frequency of emission of messages of notifying and more generally emissions that concern activities of maintenances.
- The function of protocol should be distributed and no assembled and this because the centralized protocol is susceptible in congestion.
- The exploration of existing problems of routing in the wireless networks as these are presented at the transmission of such forms of communication.

- The automatic redefinition of wireless network from a failed transmission and feed in of one node.
- Guarantee of the path that will not lead to repeated loop.
- The possibility of adaptability in the topology and typology of movement of network and naturally this adaptability will be supposed to become with as much as possible smaller functional cost (overhead).
- End – to – end delay. The time that a parcel is maintained in the buffer before being decided its reject because of not discovery the path to be promoted.
- The capacity that governs the nodes who participate in the wireless network, as well as the redefinition of provision of nodes according to the mobility and capacity of their location.
- The start of transmission "Bring - Up" after a pause or inactivity of node.
- The determination of the advantages as well as the disadvantages of algorithms of routing of shorter way, of most optimal routing, as well as algorithms of deviation of flow.
- The real performance from end – to – end throughput.
- The search of optimal way.

3   Multicast Wireless Networks

Multicasting has naturally been considered the ideal technique to be used with multimedia communications, mainly because its inherent nature is to minimize the network resources needed to support this type of transmission [5]. Multicast in wireless networks is based in structure of tree. One node initiates the group and becomes the group master of the network. It works as the base node in a multicast tree and conserve a list of all nodes joining the network. This list is being kept in a dynamic table which is updated continually. Its task is to periodically send hello messages in order to be informed about the condition of the network. Every node in a group must send an acknowledgement (ACK) to inform the master node concerning the packets that have received or a negative acknowledge (NACK) if a transmission failed [6]. Nodes in a multicast network function either as destination or as relay to transmit messages to the rest of the network. In cases where a failure of acceptance of a message occurs from one node during transmissions a request of retransmission must be forwarded only to the specific node. Consequently, the other nodes of the group when they realize that a retransmission occur they ignore the content of the message and they forward it to the destination node where the failure happened.

In a multicast network an amount of messages concerns the joining or leaving a group from a node, the rearranging of the network topology and the failures that occur during transmissions. The master of the group is being informed for every condition of the wireless network and this implies the normal function of it. Focusing in an educational environment the transmission of a video conference or a multimedia presentation from an instructor facilitates the forward of the packets and reducing the consumption of the resources especially the battery power. Students and staff also can utilize multicast structure to communicate with database systems in the campus and attend e-learning courses, or to keep notes and guidance for projects and group co operations. The place restrictions does not limit the multicast transmission as the members – nodes can work dispersed within the bounds of range of communication. Wireless networks and especially multicasting function additively to the training models and enhance them to new educational forms. The ability to work with wireless multicasting technology reduces the cost of resources and increases the edutainment capacity of members.

4 Educational Models and Architectures

Wireless networks can give network access in every classroom with no or minimal renovation costs. The Wireless Classrooms require only the installation of the access points, which can be placed strategically throughout the building and can usually be installed without interruption of the regular classroom schedule. Additionally, it is a valuable factor since without any modification (or visible wiring) to the existing physical structure/classroom we can provide network connectivity [7].

The difference between wiring laboratories in a campus and wireless classrooms is in their roles and objectives. In a wireless network where mobility and roaming are supported, students can move from class to class and remain connected to the network without any interruptions. The information and educational material is available consecutively by using database technology and metadata which maximize reusability and maintenance of existing system.

As the most critical factor for the implementation of a network is cost saving it has been proven that educational environments which make use of a wireless infrastructure can be less expensive than a wiring network installation. The equipment that will be used will be limited to the minimum as it can be arranged to be transferred from classroom to classroom according to course needs. Another important factor is that wireless networks can develop and evaluate communication patterns and possible infrastructure for interconnected embedded technologies among devices.

A major advantage in a wireless network is the multicasting approaches of communication. Wiring networks have been used to exchange data and to communicate through the Internet. Wireless networks provide another type of communication especially in education where someone can multicast data to a group community. Multicast applications provide a variety of options for supporting a collaborative and individual teaching environment. A major problem in wireless networks is to minimize the unnecessary messages that transmit one computer to another especially during multicasting transmissions. Many efforts have shown remarkably results concerning the way of communication in ad-hoc wireless networks where nothing is stable. Especially in a wireless network the educational model is being enhanced and supplemented with efficiency of moving around the campus and interfering with educational material beyond time and place restrictions.

Wireless networks can be used as a platform to distribute distance learning and to provide wireless learning environment services. The distance learning and wireless learning environment could include, for example, videoconferencing between mobile phone, PC, VoIP-phone and traditional phone or streaming video content from a learning content database. Wireless networks could be used in educational purposes by including

- Access to searchable databases
- Administrative services (timetables, student records)
- Small text-based simulations
- Dictionaries, vocabularies, thesaurus
- Presentation (video, multimedia applications)
- Control of the status of a machine (i.e. robot).

An advanced-user interface will help users to log in to the backbone of the school or to the server through the access points. The wireless network will be monitored in order to permit access to the databases and facilitate users by allocating laptops or other mobile devices to the access point. The educational content can be designed properly in the same way by using modules so that to be shared in text mode or graphical or multimedia mode and help users to use any type of wireless devise.

The architecture of an educational environment using wireless technology can be based to its current infrastructure of the wiring backbone network and be enhanced in the future by replacing computers lab with wireless devices. The replacement of the existing personal computers with notebooks will maximize the usability of the classrooms by using the so far traditional laboratories. The wireless access points will be the only medium to facilitate the communication between mobile computer laboratories with both Internet and local servers. Thus, the education will be continued and enhanced even when the school is closed with the assistance of proper software which will be developed to provide courses or other helpful facilities.

In a campus area or in an educational institute the movement of nodes is very rare or not continuous. Nodes must work evenly as source, as destination and as a relay for other's packets. The model of having wireless nodes in a classroom environment and exchange data complicates the problem. Especially, in multicasting where the data transmission concerns video or multimedia presentations from a source node to a group of destination nodes who work also as relays, the utilization of the available bandwidth demand a properly management of data transmission avoiding iterations and engagements of channel such as power and useless procedures. In an ad-hoc wireless network located in a classroom the traffic carried by the nodes are relayed traffic.

Problems that occurred in wireless networks concern the knowledge of the network topology during transmissions. The lack of centralized control and the time-varying of network topology determine the use of the routing protocol that will facilitate the multicast transmission. The case of one node to leave the multicast session necessitates the determination of the location of all nodes and the routing tables that each one maintains. Furthermore, the entering of one node to the topology must rearrange the paths and the role of this node to the whole network. Such kind of problems is met in conferences where participants are moving toward the covered area. During the multicast transmission nodes are responsible to forward the packets to all destinations belong to a group community certified to receive these packets and only once. Duplicated packets must be rejected in order to release bandwidth. Each participant must receive the packets from the nearest node rejecting the request of transmission from other nodes with longer distance. Thus, the transmission depends on the ability of one node to send a packet according to other requests and noises that occurring in the channels or in the area.

5 Conclusions

Mobile wireless ad-hoc networks are highly dynamic because of node mobility, unreliable wireless links, and frequent outages. Furthermore, they are sensitive to network load and congestion. For wireless network protocol design, the key of their success is that the protocols are adaptive and generate minimal control message overhead. The wireless network is a fairly new idea which addresses to the problem of forming mobile networks in dynamic fashion. In contrast to the infrastructure network wireless networks provide true wireless features with no need of base stations. However, there is no way of assuring network coverage. It is said that these kinds of networks will be deployed in educational application where the community is dynamic according to courses and groups communications. The utilization of wireless networks compared to traditional cellular systems make wireless networks very appealing in many applications (video, audio, multimedia transmissions). The advantages of wireless networks include the continuously function of the network as there isn't a base station which is the only responsible for the transferring the messages like in cellular systems. Moreover, wireless networks don't rely on wired base stations and therefore are capable of being deployed in places with no existing infrastructures.

Wireless networks take advantage of the nature of the wireless communication medium. In other words, in a wired network the physical cabling is done a priori restricting the connection topology of the nodes. This restriction is not present in the wireless domain and, provided that two nodes are within hearing distance of each other, an instantaneous link between them is automatically formed.

The advantages in educational systems stems from the needs of dynamic networks with cost reduction in technology investments, as laptops can be transferred in every classroom thought to be necessary, with easy instalment of a group communication, with fewer requirements in a campus area and the ability to communicate all the members without being restricted of place and time. Models of education like e-learning or multicasting services give advantages to the wireless networks as the collaboration and the communication with database systems of the campus even outside the classroom and laboratories facilitate the transmission of knowledge. Many efforts have been done concerning schools and universities and the effects in faculty and students but still the utilization of multicasting wireless networks remains immature to ride high.

References

1. Panetsos, S.: Communication and Computer Network. Tziolas Publications, Thessaloniki (2007)
2. Alexopoulos, A., Lagogiannis, G.: Communication and Computer Network, Athens (2005)

3. Broch, J.: A Performance Comparison of Multi-Hop Wireless Ad-hoc Network Routing Protocols. In: Proceedings Mobicomm 1998 (1998)
4. Tschudin, C.: Active Routing for Ad-hoc Networks. IEEE Communications Magazine, 122–127 (April 2000)
5. Larson, T., Hedman, N.: Routing Protocols in Wireless Ad-hoc Networks– A Simulation Study Switch Lab Erricson, Stockholm (1998) ISSN 1402-1617
6. Stallings, W.: Data and Computer Communications. Prentice-Hall, Englewood Cliffs (2003)
7. Nair, P.: The Role of Wireless Computing Technology in the Design of Schools National Clearinghouse for Educational Facilities (October 2002),
   http://www.edfacilities.org

Context-Aware Mobile Learning

Anastasios A. Economides

Information Systems Department, University of Macedonia,
156 Egnatia Avenue, Thessaloniki, 54006 Greece
economid@uom.gr

Abstract. Recent developments on mobile devices and networks enable new opportunities for mobile learning anywhere, anytime. Furthermore, recent advances on adaptive learning establish the foundations for personalized learning adapted to the characteristics of each individual learner. A mobile learner would perform an educational activity using the infrastructure (e.g. handheld devices, networks) in an environment (e.g. outdoors). In order to provide personalization, an adaptation engine adapts the educational activity and the infrastructure according to the context. The context is described by the learner's state, the educational activity's state, the infrastructure's state, and the environment's state. Furthermore, each one of these states is described by its dimensions. Many examples illustrate the adaptation decisions.

Keywords: adaptation, adaptive learning, context-aware, knowledge society, learner profile, learner model, mobile learning, personalized learning, pervasive learning, ubiquitous learning.

1 Introduction

Recently, there is a widespread use of mobile phones and wireless networks in everyday life. Educational institutes are also starting to exploit mobile devices and networks for learning and management. As most students already possess handheld devices, several educational institutes are using wireless technology to deliver and support mobile learning [1-4]. The intersection of online learning and mobile computing – called mobile learning – holds the promise of offering frequent, integral access to applications that support learning, anywhere, anytime [5]. Mobile learning would help the development of the Knowledge Society. The objective is a society with access to knowledge and learning for everyone [6]. The mobile learner will carry multiple heterogeneous wearable and handheld devices. He will move and interact unrestricted with other learners, hardware and software resources in his neighborhood or on remote locations. He will be able to continually learn wherever he is moving without any mobility, time and other restrictions.

However, the diversity of learners' characteristics as well mobile devices and networks requires personalization for different cases. The educational activities and the provided infrastructure would be auto-configured tailored to the learner needs, interests and abilities. Multiple sources of information would be used to adapt the

M.D. Lytras et al. (Eds.): WSKS 2008, CCIS 19, pp. 213–220, 2008.
© Springer-Verlag Berlin Heidelberg 2008

educational activities and the infrastructure to every situation and condition. Most of the physical objects in the environment will be equipped with some embedded sensing and communication capabilities. They will sense, track, and monitor the surrounding environment and transmit this information to those interested for that. This information would be used to make dynamic adaptation decisions for the benefit of the learner.

This paper presents a general framework for context-aware adaptive mobile learning. It explicitly defines the context on which the adaptations would be based. An adaptation engine acquires input data and produces the adaptation results. Part of the input data into the adaptation engine is closely related to the context of ubiquitous computing. This paper defines context to include the learner's state, the educational activity's state, the infrastructure's state, and the environment's state. Several previous studies in ubiquitous computing provided various definitions of context. Location, identity, time and activity have been suggested as primary types of context [7]. Computing context (e.g. network connectivity, communication costs, communication bandwidth, nearby resources such as printers, displays, and workstations), User context (e.g. user's profile, location, people nearby, and current social situation), and Physical context (e.g. lighting, noise levels, traffic conditions, and temperature) have been also proposed as main context categories [8]. In addition to location [9], identities of nearby people and objects, as well as changes to those objects have been included in the context [10]. Context-aware has been defined as "the ability of the computer to sense and act upon information about its environment, such as location, time, temperature or user identity" [11]. Context has been also described across three dimensions: i) Environment (physical and social), ii) Self (device state, physiological and cognitive), and iii) Activity (behavior and task) [12]. Any information that can be used to characterize the situation of an entity (e.g. person, place, or object) would be considered as context [13]. Different types of information about a user can simultaneously be relevant to a given adaptation decision [14]. An ontology-based context model considered time, place, user knowledge, user activity, user environment and device capacity [15]. In parallel, a situation model gave a view on the context model describing temporal properties. It was argued that the following context parameters should be taken into consideration: variety, priority, granularity, implementation, cost-effectiveness [16]. Furthermore, it has been argued that a context aware mobile learning system should also take into consideration the learner's willingness to participate in the proposed learning activity [17].

Several architectures for context-aware applications have been proposed [18-23]. However, implementing such systems on a large scale is not free from obstacles [24]. Educational, socio-cultural, economical, and technical requirements for mobile learning applications should be considered [25]. A mechanism to support adaptation in m-learning systems has been proposed [26]. An ontology-based framework for context-aware mobile learning has been proposed [27]. Context-aware social presence mechanisms would support a learner [28]. Instant messaging would provide the learner with continuous access to social networks. A three-tier web-based architecture has been proposed for context-aware m-learning [29]. Similarly, "SmartContext" was an ontology based context model which included a standardized context template, a context reasoning ontology and a context middleware [30]. A flexible e-learning model would take into consideration the learner's knowledge state and learning preferences [31] to create personalized learning paths [32]. Furthermore, the users may prefer informal communication and learning [33]. The architecture of a context-aware schedule tool for learning Java has been proposed in [34]. A context-aware system consisting of three components has been proposed [35]. Also, the user's vision and speech would be monitored [36].

In this paper, an adaptation engine adapts the learner's educational activity or/and infrastructure according to the context. The adaptation decisions would be either deterministic or probabilistic [37]. The next section 2 presents the context on which the adaptations would be based.

2   Context Model

The context is defined to consist of the learner's state, the educational activity's state, the infrastructure's state, and the environment's state. Next, each one of these states is further described by its dimensions. Each dimension would be further analyzed to its variables. It is obvious that the more information is available about each dimension, the more accurate but complicated the model becomes. The proper type and number of dimensions remains an open research issue. Adding additional dimensions will increase the complexity of the model and the requirements to collect additional information. There may be a balance between the number of dimensions, model complexity, and the accuracy of the model. Techniques for modifying the weights associated with different dimensions dynamically to better represent the context are open research issues. The same stands for the variables in each dimension.

2.1   Learner's State

The Learner's state is described by the following dimensions (with examples):

Demographics, e.g. the educational activity should be adapted to a learner who has grown up in a loose time orientation culture. In this case the learner may not be punctual with deadlines and scheduling, and therefore the educational activity should adapt to afford loose deadlines.

Education & Profession, e.g. if the learner has practicing experiences, then the educational activity should be adapted to provide him with pragmatic cases, real life projects, and experiments.

Preferences & Interests, e.g. if the learner prefers audio communication, then the educational activity and the infrastructure should be adapted to increase the audio communication (e.g. speak the instructions).

Objectives, Aims & Plans, e.g. the educational activity should be adjusted to the short and long term objectives of the learner.

Health, e.g. if the learner is overweight, then the educational activity and the infrastructure should be adapted to his weight.

Physical Abilities, e.g. if the learner has movement disability, then the educational activity should be adjusted to take place in a given space.

Cognitive Abilities, e.g. if the learner learns inductively, then the educational activity should proceed step-by-step in an inductive way.

Social Abilities, e.g. if the learner has leadership abilities, then the educational activity may assign him the coordinator's role in a group task.

Feelings & Emotions, e.g. if the learner is bored, then the educational activity may become more intriguing.

Intentions, Wills & Values, e.g. if the learner underestimates his abilities, then the educational activity may tailor the project to his performance level, in order that he becomes motivated and successful.

Time & Schedule, e.g. if the learner is required to complete a project in a given deadline, the educational activity may remind him some time in advance as well as alert him on the deadline.

Location, e.g. If the learner approaches a specific object, then the educational activity may give him further instructions and directions.

Mobility, e.g. the educational activity may guide and teach the learner through a botanical garden.

Current Needs & Desires, e.g. if the learner is thirsty, then the educational activity may suggest him of drinking locations.

Wearable & handheld hardware, software and other resources, e.g. if the screen of the learner's handheld device is small, then the educational activity may be adapted to show the summary and the main points instead of the full content.

Tasks, Results & Achievements, e.g. if the learner is performing excellent, then the educational activity may increase the difficulty level.

Restrictions, e.g. if there are access restrictions to some resources for the learner, then the educational activity should consider these.

2.2 Educational Activity's State

The Educational Activity's state is described by the following dimensions (with examples):

Subject, e.g. if the subject of the educational activity is related to drawing, then wizards and auto-shapes facilities may be activated.

Requirements, e.g. if the educational activity requires video delivery, then the infrastructure should adapt to reserve high bandwidth and storage capacity.

Purpose, if the educational activity purpose is to assess the learner's knowledge, then a test may be taken by her.

Expected Outcomes, e.g. if the educational activity outcome is to increase the learner's synthesis ability, then it may ask the learner to assemble parts into an integrated system.

Pedagogical Theory, e.g. if the teacher wants the educational activity to be based on collaboration, then the educational activity may set up learner teams and ask them to complete a collaborative project.

Management, e.g. if the educational activity is coordinated by an examiner, then its tasks may have strict deadlines and access restrictions may be imposed too.

Content, e.g. if the learner is an activist type, then the educational activity may be tailored around real cases and experiments.

Presentation, e.g. if the learner is a visual type, then more visual than audio objects may be presented to her.

Structure & Sequencing, e.g. if the learner is a sequential learner, then the educational content may be presented inductively and step by step.

Resources, e.g. if the educational activity helps the learner, then it may provide to him further bibliography and links on the Web.

Participants & Teams, e.g. if the educational activity establishes teams, then the infrastructure should try to keep on connectivity among the team members during the whole activity duration.

Achievements & Results, e.g. if the educational activity records the learner's progress, then it may become easier or harder depending on the learner's achievements.

2.3 Infrastructure's State

The Infrastructure's state is described by the following dimensions (with examples):
Devices, e.g. if the learner walks on a mountain, then adjustment of the antenna range or/and the communication technology may be needed.

Networks, e.g. if the communication jitter is high and the quality of video transmission is low, then alternative communication channels or alternative media should be selected.

Hardware and Software Resources, e.g. if the learner is close to an energy charger and his battery lifetime is short, then the system may notify him about the available charger.

Adaptable Activities, e.g. if there is interference with other adaptable activities in the vicinity of the learner, adjustments on the antenna range or the communication protocols may be done.

2.4 Environment's State

Finally, the Environment's state is described by the following dimensions (with examples):

Terrain, e.g. if the learner moves from outdoors to indoors, then a different network technology may be selected.

Weather, e.g. if there is a lot of sunlight, then the screen should be adjusted to not reflect the light.

Environmental Characteristics, e.g. if there is a lot of noise in the environment, then the audio volume may be increased or text communication may be enabled.

Neighbors, e.g. if there are available neighbors, then the network can use them as intermediate nodes in order to connect two communicating faraway learners.

Non-adaptable Activities, e.g. if other non-adaptable activities are running, then they should be considered in the battery consumption.

3 Conclusions

The paper presents a general framework for context-aware adaptive mobile learning. The mobile learner learns and performs an educational activity as he moves in an environment. The goal is to help the mobile learner, to increase his satisfaction and learning, to decrease his limitations and restrictions in order to be unconcernedly engaged in learning. The learner is supported by an adaptation engine that adapts the educational activity and/or the infrastructure according to the context. This paper explicitly defines the context to consist of the learner's state, the educational activity's state, the infrastructure's state, and the environment's state.

The presented framework may help designers and developers of mobile learning systems at their decisions. It may help them to identify requirements, open problems, challenges and opportunities, to share ideas and methods, to take a holistic approach in developing systems and thoroughly evaluate them. In order to expand students' and citizens' opportunities, government would consider adopting lifelong mobile learning into the educational system. People would learn not only in formal situations (e.g. in class) but everywhere (e.g. while working, collaborating, walking, playing) anytime.

Hopefully, this study would stimulate future research and development efforts. An initial step would be the implementation of a simple case. The adaptation engine would accept as input the learner's location and would select the team members in an outdoors collaborative activity [38, 39]. The ultimate goal will be the implementation of adaptation engines that use the full context and produce the full adapted educational activity and infrastructure, as presented in the Context model section. Another idea for future work would be the harmonious integration of the input data, as well as the explicit decisions under various input data combinations.

References

1. Davis, S.: Observations in classrooms using a network of handheld devices. Journal of Computer Assisted Learning 19, 298–307 (2003)
2. Waycott, J., Kukulska-Hulme, A.: Students' experience with PDAs for reading course materials. Personal and Ubiquitous Computing 7, 30–43 (2003)
3. Sung, M., Gips, J., Eagle, N., Madan, A., Caneel, R., Devaul, R., Bonsen, J., Pentland, A.: Mobile-IT education (mit.edu): m-learning applications for classroom settings. Journal of Computer Assisted Learning 21, 229–237 (2005)
4. Economides, A.A., Nikolaou, N.: Evaluation of handheld devices for mobile learning. International Journal of Engineering Education (IJEE) 24(1), 3–13 (2008)
5. Tatar, D., Roschelle, J., Vahey, P., Penuel, W.R.: Handhelds go to school: Lessons learned. IEEE Computer 36(9), 30–37 (2003)
6. Lytras, M.D., Sicilia, M.A.: The knowledge society: A manifesto for knowledge and learning. International Journal of Knowledge and Learning 1(1/2), 1–11 (2005)
7. Schilit, B.N., Theimer, M.M., Welch, B.B.: Customizing mobile applications. In: Proceedings of the USENIX Symposium on Mobile and Location-Independent Computing (USENIX Association), August 1993, pp. 129–138 (1993)
8. Schilit, B., Adams, N., Want, R.: Context-aware computing applications. In: Proceedings of IEEE Workshop on Mobile Computing Systems and Applications, Santa Cruz, California, December 1994, pp. 85–90. IEEE Computer Society Press, Los Alamitos (1994)

9. Becker, C., Durr, F.: On location models for ubiquitous computing. Personal Ubiquitous Computing 9, 20–31 (2005)
10. Schilit, B.N., Theimer, M.M.: Disseminating active map information to mobile hosts. IEEE Networks 8(5), 22–32 (1994)
11. Ryan, N., Pascoe, J., Morse, D.: Enhanced reality fieldwork: the context-aware archaeological assistant. In: Computer Applications in Archaeology 1997, British Archaeological Reports, Oxford (October 1998)
12. Schmidt, A., Beigl, M., Gellersen, H.W.: There is more to context than location. Computers and Graphics Journal 23(6), 893–902 (1999)
13. Dey, A.K., Abowd, G.: Towards a Better Understanding of Context and Context-Awareness. In: 2000 Conference on Human Factors in Computing Systems (CHI 2000), The Hague, The Netherlands, April 3 (2000)
14. Tamminen, S., Oulasvirta, T.K., Kankaninen, A.: Understanding mobile contexts. Personal and Ubiquitous Computing 8, 135–143 (2004)
15. Bouzeghoub, A., Do, K.N., Lecocq, C.: A situation-based delivery of learning resources in pervasive learning. In: Duval, E., Klamma, R., Wolpers, M. (eds.) EC-TEL 2007. LNCS, vol. 4753, pp. 450–456. Springer, Heidelberg (2007)
16. Bayoumi, F.: Context aware systems: Present and Future. In: Proceedings of the IASTED European Conference, Internet and Multimedia Systems and Applications, Chamonix, France, pp. 208–213 (2007)
17. Uday Bhaskar, N., Govindarajulu, P.: A design methodology for acceptability analyzer in context aware adaptive mobile learning systems development. IJCSNS International Journal of Computer Science and Network Security 8(3), 130–138 (2008)
18. Dey, A.K.: Understanding and using context. Personal and Ubiquitous Computing 5, 4–7 (2001)
19. Jameson, A.: Modelling both the context and the user. Personal and Ubiquitous Computing 5, 29–33 (2001)
20. Petrelli, D., Not, E., Zancanaro, M., Strapparava, C., Stock, O.: Modelling and adapting to context. Personal and Ubiquitous Computing 5, 20–24 (2001)
21. Indulska, J., Sutton, P.: Location management in pervasive systems. In: Johnson, C., Montague, P., Steketee, C. (eds.) Workshop on Wearable, Invisible, Context-Aware, Ambient, Pervasive and Ubiquitous Computing, Conferences in Research and practice in Information Technology, vol. 21. Australian Computer Society (2003)
22. Lonsdale, P., Baber, C., Sharples, M., Arvanitis, T.N.: A context awareness architecture for facilitating mobile learning. In: Proceedings MLEARN 2003 (2003)
23. Biegel, G., Cahill, V.: A framework for developing mobile, context-aware applications. In: Proceedings of the Second IEEE Annual Conference on Pervasive Computing and Communications (PERCOM 2004). IEEE, Los Alamitos (2004)
24. Raisinghani, et al.: Ambient intelligence: changing forms of human-computer interaction and their social implications. Journal of Digital Information, Article No. 271, 5(4) (2004)
25. Economides, A.A.: Requirements of mobile learning applications. International Journal of Innovation and Learning 5(5), 457–479 (2008)
26. Martin, E., Carro, R.M., Rodriguez, P.: A mechanism to support context-based adaptation in m-learning. In: Neijdl, W., Tuchtermann, K. (eds.) EC-TEL 2006. LNCS, vol. 4227, pp. 302–315. Springer, Heidelberg (2006)
27. Berri, J., Benlamri, R., Atif, Y.: Ontology-based framework for context-aware mobile learningh. In: IWCMC 2006, Vancouver, British Columbia, July 2006, pp. 1307–1310. ACM, Canada (2006)

28. Kekwaletswe, R.M., Ng'ambi, D.: Ubiquitous social presence: Context-awareness in a mobile learning environment. In: Proceedings of the IEEE International Conference on Sensor Networks, Ubiquitous, and Trustworthy Computing (SUTC 2006), pp. 1–6. IEEE, Los Alamitos (2006)
29. Basaeed, E.I., Berri, J., Zemerly, M.J., Benlamri, R.: Web-based context-aware m-learning architectyre. International Journal Interactive Mobile Technologies 1(1), 5–10 (2007)
30. Hu, B., Moore, P.: "SmartContext": An ontology based context model for cooperative mobile learning. In: Shen, W., Luo, J.-Z., Lin, Z., Barthès, J.-P.A., Hao, Q. (eds.) CSCWD. LNCS, vol. 4402, pp. 717–726. Springer, Heidelberg (2007)
31. Albano, G., Gaeta, G., Salerno, S.: E-learning: A model and process proposal. International Journal of Knowledge and Learning 2(1/2), 73–88 (2006)
32. Albano, G., Gaeta, G., Salerno, S.: IWT: An innovative solution for AGS e-learning model. International Journal of Knowledge and Learning 3(2/3), 209–224 (2007)
33. Groth, K., Bogdan, C., Lindqvist, S., Sundblad, Y.: Simple and playful interaction for informal communication and learning. International Journal of Knowledge and Learning 3(2/3), 191–208 (2007)
34. Yau, J., Joy, M.: Architecture of a context-aware and adaptive learning schedule for learning Java. In: Seventh IEEE International Conference on Advanced Learning Technologies (ICALT 2007), pp. 1–5. IEEE, Los Alamitos (2007)
35. Yau, J., Joy, M.: A context-aware and adaptive learning schedule framework for supporting learners' daily routines. In: Second International Conference on Systems (ICONS 2007), pp. 1–6. IEEE, Los Alamitos (2007)
36. Porta, M.: E-learning and machine perception: In pursuit of human-line interaction in computer-based teaching systems. International Journal of Knowledge and Learning 3(2/3), 281–298 (2007)
37. Economides, A.A.: Adaptive mobile learning. In: Proceedings IEEE WMUTE- 4th International Workshop on Wireless, Mobile and Ubiquitous Technologies in Education (2006), Athens, Greece, November 2006, pp. 26–28. IEEE, Los Alamitos (2006)
38. Vasiliou, A., Economides, A.A.: MANET-based outdoor collaborative learning. In: Proceedings 3rd International Conference on Interactive Mobile and Computer Aided Learning (IMCL 2008), Amman, Jordan (2008)
39. Vasiliou, A., Economides, A.A.: Mobile collaborative learning using multicast MANETs. International Journal of Mobile Communications (IJMC) 5(4), 423–444 (2007)

Reliable Personalized Learning Paths: The Contribution of Trust to E-Learning

Vincenza Carchiolo, D. Correnti, Alessandro Longheu, Michele Malgeri, and Giuseppe Mangioni

Dipartimento di Ingegneria Informatica e delle Telecomunicazioni
Facoltà di Ingegneria - Università degli Studi di Catania - Italy

Abstract. The personalization of learning paths according to personal profiles is one of the major advantages of computer assisted learning. However, the choice of most suitable learning resources is sometime a controversial question due to different e-learning providers assessment about each other and their learning resources. In this work an approach to address this issue is presented, by exploiting the idea of trustworthiness associated to both learning objects as well as to peers in a P2P e-learning scenario. We test our proposal on an e-learning network based on MERLOT and ARIADNE data. Results show the effectiveness of trust in e-learning context.

1 Introduction

One of the major and well-known advantages of computer assisted learning is the possibility of learning according to personal profiles, following tailored learning paths through available resources [1] [2]. However, the choice of most suitable learning resources, as well as their sequence according to precedence-succession relationships is sometime a controversial question due to different e-learning providers assessment about each other and their learning resources.

This question has become more and more important due the evolution of *e-learning* paradigm, since from the first scenario, where students accessed a remote centralised system with materials arranged and managed by a single authority, to the current Web 2.0 scenario [6], which promotes users' participation through blogs, wikis and folksonomies, making learners *knowledge prosumers*, i.e. both consumer and producer, finally leading to the question "should I trust this material? And who gave it to me?"; this behaviour is naturally supported by the well known Peer-to-Peer (P2P) paradigma [15]

To address the question of the reliability of information and his provider we associate the concept of trust (we considered in general e.g. [3]) to both learning objects as well as to peers in a P2P e-learning scenario. In particular, trust relationships among peers allows to select which ones of them can be considered more authoritative in answering a query within a given topic (described by shared ontologies). Trust about learning objects instead expresses their reliability, also helping in finding the best personalized learning path, expecially when

M.D. Lytras et al. (Eds.): WSKS 2008, CCIS 19, pp. 221–228, 2008.

contradictory information are collected from different peer. We test our proposal on an e-learning network based on real data set with additional trustworthiness information. Results of simulations performed over these data sets shows the effectiveness of trust in e-learning context.

The paper is organised as follows: first, in section 2 we describe related works, then in section 3 we introduce the e-learning P2P trust-based network model. In section 4 we presents the data set for experiments, derived from real data set, together with the algorithm used to search for personalized learning path and we show preliminary results of our approach. Finally, in sections 5 we consider future issues related to the topics discussed throughout the paper.

2   Related Work

In literature can be found several proposal about adaptive e-learning systems [14,16,17]. Some of them are cited in the following. Ariadne [5] foundation propose the *Knowledge Pool System* to manage and reuse learning resources. Ariadne is based on P2P model inspired by IEEE LOMster [7] ALFanet [13] is an adaptive e-learning system providing support in users adaption for both information and contents format. Edutella [11], is a p2p network designed for distributed environments. The project define a framework that provides mechanism to manage peer access, a reference model called "Edutella Common Data Model" allowing sharing of queries and messages, but each peer refers only to local data representation and query model [12].

Above systems adopt different approaches when building learning paths, but to our knowledge none of them actually exploits trust for this.

3   The Proposed Model

3.1   The Learning Network

The network model we adopt for the construction and retrieval of personalized and reliable learning paths can be considered a Peer-to-peer (P2P) overlay network since anyone (lerner, teacher, content creator and so on) can share his resources and judge other peers and their resources by providing trustworthiness. Formally, this P2P overlay network can be modeled as a directed graph $\mathcal{G} = (\mathcal{N}, \mathcal{E})$, where $\mathcal{N}$ is the set of nodes and $\mathcal{E}$ is the set of edges.

In particular, $\mathcal{N} = \{ A \mid (A \in \mathcal{P}) \vee (A \in \mathcal{R}) \}$, where $\mathcal{P}$ is the set of peers and $\mathcal{R}$ is the set of resources, and a node $A \in \mathcal{N}$ is either a peer or a resource. A peer is a learner, a content creator, an educational institution, an agent or any other entity that is devoted to assign trustworthiness to other peers and resources, and to store and suggest learning paths, whilst a resource is a Learning Object (LO) as intended within the SCORM standard [18], and that is assigned a trustworthiness by peers (its creator plus any other peers accessing that resource). A resource $R \in \mathcal{R}$ is described as $R = \{ n_R, d_R, pre_R, obj_R \}$ where n_R is a name, d_R a description and pre_R and obj_R the set of prerequisite and objectives, that are those concepts respectively needed before and gained after learning that resources; they are both needed to compose the sequence of resources (LOs) to be learned and are expressed as keywords belonging to a given shared ontology. The set of edges $\mathcal{E} = \{ e \mid (e \in \mathcal{T}) \vee (e \in \mathcal{S}) \}$ includes:

- $\mathcal{T} = \{ (A, t_X^A, X) \bigcup (A, (t_Y^A, time_Y, diff_Y), Y) \mid (A, X \in \mathcal{P}), (A \neq X), (Y \in \mathcal{R}), (t_X^A \in [-1, 1]), (time_Y > 0), (diff_Y \in \{low, mid, high\}) \}$, being $\mathcal{T}$ the set of trustworthiness edges, and each element is a triple that represents either a peer-to-peer or peer-to-resource edge labelled with t_X^A or t_Y^A, respectively, expressing the peer-to-peer edge the reliability t_X^A a peer X is given by another node A, and the peer-to-resource edge the usefulness t_Y^A of the resource Y for learning purposes (i.e. whether it is coherent, correct and understandable), as stated by A. $time_Y$ represents the estimated time needed to learn that resource's contents, for instance expressed in minutes, while $diff_Y$ represents the difficulty in learning resource's contents, here expressed using a (common) discrete set of values as $\{low, mid, high\}$.
- $\mathcal{S} = \{ s_{A \rightarrow X} : (A, X) \mid (A \in \mathcal{R}) \wedge (X \in \mathcal{R}) \wedge (A \neq X) \}$, being $\mathcal{S}$ the set of precedence-succession relationships among resources, i.e. the edge $s_{A \rightarrow X}$ from A to X means that the resource A should be learned before the resource X. Note that different, even contradictory learning paths can be provided by distinct peers.

In our discussion and further simulations, we consider an existing learning trust-based network, see section 4 for more details. Besides, since the model introduced above describes an overlay network, we do not consider lower-levels issues, e.g. resource storage management and replication.

3.2   Searching for Learning Paths

In order to find personalized and reliable learning paths, the model allows a peer in the network to send a query over the network. The structure of the query issued by a learner L is $\mathcal{Q}_L = \{ pre_L, obj_L, time_L, diff_L, trust_L \}$, where pre_L and obj_L are two list of keywords (referring to the same ontology shared by all peers) expressing prerequisite and objectives, i.e. those concepts learnt by L and L wants to learn, respectively. The $time_L$ represents the desired total time available for the learner and $diff_L$ is the mean level of difficulty required; such needs will provide learner's personalization in the learning path. Finally, $trust_L$ is the threshold for trustwothiness to be used when searching resources among peers (it allows L to specify what resources and what peers should be considered as reliable). The result of the query, when exists, is a sequence of n resources (LO) $\mathcal{R}_L = \{ R_1, ..., R_i, ..., R_n \}$ where $pre_{R_1} \subseteq pre_L$ (the learner is able to start learning) and $obj_L \subseteq obj_{R_n}$, that is L will learn desired objectives, and $pre_{R_i} \subseteq obj_{R_{(i-1)}}$ to build the learning path.

A relevant question is who and how answers $\mathcal{Q}_L$; in the following, only local view of the network is considered for a given peer. The algorithm for searching learning paths is based on the following functional blocks (modeling a peer):

- LOR stands for Local Object Repository, simply it contains references to all resources the peer accessed, thus being considered *local*.
- local resolver: it tries to locally solve Q_L using all the resources linked in local LOR. It is in charge to send Q_L to the resolver whenever either no or partial solutions have been locally found, further composing results when resolver gives more responses, in order to select the best learning path in terms of personalization and reliability.
- resolver: it is the core of the system, receives from local resolver (or from other peers) Q_L and tries to solve it using LOR: when succesfully, it returns the solution R_L, whilst it propagates Q_L (eventually modified) to a proper subset of neighbour peers' resolvers.

Searching for learning paths operates through the following steps:

1. The peer-learner L needs to solve a query Q_L hence calls the local resolver to search for local solutions R_L; the local resolver propagates Q_L to the underlying resolver together with the list of all peers contacted so far (at first step, the list is clearly empty), and waits for a response. To avoid search indefinitely, a time-to-live (TTL) is established for each contacted peer; as TTL goes to 0, Q_L will no further propagated along the network.
2. the resolver uses pre_L, obj_L and $trust_L \in Q_L$ to search for resources within the LOR having those prerequisite and/or those objectives and with a trust not below $trust_L$, and also with a required time not greater than $time_L$ and finally with difficulty not greater than $diff_L$; the former group of resources forms the set P_L whereas the latter is named O_L.
3. the resolver searches for all paths connecting each element in P_L with O_L, according to prerequisite-succession relationship, discarding unreliable resources (using $trust_L$), keeping the cumulative time needed for the path being built under the $time_L$ value, and finally guaranteeing that difficulty for each resource along the path is less than or equal to $diff_L$. If some path with all these contraints is found, a local solution has been found, and the corrisponding set of resources is the R_L learner L was looking for. Note that acutally different R_L could be found; if so, the resolver provide L with all of them, since they satisfy all conditions L specified in Q_L (L will choose one).
4. If no path is found at all, the local search was unsuccessfully, hence the resolver simply decreases TTL, add the peer id to the list of visited peers and propagates Q_L along the network (see below)
5. the resolver could find a *partial* solution, i.e. a $\overline{R_L} = \{ R_1, ..., R_i, ..., R_k \}$ where $pre_{R_1} \subseteq pre_L$ and $pre_{R_i} \subseteq obj_{R_{(i-1)}}$ for $i < k$, but $obj_{R_k} \subseteq obj_L$ (more $\overline{R_L}$ could be found). In this case, the sets P_L and O_L are properly updated in order to exploit partial results in further query propagations [4], the TTL is decreased, the peer id is added to the list, pre_L and $obj_L \in Q_L$ are modified to take into account new prerequisites and/or objectives coming from partial solutions, and the modified Q_L is sent along the network together with P_L and O_L.
6. Whenever needed, the propagation of Q_L occurs considering propagating peer's neighbours, and choosing those of them which are *similar* to

propagating peer and also *trusted* by him. In particular, it is reasonable that a learner L tends to ask first to a neighbour peer X which gave the same opinion about resources accessed by both peers, thus we consider similar peers L and X if they assign similar trustworthiness to the same set of resources (whenever present). To quantify this aspect, we introduce a similarity distance

$$Sim_{(L,X)} = \frac{\sum_j (t_{L,j} - \overline{t_L}) * (t_{X,j} - \overline{t_X})}{\sqrt{\sum_j (t_{L,j} - \overline{t_L})^2 * \sum_j (t_{X,j} - \overline{t_X})^2}} \tag{1}$$

where j ranges over all resources accessed by both L and X and $\overline{t_L}$ is the mean trust given by L to his pointed resources (the same applies to X). The overall evaluation $Eval_{(L,X)}$ of similarity $Sim_{(L,X)}$ and trust t_X^L (at this stage, a weighted linear combination) is used to select the *best* peer among L's neighbours for propagating the query Q_L. A set of best peers is actually chosen, i.e. those with $Eval_{(L,X)}$ over a given threshold. Note that here similarity and trust are separate concepts, i.e. we do not address (possible) reciprocal influences.

7. each contacted peer searches for a learning path and answers to its requesting peer. Each intermediate peer that propagated Q_L hence can receive several response; if at least a complete solution R_L come from one of the best neighbours, that solutions are considered, whereas if only partial solutions are returned, they must be integrated among them and also with local partial solution in order to build a learning path satisfying Q_L. If distinct partial solutions involves the same set of resources, corresponding learning paths could be in contrast; in this case, trust is again used to choose the *best* path, in particular we take into account both the trust assigned to peers that provided such solutions and trust they gave to resources they suggested, combining them using fuzzy rules [4]. The choice of best path is not needed if partial solutions do not share any resource. Next, the peer receiving partial solutions tries to build a learning path exploiting precedence/succession relationships of the suggested resources, and returns the answer back to its requesting peer until L get his answer.

4   Simulation

4.1   The Data Set

The model we introduced in section 3 has several characteristics we did not notice in current real data sets, expecially for what concerns the integration of trust within e-learning, however since different data sets (networks) within trust context and, separately, within e-learning are actually available, we exploit them by properly integrating their data in order to get to a data set with all features described in the proposed model. We preferred this choice rather than build a synthesized data set from scratch in order to perform simulations based on real data.

Several data set have been used; in the following we briefly describe them:

– Merlot [8] was our main source of information. Merlot is "a leading edge, user-centered, searchable collection of peer reviewed and selected higher education, online learning materials" currently, over 60000 users and 20000 resources are present into the system. Merlot dataset contains information about difficulty level and also somehow about prerequisites/objectives (we described them using Merlot categories [4]). Other information we introduced in the model are not present, so we enhanced Merlot data set with data coming from other data sets; all these values are generated always in accordance with the statistical distribution of the data set they come from, and also satisfying some constraints based on heuristic (described in the following) in order to keep data realistic.
– Ariadne[5] is an european project providing a distributed LOR accesible through WebServices. We used Ariadne to get information about the distribution of time spent by people while learning, in order to assign these values to resources. In addition to this, we adopt the heuristic that when associating time evaluation different peers give to the same resources, standard deviation is limited, reflecting the (realistic) case of avoiding scattered values of "required time" to the same resource.
– Epinions is a social network mainly used to figure out reputation [10]. Epinions data set was used to evaluate peer-resources trustworthiness. The heuristic we added is that trust is positive, modeling the realistic fact that a "bad" resource is not inserted into the system, rather than being inserted with a negative trustwothiness. Note that Merlot allows to provide a comment about a resource, someway similar to a trustworthiness but too few values have been provided for this field and the comment is simply a string, thus unsuitable for combining trustworthiness values.
– Advogato[9] is an online community site dedicated to free software development, where users can certify each other on different levels (we name trustworthiness values). Advogato's data set has been exploited to assign peer-to-peer trust values; no heuristic has been imposed for these values.

4.2   Simulation Results

A first set of simulation has been performed. In particular, we considered that Merlot data set presents some nodes (about 800 over 60000) being a sort of "superpeers", i.e. nodes pointing to many resources; this could be considered a reasonable scenario within e-learning context where few "gurus" provide many resources, while many others access them. Due to this consideration, queries are not sent to all 60000 nodes, rather to a subset of about 10000 nodes (including superpeers and "ordinary" nodes); note that the algorithm anyway operates over the entire set of 60000 nodes. In particular, we establish a set of significant query, i.e. whose pre_L and obj_L fall into the same Merlot category and are not directly related, so that a learning path is needed to link them; each of these 10 queries originates from each of 10000 peer of the network subset, and we count the

Query ID	Number Of Answering Node
1	9112
2	8864
3	8998
4	8438
5	8893
6	9114
7	9140
8	8399
9	6976
10	8744

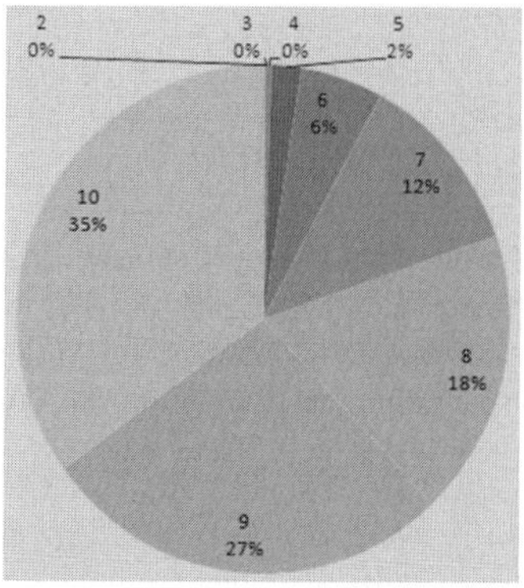

Fig. 1. # of nodes answering sample queries

number of peers that receive an answer for that query exploiting resources over 60000 nodes.

In fig. 1 we report on the left the number of answering nodes for each query (named with IDs); this measures the effectiveness of our algorithm over the data set, and these preliminary results are encouraging, since the worst query is q_9 with about 70% (7000 over 10000) nodes with successful answer; others are better. On the right we show the capability of nodes of resolving queries; the main consideration we derive is that most nodes actually answers most queries (the max is 10), thus being a superpeer is not required, being even an "ordinary" node able to answer queries.

5   Conclusions and Future Work

In this paper, the search of personalized and reliable learning paths within computer assisted learning context has been considered, in particular we proposed an overlay P2P network model that exploits the idea of trustworthiness associated to both learning objects as well as to peers (learners, contents providers). The model has been introduced, together with first simulation results showing the effectiveness of trusting in finding reliable learning resources.

Other issues to be addressed are (1) to perform further experiments to refine the validation of both the model and the data set, (2) consider dynamic issues, i.e. both the transient of the network, when trustworthiness is being assigned, and the evolution of network (peers and/or resources that join/leave the network, or changes in trust), and (3) analyze whether and how trust about resources is influenced by assigned time and difficulty, and whether and how trust about a peer interacts with trust about resources pointed by him.

References

1. Brusilovsky, P., Vassileva, J.: Course sequencing techniques for large-scale web-based education. nternational Journal of Cont. Engineering Education and Lifelong Learning 13(1-2), 75–94 (2003)
2. Carchiolo, V., Longheu, A., Malgeri, M., Mangioni, G.: A model for a web-based learning system. Information Systems Frontiers 9(2-3), 267–282 (2007)
3. Carchiolo, V., Longheu, A., Malgeri, M., Mangioni, G., Nicosia, V.: Applying social behaviours to model trusting. In: Advances in Intelligent and Distributed Computing, proc. of the 1st International Symposium on Intelligent and Distributed Computing IDC 2007, Craiova, Romania, October 2007. Studies in Computational Intelligence, vol. 78. Springer, Heidelberg (2007)
4. Correnti, D.: Trust and e-learning: a proposal. Technical report, Dipartimento di Ingegneria Informatica e Telecomunicazioni - Univ. Catania (2008)
5. Ariadne Foundation. Ariadne
6. Gibson, B.: Enabling an accessible web 2.0. In: W4A 2007: Proceedings of the 2007 international cross-disciplinary conference on Web accessibility (W4A), pp. 1–6. ACM, New York (2007)
7. Learning Technology Standards Commitee IEEE. Learning object metadata, wg12 (2007), http://www.ieeeltsc.org/working-groups/wg12LOM
8. Koning-bastiaan: MERLOT position paper. In: Int. CORDRA Workshop (2005)
9. Levien, R.: Advogato data set (2004)
10. Massa, P., Avesani, P.: Controversial users demand local trust metrics: An experimental study on epinions.com community. In: AAAI, pp. 121–126 (2005)
11. Nejdl, W., Wolf, B., Qu, C., Decker, S., Sintek, M., Naeve, A., Nilsson, M., Palmer, M., Risch, T.: Edutella: a p2p networking infrastructure based on rdf, pp. 604–615. ACM Press, New York (2002)
12. Nejdl, W., Wolf, B., Qu, C., Decker, S., Sintek, M., Naeve, A., Nilsson, M., Palmér, M., Risch, T.: Edutella: a p2p networking infrastructure based on rdf. In: WWW 2002: Proceedings of the 11th international conference on World Wide Web, pp. 604–615. ACM, New York (2002)
13. Santos, O.C., Barrera, C., Boticario, J.: An overview of alfanet: An adaptive ilms based on standards. In: De Bra, P.M.E., Nejdl, W. (eds.) AH 2004. LNCS, vol. 3137, pp. 429–432. Springer, Heidelberg (2004)
14. Sasakura, M., Yamasaki, S.: A framework for adaptive e-learning systems in higher education with information visualization. In: IV 2007: Proceedings of the 11th International Conference Information Visualization, Washington, DC, USA, pp. 819–824. IEEE Computer Society Press, Los Alamitos (2007)
15. Steinmetz, R., Wehrle, K. (eds.): Peer-to-Peer Systems and Applications. LNCS, vol. 3485. Springer, Heidelberg (2005)
16. Stiubiener, Ruggiero, Rosatelli: An approach to personalisation in e-learning. In: VII IEEE International Conference on Advanced Learning Technologies, pp. 189–193. IEEE Computer Society Press, Los Alamitos (2007)
17. Tan, A.-H., Teo, C.: Learning user profiles for personalized information dissemination. In: Neural Networks Proceedings, 1998. IEEE World Congress on Computational Intelligence. The 1998 IEEE International Joint Conference on, vol. 1, pp. 183–188 (1998)
18. ADL Technical Team. Scorm 2004 3rd edition documentation suite (2004), http://www.adlnet.gov/scorm/index.aspx

Advanced Tool to Develop the Assessment Process in Collaborative e-Learning Environments

Roberto Barchino, José-María Gutiérrez, Mario Triguero,
Luis de-Marcos, and Lourdes Jiménez

Computer Science Department. University of Alcalá
Ctra. Barcelona km 33.6. Alcalá de Henares, Spain
{roberto.barchino,josem.gutierrez,mario.triguero,luis.demarcos,
lou.jimenez}@uah.es

Abstract. This work presents a new method of assessment configuration based in a Markup Language. The work aims to obtain an interoperable and reusable design of assessment plans. This configuration allows the establishment of basic assessment attributes in learning process. These attributes can be exported and imported by a Learning Management System – LMS to achieve the configurations' reusability. The main objective of the assessment configurations is to reduce the required time to configure assessment activities, simplifying and automating them.

Keywords: e-Learning, assessment, learning management system (LMS), test, learning technology.

1 Introduction

Information Technologies have widely spread in our society and its influence in the learning process is very important at present time. This influence has lead to the rise of new specific techniques for teaching and learning, called e-learning. The used technological key in e-learning is Internet and it is used to perform most of the activities of the learning process, as proposed in the Learning Technology System Architecture (LTSA) from the Learning Technology Standards Committee of IEEE [1]. Figure 1 shows a diagram including main elements, relations and actions of the architecture.

This architecture defines the basic entities found in e-learning systems: learners, teachers, contents and assessments; and it defines the term "assessment" as the evaluation reached by the learner, being the degree of assimilation of knowledge and abilities. These knowledge and abilities must be established a priori and the achieved level must be obtained through some evaluation tools.

There are some modeling languages for e-learning systems. These languages offer semantic notations for the creation of learning objects which can be reused. Most of them are focused on the creation of teacher tools to design the whole process. The European Committee for Standardization in the Learning Technologies Standard Observatory presents the most important languages [2] which are: OUNL EML, IMS Learning Design, PALO, CDF, LMML, TARGETEAM and TML/Netquest.

M.D. Lytras et al. (Eds.): WSKS 2008, CCIS 19, pp. 229–236, 2008.
© Springer-Verlag Berlin Heidelberg 2008

As the focus of these languages is the whole learning process, the assessment process remains undefined in many of its characteristics. For the assessment process through Internet, the same activities set for Computer-Assisted Assessment (CAA) can be applied in question presentation, answer check, score, examination interpretation and analysis. So, it can be said that CAA reinforces the classic evaluation process trying to apply—as itself—the use of Information Technologies as support. Also, Internet assessment systems, as a type of CAA, make this affirmation suitable.

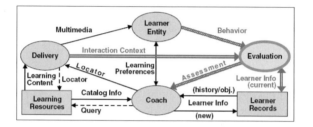

Fig. 1. Learning Technology System Architecture

To help in the creation of assessment process, IMS Global Learning Consortium, Inc., proposes the most relevant specification, QTI (Question & Test Interoperability) [3]. QTI defines a model to represent questions and test data and their corresponding results. The reuse of the data is aided by the definition of a XML-based language to represent it. Nevertheless, the specification focuses on a really low level and detailed part of the process, which is only useful to represent the involved data in the assessment, not the process itself.

To fill the existing gap between the global definition of a learning process and the detailed specification of the evaluation contents, and to achieve the possibility of modelling the assessment process as a unique reusable piece, we propose a new method of assessment configuration. Figure 2 represents the relation between the assessment configuration based on assessment attributes using this tool and the lower level QTI elements.

2 Assessment Configuration

In order to achieve an effective assessment configuration and to allow its reuse in further learning processes, the proposed language must be abstract enough. Looking into these concepts with more depth, we find that:

- Reusable: capability of being reused in some different learning processes without making any change or adjustment (if the configuration fits the specific necessities)
- Effective: capability of the modelled assessment to represent the established objectives and to obtain the degree of achievement from the learners.

In our experience, four assessment types are usually found in every learning process:

- Initial Assessment: Carried out before the real beginning of the course. This assessment aims to record the initial learners' knowledge level related to the subject of the course.
- Final Assessment: Carried out after the end of the course. The objective is to check if the learners reached the desired level of knowledge.
- Module Assessment: Made at the end of every chapter in the course. This test can help to make a continuous evaluation or it can be used to help the learners check their evolution.
- Free Assessment: Without time limit, this type of evaluation allows the learners to check their progress and the level of their reached knowledge. Also, they can find problems and ask for help if needed.

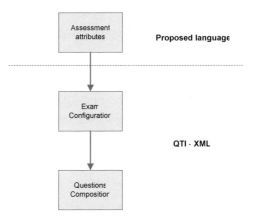

Fig. 2. Abstraction Level

2.1 Assessment Attributes

The required attributes to represent the characteristics of every one of these types of evaluation have been identified. The analysis has lead to a group of parameters available to the learning manager in order to program the activities. These attributes are:

- Type of exam. This allows establishing general characteristics of the exam such as direct questions or multiple choice questions.
- Number of answers for each question. This attribute identifies the whole number of offered answers for each question. The exam will use the same number of answers.
- Number of correct answers for each question. This attribute, which is also global, sets the number of right answers, to allow creating single or multiple choice tests.
- Number of questions per exam.
- Maximum result. Associated to the best combination of answers.
- Minimum result. Associated to the worst combination of answers.

- Needed percentage for success. The percentage of correct answers needed to pass, which is considered by the learning manager.
- Duration. The time frame in which the exam will be available in the Learning Management System - LMS.
- Relevant. Attribute which identifies the needed results for scoring the final results of the course.
- Mandatory. Attribute which establishes if the exam must be fulfilled or not to achieve success in the whole course.
- Number of tries. This number can be configured by the learning manager.
- Exam can be continued. With this option, the learning manager can establish if the exam can be answered in different sessions.
- Correct answers showed. It determines wheter the students have access to the correct answers for the exam.
- Evaluation weight. In this attribute, the manager establishes the weight of each exam in the learning process.

Since the manager configures the platform using the attributes, in our case the LMS EDVI [4] [5] [6] completes the related activities to implement the described assessment (with automatic implementation of the required tests to perform the assessment). The user interface to set the attributes is shown in figure 3 (in Spanish).

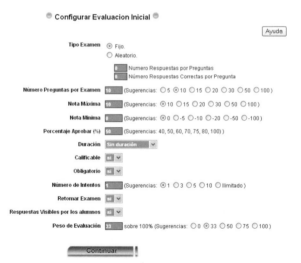

Fig. 3. Configuration Assessment Interface

3   Definition Language

The language proposed is defined as a XML dialect. One main objective in the language definition has been to allow the import and export of assessment configurations by the LMS. These configurations are intended to be compatible with the

Table 1. CAML.xsd file

```xml
<?xml version="1.0" encoding="UTF-8"?>

<xsd:schema xmlns:xsd="http://www.w3.org/2001/XMLSchema" xmlns:ns=http://cc.uah.es/barchi/CAML
xmlns="http://cc.uah.es/barchi/CAML" targetNamespace=http://cc.uah.es/barchi/CAML
elementFormDefault="qualified">

        <xsd:element name="assessment">
                <xsd:complexType>
                        <xsd:sequence>
<xsd:element name="test" type="reg-test" maxOccurs="4"/>
                        </xsd:sequence>
                </xsd:complexType>
        </xsd:element>

        <xsd:complexType name="reg-test">
                <xsd:sequence>
 <xsd:element name="availability" type="ns:type_availability"/>
<xsd:element name="questions-number"      type="xsd:integer"/>
<xsd:element name="answers-number"        type="xsd:integer"/>

<xsd:element name="correct-answers-number" type="xsd:integer"/>
<xsd:element name="maximum-qualification" type="xsd:integer"/>
<xsd:element name="minimum-qualification"  type="xsd:integer"/>
<xsd:element name="percentage-pass"        type="xsd:integer"/>
<xsd:element name="times-number"           type="xsd:integer"/>
<xsd:element name="weight-test"            type="xsd:integer"/>
                </xsd:sequence>

<xsd:attribute name="test-sched" type="type_sched"  use="required"/>
<xsd:attribute name="score"      type="type_yes-no" use="optional" default="no"/>
<xsd:attribute name="mandatory" type="type_yes-no" use="optional" default="no"/>
<xsd:attribute name="session"    type="type_yes-no" use="optional" default="no"/>
<xsd:attribute name="visible-answers " type="type_yes-no" use="optional" default="no"/>
<xsd:attribute name="type-questions"   type="tipo_fixed-random" use="optional" default="random"/>
        </xsd:complexType>

        <xsd:complexType name="type_availability">
                <xsd:sequence>
<xsd:element name="since" type="xsd:date"/>
<xsd:element name="to"      type="xsd:date"/>
        </xsd:sequence>
        </xsd:complexType>

        <xsd:simpleType name="type_yes-no">
                <xsd:restriction base="xsd:string">
                        <xsd:enumeration value="yes"/>
                        <xsd:enumeration value="no"/>
                </xsd:restriction>
        </xsd:simpleType>
        <xsd:simpleType name="type_fixed-random">
                <xsd:restriction base="xsd:string">
                        <xsd:enumeration value="fixed"/>
                        <xsd:enumeration value="random"/>
                </xsd:restriction>
        </xsd:simpleType>
        <xsd:simpleType name="type_sched">
                <xsd:restriction base="xsd:string">
                        <xsd:enumeration value="initial"/>
                        <xsd:enumeration value="final"/>
                        <xsd:enumeration value="free"/>
                        <xsd:enumeration value="module"/>
                </xsd:restriction>
        </xsd:simpleType>
</xsd:schema>
```

Table 2. Example of Assessment Configuration

```xml
<?xml version="1.0" encoding="UTF-8"?>

<assessment xmlns='http://cc.uah.es/barchi/CAML'
            xmlns:xsi='http://www.w3.org/2001/XMLSchema-instance'
            xsi:schemaLocation='http://cc.uah.es/barchi/CAML CAML.xsd'>


<test type-test="initial">
                    <availability>
                        <since>2006-11-09</since>
                        <to>2006-11-15</to>
                    </availability>
<questions-number>10</questions-number>
<answers-number>3</answers-number>
<correct-answers-number>1</correct-answers-number>
<maximum-qualification>10</maximum-qualification>
<minimum-qualification>0</minimum-qualification>
<percentage-pass>50</percentage-pass>
<times-number>5</times-number>
<weight-test>10</weight-test>
</test>

 <test type-test="module" obligatory="no" score="no" session="no" type-questions="fixed"  visible-answers="no">
                    <availability>
                            <since>2006-11-15</since>
                            <to>2006-11-15</to>
                    </availability>
<questions-number>20</questions-number>
<answers-number>5</answers-number>
<correct-answers-number>2</correct-answers-number>
<maximum-qualification>10</maximum-qualification>
<minimum-qualification>-3</minimum-qualification>
<percentage-pass>50</percentage-pass>
<times-number>1</times-number>
<weight-test>20</weight-test>
</test>

 <test type-test="free" obligatory="no" score="yes" session="yes"
      type-questions="random" visible-answers="yes">
                    <availability>
                            <since>2006-11-16</since>
                            <to>2006-11-17</to>
                    </availability>
<questions-number>216</questions-number>
<answers-number>5</answers-number>
<correct-answers-number>1</correct-answers-number>
<maximum-qualification>90</maximum-qualification>
<minimum-qualification>-10</minimum-qualification>
<percentage-pass>70</percentage-pass>
<times-number>10</times-number>
<weight-test>70</weight-test>
</test>

</assessment>
```

SCORM[1] content packaging in order to include them inside the SCORM ZIP package. Another main objective is the definitions' reuse. It will be possible to use the same assessment configuration in some learning process—related or not—and in future editions of the same process. There are two possibilities to define a XML dialect: XML Xchema[2] and DTDs [3]. The language proposed is defined using XML Schema because of its richness in types. Table 1 contains the *CAML.xsd* file that represents the dialect proposed for making the assessment definitions.

4 Example

This section includes an example of assessment configuration (table 2), as it is defined in the XML Schema. As such, this example is a well-formed and valid XML document. This example shows an assessment configuration which establishes the characteristics of three of four possible assessments: the initial assessment, module assessment and free assessment.

5 Conclusions

This paper presents Configuration Assessment Mark-up Language for helping learning managers to build assessment related tasks in e-learning systems. The proposed language allows setting assessments characteristics by the use of high level and reusable definitions. This method has been designed and implemented taking into account the results of studies made by Sunion (a learning company), which carried out several surveys to its students using EDVI as its Learning Management System (LMS).

We also describe the main results. The first result is the time savings obtained by learning managers which can be employed in other teaching activities. The second result is the student's initial knowledge about the assessment process as it is fixed in a previously defined configuration file. This issue is highly appreciated by the students as they know the relevance of activities at the beginning. This knowledge helps to decrease the number of drop-outs and increase the student's motivation.

Currently this language is being used in the inner courses of the Computer Science Department of the University of Alcala. The second planned stage includes its use in every learning process performed by this Department.

---

[1] Sharable Content Object Reference Model (SCORM) is a collection of standards and specifications for web-based e-learning. SCORM is a specification of the Advanced Distributed Learning (ADL) Initiative, which comes out of the Office of the United States Secretary of Defense. This model defines, among other questions, how content may be packaged into a transferable and reusable ZIP file.

[2] The XML Schema allows defining the elements and structure of XML documents using and XML dialect and with a wide variety of data types.

[3] The Document Type Definition allows defining the contents and structure of XML documents using a specific syntax and including a limited and simple set of data types.

Acknowledgements

This research is funded by the University of Alcalá FPI research staff education program and by the Spanish Ministry of Industry, Tourism and Commerce Plan Avanza program (grants PAV-070000-2007-103 and TSI-020100-2008-23).

References

[1] Learning Technology System Architecture – LTSA Home Page. Current LTSA specification (2006), http://edutool.com/ltsa/
[2] European Committee for Standarization. Information Society Standarization System. Learning Technologies Standards Observatory (2007),
    http://www.cen.eu/cenorm/homepage.htm
[3] IMS Global Learning Consortium: Question and Test Interoperability Specification (2007), http://www.imsglobal.org/question/index.html
[4] Barchino, R., Hilera, J.R., García, E., Gutiérrez, J.M.: EDVI: Un Sistema de Apoyo a la Enseñanza Presencial Basado en Internet. VII Jornadas de Enseñanza Universitaria de la Informática – JENUI-2001. Palma de Mallorca. España (2001)
[5] Barchino, R., Jiménez, M.L., Gutiérrez, J.A.: EDVI Pro 2004: Un Sistema de Apoyo a la Enseñanza Presencial Basado en Internet. In: 3ra. Conferencia Ibero-Americana en Sistemas, Cibernética e Informática – CISCI 2004. Orlando. EEUU (2004)
[6] Barchino, R., Oton, S., Gutiérrez, J.M.: An Example of Learning Management System. In: IADIS Virtual Multi Conference on Computer Science and Information Systems MCCSIS – 2005 (2005)

Collaborative Work and Multi-criteria Organization of Web Educational Resources: A Theoretical Framework

Alivizos Sofos and Apostolos Kostas

University of the Aegean, Primary Education Department, Dimokratias 1,
85100 Rhodes, Greece
lsofos@rhodes.aegean.gr, apkostas@aegean.gr

Abstract. In this paper we quote a theoretical framework of information organization for the systemization of web-based educational resources. Based on this framework we present an ongoing experimental system aiming at the establishment of alternative communication and collaboration scenarios among educators. For an objective substantiation of information, various evaluation criteria have been developed such as Functional, Pedagogic and Didactic ones.

Keywords: Learning, Collaboration, Evaluation, Knowledge.

1 Introduction

Human Learning is one of the most fascinating and complicated phenomenon, taking place through the whole Human Life Cycle. *Media Didactic*, as a sub-domain of Pedagogy and Didactic, heavily quotes the learning process with a variety of models, which are classified in the context of three main theories: *Behaviorism*, *Gnosticism* and *Constructivism* (Table 1).

A common place of these theories is comprised by the acknowledgement that:

(a) Learning is the outcome of practice
(b) Individual's capabilities deployment is activated through its environment
(c) Learning process is time-consuming and heavily depends on the growth level of the individual [1]. Knowledge of various learning models by the educators forms a critical success factor for the teaching process with new Information and Communication Technologies (ICT), as well as a foundation for their work during design and analysis of content and activities.

Learning models could be systematized on the basis of either the individual, or the environment. In our work, we quote learning as a procedure, during which an individual actively effects with its environment and with other individuals, thus *learning*, *activity theory*, *distributed cognition*, *connectivism* and *flexible learning*.

2 Theoretical Aspects

Current research on learning, acknowledges that learning is directly related on specific situations and conditions of actions of the individual and each individual

M.D. Lytras et al. (Eds.): WSKS 2008, CCIS 19, pp. 237–244, 2008.

Table 1. Learning Theories

	Behaviorism	Gnosticism	Constructivism Social Constructivism
Learning Paradigm	Action/Reaction	Activities/Problem solving	Construction
Pedagogy Strategy	Educator Oriented	Support	Support and Collaboration
Main Idea	Behavior	Cognition	Reaction
Educator	Authority	Tutor	Coach
Aims	Input/Output Relation	Discovery Learning and Problem Solving	Complex and Authentic Situation
Learning	Passive Learning Pool	Linear Information Processing System	Closed Information Processing System
Evaluation	Record: Performance, Evaluation, Facts	Knowledge (verification of medal conceptions)	Ability to Recognize Problem Dimensions and Solutions
Learning Content	Small Monogrammed Units	Complex Environments	Unstructured Reality, Communication Environment
Theoretical Approaches	Linear Programmable Teaching [2] Programmable Teaching with Crowder Multiple Choices [3] Didactic Design [4]	Structural Construction [5] Cybernetics [6] Discovering Learning [7] Information Processing [4] Connectionism [8]	Social-cultural Theory [9] Situated Learning [10] Cognitive Apprenticeship [11]

possesses experiences as a knowledge, which can be utilized during collective dialogue and communication within the community [11]. This theoretical foundation explains how individuals are learning within certain circumstances and groups and how these individuals are evolved by transforming their own cognitive concepts. Moreover, research on Symbolic Reaction has lead to a most likely explanation of the above fact, from a sociological respective [12], where the individuals construct their own subjective world within various cultural and social reactions and communication procedures. During these learning and evolving procedures, individuals gain the capability of autonomous assimilation, evaluation and utilization of knowledge.

The above approach and according to [13], leads to a theoretical direction known as *Interactive Constructivism*, which actually states that the provocation of action and reaction situations are taking place not within interpersonal level but within the environment, while at the same time, these situations are stimulating the constructivistic potentials of the individual, i.e. acquisition of knowledge and skills. Individual's overall progress is taking place during this interpretative construction procedure, where individuals process, in a subjective manner, the requirements, i.e. stimulations from the outer environment, the communication and the collaboration with others, such as groups or communities of interest or practice. Within such communication correlations, individuals are working on a common subject around which are self-organized and exchanging estimations and approaches. One of the main goals of a community of practice is the "smart" evolution and learning of the individuals via their participation in activities of common interest. In some cases, such as the *virtual communities*, a network of relations could be formatted based on a common social identity. On the educational domain of interest, usually small groups of educators are formatted while working on the basis of predefined subjects and time-schedules [14]. According to [15] there are differences between the learning communities models (Fig. 1), which are related with the (a) learning type (formal or informal), (b) underlying technology infrastructure (platforms or simple means such as forums, chats, etc.), (c) motives of the participants and (d) functional operations of the learning community.

3 System Model

The proposed system in this work follows the Knowledge Management Model of Munich [16], which has been designed as a regulating system (Fig. 2).

Goals
Targeting of goals by the community members is the reference point for the upcoming work and communication, where the point of interest for the community is being established, as well as the type and functionality of the collaboration environment. In our system, this reflects to the configuration phase of the web-based environment where a preliminary user requirement analysis has taken place among the participants educators in order to focus on their main interests, thus resulting to the following requirements list:

- design, development and use of pedagogic criteria for the *evaluation* of educational resources on the Web
- *documentation* and *publication* of educational content on the Web
- *access* to the recorded educational content
- evaluation of educational recourses using *pedagogic criteria*
- evaluation of educational recourses using *personal opinions* and *educational experiences*
- communication and common sharing of experiences and views between the participants

In general, the overall point of interest for the community is the deeper understanding of educational resources via a multi-criteria analysis, the establishment of an educational "orientation" for those resources and the establishment of a communication framework between the educators.

Knowledge Presentation
Knowledge presentation causes the necessity of *information recording*, in our case of *web–based educational resources*, in the form of an objective substantiation of information. This substantiation follows the *User-Centric* model of information organization [17], based on the process of multi-criteria evaluation [18], where for each information unit, such as web page, document, etc., certain categories and subcategories of standardized criteria (Table 2) has been determined, forming a micro-level where users are interacting with the system. These criteria where developed based on bibliography research ([19], [20], [21, [22], [23], [24], [25], [26]) and on focus groups with educators, as well. Within this context, **Taxonomy** is being used, referring to the process of an exhaustive and mutual excluding arrangement of information entities, on the basis of their similarities/dissimilarities. Main outcome of this process is the *taxonomy* of our system, namely a list of categories/subcategories of educational interest, hierarchical

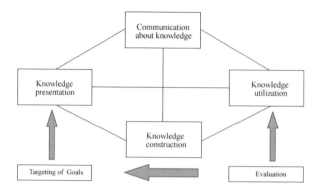

Fig. 1. Munich KM Model with its fundamental attributes: Goals, Knowledge Presentation, Communication, Knowledge Construction, Exploitation of Knowledge, Evaluation

and evolutionary structured, subjective and subject to alterations. *Information* is perceived as the *composition of signs*, either equivalent to a message or representing an intellectual unity. **Knowledge** is perceived as a process (not as a final outcome) that transforms information relative to a domain of interest, according to the sensible-emotional background of the individual, resulting to the construction of a subjective meaning [12]. Finally, a differentiation of knowledge in two levels is taking place, namely **Implicit**, which contains cognitive and technical knowledge and is not easy populated and **Explicit**, which is populated on a well-formed communication code [27].

Table 2. Main Categories of Evaluation Criteria

Functionality	Pedagogy	Didactic
Legal Authority	Content	Media Operations
Transparency	Structure/Design	Media Dimensions
Efficiency/Ergonomic	Reference Group	Learning States
Media Elements	Educational Levels	Didactic Transformations
Navigation	School Subjects	Descriptive Re-thinking

Communication

It refers to the personal/team knowledge level, where suggesting annotations, comments, remarks and criticism over the transmitted knowledge, subjective evaluation and exchange of experiences over web educational resources are taking place. This leads to the expansion of the traditional educational and training environments and creation of collaborative ones, where participants are codifying their personal knowledge and experiences, communicate with each-other and test the knowledge directly on the didactic process. In this context, *collaboration* within the system (Fig. 3) is perceived as the communicative load between educators. *Specific interest of individuals on a common scientific field* is the reference point and constitutes a *network* [14]. Knowledge distribution and management is effectively promoted within a network of learning, which in social sciences is defined as a set of individuals that develops relations in a specific manner and thus composes a system. In these *social networks*,

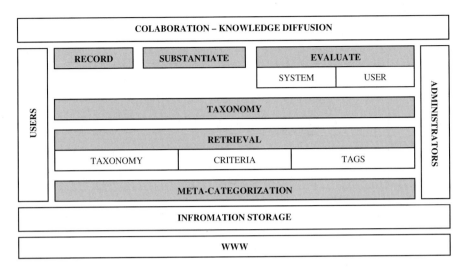

Fig. 2. System Organization

information is created and activated in particular nodes of the Web, which addresses certain needs in the framework of a specific problem [28].

Knowledge Construction

It is the result of the communication process. New knowledge does not consist of new elements only, but of communication tools, inter-evaluation and comments on testified experiences. This leads to the creation of a collective-dialogical framework of meta-information, which can help educators select content. Given that the system rationalizes content through the evaluation, rating, annotation and commenting processes, it actually provides a transformation of the *formal* knowledge to that of *informal* knowledge, which can be shared among web community members.

According to the theoretical model of *situated cognition and distributed knowledge* [29], [30], knowledge is deducted through collective procedures. Distributed knowledge refers to the fact that personal knowledge must be perceived in the framework of a team. Representation of the individual's constructions and meanings are positioned within the community in a state of potential acceptance, aiming at the development of a common *"language of representations and knowledge"* [31]. More specific, within the system a systematic substantiation of the taxonomy is taking place, with information categorization, presentation and reformation on the basis of new content [32], [33]. This methodology lead to a transformation process [18] where initial information, after having been documented, reverts to formal knowledge in the domain of interest (Fig. 4). System content remains in relatively low level until information is been classified, rated, annotated and content are enhanced with new meta-information of added value. This new content adds explicit as well as implicit knowledge to the system. This process comprises a basic dimension of knowledge construction for every form of social organization (physical or virtual) and can be integrated in electronic environments like a community of learning.

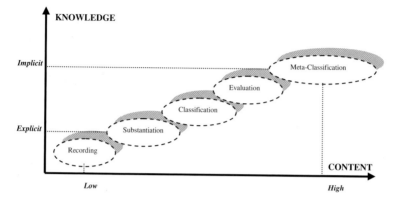

Fig. 3. From information to knowledge

Exploitation of Knowledge

It is related with the application of knowledge for achieving personal goals. Recording of individual's experiences, which are gained through this knowledge exploitation, forms a very important material that feedbacks the members of the collaboration environment. In our case, knowledge consists from the substantiated classified content which refers to educational resources and the annotations, comments, rating and personal experiences on it. This enriched content can be used form the educators either as an *educational archive* or as a *source* for the creation of activities and educational content within the classroom.

Evaluation

Evaluation process has a central role especially on those collaboration environments that evolves to a community of learning. Preliminary goals of the community members are evaluated against their accomplishments and new goals are reformulated aiming to the fulfillment of current needs and interests of the team. Evaluation in out framework refers to the process of evaluating, not the content itself, but the strategy and methodology that educators or a focus group of educators followed for the discovery and substantiation of a number of resources on a certain domain of interest. For example, exploitation of the produced knowledge on recourses for physical sciences for primary education, may lead to the conclusion that the quality is inappropriate, because either the original information was collected based on a wrong methodology, or that the substantiation process was wrong. This creates reaction and feedback to the system, in order for the educators to regulate their strategy.

4   Research Considerations

The proposed framework is negotiating learning, knowledge construction and interaction within a community of educators. A theoretical model was formulated covering aspects of learning within a community of educators. Moreover, a model of knowledge management was presented and analyzed. More specific, our work is exploiting aspects on:

(a) **Media Didactic**, like analysis and application of *complex evaluation criteria on educational content*, exploitation of *types, quality and media elements* of educational resources for the primary education and their *application to the classroom teaching*, estimation of the *added value* of the web-based materials *against* classical educational materials, like school handbook, images, etc.

(b) **Information Organization**, like analysis of relation between the taxonomy structure and the meta-classification of content based on user annotation, commenting, and rating.

(c) **Community Interaction,** like educators profile, public dialogue on educational content, "reputation" of educational resources on the Web and patterns of self-organizing knowledge groups between participants.

In the current pilot phase, this model is implemented as an experimental web environment in the University of the Aegean, Department of Primary Education, where we observe (a) content evolution through the substantiation of information, (b) the process of knowledge construction from information through the transformation process, (c) participating activation dynamics within the community of interest of the participants educators and (c) the potential of evolving to a network of knowledge.

References

1. Kron, F.W., Sofos, A.: Media Didactic. Gutenberg, Athens (2007)
2. Skinner, B.F.: Wissenschaft und menschliches Verhalten. Kindler Verlag, München (1973)
3. Klaus, D.: Eine Analyse der Programmierungstechniken. In: Glaser, R. (Hrsg.) (ed.): Programmiertes Lernen und Unterrichtstechnologien, Deutsche Ausgabe Flechsig, K.-H./Schultze, W. Cornelsen Verlag, Berlin (1971)
4. Gange, R.M.: Die Bedingungen des menschlichen Lernens. Beltz Verlag, Hannover/Dortmund/Darmstadt/Berlin (1980)
5. Piaget, J.: Theorien und Methoden der modernen Erziehung. Fisher Verlag, Wien/Zürich/München (1972)
6. Cube, F.v.: Kybernetische Grundlagen des Lehrens und Lernens. Kettler Verlag, Stuttgart (1965)
7. Bruner, J.S.: Der Prozess der Erziehung 5. Schwan Verlag, Aufl. Berlin/Düsseldorf (1980)
8. Maturana, H.R., Varela, F.J.: Der Baum der Erkenntnis. Die biologischen Wurzeln menschlichen Erkenntnis. Goldmman Verlag, Bern (1987)
9. Vygotsky, L.: Notion and Language. Knowledge Publications, Athens (1988)
10. Mandl, H., Gruber, H., Renkl, A.: Situiertes Lernen in multimedialen Lernumgebungen. In: Klimsa, I. (ed.) Information und Lernen mit Multimedia und Internet, pp. 139–150. BeltzPVU, Weinheim (2002)
11. Brown, J.S., Collins, A., Duguid, P.: Situated Learning and the Culture of Learning. Education Researcher 18(1), 32–42 (1989)
12. Kron, F.W.: Grundwissen Padagogik' 6. Auf. Reinbardt, Munchen (2001)
13. Oevermann, U.: Sozialisationstheorie. Ansätze zu einer soziologischen Sozialisationstheorie und ihre Konsequenzen für eine allgemeine soziologische Analyse. In: Lüschen, G. (ed.) Deutsche Soziologie seit 1945. Entwicklungsrichtungen und Praxisbezug. Kölner Zeitschrift für Soziologie und Sozialpsychologie, pp. 143–168 (1979)

14. Doering, N.: Sozialpsychologie des Internets. Die Bedutung des Internets fuer Kommunikationsprozesse, Identitaet, soziale Beziehungen und Gruppen. Bern, Toronto, Seatle, Horgefe, Goettingen (1999)
15. Seufert, S.: Virtuelle Lerngemeinschaften: Konzept und Potenziale für die Aus-und Weiterbildung. Ergebnisbericht des Bundesinstitut für Berufsbildung (BIBB) (2002)
16. Reinmann-Rothmeier, G., Mandl, H., Erlach, C.: Wissensmanagement in der weiterbildung. In: Trippelt, R. (ed.) Handbuch Erwachsenenbildung/Weiterbildung s, pp. 753–768. Leske + Budrich, Opladen (1999)
17. Sofos, A., Kostas, A.: Models of Information Organization: A Web-based Environment for Multi-criteria Organization of Educational Resources. In: 4th International Conference in Open and Distance Learning (ICODL2007), Athens, Greece. Open Access and Distance Education, Forms of Democracy in Education (2007)
18. Sofos, A., Kostas, A.: Development of Pedagogy Criteria for the Substantiation and Evaluation of Educational Resources on the Web. In: 4th National Conference ICT in Primary Education, Pireus, Greece (2007)
19. Dragulanescu, N.: Website Quality Evaluations: Criteria and Tools. The International Information & Library Review 34(3), 247–254 (2002)
20. Olsina L., Lafuente G., Rossi G.: Specifying Quality Characteristics and Attributes for Websites, Retrieved on 10 September 2006 (2001),
    http://plinks.ebscohost.com/ehost/results;vid=4&hid=1&sid=7f
    679419-0354-45cc-834c-895796963fb3%40sessionmgr4
21. Beck, E. S.: The Good, The Bad & The Ugly or, Why It's a Good Idea to Evaluate Web Sources (2006), Retrieved on 10 September 2006,
    http://lib.nmsu.edu/instruction/evalcrit.html
22. Lesley University, Evaluating Web Sites Criteria for the Classroom (2005), Retrieved on 01 September 2006, http://www.lesley.edu/library/guides/
    research/evaluating_web.html
23. Kapoun, J.: Teaching undergrads WEB evaluation: A guide for library instruction. C&RL News, pp. 522–523 (1998)
24. McInerney, C.R., Bird, N.J.: Assessing Website quality in context: retrieving information about genetically modified food on the Web, Retrieved on 10 September 2006 (2005),
    http://informationr.net/ir/10-2/paper213.html
25. Payton, T.: Web Evaluation, Retrieved on 10 September 2006 (1997),
    http://www.siec.k12.in.us/west/edu/rubric3.htm
26. McLachlan, K.: WWW cyberguide ratings for content evaluation, Retrieved on 10 September 2006 (2002), http://www.cyberbee.com/content.pdf
27. Polyani, M.: The Tacit Dimension. Lawrence Elbaum Associates, London (1967)
28. De Paula, R.: Active Learning Networks: Designing for Computer Supported Social Networks in Special Education Environments. In: ECSCW 2003 Workshop on Social Networks, Helsinki (2003)
29. Kerres, M.: Multimediale und telemediale Lernumgebungen. Konzeption und Entwicklungen. München (1998)
30. Komis, B.: Introduction to Educational Applications of Information and Communication Technologies. New Technologies Publications, Athens (2004)
31. Schmidt, S.: Geschichten und Diskursen. Abschied vom Konstruktivismus. Hamburg (2003)
32. Baile, D.K.: Typologies and Taxonomies An Introduction to Classification Techniques. SAGE Publications, Thousand Oaks (1980)
33. DELPHI: Information Intelligence-Content Classification and the Enterprise Taxonomy Practice, DELPHI Group Report (2004)

Knowledge, Knowledge Security, and Meta-knowledge

Bogdan D. Czejdo[1] and Tadeusz Morzy[2]

[1] Department of Mathematics and Computer Science
Fayetteville State University
Fayetteville, NC 28301, USA
bczejdo@uncfsu.ed
[2] Institute of Computing Science
Poznan University of Technology
Poznan, Poland
tmorzy@put.poznan.pl

Abstract. One of very important activities in an Information Security course is the case analysis of information security violations. This paper addresses several aspects of knowledge security violations. The case study describes the type of knowledge that was stolen and the process of knowledge security violations. The meta-knowledge about knowledge security violation is also identified.

Keywords: Knowledge Representation, Knowledge Security, Meta-Knowledge.

1 Introduction

One of very important activities in an Information Security course is to analyze cases of information security violations. The case study included in our Information Security course was based on the article "Cyberthieves stole 1.3 million names, Monster says" published by USA Today [1]. This case study was very useful for variety of reasons. Firstly, it described the type knowledge that was stolen. Next, it described the important process of knowledge security violation and did it in a very concise way. Lastly, the meta-knowledge about knowledge security violation could be created relatively easy based on its concise description.

Very intensive practical and theoretical research continues in the Knowledge Representation area [6, 7, 8, 16, 17]. This research includes continuing efforts to find the best representation of abstract concepts and the relationships between them. There are many challenges in that research, one of them is that it is very difficult to find a uniform modeling language to describe different types of abstract concepts.

In this paper, we use the notation of Universal Modeling Language (UML) [2, 12] mostly for ontology modeling. The UML, though created and used for database and software design, is not specific to software design. This kind of modeling has been already used for a long time to represent a variety of ontologies [13]. The UML ontology modeling is characterized by concise graphical notation, availability of simple tools, and the possibility to use informal specifications if necessary. It can be very useful for ontology specifications, especially in the initial phase when all details are not clear, and as one of the graphical interfaces for ontologies. Therefore, UML

M.D. Lytras et al. (Eds.): WSKS 2008, CCIS 19, pp. 245–252, 2008.
© Springer-Verlag Berlin Heidelberg 2008

diagrams can still play an important role for ontologies even though new notations such as OWL [15] and new tools such as SWOOP and Protégé allow for powerful operations on ontologies including queries not readily available in typical UML tools.

In our previous research we have found that creating a proper model for higher-level abstract concepts might require UML extensions [3, 4, 5]. Even with these extensions, however, the managing the complexity of real life knowledge bases is unsatisfactory. For example, building complex knowledge bases can be accelerated, by appling phases in modeling. By making clear the differences between phases we can apply the step-by-step reasoning required to create a complex knowledge.

Such knowledge bases can be an excellent educational tool. The system can be very useful for students as well as teachers. If, teachers could generate questions based on such knowledge bases and analyze the answers based on such system. The analysis can help the teachers understand the student precision level. It can also help to control the scope of additional background knowledge required i.e. knowledge beyond existing knowledge bases.

In this paper, we discuss modeling based on UML. First, we discuss how to create an ontology that can be used to capture the structure of the database from a sample domain specified in a natural language. Next, we capture knowledge of the whole system including the database. We also describe queries based on diagrams.

2 Knowledge Processing Methodology

Our Knowledge Processing Methodology is applicable for situations to describe systems with the ability to store some information. Such methodology is especially

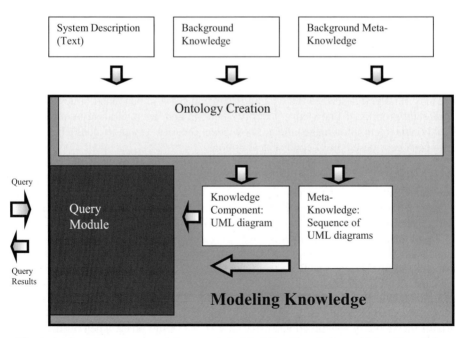

Fig. 1. An Overview of a general framework for Modeling Knowledge and Meta-Knowledge

useful when discussing Information Security problems hence we need to identify the stored information (knowledge).

The general framework of our methodology is shown in Fig 1. It involves relatively independent modules: Ontology Creation Module and Query Module.

Ontology creation involves, generally, concepts and relationship identification. Such ontology can be represented by a diagram e.g. UML. UML diagrams can be used for different purposes: to capture the knowledge or knowledge about the knowledge (meta-knowledge). We refer to these components as Knowledge Component and Meta-Knowledge Component. In our case study, we simplify the Knowledge Component to a simple Database Component.

3   UML Diagram as a Database Model

Let us start with typical use of UML diagrams as database models. As our running example we will use the newspaper article entitled "Cyberthieves stole 1.3 million names" [1]. Let us consider the first sentence (Text Fragment 1) from this article "Monster Worldwide acknowledged Thursday that intruders swiped sensitive data for at least 1.3 million job seekers from its popular employment website". The goal here is to extract from the text an information (knowledge) describing database structure i.e. maintained by Monster Worldwide and subject of an attack. We see that the database contains data about Job Seekers but the complexity of database is initially unknown.

Let us consider the second statement (Text Fragment 2) "The company issued a statement saying it shut down the "rogue server" where the stolen data was being stored and that only names, addresses, phone numbers and e-mails were found". This text fragment clarifies that the database contains at least names, addresses, phone numbers and e-mails of job seekers. We can represent such a database by a simple class diagram containing only one class Job Seeker Data.

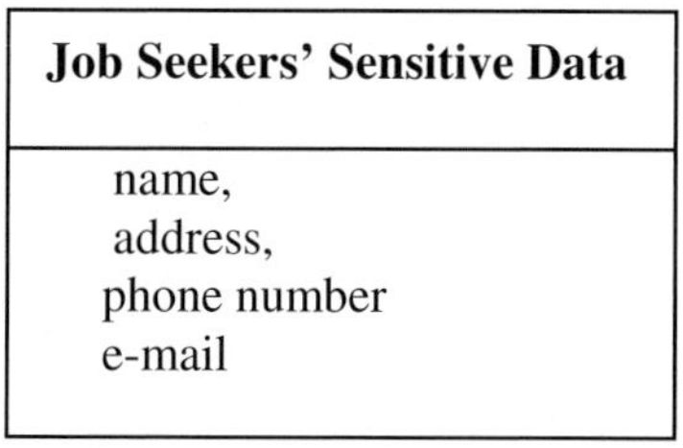

Job Seekers' Sensitive Data
name, address, phone number e-mail

Fig. 2. UML diagram showing database structure

There are many issues related translation of class UML diagrams into implementation models [14] but in our case the UML diagram clearly determines implementation i.e. by one relation. The most important in our paper, however, is that it can be treated as an object that can be assigned some properties and operations in a meta-model.

4   UML Diagram as Ontology

UML diagram can be also very useful in the process of ontology building because of their diversity and extendibility capability. Among UML diagrams, state diagram and class diagrams are most useful. The UML state diagrams model efficiently different states of relatively simple objects. When we want to describe state changes of complex systems a combination of techniques is typically applied. In this paper we concentrate on modeling state changes of systems containing databases. The small and typically cumulative changes are represented by sequence of relationships. The larger changes of the class diagram involving some deletions or de-emphasizing of it components are modeled by sequence of UML diagrams .

To apply such methodology we need to identify class diagrams representing the initial state of the system and other states of the system. Typically, there are two states: before an event and after the event. There are also situations with many events and many states. Less complex situations might require only one state.

In our case study we can identify two main states: before the cyber attack and after the cyber attack. Let us consider the Text Fragment 1 again: "Monster Worldwide acknowledged Thursday that intruders swiped sensitive data for at least 1.3 million job seekers from its popular employment website". The first sentence mentions an entity "Monster Worldwide" that apparently has Website containing sensitive data for job seekers. We can partition this text fragment into 3-tuples: object-relationship-object as follows (relationship is underlined):

1.   Monster Worldwide <u>has</u> Employment Website.
2.   Employment Website <u>contains</u> sensitive data.
3.   Sensitive data <u>are for</u> job seekers.
4.   <u>There are</u> 1.3 job seekers.

The above 3-tuples can be represented by a diagram shown in Figure 3. Each entity (object or object class) is represented by a rectangle with the label e.g. rectangle with the "Monster World" label. Each simple relationship is represented by a line with a label e.g. "contains". If an entity has an explicit property it is listed in a separate rectangular adjacent to the original entity rectangle e.g. "at least 1.3 mln" for the entity "Job Seeker". There are many types of properties: cardinality of a set as "at least 1.3 mln" as in our example. Later we will see how to add static properties such as "heavy" and dynamic properties such as "guarantees safety".

One or more classes can refer to the database previously designed. In our case it is the **Job Seekers' Sensitive Data** entity.

Each diagram can be used to answer queries. The queries can be simple or complex. The simple queries can ask for the entity name, entity property or relationship name called shortly entity, property and relationship queries respectively. The first three queries given below are entity queries:

1.   What does Monster Worldwide <u>have</u>?
2.   What does Employment Website <u>contain</u>?.
3.   Whose sensitive data <u>are for?</u>

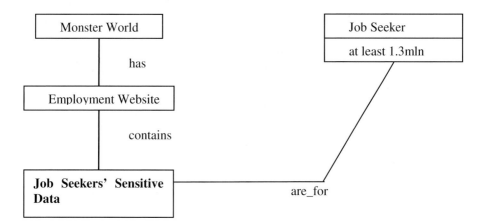

Fig. 3. An initial diagram for Monster World System described by 2 Text Fragments

The answers for these queries give us back the initial 3-tuples. There are also properties queries as shown below:

> 4.   How many job seekers <u>are</u> there?

We can also construct relationship queries as shown below:

> 5.   Who <u>has</u> Employment Website?

5   Refining UML Diagrams Using Background Knowledge and Meta-knowledge

The initial diagram can be significantly extended to include more "knowledge" and allow to automatically answer more queries. The most important in this modification process is to apply background knowledge to our modification process. Our background knowledge and meta-knowledge can include information that allows us to:

- Classify the existing relationships.
- Classify the existing entities.
- Add new relationships between entities.

An important part of our background meta-knowledge is classification of the existing relationships into 3 types: *is_a, is_part_of, is_property_of* and a *generic relationship*. Each type has a set of allowed labels attached to each direction of the relationship i.e. is_a relationship has subset of labels {is_a, is_subtype_of, is_type_of, is_subset_of} referred to as type labels attached to one direction and labels {has_subclass, has_subset, has_subtype} attached to another direction.

Our background knowledge can allow us to classify the existing relationships. In our case the relationships "has" and "contains" can be assigned *is_part_of* type. We will represent such relationships by a line with diamond as shown in Fig. 4.

The type labels can be used for specifying the reverse 3-tuples (reverse relationship) e.g. the relationship {Monster Worldwide has Employment Website} corresponds to a reverse relationship {Employment Website is part of Monster Worldwide} because is part of is a type label of the other direction of the relationship type has .

Alternatively, the reverse relationship names can be specified by using our background knowledge about passive verbs e.g. the relationship contains corresponds to reverse relationship is contained by.

Our background knowledge can also include information allowing us to classify the existing entities. In our case we assume that the background knowledge contains entities: company and people. It is easy to determine that the entity "Monster World" is a company and "Job Seekers" are people. We will represent such knowledge by expanding the diagram accordingly i.e. adding new rectangles representing entities Company and "Job Seekers" and appropriate relationship of the subclass type (line with a arrowhead) as shown in Fig. 4.

Our background knowledge can includes information allowing us to add new relationships between existing entities. In our case it is easy to realize that Employment Website of Monster World must be accessed by Job Seekers. We will represent such knowledge by adding new relationships of the general type (general associations lines with no arrowheads) as shown in Fig. 4.

There are several issues related with proper integration of background knowledge. One of the issues is related with contradictions between extracted knowledge and the background knowledge. In general, we can find statements supporting our background knowledge, negating it or neutral. The discussion about rules for such modeling process is beyond the scope of this paper.

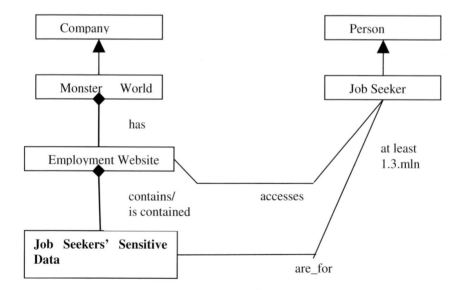

Fig. 4. Diagram for Monster World System after first modification

6   UML Diagram(s) for the Next State(s)

Let us consider the third statement (text fragment 3) "Crooks begin sending out e-mails asking recipients to click on a Web link for services offered by Monster. They also post pop-up ads on Monster. Clicking on the link injects virus into their PCs "

The process of extraction of text knowledge can continue. Questions about the first phase of stealing sensitive data (EVENT 1 through EVENT 4) can be identified (Queries 6-11):

6. Did the thieve have a computer (Rogue Server)?

Yes.

7. What did thieves create and put (and apparently paid for) on the legitimate Employment Web Site (that is a component of Monster Worldwide)? (**EVENT 1**)

Pop-up containing virus.

8. What did Job Seekers and Recruiter do using their PCs? (**EVENT 2**)

Open pop-up infected with virus using their own cPCs.

9. What did the virus (that was part of pop-up on Employment Web Site) do? (**EVENT 3**)

Turn control of their PCs to thieves and sending sensitive data from PC internal memory

10. How did thieves steal all Employment Web Site data? (**EVENT 4**)

Using Username and Password to Employment Web Site of recruiter.

Similarly we can create questions about the second phase of stealing sensitive data (EVENT 5 through EVENT 7):

11. How did thieves use the stolen email addresses? (**EVENT 5**)

They sent well directed emails pitching job-finding services with pop-ups containing the virus.

12. What did the virus (that was part of pop-up in emails) do? (**EVENT 6**)

Turn control of their PCs to thieves and create "zombies".

Based on this analysis the UML diagrams can be created similar to these shown in Figures 3 and 4.

7   Summary

Important activities in many courses include not only identification of data structure but also but also analysis of more abstract knowledge about such data. Our case study was done for Information Security course and was based on the article "Cyberthieves stole 1.3 million names, Monster says" published by USA Today [1]. We used the notation of Universal Modeling Language (UML) for both data modeling and ontology modeling. This way we could take advantage of a uniform structures for the purpose of their integration.

References

1. US News Today Cyberthieves stole 1.3 million names, Monster says, 8/24/ (2007), http://www.usatoday.com/tech/news/computersecurity/infotheft/2007-08-23-cyberjobs_N.htm
2. Booch, G., Rumbaugh, J., Jacobson, I.: The Unified Modeling Language User Guide. Addison Wesley, Reading (1999)
3. Czejdo, B., Mappus, R., Messa, K.: The Impact of UML Diagrams on Knowledge Modeling, Discovery and Presentations. Journal of Information Technology Impact 3(1), 25–38 (2003)
4. Czejdo, B., Czejdo, J., Lehman, J., Messa, K.: Graphical Queries for XML Documents and Their Applications for Accessing Knowledge in UML Diagrams. In: Proceedings of the First Symposium on Databases, Data Warehousing and Knowledge Discovery, Baden, Germany, pp. 69–85 (2003)
5. Czejdo, B., Czejdo, J., Eick, C., Messa, K., Vernace, M.: Rules in UML Class Diagrams. Opportunities of Change. In: Proceedings of the Third International Economic Congress, Sopot, Poland, pp. 289–298 (2003)
6. Delteil, A., Faron, C.: A Graph-Based Knowledge Representation Language. In: Proceedings of the 15th European Conference on Artificial Intelligence (ECAI), Lyon, France (2002)
7. Dori, D., Reinhartz-Berger, I., Sturm, A.: OPCAT—A Bimodal CASE Tool for Object-Process Based System Development. In: Proceedings of the IEEE/ACM 5th International Conference on Enterprise Information Systems (ICEIS 2003), Angers, France, pp. 286–291 (2003), http://www.ObjectProcess.org
8. Lehrnan, F. (ed.): Semantic Networks in Artificial Intelligence. Pergamon, Oxford (1999)
9. Mayer, R.E.: Multimedia Learning. Cambridge University Press, New York (2002)
10. McTear, M.F. (ed.): Understanding Cognitive Science. Ellis Horwood, Chichester (1998)
11. Novak, J.D., Gowin, D.B.: Learning How to Learn. Cambridge University Press, New York (1984)
12. Rumbaugh, J., Jacobson, I., Booch, G.: The Unified Modeling Language Reference Manual. Addison-Wesley, Reading (1999)
13. Rumbaugh, J.: Objects in the Constitution: Enterprise Modeling. Journal of Object Oriented Programming (1993)
14. Schulte, R., Biguenet, J.: Theories of Translation. The University of Chicago Press, Chicago (1992)
15. Smith, M.K., McGuinness, D., Volz, R., Welty, C.: Web Ontology Language (OWL) Guide Version 1.0. W3CWorking Draft (2002)
16. Sowa, J.F.: Conceptual Structures: Information Processing in Mind and Machine. Addison-Wesley, Reading (1984)
17. Sowa, I.F.: Knowledge Representation: Logical, Philosophical, and Computational Foundations. Brooks Cole, Pacific Grove (1999)

Content Requirements Identification towards the Design of an Educational Portal

Charalampos Z. Patrikakis[*], Maria Koukouli, Constantina Costopoulou, and Alexander B. Sideridis

Informatics Laboratory, Agricultural University of Athens, 75,
Iera Odos Str., 11855, Athens, Greece
{bpatr,mkou,tina,as}@aua.gr

Abstract. This paper presents the requirements for the provision of a multilingual educational platform, as these emerge out of the usage and exploitation of digital educational content related to Organic Agriculture (OA) and Agroecology (AE). The results come as an intermediate output of an actual platform implemented in the context of the EU eContentplus program Organic.Edunet, which aims at deploying a multilingual online environment (the Organic.Edunet Web portal), populated with quality content from various content producers.

Keywords: learning resources, content requirements, educational portal.

1 Introduction

The demand for food quality and safety as well as the overall need for sustainable development has generated new opportunities for the agricultural sector, while frequent food scares in combination with the unknown consequences from the cultivation and consumption of genetically modified organisms, are constantly raising consumers' concern and doubts about food safety. In this context, Organic Agriculture (OA) has evolved not only as an agricultural movement but also as an action that contributes in the environmental protection. Agricultural universities around the world have included OA-related and Agroecology (AE) courses in their educational programs, in order to prepare agricultural professionals in this field.

The need for related information and the ability of providing this information over the internet have led to a constant increase in production of digital content for supporting the goals of this initiative. However, there is a large number of dispersed resources, individually listed in separate sites, and with no clear plan for their educational exploitation. An initial collection step has been performed by the BIOAGRO eContent project No EDC-11293, which in a repository of the BIOAGRO web portal (http://www.bioagro.gr) included an initial pool of multilingual OA content resources that could support educational purposes.

The rest of the paper is organized as follows. In section 2, the content identification requirements capturing process is described, starting from the rationale and

---

[*] Corresponding author.

M.D. Lytras et al. (Eds.): WSKS 2008, CCIS 19, pp. 253–260, 2008.
© Springer-Verlag Berlin Heidelberg 2008

continuing through the description of the selected instrument used for capturing these requirements. The findings of the requirements capturing process are presented in the next section, while some conclusions and recommendations are given in the subsequent section. The paper concludes with the next steps towards the identification of requirements of the Organic.Edunet platform.

2 Content Identification Requirements

In the context of the Organic.Edunet project, a set of Learning Resources (LRs) related to OA and AE will be compiled. The term LR refers to any digital content resource that belongs to one of the Organic.Edunet content collections (own or public), and will be included in the learning repositories of the project. This term follows the IEEE Learning Technology Standard Committee definition for Learning Object that has been defined as: "any -digital or non-digital- entity that may be used for learning, education or training" [5]. In addition, the term content collection refers to a set of Organic.Edunet LRs that are contributed to the project by a particular content provider.

The Organic.Edunet LRs collection will be built upon contributions from the content providers, enhanced with publicly available information. More specifically, a total of about 6500 LRs are expected to be available in the project, together with about 1800 more produced out of publicly available content taken from other initiatives such as Organic ePrints [8], the Corporate Document Repository [3], the UK's Soil Association [10], Spanish Society for Organic Farming (SEAE) [1] and FAO's WAICENT Information Finder [4] and LEAD's Virtual Research and Development Centre [6]. The LRs collection will consist of text, presentations, educational games, best practice guides, lecture slides, worksheets, methodological guidelines, movies and graphs that will be contributed from 8 partners covering the whole of Europe (Austria, Estonia, Greece, Norway, Hungary, Romania, Spain and UK). As regards the format, this will cover a large range of supported types including Word, Excel and Powerpoint files, PDF files, HTML documents Flash files, Stand alone applications, JPG images and MPEG videos.

3 Content Analysis Rationale

In order to analyse the content, a set of quantifiable and non-quantifiable characteristics were analysed. The selection of characteristics was largely affected by the elements of IEEE Learning Object Metadata (LOM) standard [5]. The selected characteristics classified in four main categories namely, content characteristics and coverage of topics, media type and format, ownership and availability, and special requirements.

4 Content Requirements Capturing Instrument

In order to create a common platform for evaluating the different LRs, a special Content Requirements Capturing Instrument (CRCI) has been developed in the form of a Microsoft Excel application. Through the use of CRCI, the status of all available LRs has been recorded and quantified with respect to the aforementioned characteristics. The CRCI was implemented in the form of an excel file containing 12 different sheets, each one requesting information about a different characteristic of the content collections of the project. Guidelines have also been provided, with examples of possible ways to fill in the requested information.

4.1 Content Requirements Collection Process

The CRCI instrument was distributed among the content providers of the project. The participants were supported throughout this process by internal communication in order to complete all necessary details for their content that will be contributed to the project. The results of the survey were collected and analysed in order to provide a clear view of the status of the existing content and provide the necessary information and guidelines to the consortium for the future planning on the design and implementation of the system.

4.2 Issues Related to the Use of the Instrument

Before the presentation of the results of the content collection, it should be noted that not all partners were able to complete all the cells in the same way, due to particularities of the content that each one possessed. However, in the vast majority of cases, numeric (and therefore quantifiable) input was provided, while in cases where the proposed cases were inadequate to capture the exact cases of the LRs, the excel file was enriched with the extra cases. Furthermore, the adoption of exclusive selection of categories has been assessed and was rejected, since the expected result of the capturing of content requirements is the full identification with respect to the selection of user scenarios. Therefore, the complete description of each LRs collection was the ultimate goal. For this, some LRs could meet the criteria for inclusion in more than one category, and therefore, the use of sums in some sheets in order to produce total numbers is not of any use.

5   Content Identification Results

5.1 Content Characteristics and Coverage of Topic

Subject Coverage: The most important identification in regard to the educational content is the different topics that the Organic.Edunet collection will cover. As regards OA, a total of 31 different categories of OA topics were identified. From the above categories, the most populated category is that of "Organic Field Crops" (340 LRs), followed according to the number of available LRs by the category "Organic Vegetables" 266 LRs). On the other hand, there are some categories (very specific) that include only a few LRs, such as the "Organic Olive Oil" category. As regards AE, more than 20 different categories of topics were recorded. The most populated category is that of "Related Fields of Biology" (2,274 LRs), followed by the "Environmental Science" category (1,480 LRs).

Type of LRs: The following categories have been used for the classification of the LRs in different types, according to the vocabulary of types that is used in the Learning Object Exchange application profile of the MELT *eContentplus* project [7]. These type categories are: Application, Assessment, Case study, Demonstration, Educational game, Enquiry-oriented activity, Exam, Experiment, Glossary, Guide, Lecture (course/seminar), Narrative text, Open activity, Paper/Article, Presentation, Role play, Simulation, Web resource, and Other.

As a result the vast majority of the LRs are web resources (about 70% of the total) and presentations (about 24% of the total). The type of web resources, including 4622 LRs out of the total estimation of about 6789 LRs is the largest in size. The only exception here is that of educational games, and experiments where a good number of them is available from three of the partners.

Content Use: In regard to the potential use of the content, three possible uses were identified: Informational use, Use for research purposes and Use for training/teaching purposes. In regard to the total of LRs per category, (omitting the LRs that is of web resource types which cannot be easily classified), we have the following results: for informational purposes: 822 LRs, for research purposes: 1170 LRs, and for training/teaching purposes: 2175 LRs. Consequently, the majority of LRs is related to teaching/training purposes, followed by LRs related to research purposes, while the LRs designed for informational purposes comes last.

Audience: The audience was categorized in 5 groups and the results for the total of LRs addressed to each group are 860 LRs for Academic staff / researcher, 1090 LRs for Teachers, 1120 LRs for Students, 460 LRs for Professionals related to OA/AE (non academics) and 990 LRs for the General public. At this point, it should be noted that there are cases where one resource is assigned to more than one group. We see that the majority of the LRs is focused mainly on educational purposes rather that covering the needs of professionals. This is expected, due to the educational nature of the project.

Metadata: Only a few of the content collections have some metadata associated with their resources. The majority follows the IEEE LOM Application Profile [5], while part of the content is following custom, simple metadata scheme built upon Dublic Core. As regards the languages in which the metadata is available, all three collections have metadata in English, while part of the content is also available in Greek, Romanian and German.

Quality procedures: The answers from the partners indicate that some of the partners have some rather implicit Quality Assurance (QA) mechanism, while wherever explicit QA exists it is often performed unsystematically. The use of volunteers and internal moderators is a followed approach by some partners, while external evaluators are involved in some cases. Even though general directives are proposed, no common framework already exists. Regarding the content that is based on web links, a quality ensuring mechanism for determining broken links, through running weekly link controls and remove/update broken links is deployed.

5.2 Media Type and Format

In the following paragraphs, the content collections analysis is presented, with respect to media type and format in which LRs are available.

Storage type: The classification of all the available LRs according to their storage type is necessary for the design of the system. In order to have a clear view on which are the storage types of the collected LRs, a list with all the possible media format with a short description for each one was provided to the participants, offering them the necessary guidelines for describing their content. The list provided is the following: CD-Rom / DVD, Database Server, Electronic Document, Paper only Document, Website and Other. The survey indicates that the majority of information can be stored in a database server.

Format: During this procedure we identified the different media types of the LRs. These were selected using the definitions in RFC 2048 [8]. The majority of content is reported as images, followed by applications. Elaborating further on the format of the content, we can conclude that the jpeg format (which is a quite common format) is dominant. Following that, the Ms-word (.DOC), PowerPoint (.PPT/.PPS), text/html (.TXT .HTM/.HTML) and Acrobat (.PDF) format are the most popular for the provided content. It can be concluded that the content (apart from the web resources related) is available in its majority in the form of images.

Size: The analysis of content in respect to the storage capabilities revealed that the total of content does not have excessive requirements for storage. The amount of 3.3 GBs reported (expected of course to be much larger when metadata is added and is integrated in some repository server) is by far adequately covered by any medium or even small scale storage system.

5.3 Ownership and Availability Analysis

In this section, the availability and usability aspects of the content collection are addressed, and the corresponding results are presented.

Ownership: As far as the ownership of the content is concerned, the resources have been classified into four categories: a) LRs for which the content provider is the sole IPR owner, as well as the creator/author, b) LRs for which content provider is the sole IPR owner, but not the creator/author, c) LRs for which the content provider is one of the IPR owners but not the only one (co-ownership), d) LRs for which the content provider is not the IPR owner (public resources).

As a result, the resources have been classified in all four categories, with the vast majority being content for which the partners have the rights. This ownership originates either from the production of the content by the partners, or because it has eventually come to their possession. It should be noted here that for the particular case of one partner, ownership refers to the metadata records that describe the resources in this collection, and not the resources themselves.

Time of production: In regards to the time of production, the existing LRs categorisation was done according to 12 different categories. Each category represents a year from 2001 up to the year 2010 (in the case of LRs that are expected to be delivered in the course of the project), while the content for the years 1997-2000 was included in one category, as also the content older than 1997. Note that the time of production refers to the time that the actual LRs were produced and not the time that the related information is made available in the Organic.Edunet platform, which is recorded in another part of the analysis.

The results shows that the majority of the LRs will be less than 5 years old, even at the end of the project (in three years from the start) and in addition content providers have decided to revisit their existing resources, so that they meet current needs and state-of-art. This is why the expected time of production of some resources appears to be after 2007 when the project launched. Thus, the existing content by the project's partners is contemporary, and even at the end of the project it will continue to be considered as "current". However, the issue of aging content, though it seems that it will not appear during the lifetime of Organic.Edunet, is important for the future. Therefore, special mechanisms need to be designed to ensure that quality criteria in regards to the time of production of included content are met.

Availability time: In regards to time that the LRs will be available to the project, four categories have been defined, corresponding to the years 2007 up to 2010. These years cover the duration of the project. The time of availability has been decided to be recorded so that an estimation of the LRs availability for inclusion to the system can be made and to avoid having all the LRs been introduced to the system at the end of the corresponding content population tasks.

The analysis indicates that the availability of the content is at the present satisfactory, with most of the content been available even from the very early stages of the project. Therefore, the content population tasks can be designed without the risk of not having content to be used for evaluation of the design and implementation of content population mechanisms.

5.4 Special Requirements

In regards to special requirements that may apply to the content of the partners, they were asked to provide these requirements based on 3 categories: a) Special requirements in regards to platform, b) Special requirements in regards to copyright issues, c) Other requirements.

6 Recommendations on the Platform Design and Deployment

Taking into account the analysis of the existing content collections, a set of recommendations towards the definition of an educational framework built over the corresponding LRs has been defined. These are listed in the following paragraphs.

As regards the metadata framework definition, the evaluation of existing content has revealed that a large number of resources have no associated metadata. For the rest, the IEEE LOM application profile seems to prevail. Therefore, the need for simplicity as well as the need for reuse of existing metadata, indicate that IEEE LOM application profile is the best candidate for the implementation of the metadata framework.

Based on the study of the overall characteristics of the collections, we can identify the following suggestions for IPR licencing: Since the majority of the resources are distributed for free use by interested communities, focus should be given to the adoption of Open Licencing Schemes. Nevertheless, the permitted licences for using, reproducing, and/or repurposing part or whole of the resources, should be reflected in their metadata, following some commonly accepted format like Creative Commons.

Since most of the content to be provided is already available in repositories (for case of the public content, even available through web portals), the only need is the provision of a LRs repository that will be able to store only newly produced content, together with the necessary web based front end for accessing the information. This translates to the need for a web portal through which users will be able to access the LRs and also to address search queries.

Several topics related to quality assurance have been raised during the analysis, with most important being the issue of web links checking and maintenance, and the issue of resources' currency. Both should be taken into consideration. In addition, compatibility with (or even enhancement) of the existing quality assurance mechanisms for the non publicly available content should be considered, so that a common quality assurance standard is applied to all LRs.

7 Next Steps towards Platform Definition

After the completion of the content requirements phase, the next phase towards the complete definition of the platform architecture and functionality is the provision of user requirements. A specially designed questionnaire, taking into account the findings of the first phase (content requirements identification) has been published, in which all potential users are called to provide feedback on the possible uses of the Organic.Edunet portal in relation to existing courses, and the possible ways in which the use of ICT enhanced training could assist in the teaching of OA and AE related topics.

The content identification process described in this paper, can be easily extended so as to satisfy general needs for a content identification framework towards the implementation of digital data repositories. Currently, the work presented in this paper is being enhanced in order to include all the necessary parameters that fully describe such a framework. Issues such as ethical and privacy concerns, legal implications, information accuracy, security e.a. are among the enhancements under consideration.

Acknowledgments. The work presented in this paper has been funded with support by the EC, under the eContentplus project No ECP-2006-EDU-410012 "Organic.Edunet". This publication reflects the views only of the authors, and the Commission cannot be held responsible for any use which may be made of the information contained therein. The authors would like to thank N. Manouselis, Ch. Thanopoulos, Prof. Gh. V. Roman, M. Toader, L. I. Epure, V. Ion, M. Mihalache, A. M. Truta, M. E. Dusa, J. Wickham, M.Hofer, Prof. G. Lieblein, T. A. Breland, A. S. Holm, Dr. U. Ehlers, Ass. Prof. S.Sanchez-Alonso, J. C. Tello, Prof. L. Radics, for their contribution in the work presented.

References

1. AGRO-ECOLOGÍA. (n.d.). Retrieved 5 17, 2008, from Sociedad Española de Agricultura Ecologica, http://www.agroecologia.net/
2. Bio@gro, Metadata Models for Bio@gro Content Objects (BCOs) Description, Bio@gro Technical Report (2005)
3. Corporate Document Repository. (n.d.). Retrieved 6 21, 2008, from FAO, http://www.fao.org/documents/

4. FAO WAICENT Information Finder. (n.d.). Retrieved 3 14, 2008, from FAO,
   `http://search.fao.org/opensearch?query=organic&lang=en`
5. IEEE LOM, Draft Standard for Learning Object Metadata, IEEE Learning Technology
   Standards Committee, IEEE 1484.12.1- 2002, 15 July 2002, HYPERLINK,
   `http://ltsc.ieee.org/wg12 http://ltsc.ieee.org/wg12`
6. LEAD Virtual Research and Development Center. (n.d.). Retrieved 12 10, 2007, from
   LEAD, `http://lead-en.virtualcentre.org/`
7. MELT eContentPlus project web site. (n.d.). Retrieved 6 20 (2008),
   `http://info.melt-project.eu`
8. Organic ePrints. (n.d.). Retrieved 6 21, 2008, from Organic ePrints,
   `http://orgprints.org/about.html`
9. RFC 2048 - Multipurpose Internet Mail Extensions (MIME)
10. Soil Association. (n.d.). Retrieved 6 10, 2008, from Soil Association,
    `http://www.soilassociation.org`

Training Adults on Traditional vs. Web 2.0 IS Topics: The Trainees' View

Efthimios Tambouris[1,2] and Konstantinos Tarabanis[1]

[1] University of Macedonia, Egnatia 156, Thessaloniki, Greece
[2] Informatics and Telematics Institute, Center for Research and Technology Hellas
(ITI-CERTH), 6th km Charilaou-Thermi, Thessaloniki, Greece
{tambouris,kat}@uom.gr

Abstract. In this paper we present the trainees' view with regards to training on traditional versus contemporary (mainly Web 2.0) Information Systems solutions. The training program was performed within the Digital Enterprise Research Network (DERN); a network of five organisations (three universities and two IT companies) in Greece aiming to promote long-life learning in the field of Business Administration emphasizing the use of ICT technologies, in line to the needs of the Knowledge Society. The program trained twenty trainees for 120 hours equally divided between lectures and workshops. In this paper we first present the profile and motivation of trainees. We thereafter survey their views with regards to expectation and value of traditional and contemporary training topics. The early results suggest that trainees expect and value traditional topics higher than contemporary ones.

Keywords: Web 2.0 training, IS training.

1 Introduction

DERN (Digital Enterprise Research Network) aims at building a research network among some of the most important academic, research and technological bodies and enterprises of Greece [1]. The interest focuses on the use of traditional and contemporary ICT technologies in business administration.

During the life-time of the project five training programs will be performed. The first training program, titled "The use of ICT in Organizations: past and future" was performed by the Information Systems Laboratory at the University of Macedonia between winter 2007 and summer 2008. It was a 120-hour program aiming to familiarize the trainees with traditional and contemporary (mainly Web 2.0) use of ICTs in organizations.

In this paper, we present our early experiences after finalizing this training program. We mainly concentrate on investigating the perception of trainees with regards to the topics covered in the program. More specifically, it was decided that 21 different topics would be covered. These could be categorized as shown in Table 1.

In the tables presented in this paper, contemporary topics are listed in italics to be easily distinguished from traditional ones.

M.D. Lytras et al. (Eds.): WSKS 2008, CCIS 19, pp. 261–266, 2008.
© Springer-Verlag Berlin Heidelberg 2008

Table 1. Categorization of topics taught

	TRADITIONAL	CONTEMPORARY
CONCEPTS/ AREAS	Information systems in general, Enterprise Architecture, eBusiness	*eGovernment, eParticipation*
ORGANISATION/ BUSINESS VIEW	Process modelling, Project management, Research in information systems, Business process reengineering	*The use of Web 2.0 technologies in organisations*
PLATFORMS/ TECHNOLOGICAL VIEW	Enterprise Resource Planning (ERP), Unified Modeling Language (UML), Customer Relationship Management (CRM), Content Management Systems (CMS), Business Process Modeling Notation (BPMN), Portal platforms	*Mashups, Wikis, blogs*

The two main categories are traditional topics and contemporary topics. The former include topics normally found in any Information Systems (IS) course [2][3]. The latter include mainly Web 2.0 concepts, principles and technologies [4]. The main idea of Web 2.0 is referred as "Web as a platform", meaning that umbrella software services run in a browser, communicating with network and other servers [5]. Web 2.0 principles and solutions attract significant attention in the last few years and are promising a new look at Enterprise Information Systems. It is a fact that the diffusion of Web 2.0 is actually changing the way people develop collaboratively and consume information and knowledge [6]. The potential of Web 2.0 in education and training is under current research and practice (e.g. [6][7][8]).

It should be noted that DERN is inline with the needs of the Knowledge Society. Knowledge and learning are perceived as the *"new battlefields of our society"*, since *"knowledge society is a new strategic position of our society where the social and the economic perspective are concentrated on the exploitation of emerging technologies"* [9]. One can easily understand that a training program aiming to familiarize trainees with contemporary ICTs and their utilization in organizations contributes to building the knowledge society.

In fact, the term "Knowledge Society" originates from the "Information Society". The recommendations of the high-level expert group (HLEG) on Information Society [10], refer to actively stimulating the acquisition of knowledge and skills by a. establishing an education network, b. giving financial incentives for training, c. improving and disseminating knowledge on learning methods and d. producing high-quality, low-cost learning materials. DERN is exactly such a network that meets all four requirements.

The aim of this paper is to investigate the opinion of trainees with regards to the comparative need and usefulness of traditional and contemporary IS solutions in a relevant training program.

The rest of this paper is organized as follows. In section 2 we briefly present the training program. In section 3 we outline the profile of candidates along with the profile of the selected trainees. In section 4 we present the results of our survey while in section 5 we discuss these results and conclude.

2   Trainees Profile

Twenty persons were selected to attend the training program. The profile of selected trainees was as follows:

- Academic background: All candidates had a degree; 6 out of 20 (30%) had a University or Technological Educational Institute degree; 8 out of 20 (40%) had a postgraduate degree while 6 (30%) were postgraduate students (the number of students increased since the application period)
- Working experience: 11 out of 20 (55%) were working during the training course; 4 out of 20 (20%) had no working experience; while 5 out of 20 (25%) used to work but were currently not employed.

It should be noted that the profile of candidates was different than anticipated. More specifically, our original expectations, which were in line with the scope of the specific program, were supportive of candidates with less academic qualifications and more relevant working experience to apply.

3   Trainees' Survey Results

The survey was conducted using questionnaires, which were filled in anonymously by all twenty trainees. The main results follow.

First, we questioned the motivation for trainees to attend the program. We provided seven alternatives and the trainees were asked to choose and rank the tree most important. The results are presented in table 2, where for simplicity ranking is not shown.

Table 2. Motivation for attending the program (20 is the maximum; 0 is the minimum)

MOTIVE	# Trainees
To learn new things	17/20
To enhance existing knowledge	15/20
To use the acquired knowledge in the market	13/20
To increase my qualifications	8/20
To get the financial support	5/20
To meet new people, Because I am currently unable to find a job	1/20

The results were encouraging for our purposes. It seemed that the main purpose for attending the program was learning new things followed by enhancing existing knowledge. This was encouraging as it suggested that trainees had a positive attitude towards contemporary solutions.

Second, we asked the trainees whether, before the start of the program, they anticipated each of the 21 topics to be taught in this seminar. The results are presented in the second column of Table 3.

Finally, we asked the trainees, after the end of the program, which of the topics taught they considered as most useful. Each trainee was asked to rank all topics using

Table 3. Training topics anticipated by trainees before the start of the program and their Usefulness (1 indicates the most useful and 21 the least useful)

TOPIC	% of train- ees antici- pating the topic	Usefulness
Information systems in general	80%	6
Process modelling	80%	7
System analysis and design	75%	8
eBusiness	75%	9
UML	60%	11
ERP	55%	11
Enterprise Architecture	50%	10
CRM	50%	12
Data modelling	45%	8
eGovernment	45%	10
Project management	40%	11
Business process reengineering	35%	8
Research in information systems	35%	10
CMS, BPMN	30%	13
Mashups	30%	17
The use of Web 2.0 technologies in organisations	25%	10
Wikis	25%	17
Portal platforms	25%	15
blogs	25%	16
eParticipation	20%	10

a scale from 1 (most useful) to 21 (less useful). The average of ranking is presented in the third column of Table 3. A score close to 1 indicates a highly useful topic while a score close to 21 indicates a less useful topic (compared to others).

The results presented in the second column suggest that the trainees anticipated a more traditional curriculum. Also it can be easily derived that they expected bigger focus on concepts and the organizational view rather than platforms and a technological view.

The results presented in the third column suggest that traditional topics are still perceived as more useful as compared to contemporary ones. Also, knowledge of concepts and areas as well knowledge of the organizational/ business view is perceived more important than knowledge of platforms and the technological view.

4   Discussion and Conclusions

In this paper, we present our early experiences with regards to the trainees' perceptions of an Information Systems training program that comprises both traditional and contemporary (mainly Web 2.0) topics. This program consisted of 120 hours equally divided between lectures and workshops. The program was advertised through the university normal channels (website, careers office, posters etc) and attracted 41 candidates from which 20 were finally selected.

An examination of the candidates' profiles suggests that their academic qualifications were significant. This can be interpreted in two ways. First, people with qualifications understand the significance of further qualifications and specialization and therefore are those interested in further training. Another interpretation is that the channels selected by the University for advertising the program were such that people with academic qualifications were more likely to learn about it. It is therefore essential that training programs are advertised properly in order to attract the attention of the appropriate candidates.

The topics that were chosen to be taught in this training program were determined at the outset. This was a requirement from the financing body and poses certain constraints on the flexibility of the program. Indeed, it is known that an adults' training program should consider the profile of trainees; something that was not possible in this case.

A survey was conducted to better appreciate the views of the trainees with regards to the topics taught. The main results of this survey are summarized below.

First, the main motive for trainees to attend the program was to learn new things closely followed by the motive to enhance existing knowledge. The main motive seems to significantly affect some of the other results below.

Second, before the start of the program, trainees anticipated mostly traditional topics rather than contemporary. This is quite strange given the fact that they main motive was to learn new things. One possible interpretation is that they are used for universities to provide traditional courses and therefore they anticipated the same to happen again. Furthermore, trainees mainly anticipated that the focus would be on overviews of areas and concepts, followed by organizational/ business view and not technological solutions.

Finally, after the end of the program, trainees suggested that the most useful topics were those related to traditional rather than contemporary solutions. Furthermore, in general they ranked as more useful those topics they were anticipating to be taught. This again contradicts to the result indicating that the main motive was to acquire new knowledge; indeed, it seems that enhancing existing knowledge happened more efficiently. This is however inline with research on adults education which suggests that although acquiring new knowledge is relatively easy to achieve, this is not the same with changing attitude especially when new attitudes contradict prior knowledge [11]. In that respect, it can be assumed that trainees were biased towards certain topics from the beginning. However, this fact can be also explained by assuming that trainers failed to emphasize the importance and usefulness of contemporary issues in Information Systems. A notable exception is the use of Web 2.0 in organizations. In this case, trainees did not anticipate this topic would be taught but nevertheless at the end, they rated relatively high its usefulness.

In summary, the survey suggested that contemporary technologies in the use of ICT is modern organizations are still not considered as essential in a training course and their usefulness is questioned. This might be a lesson to be considered by others looking into the same area. It should be noted however that these results are only indicative and generalization to the whole population of trainees should not be attempted. We believe that further research is needed in this area to clearly determine the trainees' attitude towards learning about contemporary, Web 2.0 solutions. It should be finally noted that due to time restrictions the final paper, if accepted, will also include a statistical analysis of the results trying to also determine relationships between different answers.

Acknowledgments. The DERN project is co-financed by the General Secretariat of Research and Technology of Greece. In the project there is equal representation from the academia (Information Systems Laboratory/ University of Macedonia; Institute of Communication and Computer Systems/ National Technical University of Athens; and the Athens University of Economics and Business - ELTRUN/OIS) and the industry (FORTHnet S.A. and ALTEC S.A.).

References

1. DERN (Digital Enterprise Research Network), `http://islab.uom.gr/dern`
2. ACM, IS 2002 Model Curriculum and Guidelines for Undergraduate Degree Programs in Information Systems,
`http://www.acm.org/education/education/curric_vols/is2002.pdf`
3. ACM and AIS, MSIS 2000 Model Curriculum and Guidelines for Graduate Degree Programs in Information Systems,
`http://www.acm.org/education/education/curric_vols/a1-gorgone.pdf`
4. O'Reilly T.: What is Web 2.0: Design Patterns and Business Models for the next generation of software,
`http://www.oreillynet.com/pub/a/oreilly/tim/news/2005/09/30/what-is-web-20.html`
5. Anderson, P.: What is Web 2.0? Ideas, technologies and implications for education, JISC Technology and Standards Watch (February 2007)
6. Sigala, M.: Integrating Web 2.0 in e-learning environments: a socio-technical approach. International Journal of Knowledge and Learning 3(6), 628–648 (2007)
7. Safran, C., Helic, D., Gütl, C.: E-Learning practices and Web 2.0. In: Conference ICL 2007, Villach, Austria, September 26 -28 (2007)
8. Parker, K.R., Chao, J.T.: Wiki as a Teaching Tool. Interdisciplinary Journal of Knowledge and Learning Objects 3, 57–72 (2007)
9. Lytras, M.D., Sicilia, M.A.: The Knowledge Society: a manifesto for knowledge and learning. International Journal of Knowledge and Learning 1(1/2), 1–11 (2005)
10. Tuomi, I.: From Periphery to Center: Emerging Research Topics on Knowledge Society, Tekes, Technology Review 116/2001, `http://www.tekes.fi/julkaisut/emerging_research_topics_on_knowledge_society.pdf`
11. Rogers, A.: Teaching adults. Open University Press (1996)

ERA - E-Learning Readiness Analysis:
A eHealth Case Study of E-Learning Readiness

J. Schreurs[1], George Sammour[1], and U. Ehlers[2]

[1] Hasselt University, Diepenbeek, Belgium
Jeanne.Schreurs@uhasselt.be,
George.sammour@uhasselt.be
[2] University of Duisburg-Essen, Germany
ulf.ehlers@web.de

Abstract. Electronic learning is seen as a good solution for organisations that deal with fast changing knowledge and for reducing the cost of training. E-learning is a good opportunity for companies but needs to be well prepared because it takes often high investment costs. That is why it is important for a company to know if it is e-ready. E-readiness is already well covered in literature and several models are suggested. We used these models to develop an e-learning readiness measurement instrument and questionnaire. We used our instrument to check whether the Flemish hospitals were e-ready for e-learning.

1 Introduction

The promises of e-learning for organisations are manyfold. Too often they fail to take effect. The reason is a not sufficient readines to take up e-learning in an organisations and absob the innovation effects coming along with it. In this paper we suggest e-learning readiness as a key factor influecing the uptake of e-learning in organisations. We present ERA an e-learning readyness analysis toool and discuss results its application from a case study in the healthcare sector.

In the globalised world of the 21st century, organisations are confronted with a challenging economic competition. Employees need to be equipped with new competences to adapt to constantly changing work and life conditions in knowledge-based economies and societies. Organisations are aware of the value of knowledge and learning for their continual development and for the acquirement of a competitive advantage, which relates to innovation and fulfilment. Especially the healthcare sector is a fast changing environment and it is clear that its performance depends on the ability of staff to update their competences fast in order to adapt to a constant changing environment (S.Psycharis 2005, Bernhardt et al., 2003). Looking at e-learning in today's organisations, it can be defined as the delivery of instructional content or learning experiences enabled by electronic technology and it is one of the major innovations that is diffusing corporate settings. E-learning requires that the learners use the internet, collaborate with peers and interact with the trainer for support. Experienced e-learners can even use technology to monitor their training and ultimately become responsible managers of their own personal and career development. The number of e-learning initiatives in corporate training scenarios is steadily increasing.

M.D. Lytras et al. (Eds.): WSKS 2008, CCIS 19, pp. 267–275, 2008.

Reasons are related to the cost of training and reports show that e-learning contributed to saving travel costs and downtime for workplaces. Advantages such as asynchronous training, training at individual pace, just-in-time training, and cost-effectiveness lure organizations to e-learning (Powell 2000). The opportunity to learn via technology presents an exciting prospect to train even learners with little previous access to computer-based training. E-learning is a good opportunity for organisations that deal with fast changing knowledge but companies needs to be well prepared because it takes often high investment costs.

2   Introducing E-Learning Readiness

Organizations have to be ready to adopt e-learning and benefit from its advantages. Such *e-readiness* can be defined as "how ready the organisation is on several aspects to implement e-learning". E-learning-readiness should be determined before organizations introduce e-learning. Readiness includes learners' ability to adapt to technological challenges, collaborative training and synchronous as well as asynchronous self-paced training. It also depends on their motivation and their discipline to learn in a self-driven mode and to respond to online instructions. E-readiness makes up the e-maturity of the organization which also is represented in the readiness of learners. It includes the availability of infrastructure, clear training objectives, trainer support and guidance and knowledgeable leadership. Therefore, e-learning not only requires readiness from the learner but also from the trainer and the organization to successfully engage e-learning (Bowles 2004).

2.1   Strategy to Improve Learners' Online Experience

In the study of Ipsos Mori (Ipsos Mori 2006), key components of e-learning readiness have been identified: social context, content delivery, technology access, learning style, collaboration capacity, organisational learning environment and personal motivation. Over two-thirds of employees would like to see their organisation make more use of e-learning. Three in four feel e-assisted training could be useful to them as trainers or to other trainers in their organisation. Employers who are more sceptical say that they are limited by resources; half feel they don't have the budget while three in five believe that employees will just not be interested. The key reason why some employers are sceptical about the potential of e-learning is that of technical resources. One of the main barriers to effective e-learning is the lack of accessible computers at the workplace. To improve learners' online experience, strategies need to be found that address the 5 areas of difficulty encountered by people which diminish the quality of their experience and may make people less inclined to e-learning. (Ipsos MORI 2006). The five areas of difficulty are the technical means, autonomy in web use, e-skills, level of social support, variation in motivation Some cross-cutting components are influencing how people perceive barriers to e-learning and therefore how ready they feel they are to participate in it Influencing components are the organizational culture, self-belief, computer competence and computer training.

2.2   E-Readiness Assessment

Literature on organizational readiness for e-learning provides managers with questions, guidelines, strategies, models and instruments for assessing the readiness of their companies. E-readiness can be assessed by evaluating an individual's technical experience and competency to interact with computers. This competency should be supported by the individual's capability to direct his or her own training through appropriate knowledge, skills, attitudes, and habits. Aydain and Tasci (Aydin, 2005) suggests a questions tool with 7 categories: human resources, learning management system, learners, content, IT, finance and vendor. Another categorization results from *Chapnic (*Chapnic 2005): psychological, sociological, environmental, HR, financial readiness, technological skill (aptitude), equipment, content readiness.

2.3   Model to Measure E-Learning Readiness

How to find a comprehensive concept to measure the e-readiness of organisations? Which criteria can be included? If we examine the models described above closely we see certain common parameters that always come back. Psycharis suggests three large categories (Psycharis 2005): resources, education and environment. Each category contains certain criteria. In the category resources the technological readiness, the economic readiness and the human resources readiness are investigated. Education means the readiness of content and the educational readiness. Environment includes entrepreneurial readiness, leadership readiness and readiness of culture.

- **Resources:** First of all we want to investigate the **technological readiness,** about the available technological systems that are provided and the way they are used. The **economic readiness** examines the willingness of the organisation to invest in e-learning. Implementing e-learning brings along large costs and the organisation needs to be prepared to make the necessary investments in infrastructure but also foresees a degree of administration support. The **human readiness** refers to the knowledge and the skills of the employees being the e-learners. An important question is if staff has the necessary basic skills and if they do feel at ease with used technology, necessary investments in infrastructure but also foresees a degree of administration support. The **human readiness** refers to the knowledge and the skills of the employees being the e-learners. An important question is if staff has the necessary basic skills and if they do feel at ease with used technology.
- **Education:** Whether or not an organisation is ready from an educational point of view will be determined by the measurement of the readiness of the content. Is the educational content easily available, is it structured good and is it reusable? But also the educational readiness is important. It is about the learning styles and the educational needs of the employees.
- **Environment:** The criteria of this category are the entrepreneurial readiness and the readiness of the culture. So the Flemish hospitals of our case all have their own authority on decision making on how how they train their staff.

2.4   Building ERA – The E-Learning Readiness Analysis Instrument

Studying the already existing theory and using our insights of e-learning and quality aspects of e-learning we developed an e-learning readiness measurement instrument

(Schreurs 2008). We developed a structure for the instrument and developed a set of questions based on our self assessment quality questionnaire. This questionnaire can slightly be changed, and adopted according to the sector in which it is used – if necessary.

1. Learner characteristics	3. Management
• ICT skills of the trainees • Motivation for use of e-learning of the trainees • Do they have a preferred learning style? (prefer presentations including audio, video, ….)	• Investment in physical environment • Organization of e-learning in-house • Investment in good user systems • Investment in e-learning infrastructure • Learning time during working hours?
2. Available facilities for e-learning	4. E-learning solutions/ courses /processes
• ICT aspects / infrastructure • Learning management system	• Information about available course • ICT aspects • Support learning activity • Maintenance of systems • Organization of learning activity itself • Support of the learner

3 Applying ERA to Hospitals: The Agfa Case

A study on the adoption of e-learning for public health nurse continuous education showed an affirmative intention towards adopting e-learning as their way of continuing education (Shu Yu et al. 2006). Reasons for adopting e-learning include achieving lifelong learning, fulfilling personal interests, the orientation on concrete job needs, demands for information diversity, flexibility in time and space, the possibility of self-regulatory learning, cost-effectiveness, and less impact on family duties. Reasons to reject e-learning include poor computer literacy, lack of personal access to computers with and without internet access, heavy workload, lack of motivation, low self-control. On the whole, employees are keen to see e-enabled training and staff is interested in e-learning. Three in five employees think e-learning is a practical option in their own organisation (ibid.). Healthcare workforce is e-ready.

3.1 The Case: eHealth Services of Agfa

In collaboration with the company Agfa healthcare, we were investigating the e-learning readiness of 10 Flemish hospitals being the customers of Agfa. Agfa HealthCare is a leading provider of integrated IT solutions and state-of-the-art diagnostic imaging for hospitals and other healthcare centers. The mission of Agfa Healthcare is to support the transformation process to ICT solutions being improving the medical care services of the hospitals. Recently Agfa Healthcare provides e-learning services to its customers, the hospitals. All ICT solutions will be complemented with an optional e-learning component. The e-learning component can be accessed via an e-learning portal of Agfa. By the way the hospital can also change from traditional classroom learning to e-learning. The e-learning course functions also as a help tool afterwards.

3.2   Applying ERA: An eHealth Case

Agfa is convinced of the advantages of using their e-learning solution for the hospitals, replacing the traditional classroom learning - but are hospitals ready to change? For the analysis we first selected the relevant criteria from our e-learning readiness measurement instrument We developed a questionnaire of 80 questions that should assess the e-readiness of the hospitals in several areas. The development of the questionnaire has been based on earlier mentioned criteria in combination with quality questionnaires of e-learning which we developed earlier (Schreurs et al. 2008). We checked first for the preferred situation by the doctor radiologist, the head of nursery of the department and the ICT director. Secondly we asked to do a self-assessment of their skills, motivation, experiences, and alike. Thirdly we asked for the evaluation of the hospital ICT infrastructure to be used for e-learning. Furthermore we also asked a judgement from AGFA in which way they are facilitating the e-learning application for the hospital.

3.3   Results: E-Learning Readiness in Hospitals

The results of our analysis of 10 hospitals were quite homogeneous and will be reported in summary below, referring to general aspects as well as specific experiences from the case study.

Table 1. e-learning readiness measurement instrument, measuring e-readiness in a hospital

Criteria /subcriteria	How important for you (scale: 1 to 4)			Evaluation of skills level of learner (scale: 1 to 4)		Quality of e-learning facilities (scale: 1 to 4)		Evaluation facilities by AGFA
	doctor	nurse	ICT	doctor	nurse	ICT	Mgmt Doctor	AGFA
Enabling Learning Resources								
Information on available learning opportunities	x	x						x
The electronic online Learning Environment								
ICT and the learning system					x	x		x
System functions facilitate learning activities					x			x
Maintenance of facilities					x			x
The physical learning environment provided for online session	x	x					X	
Investment in e-learning solutions								
Investments in local central ICT learning infrastructure for implementation of e-learning					x		X	
Learners in this new learning environment								
ICT skills of learners				x	x			
Motivation of learners				x	x			
Learning styles of learners				x	x			
Enabling Learning Processes								
E-learning activities	x	x	x					x
Course progression								
Teaching approach/Course design								
Personalising the learner's e-learning course								
Personalising your own learning								
Learner Support	x	x	x					x
ICT Support								
Online support								
The resulting Learning Results								
Knowledge Increase	x	x						
Using skills learned	x	x						

- **Learner characteristics:** Most employees don't have experience using an e-learning course, although most of them work regularly with pc and have knowledge of the standard packages. It is very important that the first time they use e-learning, they will be guided and they prefer a classroom session organised in advance to coach and enhance the use of the system. It is recommendable that the key-users will be thoroughly coached when they have no experience with e-learning. The learners are not more motivated for e-learning, than for a traditional course. It can be explained by the fact that most of them still have no experience with e-learning. It is an opportunity for Agfa to clarify the advantages of an e-learning solution. On point of the preferred learning styles, we see that video fragments are regarded necessary in an e-learning course and the insertion of simulation modules in the e-learning system creates a large surplus value. So we can say that if those two items are integrated in the system, the readiness of the users will increase. However results also show that they don't prefer audio above written documents.

- **Available facilities for e-learning:** First we consider the ICT aspects and their scores. We checked the expected ICT situation, the current situation and the AGFA approach. A first remarkable result is the similarity between the expected situation of the hospitals and the solution for facilitating e-learning as delivered by AGFA. The results from AGFA can be seen as the requirements of ICT infrastructure of the hospitals. We see a good match between the expected situation and the prospected situation by Agfa. Though there is a discrepancy between thye expected situation and the actual situation. Hospitals are aware that the current situation of the ICT infrastructure is often not sufficient to meet the requirements. Some additional investments are required. We find another remarkable result with the underlying system functions to facilitate e-learning. There is a great discrepancy between the required underlying system functions (average score of 3.2) and the way Afga wishes to facilitates them (average score of 1.0). Agfa has to consider to built in underlying system functions. The same results are denoted for the maintenance of ICT facilities: an average score of the expected situation resulted in 4.0 which is remarkable higher than the average score of 2.5 of AGFA. The reason for the difference lies mainly in the range of scores of the indicator : adjustment of the learning system to new versions of system software. Also here Agfa should consider the incorporation of this facility in the packet.

- **Management:** The wishes of all staff are quite similar as for the physical aspects. The expectations are rather high. Which is good in the case for Agfa because their physical learning environment is already on a high level. The duration of the learning hours in working time is preferable above the willingness to work at home. The current ICT infrastructure isn't good enough in most cases. ICT is fairly prepared to make investments to upgrade to the necessary level to making e-learning possible and successful.

- **E-learning solutions/courses:** On the information of training supply they all agreed, the composition of the e-learning packet must be clear. Accordingly Agfa can satisfy his customers by composing clearly structured packet. The personalisation of the e-learning course gives a remarkable difference. Hospitals want a reasonable personalisation of the course in contrast with Agfa, who clearly not wishes to incorporate personalisation. If Afga would add to the readiness to e-learning of the hospitals it should consider personalisation. The self management of the learning process gives also a difference between hospitals and Agfa but in the opposite direction. On this matter Agfa thinks it is very important in contrast with the hospitals who rate it low. Support of the trainee is considered important for all persons in hospital this for as well ICT as online support; Also here Agfa considers this as being of minor importance. It creates again a new opportunity for Agfa to add to the readiness of the company if the wish to compromise in this matter. The learn results that are put forward being enlargement of knowledge and apply what is taught is important to radiologist and they expect a thorough knowledge. Case versus results found in the literature.Out of the literature we found some findings on readiness to e-learning in the social care sector. SCIE concluded seven components of good e-learning delivery from a study of international e-learning experiences. The results suggest that without these components put in place by organisations, barriers will form and inhibit the e-learning experience. We will first refer to them short and then compare them with the result of our case study.

- **Situational component:** This component includes elements of basic 'know how', but goes beyond this in that it includes elements that influence how e-learning is facilitated within an organisation. In the reported case most employees did not have experience using an e-learning course, although most of them work regularly with pc and have knowledge of the standard packages, as stated earlier it is very important that the first time they use e-learning, they will be guided well.

- **Content suitability component:** The subject materials that are made available to e-learners are important too. In the reported case the results all agreed upon that the composition of the e-learning packet must be clear. Hospitals value high the presentation of the course, the progress of the course, the personalisation of the course and in a lesser extent the self-management of the process.

- **Technological component:** There are three distinct technological elements which organisations need to address if they are to be ready to deliver e-learning. These include the hardware available to staff, the internet connectivity and how flexible the system is to engage with all the webbased material. In the reported case the physical conditions seem to be evaluated of great importance to the employees and score in general well in Flemish hospitals.

- **Learning style component:** How well an organisation matches the learners it has to diversify the types of training and learning resources it can offer. In the reported case it became apparent that if taking a look at the preferred learning styles in our questionnaire, we see that video fragments are regarded necessary in an e-learning course and the insertion of simulation modules in the e-learning system creates a large surplus value. So we can say that if those two items are integrated in the system, the readiness of the users will increase.

- **Instructional and network component:** This component identifies the elements required for a collaborative e-learning approach. In the reported case supporting system facilities are wanted by the hospitals but are not facilitated by supply. Here an opportunity can be taken by supply to increase the readiness.

- **Organisational component:** Here we consider the organisational culture or attitude to e-learning, the learning environment it fosters, the applicability of training to the work of the organisation and the way in which it evaluates the impact of training. In the reported case this component wasn't of great importance for our research because the decision on whether and how the training is organised was a decision of authorised staff employee.
- **Personal component:** The organisation's ability to influence staff motivation. In the reported case e-learning is not yet be seen as being more motivational then traditional learning. So the advantages of e-learning have to be well pointed out for. A challenge for the Flemish market;

4   Conclusions

Everyone is aware that e-learning can offer advantages. Obstructions for implementing can be among others high costs and because of these obstructions, there is still a lot of reservation towards e-learning. An organisation can check how ready it is on several aspects to implement e-learning, this is called e-readiness. In this paper we wanted to see whether the Flemish healtsector was e-ready. The theory offers several models and approaches. We used our own to see whether the results of the research corresponded with the theory. It seems results follow theory but that it needs efforts from both sides to increase the readiness. E-readiness requires a team effort from as well demand as supply, from trainer as trainee.

References

Aydin, C.H., Tasci, D.: Measuring readiness for e-learning: reflections from an emerging country. Educational Technology & Society 8(4), 244–257 (2005)

Bernhardt, J.M., Runyan, C.W., bou-saada, I., Felter, E.M., et al.: Implementation and evaluation of a web-based continuing course in injury prevention and control. Health promotion Practice 4(2), 120–128 (2003)

Bowles, M.: Relearning to e-learn: strategies for electronic learning and knowlzdge. Melbourne University Press (2004)

Chapnic, S.: Are you ready for e-learning? Learning Circuits: ASTD's Online Magazine All abouit e-learning (2005)

Chorng-Shyong, Jung-Yu, Yi-Shun: Factors affecting engineers acceptance of asunchronous e-learning systems in high-tech companies. Information & management 41(6), 795–804 (2004)

Moolman, H.B., Blignaut, S.: Get set! E-ready, ...e-learn! The e-readiness of warehouse workers. Technology & Society 11(1), 168–182

Mungania, P.: The Seven E-Learning Barriers Facing Employees. The Masie Centre (2003)

E-Readiness in the Social Care Sector

Powell, G.C.: Are you ready for web-based training? Educational Technology & Society 3(1), 52–55 (2000)

Psycharis, S.: Presumptions and actions affecting an e-learning adoptionby the educational system. In: Implementation using virtual private networks, Eurodl (2005), http://www.eurodl.org/materials/contrib/2005/Sarantos_Psycharis.htm

Schreurs, J., Husson, A.M., Merison, B., Morin, E., Van Heysbroeck, H.: SEVAQ: a unique multi-functional tool for assessing and improving the quality of e-courses. International Journal of emerging technologies in learning (IJET) 3(1) (2008)

Yu., S., Chen, I.-J., Yang, K.-F., Wang, T.-F., Yen, L.-L.: A feasibility study on the adoption of e-learning for public health nurse continuing education in Taiwan. Nurse Education today 27(7), 755–761 (2007); Study from Ipsos MORI; Social Care Institute for excellence. E-readiness in the social sector (December 2006)

Applications and Exploration of ICT in Teaching History and Foreign Languages: Students and Teachers Attitudes, Perceptions and Evaluation

Anastasia Pamouktsoglou[1], John Antonopoulos[2], and Ourania Kalouri[3]

[1] Pedagogical Institute
anpam@otenet.gr
[2] Historian
jeanantonopoulos@otenet.gr
[3] ASPETE
rkalouri@otenet.gr

Abstract. The way of teaching history and foreign languages, at high school level, is changing rapidly. New needs for educational material arise from these changes. The technological development because of its effects on teaching practices as well as on the methodology of learning and teaching can be of great support to confront these needs. In this paper we present some of the issues related to the changes mentioned above we focus on the role of the new virtual learning environments towards this direction and the students and teachers perceptions and evaluation about this teaching approach.

Keywords: trainee teachers, ICT, initial training.

1 Introduction

The way of teaching history and foreign languages, at high school level, is changing and the ends of 20 century rapidly. New technologies (ICT) and mostly the engaged of the three branches commuters, Communications and Media, are catalyst for the society (Ypepth,-P.I., 2000, p.343). New needs for educational material arise from these changes. First, one must take into account of the relationship between teaching and society. This issue has many aspects. For example in the curricula there is an increased competition among the different disciplines. Thus, history and foreign languages teaching should constantly justify the role it plays in the curriculum and its educational value. Also becoming a widely taught subject, it must also face the increased heterogeneity of students and adapt to their cultural diversity and needs.

Second, one must take into consideration the evolution of learning theories and that of ICT. Finally, another point of interest is the relationship between the technological developments because of its effects on school practices as well as on the methodology of learning and teaching can be of great support to confront these needs. In this paper we present some of the issues related to the changes mentioned above we focus on the role of the new virtual learning environments towards this direction and the students and teachers perceptions and evaluation about this teaching approach.

M.D. Lytras et al. (Eds.): WSKS 2008, CCIS 19, pp. 276–281, 2008.

Although it is hard to determine the beginnings of interdisciplinary, its proto ideas are impeded in the works of Plato: «At the age of twenty, [some of our children] will be selected for promotion, and will have to bring together the disconnected subjects they studied in childhood and take a comprehensive view of their relationship with each other and with reality» (Plato, The Republic, Bk.VII). It is obvious that Plato is aware that specialized instruction in a number of diverse subjects, if unchecked, tends to stress the mutually exclusive aspects of such subjects (and perhaps even thereby promote a high degree of what the twentieth century has come to term "mental fragmentation" (Raptis et.al., 2001). Therefore he demands that all students selected for promotion must be compelled to explore the interrelationship of the various subjects, which comprise their preliminary education. Nevertheless the term interdisciplinary did not turn up until this century and it is used in order to cope with the complexity of scientific research as well as to define questions bordering several disciplines (holistic approach of knowledge) (DEPPS, 2003: Kleine, 1990). Also, interdisciplinary courses are widely commended to help students acquire the mental agility and critical thinking skills needed for success in the modern world.

2   Current Issues in the Teaching in a Multicultural and Multilingual Age

Today's Europe is unarguably multicultural and multilingual. The forces of globalisation and migration, expectations of mobility and the availability of cheap travel mean that cultures are mixing at a rate not seen before in history.

Wherever you look in Europe, the figures are startling. Already 12 million French do not have the French language as a mother tongue. And the process is continuing: 4 million asylum-seekers sought refuge in Western Europe during the 1990s (Council of Europe, 2003).

In Greece, twelve percent of schoolchildren speak another language in addition to Greek language. As the country is meeting the challenge of a multicultural society for the first time and this is expected to rise by 2020.

Frequently, assimilation is the priority for migrants, even to the point of refusing to let their children study the "home" language at school. One of the most important challenges for language educators is to be able to convince learners that multilingualism is possible and realistic – learning one language does not mean that you have to reject another. And, of course, for this to be feasible, the organisation of curricula needs to be less restrictive. The present pattern of choice around Europe – typically, English taught as a first foreign language, with one – frequently French - of the others major European languages as a second foreign language – does not appear to be an adequate response to this diversity, nor does it take account of the vast repertoire of language knowledge present in the European population.

The issue of teaching as a human activity is directly related to the evolution of learning theories (constructivist approach of teaching). Also the fundamental principle of constructivism is that learning is a constructive activity that students themselves have to carry out. From this point of view, the task of the educator is not to dispense knowledge but to provide students with opportunities and incentives to build it up (Von Glasserfeld, 1996).

According to Piaget's socio-historical approach the individual is responsible for his thinking and his knowledge and he is the central element of meaning making. On the other hand Vygotsky's constructivist perspective (socio-cultural approach) places communication and social life at the center of meaning making, so the individual can construct knowledge facilitated by a teacher or some of his peers. Following the original work of Vygotsky, it is now widely acknowledged that the conversation, questioning, explanation and negotiation of meaning of an adult and a learner's peers play an important role for learning. Vygotsky and his followers emphasise the central position of language and dialogue in human culture and cognition; they argue that learning occurs as people participate in shared endeavours with others (Raptis & Rapti, 2001, pp. 77-80). Therefore social environment plays an important role in the representation of scientific concepts. Also research that has been realized (Καλούρη & Αντωνόπουλος, 2002) has proved the interest of students and their improved output through the figurative depiction of history.

From one other way ICT and the widespread availability of the Internet offers opportunities for breaking down the barriers of the language classroom, making authentic language and real time information readily available; learners all around the world can communicate with each other. This work for the development of European citizenship, as an educated European citizen can understand several languages, is able to study and travel in many countries, and respects different nationalities and national cultures.

As Raptis and Raptis (2001) points out, the Internet takes teaching materials outside of the classroom and into the school communities. This in turn ensures that entirely new relationships between teachers and pupils, teachers and parents and between teacher and teacher will be forged. We can expect that teachers will soon be required to adopt the role of mediator between student and knowledge.

The use of computers and multimedia applications turns the schoolteacher into cultivator, as marked Mialaret, that can "coordinate" the reception of information from the students and guide complex activities (Mialaret, 1991). There is an increasing awareness amongst educationalists, researchers and administrators that the introduction of the new media into educational institutions calls for a change in learning and teaching patterns. They believe that the new media:

- call for and facilitate more independence on the part of the learner, more self directed activities and the organisation of learning processes;
- encourage interactive work;
- facilitate direct feedback;
- call for a change in the role distribution of teacher / learner, where learners take on
- teaching functions;
- enable contents to be continually updated with minimum efforts;
- provide faster access to teaching materials;
- provide greater opportunities for individual forms of learning;
- but also demand more social learning in group and teamwork. (Mialaret, 1991).

3   Methodology

The concept of ICT in education is seen as a system that enables information gathering, management, manipulation, access, and communication in various forms (DEPPS, 2003).

In line with this, the Ministry of Religion Education has formulated three main policies related to ICT in education (Ypepth, 2003):

- ICT is for all students. ICT is used as an enabler to reduce the digital gap between the schools.
- ICT is used as a teaching and learning tool, as part of a subject, and as a subject itself.
- ICT is to be used to increase efficiency, productivity, and effectiveness of the teaching.

In relation to these three policies, the Ministry of Religion Education tray to have all primary and secondary schools to be wired and fully equipped with ICT. A website known as Ekpaidevtiki Pili (educational Portal), was set up by the Ministry of Education to help increase the use of ICT in education and to provide links to help teachers and students access educational information readily. Realizing that teacher ability is a vital component for the success of ICT in implementation in schools.

3.1 Objectives of the Study

The study attempted to assess trainee teachers' confidence to integrate ICT in teaching based on the following:

- Gender
- Program of studies
- Academic performance, and
- Teaching experience

The study was conducted during their final semester. The methods were: a survey (using a questionnaire) and interviews (one-to-one). The interviews (n = 38) were based on semi-structured schedules. The target population was trainee teachers in faculties of Athens University in 2005-06, and random sample was 836 people. Qualitative dimensions of the data included perceptions and opinions.

The use of new forms of technology in the teaching of foreign languages and history demands that the educators embrace new abilities and new roles, in a technological but also a pedagogical and educational aspect.

The acquisition of technical knowledge and dexterities by the teacher is naturally not sufficient unless it is at the same time supported by an ability to learn and apply the corresponding pedagogic and instructive methods.

In order for the teacher to be able to use multimedia technology for his teaching purposes, he should have some relevant training that will allow him to analyze, evaluate and incorporate new technology to the teaching procedure. He should be able to choose, among the various information sources offered for teaching, the ones that correspond the best to the needs of the subject to be taught, but also to the needs and the particular traits of his students.

Teachers were asked to make a self-reflection on their ability to integrate ICT in teaching history and foreign languages. Also trainee teachers were asked to do a self-reflection on their confidence to integrate ICT in teaching. Their confidences were assessed using statements on their ability to integrate ICT with teaching. The study shows that trainee teachers were quite confident integrating ICT with teaching (M = 2.90).

The study shows that male teachers score significantly higher (M = 47.0) than female teachers (M = 41.5). Also trainee teachers who had several years experience in ICT scored significantly higher than those who hadn't.

The findings from the discussions with trainee teachers indicated that they generally viewed their lack of training in computers as the strongest inhibitor of usage. In contrast, some of the trainee teachers believed that they had learned a great deal about computers from friends. Also, some of them criticized the type of training. "All of as should be taught basic computer and word processing skills as part of their course. I am expected to use a computer but have never been shown how to do so".

Furthermore some teachers said that: "we need to become completely computer-literate and have the confidence to use the available technology adequately'. 'I should have been able to cope with the most common problems arising from the use of computers, in my lesson".

The findings, from the questionnaire survey indicated that a number of trainee teachers (49%) attributed their failure to acquire and develop computer skills to lack of support in terms of training, information and help from staff.

Our study shows that, in general, teachers and students are quite confident in using ICT for teaching. Their readiness to use ICT in teaching was no so good enough and they are not quite ready to answer questions about ICT and the use of new software in teaching of languages and history.

At the end the following conclusions can be made:

- Teachers were quite confident with their ability to integrate ICT training teaching.
- Male trainee teachers were more confident than female teachers, with the ability to integrate ICT in teaching.
- They believed that they had learned a great deal about computers from friends.
- The trainee teachers attributed their failure to acquire and develop computer skills to lack of support in terms of training, information and help from staff.
- They believes that they may be are good and effective teachers because they trying the best to teach the goals of learning for the best of their pupils.

We here remind that a computer is no more than a tool, and the role of the teacher towards his students is always of vast importance. Computers and new technology can contribute to more effective learning, and even more to the incitement of students. But the teachers are the one who have to determine the specific role new technology will acquire in the educational process.

However, teachers use ICTs for a number of purposes in their lives, and the sociocultural framework alerts the researcher to evidence of alternative figured worlds and corresponding budding identities that can be seen to be nested within the answers of student tech teachers. In tech teacher education it is imperative that such figured worlds are cultivated, allowing for the development of teachers' identities as potential architects of 'new worlds'.

References

1. Badura, A.: Social Learning Theory. Prentice-Hall Inc., Englewood Cliffs (1997)
2. Council of Europe, The Information Society. A Challenge for Education Policies (Strasbourg, Council of Europe) (1989)
3. Flake, J.L.: The World Wide Web and Education. Computers in the schools 12(1/2), 89–100 (1996)
4. Kaput, J.J.: Technology as a Transformative Force in Education: What Else Is Needed to Make it Work? Paper for the NCTM 2000 Technology Working Group in May (1998)
5. Kline, J.: Interdisciplinarity-History, Theory and Practice (1990)
6. Ministry of Education and Religion, Diathematikon programma. Government paper 303 & 304/13-3-2003 (Athens, Ministry of Education and Religion (in Greek) (2003)
7. Olson, J.K.: Changing our ideas about change. Canadian Journal of Education 10, 294–307 (1995)
8. Papert, S.: The Children's Machine: Rethinking School in the Age of the Computer. Basic Books, New York (1993)
9. Prawat, R.: Learning community, commitment and school report. Curriculum Studies V 28(1), 91–110 (1996)
10. Raptis, A., Rapti, A.: Learning and Teaching in the era of Informatics, 2nd edn. Raptis, Athens (2001)
11. Vygotsky, L.S.: Thought and Language. MIT Press, Cambridge (1962)
12. Von Glaserfeld, E.: Aspects of Constructivism (Introduction to) Constructivism: Theory, Perspective and Practice (ed.) Fosnot, Teachers College, Collumbia University (1996)
13. Καλούρη-Αντωνοπούλου Ο. - Αντωνόπουλος, Ι. (2002), Οι αντιδράσεις των μαθητών της Γ΄ Γυμνασίου απέναντι στην εικαστική απεικόνιση της ιστορίας. Μηχανισμοί προσέγγισης και κατανόησης του παρελθόντος μέσα από τα έργα τέχνης στο αντίστοιχο μάθημα, Πρακτικά (ηλεκτρ.) 3ο Διεθνές Συνέδριο Ελληνικής Παιδαγωγικής και Εκπαιδευτικής Έρευνας, Παιδαγωγική Εταιρεία Ελλάδος.

Learning to Invent: Let the New Knowledge Come

Carel S. de Beer

University of Pretoria, Department of Information Science, Pretoria, South Africa
fanie.debeer@up.ac.za

Abstract. The object of this paper is to present an alternative classroom situation, a departure from the classical situation based on platonic dialogue coupled with an instrumentalist model of communication. The strength of that approach lies in the apparent impact of reproduction and repetition – which, however, undermine inventiveness, more specifically the invention of new knowledge. I propose an alternative based on the work of Beuys, Deleuze and Kandinsky, Serres, and Ulmer. In terms of this alternative reality is playfully perceived as multiple and notably creates space for inventiveness. The development and cultivation of a disposition of inventiveness should enable us to invent new knowledge required for continuously developing challenging situations.

Keywords: Euretics, instructed third, invention, multiplicity, rhisomatic thought, social sculpture.

1 Introduction

The object of this paper is to propose an alternative classroom situation, a completely different one from the traditional model with its basis of platonic dialogue and its assumption that teaching/learning should take place face to face – in other words, repetitively. This platonic dialogue can no longer be our model. The assumptions that govern the representation and communication of knowledge, based on the classical perception of communication (which in turn is governed by a functionalist, instrumentalist approach), are completely inadequate. We need to move on to an alternative way of dealing with knowledge and reality in a life situations, and more specifically in teaching/learning situations. This conviction is reinforced by theoretical reflection in the light of experimental work that has been done in different parts of the world. Implications for the practical teaching/learning situation will briefly be worked out in this paper. It is a question of finding a method that will transcend itself by making it possible to think euretically or inventively – not repetitively, but in terms of discovery and invention. Euretics comprises a method of research and teaching that applies to the practice of teaching the tendency to a generative use of theory. This implies inventing an alternative teaching practice rather than interpreting or criticising one that exists. Rather than assuming fixed subject matter with a fixed meaning which merely has to be packaged and reproduced in lectures, seminars and the like, we need to assume heterogeneous matter that contains the raw material for the composition of discourses. This would have the potential to mobilise students.

M.D. Lytras et al. (Eds.): WSKS 2008, CCIS 19, pp. 282–290, 2008.

What is proposed is a self-education process – one that produces results which will surprise both teacher and student. We need to implement a pedagogics of inventiveness from which the institution itself may learn, one that can affect the social conditions for learning and reorganise the classification of knowledge. Basically it means exploring methods of creating ideas at a time when we are overwhelmingly convinced that we know all about the creation of ideas – that the creation of new ideas and knowledge is not particularly relevant. It means using theory in the service of inventiveness, creating a new poetics, actualising theory in practice.

This may be done by, for example, selecting a particular theorist and asking: if so-and-so is right – say, about the nature of language, epistemology and institutions – then how can and should works be created (in whatever field – philosophy, information, architecture, law, anthropology)? This draws data from other disciplines into one's own, not as evaluation standards or schemes of interpretation but as tools for creating something different. It is not so much a question of probing the author's or teacher's meaning as of trying to use it as the raw material of something distinctive. Much more is at stake in learning than precise messages can convey.I am greatly indebted to Michel Serres and Gregory Ulmer whose wonderful insights I could have shared over a long period of time, through their precious works and personal encounters that served as a great inspiration for my own thinking in the direction of the importance of invention and inventiveness in the context of a knowledge society. In the educational situation or the classroom one should playfully consider the multiple nature of reality as suggested (for instance) by artists such as Beuys and Kandinsky and by the philosopher Deleuze and the psychoanalyst Guattari, as well as the philosopher Michel Serres and the literary theorist Gregory Ulmer. In other words, we need to look beyond the rigid, the serious, the singular, that which controls. The suggestion is that theory should be seen as a hobby, a game; that a self-chosen artistic skill should be applied to the investigation of philosophical questions. Marx, Freud and others have borrowed the non-Western concept of fetishism to describe modern behaviour. The objects that surround us are fetishes, which mean that they are charged with social and psychological significance. We think through and by means of these objects at the most detailed level, so that by examining objects in terms of theory seen as a hobby we can eavesdrop on modern culture.In proposing the strategy of inventiveness, or a kind of euretic classroom, in which discovery and invention will be prominent, the following examples from the fields of the Arts and Philosophy have been selected in order to discuss and illustrate it.

2 Joseph Beuys's Concept of Social Sculpture

Beuys demonstrates how to do theory as sculpture. A theory of social organisation is basically a theory of social sculpture. On a lecture tour to the USA Beuys discussed his Energy plan for western man, in which he expounded his ideal of social sculpture. What it amounts to is the active mobilisation of each individual's latent creativity and then, as a consequence of this, shaping the society of the future in terms of the total energy of this individual creativity. He pointed out that humanity is a dynamic thing and that we as spiritual beings must take an active part – intellectually, volitionally and emotionally – in the dynamics of the changes associated with it. Our organically instinctive emotional forces must be combined with our intellectual forces. Our vision of the world must be expanded to include all those invisible energies with which we have lost touch. What it amounts to is the active mobilisation of each individual's latent creativity and then, as a consequence of this, shaping the society of the future in terms of the total energy of this individual creativity. He pointed out that humanity is a dynamic thing and that we as spiritual beings must take an active part – intellectually, volitionally and emotionally – in the dynamics of the changes associated with it. Our organically instinctive emotional forces must be combined with our intellectual forces. Our vision of the world must be expanded to include all those invisible energies with which we have lost touch.During a subsequent visit to the USA, on the occasion of an exhibition in the Guggenheim Museum, he accepted "creative responsibility" for organising and placing the works in such a way that, rather than a simple presentation of his art, the exhibition as such should be an "autonomous work of art". The following statement appeared in the introduction to the catalogue: "My objects are to be seen as stimulants for the transformations of the idea of sculpture, or of art in general. They should provoke thoughts about what sculpture can be and how the concept of sculpting can be extended to the invisible materials used by everyone: Thinking Forms – how we mould our thoughts or / Spoken Forms – how we shape our thoughts into words or / Social sculpture – how we mould and shape the world in which we live: Sculpture as an evolutionary process; everyone an artist" (Tisdall, 1979).

These ideas are charged with suggestions as to intervention in the educational system.Beuys's sculptural practice constitutes a theory about the concept of creativity as such in all human productivity. Our educational system as a whole is based on reading and writing. Beuys presents us with an individual form of writing – on the other side of the book. The best way to appreciate the nature of this writing is to see it not as art, science or philosophy but as pedagogics: "To be a teacher is my greatest work of art". The relationship of ideas to objects in the practice of Beuys contains suggestions on reversing the pedagogical process. As in psychoanalysis, it suggests a register of concepts unlike those of the rational intellect. The status of the subject of knowledge and the nature of the process of knowing (which, on the whole, are naively taken to be self-evident) become crucially important. Beuys approached art not by the common route – the skilled production of a "beautiful object" – but by way of "epistemological considerations".And how does Beuys teach? All the elements of a "new pedagogics" are at work here: speech, discourse, mimetics, models, objects, actions. In his actions, standard school equipment such as blackboard, chalk, desks, pointers, lectures and erasers all form part of a system of pedagogics. The eraser, which is made of felt, has all the associations of this primary material and makes a good example. "Felt is an insulator, as a protective covering against other influences, or conversely as a material that permits infiltration from outside influences. Then there is the warmth character, the greyness which serves to emphasize the colours that exist in the world by a psychological after-image effect, and the silence as every sound is absorbed and muffled" (Beuys, 1979:120). The blackboard is another example. Beuys's writing rests on assumptions as to how ideas are generated and, more particularly, how they are communicated or rather disseminated. The principle: a letter does not always reach its destination; or, the letter's destination is not determined by the old notion of identity. One of his commonest "multiples" is a postcard, which indicates not only a scene or a message but more specifically the phenomenon of "transmission" or "transfer". The effect of the multiples is to characterise the reception of the scene of writing as a mnemonic. Bueys meant one of his other works, The Fettecke [Fat corner] to represent the dissemination of ideas. We need to remember, however, that objects of art do not "convey messages": they mobilise the observer/spectator. They encourage and inspire inventions.

3 Deleuze on Nomadic and Rhisomatic Thought

Deleuze's intellectual experiment in which he employs the properties of felt as a way of thinking about certain abstract questions, follows the same line as Beuys's work. Deleuze and Guattari characterise the difference between the State apparatus and a "war machine" (contrasting notions of social organisation and of science) as the difference between woven material and felt. "Felt is a supple solid product that proceeds altogether differently, as an anti-fabric. It implies no separation of threads, no intertwining, only an entanglement of fibres obtained by fulling (for example, by rolling the block of fibres back and forth). What becomes entangled are the microscales of the fibres. An aggregate of intrication of this kind is in no way homogeneous: it is nevertheless smooth, and contrasts point by point with the space of fabric" (Deleuze & Guattari, 1988:475). At the level of interpretation there may be differences as to whether felt is homogeneous or not, but in euretic or inventive terms the procedure is the same. An art skill material is scrutinised or questioned to obtain an insight into theoretical questions, and supplementation of the prevailing Western culture is sought in a nomad culture.

An important facet of Deleuze's work has to do with generating a nomadic mobility between the thousands of plateaus in which reality manifests itself. The image of the nomad is an apt one for this movement between plateaus. The crux of the matter, invariably if not always overtly expressed, lies in our assumptions about the nature of reality. If we assume the existence of a first principle ("being", the self, the concrete, etc.), then everything is interpreted in these terms. But the pursuit of, or faith in, an abstract first abstract principle can stifle all life; and that, unfortunately, is what the prevailing educational system does. It stifles instead of cultivating life. That is why Deleuze stresses the multiple (the thousand plateaus) rather than the unity. However, it is not enough to acquire this insight into the multiple: it first has to be created.Of course, the idea of a first principle establishes a hierarchical order and hegemonic categories. The idea of the multiple makes it possible to pursue a non-hierarchical pedagogic discourse. It enables us to think about literally everything in one uninterrupted line. Every single thing, not only the highest and first, is drawn in at the same level: short stories, eyesight, birdsong, the state, and so forth – all in one breath, as it were. None of them excels the others: all are at the same level.

There is no question either of fixities or of a first. This permits Deleuze to differentiate between two forms of thought. (See Deleuze 1984, 1994). The dogmatic form is characterised by the love of truth, the rejection of forces leading away from the truth; by adherence to method. In this form of thought, we are never referred to the actual forces that shape thinking and are assumed by the intellect to constitute thinking. On the other hand we have a new form of thought that centres not on truth but on meaning and value. The categories of this form of thought are not truth and falsity but nobility and baseness, depending on the forces that preoccupy the intellect. Here falsity and error are not the enemies of thought: they may even be reversed into affirming powers. The enemy of thought, the symptom of its degeneracy, lies elsewhere: folly, which is the great antagonist of mature, considered, noble thought.

The choice between these two thought forms is the choice with which education is now confronted. What thought requires is not so much a method as a paideia, a moulding, a culture! And that, indeed, is the choice. Teaching as ped-ago-gics (e-duca-tion) has the primary task of eradicating and arresting degeneracy of thought, of shaming folly; unmasking degeneracy and the follies that arise from it (and the bewildering alliance that results between victims and perpetrators). It criticises all mystification (whatever its purpose), unmasks all fiction (the impetus behind reaction). It transforms thought into aggressive, energetic, affirming action. It leads students into freedom – freedom from every dogmatic thought form, freedom from caricatures of criticism, freedom to conceive multiplicity. The first of the two thought forms arrests every kind of inventiveness; the second sets it free to burst into flower.The concept of multiplicity (a swarming world of anonymous, impersonal, proto-individual nomadic singularities opening up ahead of us), as used by Deleuze, is designed precisely to achieve an adequate and positive theory of implementation of invented knowledge (theory of practice).

4 Kandinsky's "Multiplicity" as a Theory of Spiritual Development and Orientation

Deleuze's "immanent reduction" may be explained in terms of Kandinsky's painting. One of the classical problems of intercourse with the world and with reality and knowledge (but also the most intractable) is the problem of representation. Deleuze's immanent reduction is a determined onslaught on this problem and Kandinsky's art is an ally in the attempt. It is not really possible to represent multiplicity. Kandinsky's art illustrates this well. He also wrote: "Cezanne made a living thing out of a teacup, or rather, in a teacup he realized the existence of something alive. He raised still-life to the point where it ceased to be inanimate. He painted things as he painted human beings, because he was endowed with the gift of divining the internal life in everything. He achieved expressive color and a form that harmonizes this color with an almost mathematical abstraction. A man, a tree, an apple, are not represented, but used by Cezanne in building up a painterly thing called a 'picture'. The same intention actuates the work of one of the greatest of the young Frenchmen, Henri Matisse. He paints 'pictures' and in these 'pictures' endeavours to render the divine. To attain this end he requires nothing but the subject to be painted (human being or whatever it may be) and means that belong to painting alone, color and form" (Kandinsky, 1966:36). Compare Foucault's little book on Matisse, This is not a pipe. This is not about representative art. It is also strongly reminiscent of Beuys, in whose view eraser, blackboard and suchlike, together with students, suffice for a complete pedagogic or training act.

We need to remember that the theory of multiplicity as first opponent contains the general unconsidered concept of representation – in other words, the representation of something. As Kandinsky puts it: "One of the first steps away from representation and towards abstraction was, in the pictorial sense, the exclusion of the third dimension – in other words, the tendency to restrict the picture to a single level. There is also a need to alter the proportions of the pictorial space and the objects that occupy it, which means that he goes beyond the mere elimination of orthogonal perspective space or optical destruction of the pictorial level: the pictorial level virtually "disappears" and the elements are suspended in the space –which, however, has no precise boundaries (especially as to depth)" (Overy, 1969:121). Compare, too, his book about the spiritual dimension of art (Kandinsky, 1966). A Kandinsky is a multiple, writes Deleuze.

Only by intellectual (noetic) acts can reality as a multiple be composed in a symphonically rhythmic style. One might go even further: an inappropriate combination of colour and form is not necessarily jarring since it may, by operations of the intellect combined with manipulation, uncover fresh harmonious possibilities. New inventive horizons beckon. It should also be remembered, writes Kandinsky, that each represented object generates certain inner vibrations that lead to new modes of expression –inventiveness, in other words. Kandinsky (1966:77) concludes his book with this statement: "We have before us an age of conscious creation, and this new spirit in painting is going hand in hand with thought towards an epoch of great spirituality". Using the vocabulary of this paper, one might speak of an epoch of inventiveness or heuretics. (Cf Ulmer 1994). The authors we have considered all investigate artistic materials with a view to gaining insights into theoretical questions. All of them assign a special place to the human intellect. All understand and articulate reality in terms of multiplicity. All explore a nomadic culture in search of an indirect way of supplementing the Western intellectual framework. For all of them, the whole activity is an exercise in paideia or education in the full sense of the word.

5 Michel Serres: The Instructed Third

One encounters in the work of Michel Serres (1995, 1997) the exploration of numerous pathways in philosophy, science and literature to argue that the best contemporary education requires knowledge of both science's general truth and literature's singular stories. He heralds a new pedagogy that claims that from the cross-breeding of the humanities and the sciences a new educational ideal can be born: the educated third, or, the troubadour of knowledge. Whomever is called "the instructed third", is competent and very able to link the sciences (the instructed first) with the humanities (the instructed second), while taking him/herself the third position, that is the position between the two, with the ability to move from the one to the other and back again - a kind of traveller or voyager, hence the troubadour. The "instructed third" is the person who knows how to weave together the truth of the sciences with the peace of judgement. His Instructed third is a book on education in the largest possible sense: the all-encompassing formation of human thought as invention. According to Serres inventive creativity is the only activity worthy of cognitive thought. In the age of knowledge and information his contributions on the 'atlas of knowledges' and on the angels as 'a contemporary myth' regarding the sending of messages are of vital importance.

In his articulation of a new legend of the angels (Serres 1995) he emphasises that our sciences and technics provide hundreds of ways of communication, too many universal (world) networks, a city without boundaries, unstoppable displacements that designs the map of a new universe and inducing planetary problems, brought to us without end by thousands of messages. But this universal messagerie is simultaneously accompanied by undecidable injustices, growing misery, hunger and war, a revolting inequality. Do we not notice everywhere around us a new legend of the angels with exchangers and announcers, networks and passages, downfalls and demons, powers and dominations, a quest for misery...? A warning that should be taken heed of in the knowledge society.

6 Gregory Ulmer: Internet invention

This complementary view, that relates unrelated areas, ideas, and forms, is well-developed by Gregory Ulmer (2003) in his Internet invention. Apart from his very illuminating exploration of the value of Beuys and Kandinsky for the learning of inventiveness (See Ulmer 1885), he devotes plenty of attention, perhaps not adequately acknowledged, to the role of electronic media in the cultivation of inventiveness. As a matter of fact the very idea of a knowledge society is in a direct sense linked to the impact of electronic media developments on the creation, dissemination and utilization of knowledge. His development of what he calls a 'teletheory' with the emphasis on theoretical developments for the age of the video is extremely relevant here. (Ulmer 1989). In line with this he also proposes 'heuretics' as "the use of theory to invent forms and practices, as distinct from 'hermeneutics' which uses theory to interpret existing work" (Ulmer 2003:4-5). Internet invention concerns how the new technologies might affect our working conditions and teaching practices [and certainly also learning experiences], and what we might do to reduce the negative aspects and enhance the positive. According to his understanding "the one negentropic force in the world is human intelligence (creativity): we should consider this moment as a time for invention."

7 Discussion

From these five theoretico-practical explorations we derive the following suggestions:

With regard to the inventive or euretic classroom: it does something other than convey and receive precise messages. It is concerned with inference rather than communication. A course is designed to create gaps in texts – in the totality of information – and to provide the means, designs and rhetoric to fill these gaps. That is the function of composition. As Bernard Stiegler(2003:37) emphasises, we are in a natural sense inclined to oppose things in stead of composing them. The result of such a decomposition is diabolic and as such a very dangerous strategy of disturbance and disintegration in the context of learning as well as teaching in the knowledge society. Compositional thinking is in line with the image of thought explored and promoted by Gilles Deleuze and as such an absolute condition for inventiveness. The inventive or euretic assignment derives a basic principle of composition from Alice in Wonderland: the appropriation of Alice (or some other now mythical figure) as an organisational principle, as though

Alice were a kind of index or mnemonic system. These figures are neither symbol nor allegory: they are inventio and memoria. (Cf Deleuze 1990 on sense and non-sense, in a book devoted to or at least inspired by Alice in Wonderland). With regard to the student of euretics, the student who really wants to invent: How can students use this formula for encounters in wonderland in order to liberate, organise and mobilise any amount of information, any terrain of knowledge? The point at issue is not the specific content of a package; the point is that the holders or possessors of the information are the ones who unpack it. The student as a reader is confronted with the totality of information or with a specific amount of it; this happens in the euretic classroom, which provides the area or space of inventive encounters. Students compose a scene out of the items – a mnemonic scene – or they dramatise an event, depict a place, bearing in mind throughout that the procedure is also a method of inventiveness, a manner of writing, a theoretical experiment.

What this paper is suggesting, then, is that the euretic classroom should trade re-production for inventiveness, strict methodology (dogmatic thinking) for a theoretical indulgence in hobbies (anti-method), sterile memorisation for playful writing, and stark and dull research for the entrancing gardens of wonderland. (Ulmer 1991).All this calls for intellectual exercise according to the new perception of thinking; in other words, mobility between a thousand plateaus and through multiples of multiplicity. But … "Learning to think: our schools no longer have any idea what this means" (Nietzsche). This stratum of meaning simply has to be restored to our students (schools). Our competence to do so depends on the extent to which we are still vic-tims of the dogmatic perception of thought or intellect. We conclude with Deleuze's sketch, into which students need to be inducted or introduced: "Empedocles and his volcano – this is an anecdote of a thinker. The height of summits and caves, the laby-rinths; mid-day – mid-night; the halcyon aerial element and also the element of the subterranean. It is up to us to go to extreme places, to extreme times, where the high-est and the deepest truths live and rise up. The places of thought are the tropical zones frequented by the tropical man, not temperate zones or the moral, methodical or mod-erate man" (Deleuze, 1983:110; 1994: 129-167). That is the domain or space of the inventive or of the euretic experience, the space in which new knowledge emerge on a regular scale!

Bibliography

Beuys, J.: Drawings. Prestel Verlag, Munich (1979)
Deleuze, G.: Nietzsche and philosophy. Athlone, London (1983)
Deleuze, G., Guattari, F.: A thousand plateaus: capitalism and schizophrenia. Athlone, London (1988)
Deleuze, G.: The logic of sense. Columbia University Press, New York (1990)
Deleuze, G.: Difference and repetition. Athlone Press, London (1994)
Kandinsky, W.: Concerning the spiritual in art. George Wittenborn, New York (1966)
Overy, P.: Kandinsky, the language of the eye. Elek, London (1969)
Serres, M.: Angels: a modern myth. Flammarion, Paris (1995)
Serres, M.: The troubadour of knowledge. The University of Michigan Press, Ann Arbor (1997)
Serres, M., Latour, B.: Conversations on science, culture and time. The University of Michigan Press, Ann Arbor (1995)
Stiegler, B.: Aimer, saimer, nous aimer. Galilée, Paris (2003)

Tisdall, C.: Joseph Beuys. Hudson & Thames, London (1979)

Ulmer, G.: Applied Grammatology. The Johns Hopkins University Press, Baltimore (1985)

Ulmer, G.: Teletheory: grammatology in the age of video. Routledge, New York (1989)

Ulmer, G.: The euretics of Alice's valise. Journal of Architectural Education 45, 3–10 (1991)

Ulmer, G.: Heuretics: the logic of invention. The Johns Hopkins University Press, Baltimore (1994)

Ulmer, G.: Internet invention: from literacy to electracy. Longman, New York (2003)

The New Informatics Technologies in Education Debate

Prudenciano Moreno-Moreno[1] and Cornelio Yáñez-Márquez[2]

[1] Universidad Pedagógica Nacional, Área I. Política Educativa
Carretera al Ajusco No. 24, Col. Héroes de Padierna, México, D. F., 14200, México
pmoreno@ajusco.upn.mx
[2] Centro de Investigación en Computación, Instituto Politécnico Nacional
Av. Juan de Dios Bátiz s/n, México, D.F., 07738, México
cyanez@cic.ipn.mx

Abstract. The current paper is focused on the evolution and future of discussions on the application of Information Technologies on education and pedagogy from a conceptual perspective. The analyzed debate revolves around those who back New Communication and Information Technologies (NCITs) as a technical-functional expression of modernity (the Accolatory); and the opposites (the Dismissive), both postmodern —simply critics and skeptics— and antimodern, decidedly contrary to the use of NCITs. Finally, we conclude with a proposal of conciliation of all the above positions into a new educative vision, transmodern or metamodern, based on the advances of the so-called "Integral Theory of the Whole".

1 Introduction of Computational and Informatics Education

The invention of the computer precedes its introduction in educative processes. Computer technologies induce curricular changes between the decades of the 1960s and 1970s, with the notion of "kind of skill" and changes in the production of knowledge [1]. Also, the concept of Computational Education (CE) appeared before that of Informatics Education (IE).

In the 1960s and 1970s, the CE is for all kinds of alumni; thanks to the efforts of Mathematics teachers, ensuing the arising of the *new mathematics*. According to the British Computer Society Committee, the introduction of CE was stimulated by the growing potential of the computer industry. Thus what was termed as new mathematics is the result of a particular kind of computational development.

The former mathematical model was that of logic abstraction; the new one is about solving real problems in the productive and services world, via computers. This affected the design of computers as special experiments in education: IBM introduced educative computers to the United Kingdom (UK) in 1966, apart from commercial ones. However, Tinsley [2] argued that in practice, computers were used as *calculators* in the mathematical context of the 1960s.

Later on began a change of paradigm from a *technical* approach to a *conceptual* approach. This latter development gave rise to a wide debate, not just technical, over computers and their trajectory, possibilities, limits and global perspectives.

M.D. Lytras et al. (Eds.): WSKS 2008, CCIS 19, pp. 291–296, 2008.

Some indicators of this change: for instance, the revision of computers in high school by the OECD Centre for Educational Research and Innovation, with the critique that CE had been reduced to teaching Mathematics and creating talented students in said area; hence the need to broaden CE horizons. In 1967, several publications on CE development and social work division influenced the National Counsel for Educative Technology, which divided CE into two areas: computers for education and education about computers. The former includes Computer Assisted Learning, which gives the student the impression of receiving individual attention and does learning by discovery.

The focus changed from technical-mathematical on hardware to information processing in the 1970s. Particular attention received some specific application areas such as: supermarkets, airline ticket registering, and large databases.

By 1973 [1] the computers graduating student profile is being discussed, being the first real effort to expand CE. The learning methods associated with CE were those of Dewey (learning by discovery), Piaget (problem solving), Isaacs (concrete experience), and Whitehead (student participation).

By the early 1980s, Longworth in UK saw that Mathematics teachers (dominant in CE) were oblivious to the socio-cultural implications of computing, and that Humanities teachers were reluctant to get involved in what they saw as a scientific topic. Longworth was very important to breaking interdisciplinary boundaries and to clarify that information processing can articulate the curriculum.

As a consequence of curricular development and the passage from computer science (as a unitary discipline) to information processing with applications and implications of a broad usage, the transition from CE technical aspects to IE was made. Informatics (in the early 1970s) was seen as a cognitive corpus, separated from computer science. By 1975, CE had been transformed into Informatics.

Even with this broader orientation, which was consolidated in the decades of the 1980s and 1990s, and characterized by a vision of computer as a tool to think and work, it has not moved along with informatics. The latter was shown in the document National Curriculum Technology which is based on the "Tools / Skills" education model. This evolved into an educative debate, developed in parallel to CE and IE, which continues nowadays with relevant context changes.

2   The Accolatory

Understanding of NCITs introduction in education started with divergent scenarios: the voices represented in the Accolatory, technology determinists based on cognitive psychology; and the Dismissive voices, representing the social critics to NCITs in an extra-scholar political-philosophical level, while the former situated themselves in a pragmatic, scholar level.

The Accolatory make a semi-evangelic defense through several journals, using a high-tech language. They even propose the absurd idea that in the XXI century, the best teaching-learning system will be the interactive use of computers.

The demands made to NCITs in education would be: 1) Teaching better than preceding systems; 2)Teaching what other systems cannot do; 3) Creative interaction; 4) High-level intellectual activity (logic thought); 5) Better variety than conventional pedagogy; and 6) High levels of skill and understanding.

Stonier and Colier [1] made the noisiest defense of the computer-education relationship. Under the concept of *homo sapiens cerebrus*, we were witnessing a revolutionary stage of history, where the brain powers increase thanks to computers and automated information. The latter was endorsed also by Golden [1].

Seymour Papert [2], one of the most brilliant defendants of CE, was inspired by Piaget to argue that the programming language Logo allows independent learning and problem solving skills, as well as creativity and self-confidence.

3 The Dismissive

This is an ironic term directed at critics of the use of computers in education. Baker [1], a strong critic of NCITs in the UK, has argued that:

1. There is a marginalization of teachers, besides software development does not take into account the educative use.
2. Computers are actually intruders in curricula since educative progress is not an unavoidable consequence of technological progress.
3. The conventional format of basic games persists; fun is considered an end in and of itself. It is questionable whether software is a springboard for learning, given that a large number of programs are trivial, allowing only stereotypical, rigid, strict, and mechanical feedback.
4. Computers have been idolized as a super brain, as an important source of knowledge: unjustified centrality in curricula, when there is even the danger of forming passive and isolated individuals.

The defense argues that there can be learning by discovery via complex data bases and simulated experiments to be reproduced in the lab. However Baker counter-argues by saying that the type and quality of occurring interaction is unknown, since computers can produce silence. Karger admits to the technological potential, but questions the urgency of introducing the child in it [2].

As there are technological determinists, there are social determinists too, like Noble and Williams, who consider technology as part of the mental machinery of domination and alienation of the hegemonic capitalistic system [1].

However, in Beynon [2] the question is still: how can technology restructure and enlarge educational power? Answers are still problematic: by artificial intelligence as a metaphor of brain processes model construction, and by the influence of computers on the development of cognitive psychology.

At the International Conference on Technology and Education (1988) [3], the cognitive psychology / artificial intelligence predominated, emphasizing technical over the socio-cultural aspects. This has been a recurring complaint of the Dismissive, for CE as well as for IE: the predominance of the technocentric approach. According to Streibel [4], it forces us to work (or act) as rule-governed information processors, as well as building thoughts as solutions to cognitive problems; when the resolutions are received by formal calculus and rational analysis.

Medway [1] observes the building of a systematical design process, mean-end oriente. Even if we are active and intuitive in our vision of the world, we would have to reduce problems to procedural and measurable structures, restricting thought to cognitive operations, to a mere normative dimension, lacking the interpretative one.

4   The Situation in the 1990s and the XXI Century

Etchevery [5] criticized Argentinean parents for thinking that educative technology is the solution to low quality in teaching (96% of them believe in it being mandatory). He also states that in 1996, United States (US) citizens considered informatics education more necessary than History, Exact and Social Sciences, and Humanities. Also, in the US, the programs for informatizing schools have gone from 40 to 100 thousands of millions of dollars, from 1997 to 2000.

The criticism of Etchevery focuses on the fact that Internet does not stimulate intellect, since the public selects banalities over complex contents. He relies on a quote by the multimillionaire founder of Apple, Inc., Steve Jobs: "what is wrong in education cannot be solved with technology" [5].

The debate tends to take fairer proportions with the intervention of authors such as Aguirregabiria [6], when without opposing the technological solution he states the need to classify the educative project.

He characterizes learning into: 1) Learning with the computer; 2) Learning through the computer; 3) About the computer; 4) Informatics of teaching; and 5) Teaching to integrate informatics in the curriculum.

He divides the different waves of educative informatics as follows:

1. 1960s – 1975. Triumph of the philosopher's stone by intelligent artifacts (CAI).
2. 1975 – 1990. Micro-computers (1977) and access to documental information.
3. 1990 – 2000. NCITs; compact discs (CD), video (laser vision), teleconferences, email, virtual classroom.
4. 2001 – 2020. A million scientific-technological journals and the electronic library; technological convergence, multimedia, telematics.
5. 2020 – 2060. Biochips, nanotechnology.

Aguirregabiria states that computers can be seen as didactic machines in the following aspects: interactive text books, intellectual agent, multifunctional instrumental cognitive tool, expression means, and communicative empowerment prosthetic of cognitive access.

Carvajal [7] concurs too with the notion of the technological dimension being a first order component of educative and cultural transformations. He conceives NCITs as an exogenous element which intrudes in the educative institution, opening new questions in that space, but affecting firstly as an increasing need in children, young, and adults alike, to *alphabetize* themselves in computers. "It has been said that computer alphabetization would take its place along reading, writing, and arithmetic, as a fourth key subject of basic education" [7].

However, the Accolatory also reappear in Serres thesis [8] for whom NCITs are influencing the formation of a pedagogic society. On the other hand, the Dismissive reappear with Archambault [9] who fears the NCITs as a Trojan horse for the industrialization and mercantilization of education, and Tremblay [10] by the context of neoliberal economy, competitive market, and the direct payment of product and services of formation which clients receive. Therefore, the prophecies which foretold a pedagogic revolution have not been fulfilled, while the stronger tendencies are the industrialization and mercantilization of symbolic activities.

5   Conclusions

After the journey along the surge and development of the debate on the introduction of computers in education, it can be seen that later authors take a more balanced stance. This is the case of A. Piscitelli [11] who although criticizing the neodismissive, recognizes also that "the introduction cycle of new information technologies in school has been as predictable as useless, and maybe that is why the results inside the classrooms have been so meager" [11].

For this author, by just analyzing how schools have boarded the transmission and creation of new competences, skills, and learning capacities, we can understand the technology-education relationship.

The author recommends advancing on the following points: 1) Equipping for digital alphabetizing; 2) Contents (curriculum); 3) Docent formation; and 4) Internet connection in schools, opting for an equidistant point between technophobia and technophilia, distinguishing also 3 kinds of usage: banal, enabling, and empowering.

Among the latter two we could find as an example the program "Math Visual", which was created by a group of engineers, as an informatics program for learning, practicing, examining, and solving Mathematics problems by sequences. The design team intends with this software to attack *mathemaphobia* in the areas of Algebra, Arithmetics, Geometry, and Trigonometry [12].

In this order, also the program *Eciclomedia* by SEP for grade schools: a CD with pictures, videos, sounds, and virtual tours, which digitizes the text book contents. Another, the first virtual reality laboratory in Latin America, located in DGSCA-UNAM.

Future advances of NCITs (digital cities, quantum computing, semantic web, and the convergence of biochip to store in artificial memory the brain contents) will continue to impact strongly on education. However, such impact will continue to be reduced to an informatics usage as a cognitive tool, but it will not broaden to a change of *pedagogic vision*, which is the nucleus of educative theory. These points do not touch each other.

Therefore it is necessary to involve IE into the integral knowledge paradigm of the XXI century: the integral theory of the whole [11, 13-15]. This is done in order to put it into perspective and allow the union of what the Accolatory and the Dismissive kept apart, pedagogic vision and technological vision, and integrate them both in a broader model of transmodern science, a conception which transcends technology as a mere analytical instrument and knowledge base, to another where its role can be seen as a part of an educative formation of wider base.

Acknowledgments. The authors would like to thank the Instituto Politécnico Nacional (Secretaría Académica, COFAA, SIP, and CIC), the CONACyT, and SNI for their economical support to develop this work.

References

1. Capel, R.: Historia social de la educación computacional: oportunidad fallida? En Under satnding Technologies in education. Falmor Press, UK (1991)
2. Beynon, J.: Learning to real technology. Under standing Technologies in education. Falmor Press, U K (1991)

3. International Conference Technology and Education. University Press, London, UK (1988)
4. Streibel, W.: Tecnocentric approach and concept of "tool/skill". Falmor Press, UK (1985)
5. Jaim Etchevery, G.: La tragedia educativa. Ed. FCE Buenos Aires, Argentina (2000)
6. Aguirregabiria, Mikel (Coord.) Tecnología y educación. Ed. Narcea, España (1998)
7. Carvajal Romero, J.: Internet, lo educativo y la educación;complejo discursivo. En el libro de Josefina Granja Castro (comp.).Miradas a lo educativo. Ed. Plaza y Valdes, México (2003)
8. Serres, M.: La societé pedagogique". Le Monde de LËducation (September 1998), http://www.globenet.org/arbor/biblio/textes/M-Serres/serres.htm
9. Archambault, J.P.: L Ecole et les technologies de L information;mercantilización pedagogie, http:crdp.ac-paris.fr/b/res/jpamarchand.pdf
10. Tremblay, G.: Redes de comunicación, aprendizaje y sociedad. En el libro de Delia Crovi Druetta (Coord.) Hacia la sociedad de la información y el conocimiento. Memorias de PANAM II, FCPS-UNAM. México (2004)
11. Piscitelli, A.: Internet: la nueva imprenta del siglo XXI, Paidos, España (2005)
12. Gutierrez, G.: Cura para la matemafobia. En Revista Ciencia y Desarrollo, Nueva Epoca 30(#176) (Mayo-Junio 2004)
13. Lazlo, E.: La ciencia y el campo akásico. Una teoría integral del todo. Ed. Nowtilus, España (2005)
14. Wilber, Ken.Una teoria del todo. Ed. Kairos, España (2002)
15. Kapra, F.: El turning point.Hacia un nuevo paradigma del conocimiento en el siglo XXI. Ed. Paidós, España (1997)

King Saud University Drive toward the Knowledge Society: *A STOPE View*

Ali Al-Ghamdi and Saad Haj Bakry

King Saud University, P.O Box 800, 11421, Riyadh, Saudi Arabia
asghamdi@ksu.edu.sa, shb@ksu.edu.sa

Abstract. The drive toward the "knowledge society (KS)" is becoming an important issue for development. As influential knowledge organizations, universities have an essential role to play in this regard. The ambitious university, "King Saud University (KSU)", recently initiated development programs, for the promotion of its knowledge leadership at the national Saudi level, and beyond. This paper is concerned with introducing these programs for the purpose of sharing their drive and activities, and learning from potential feedbacks. The presentation of these programs is associated with the elements of a recent KS ecosystem framework. The framework integrates the knowledge activities of knowledge generation, diffusion, and utilization, into a "knowledge circle (KC)" that can support sustainable development; and it considers the activation of the circle to be associated with the domains of "strategy, technology, organization, people and environment (STOPE)". The paper hopes to initiate discussions on how to prepare universities for the third millennium.

Keywords: Universities, King Saud University, Knowledge Society; Knowledge Activities; Knowledge circle; STOPE view.

1 Introduction

This introductory section emphasizes the role of universities in the drive toward a dynamic knowledge society. It also addresses the objectives and the content of the paper.

1.1 Universities and the Knowledge Society (KS)

In the year 2000, at the turn to the 21st century, the "European Union (EU)", in its Lisbon strategy, identified the university as an important moving force for achieving the central Europeans goal of establishing the knowledge society [1]. In a recent paper [2], the knowledge society ecosystem has been viewed according to the framework given in Figure 1. The framework emphasizes that the knowledge activities of "knowledge generation, diffusion and utilization" should be integrated, in a "knowledge circle (KC)", so that they can provide efficient and effective sustainable support to development. In addition, the framework illustrates that the KC can be activated through the issues associated with the main domains of "strategy, technology, organization, people and environment (STOPE)".

M.D. Lytras et al. (Eds.): WSKS 2008, CCIS 19, pp. 297–307, 2008.

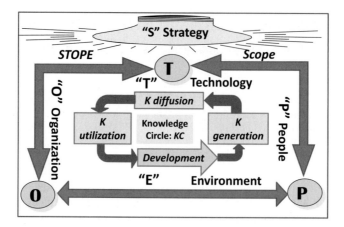

Fig. 1. A view of the knowledge society ecosystem [2]: Universities should activate KC through supporting STOPESTOPEScopeO

Considering the framework of Figure 1, the EU wants universities to be an important force in driving KC toward enhancing development; of course taking the issues of the STOPE domains into account. In this respect, all KC activities need to be considered in an integrated manner, with emphasis on knowledge generation, through research and innovation, as this is the main driving force of the KC.

1.2 Driving the Knowledge Circle (KC)

As the main driving force of the KC, research and innovation have been widely recognized as essential activities in distinguished and ambitious universities. There are many examples in support of this; and these examples stem from three main issues: classification and ranking of universities, membership of associations of distinguished universities, and expert definitions of what a university is, or should be.

With regards to the first type of examples, Carnegie classification of higher education (HE) institutions places universities with research degrees on top of its classes, and it calls them: doctorate granting (DR) institutions [3]. In addition, research output and citations are important factors in ranking universities according to the widely known ranking systems of: Times Higher World University Ranking; Academic Ranking of World Universities (known as the Shanghai system); and Ranking of World Universities on the Web (known as Webometrics) [4].

Considering associations of distinguished universities, in the United States and Europe, there are two important ones: Association of American Universities (AAU) [5]; and the League for European Research Universities (LERU) [6]. While AAU has a total membership of "sixty American universities" and "two Canadians"; LERU has "twenty". Research and innovation that drive the KC is an essential factor in the membership of these privileged associations.

HE experts have their own views of universities and their role in knowledge activities in general, and research and innovation in particular; two important examples are presented here. Rhodes, the former, long time, president of Cornell university, considers a research university to be "a substantial institution: seriously engaged in

research and scholarly apprenticeship and partnership that lead to the PhD; and sufficiently competitive in the quality of its work to attract both graduate students and
research support [7]". On the same issue, another expert, Taylor in an OECD (Organization of Economic Cooperation and Development) paper, states that "the key
characteristics of leading research universities are: presence of pure and applied research; delivery of research-led teaching; breadth of academic disciplines; high proportion of postgraduate research programs; and high level of external income; and an
international perspective [8]".

1.3 Presented Work

Recognizing the need for the activation of the KC, and the establishment of the KS,
KSU, with its ambitious vision, initiated a new development drive toward the KS. The
coming sections of this paper address this drive. The next section introduces the university and the directions of its drive. This is followed by presenting KSU new development programs that translate the drive into action. The presentation structures these
programs according to the element of the KS ecosystem of Figure 1. The work is then
concluded with some comments and observations.

2 King Saud University (KSU)

KSU is a Saudi university, and Saudi Arabia spreads over an area of "2.15 million
square kilometers", with a population of around "24 million, in mid 2007", "27 % of
which are non-Saudis" living in the country [9]. It has "20 universities", and "14 colleges" offering degree programs. This section introduces KSU by providing a brief
history of its past development, addressing its current state, and highlighting its future
vision toward building the KS.

2.1 A Brief History

King Saud University is the oldest and largest university in Saudi Arabia. Its foundation
goes back to 1957, when it started with one college, the College of Arts. Soon after, new
colleges were established: the College of Science in 1958, the Colleges of Pharmacy
and Administrative Sciences in 1959; and series of other colleges later. Currently, the
university covers practically all higher education disciplines. It may be important to
state that, in the early days, the university admitted only male students; but in 1962, only
five years after its establishment, it started admitting female students [10].

2.2 The Present State

At present, the university has around "20 colleges", with over "100 academic departments". Each college has a research center, with all centers associated with the dean-
ship for research. The university also has three other specialized research centers
working on subjects of local interest. In addition, an institute for consulting and research studies is available, and is known as "King Abdullah Institute for Consulting
and Research". The numbers of students and staff of the university are given in
Table 1 [10].

2.3 KSU: Knowledge Society University

In 2007, the university moved forward toward activating its role in driving the KC and contributing to the development of the KS. This movement was briefly and elegantly described by Professor Abdullah Al-Othman, the university Rector, who said: "we are in KSU not only King Saud University, but also Knowledge Society University". A vision and a mission that translate this movement into specific directions are given in Table 2.

Table 1. Students and staff at King Saud University (KSU)

King Saud University: *KSU* (2007)				
WHO	DEGREE PROGRAM	NUMBERS		
		Males	Females	Total
Students	Bachelor	28536	20800	49336
	Master	2206	1467	3673
	Doctorate	361	152	513
Academic staff: from Professor t Demonstrators		2310	826	3136

Table 2. KSU drive toward the knowledge society (KS)

KSU: *Knowledge Society University*	
Vision	Mission
To be a leading enabler of a dynamic and prosperous knowledge society	To activate the *knowledge circle* of knowledge *generation, diffusion and utilization, through*: setting-up suitable *strategies*; emphasizing promising *technologies*; enhancing *organization* and management; preparing, and supporting *people*; and establishing cooperative *environment*, *with* national and international *partnerships*

3 KSU Development Drive

An approach for presenting the KSU development programs is introduced here. The approach is based on the KC-STOPE framework of Figure 1. Following the approach, the programs are then described, together with the management units established in support of these programs.

3.1 KC-STOPE Approach

Figure 2 presents the KC-STOPE approach according to which the KSU development programs and support units, concerned with the knowledge society, can be viewed and assessed. The approach is associated with three main dimensions:

- The KC, which integrates the knowledge activities in order to support development efficiently and effectively.
- The STOPE scope, which enables viewing the development issues in an organized wide-scope manner, according to the well-defined domains of strategy, technology, organization, people, and environment.
- Development assessment of quality and progress, with performance measures, for continuous learning and improvement.

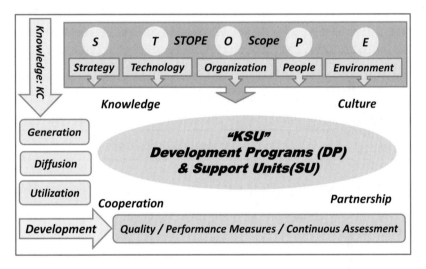

Fig. 2. KC-STOPE approach concerned with KSU drive toward the KS

The development programs and support units [10] activate the KC, and drive development, as explained in the following points:

- they promote "knowledge generation" by supporting research and innovation; and
- they enhance "knowledge diffusion", through building the knowledge culture that makes such diffusion based on interaction and innovation;
- they enable "knowledge utilization", that is making use of the innovative ideas and innovative skills resulting from the activities above, by creating suitable conditions.

While all development programs and support units are associated with all the domains of the STOPE scope, with different degrees of correlation, each of them can be related to a key domain that emphasizes it primary function.

The programs and units are addressed in the following, according to their related key domains. Since these programs and units are in their early stages, the development assessment dimension of Figure 2 is left for future consideration.

3.2 The "Strategy" Domain

KSU strategic directions toward the knowledge society are summarized in the vision and mission of Table 2. One development program and one support unit are associated with the strategic issues, as given in Table 3.

- The program, "National Plan for Science and Technology" coordinates the university directions and activities with the national plans of Saudi Arabia.
- The support unit, "Strategic Studies" is concerned with initiating development programs for the university, like the programs already in action.

Table 3. Development programs and support units emphasizing the "strategy" domain

| Knowledge | STOPE Scope: Focus on *Strategy* | | | |
	Strategy	T	O	P	E
Generation Diffusion *Utlization*	National Plan for Science and Technology Program			
	Strategic Studies Unit			

3.3 The "Technology" Domain

This domain is concerned with the "knowledge sensitive" technologies that enjoy promising features for supporting the knowledge economy, and contributing to the world development. In addition, technologies concerned with the current needs of Saudi Arabia, or with its future development potentials, are also taken into account here. In this context, three programs were initiated, as given in Table 4, and explained in the following.

- "King Abdullah Institute of Nanotechnology": it is concerned with the development of an internationally emphasized and highly promising technology.
- "Centers for Research Excellence" program: it has already started two centers in the subjects of: "Biotechnology"; and "Material Engineering".
- "Research Chairs" program: each of these chairs is supported by an enterprise, or an individual. Over "30 chairs", in various subjects of priority to Saudi Arabia, have already started, and many more are on the way.

3.4 The "Organization" Domain

Since this domain deals with organization, most support units come under this category. These units are mainly concerned with supporting the activities of the development programs. Table 5 presents these units, which are also introduced in the following.

Table 4. Development programs emphasizing the "technology" domain

Knowledge	STOPE Scope: Focus on *Technology*				
	S	Technology	O	P	E
Generation **Diffusion** **Utlization**		King Abdullah Institute of Nanotechnology			
		Centers for Research Excellence Program: *Biotechnology Center* *Material Engineering Center*			
		Research Chairs Program: over 30 started (June 2008)			

Table 5. Support units concerned with the "organization" domain

Knowledge	STOPE Scope: Focus on *Organization*				
	S	T	Organization	P	E
Generation **Diffusion** **Utlization**			Computer and Information Systems Unit		
			Reports Unit		
			Linguistic Follow-up & Translation Unit		
			Technical Design Unit		
			Quality Monitoring Unit		
			Conferences and Events Unit		
			Daily Follow-Up Unit		
			Knowledge Generation (Support) Unit		

- "Computer and Information Systems" unit: it is responsible for providing IT support to the development programs and other support units, including web publishing and services.
- "Reports" unit: it is concerned with all necessary documentations.
- "Linguistic Follow-up and Translation" unit: it is responsible for ensuring the language quality of reports, in addition to translations.
- "Technical Design" unit: it is in charge of the artistic appearance of publications.
- "Quality Monitoring" unit: it ensures management quality; and it works toward compliance with ISO 9001.
- "Conferences and Events" unit: it is in charge for the organization of conferences, workshops and other events.
- "Daily Follow-up" unit: it is concerned with monitoring the important activities, and communicating them to the media.
- "Knowledge Generation (support)" unit: it encourages the creation of promising ideas, and works toward their support.

3.5 The "People" Domain

The development programs concerned mainly with people are listed in Table 6, and are described in the following.

- "Prince Sultan International Program for Distinguished Research Scholars": it is concerned with attracting the best graduates, not only from Saudi Arabia, but also from other parts of the world, to join postgraduate studies, and consequently support the human intellectual capabilities of research and innovation in the university.
- "Future Scholars" program: it provides opportunities for the gifted, and support their capabilities.
- "Attracting Outstanding Faculty" program: it is concerned with enriching the university with outstanding academics.
- "Prince Nayef Program for Intellectual Security Studies": it is concerned with the intellectual security, from an Islamic perspective, which emphasizes the protection of man's: religion, soul, progeny, intellect and money.
- "Alumni" program: it works toward establishing a life-long partnership with those who graduate from the university.

Table 6. Development programs emphasizing the "people" domain

Knowledge	STOPE Scope: Focus *People*				
	S	T	O	People	E
Generation Diffusion Utlization				Prince Sultan International Program for Distinguished Research Scholars	
				Future Scholars Program	
				Attracting Outstanding Faculty	
				Prince Nayef Program for Intellectual Security Studies	
				Alumni Program	

3.6 The "Environment" Domain

Table 7 lists the "nine programs" that mainly support the university environment, and enhance the knowledge activities. The programs are also described in the following:

- "Riyadh Technology Valley": it is a technology park that promotes building partnerships between the university and public and private sector organizations.
- "Riyadh Knowledge Corridor" program: it integrates key knowledge organizations in Riyadh City and enhances their interaction with regards to education, research, economy and intellectual activities.
- "KSU Endowment" program: it provides a new source of support to the university.

- "Attracting Nobel Laureate" program: it builds partnership with Nobel Prize winners in different fields, and this would lead to promoting the environment of innovation in the university.
- "International Scientific Twinning" program: it establishes partnerships with outstanding universities, and other knowledge organizations, in specific fields for enhancing scientific achievements.
- "Arab Cooperation" program: it works toward pan-Arab cooperation in promoting knowledge activities and development.
- "Innovators (support)" program: it assists innovators, and promotes the culture of innovation.
- "Intellectual Property" program: it protects, licences and supports the management of intellectual property.
- "Knowledge Society" program: it is concerned with building the knowledge culture, within and beyond the university.

Table 7. Development programs emphasizing the "environment" domain

Knowledge	STOPE Scope: Focus on the *Environment*				
	S	T	O	P	Environment
Generation Diffusion *Utlization*					Riyadh Technology Valley
					Riyadh Technology Corridor Program
					KSU Endowment Program
					Attracting Nobel Laureate Program
					International Scientific Twinning Program
					Arab Cooperation Program
					Innovators (Support) Program
					Intellectual Property Program
					Knowledge Society Program

The above development programs and support units work in an integrated manner under one deputy rector of the university. Their work is still in its early stages, and expectations are high. In the future continuous performance assessments will be conducted, so that feedback is derived for future improvements.

4 Discussions and Conclusions

In brief, the new KSU development programs cover a spectrum of issues associated with the STOPE scope, including the following:

- strategic aspects, which are related to the national strategy of the country;
- technology issues, which emphasize knowledge sensitive technologies, and technologies of national priority;

- organization services that support the work and performance of the development programs;
- people considerations, concerned with attracting capable scholars, supporting potential skills, and protecting intellectual security; and
- environment aspects, associated with enhancing cooperation, building partnerships, inspiring innovation, supporting the knowledge culture, all with national and international dimensions.

The new programs represent the KSU drive toward the KS, and this matches the target set by EU Lisbon strategy, for the European universities to be "an important moving force toward establishing the KS". In addition, looking at university ranking systems, where research output is an essential ranking factor, the development programs support research in different ways that would lead to enhanced output, both in quality and in size, and consequently lead to an advanced world rank for KSU. Furthermore, considering Rhodes and Taylor definitions of distinguished universities, the development programs lead to satisfying these definitions in the following ways:

- supporting research and graduate programs;
- attracting external sources of support;
- creating partnerships; and
- enhancing the international perspective for both students and staff.

The development programs described in this paper represent the current state of KSU drive toward the KS; the drive would continue and other programs would be on the way. Assessment of outcomes is in mind, in the future, for accumulating experience, correcting problems, and achieving improvements. Finally, the authors of paper welcome comments and views, and call for discussions concerned not only with the KSU development programs presented here, but also with the role of universities in the third millennium, both at their national levels, and at the universal level.

References

1. Katsikas, S.K.: The university in the third millennium: which reforms are needed. Organization of Economic Cooperation and Development (March 2008),
   http://www.oecd.org/dataoecd/
2. Bakry, S.H., Al-Ghamdi, A.: A framework for the knowledge society ecosystem: a tool for development. The International Journal of Arab Culture, Management and Sustainable Development (to appear)
3. EDUCAUSE: 2005, Core Data Service: Fiscal Year 2004 (May 2006),
   http://www.educause.org
4. Ranking of World Universities and Departments, Social Capital Gateway (Accessed May 2008), http://www.socialcapitalgateway.org/eng-rankig.htm
5. Association of American Universities (AAU) (Accessed June 2008),
   http://www.aau.edu/aau/aboutaau.cfm
6. League of European Research Universities (LERU) (Accessed June 2008),
   http://www.leru.org
7. Rhodes, F.H.T.: The Role of the American University: The Creation of the Future. Cornell University Press, Ithaca (2001)

8. Taylor, J.: Managing the unmanageable: the management of research in research-intensive universities. Higher Education Management and Policy 18(2) (2006), OECD
9. Saudi Ministry of Economy and Planning (Accessed June 2008), www.mep.gov.sa
10. King Saud University (2008) Accessed in June 2008 and printed brochures, http://www.ksu.edu.sa

Metadata and Knowledge Management Driven Web-Based Learning Information System

Hugo Rego, Tiago Moreira, Erla Morales, and Francisco José Garcia

University Of Salamanca, Plaza de la Merced s/n
37008 Salamanca, Spain
hugo_rego05@yahoo.com, thm@mail.pt, {solis15,fgarcia}@usal.es

Abstract. AHKME e-learning system main aim is to provide a modular and extensible system with adaptive and knowledge management abilities for students and teachers. This system is based on the IMS specifications representing information through metadata, granting semantics to all contents in it, giving them meaning. Metadata is used to satisfy requirements like reusability, interoperability and multipurpose. The system provides authoring tools to define learning methods with adaptive characteristics, and tools to create courses allowing users with different roles, promoting several types of collaborative and group learning. It is also endowed with tools to retrieve, import and evaluate learning objects based on metadata, where students can use quality educational contents fitting their characteristics, and teachers have the possibility of using quality educational contents to structure their courses. The metadata management and evaluation play an important role in order to get the best results in the teaching/learning process.

Keywords: Metadata Management, e-Learning, Knowledge Management, IMS Specifications.

1 Introduction

In learning environments, information has to be perceived and processed into knowledge. One of the problems that have emerged from this transformation was how to represent knowledge. So standardization was indispensable, because it provides a semantic representation of the knowledge through ontologies in which concepts are clearly and unambiguously identified, providing a set of semantic relation types which allow representing meaning by linking concepts together [8][2].

Here we present AHKME a system that supports both knowledge representation and management (KM) based on metadata described by the IMS specifications, which goals and main contributions are: the learning object management and quality evaluation, where we tried to introduce some intelligence to these processes through intelligent agents; the usage of the IMS specifications to standardize all the resources of the platform; and the interaction of all subsystems through the feedback between them allowing the platform to adapt to students/teachers characteristics and to new contexts. As we know, the timely and correct management of knowledge became a sustainable source of competitive advantage, as well as a way to connect people to quality knowledge as well

M.D. Lytras et al. (Eds.): WSKS 2008, CCIS 19, pp. 308–313, 2008.

as people to people in order to peak performance. In the educational area KM and advanced systems can be used to explore how technologies can leverage knowledge sharing and learning and enhance performance[3][5]. We are trying to implement a system that adapts to students and teachers characteristics and to new contexts, using KR and KM by capturing user behavior and interaction with the system, allowing decision makers to check which resources, course formats and learning strategies have best or worst results in determined contexts, helping them to define strategies on how to address certain types of students and contexts.

In this paper we will start to present an analysis of standards and specifications in order to find the one to develop our system. We will give an overview and context the system and focus on the tools that provide learning objects management and quality evaluation through metadata. Finally we'll present some conclusions and future work.

2   Standards and Specifications Comparative Analysis

In order to structure content and information using nowadays pedagogical models there has been the development of several standards and specifications like *Sharable Content Object Reference Model* (SCORM) [1], a project from *Advanced Distributed Learning* (ADL) and the IMS specifications [7] developed by the IMS consortium.

The use of standards help to achieve more stable systems, reduces the development and maintenance time, allows backward compatibility and validation, increases search engine success, makes everything cross systems, among many other advantages [10].

In order to choose the specifications that would best fit our needs we have started to analyse the support of several features, like described on table 1.

Table 1. Standards and specifications comparative analysis

Features		IMS	AICC	SCORM	Dublin Core
Metadata		✓		✓	✓
Learner Profile		✓			
Content Packaging		✓	✓	✓	
Q&T Interoperability		✓			
DR Interoperability		✓			✓
Content structure		✓	✓	✓	
Content Communication			✓	✓	
Learning Design		✓			
Accessibility		✓			
Bindings	XML	✓		✓	✓
	RDF	✓			✓
Learner registration		✓			

We have analyzed the IMS Specifications, AICC, SCORM and Dublin Core [4], from which we have chosen the IMS specifications, since they allow most of the aspects we've analyzed and that we considered important to reach our goals.

3 AHKME Description

AHKME is an e-learning system that is divided in four different subsystems (Learning Object Manager and Learning Design, Knowledge Management, Adaptive, Visualization and Presentation subsystems), that were structured taking into account a line of reasoning, where first we have the process of LOs creation and management, which is followed by the course creation process through the learning design (LD). In parallel with these two processes the KM subsystem evaluates the quality of the available LOs and courses. Then they pass through an adaptive process based on the students' characteristics to be presented to them, as seen on figure 1.

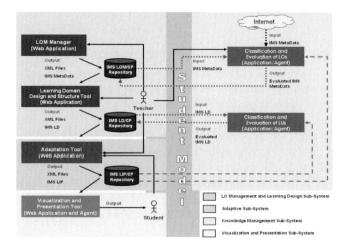

Fig. 1. AHKME's structure

We will now focus on the components of the system that provide the management and evaluation of learning objects through their metadata, the Learning Objects Manager and the Knowledge Management subsystem.

3.1 Learning Objects Manager

The Learning Objects Manager tool allows teachers to define/create metadata to describe LOs. It uses the IMS *Learning Resource Metadata* (IMSLRM) specification [7] that is based on the IEEE LOM standard that allows the management/representation of knowledge through LOs [6].

This tool allows the user to edit LOs and associate descriptive metadata to them. It passes the information into a XML manifest, that gathers all the XML files with their metadata and all the resources used by a LO. Besides it has an information packaging feature that gathers their manifests with the LOs and their stores them in a MySQL database, what enables the management of these packages that will be used in the design of courses. The information packaging enables the creation of packages of LOs and courses with their metadata, so they can easily be transported and reused in other systems, going towards reusability and interoperability, using the IMS CP specification [7]. The tool's architecture is described on figure 2.

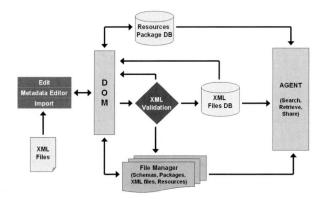

Fig. 2. LO Manager Architecture

All the files and packages in the platform pass through a validation process to check if they're in conformance with the IMS specifications, and all the communication between tools and databases is done through XML Document Object Model.

The LOs are in constant evaluation made by the knowledge management subsystem that has tools that communicate with the LO Manager.

The main advantage of using the IMS specification for LOs is that through the association of descriptive tags, we can better index them, find them, use and reuse them.

In order to facilitate the insertion of metadata we provide an automation of this process, advising the most commonly used values for the elements on the LO cataloguing in order to describe the LO's through the most adequate metadata elements.

3.2 Knowledge Management Subsystem

Knowledge management and e-learning are two concepts that are strictly related, as e-learning needs an adequate management of educational resources to promote quality learning, to allow students to develop in an active and efficient way, that's why we have decide to create a subsystem which main objective is to assure quality to the information in the platform through the evaluation of LOs and courses.

3.2.1 LO Evaluation

To archive a LOs' optimal evaluation, it is necessary to consider quality criteria, for this reason the weighted criteria presented in Table 2 were proposed [9] where the final evaluation value is the sum of all the classifications of each category multiplied by their weight and has the following rating scale:0=not present;1=Very low; 2=Low;3=Medium;4=High;5=Very High. To use these criteria we have made a match between the IMSLRM educational category elements and the categories described on Table 2. For now we have just considered the educational category because it has most of the LOs' technical and educational aspects we found important to evaluate.

With these criteria, we're developing two different tools to evaluate LOs' quality. One tool allows teachers and experts to analyze, change and evaluate LOs through a Web application and after the individual evaluation, all persons involved gather in a

Table 2. Evaluation criteria categories and matching with the IMSLRM educational category

Eval. criteria categories	Weight	IMSLRM Ed. elements	Description
Psychopedagogical	30%	intended end user role; typical age range; difficulty	Criteria that can evaluate, for example, if the LO has the capacity to motivate the student for learning;
Didactic-curricular	30%	learning-resource type; context; typical learning time; description	Criteria to evaluate if the LO helps to archive the unit of learning objectives, etc;
Technical-aesthetic	20%	semantic density; language	Criteria to evaluate the legibility of the LO, the colors used, etc;
Functional	20%	interactivity type; interactivity level	Criteria to evaluate LOs accessibility among other aspects to guarantee that it doesn't obstruct the learning process;

sort of online forum to reach to the LO final evaluation [9].The other tool is an intelligent agent that automatically evaluates LOs that acts when some kind of interaction is made on the LOs in order to readjust its quality evaluation. For example, if students have difficulties in using a LO, the quality evaluation will be recalculate in order to reflect them. Thus, the agent starts to import the LO to evaluate and others already evaluated, then applies data mining techniques (decision trees) to its educational characteristics defined in the IMSLRM specification to calculus its final evaluation.

With these tools LOs are constantly being availed of their quality, playing an important role in the LOs reusability for different contexts. Meanwhile we are testing these tools in order to verify their reliability.

4   Conclusions

In this article we've presented how the platform AHKME uses metadata annotation for learning resource management and evaluation.

The IMS specifications, which use the combination of metadata and XML potentialities, are excellent to represent knowledge, dividing information in several meaningful chunks (LOs) providing their description through metadata and storage in XML files, therefore permitting their cataloguing, localization, indexation, reusability and interoperability, through the creation of information packages. These specifications grant the capacity to design learning units that simultaneously allow users with different roles promoting several types of both collaborative and group learning.

Through knowledge management we have a continuous evaluation of contents, granting quality to all the resources in the platform for teachers and students to use.

AHKME's main contributions are: the LO management and quality evaluation; the usage of the IMS specifications to standardize all the resources in order to reach interoperability and compatibility of learning components, and the interaction of all subsystems through the feedback between them allowing the platform to adapt to the students and teachers characteristics and to new contexts, using KR and KM to grant success to the teaching/learning process, being able to be applied in several kinds of matters, students, learning strategies in both training and educational environments.

Thus, it's very important to have the resources well catalogued, available and with quality to create quality courses, but quality courses don't just depend on quality resources, but also in the design of activities to reach learning objectives.

In terms of future work, we will add the level B of the IMS LD specification in the learning design tool, to include properties and generic conditions. In the adaptive subsystem we will add some functionality according to the IMS Question and Test Interoperability and Enterprise specification. In the KM subsystem we will add the feature of course quality evaluation through the development of some tools.

Acknowledgments. This work has been partly financed by Ministry of Education and Science as well as FEDER KEOPS project (TSI2005-00960). We would like to thank the GRIAL Research Group.

References

1. ADL: Sharable Content Object Reference Model (SCORM)® 2004 3rd edn. - Overview Version 1.0. Advanced Distributed Learning (2006)
2. Berners-Lee, T., Hendler, J., Lassila, O.: The Semantic Web. Scientific American 284(5), 34–43 (2001)
3. Chatti, M.A., Jarke, M., Frosch-Wilke, D.: The future of e-learning: a shift to knowledge networking and social software. Int. J. Knowledge and Learning 3(4/5), 404–420 (2007)
4. Dublin Core Metadata Initiative (2005), http://dublincore.org
5. Grace, A., Butler, T.: Learning management systems: a new beginning in the management of learning and knowledge. Int. J. Knowledge and Learning 1(1/2), 12–24 (2005)
6. IEEE LTSC Working Group 12: Draft Standard for Learning Object Metadata. Institute of Electrical and Electronics Engineers, Inc. (2002)
7. IMS Specifications, IMS Global Learning Consortium Inc. (2004), http://www.imsglobal.org
8. Mendes, M.E.S., Sacks, L.: Dynamic Knowledge Representation for e-Learning Applications. In: Proceedings of the 2001 BISC International Workshop on Fuzzy Logic and the Internet, FLINT 2001, Memorandum No. UCB/ERL M01/28, University of California Berkeley, USA, August, pp. 176–181 (2001)
9. Morales, E., García, F.J., Moreira, T., Rego, H., Berlanga, A.: Units of Learning Quality Evaluation. In: SPDECE 2004 Design (Guadalajara, Spain). CEUR Workshop Proceedings, vol. 117 (2004), http://ceur-ws.org/ ISSN 1613-0073
10. Totkov, G., Krusteva, C., Baltadzhiev, N.: About the Standardization and the Interoperability of E-Learning Resources. In: CompSysTech 2004 - International Conference on Computer Systems and Technologies, Bulgaria (2004)

Case-Based Reasoning: A Recent Theory for
Problem-Solving and Learning in Computers and People

Michael Gr. Voskoglou

Professor of Mathematical Sciences
Higher Technological Educational Institute
263 34 Patras – Greece
voskoglou@teipat.gr

Abstract. In this paper we present the Case-Based Reasoning (CBR) approach, which over the last few years has grown from a rather specific and isolated research area into a field of widespread interest both from academic and commercial stand, and has been developed to a theory of problem-solving and learning for computers and people.

More explicitly, following an introduction with the basic concepts and a brief historical background of CBR, we focus on the steps of the CBR process, the several types of the CBR methods and the applications of CBR to a wide range of domains. Finally, in our conclusions' section, we underline the differences between CBR and the classical rule-induction algorithms, we discuss the criticism for CBR methods and we focus on the future trends of research for CBR.

1 Introduction

Case-Based Reasoning (CBR) is a recent approach to problem-solving and learning, that has got a lot of attention over the last few years. Broadly construed, CBR is the process of solving new problems based on the solutions of similar past problems. The CBR systems expertise is embodied in a collection (library) of past cases rather, than being encoded in classical rules. Each case typically contains a description of the problem plus a solution and/or the outcomes. The knowledge and reasoning process used by an expert to solve the problem is not recorded, but is implicit in the solution.

A lawyer, who advocates a particular outcome in a trial based on legal precedents, or an auto mechanic, who fixes an engine by recalling another car that exhibited similar symptoms, are using CBR; in other words CBR is a prominent kind of analogy making.

CBR is liked by many people, because they feel happier with examples rather, than conclusions separated from their context. A case-library can also be a powerful corporate resource allowing everyone in an organization to tap in the corporate library, when handling a new problem. CBR allows the case-library to be developed incrementally, while its maintenance is relatively easy and can be carried out by domain experts.

CBR is often used where experts find it hard to articulate their thought processes when solving problems. This is because knowledge acquisition for a classical knowledge-based system would be extremely difficult in such domains, and is likely to produce incomplete or inaccurate results. When using CBR the need for knowledge acquisition can be limited to establishing how to characterize cases.

M.D. Lytras et al. (Eds.): WSKS 2008, CCIS 19, pp. 314–319, 2008.

Some of the characteristics of a domain that indicate that a CBR approach might be suitable include:

- Records of previously solved problems exist
- Historical cases are viewed as an asset which ought to be preserved.
- Remembering previous experiences is useful; experience is at least as valuable as textbook knowledge.
- Specialists talk about the domain by giving examples.

CBR has recently been developed to a theory of problem-solving and learning for computers and people. This evolution traces its roots to the work of Roger Schank and his students at Yale University – U.S.A. in the early 1980's [6]. The basic ideas and the underlined theories of CBR have spread quickly to other continents. In Europe we are now within a period of highly active research in CBR, to a large extend focused towards the utilization of knowledge level modeling in CBR systems. From Japan, India and other Asian countries, there are also activity points. In Japan the interest is mainly focused towards the parallel computation approach in CBR.

In the 1990's , interest in CBR grew in the international community, as evidenced by the establishment of an International Conference on CBR in 1995, as well as European, German, British, Italian and other CBR workshops.

2   The Steps of the CBR Process

CBR has been formalized for purposes of computer and human reasoning as a four step process, known as the *dynamic model of the CBR cycle*. These steps involve:

1. RETRIEVE the most similar to the new problem past case, or cases.
2. REUSE the information and knowledge in that case to solve the problem.
3. REVISE the proposed solution.
4. RETAIN the parts of this experience likely to be useful for future problem-solving.

In more detail, an initial description of a problem defines a *new case*. This new case is used to RETRIEVE the most similar case, or cases, from the library of *previous cases*. The subtasks of the retrieving procedure involve:

- Identifying a set of relevant problem descriptors.
- Matching the case and returning a set of sufficiently similar cases, given a similarity threshold of some kind
- Selecting the best case from the set of cases returned..

Some systems retrieve cases based largely on superficial syntactic similarities among problem descriptors, while advanced systems use semantic similarities.

The retrieved case (or cases) is combined, through REUSE, with the new case into a *solved case*, i.e. a proposed solution of the initial problem. The reusing procedure focuses on identifying the differences between the retrieved and the current case, as well as the part of the retrieved case which can be transferred to the new case.

Through the REVISE process this solution is tested for success, e.g. by being applied to the real world environment, or a simulation of it, or evaluated by a teacher, and repaired, if failed. This provides an opportunity to learn from failure.

During RETAIN, useful experience is retained for future reuse, and the case base (schema, or script, or frame in the language of the cognitive science) is updated by a new *learned case*, or by modification of some existing cases. The retaining process involves deciding what information to retain and in what form to retain it, how to index the case for future retrieval, ant integrating the new case into the case library.

A *task-method decomposition* of the four main steps of the CBR process to sub-steps, where related problem-solving methods are also described, is given – in the form of a decision tree - in Aamond & Plaza [1], Figure 2.

The *general knowledge* usually plays a part in the CBR cycle by supporting the CBR process. This support however may range from very weak (or none) to very strong, depending on the type of the CBR method (see section 3 below). By general knowledge we here mean general, domain-dependent knowledge, as opposed to specific knowledge embodied by cases. For example, in the case of a lawyer, mentioned in our introduction, who advocates a particular outcome in a trial based on legal precedents, the general knowledge is expressed through the knowledge of the existing relevant laws and the correlations among them and the case of the trial. A set of rules may have the same role in other CBR cases.

3   Main Types of the CBR Methods

The CBR paradigm covers a range of different methods for organizing, retrieving, utilizing and indexing the knowledge in past cases. Actually CBR is a term used both as a generic term for the several types of these methods, as well as for one such type, and this has lead to some confusion. The main types of CBR methods are listed below.

- *Exemplar-Based Reasoning.*

In the exemplar view a concept is defined extensionally as the set of its exemplars. In this approach solving a problem is a *classification task*, i.e. finding the right class for the unclassified exemplar. The set of classes constitutes the set of *possible solutions* and the class of the most similar past case becomes the solution to the classification problem. Modification of a solution found is therefore outside the scope of this method.

- *Instance-Based Reasoning.*

This is a specialization of exemplar-based reasoning. To compensate for lack of guidance from general background knowledge, a relatively large number of instances is needed in order to close in on a concept definition. The representation of the instances is usually simple (e.g. feature vectors), since a major focus is to study *automated learning,* with no user in the loop, e.g. see [2]

- *Memory-Based Reasoning.*

This approach emphasizes a collection of cases as a *large memory*, and reasoning as a process of accessing and searching in this memory. The utilization of *parallel processing* techniques is a characteristic of these methods and distinguishes this approach from the others ; e.g. see [5].

- *Case-Based Reasoning.*

The typical CBR methods have three characteristics, wich distinguish them from the other approaches listed here. First, they assume to have a *complexity* with respect to their internal organization, i.e. a feature vector holding some values and a corresponding class is not what we would call a typical CBR description. Second, they are able to *modify*, or adapt a retrieved solution when applied in a different problem-solving context, and third they utilize *general background knowledge*, although its richness and role within the CBR processes vary. Core methods of typical CBR systems borrow a lot from cognitive psychology theories.

- *Analogy-Based Reasoning.*

This term is sometimes used as a synonymous of the typical CBR approach , however is often used also to characterize methods, that solve new problems based on past cases of *different domains* (e.g. see [3]), while typical CBR methods focus on single-domain cases (a form of intra-domain analogy). The major focus of study in the analogy-based reasoning has been on the *reuse* of a past case, what is called the *mapping problem*: Finding a way to transfer, or map, the solution of an identified analogue (called *source,* or *base problem),* to the present problem (called *target problem)*; e.g. see [8].

Throughout this paper we are using the term CBR in the generic sense.

4   Tools and Applications of CBR

A CBR tool should support the four main processes of CBR: retrieval, reuse, revision and retention. A good tool should support a variety of retrieval mechanisms and allow them to be mixed when necessary. In addition, the tool should be able to handle large case libraries with the retrieval time increasing linearly (at worst) with the number of cases CBR first appeared in commercial tools in the early 1990's and since then has been sued to create numerous applications in a wide range of domains including:

- *Diagnosis*:

CBR diagnostic systems try to retrieve past cases, whose symptom lists are similar in nature to that of the new case and suggest diagnoses based on the best matching retrieved cases. Most CBR systems of this type are medical diagnostic systems

- *Help-desk:*

CBR diagnostic systems are used in the customer service area dealing with handling problems with a product or service, such as the Compaq SMART system

- *Assessment:*

CBR systems are used to determine values for variables by comparing it to the known value of something similar. Assessment tasks are quite common in the finance and marketing domains.

- *Decision support:*

In decision making, when faced with a complex problem, people often look for analogous problems for possible solutions. CBR systems have been developed to supporting this problem retrieval process (often at the level of the document retrieval) to find relevant similar problems. CBR is particularly good at querying structured, modular and non-homogeneous documents. A number of CBR decision support tools are commercially available, including k-Commerce from eGam, Kaidara Advisor from Kaidara and SMART from Illation.

- *Design:*

Systems to support human designers in architectural and industrial design have been developed. These systems assist the user in only one part of the design process, that of retrieving past cases, and would need to be combined with other forms of reasoning to support the full design process.

Several commercial companies offer *shells* for building CBR systems. Just as for rule-based systems shells, they enable you to quickly develop applications, but at the expense of flexibility of representation, reasoning approach and learning methods. Four such shells are reviewed in Harmon [4] : ReMind from Cognitive Systems Inc., CBR Express/ART-IM from Inference Corporation, Esteem from Esteem Software Inc., and Induce-it (later renamed to CasePower) from Inductive Solutions Inc. On the European scene Acknosoft in Paris offers the shell KATE-CBR as part of their Case-Craft Toolbox, Isoft, also in Paris, has a shell called ReCall, TecchInno in Kaiserslauten has S3-Case, a PATDEX-derived tool that is part of their S3 environment for technical systems maintenance.

Some academic CBR tools are freely available, e.g. the PROTOS system, which emphasized on integrating general domain knowledge and specific case knowledge into a unified representation structure, is available from the University of Texas, and code for implementing a simple version of dynamic memory is available from the Institute of Learning Sciences at Northwestern University.

5 Discussion and Conclusions

Summarizing the paper we can say that CBR emphasizes problem-solving and learning as two sides of the same coin: Problem-solving uses the results of past learning episodes, while it provides the backbone of the experience from which learning advances.

The key difference between CBR and the classical rule-induction algorithms, which are procedures for learning rules for a given concept by generalizing from examples of that concept, lies in when the generalization is made. In fact, while CBR starts with a set of cases of training examples and forms generalizations of these examples by identifying commonalities between a retrieved case and the target problem, a rule-induction algorithm draws generalizations before the target problem is even known, i.e. it performs eager generalization.

All inductive reasoning, where data is too scarce for statistical relevance, is inherently based on anecdotal evidence. Critics of CBR argue that it is an approach that accepts anecdotal evidence as its main operating principle, but without statistically relevant data for backing an implicit generalization, there is no guarantee that the generalization is correct. Our personal opinion is that the above criticism has only a theoretical base, because in practice the CBR methods give satisfactory results in most cases.

We shall close with some comments on the development trends in CBR methods that can be grouped around four main topics: *Integration with other learning methods, integration with other reasoning components, incorporation into massive parallel processing, and method advances by focusing on new cognitive aspects.*

The first trend forms part of the current trend in research towards *multistrategy learning systems.* This research aims at achieving an integration of different learning methods into a coherent framework, where each learning method fulfills a specific and distinct role in the system, e.g. case-based learning and induction as is done in MMA and INRECA systems.

The second trend aims at using the different sources of knowledge in a more thorough, principal way, like what is done in the CASEY system with the use of causal knowledge. This trend, which is very popular in the European continent, emphasizes the increasing importance of knowledge acquisition issues and techniques in the development of knowledge-intensive CBR systems.

The massive memory parallelism trend applies CBR to domains suitable for shallow, instance-based retrieval methods on a very large amount of data. This direction may also benefit from integration with neural network methods, as several Japanese projects currently are investigated (e.g. see [5]).

By the fourth trend, method advances on focusing on the cognitive aspects, in particular in the follow-up work initiated on creativity (e.g. see [7]) as a new focus for CBR methods. It is not just an "application type", but a way to view CBR in general, which may have significant impacts on the CBR methods in future.

Conclusively CBR has blown a fresh wind and a well justified degree of optimism into Artificial Intelligence in general, and knowledge based decision support systems in particular. The growing amount of on going CBR research has the potential of leading into significant breakthroughs of Artificial Intelligence methods and applications.

References

1. Aamodt, A., Plaza, E.: Case-Based Reasoning: Foundational Issues, Methodological Variations, and System Approaches. A. I. Communications 7(1), 39–52 (1994)
2. Aha, D., Kibler, D., Albert, M.K.: Instance-Based Learning Algorithms. Machine Learning 6(1) (1991)
3. Hall, R.P.: Computational approaches to analogical reasoning: A comparative analysis. Artificial Intelligence 39(1), 39–120 (1989)
4. Harmon, P.: Case-based reasoning III. Intelligent Software strategies VIII(1) (1992)
5. Kitano, H.: Challenges for massive parallelism. In: Proceedings of the 13th Intern. Conference on A.I., pp. 813–834. Morgan Kaufman, Chambery (1993)
6. Schank, R.: Dynamic memory; a theory of reminding and learning in computers and people. Cambridge Univ. Press, Cambridge (1982)
7. Schank, R., Leake, D.: Creativity and learning in case-based explainer. Artificial Intelligence 40(1-3), 353–385 (1989)
8. Voskoglou, M.: Analogical problem solving and transfer. In: Gagatsis, A., Papastavridis, S. (eds.) Proceedings 3rd Mediterranean Conf. Math. Educ., Athens, pp. 295–303 (2003)

SOLERES-HCI: Modelling a Human-Computer Interaction Framework for Open EMS

Luis Iribarne[1], Jose A. Asensio[1], Nicolas Padilla[1], and Rosa Ayala[2]

[1] Applied Computing Group, University of Almeria, Spain
{luis.iribarne,npadilla,jacortes}@ual.es
[2] Environmental and Computers Group, University of Almeria, Spain
rmayala@ual.es

Abstract. Organizations and administrations working on environmental information for specific behaviors of soil or planning management of natural resources need to have innovator systems of quality information in order to guarantee the success of theirs daily activities. Experts managing the system consider that not only it is important to have reliable and updated information in order to help to make the most suitable decisions. Due to the variety of final users that cooperate and interact with the decision making system (for instance, politicians, technicians, administrators, etc.) it is also important to have real-time query systems that facilitate the human-human and human-computer interaction and coordination not only with user interfaces that adapt to the users' profiles habits, but also with intelligent software agents. In this work we advance some ideas about the HCI framework of the SOLERES project, an *Environmental Management System* (EMS) that fixes, defines and experiences solutions to problems previously described.

Keywords: Human-Computer Interaction, Modelling of Systems, Software Agents, Environmental Management Systems.

1 Introduction

Organizations and administrations that work with environmental information need to have innovative quality information systems in order to guarantee the success of their everyday activities. In this social-technical systems —also known as *Environmental Management Systems* (EMS)— appears a variety of final users (i.e., politicians, technicians, administrators, etc.) that cooperate with each other and interact with the system for decision-making, problems resolution, etc.

To design this kind of systems as a support adapted to working groups, we will need to develop a framework that helps us to understand:

(a) The complex relationships that happen in this environment,
(b) The underlying technology that is used,
(c) The organization of the work,
(d) The tasks of the organization, and
(e) The requirements for the accomplishment of the tasks.

M.D. Lytras et al. (Eds.): WSKS 2008, CCIS 19, pp. 320–327, 2008.

Therefore, it is important to have:

(a)   Exploitation (environmental) information systems to facilitate the human-human and human-computer interaction and coordination,

(b)   Intelligent user interfaces that adapt to the users profiles' habits and,

(c)   Intelligent software agents that intercede on behalf of the users in the search processes helping in the interpretation tasks, the decision-making tasks and prediction/prevention tasks.

This framework must consider the use of open standards, both at the application domain (i.e. ISO 14000 family for EMS) and the modeling of the system (i.e. XML, UML, etc). The use of standards makes the systems more adaptable to the technological advances and to the endless market changes. These standards facilitate the modelling of the system by means of formal methods, which provide mechanisms and tools that guarantee the users a correct deployment and use of the system to be modeled.

In our case, we are applying these R&D lines in the SOLERES project, *a spatio-temporal information system for environmental management*. This system is supported by the application, integration and development (extension) of multidisciplinary works in satellite images, neural networks, cooperative systems based on multi-agent architectures and intelligent agents and software systems with commercial components (Figure 1). The general idea of the project is the study of a framework for the integration of the aforesaid disciplines using the "Environment" as the application domain, specifically ecology and landscape connectivity.

Fig. 1. Main R&D areas of the SOLERES System

In this paper we will focus on describing SOLERES-HCI: the part of environmental information system that uses a human-computer interaction based on intelligent user-interfaces, and implemented by means of trading and software agents.

The rest of the paper is structured as follows. Section 2 briefly describes some of the more common techniques used in environmental information systems. Section 3 continues with our SOLERES-HCI proposal. Finally, in Section 4, we complete the paper explaining some conclusions and future work.

2   Environmental Management Systems in Knowledge Society

At present, processes and quality products prevail in every discipline. Standardization organizations develop recommendations to help the engineers in different phases of action. In the scope of environmental management systems there are the international standards of the ISO 14000 family.

The basic principle of the system modelling is the use of engineering standard specifications and implementations that adapt to such specifications. Using open computer techniques has the potential to reduce costs, have less dependence on owner solutions, shorter development times, better-tested products, increase of portability and of stable technologies. Moreover, the fact of using standards make the systems (modeled with these standards) more adaptable to technological advances and to the endless market changes.

Figure 2 shows a group of Information Technology materials and methods that support an **environmental management system** (EMS). As the reader can see, an EMS is supported by standard techniques of:

— W3C (*World Wide Web Consortium*. http://www.w3c.org),
— OMG (*Object Management Group*, http://www.omg.org) or
— ISO (*International Organization for Standardization*, http://www.iso.org).

For instance, the ISO 14000 standard family guarantees the building of appropriate environmental management systems [4] [17], or ISO 9000 standard family guarantees quality features. W3C and OMG support other techniques of system modelling such as UML (*Unified Modelling Language*), XML (*eXtensible Markup Language*), OCL (*Object Constraints Laguage*), CIM (*Computation Independent Model*), among others (not included in the figure either for space limitations) [5] [6] [13].

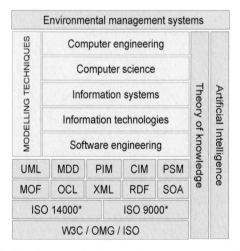

Fig. 2. Technologies used for modelling EMS

In order to model an EMS, we can use some other modelling techniques typical of five disciplines of Computing, internationally defined in the ACM/IEEE CC, from computer engineering to software engineering. Furthermore, because of the wide range of information that an EMS may contain and the variety of users that may interact with each other and with EMS (administrators, politicians, operators, final users, work groups, etc.) there are modelling techniques based on artificial intelligence and theory of knowledge [15] (though not always). In this paper we will only focus on those techniques concerning human-computer interaction perspectives.

3 Modelling SOLERES-HCI

SOLERES-HCI is the framework of the SOLERES environmental information system, specialized in the human-computer interaction. This level of the information system is defined by means of the paradigm of *Computer Supported Cooperative Work* (CSCW) and implemented by using innovative technology of intelligent agents and multi-agent architectures [18].

Figure 3 shows the partial meta-model of the SOLERES information system. The framework concerns the modelling and implementing of an "Information Exploitation and Searching System" based on intelligent-agents.

For the process of data exploitation it is necessary to identify and structure the type of queries and the sort of information susceptible to be consulted, by using techniques of hierarchical decomposition (for instance, trees, cut and pruning).

Firstly, as previously mentioned, the system is designed to be used for environmental decision-making tasks and in cooperation among different people (system's users) organized following different organized models (i.e. depending on their hierarchy or profile). There may be politicians, technicians or administrators, among others, who need to interact between them and with the system.

This human-computer interaction and human-human interaction is guided by a cooperative system for the decision-taking tasks in group supported by a multi-agent architecture (next layer). Therefore, each user of the cooperative system has an intelligent agent (*Userbot*), which operates at two ways:

(a) Managing the user interface presentation and interaction (*UI Agent*), and
(b) Managing the environmental queries (*EMS Agent*).

The *UI Agent* adapts the user interface to his/her needs by identifying his/her interaction habits with the user interface, by recognizing his/her preferences and, in short, by changing in the course of time (*evolution* and *adaptation* issues). This *UI Agent* mediates between the user and:

(a) The rest of the system's users (having their own *UI Agent*),
(b) The information search system directly, or
(c) An environmental software agent (*EMS Agent*).

The *EMS Agent* refers to a virtual consultant or virtual supervisor who cooperates with other agents within a previously established multi-agent architecture and respects a model of organization and cooperation (that is our project's aim). The purpose of this cooperation and therefore, each EMS's job, is to facilitate the tasks of information

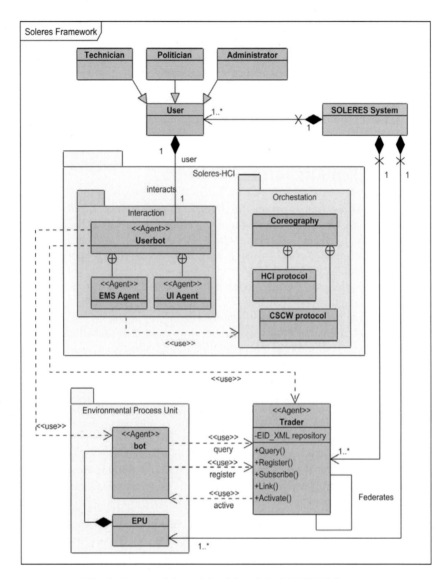

Fig. 3. Meta-model (partial) of the whole SOLERES System

exploitation: they interact with the information search system (next level which we will give details from later on) and filter the irrelevant information. The use of this sort of systems is useful because of its natural capacity to represent and implement organizational and social aspects that can help us to identify and/or solve problems.

Both UI and EMS agents follow protocol models for orchestration the cooperative system: the cooperation between agents. UI agents use HCI choreography (protocol) and EMS agents use CSCW choreography.

Given the magnitude of the information available in the information system, and due to the fact that this information may be provided by different sources, at different times or even by different people, the information system that we try to model must follow the development guidelines of the **open and distributed systems**. Therefore, the environmental information may be distributed and consulted, and geographically located in different places, in what we call an *Environmental Process Unit* (EPU).

The general system is formed by a cooperative group of EPUs based on knowledge; this group operates individually by using an intelligent agent (*bot* in the figure) in order to get better solutions (consults on ecological maps). We bring up the distributed cooperation of these EPUs through the development of a trading agent. We adopt the ODP trader specification [9] and extend it to the agent behaviour. A trader is used as a middleware solution to identify, locate and register objects in an open and distributed system. In our case, the trading agent mediates between HCI requests and EPU services, and it manages a Environmental Information repository of XML metadata templates [3].

The internal description of the EPU falls outside the scope of this paper. The reader will find more information about the trading implementation, EPU and SOLERES project at http://www.ual.es/acg/soleres.

4   Conclusions and Future Work

In this work we present the modelling of the *human-computer interaction framework* for the SOLERES system: an information system for environmental management (EMS). The framework is modelled by considering the coordination and orchestration of several interaction agents: user-interfaces and EMS agents. Both agents (UI/EMS) connect a trading agent, which mediates between the users and the EMS core.

As a future work, there are specific objectives that we want to address. Firstly, we plan to study the design of intelligent user interfaces by using algorithms of real-time UI-COTS services composition. We try to examine this component and its market placement (i.e., how many, which types, how to define them, what kind of existing repositories, etc.).

Secondly, we want to develop trading services of UI-COTS components [7] [8] and applications in *Cooperative Systems* (specifically in environmental information). For this, we want to achieve the following activities:

(a) Define a trading model,
(b) Identify and structure the type of information and
(c) Define the types of queries by using hierarchical decomposition techniques.

In addition, we plan to study the social and psychological implications for the building of cooperative, adaptive and evolutive HCI. Due to the variety of information behaviour and technology in the SOLERES framework, it may serve as an experimental centre for investigating information behaviour and information use in social and technological context [11] [16].

On the other hand, as we advanced before the SOLERES project concerns the paradigm of open information systems. In attention to this, we are mapping the data modelling of the SOLERES EMS following *Semantic Web* issues. In [10] the author describes five keys converging actions of semantic Web and IS research:

(a) Expression of meaning/managing of knowledge content;
(b) Ontological evolution/diversification personalization;
(c) Information flow and collaborative life/context;
(d) Policy aware infrastructure/interoperability standards; and
(e) Web of trust/communities.

In our context, in the SOLERES project, we are focusing our studies on the three first ones. Therefore, we want to develop ontological HCI issues for connecting the knowledge, user and data layers. In addition, we are planning to improve our searching system to accommodate multi-variable *soft & matchmaking* algorithms considering optimisation mechanisms in a similar way to [12], but only in open distributed IS and not in web.

Finally, we want to implement an experimental prototype of the modelled HCI framework by using open and distributed paradigms based on Web Services and EMS ontology approaches.

Acknowledgments. This work has been partially supported by the EU (FEDER) and the Spanish MEC under grant of the project I+D TIN2007-61497 "*SOLERES. A Spatio-Temporal Environmental Management System based on Neural-Networks, Agents and Software Components*".

References

1. Almendros, J., Iribarne, L.: Designing GUI components from UML use cases. In: IEEE International Conference on the Engineering of Computer-Based Systems, pp. 210–217. IEEE Computer Socciety, Los Alamitos (2005)
2. Almendros, J., Iribarne, L.: Visual Languages for Interactive Computing. In: User Interaction and Interface Design with UML, pp. 202–222. Idea Group Inc., Hersey (2007)
3. Asensio, J.A., Iribarne, L., Padilla, N., Ayala, R.: Implementing trading agents for adaptable and evolutive COTS components architectures. In: Proceedings of the International Conference on e-Business, Porto, Portugal, 26-29 July (in press, 2008)
4. Corbett, C., Russo, M.: ISO 14001: Irrelevant or invaluable? ISO Management Systems, pp. 23–29 (2001)
5. Cranefield, S., Purvis, M.: Integrating environmental information: incorporating metadata in a distributed information system's architecture. Advances in Environmental Research 5(4), 319–325 (2001)
6. Dupmeier, C., Geiger, W.: Theme park environment as an example of environmental information systems for the public. Environmental Modelling and Software 21(11), 1528–1535 (2006)
7. Iribarne, L., Troya, J., Vallecillo, A.: A trading service for COTS components. Computer Journal 4(3), 342–357 (2004)
8. Iribarne, L., Troya, J., Vallecillo, A.: Trading for COTS Components to Fulfil Architectural Requirements. In: Cesare, S.d., Lycett, M., Macredie, R.D. (eds.) The Development of Component-Based Information Systems, ch. 11, M.E. Sharpe, Inc. (2005)
9. ISO, Information Technology – Open Distributed Processing – Trading Function: Specification. ISO/IEC 13235-1, ITU-T X.950 (1997), http://www.iso.org

10. Lytras, M.: Semantic Web and Information Systems: An Agenda Based on Discourse with Community Leaders. International Journal on Semantic Web and Information Systems (IJSWIS) 1(1), i–xii (2005)

11. Nahl, D.: Social-Biological Information Technology: An Integrated Conceptual Framework. Journal of the American Society for Information Science and Technology 58(13), 2021–2046 (2007)

12. Panagis, Y., Sakkopoulos, E., Garofalakis, J., Tsakalidis, A.: Optimisation mechanism for web search results using topic knowledge. International Journal of Knowledge and Learning (IJKL) 2(1/2), 140–153 (2006)

13. Pinet, F., Duboisset, M., Soulignac, V.: Using UML and OCL to maintain the consistency of spatial data in environmental information systems. Environmental Modelling and Software 22, 1217–1220 (2007)

14. Purvis, M., Cranefield, S., Ward, R., Nowostawski, M., Carter, D., Bush, G.: A multi-agent system for the integration of distributed environmental information. Environmental Modelling and Software 18(6), 565–572 (2003)

15. Russ, M., Jones, J.K.: Knowledge-based strategies and information system technologies: preliminary findings. International Journal of Knowledge and Learning (IJKL) 2(1/2), 154–179 (2006)

16. Smith, K., Shanteau, J., Johnson, P.: Psychological investigations of competence in decision making. Cambridge Series on Judgment and Decision Making (2004) ISBN-13: 9780521583060

17. Stapleton, P.: ISO 14004 revision will promote use of environmental management systems by the EMS. ISO Management Systems, 21–25 (2002)

18. Tweedale, J., Ichalkaranje, N., Sioutis, C., Jarvis, B., Consoli, A., Philips-Wren, A.: Innovations in multi-agent systems. Journal of Network and Computer Applications 30, 1089–1115 (2007)

Improving the Learning Process of Engineering Students by Deployment of Activating ICTs

Seppo Virtanen

Department of Information Technology, University of Turku
FI-20014 Turku, Finland

1 Introduction

During the first decade of the 21st century the academic learning environment and the university-level educational system of Finland has seen several challenging, if not radical, changes and reforms. In terms of the students and their everyday studying, the most important reforms have been transition to the two-phase degree program through the so called Bologna process, the establishment of maximum allowable study time limits and the diminishing real value of state monetary study support. Especially among engineering students it is nowadays very common that the students seek employment in corporations in the field of their study already after the first year of their studies. This way the students wish to obtain financial security, hope to find a corporate sponsor for their Master's theses, and even to lay foundations for permanent employment once they have completed their degree. Very often the initial, perhaps part-time, work in the technology sector gradually yet quickly becomes a full-time job, and causes difficulties in allocating adequate time for academic studies. Especially for an average student that obtains mid-range grades through hard work the situation is becoming very challenging: there is not anymore enough time left to be allocated to course work after all job responsibilities have been taken care of.

According to the author's experience as a university educator, in the past five years active lecture participation by students has decreased significantly, and at the same time lecturers receive more and more requests to organize courses in the evening (after 4 pm). On many courses with over 100 registered participants it is not uncommon to have only about 30-40 students listening to lectures. This is contrary to the situation five years ago, when the attendance in a similar situation would have been 70-80 students. This development has had a severe influence on the average grades received on exams, as shown in next section.

One could argue that students should not be encouraged to take jobs in their field in the early phases of their academic studies at all to ensure proper marks in reasonable degree study time. The purpose of this article, however, is not to support or discourage the previous argument. Instead, this article acknowledges the current situation and tries to find remedies to the decreasing grades in traditional lecture courses. This article presents an experiment of activating student participation and self-study by reducing the number of daytime lectures into half and requiring online independent work and group work with obligatory reporting. The results of the experiment were very promising.

M.D. Lytras et al. (Eds.): WSKS 2008, CCIS 19, pp. 328–333, 2008.

Table 1. Lecture outline of annual intermediate level 5 ECTS course *computer networks and security* at University of Turku. Each lecture is 2 hours.

Lecture	Topic	Key Content
1	Introduction	Introductory topics on networks and protocols
2	Reference Models	OSI model, TCP/IP model, ATM model
3	Basic concepts	Propagation, checksums, packet switching
4-5	Physical layer	Basics of transmission tech, SDH, ATM, DSL
6-7	Data link layer	802.3, 802.11, 802.2, 802.16; LAN cabling
8-9	Network layer	Dynamic and static routing, Internet, IP, IPv6
10-11	Transport layer	E2E connections, TCP, UDP, congestion ctrl
12	Application layer	World Wide Web, HTTP, SMTP, FTP, P2P
13-14	IT Security	Cryptography basics, email security, SSL/TLS
14-15	IT Security	IPSec, system security, firewalls, intrusions
16	Conclusion	Concluding remarks of the course

The rest of this article is structured as follows: in section 2 long-term results from a conventional lecture course are discussed. Section 3 presents the course implementation used in the experiment to encourage the students to take more responsibility of their course work. Results of the experiment are also discussed. In section 4 concluding remarks of the article are provided.

2   Observations from a Traditional Lecture Course

Engineering students at the department of Information Technology in University of Turku are required to take an obligatory intermediate-level course on computer networks and information security in their second year of studies. The course has had the same structure and implementation since 2003, although the course name changed in 2006: earlier the course name was *computer networks*, and since 2006 it has been *computer networks and security*. The content of the course naturally evolves every year as technology advances, and also topic-level emphasis may vary annually depending on the developments in the field since the previous implementation of the course. The course outline is provided in Table 1.

Course literature consists of books [1,2], material gathered by the lecturer, and, for certain topics, online resources. The course gives 5 ECTS credits, it is lectured in Finnish and it consists of 32 hours of lectures. Typically the course is organized during an eight-week teaching period with four hours of lectures each week (gathered into 2 two-hour sessions). There are no obligatory exercise sessions, which compensates for the 4 hours of extra lectures: normally a 5 ECTS course has 28 hours of lectures and additional exercise sessions. The first exam is typically within two weeks of the last lecture. Figure 1 shows the distribution of grades obtained by participants in the five year period 2003-2008. The data is gathered from the first exam arranged after the end of the course each year. There is no data for 2005 because then the course was moved from the fall semester to the spring semester (the course was organized in fall 2004 and the next time in spring 2006).

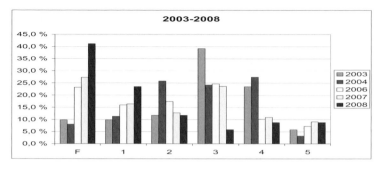

Fig. 1. Grades in a 2nd year course on computer networks and security between 2003-2008. F=fail, 1=lowest mark, 5 = highest mark.

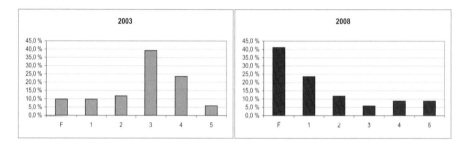

Fig. 2. Detailed views of the data shown in Figure 1 for 2003 and 2008

The detailed views provided in Figure 2 allow one to clearly observe that in 2003 the exam results formed a Gaussian-like distribution (although a linear grading scheme is applied) with only 10% of participants failing the exam (grade F), whereas in 2008 the curve is saddle-shaped with more than 40% of participants failing. In 2003-2008 there is an observable shift of mid-range grades towards the lowest grades and even failures as can be observed in Figure 1. At the same time the percentage of students receiving the highest mark has remained almost the same (there is even a slight increase). The shift towards low-end grades seems to have concerned most the type of students that earlier obtained a mid-range grade through diligent self-study and active participation in course work and lectures.

The course implementation has not changed dramatically in the five-year observation period, it has only gone through the type of evolution any course would in five years to stay up to date. Also course feedback from students has remained about the same from one year to another. From these facts it is within reason to also conclude that student interest toward the course topic should have remained about the same from on year to another. Thus, the likeliest reasons for decreasing grades on the course can be identified as reduced effort on coursework by students, and academically less qualified students. The latter alternative certainly is an important factor, but as seen in Figures 1 and 2, the percentage of course participants receiving the highest mark has remained about the same or even slightly increased during the five year period, hinting that the academic qualifications of students would also have remained about the same. The next section focuses on the former alternative and presents an experimentation with a different kind of course implementation, where the number of lectures has been reduced while there is an increased amount of independent and group work facilitated by ICTs and controlled by regular reporting to the lecturer.

3   Using ICTs to Activate Participation in Coursework

The Technology Industries of Finland Centennial Foundation decided in 2007 to fund the author's proposal of starting a new information security minor subject curriculum with a grant of 200.000 eur. The new curriculum consists of 8 new advanced-level (4th-5th year studies) IT security courses, 5 ECTS each. The first course was run in spring 2008 and was titled *human element in information security*. Based on previous experiences in decreasing grades, a decision was made to reduce the number of lectures and deploy activating ICTs as a replacement. It was run in a 7-week teaching period with 2-hour lectures once per week, with lecture topics as seen in Table 2. Course literature consists of books [3,4,5], scientific articles and online resources. In addition to lectures, the course consisted of independent and group work, weekly reporting and a learning journal.

The Moodle framework [6] was chosen as the learning platform for the course. The platform was used for storing and distributing all information and material of the course, and for dispatching and returning all course related assignments. In Moodle the course participants were divided into 4-6 person groups, and each group was given their own electronic discussion area. Early each week, an independent reading assignment of electronic documents (IT security reports, surveys and scientific articles) related to the weekly lecture topic was given in Moodle to all participants. During the same week, each student group was required to have a meeting of at least one hour to discuss 2-4 topics provided by the lecturer in the Moodle pages based on the weekly reading assignment. Each week the group was required to have a different chairman who had to call the meeting and write minutes of it. The minutes were required to be posted on the Moodle discussion area of the group by the end of the week. The students could decide among themselves when and where to meet as long as everyone was present in the meeting and the minutes were posted in the discussion area: some groups had their meetings in e.g. negotiation rooms at the department whereas some others met in local pubs.

Instead of requiring an exam, the students were required to write a weekly report of 1-2 pages discussing topics provided by the lecturer for groupwork meetings. The reports needed to be submitted in the Moodle system every Sunday by 23:59. For the lecturer it is quite convenient to allow a computer based learning environment to automatically enforce all course deadlines and maintain a course event calendar for the participants. Also, to see with one glance which students have returned their weekly assignments is of great assistance.

Table 2. Lecture outline of advanced level 5 ECTS course *human element in information security* at University of Turku. Each lecture is 2 hours.

Lecture	Topic	Key Content
1	Introduction, Social engineering	Introductory topics on people and information security, introduction to social engineering
2	Privacy, security	Surveillance society, privacy issues
3	Privacy, security	Chinese practices of Internet control
4	Social engineering	Identifying and deferring social engineering
5	Security policies	Defining security policies
6	Security policies	Deploying security policies, personnel security
7	Summary session	Psychology of computer criminals, Y2K - lessons learned for security, course summary

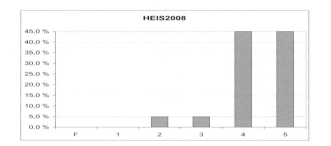

Fig. 3. Grades in a 4th year course on information security in 2008

At the end of the course, a learning journal was returned and graded. The learning journal consisted of an introduction, topic sections based on the weekly reports, and a conclusion. The learning journals were returned in Moodle within two weeks of the last lecture. The learning journals were graded for *content* and *structure and presentation*. The *content* grade was the basis for evaluating the overall grade. For this grade, the assessment areas were evolvement of the student's perception of the course topics during the course (as seen in the weekly reports), depth of analysis in the given discussion and writing topics, and finally expression of criticism towards the provided reading material. If all areas were assessed to be *excellent*, the *content* grade was 5, and if two or more of these areas were assessed to be *very good*, the *content* grade was 4. For the *content* grade of 3, all areas had to be assessed as at least *good*. In grades 2 and less the criteria was that the learning journal was *satisfactory* but not *good*.

In cases where the content assessment was somewhere between grades, a well crafted structure and well written presentation accompanied with good lecture and group meeting attendance gave a higher overall mark: for example a strong 3 for *content* and an assessment of 4 or 5 for *structure and presentation* would yield an overall grade of 4. The assessments and detailed feedback for each student were provided in the Moodle system after the grading had been finalized. Figure 3 shows final grades of the participants. It is noteworthy that all participants of the course received at least a *satisfactory* grade (grade 2).

4   Conclusion

Long term results in terms of grades and learning outcomes in a traditionally implemented lecture course have deteriorated during the past few years in the author's department as can be seen in Figures 1 and 2. In a new course launched in spring 2008 an experimentation was made in which about 50% of lectures were replaced by independent and group work assignments using ICTs, and the traditional written exam was replaced with a learning journal that was composed throughout the course (by returning weekly reports). All assignments and their deadlines were monitored and enforced by a computer based learning environment. The results presented in Figure 3 clearly indicate that reducing the amount of daytime lectures to about one half of the usual amount, and instead using ICTs to activate the students to work independently and in groups produced promising learning results. Although the results presented in Figure 2 and Figure 3 are not directly comparable because the results are obtained for different courses, the results are certainly promising. The participants for both courses come from the same department, and therefore it is concluded that the transferral of the ICTs and strategies employed in the experiment should be considered for use also in the next implementation of the traditional lecture course. Course feedback from students was extremely positive in terms of the activating ICTs, and especially the weekly group discussions based on scientific articles were seen as a key contributor to the overall learning process.

In broader scope, the results of the experiment can be seen to implicate that promoting methods based on 24-hour accessible online environments instead of methods requiring physical presence at a predefined date, time and location, is a preferable approach for the knowledge society: not only in terms of education but also in terms of deploying advanced systems for societal functions that traditionally are performed in physical interaction.

References

1. Tanenbaum, A.S.: Computer Networks, 4th edn., Pearson (2003)
2. Stallings, W.: Network Security Essentials, 2nd edn., Pearson (2003)
3. Mitnick, K., Simon, W.: The Art of Deception. Wiley (2002)
4. Greene, S.: Security Policies and Procedures. Pearson (2006)
5. Bosworth, S., Kabay, M. (eds.): Network Security Handbook, 4th edn. Wiley (2002)
6. Dougiamas, M., Taylor, P.: Using learning communities to create an open source course management system. In: Proc. World Conf. on Educational Multimedia, Hypermedia and Telecommunications (2003)

Modeling Student's Mood during an Online Self-assessment Test

C.N. Moridis and A.A. Economides

Information Systems Department University of Macedonia, 156 Egnatia Avenue
Thessaloniki, 54006 Greece
papaphilips@gmail.com, economid@uom.gr

Abstract. Student's emotional state is crucial during learning. When a student is in a very negative mood, learning is unlikely to occur. On the other hand too positive mood can also impair learning. Thus a key issue for instructional technology is to recognize student's mood, so as to be able to provide appropriate feedback. This paper introduces a model of student's mood during an online self-assessment test. The model was evaluated using data emanated from experiments with 153 high school students from 3 different regions of Greece. The results confirm the model's ability to estimate a student's mood.

Keywords: computerized testing; computer based assessment; affective computing; affective learning; modeling mood; mood recognition.

1 Introduction

Educational learning and success are among the most significant topics across the life span in knowledge society, particularly since educational and professional careers, social relations, and the distribution of many kinds of resources are largely dependent on individual achievement. This indicates that learning and achievement are exceptionally essential and therefore key sources of human emotions nowadays, instigating a variety of self-referenced, task-related, and social emotions [1]. As a result, students receive emotional pressure from many different sources (teachers, schoolmates, parents, themselves etc.) to perform well in a learning task. Consequently, student's failure to accomplish a learning task may be due to emotional pressure. Faced with frustration, despair, worry, sadness, or shame, people lose access to their own memory, reasoning, and the capacity to make connections [2].

Research community is increasingly acknowledging that emotions play a crucial role in human learning procedures. During the last decade, artificial intelligence in education is trying to integrate emotional factors into computerized learning systems. If the system can reason about the emotional state of a user from the input that the system receives, appropriate feedback could be displayed in a way adapted to the emotion or the mood of the user. Besides, the learning flow corresponds to the archetype of human behavior that action and feedback promote understanding and adoption to the environment [3].

M.D. Lytras et al. (Eds.): WSKS 2008, CCIS 19, pp. 334–341, 2008.

A person's emotions could be predictable if their goals and perception of relevant events were known [4]. Implemented in a computational model this can be achieved by using agents, artificial intelligence techniques, reasoning on goals, situations, and preferences [5].The student's recognized emotional state would be properly managed from the computer-aided affective learning system, based on pedagogical models, which integrate our knowledge about emotions and learning. The system would assess whether the learning process is developing at a healthy rate. If there is a positive development, the system should help the learner maintain this emotional state. If not, the system should induce the learner to an emotional state beneficial to learning.

Students' detrimental to learning emotional states could be healed through a self-assessment system. Our aim is to develop an online multiple choice questions platform that would help students to identify and improve their weaknesses. A flexible e-learning system would take into consideration the student's knowledge state and learning preferences [6] to generate individualized learning paths [7]. In addition, the system would try to introduce students to an emotional state beneficial to learning, providing adequate feedback [8]. The emotional feedback can occur before and after the test, during the test, and before and after a student's answer to a question. In all these cases emotional feedback can be provided either automatically according to the student's emotional state, either by the student's or the teacher's request. Emotional feedback can be implemented by using beneficially positive emotions, while preventing, controlling and managing negative emotions. Moreover, the emotional feedback can also be implemented using negative emotions in order to increase the student's devotion and engagement. These "strategies" can be applied using humor and jokes, amusing games, expressions of sympathy, reward, pleasant surprises, encouragement, acceptance, praises but also through criticism and punishment [9]. Thus, students would receive psychological and cognitive assistance through their preparation for the exams.

For this purpose we need a method in order to provide a measurement for the evaluation of student's mood with respect to each question the student is about to answer, and determine the system's feedback to the student. Modeling multiple variables is important as students have complex characteristics that ultimate affect their performance. However, adding additional variables will not always increase the accuracy of the student model [10]. After several assumptions, we developed and evaluated a model in order to provide a measurement for the estimation of student's mood while undertaking a self-assessment multiple choice questions test. To evaluate the model, we created a suitable online test of multiple-choice questions about basic computer knowledge and experimented with 153 high school students from 3 different regions of Greece. The results verified our assumptions and proved the model's ability to approximate students' mood at a satisfactory level.

2 Our Approach

We explored several research questions in the context of an online multiple choice questions self-assessment test, providing a measurement for evaluating students' mood during the test. One assumption was that students' goal does influence students' mood during the test in relation to the remaining questions and their record. That is to say, that if a student knows that he has already failed to reach his goal during the test, because the remaining questions are less than the questions he has to answer correctly in order to reach his goal, then there is a high possibility to be in a negative mood. In addition to that we assumed that student's mood is also influenced by his success or failure to answer the questions just before the current one. For instance, if a student has failed to provide a correct answer to all of the 5 previous questions, there is a high possibility to be emotionally negatively influenced, but if a student has managed to provide a correct answer to all of the 5 previous questions, there is a high possibility to be emotionally positively influenced. With the purpose of checking these assumptions we formulated this model:

$$R(q) = N - q, R(q) \in (0, N) \tag{1}$$

where R is the number of questions remaining before the end of the test, N is the total number of questions, and q is the number of the current question.

$$D(q) = I - r(q), \tag{2}$$

where $D(q)$ is the number of questions that the student still needs to answer in order to reach his goal, I is the student's goal, and $r(q)$ is the number of student's correct answers up to the current point.

$$H(q) = R(q) - D(q), \tag{3}$$

where $H(q)$ is a number that shows whether the remaining questions are enough for the student to reach his goal. For example, $H(q) = -4$ would mean that the student has already failed to reach his goal for 4 questions.

$$M(q) = H(q)^{+rr(q)}_{-wr(q)} \tag{4}$$

where $M(q)$ is the student's mood, $rr(q)$ is the number of correct answers in a row just before the current question, and $wr(q)$ is the number of wrong answers in a row just before the current question. So, if there are one or more correct answers in a row just before the current question, we add them to $H(q)$, while if there are one or more wrong answers in a row just before the current question, we subtract them from $H(q)$. The model also provides minimum and maximum values for M, which are given from the formulas shown bellow:

$$\max M = 2N, \tag{5}$$

$$\min M = -2N \tag{6}$$

2.1 Calculating the Agents Feedback to Student's Mood

Since, according to (5) and (6) we know the maximum and minimum values that M can take into the system, we can use a set of discrete values in order to approximate the real value of M. In this way, each discrete value of input M is mapped to a discrete output value which corresponds to a set of certain actions the agent will perform as a feedback to the student. Thus, we can calculate the agent's feedback to the student using the formula shown bellow:

$$feedback(M, L) = A, \qquad (7)$$

where L is the discrete level to which M is assigned, and A is a set of actions that can be triggered from the M, L pair. In order to provide the agent with a much richer and varying behaviour, we can attach more than one possible action to each M, L pair. These actions could be triggered randomly or based on the frequency of their appearance. It would be preferable, if the agent wouldn't repeat the same action for the same M, L pair.

3   Experiment Method

3.1   System Architecture

We build the online multiple choice questions test in a Windows XP machine using JavaScript with Perl CGI on Apache web server with MySQL. Common Gateway Interface (CGI) is used to provide dynamic web pages to students and the Perl programming language is a common choice for various reasons including simple and powerful string manipulation, Web server integration (i.e., Apache web server), and data manipulation [11]. Many students took the online test simultaneously, thus MySQL which is designed for multiple users accessing the files through a single server process was a very convenient choice for this kind of work [12].

The student's terminal sent a standard HTTP request encoded with special variables (commonly called CGI variables) and their values. The apache web server received the HTTP request and determined that the request was destined for a CGI program and not for a HTML file. The perl interpreter accepted the input from the server, parsed the variables, contacted the MySQL database for reading and recording data, applied some programming logic to the data, and returned a document back to the web server.

3.2   Participants

High schools students (N = 153) were recruited from 3 different regions of Greece (60 students from Athens, 50 students from Thessaloniki, and 43 students from Mitilini). Respondents consisted of 56% females and 44% males. The average age of participants was 16.8 (SD = 1.98) with 90% of the sample ranging from 15 to 19 years.

3.3   Materials

The multiple choice questions were focused on basic computer knowledge and skills, based on material taught in lectures. The context of questions was pre-specified by the teachers prior to the study. The test was constituted from 45 questions. The order of questions presented was randomly altered among students.

3.4 Procedure and Data Collection Methodology

The duration of the experiment was approximately 45 minutes and took place during the regular schedule of laboratorial courses. Students were told that this is a general education test concerning computer knowledge that would help them assess their knowledge about computers. At the beginning of the test, the system asked students how many correct answers would make them feel satisfied considering the level of their knowledge, making them set their personal goal. Throughout the test, a student choused his answer among 4 possible answers and confirmed his choice by clicking the "submit" button. After each question the system informed the student whether his answer was right or wrong and presented his score. Then the student could proceed to the next question by clicking the "next" button. During these 45 questions a slide bar appeared asking the student to move it according to his mood concerning the test, from -100(extremely negative mood) to +100(extremely positive mood).

The slide bar appeared 5 times during the test at a different instant for each student, as shown in Table 1. Accordingly, every 9 students we had checked once students' mood after every question of the test, so that the 153 participants gave us the chance to check students' mood after every question 17 times. Thus, the data set consisted of 765 instances (5 instances of each student).

Table 1. The slide bar sequence which was repeated every 9 students

Student	Question after which the slide bar appeared				
1st student	1st	9th	18th	27th	36th
2nd student	2nd	11th	20th	29th	38th
3rd student	3rd	12th	21st	30th	39th
4th student	4th	13th	22nd	31st	40th
5th student	5th	14th	23rd	32nd	41st
6th student	6th	15th	24th	33rd	42nd
7th student	7th	16th	25th	34th	43rd
8th student	8th	17th	26th	35th	44th
9th student	10th	19th	28th	37th	45th

Following each completed interaction, 10 parameters were calculated and recorded: (1) The number of the current question, (2) the number of questions remaining before the end of the test, (3) the number of questions that the student still needs to answer in order to reach his goal, (4) the number that shows whether the remaining questions are more or less than the number of questions that the student has to answer so as to reach his goal, i.e., student's hope to reach his goal, (5) the number of correct answers in a row just before the current question, (6) the number of wrong answers in a row just before the current question, (7) the number of correct answers up to the current question, (8) the number of wrong answers up to the current question, (9) the score, and (10) the mood that the student indicated by moving the slide bar.

4 Results

Initially we evaluated the model based on it's divergence from the mood that students pointed out on the slide bar. The mean error was normalized from 0 to 1. Nevertheless, this is a quantitative way of evaluation, while it is difficult to be highly accurate in predicting students' mood, which is an extremely sensitive variable.

Though in a quantitative evaluation, the linear correlation coefficient between the user declared mood and the mood estimated by the model, is strong ($r = 0.71$). Experiments in Human Computer Interaction (HCI) involve people, who would be unpredictable. Thus, we consider that a mean error of 0.1 with a standard deviation of 0.1 and having a normal error distribution is a pretty fine performance in predicting a student's mood. A confidence level of 90%, gives us a confidence interval of 0.01, which means that the range for true population mean error is 0.09 to 0.11.

It is obvious that the more close to his goal the student is throughout the test, the more positive his mood becomes. On the contrary, as long as the student's distant from his goal gets bigger as he proceeds into the test, the more negative his mood becomes.

Another important issue is that adding or subtracting the number of correct or wrong answers in a row just before the current question increases the model's efficacy (Table 2). We compared $H(q)$ alone with the entire model, which is $H(q)$ plus $rr(q)$ (the number of correct answers in a row just before the current question) or minus $wr(q)$ (the number of wrong answers in a row just before the current question). This shows that student's success or failure to recently previous questions influences his mood positively or negatively towards the current question.

Table 2. Comparing $H(q)$ with the entire Model shows that taking into account the number of correct or wrong answers in line just before the current question increases the model's efficacy

Models	R	Mean error	SD	Mean success recognizing whether student is in a positive or negative mood	Mean success recognizing whether student is in a positive mood	Mean success recognizing whether student is in a negative mood
$H(q)$ alone	0.64	0.11	0.1	77%	79%	80%
$M(q)$	0.71	0.1	0.1	82%	85%	82%

Trying to determine the exact percentage of student's positive or negative mood is a difficult task. However, if we try to determine just whether a student is in a positive mood or in a negative mood, things are getting much easier. So, in a qualitative evaluation, we would judge the model by its success in predicting whether a student is in positive or negative mood, no matter how positive or how negative this mood is. Using this model we can have a safe prediction of student's mood in terms of whether this mood is positive or negative (Table 2). A problem that is difficult to be solved from a quantitative point view, becomes more approachable from a qualitative point of view.

5 Conclusions

We have presented a model for recognition of student's mood during a computer based self-assessment test, with respect to each question the student is about to answer. We showed that this model is accurate enough and easy to implement. A relatively large number of students took an online test. The system informed the student after each question, whether he had provided a correct or a wrong answer and presented his score. The recorded data was used as input to the model. The system also presented a slide bar 5 times during the test at a different sequence for each student, asking the student to declare his current mood concerning the test.The evaluation of the model was based on students' feedback concerning their mood during the test. The present study is unique for a number of reasons. First, it demonstrated the ability to find good statistical fits on the model to predict the students' mood based on students' goal and record during the test. Second, it made obvious that student's verification or rebuttal of hope to reach his goal configures his mood during a test. Third, it demonstrated that student's success or failure to recently previous questions influences his mood positively or negatively towards the current question. Fourth, it showed that it may be helpful to see HCI problems from a qualitative point of view rather than from a quantitative point view.

In the future, we plan to use our mood-recognizer models for providing feedback to students' mood while taking a self-assessment test, so as to help the students improve their knowledge and acquire a positive attitude towards learning.

References

1. Pekrun, R., Goetz, T., Titz, W., Perry, R.P.: Academic Emotions in Students' Self-Regulated Learning and Achievement: A Program of Qualitative and Quantitative Research. Educational Psychologist 37(2), 91–105 (2002)
2. Goleman, D.: Emotional Intelligence. Bantam Books, NY (1995)
3. Lytras, M.D., Sicilia, M.A.: The knowledge society: A manifesto for knowledge and learning. International Journal of Knowledge and Learning 1(1/2), 1–11 (2005)
4. Ortony, A., Clore, G.L., Collins, A.: The cognitive structure of emotions. Cambridge University Press, Cambridge (1988)
5. Conati, C.: Probabilistic assessment of user's emotions in education games. Journal of Applied Artificial Intelligence, special issue on managing cognition and Affect in HCI 16(7-8), 555–575 (2002)
6. Albano, G., Gaeta, G., Salerno, S.: E-learning: A model and process proposal. International Journal of Knowledge and Learning 2(1/2), 73–88 (2006)
7. Albano, G., Gaeta, G., Salerno, S.: IWT: An innovative solution for AGS e-learning model. International Journal of Knowledge and Learning 3(2/3), 209–224 (2007)

8. Economides, A.A.: Personalized feedback in CAT. World Scientific and Engineering Academy and Society (WSEAS) Transactions on Advances in Engineering Education 2(3), 174–181 (2005)

9. Economides, A.A.: Emotional feedback in CAT (Computer Adaptive Testing). International Journal of Instructional Technology & Distance Learning 3(2) (2006)

10. Triantafillou, E., Georgiadou, E., Economides, A.A.: Applying Adaptive Variables in Computerised Adaptive Testing. Australasian Journal of Educational Technology 23(3) (2007)

11. Guelich, S., Gundavaram, S., Birznieks, G.: CGI Programming with Perl, 2nd edn. O'Reilly, Cambridge (2000)

12. Kofler, M.: The Definitive Guide to MySQL 5, 3rd edn. Apress, Berkeley (2005)

Enhancing Motivation, School Competence and Self-perception of Physics in the Environment of the Cognitive Tutor CTAT during Physics Instruction

Evi Makri-Botsari[1] and Sarantos Psycharis[2]

[1] School of Pedagogical and Technological Education (ASPETE)
maeducation@aspete.gr
[2] University of the Aegean, Department of Education and School of Pedagogical and Technological Education (ASPETE)
sarpsy@otenet.gr

Abstract. Recently, a number of factors have prompted change in the teaching –learning sequences in general and in particular in Physics. These factors include: 1) results from physics education research, 2) ICT as a teaching tool, and 3) concerns about the physics content knowledge.

These factors provide the impulse to scientists in education research to focus on conceptual understanding and the cognitive skills required to understand and apply physics concepts, interactive engagement methods, teaching physics in different contexts and the use of ICT in the teaching learning sequence. Intelligent tutoring systems and Cognitive tutors are highly interactive learning environments based on cognitive psychology theory of problem solving and learning and they have been proved to improve classroom instruction.

In this paper we investigate the use of the cognitive tutor authoring tool (CTAT) in order to address issues concerning: the influence of CTAT on structures like: academic Intrinsic Motivation ,General School Competence, Competence of Physics, and Self esteem. Data were collected with respect to the above mentioned variables and our results provide indications that the teaching process through CTAT influences academic motivations, competence in physics and scholastic competence.

Keywords: Cognitive tutors, motivation, school competence, self-perception , physics.

1 Introduction

Recently, a number of factors have prompted change in the teaching in general and obviously in the teaching of physics like: 1) results from educational research, 2) ICT as a teaching tool, 3) concerns about the physics content knowledge (Thacker, 2003).

Intelligent tutoring systems are highly interactive learning environments that have been shown to improve upon typical classroom instruction(Murray 1999, VanLehn 2006) ,they have been successful in raising student achievement (Koedinger et.al 2003) and have been disseminated widely. Intelligent Tutors are based on artificial Intelligence technology to provide interactive instruction that adapts to individual

M.D. Lytras et al. (Eds.): WSKS 2008, CCIS 19, pp. 342–353, 2008.

students' needs and personality's characteristics and, most typically, support student's practice in learning complex problem solving and reasoning. Cognitive Tutors are a type of intelligent tutor based on cognitive psychology theory of problem solving and learning.   Cognitive Tutors also provide a rich problem-solving environment with tutorial guidance in the form of step-by-step feedback, specific messages in response to common errors, and on demand instructional hints. They also select problems based on individual student performance (Koedinger & Aleven 2007). Cognitive Tutors grew out of an attempt to apply and test the ACT-R theory of cognition and rely on cognitive psychology research in their design and development (Anderson et al. 1995). Physics education research is a growing field of physics and its field covers students' understanding of physics concepts (Thacker et.al 1999, Park et.al 2001), assessment of students' understanding (the design of instruments to probe students' understanding and interpretation of the results)   instructional methods, and cognitive structures as related to students' learning (Alsop 2000, Greca & Moreira 2000) .The results of research on students' conceptions before instruction and in the process of learning physics concepts (including studying the cognitive processes involved and the development of models of students' reasoning), can be used as the basis for the development of curricula and instructional (Snyder 2000,Taber 2000). During the last three decades, numerous researchers have highlighted the importance of motivational variables within the school setting (Ryan, Deci, 2000). Low school performance and dropouts is attributed by the teachers to the lack of motivation at school and most classroom teachers would like to find ways to enhance students' motivation to learn. A number of studies have revealed that students who are intrinsically motivated show significantly higher school achievement and higher self perception's levels of school competence   (Fontaine, 1994, Harter & Connell, 1984, Makri-Botsari, 1999, Deci, Koestner, & Ryan 2001), higher intellectual ability (Gottfried, 1990), and more favorable perceptions of their academic competence.

Studies focussing on the interrelationships between motivation to learn and lifelong learning (Venkatesh, 1999, Makri-Botsari& Megari, 2001c), have further revealed that intrinsic motivation to learn is a necessary condition for promoting lifelong attitudes and skills, and leads to sustained behavior. An intrinsic motivation for schoolwork is an important element in keeping adolescents in school and in promoting lifelong learning.

The question of how academic intrinsic motivation and hight academic achievement can be increased has been of central interest to educators and psychologists. Toward this direction, teachers and teaching practices are considered to be critical factors that can contribute to the development of an intrinsic interest in school learning. (Weiler, 2004).

According to the theory of Carl Rogers (Rogers, 1961, 1974), each person has a basic need to maintain, protect and enhance his/her self-concept, employing the sole motivating power, that of self-actualization. So individuals are always motivated. This view of motivation as an ever-present internal drive, which can be dispensed in a variety of ways, is a tremendous advantage for the teacher. For Rogers, teachers are most likely to directing this motivation to educational ends and personal development, if their students see them as caring, supportive and accepting. Particular teacher attitudes associated with the transition to junior high school, such us teachers' greater emphasis on grades, their greater focus on competition and decreasing personal interest in students, impact perceived scholastic competence, which in turn, influences motivation. (Makri-Botsari, 2001b).

Several research studies have revealed that teaching practices which focus not only on the development of skills, but also on the enhancement of students' self-esteem, are more effective (Davis & Brember, 1999, Deci & Ryan 2004, Yeung & Wong 2004, Swann, Chang-Schneider & Larsen McClarty, 2007).

Self-esteem and self-perception, the two aspects of self-concept have been studied as important variables in the development of human being. During adolescence, self-awareness becomes particularly acute and questioned, after a period of stability during late childhood. Related to self-perception, self-esteem seems to suffer also from this process of self-evaluation and questioning. Self-esteem, defined here as a differentiated and evaluative process of self-definition is often related, in the investigation, with academic performance, scholastic competence and academic motivation.

2 The CTAT Authoring Tool

Cognitive Tutor CTAT is based on   the ACT-R theory of cognition and learning and interprets student problem-solving behavior using a cognitive model that captures, in the form of production rules, the skills that the student is expected to learn (Koedinger et.al ,1997) The tutor applies an algorithm called "model tracing" to monitor a student involved in a problem and   compares the students' actions against those that are appropriate according to the model.

That is, an Instructor-author demonstrates to the system how students are expected to solve each assigned problem and what errors they are expected to make while no AI programming is needed. The Cognitive Tutor Authoring Tools comprise three separate applications: an external GUI Builder (typically, NetBeans or Macromedia's Flash), a set of core tools for demonstration-based task analysis and for testing and debugging cognitive models, and an external editor for cognitive models (typically Eclipse)

Two of the main characteristics of the CTAT (used in our work) are:

- the Behavior Recorder – a central tool with three key functions. First, it records examples of correct and incorrect behavior demonstrated by the author, in the Student Interface, in the form of a Behavior Graph. Second, it implements the example-tracing Function and third provides support for planning and testing of cognitive models.
- the Working Memory Editor – used for cognitive model development: it allows an author to inspect and modify the contents of the cognitive model's "working **memory," which is frequently needed during model development.**

3 Methodology

At the first stage of the research, 5 teachers were trained by the authors on the use of CTAT. Training period lasted for 4 weeks, 5 hours per week and teachers were trained in the five applications of the unit of Mechanics and Thermal Energy, according to the official curriculum.

Teachers had the responsibility of teaching physics in Grade 8 and they were experienced teachers on the use of ICT in education, but their experience was limited in specific software like Interactive Physics and Modellus. In our research participated 124 students, 68 girls and 56 boys.

During the training period, teachers made interventions on the applications created by authors of the article, mainly on the aspects to be involved in the teaching-learning sequence, on the alternative solutions to be included and in the form of feedback should be provided by CTAT.

Before the instruction, a first evaluation was implemented in students' self-perception of scholastic competence, self-perception of competence in physics, self-esteem and academic motivation while after the instruction a second evaluation was done.

3.1 Self-perception of Scholastic Competence

The instrument used to tap perceived scholastic competence was a subscale of the *Self-Perception Profile for Adolescents* (Harter, 1988), as adapted by Makri-Botsari (2001a) for use with Greek students. This scale contains nine separate subscales tapping eight specific domains of self-concept, as well as global self-worth or self-esteem.

Questions are written in a "structural alternative format" designed to reduce the tendency to give socially desirable responses. A sample item reads as follows: Some teenagers do very well at their classwork BUT Other teenagers don't do very well at their classwork. The respondent is first asked to decide whether he/she is more like the teenagers described in the first, or the second, part of the statement. After making this choice, the subject is then asked to check one of the two boxes on the side of the statement selected, indicating whether that description is only "Sort of True for Me" or "Really True for Me".

Items are scored along a four-point continuum in which an endorsement of "Really True for Me" of the more positive description would receive a score of 4,"Sort of True for Me" of the more positive description would receive a 3,"Sort of True for Me" of the more negative description would receive a 2, and "Really True for Me" of the more negative description would receive a 1.

3.2 Self-esteem

Self-esteem was assessed using the subscale for Self-esteem.

3.3 Self-perception of Competence in Physics

In order to asses *Self-Perception of Competence in Physics* we created a new subscale which contains questions in the same "structural alternative format". A sample item reads as follows: Some teenagers do very well at Physics' exams BUT other teenagers don't do very well at Physics' exams.

Some teenagers find it hard to comprehend anything that is related to Physics, BUT other teenagers comprehend easily anything that is related to Physics.

3.4 Academic Motivation

The instrument used to tap *academic motivation* was the *Scale of Intrinsic versus Extrinsic Orientation in the Classroom* (Harter, 1981). This scale identifies five aspects of classroom learning along an intrinsic to extrinsic continuum: preference for challenge versus preference for easy work assigned, curiosity or intrinsic interest in the subject material versus getting grades/pleasing the teacher, independent mastery versus dependence on the teacher, independent judgment versus reliance on teacher's judgment, and internal criteria for success/failure versus external criteria for success/failure.

The question format of this instrument directly pits these orientations against one another, as alternative choices. Sample questions for the preference for challenge and the curiosity/interest subscales were: (a) *Preference for challenge-* "Some students like hard work because it's a challenge" b u t "Other students prefer easy work that they are sure they can do"; (b) *Curiosity/interest-* "Some students do their schoolwork because the teacher tells them to" b u t "Other students do their schoolwork to find out about a lot of things they've been wanting to know". The respondent is first asked to decide whether he/she is more like the children described in the first, or the second, part of the statement. After making this choice, the subject is then asked to check one of the two boxes on the side of the statement selected, indicating whether that description is only "Sort of True for Me" or "Really True for Me".

Items are scored along a four-point continuum in which an endorsement of "Really True for Me" of the more intrinsic orientation would receive a score of 4, "Sort of True for Me" of the more intrinsic orientation would receive a 3, "Sort of True for Me" of the more extrinsic orientation would receive a 2, and "Really True for Me" of the more extrinsic orientation would receive a 1.

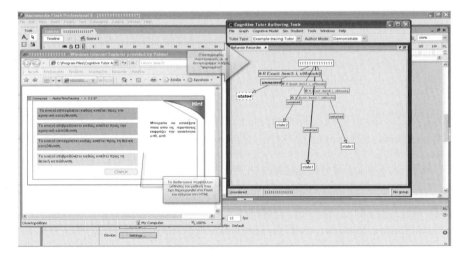

Fig. 1. One of the activities created by CTAT in the course of Mechanics (in Greek)

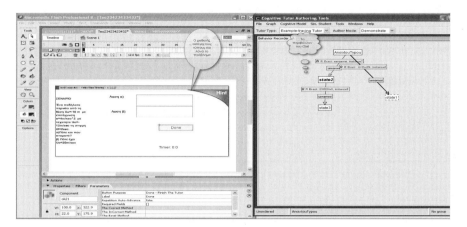

Fig. 2. The interface used by students when participating in problem solving(left) and the behaviour recorder (right)

For the purposes of the present investigation, only the first two subscales (preference for challenge and curiosity/interest) were considered. A given child's scores from these two subscales were combined into one variable, which is labeled as *academic intrinsic motivation*. Bear in mind that while this variable is labeled in terms of the intrinsic pole, represented by high scores, a low score on this variable designates an extrinsic orientation.

All students engaged in problem solving situations created in the environment of CTAT by the authors of the paper including the interventions of teachers. The technical part was implemented using the component of Flash connected to CTAT.

4   Results

4.1   Sex Effects on Motivational Orientation

Preference for challenge and curiosity/interest mean scores by sex are presented in Table 1. There it can be seen that, in general, means are above the midpoint (2.50) of the scale indicating that children in the age range considered here are rather intrinsic in their orientation. However, there are differences associated with both gender. Moreover, boys' preference for challenge scores were significantly and substantially higher than their curiosity/interest scores (t[56]=4.786, p<.001), while girls showed slightly higher curiosity/interest in the subject material than preference for challenge (t[68]=2.357, p=.020).

4.2   Grade and Sex Effects on Motivational Orientation

Preference for challenge and curiosity/interest mean scores by sex are presented in Tables 1A and 1B.(A stands for before and B stands for after).

Table 1A. Preference for Challenge and Curiosity/ Interest Mean Scores by Sex *before* Intervention

Dimension	Grade		
	8th		
	Boys	Girls	Total average
Preference for Challenge	2.93	2.59	2.76
Curiosity/ Interest	2.69	2.61	2.65

Table 1B. Preference for Challenge and Curiosity/ Interest Mean Scores by Sex *after* Intervention

Dimension	Grade		
	8th		
	Boys	Girls	Total average
Preference for Challenge	3.00	2.82	2.91
Curiosity/ Interest	2.90	3.01	2.99

4.3 General School Competence, Competence of Physics and Self Esteem Mean Scores by Sex

The Mean Scores of self perceptions of General School Competence, Competence of Physics and Self esteem by Sex are presented at Tables 2A and 2B.

Table 2A. General School Competence, Competence of Physics and Self esteem Mean Scores by Sex *before* Intervention

Scale	Boys	Girls	Total average
General School Competence	2.72	2.90	2.55
School Competence of Physics	2.70	2.43	2.56
Self esteem	3.15	3.03	3.06

Table 2B. General School Competence, Competence of Physics and Self esteem Mean Scores by Sex *after* Intervention

Scale	Boys	Girls	Total
General School Competence	2.78	2.92	2.85
School Competence of Physics	2.90	2.85	2.87
Self esteem	3.18	3.08	3.13

The Pearson r correlations between the variables we examined are presented in Table 3.

Table 3. Pearson r Correlations between General School Competence, Competence of Physics and Self esteem and academic Intrinsic Motivation[1]

Variable	1	2	3	4
1. Competence of Physics	1.000			
2. General School Competence	0.381	1.000		
3. Self esteem	0.212	0.311	1.000	
4. Intrinsic Motivation	0.270	0.336	0.227	1.000

4.4 χ^2

The causal links between sex, general school competence, competence in physics, self-esteem and academic intrinsic motivation were examined using maximum likelihood analysis of structural equations (Jöreskog & Sörbom, 1989). As indices of the model goodness of fit were used the: chi-square (χ^2) statistics, the adjusted goodness of fit index (AGFI) and the root mean square residual (RMSR).

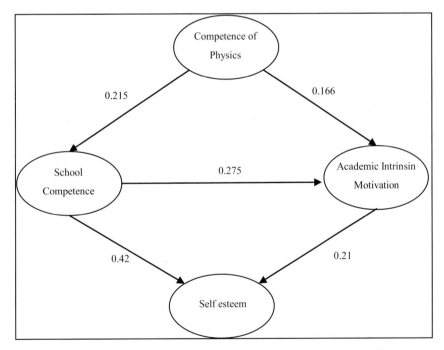

Fig. 3. Path Diagram of the Relation between General School Competence, Competence of Physics and Self esteem and Academic Intrinsic Motivation

---

[1] All correlation are significant at level p<.01, unless otherwise stated.

The measures of the overall fit of the whole model were: χ^2 (6) = 9.93, p = .122, AGFI = .961, RMSR = .036.

It is remarkable that after intervention the scores in physics increased. In some cases, especially for girls, the increase was up to 60%.

5 Conclusions

In our paper various questions come to the fore: Are there significant correlations between motivations and learning outcomes? What is the relationship between competence of physics, school competence and self-esteem? Is CTAT an effective tool to increase the above mentioned structures? Results of our research strongly indicate that the use of CTAT in the teaching-learning sequence affects scholastic competence, competence in physics as well as the academic motivations.

Through our research we reached the same conclusions with other researchers, according to which boys seem to perceive themselves more competent at Maths and Natural Sciences than girls (Chissick, 2002). Remarkably interesting is the fact that girls' competence of Physics was substantially increased after the intervention.   It seems that through that procedure, the competitive environment impact between boys and girls, which is led by social stereotypes of gender, is suppressed. According to the latter, girls are presumed to have better performance at literature lessons than at Maths and Natural Science courses.

Learning occurs only when what is being presented is meaningful enough to the student that he or she decides to actively engage in the learning experience. (Pierce, Cameron, Banko & So, 2003)

The relationship between self-esteem ,academic achievement and scholastic competence has been widely researched. Self-esteem seems to be a very important personal characteristic related to many aspects of healthy behaviour. (Skaalvik & Hagvet 1990)

Since children and adolescents spend most of their growing and developing years in school, it is therefore natural that the researchers all over the world feel interest in finding out the nature of the relationship between self-esteem, academic performance, scholastic competence and academic motivation.

We are in the process to continue our work to incorporate the issue of metacognition because we consider that a crucial factor affecting the problem solving is the way students make decisions and this is related to cognitive structures.

References

1. Alsop, S.: Meeting the needs of lifelong learners: recognizing a conative dimension in physics education. Phys. Educ. 35, 202–208 (2000)
2. Anderson, J.R., Corbett, A.T., Koedinger, K.R., Pelletier, R.: Cognitive tutors: Lessons learned. The Journal of the Learning Sciences 4(2) (1995)
3. Bliss, J., Ogborn, J.: Students' reaction to undergraduate science. Heinemann Educational Books, London (1977)

4. Chi, M.T.H., Bassok, M., Lewis, M.W., Reimann, P., Glaser, R.: Self-explanations: How students study and use examples in learning to solve problems. Cognitive Science 13(2) (1989)
5. Chissick, N.: Factors affecting the implementation of Reforms in School Mathematics. In: Proceedings of the Annual Meetinh of the international group for the Psychology of Mathematics Education, Norwich, England (2002)
6. Davis, J., Brember, I.: Self-esteem and national tests in years 2 and 6: A 4-year longitudinal study. Educational Psychology 19, 337–345 (1999)
7. Deci, E.L., Koestner, R., Ryan, R.M.: Extrinsic rewards and intrinsic motivation in education: Reconsidered once again. Review of Educational Research 71, 1–27 (2001)
8. Deci, E.L., Ryan, R.M.: Overview of self-determination theory: An organismic dialectical perspective. In: Deci, E.L., Ryan, R.M. (eds.) Handbook of self-determination research, pp. 3–33. The University of Rochester Press, Rochester (2004)
9. Fontaine, A.M.: Self-concept and motivation during adolescence: Their influence on school achievement. In: Oosterwegel, A., Wicklund, R.A. (eds.) The Self in European and North-American Culture: Development and Processes, pp. 205–217. Kluwer Academic Publishers, Amsterdam (1994)
10. Frederick-Recascino, C.M.: Self-determination theory and participation motivation research in the sport and exercise domain. In: Deci, E.L., Ryan, R.M. (eds.) Handbook of self-determination research, pp. 277–294. The University of Rochester Press, Rochester (2004)
11. Girep-Research Group on Physics Teaching (December 30, 2002) http://www.pef.uni-lj.si/~girep/
12. Greca, I.M., Moreira, M.A.: Mental models, conceptual models, and modeling. Int. J. Sci. Educ. 22, 1–11 (2000)
13. Gottfried, A.E.: Academic intrinsic motivation in young elementary school children. Journal of Educational Psychology 82, 525–538 (1990)
14. Harter, S.: A new self-report scale of intrinsic versus extrinsic orientation in the classroom: Motivational and informational components. Developmental Psychology 17, 300–312 (1981)
15. Harter, S., Connell, J.P.: A model of children's achievement and related self- perceptions of competence, control and motivational orientation. In: Nicholls, J. (ed.) Advances in Motivation and Achievement, pp. 219–250. JAI Press, Greenwich (1984)
16. Harter, S.: Manual for the Self-Perception Profile for Adolescents. University of Denver Press, Denver (1988)
17. Hattie, J.: Self-concept. Erlbaum, Hillsdale (1992)
18. International Commission on Physics Education (December 30, 2002), http://www.physics.umd.edu/ripe/icpe/
19. Johnson, B.: Teacher as researcher. Clearinghouse on Teacher Education. ERIC Document Reproduction Service No. ED 355205, Washington D.C (1993)
20. Koedinger, K.R., Anderson, J.R., Hadley, W.H., Mark, M.A.: Intelligent tutoring goes to school in the big city. International Journal of Artificial Intelligence in Education 8 (1997)
21. Koedinger, K.R., Aleven, V., Heffernan, N.: Toward a rapid development environment for Cognitive Tutors. In: Hoppe, U., Verdejo, F., Kay, J. (eds.) Artificial Intelligence in Education, Proc. of AIED 2003. IOS Press, Amsterdam (2003)
22. Koedinger, K.R., Aleven, V.: Exploring the Assistance Dilemma in Experiments with Cognitive Tutors. Educational Psychology Review 19 (2007)
23. Makri-Botsari, E.: Academic intrinsic motivation: Developmental differences and relations to perceived scholastic competence, locus of control and achievement. Evaluation and Research in Education 13, 157–171 (1999)
24. Makri-Botsari, E.: The Way I Perceive Myself – III: A Scale for Assessing Self-Perception and Self-Esteem of Junior High School Children. Greek Letters, Athens (2001a) (in Greek)

25. Makri-Botsari, E.: Causal links between academic intrinsic motivation, self-esteem, and unconditional acceptance by teachers in high school students. In: Riding, R., Rayner, S. (eds.) International perspectives on individual differences. Self-perception, vol. 2, pp. 209–220. Ablex Publishing, CT (2001b)
26. Makri-Botsari, E., Megari, E.: Lifelong Learning and Intrinsic Motivation. In: Haris, K., Petroulakis, N., Nikodemos, S. (eds.) Continuing Education and Lifelong Learning: International Experience and Greek Perspective, Atrapos, Athens, pp. 316–329 (2001c) (in Greek)
27. Makri-Botsari, E., Psycharis, S.: An e-Learning Model in the Educational System: Determinants and Parameters of its Application in Teacher Training. In: Hatzidimou, D., Vitsilaki, C. (eds.) The Schooll in the Information and Multicultural Society, pp. 321–332. Kyriakidis Publications, Thessalonica (2006)
28. Marsh, H.W.: The structure of academic self-concept, the Marsh/Shavelson model. Journal of Educational Psychology 82, 623–636 (1990)
29. Miltiadou, M., Savenye, W.C.: Applying Social Cognitive Constructs of Motivation to Enhance Student Success. Online Distance Education (2004),
    http://www.aace.org/pubs/etr/issue4/miltiadou2.pdf
30. Murray, T.: Authoring intelligent tutoring systems: An analysis of the state of the art. International Journal of Artificial Intelligence in Education 10 (1999)
31. Park, J., Kim, I., Kim, M., Lee, M.: Analysis of students' processes of confirmation and falsification of their prior ideas about electrostatics. Int. J. Sci. Educ. 23, 1219–1236 (2001)
32. Pajares, F., Miller, M.D.: Role of self-efficacy and self-concept beliefs in mathematical problem solving: A path analysis. Journal of Educational Psychology 86, 193–203 (1994)
33. Pajares, F., Schunk, D.: Self-beliefs and school success: Self-Efficacy. In: Riding, R., Rayner, S. (eds.) Self-Concept and school achievement, pp. 239–266. Ablex Publishing, London (2001),
    http://www.emory.edu/EDUCATION/mfp/PajaresSchunk2001.html
34. Pierce, W.D., Cameron, J., Banko, K.M., So, S.: Positive effects of rewards and performance standards on intrinsic motivation. The Psychological Record 53, 561–578 (2003)
35. Pintrich, P.R., Schunk, D.H.: Motivation in education: Theory, research, and practice. Prentice Hall, Englewood Cliffs (1996)
36. Prosser, M., Walker, P., Millar, R.: Differences in students' perceptions of learning physics. Physics Education 31(1) (1996)
37. Psycharis, S., Makri-Botsari, E., Paraskeva, F.: Computer simulation: Before or after the instruction? A didactic approach for teaching the process of matter phase changes to students. International Journal of Learning 12(8) (2006) (ISSN: 1447-9494.2006)
38. Rogers, C.: On Becoming a Person. Houghton Mifflin, Boston (1961)
39. Rogers, C.: In retrospect. American Psychology 29, 115–116 (1974)
40. Ryan, R.M., Deci, E.L.: Intrinsic and extrinsic motivations: Classic definitions and new directions. Contemporary Educational Psychology 25, 54–67 (2000)
41. Skaalvik, E.M., Hagvet, K.A.: Academic achievement and self-concept: na analysis of causal predominance in a developmental perspective. Journal of Personality and Social Psychology 58(2), 292–307 (1990)
42. Snyder, J.L.: An investigation of the knowledge structures of experts, intermediates and novices in physics. Int. J. Sci. Educ. 22, 292–979 (2000)
43. Swann, W., Chang-Schneider, C., Larsen McClarty, K.: Do People's Self-Views Matter? Self-Concept and Self-Esteem in Everyday Life. American Psychologist 62(2), 84–94 (2007)
44. Taber, K.S.: Multiple frameworks?: evidence of manifold conceptions in individual cognitive structure. Int. J. Sci. Educ. 22, 399–417 (2000)

45. Thacker, B.A., Ganiel, U., Boys, D.: Macroscopic phenomena and microscopic processes: student understanding of transients in direct current electric circuits. Phys. Educ. Res., Am. J. Phys. Suppl. 67, 25–31 (1999)
46. Thacker, B.: Recent advances in classroom physics. Reports Progress in Physics 66 (2003)
47. VanLehn, K.: The behavior of tutoring systems. International Journal of Artificial Intelligence in Education 16 (2006)
48. Venkatesh, V.: Creation of favorable user perceptions: Exploring the role of intrinsic motivation. Management Information Systems Quarterly 23, 239–263 (1999)
49. Weiler, A.: Information-Seeking Behavior in Generation Y Students: Motivation, Critical Thinking, and Learning Theory. The Journal of Academic Librarianship 31(1), 46–53 (2004)
50. Yeung, A.S., Wong, E.: Teacher Self-concept Enhancement: Effects of an In-Service Training Program in Hong Kong. The Hong Kong Institute of Education, Hong Kong (2004)
51. Zimmerman, B.J., Bandura, A.: Impact of self-regulatory influences on writing course attainment. American Educational Research Journal 31, 845–862 (1994)

An Examination of Assessment Practices in Colleges of Business at Various Middle East Countries[*]

Nitham M. Hindi, Mohammad K. Najdawi, and Hend Abdulrahman Mohamed Jolo

College of Business and Economics
Qatar University
Doha, Qatar
nhindi@qu.edu.qa, monaj@qu.edu.qa, hjolo@qu.edu.qa

Abstract. This study reports the results of a survey conducted during 2007 which was mailed to deans of schools of business at institutions of higher education located within the Middle East. Schools of business are now more engaged in assessment activities than a few years ago. Assessment activities are costly and the emphasis seems to be placed on assessing critical thinking, communication skills, technology/computer usage, professional knowledge, and problem solving. Colleges of business are relaying heavily on course-embedded measures, followed by indirect measures of assessment. Curriculum and instructional changes were the top-ranked uses of assessment results. Universities that are accredited by the ministry of higher education were more likely to indicate attract equipment and/or financial resources as the purpose of assessment. Finally, AACSB accredited universities were more likely to identify alumni as assessment stakeholder and were more likely to assess global issues.

Keywords: Assessment, assurance of learning, benchmarking, quality assurance, higher education assurance of learning, business assessment.

1 Introduction

Educational institutions are increasingly challenged to justify use of human and financial resources and provide assurance that educational experiences are worthwhile in terms of student learning and preparation for professional careers. The recent shift in paradigm of output based assessment (to measure students' learning) focused colleges and universities to measure the achievement of their learning outcomes. Therefore, faculty and administration personnel search for ways to assure stakeholders that college experiences add value to students. With increasing complexity and uncertainty, stakeholders are having increasingly greater performance expectations. Consequently, the concept of assessment in the Middle East appears to be receiving attention as a worthwhile approach to measurement of learning outcomes.

---

[*] This publication was made possible by support from Qatar University. Its contents are solely the responsibility of the authors and do not necessarily represent the official views of Qatar University.

M.D. Lytras et al. (Eds.): WSKS 2008, CCIS 19, pp. 354–359, 2008.
© Springer-Verlag Berlin Heidelberg 2008

Colleges of business that are either accredited by specialized business accrediting agency, pursuing such accreditation, or mandated by ministry of higher education of their countries are required to assess their degree programs. Effective assessment of student learning is a critical step toward achieving quality. The purpose of the paper is to present perceptions of business deans at selected Middle Eastern universities regarding their assessment programs. This paper proceeds as follows. The paper reviews relevant literature regarding assessment, explains the methodology utilized, discusses results, and presents summary and conclusions.

2 Literature Review

The precise meaning for the word "assessment" is somewhat absent. Terenzini [1] noted views ranging from reviews of general education to surveys of stakeholder groups and institutional self studies. Definition and process of assessment are critical. Angelo [2] defined assessment as an "ongoing process aimed at understanding and improving student learning." Therefore, the ultimate outcome of assessment is improved student learning. AACSB [3] described the assessment process to include the five activities, including identify learning goals and objectives, gather and analyze evidence, report and discuss results, identify improvement opportunities, and reflect and make changes.

Over the years, numerous factors influenced development of assessment practices that prevail in today's educational environment. Bock, Mislevy, and Woodson [4] traced inception of the relationship between assessment and accountability to the early 1960s. Hatfield and Gorman [5] observed that the basics of prevailing approaches to assessment originated in the 1930s, were adopted by business organizations after World War II, and came to the forefront in academia in the 1980s. During the 1990s, further interest in assessment evolved as accreditation organizations initiated requirements for assessment plans. In practice, external pressures combined with internal desires for continuous improvement influenced development of assessment programs. For many years, accreditation agencies stressed "inputs" and concentrated on commitment of institutional resources to assessment, rather than measurement of outcomes [6]. The most-recent AACSB standards [3] include greater emphasis on the role of assessment and assurance that various learning standards are met.

In the Middle East area, formal assessment of programs is somewhat a new concept. Shaw, Badri, and Hukul [7] reported that "although the concern for assessment currently sweeping the West is not so pronounced in the Gulf." Some universities in the Middle East assess particular portions of their operations, such as registration and advising [8], university training of occupational attainment [9], and e-learning challenges in the Arab World [10].

3 Methodology

A questionnaire was based on a recommended assessment model developed by the Accounting Education Change Commission [11]. The draft was then reviewed by administrative colleagues for content analysis. The revised questionnaire was mailed to 68 deans from various schools in the Middle East. A total of 35 deans from Middle East universities completed and returned the surveys for a response rate of 51 percent. The survey solicited relevant information concerning assessment practices from deans of business schools at colleges and universities located in the Middle East.

The three-page questionnaire asked respondents for some demographic information such as the highest degree awarded, type of institution (public/private), and the type of business accreditation (AACSB, ACBSP, regional, or Ministry of Higher Education). Then, the survey inquired whether universities and business schools had formal assessment programs and, if so, the title of the person(s) responsible for them and the how often they conducted their assessment activities.

The second page asked respondents to indicate the costs of assessment, and the existence of budget allocated for assessment. In addition, the survey requested information about curriculum/ program objectives and whether these objectives were assessed. Finally, participants were asked to identify their assessment approaches, assessment instruments, and usages of assessment. The third page of the questionnaire included questions related to purposes of assessment, stakeholders of business schools, and skills/competencies assessed. Finally, the respondents were asked to identify the major strengths and weaknesses of their assessment programs, and whether business schools planned to revise/improve the programs, and a list of anticipated improvements.

4 Results

The respondents included 20 (57 percent) public and 15 (43 percent) private universities/colleges. Nine (26 percent) of the respondents indicated that the baccalaureate degree was the highest degree offered; 9 (26 percent) colleges and universities offered masters degrees; and 17 (49 percent) institutions offered doctorate degrees. Of the 35 schools responding to the survey, 6 (17 percent) were accredited by AACSB; 1 (3 percent) schools were accredited by regional accrediting agencies; and 28 (80 percent) schools are accredited by the ministry of higher education.

Of the 35 respondents, 21 respondents (60 percent) noted that their colleges or universities had formal assessment programs. Nineteen respondents (54 percent) stated that their schools of business had formal assessment programs. Deans (17 percent) were mentioned the greatest number of times to be responsible for the university assessment programs. Twenty percent indicated their assessment is conducted annually, followed by 11 percent conducted every semester. Deans (29 percent) and assessment committee (11 percent) were most frequently mentioned as having the responsibility for the school of business assessment programs.

Six (17 percent) of the deans responded that the annual expense for schools of business assessment programs was less than $5,000. Two (6 percent) colleges or universities indicated costs in the range of $5,001-$10,000; and nine (26 percent) schools were in the range of $10,001-$20,000. Forty-three percent indicted the existence of a budget allocated for assessment activities. Forty-seven percent of those that had budget allocation their allocation were part of their college budget while another 47 percent was a university budget.

When asked about specific curriculum/program objectives, 71 percent deans responded affirmatively, but only 57 percent of the schools actually assessed these objectives. However, 49 percent of respondents plan to improve/revise their assessment programs. The top five improvements/revisions planned by the schools of business included continuously review and improve of assessment process, increase formality of assessment program, incorporate more direct measures of assessment, close the loop, and assessing learning outcomes.

Approaches to assessment included course-embedded (60 percent), indirect measures (49 percent), student selection (40 percent), and stand-alone testing (26 percent). The most widely used instruments were students' evaluation of faculty (54 percent), exit survey (54 percent), alumni survey (46 percent), employer surveys (46 percent), and faculty survey (31 percent). Over fifty percent of the respondents considered the most important stakeholders of school of business to be current students, employers, and faculty.

Most schools (57 percent) used assessment outcomes to make curricular changes, followed by instructional changes (51 percent), as a means for meeting responsibility to students (46 percent), and to meet responsibility to public (43 percent). The three most-mentioned purposes for assessment included meeting accreditation requirements (54 percent), monitoring program effectiveness (51 percent), and guiding planning and improvement efforts (51 percent). It is interesting to note that comparatively fewer schools of business used assessment to justify/attract financial resources, attract better students, or provide information relevant to policies.

Critical thinking, communication skills, technology/computer usage, professional knowledge, and problem solving were the top five skills mentioned by the deans. Least-assessed skills included multicultural/diversity issues, interpersonal skills, global issues, and reflective thinking. These skills are more difficult to measure, which may be a reason they were less frequently mentioned.

Survey participants were asked to identify the strengths and weaknesses of their assessment program. When asked to identify the strengths of assessment, participants mentioned thorough and comprehensive assessment program, the use of direct assessment measures, link to mission, goals, and outcomes, constant review of outcomes to ensure quality of curriculum/programs, and faculty commitment. Major weaknesses related to lack of time and resources, lack of systematic planning of assessment/limited scope, lack of faculty involvement, assessment measures need improvements, and the need to close-the-loop.

The chi-square non-parametric test was used to determine whether various relationships were statistically significant. Tests involved assessment variables (usage of assessment, purposes of assessment, and skills/competencies assessed) and characteristics of business schools (highest degree awarded, type of institution [public or private], and business accreditation status. While a lack of significance was noted for the majority of calculations, several significant relationships were apparent.

There was a statistically significant relationship between highest degree awarded and purposes of assessment, usages of assessment, and skills/competencies assessed. Universities that awarded master degrees were almost twice more likely than bachelor universities and more likely than doctorate granting institutions to use assessment data to make instructional changes and meet responsibility to the public. Master awarding

universities were more likely than bachelor awarding institutions and doctorate granting universities to identify the purposes of assessment to include attract better students, provide information relevant to policies, and attract equipment and/or financial
resources. Colleges that only offer master degrees were more likely than doctorate
granting universities and bachelor degrees institutions to assess life long learning,
multicultural/diversity, global issues, reflective thinking, problem solving, professional integrity (ethics), and professional knowledge. Universities that awarded the
master degrees were more likely than bachelor awarding institutions and doctorate
granting universities to utilize alumni survey, student evaluation of faculty, and scores
on standardized tests as assessment instruments. Institutions that award the master
degrees were more likely than bachelor degree and doctorate granting universities to
identify alumni, business community, and prospective students as assessment stakeholders.

There was a statistically significant relationship between type of institution (public
vs. private) and skills/competencies assessed. Public universities were more likely
than private universities to assess professional knowledge. Private universities (80
percent) were almost twice more likely than public institutions (45 percent) to indicate that their institution has a formal assessment program.

There was a statistically significant relationship between the type of accreditation
held by schools of business and the purposes of assessment and skills/competencies
skilled. AACSB accredited schools were twice more likely than institutions with accreditation by the ministry of higher education to have a university formal assessment
program. AACSB accredited schools were more likely than others to utilize alumni
survey and employer survey as assessment instruments. Universities that are accredited by the ministry of higher education were more likely to indicate attract equipment
and/or financial resources as the purpose of assessment. Finally, AACSB accredited
universities were more likely to identify alumni as assessment stakeholder and were
more likely to assess global issues.

Finally, a comparison of the stakeholders of assessment of USA and Middle East
institutions is completed. While USA and Middle East institutions consider faculty,
employers, current students, business community, and alumni to be the top five stakeholders, USA institutions considered faculty to be the most important stakeholder for
assessment while the Middle East institutions ranked employers and current students
higher than faculty.

5 Summary and Conclusions

This study examined the assessment programs used by various schools of business
located in the Middle East. Relatively few statistically significant differences in responses were apparent. Compared to other colleges and universities, Middle Eastern
institutions are more concerned with "meeting responsibilities to public" than USA
institutions. Middle Eastern institutions were more likely than USA universities to
identify "attract better students" and "attract equipment and other financial resources"
as major purposes of assessment. While 65 percent of USA institutions reported assessment activities annually, only 25 percent of Middle Eastern universities assessed
their curriculum annually. Compared to other colleges, public institutions were more

likely than private universities to assess professional knowledge. Universities that are accredited by the ministry of higher education were more likely to indicate attract equipment and/or financial resources as the purpose of assessment. Finally, AACSB accredited universities were more likely to identify alumni as assessment stakeholder and were more likely to assess global issues.

Curriculum and instructional changes were the top-ranked uses for assessment outcomes. As viewed by school of business deans, the most prevalent purposes of assessment were to meet accreditation requirements, monitor program effectiveness, and guide planning/ improvement efforts. Current students, employers, and faculty were considered to be major stakeholders of schools of business. Primary skills measured in assessment included critical thinking, communication skills, technology/computer usage, professional knowledge, and problem solving.

References

1. Terenzini, P.: Assessment with Open Eyes: Pitfalls in Studying Student Outcomes. The Journal of Higher Education 60(6), 644–664 (1989)
2. Angelo, T.A.: Reassessing Assessment. AAHE Bulletin 47(8), 10–13 (1995)
3. AACSB International - The Association to Advance Collegiate Schools of Business: Eligibility Procedures and Accreditation Standards for Business Accreditation. AACSB, Tampa (2008)
4. Bock, R., Mislevy, R., Woodson, C.: The Next Stage in Educational Assessment. Educational Researcher 11(3), 4–11, 16 (1982)
5. Hatfield, S., Gorman, K.: Assessment in Education—The Past, Present, and Future. Assessment in Business Education National Business Education Association Yearbook. No. 38 (1-10). National Business Education Association, Reston (2000)
6. Henninger, E.: Outcomes Assessment: The Role of Business School and Program Accrediting Agencies. Journal of Education for Business 69(5), 296–298 (1994)
7. Shaw, K.E., Badri, A., Hukul, A.: Management Concerns in the United Arab Emirates State Schools. International Journal of Educational Management 9(4), 8–13 (1995)
8. Abouchedid, K., Nasser, R.: Assuring Quality Service in Higher Education: Registration and Advising Attitudes in a Private University in Lebanon. Quality Assurance in Education 10(4), 198–206 (2002)
9. Nasser, R., Abouchedid, K.: Graduates' Perception of University Training in Light of Occupational Attainment and University Type: The Case of Lebanon. Education + Training 47(2), 124–133 (2005)
10. Abouchedid, K., Eid, G.: E-Learning Challenges in the Arab World: Revelations from a Case Study Profile. Quality Assurance in Education 12(1), 15–27 (2004)
11. Gainen, J., Locatelli, P.: Assessment of the New Curriculum: A Guide for Professional Accounting Programs. American Accounting Association, Sarasota (1995)

A Survey on Learning Profiles of the Educators of Roma in Greece in Order to Develop the Proper E-Learning Environment for Their Training

Maria Pavlis Korres, Elena García Barriocanal, and Piera Leftheriotou

Computer Science Department
University of Alcalá, Spain
eumarcor@otenet.gr

Abstract. With the use of new technologies in education, the barriers of time and place can be overcome and the cost can be reduced. The e-training of educators is an interesting and challenging field where personalized learning environments are offered to different groups of educators according to their particularities. This paper is dealing with educators of Roma[1] (Gypsies) in Greece and provides an outline of their learning profile, allowing the appropriate e-Learning tools to be used in developing the most effective e-Learning environment for their training.

Keywords: Learning styles, educators of Roma, learning profile, computer-supported collaborative learning.

1 Introduction

Effective design of online courses should be based on instructional design decisions that will have the best impact on learning. These may include decisions related to the structure of course delivery, teacher-student communication, appropriate assignments and activities that are conducive to online learning, and effective use of online resources.

In our days it is evident more than ever, that in the educational procedure, the single one-size-fits-all approach is dysfunctional and ineffective [1]. To set up the learner's profile and to direct the learning process according to this profile is one of the most actual trends [2], [3]. Personalized e-Learning is seen as a key element for next generation educational programmes [4], aiming to maximize the potential of each learner; more specifically, it offers the vision (and the opportunity) of dynamically composed courses which are tailored to an individual's specific needs, prior knowledge, experience, computing environment, connectivity and communication preferences [5].

The target profile definition is also critical from an engineering viewpoint. Once a collection of learning needs is available, the process of design starts [6].

---

[1] We use the name Roma instead of Gypsies, as this is a name commonly accepted for all members of the Gypsy origin in Greece while the name Gypsy is often used by non-Gypsies with contempt and several negative meanings.

M.D. Lytras et al. (Eds.): WSKS 2008, CCIS 19, pp. 360–370, 2008.

In this context, the set up of profile of Educators of Special Groups[2] (ESG) using technology-enhanced learning is very significant for the designer of Learning Objects (LOs) addressed to them for their training [7].

Firstly, as the educators are adults, the principles of Adults' Education must be followed in order to have the best educational outcome [8], [9], [10]. Secondly, as educators are going to educate members of a Special Group, the type and the level of compatibility between educator and learner must be assessed in order to determine the content of the appropriate Learning Objects [11], [12], [13]. Thirdly, the presentation of LOs must be adapted to the learning style, preferences, competencies, orientations and approaches to studying and learning of each educator.

The aim of this paper is to identify the main parameters which synthesize the learning profile of ESG for Roma, parameters which define the presentation of LOs and must be taken into consideration in the development of an effective e-Learning environment.

2 The Parameters Which Define the Presentation of Learning Objects

Educators differ from one another in a wide variety of ways, including the types of instruction to which they respond best (learning styles), their competencies, the ways they approach their studies (orientations to studying, and approaches to learning), their attitudes towards the nature of knowledge and their role in constructing it (levels of intellectual development). Personalized LOs aim to correspond to the parameters mentioned above, which define, to a smaller or greater extent, the presentation of the LOs in order to lead to a more effective and efficient learning procedure.

On the contrary the design of LOs with only a universal type of learner in mind could end up in frustration of the learner and possible failure of the educational process [1].

In a traditional class it is almost unachievable for the educator to balance all the individual needs of the learners concerning the content and the presentation. In an e-Learning environment tailoring the LOs according to the learners' profiles is a complex but feasible task [7].

To avoid confusion, please note that as the educators are considered as learners in the context of this paper, the terms learner and educator have the same meaning.

2.1 Learning Styles

Educators as adults are engaged in a continuing process of lifelong learning, and they have already acquired ways of coping with this. "Over the years, each of our adult student participants has developed their own strategies and patterns of learning, which they have found help them to learn most easily, most quickly and most effectively" [14].

---

[2] With the term *special group* we refer to the social group whose characteristics (social, cultural, ethnic, linguistic, physical etc.) cause to its members social exclusion, marginalization and stigmatization (i.e. immigrants, Gypsies, repatriated-refugees, prisoners/ex-cons, ex-addicts, persons with special needs) [11].

With the term learning styles we refer to the "characteristic cognitive, affective and psychological behaviors that serve as relatively stable indicators of how learners perceive, interact with, and respond to the learning environment" [15]. The concept of learning styles has been applied to a wide variety of learners' attributes and differences. Some learners are comfortable with theories and abstractions; others feel much more at home with facts and observable phenomena; some prefer active learning while others lean towards introspection; some prefer visual presentation of information and others prefer verbal explanations. No learning style is either preferable or inferior to another, but is simply different with different characteristics, strengths and weaknesses [15].

In every group of educators there is a wide range of learning styles and it is important that the learning environment is structured around the participants' individual learning styles instead of imposing designer's own learning style upon them. At the same time the goal of instruction should be to help learners develop skills associated with other learning style categories, since the learners will need all of these skills and competencies to function effectively as professionals.

Many model standards and instruments have been developed in order to support effectively the instructional design towards the direction of personalized educational material, such as the IMS Learner Information Packaging [16], PAPI Learner (IEEE P 1484.2) [17], the Myers-Briggs Type Indicator® (MBTI), the Kolb Learning Style Inventory® (McBer and Company, Boston), or the Index of Learning Styles® (ILS) of Felder and Soloman.

While numerous studies have investigated the impact of learning styles in community college courses for educators in public schools and pre-service student teachers, very little research has been focused on the relevance of learning styles to internet-based courses in higher education [18]. The few findings of a relationship between learning style and course enjoyment provide some support for consideration of learning styles in online course design. Some authors [19], [20] have noted that it is increasingly important to identify student learning styles and adapt online course design to accommodate these styles. [18] has provided specific suggestions for using Kolb's theory of learning styles as a basis for designing online course instruction.

Kolb and others argue that every individual develops one or more preferred learning styles through experience. It is important to stress that we all tend to use all of these styles – we do not confine our learning efforts to one only. But we prefer to use one or perhaps two modes of learning above the others; we feel stronger at learning through one approach rather than through any of the others [14]. Adults feel most comfortable using their own learning strategies.

According to [14] it is through a variety of learning activities engaged in over many years, that adults have developed a particular blend of learning styles which is stronger in its demand than any such blend in children. The preferred learning styles of children have not yet become established; by adulthood, these become more crystallized.

In the case of educators of special groups and more specifically educators of Roma in Greece, a survey has been implemented in order to identify the learning styles of the learners and to structure an effective learning environment based on those styles. Elements from more than one of the existing instruments have been combined. Kolb's categorization of learning styles (active learners, reflective learners, experimental learners and theorizing learners) [21] and along with his Learning Style Inventory have been taken into account as well as Felder's and Soloman's categorization of learning styles (active and reflective learners, sensing and intuitive learners, visual and verbal learners and sequential and global learners) and their Index of Learning Styles [22].

3 The Survey

The survey was conducted in the framework of a case study in order to develop a pilot educational material for educators of Roma in Greece, aiming at the collection of information on computer skills and the learning styles, preferences and approaches of studying of the educators in order to develop the appropriate e-Learning environment according to their learning profiles.

The needs assessment within the frame of which the survey was implemented was dealing also with the content of the educational material, but this is beyond the object of this paper.

The survey was also intending to have the educators participate in the design of the educational material, a fact that is in line with the principle of adults' education for active participation of learners throughout the educational procedure [8], [9], [14]. As adults are conscious of which learning strategies are the best for them [14], it is important that they participate in the choice of these strategies so that these shall be included in the design of the educational package addressed to them.

3.1 The Sample and the Method

The sample (non probability sample/purposive sampling) was consisted by 30 educators, half of which will participate in the pilot implementation of the educational material.

Sixteen of the educators already had experience working with Gypsies and in this paper we shall refer to them as *inservice* educators. Ten of them participate in the educational programme "Integration of Gypsy children in School" of the University of Thessaly, Greece and six educators work in the Health Center for Gypsies in the Municipality of Tyrnavos in Thessaly. The rest fourteen of the educators have no experience working with Gypsies but they are potential future educators and we shall refer to them as *preservice* educators. All of them are undergraduate students in Department of Nursery Education of the University of Patras, Greece.

The students of Nursery Education Department were chosen because these are the first educators the Gypsy children will have their initial educational experience with. It was also crucial to detect possible differences in educational needs between preservice and inservice educators so that these could be taken into account in the design of the educational environment.

The method which has been used for the collection of the information was a questionnaire which was completed by the educators during individual or group meeting with the researchers [24], [25]. In the design of the questionnaire many techniques based on social relations research methods have been used [23], [24], [25] such as Likert-type scale, Gutman's technique. The Statistical Package for Social Sciences (SPSS version 11.5) has been used for the data analysis.

As educators of Roma are adults the hypotheses were that they prefer active learning and they prefer that the outcome of the learning procedure would have a practical application [8], [9], [14]. The collaborative learning tools which an e-Learning environment provides could be appropriate for their needs. Another hypothesis was that preservice educators which are younger than the inservice ones are more familiar with modern technologies and e-Learning than the inservice educators, as they take courses in the university on using computer etc.

The survey was focused on the definition of the learning profile of educators of Roma in order to provide the proper educational material for each of them.

3.2   The Main Axes of the Survey

The survey has been focused on the definition of operational variables which concern the running of the project (e-Learning training of educators) and the definition of the presentation of the educational material.

The operational variables measure the accessibility of educators to Personal Computers (PC), the computer skills of the educators and the educators' familiarity with e-Learning.

In order to define the presentation of the LOs the survey tried to identify educators' learning styles and approaches to studying.

Through the research it was investigated which of the collaboration tools (e-mail, online discussion, textual chat and instant messaging, video conferencing etc.) [26] the educators prefer to use during the educational procedure.

The challenge in online education is to select appropriate tools and activities that engage meaningful interaction and collaboration. [27] argues that in the context of Computer-Supported Collaborative Learning (CSCL), instructional design should aim to facilitate skills that are transferable to the "real-world", such as metacognitive communication, learning, and participation—the highest level of learner engagement. This requires that CSCL course designs include the formation of a learning community where assessment is focused on the process of collaboration rather than the end product of the collaboration. Learner participation has been identified as both a primary indicator and problematic issue affecting its success [28].

4   Results of the Survey

The vast majority of the sample were women (76,7%) and people aged 20-30 years old (73,3%) while no one was over 55 years old.

96,7% of the sample have access to Personal Computer (PC) and 83,3% have a PC at home. 30% of the sample have also access to computers at work, while 33,3% stated that have access elsewhere too.

Concerning their computer skills the majority of the sample is familiarized with computer software as Microsoft Word (73%) although the 46% do not know of or have low level skills concerning spread sheets. 86,6% have adequate skills in using e-mail and 93,3% in using web browsers. The use of instant messaging services is adequate up to 53,3%.

More precisely the analysis among preservice and inservice educators shows that preservice educators are more familiarized with computers and have higher level skills than the inservice teachers with the exception of their skills in spread sheets as it is shown in Fig.1. According to the study of [26] the highest rates for PC and Internet usage are noted among people in the age group of 16-24. The following Fig.1 is indicative:

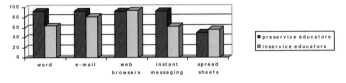

Fig. 1. Educators' efficiency in computer skills

Only 13,3% of the sample have attended distance learning. 6,6% have attended e-Learning in combination with live meetings and only 3,3% have attended pure e-Learning, while 3,3% have attended distance learning by correspondence. It is notable that 46,7% of the sample - actually the preservice educators - have attended a demonstration of the Moodle e-Learning platform in the frame of a computer science course in the University. 50% of them found this demonstration satisfactory.

70% of the sample stated that they are willing to attend e-Learning courses. This reflects that the use of new technologies in training and learning are still very low in Greece comparing to the other European countries [29], [30], but it is worth noting that the average annual growth rate of the Greek households with internet access has been increased by 11,7% during the period 2005-2007 [29].

The questions about the learning style of the educators did not reveal any significant difference between preservice and inservice educators. 50% of the sample stated as first choice that they learn better by reading, 23,3% by writing, 16,7% visually and 10% learn better by listening. As second preferable choice of way of learning 36,7% learn better visually, 20% by listening, 13,3% by reading and 13,3% by writing. The above preferences of way of learning as first and second choices are depicted in the following Fig.2:

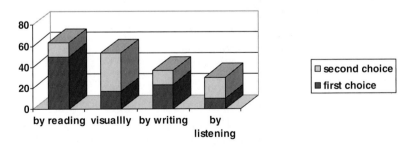

Fig. 2. Preferences on way of learning

The educational material will be developed in line with the preferences of the educators regarding the way of learning. All the learning styles will be considered without exception, as there is neither any totally rejected nor any exclusively preferred, although there will be a bias towards dominant learning preferences.

56,7% of the sample prefer working in a group, while 43,3% prefer working individually. It is interesting to note the difference between the preferences of preservice and inservice educators in Fig.3 below: 31,3% of the inservice educators prefer to work individually while 68,7% prefer working in a group. 57% of the preservice educators prefer to work individually while 42,9% prefer to work in a group.

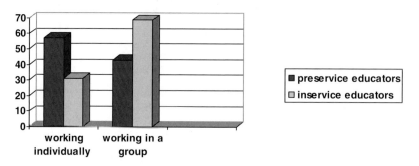

Fig. 3. Preferences on working individually or in a group

The vast majority of the sample (80%) prefers to study by guidance. All of the preservice educators prefer to study by guidance, and this could be justified by the fact that the preservice educators of the sample are students in the formal educational system which does not encourage self-directed learning.

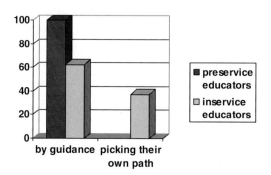

Fig. 4. Preference of the way of studying

Among the inservice educators 37,5% prefer self-directed learning, a fact that can be interpreted as one of the characteristics in adult education. As adults mature they are moving away from the formal education system and towards self- directed learning [8], [14].

Greeks are not familiarized with pure e-Learning as a teaching method and the majority of the courses take place in the conventional classroom [30]. It is consistent with this that 60% of the sample prefer the face to face teaching method while 40% prefer the combination of face to face teaching method with e-Learning.

Regarding the educators' preferences on what an e-Learning environment should contain the most popular tools are e-mailing with the educator, group activities and use of multimedia. Concerning their participation in on-line discussions they prefer to participate in small talking groups (3-5 persons) than in one single group of the whole course.

The following table shows in detail which learning tools they prefer to use in an e-Learning platform.

Table 1. Preferences on learning tools

What they like an e-Learning platform to contain	Average %
E-mail with the educator	56,6%
Group activities	46,7%
Use of multimedia	46,7%
Participation in a restrict forum of 3-5 persons	30%
Teleconferences	26,7%
Individual activities	26,7%
E-mail with other learners	26,7%
Forum with the whole group	16,7%

An interesting fact is that although preservice educators have previously stated that 57,1% of them prefer to work individually and 42,9% in groups, in the questions related to the e-Learning platform activities they state that they prefer more group activities by a large majority (42,9%) compared to individual activities (21,4%). This could be explained by the fact that in formal education younger preservice educators are mainly used to individual educational procedures while at the same time they use the internet mainly for entertainment through group activities (games, chat rooms) [29] .

Group activities must be included in the development of the e-Learning environment as a learning group is a valuable tool for promoting adult learning. There are sound educational advantages in group learning [14].

The inclination of the educators towards practical applications is in line with the principles of adult education [8], [9], [14].

The survey showed that 60% favour e-Learning material to contain theoretical data, while 83,4% favour practical applications of the theory.

In a relevant question aiming to assess the participants approach on the mode they would like to study participating in an e-Learning platform for a certain time period (3 months), 36,7% would prefer to elaborate on a certain parameter, 26,7% would prefer to get involved with more than one parameters, 23,3% would prefer to focus mainly on theoretical data while 80% would focus mainly on practical applications.

An interesting practical application may be to incorporate Problem-Solving activities in the e-Learning environment, resulting in the promotion of the educators' problem-solving skills (cognitive and metacognitive skills) [31].

As evaluation is very important in education and more precisely in adult education [14] in the questionnaire were some questions concerning the type of evaluation which the educators prefer to be included in an e-Learning platform.

The following figure shows what kind of evaluation educators prefer to be included in an e-Learning platform.

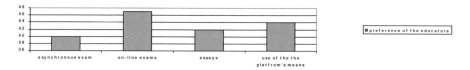

Fig. 5. Preferences on the type of evaluation

Furthermore the first choice of the educators concerning their evaluation type was:

Table 2. First choice of evaluation type

First choice of the educators for evaluation method	Average %
Asynchronous written exam	30%
Quantitative and qualitative evaluation of the use of the platform means (e.g. e-mail, participation in the forums)	23,3%
On-line exam by using multimedia	20%
Evaluation through essays	16,7%
On-line exams by using instant messaging services	6,7%

As shown in the tables above, educators are very open to new forms of evaluation existing in an e-Learning platform but they still rate the asynchronous written exam, i.e. their familiar way of evaluation, as their first choice.

5   Conclusions

The survey within the framework of the case study concerning the educators of Roma in Greece has shown that educators have sufficient access to computers and they are familiar with computers and their use so that they can attend an e-Learning course for their training. Although the majority of educators have not attended distance learning, they are willing to attend. Educators have different learning styles which synthesize their learning profiles. Educators prefer active participation learning techniques, collaborative learning tools and they want their educational outcome to have practical application. These are in line with adults' education principles as well as with the demands of the e-Learning design based on the needs assessment of the learners and provide a sound base for the development of an e-Learning environment. Taking into account the above results and incorporating them in the structure of the e-Learning environment, as well as the presentation of the LOs which will be addressed to ESG, the quality of online course delivery could be improved but also educators' learning could be enhanced.

References

1. Martinez, M.: Designing Learning Objects to Personalize Learning. In: The Instructional Use of Learning Objects, on line version, `http://reusability/org/read` (2000)
2. Trandafir, I., Borozan, A. M.: e-Learning systems personalization - new requirements and solutions (2007) (Retrieved in February 15 2008), `http://www.ici.ro/sinpers/doc/art-ie-1`
3. Wilson, R., Villa, R.: Survey on Methods and Standards of Student Modelling. University of Stathclyde Glasgow, UK (2002), `http://www.crmpa.it/diogene/archive.html`
4. Brusilovsky, P.: Adaptive Navigation Support. In Adaptive Hypermedia to the Adaptive Web and Beyond. Psychology Journal 2(1), 7–23 (2004)
5. Dagger, D., Conlan, O., Wade, V.: eLearning Without Borders - A Support Framework for Reusing Educational Strategies. In: Proceedings of e-Ducation Without Borders (2005), `https://www.cs.tcd.ie/Owen.Conlan`
6. Sicilia, M.A.: Learning about whisk(e)y: an example of multi-view learning object/learning activity design. In: III Simposio Pluridisciplinar Sobre Objetos Y DiseÑos De Aprendizaje Apoyados En La TecnologÍA, Oviedo, Spain (2006)
7. Pavlis Korres, M., Garcia Barriocanal, E.: Development of personalized learning objects for training adult educators of special groups. Journal of Knowledge Management 12(6) (2008)
8. Knowles, M.: Andragogy in Action. Applying modern principles of adult education, Jossey Bass, San Francisco (1984)
9. Jarvis, P.: Adult and continuing education. Theory and practice, Routledge, London, New York (1995)
10. Cross, K.P.: Adults as Learners. Jossey-Bass, San Francisco (1981)
11. Pavlis Korres, M.: On the requirements of Learning Object Metadata for Adults' Educators of Special Groups. In: Conference Proceedings of the 2nd International Conference on Metadata and Semantics Research, Corfu, Greece (2007)
12. Banks, J., Banks, C.: Multicultural education, Issues and Perspectives, 4th edn. John Willey and Sons Inc. (2001)
13. Irvine, J.: Educating teachers for Diversity. Teachers College, Columbia University, New York (2003)
14. Rogers, A.: Teaching Adults, 3rd edn. Open University Press (2007)
15. Felder, R.M., Brent, R.: Understanding Student Differences. J. Engr. Education 94(1), 57–72 (2005)
16. IMS LIP Specification, `http://www.imsproject.org/`
17. IEEE LTSC PAPI Specification, `http://www.ieee.org/`
18. Richmond, A.S., Cummings, R.: Implementing Kolb's learning styles into online distance education. International Journal of Technology in Teaching and Learning 1(1), 45–54 (2005)
19. Maddux, C.D., Ewing-Taylor, J., Johnson, D.L.: Distance education: Issues and concerns. The Haworth Press, New York (2002)
20. Thiele, J.E.: Learning patterns of online students. Journal of Nursing Education 42(8), 364–367 (2003)
21. Kolb, D.A.: Learning Style Inventory Technical Manual. McBer, Boston (1976)
22. Felder, R.M., Brent, R.: Understanding Student Differences. J. Engr. Education 94(1), 57–72 (2005)
23. Cohen, L., Manion, L.: Research Methods in Education. Routledge, London (1994)

24. Javeau, C.: L'enquete par questionnaire. Universite de Bruxelles, Bruxelles (1978)
25. Bell, J.: Doing your research project. Open University Press (1993)
26. Horton, W., Horton, K.: E-Learning Tools and Technologies. Wiley Publishing Inc., Chichester (2003)
27. Knowlton, D.S.: A Taxonomy of Learning through Asynchronous Discussion. Journal of Interactive Learning Research 16(2) (2005), Retrieved October 16, 2007, from Questia database, http://www.questia.com/PM.qst?a=o&d=5011048606
28. Hammond, M.: Issues associated with participation in on line forums - the case of the communicative learner. In: Education and Information Technologies, pp. 353–367. Kluwer Academic Publishers, The Netherlands (1999)
29. The observatory for the Greek Information Society, http://www.observatory.gr
30. Massy, J.: The European e-Learning Market. Bizmedia (2002)
31. Clark, R., Mayer, R.: e-Learning and the Science of Instruction. Pfeiffer (2003)

The Organizational Value of Tacit Knowledge Derived from Parenting

Eva Rimbau-Gilabert[1,*], David Miyar-Cruz[1], and Jose María López-de Pedro[2]

[1] Open University of Catalonia, www.uoc.edu
Av. Tibidabo 39-43, 08035 Barcelona Spain
[2] Centro Universitario Villanueva, www.villanueva.edu
C/ Claudio Coello 11, 28001 Madrid Spain
erimbau@uoc.edu

Abstract. The current interest in lifelong learning has resulted in work and personal experiences being recognized by educational authorities as valuable sources of informal learning, which may have a positive impact on society in general, and on individuals' employability in particular. This paper argues that one specific type of informal learning -that which is developed through parenting- can provide tacit knowledge that may be valuable in work situations. We provide a brief explanation of the nature and relevance of informal learning for the knowledge society. We review available literature in the field of developmental psychology which has focused on parenting as a context for personal development, and suggest that two tacit skills derived from parenting are especially valuable in work settings, namely flexible thinking and allocentric thinking. The organizational value of these skills is analyzed with an emphasis on its usefulness for knowledge workers, and general implications are discussed.

Keywords: Informal learning, parenting, adult development, flexible thinking, allocentric thinking, knowledge work.

1 Introduction

In educational circles there is currently an interest in lifelong learning, acknowledging the fact that learning does not occur only in formal education institutions. As a result, work and personal experiences are being recognized by educational authorities as valuable sources of informal learning, which may have a positive effect on society in general, and on individuals' employability in particular. Following this trend, management circles may gradually accept the value of informal learning and the tacit skills it provides.

This paper argues that one specific type of informal learning -that which is developed through parenting- can provide tacit knowledge that may be valuable in work situations. We first provide a brief explanation of the nature and relevance of informal learning for the knowledge society. We then review available literature in the field of developmental psychology which has focused on parenting as a context for personal

---

* Contact author.

M.D. Lytras et al. (Eds.): WSKS 2008, CCIS 19, pp. 371–379, 2008.

development, and suggest that two tacit skills derived from parenting are notably valuable in work settings, which we denominate flexible thinking and allocentric thinking. Finally, the organizational value of these skills is analysed with an emphasis on its usefulness for knowledge workers, and general implications are discussed.

The link that we establish between psychological and organizational literature which have hitherto remained separated, highlights that the knowledge society will only be fully developed if all types of learning and knowledge are recognized and integrated as valuable resources in organizational activities.

2 Informal Learning in the Knowledge Society

The development of the knowledge society has imposed new requirements on workers, who need to continuously acquire new skills and responsibilities, and adapt their prior knowledge. For this reason, lifelong learning has become a basic principle in education, and is described as an essential tool to face current social and economic challenges [1, 2]. The European Union authorities are aware of this demand and have underlined the need to uncover and value all forms of learning which people develop in different fields of their lives [3]. This view of ongoing learning involves three possible types of learning (formal, non-formal and informal) and highlights the requirement to establish links between them. According to the glossary developed by the European Centre for the Development of Vocational Training [4], formal learning "occurs within an organized and structured context (formal education, in-company training), and (...) is designed as learning". In contrast, non-formal learning is "embedded in planned activities that are not explicitly designated as learning, but which contain an important learning element". Finally, informal learning or experiential learning, "results from daily life activities related to work, family, or leisure". In the cases of formal and non-formal learning, there is an intention to learn, while informal learning is in most cases "non-intentional (or 'incidental'/random)".

Even though informal learning can be planned, it usually includes unexpected learning that learners obtain although they do not set out intentionally and explicitly to learn something through preplanned approaches. Although it may be unintentional or unplanned, it may still have a significant effect on the individual's knowledge and competence [5].

Much of the knowledge obtained through informal learning is likely to be tacit knowledge. Explicit knowledge refers to a person's "know what" and "know-why" [6]; it can be codified in the form of words, numbers, or symbols, and is easily passed on or communicated. In contrast, tacit knowledge refers to "practical know-how" and "know-who", and it is usually not directly taught or even openly expressed or stated [6, 7]. It includes "an individual's intuitions, beliefs, assumptions, and values formed as a result of experience (...) [and] forms a mental grid in the background of a person's mind; it acts as a filter through which new experiences are understood and interpreted" [8, p. 79]. For example, knowing how to convince others of the worth of an idea or product, how to interact appropriately with co-workers, or how to calm oneself in stressful situations, are not the kind of knowledge that is likely to be taught, but rather the kind of knowledge people obtain through experience.

This paper argues that, among activities of daily life, the family and especially the tasks associated to parenting are relevant contexts for informal learning. This is not to say that parenting is the only context for adult development and learning. Other life experiences -such as marriage, work, community involvement or social networks- may also contribute to informal learning and developmental transformation [9, 10]. However, researchers admit that parenting is accompanied by such opportunities and demands that it becomes a potentially strong stimulus affecting the development of those who are engaged in it [11].

3 Parenting as a Source of Tacit Knowledge

Traditional studies in developmental psychology, which have analyzed the relation between parenthood and child-rearing, have focused on the one-way effects of parents on their children [12]. This line of research tends to view children as blank slates to be written on with the adults' efforts, and to see development as an ascent through a series of stages away from childhood [13, p. 273].

However, there is a growing body of literature in this field which considers the effects of children on their parents and on other people engaged in raising children such as teachers or grandparents [10, 13, 14, 15, 16, 17, 18]. As Demick highlights [12, p. 329]:

> "This group of authors rejects the notion that socialization is a one-way process, and gives support to a bi-directional model of parent-child relations, in which both children and parent are active agents in each other's development. This implies that children often play a large and under-appreciated role in adult development and learning".

Researchers have identified quite diverse areas of behavioral, cognitive and emotional development associated with parenting. Among this literature, we have detected two common themes which may be especially relevant for organizational behavior researchers. We have named them "flexible thinking" and "allocentric thinking" respectively, as described below.

Before proceeding, it is important to state two disclaimers. First, we do not subscribe to the belief that parenting is preferable to childlessness. This paper is intended to stimulate scientific inquiry into the organizational implications of different tacit knowledge developed by parents vs. non-parents. Secondly, not all parents are expected to develop the potential for learning derived from child rearing. Several factors may mediate the relation between parenthood and adult development, such as varying degrees of parental involvement with their children [10], individual parental expectancies, contextual factors or perceived social support [9].

3.1 Flexible Thinking

Numerous authors on parenting seem to agree on the idea that child rearing involves a continuous learning process which enhances the development of cognitive flexibility and openness to new learning [13, 19, 20]. For example, Azar [9, p. 392] states that parenting requires "flexible and appropriate expectancies about the role and active capacities to learn 'in the moment' and modify one's thinking, affect, and behavior".

In the same vein, Dillon [13] reported that interactions with children can enable the adult to be more creative and cognitively flexible. Cognitive flexibility reflects "a person's (a) awareness that in any given situation there are options and alternatives available, (b) willingness to be flexible and adapt to the situation, and (c) self-efficacy or belief that one has the ability to be flexible" [21, p. 1]. When adults have to communicate with children, they may need to access and utilize modes of knowing which they do not use regularly. For example, they may use more personalized and specific modes of knowing in contrast to formal ones or in perceived social support [9].

Additionally, parents have been found to show higher dialectical thinking than non-parents [22, cited in 10]. Dialectical thinking is considered an essential contributor to creative thinking and is a helpful skill in every-day decision making [23]. It can be defined as "the continuous exploration of interrelationships between general rules and contextual necessities with the realization that no fixed patterns of thought or conduct, and no permanent resolutions to intractable problems, are possible" [23, p. 90].

We define flexible thinking as the combination of cognitive flexibility and dialectical thinking. It may improve the ability of parents involved in child rearing to encounter unfamiliar situations and adapt their behavior to meet contextual needs [21, p. 2], their tolerance for ambiguity, and their problem-solving skills [9].

3.2 Allocentric Thinking

The second group of developmental outcomes probably derives from the fact that parenting tasks require an "outward approach" to identify children's needs and the practices which would satisfy those needs [19, p. 323]. For example, Palkovitz, Copes and Woolfolk [24] found that fatherhood can cause men to become less self-centered and more "giving", thus increasing their allocentrism.

The concept of allocentrism is applied to individuals that behave consistently with a collectivistic set of values, as opposed to individualistic values [25, 26]. Idiocentric persons are not overly attached to any particular group; they define themselves with respect to their own needs, goals and achievements; they act consistently with their attitudes, and value self-reliance and independence. Conversely, allocentrics are more likely to define themselves with respect to the group, act consistently with group norms and value interdependence [25].

Perspective taking, or adopting another person's point of view, is an intellectual process that can be shown through empathy and through positive attribution [27]. The affective response of empathy entails that, when people engage in actively taking perspectives, they are more likely to feel concern about the others' misfortunes, to understand or identify with their experiences, and to experience pleasure at their achievements. Perspective taking involves attributing positive aspects to others' behavior and outcomes, such as recognizing the effects of external circumstances when things go wrong for the other and acknowledging the role of internal factors such as hard work and ability when things go well for the other [27]. Finally, perspective taking has also been found to be linked to giving altruistic help to the other [28].

The proposed concept of "allocentric thinking" integrates the abilities of allocentrism and perspective taking that several authors have reported to be higher in parents than in non-parents [9, 20; 29 and 30 cited in 10].

4   Organizational Value of Tacit Knowledge Derived from Parenting

The tacit skills of flexible and allocentric thinking may be useful in contexts other than the family and parenting tasks. This section discusses the possible links among the components of flexible and allocentric thinking and variables that are relevant for the field of organizational behavior.

First, flexible thinking skills may be needed in any situation where balancing apparently contradictory demands, learning, flexibility of mind, or the ability to adapt to changing needs are relevant for success. On the one hand, the capacity to think dialectically may be helpful in everyday decision-making, "when universal rules, and broad patterns of causal and prescriptive reasoning ('if this is the case then I should do that') is balanced against, and constantly intersects with, the contextual imperatives of a situation" [23, p. 90]. Complex work performed by managers and high profile workers probably provides plenty of such situations, where conflicting demands have to be balanced. On the other hand, cognitive flexibility is widely regarded as an essential ability for innovation [31]. The flexibility of existing knowledge structures –the easiness for crossing or bridging conceptual categories- may be a source of new ideas, while their rigidity may be an obstacle to creativity [32].

Secondly, allocentric thinking may be particularly significant for modern organizations, where traditional boundaries are blurred and the need to work in cooperation stands out. For example, Moates, Harris, Field and Armenakis [33] found that both supervisor and subordinate specific perspective taking were positively related to supervisors' assessment of the leader-member exchange. These authors also reported that taking the perspective of a subordinate had a positive effect on that subordinate's assessment of relationship quality. Turning from interactions within the organization to external interactions, Axtell, Parker, Holman and Totterdell's research [34] in a call center setting found a positive relationship between customer-oriented perspective taking and self-reported help to customers, and this relationship was partially mediated by empathy.

Allocentrism may increase employees' preference for tasks which involve high interdependence with other people, and which provide collective goals. Lam, Chen and Schaubroek [35] reported that allocentric values may influence the effect of participative decision making opportunities on how much employees contribute to their workgroup's performance. According to these authors, employees with allocentric values may perform better in team-based work settings than in contexts which highlight individual performance, but only if they believe that their group has the ability and skills to be successful. Allocentrism, then, may be valuable in organizations or organizational segments with a strong collectivistic culture and a sense of shared success.

To sum up, both flexible thinking and allocentric thinking may be valuable in organizational settings. However, these capacities may be more or less useful depending on contextual factors. The use of flexible thinking will probably increase performance in work settings that do not allow for the use of established rules. Allocentric thinking, in turn, is likely to prove more useful in situations where, for example, reaching valuable goals can be achieved more easily through a group than individually, or where there is high interdependence with other people. Table 1 shows how the tacit knowledge derived from parenting can contribute differently depending on the type of work to be accomplished.

Table 1. Contribution of tacit knowledge derived from parenting in different types of work

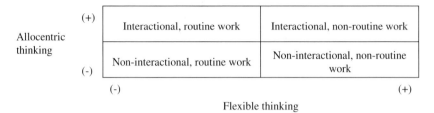

This segmentation suggests that tacit knowledge derived from parenting may be especially valuable for workers who work in collaborative groups and need to rely on their own judgment and interpretations to perform the work successfully. This type of work is typical of many knowledge workers, who may consequently obtain higher work related benefits from their parenting activities than other workers.

5   Discussion

This paper is based on the idea, posed by Azar [9, p. 392], that parenting "is basically a relational task that has some unique features, but generally involves capacities that are required for many domains of adult adjustment". Specifically, it contends that managerial circles have reasons to recognize informal learning obtained outside of educational institutions and organizational boundaries in general, and that which is derived from parenting tasks in particular.

Knowledge workers, the quintessential actors in the knowledge society, may find that the tacit skills which they can develop through involved parenting are especially useful for them. As Huws explains [36, p. 50]:

> "Their work is characterised by complex tasks and a high level of uncertainty. The result is not always clear beforehand and the search for new solutions to particular problems makes it difficult to directly control the labour process. Creativity and co-operation are crucial virtues when it comes to finding innovative solutions or 'translating' unclear customer requirements into clear product specifications".

Creativity needed for complex work is likely to be enhanced by flexible thinking, while allocentric thinking may facilitate necessary co-operation in interdependent activities. As a result, parenting may be considered a valuable experience that provides knowledge workers with capabilities that are useful for their professional activity.

If these relations between parenting and work are true, the so-called "balance" between personal and work life loses part of its meaning. The notion of balance conveys an idea of a zero-sum situation, but if parenting can be valuable for work, it may be more appropriate to think of a win-win situation. Employees' personal lives have an effect on their work, and there is evidence that when people hold multiple roles, this benefits both themselves and their employers [37]. This paper argues that people with work and parenting roles may benefit personally through the development of tacit skills, but the organization that employs them may also benefit from their improved performance in interdependent, non-routine tasks. If this hypothesis is accepted through empirical analysis, the commonly held view of life-work policies as a commitment/retention strategy may change. Life-work policies may lead to superior performance not only through the reduction of turnover and absenteeism, or through increased effort derived from higher organizational commitment (see [38]), but because they allow employees to gain useful tacit knowledge from the experience of raising a child.

However, more research is needed on the way organizations may turn tacit knowledge derived from parenting into valuable resources for organizations. Kianto [39] and O'Sullivan and Schulte's work [40] may provide theoretical ground for such research.

Finally, this paper has implications for public policies regarding parenting, education and gender. If parenting can be a valuable source of learning, parental care and paid child-care should not be considered as substitutes for one another [41], and new possibilities should be considered for child-care, whereby parents should have the flexibility of choosing the combination of both that best suits their own needs and also their offspring's well-being. In the educational field, the explicit recognition of all forms of learning should be encouraged, as a means of helping towards increasing its social and economic worth. Gender policies are another open field that stems from the consideration of parenting, and specifically fatherhood, as a source of benefits not only for individuals but also for communities and families [42]. If fathers aspire to doing more fathering than they actually do, they may face important economic, policy and cultural limitations to their involvement. Therefore, if a bigger involvement of fathers in childrearing contributes to the kind of knowledge discussed in this paper, this finding should be used to stimulate the application of efficient policies that encourage men's parenting role more actively.

References

1. Blankert, H. (pres.): Building the European Information Society for us all. Final policy report of the high-level expert group (High Level Expert Group) (1997) (retrieved on May 1, 2008),
   http://ec.europa.eu/employment_social/knowledge_society/docs/buildingen.pdf
2. O'Donoghue, J., Maguire, T.: The individual learner, employability and the workplace. A reappraisal of relationships and prophecies. Journal of European Industrial Training 29(6), 436–446 (2006)
3. European Commission: Comunication Making a European area of lifelong learning a reality, COM (2001) 678 final, Brussels (2006) (retrieved on September 12, 2007), http://ec.europa.eu/education/policies/lll/life/communicatio n/com_en.pdf
4. CEDEFOP: Glossary, in: Making Learning Visible. Thessaloniki: Cedefop (2000)
5. Skolverket, Sweden National Agency for Education: Lifelong Learning and Lifewide Learning. Stockholm, Liber Distribution, Publikationstjänst (2000) (retrieved on March 28, 2008), http://www.skolverket.se/publikationer?id=638
6. Zook, M.A.: The knowledge brokers: Venture capitalists, tacit knowledge and regional development. International Journal of Urban and Regional Research 28(3), 621–641 (2004)

7. Smith, M.C., Pourchot, T.: Adult Learning and Development: Perspectives from Educational Psychology. Lawrence Erlbaum Associates, Mahwah (1998)
8. Lengnick-Hall, M.L., Lengnick-Hall, C.A.: Human Resource Management in the Knowledge Economy. Berrett-Koehler Publishers, San Francisco (2003)
9. Azar, S.T.: Adult development and parenthood: A social–cognitive perspective. In: Demick, J., Andreoletti, C. (eds.) Handbook of adult development, vol. 423, pp. 391–415. Kluwer, New York (2003)
10. Palkovitz, R.: Parenting as a generator of adult development: Conceptual issues and implications. Journal of Social and Personal Relationships 13(4), 571–592 (1996)
11. Newman, P.R., Newman, B.M.: Parenthood and adult development. In: Palkovitz, R., Sussman, M.B. (eds.) Transitions to parenthood, pp. 313–338. Haworth, New York (1988)
12. Demick, J.: Effects of children on adult development and learning: Parenthood and beyond. In: Hoare, C.H. (ed.) Handbook of Adult Development and Learning, ch. 15. Oxford University Press, New York (2006)
13. Dillon, J.: The role of the child in adult development. The Journal of Adult Development 9(4), 267–275 (2002)
14. Ambert, A.M.: The Effect of Children on Parents. Haworth Press, New York (2001)
15. Galinsky, E.: Between generations: The six stages of parenthood. Times Books, New York (1981)
16. Knoester, C., Eggebeen, D.J.: The Effects of the Transition to Parenthood and Subsequent Children on Men's Well-Being and Social Participation. Journal of Family Issues 27(11), 1532–1560 (2006)
17. Kuczynski, L.: Beyond bidirectionality. Bilateral conceptual frameworks for understanding dynamics in parent-child relations. In: Kuczynski, L. (ed.) Handbook of Dynamics in Parent-child Relations. Sage, Thousand Oaks (2003)
18. Palkovitz, R., Marks, L.D., Appleby, D.W., Kramer Holmes, E.: Parenting and adult development: Contexts, processes, and products of Intergenerational Relationships. In: Kuczynski, L. (ed.) Handbook of Dynamics in Parent-child Relations. Sage Publishing, Thousand Oaks (2003)
19. De'Ath, E.: Teaching parenting skills. Journal of Family Therapy 5, 321–335 (1983)
20. Ellison, K.: The Mommy Brain: How Motherhood Makes You Smarter, Cambridge, MA, Perseus (2006)
21. Martin, M.M., Anderson, C.M.: The cognitive flexibility scale: Three validity studies. Communication Reports 11(1), 1–9 (1998)
22. Hoffman, L.W., Mannis, J.D.: The value of children in the United States: A new approach to the study of fertility. Journal of Marriage and the Family 41, 583–596 (1978)
23. Brookfield, S.: Adult cognition as a dimension of lifelong learning. In: Field, J., Leicester, L. (eds.) Lifelong Learning: Education Across the Lifespan, Routledge (2000)
24. Palkovitz, R., Copes, M.A., Woolfolk, T.N.: 'It's like.. You discover a new sense of being': Involved fathering as an evoker of adult development. Men and Masculinities 4(49), 49–69 (2001)
25. Hulbert, L.G., Correa da Silva, M.L.M., Adegboygea, G.: Cooperation in social dilemmas and allocentrism: a social values approach. European Journal of Social Psychology 31(6), 641–657 (2001)
26. Triandis, H.C., Chan, D.K.-S., Bhawuk, D.P.S., Iwao, S., Sinha, J.B.P.: Multimethod probes of allocentrism and idiocentrism. International Journal of Psychology 30(4), 461–480 (1995)
27. Parker, S.H., Axtell, C.M.: Seeing another viewpoint: Antecedents and outcomes of employee perspective taking. Academy of Management Journal 44(6), 1085–1100 (2001)

28. Oswald, P.A.: The effects of cognitive and affective perspective taking on empathic concern and altruistic helping. The Journal of Social Psychology 136(5), 613–623 (1996)
29. Heath, D.H.: What meaning and effects does fatherhood have for the maturing of professional men. Merril Palmer Quarterly 24, 265–278 (1978)
30. Hooker, K., Fiese, B.H.: Temporal perspectives on changes in self related to parenting. In: Symposium, Society for Research in Child Development, New Orleans, L.A (March 1993)
31. Georgsdottir, A.S., Getz, I.: How Flexibility Facilitates Innovation and Ways to Manage it in Organizations. Creativity and Innovation Management 13(3), 166–175 (2004)
32. Mumford, M.D., Baughman, W.A., Maher, M.A., Constanza, D.P., Supinski, E.P.: Processbased measures of creative problem-solving skills: IV. Category combination. Creativity Research Journal 10, 59–71 (1997)
33. Moates, K.N., Harris, S.G., Field, H.S., Armenakis, A.A.: Perspective taking and leader-member exchange in supervisor/subordinate dyads: a hierarchical linear modeling investigation. In: Academy of Management Proceedings, pp. 1–6 (2007)
34. Axtell, C.M., Parker, S.K., Holman, D., Totterdell, P.: Enhancing customer service: Perspective taking in a call centre. European Journal of Work and Organizational Psychology 16(2), 141–168 (2007)
35. Lam, S.S.K., Chen, X.-P., Schaubroek, J.: Participative decision making and employee performance in different cultures: The moderating effects of allocentrism/idiocentrism and efficacy. Academy of Management Journal 45(5), 905–914 (2002)
36. Huws, U. (ed.): The transformation of work in a global knowledge economy: towards a conceptual framework. WORKS project (2006) (retrieved on November 18, 2007), http://www.worksproject.be/documents/WP3synthesisreport-voorpublicatie.pdf
37. Fletcher, J.K., Bailyn, L.: The Equity Imperative: Redesigning Work for Work- Family Integration. In: Kossek, E.E., Lambert, S.J. (eds.) Work and Life Integration: Organizational, Cultural, and Individual Perspectives, pp. 171–192. Lawrence Earlbaum Associates, Mahwah (2005)
38. Eaton, S.C.: If you can use them: flexibility policies, organizational commitment, and perceived performance. Industrial Relations 42(2), 145–167 (2003)
39. Kianto, A.: What do we really mean by the dynamic dimension of intellectual capital? International Journal of Learning and Intellectual Capital 4(4), 342–356 (2007)
40. O'Sullivan, K.J., Schulte, W.D.: Models of human capital management: human resource management of intellectual capital. International Journal of Learning and Intellectual Capital 4(4), 453–466 (2007)
41. Folbre, N.: Rethinking the child care sector. Community Development: Journal of the Community Development Society 37(2), 38–52 (2006)
42. Flood, M.: Fatherhood and fatherlessness. Discussion paper number 59. Australia Institute (2003)

Assessing Enterprise's Knowledge Management Maturity Level

Michel Grundstein

MG Conseil, 4 rue Anquetil, 94130 Nogent sur Marne, France
Paris Dauphine University, Lamsade CNRS, UMR7024, France F-75016 Paris
mgrundstein@mgconseil.fr

Abstract. Knowledge is not manageable as if it was a data or information. Consequently, Knowledge Management (KM) must address activities that utilize and create knowledge more than knowledge by itself. With regard to this issue, we elaborated a sociotechnical approach of Knowledge Management within the enterprise, and we synthesized it into an empirical model called Model for General Knowledge Management within the Enterprise (MGKME). One purpose of this model is to serve as a template to enable assessing the Enterprise's KM maturity level.

Keywords: Knowledge Management, Knowledge Management System, Model for General Knowledge Management within the Enterprise (MGKME), Sociotechnical Approach of Knowledge Management, Enterprise's KM Maturity Model, People focused Knowledge Management.

1 Introduction

In the Knowledge Society, Enterprises are more and more concerned with Knowledge Management (KM) as a key factor for improving their efficiency and competitiveness. They need a framework that serves as a template to position their efforts and launch KM initiatives. Thus, numerous Knowledge Management (KM) frameworks have been suggested all over the world as mentioned in the European Guide to Good Practices in Knowledge Management edited by the European Committee for Standardization [1]. According to our contribution to this project, we could distinguish two main approaches underlying KM: (i) a technological approach that answers a demand of solutions based on the technologies of information and communication (ICT); (ii) a managerial approach that integrates knowledge as resources contributing to the implementation of the strategic vision of the company. Moreover, we could observe that few of them were *"people-focused"* as highlighted by Wiig [2]. With regard to these issues, we elaborated a KM Empirical Model so-called Model for General Knowledge Management within the Enterprise (MGKME).

In this article, after having set out the background theories and assumptions, we distinguish the concept of KM Empirical Model from the concept of Knowledge Management System. Then, we make a brief description of MGKME. Finally, we outline an Enterprise's Knowledge Management Maturity Model (EKMMM), transposed from the IT Governance Maturity Model suggested in COBIT® [3], and that rests on the MGKME.

M.D. Lytras et al. (Eds.): WSKS 2008, CCIS 19, pp. 380–387, 2008.
© Springer-Verlag Berlin Heidelberg 2008

2 Background Theories and Assumptions

2.1 The Definition of KM

In our research group, we consider that knowledge is not an object processed independently of the person who has to act. Thus, it appears that KM addresses activities, which utilize and create knowledge more than knowledge by itself. With regard to this question, since 2001, our group of research has adopted the following definition of KM:

KM is the management of the activities and the processes that enhance the utilization and the creation of knowledge within an organization, according to two strongly interlinked goals, and their underlying economic and strategic dimensions, organizational dimensions, socio-cultural dimensions, and technological dimensions: (i) a patrimony goal, and (ii) a sustainable innovation goal.

The patrimony goal has to do with the preservation of knowledge, their reuse and their actualization. It is a static goal. The sustainable innovation goal is more dynamic. It is concerned with organizational learning: creation and integration of knowledge at the organizational level.

2.2 The Enterprise's Sociotechnical Environment

E. Coakes [4] defines sociotechnical approach as "*the study of the relationships and interrelationships between the social and technical parts of any system*" (p. 5). From KM viewpoint, the Sociotechnical Environment constitutes the social fabric where autonomous individuals, supported by Information and Communication Technologies (ICT) and tangible resources, interact and are conversing through physical or virtual places (coffee machines, collaborative workspaces, weblogs, wikis, CoPs).

The sociotechnical approach leads to emphasizing the link between knowing and action, with due regard to the basic constraints of the social system that is to give a sense to working time. Thus, KM initiative should result in Knowledge Management System (KMS) components that take into account the individuals, both as components and users of a system that allows them to be autonomous and to achieve their potentialities.

2.3 The Value Adding Processes

Value adding processes derive from the value chain described by Porter [5] who identifies nine value-adding activities that he classifies into two main categories. The "*primary activities*" are: 1) in-bound logistics, 2) operations, 3) out-bound logistics, 4) marketing & sales, and 5) Services. The "*support activities*" are: 1) business infrastructure, 2) human resource management, 3) technological development, and 4) supplies. In this way, Value-adding processes represent the organizational context for which knowledge is essential factors of performance. It is in this context that is implanted a KM initiative.

2.4 The Managerial Guiding Principles

The Managerial Guiding Principles should bring a vision aligned with the enterprise's strategic orientations, and should suggest a KM Governance principles by analogy with COBIT® [3]. In particular, we established KM indicators. Numerous publications and books relates to that subject. From our viewpoint, we constructed two main categories of indicators in order to monitor a KM initiative: (i) a category of indicators that focus on the impacts of the initiative that favor enhancement of intellectual capital, (ii) a category of indicators that insure monitoring and coordination of KM activities, measuring the results, and insuring the relevance of the initiative.

In addition (Ref. Fig. 1), we suggest a way to get a good articulation between the Deming's cycle PDCA [6] and Argyris & Schön's Organizational learning [7].

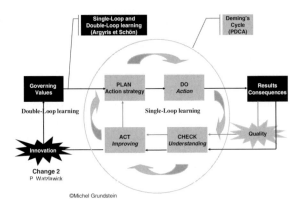

Fig. 1. Deming's cycle and Argyris & Schön's Organizational learning [8]

Firstly, we refer to the PDCA cycle of activities – plan, do, check, and act [6]; this cycle well known as the *Deming's Cycle* by Quality Management practitioners, has inspired the ISO 9004 (2000) Quality Standards in order to get a continuous process improvement of the Quality Management System. Secondly, we refer to the *Single-Loop Learning* and *Double-Loop Learning* defined in the Argyris & Schön's organizational learning theory [7].

Furthermore, we should think about the relevant infrastructures, which are adapted sets of devices and means for action. Beyond a network that favors cooperative work, it is important to implement the conditions that will allow sharing and creating knowledge. An *ad hoc* infrastructure must be set up according to the specific situation of each company, and the context of the envisaged KM initiative. The SECI spiral of conversion Model proposed by Nonaka and Takeuchi [9] and the Japanese concept of *Ba* inspire this infrastructure [10] [11].

3 KM Empirical Model Versus KM System

KM becomes a reality in the implementation of a system. The purpose of this system is to amplify the utilization and the creation of knowledge to improve the enterprise's effectiveness. This system is often called Knowledge Management System (KMS). Therefore, we have to distinguish between the notion of KM Empirical Model that is a template, and the notion of KM System - a context dependant system, which is the implementation of this template in the real world (Ref. Fig. 2).

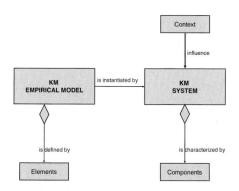

Fig. 2. KM Empirical Model and KM System [12]

To implement KMS components, Enterprises need a general model that is a pattern of reference (a template) in order to integrate KM Governance principles in their strategic vision, and to use KM as a factor that enable improving their efficiency and competitiveness. In this article, we refer to MGKME, our Model of General Knowledge Management within the Enterprise [8] that articulates the enterprise's sociotechnical environment, the enterprise's value-adding processes, and the managerial guiding principles specific to KM.

4 MGKME, a Model for General Knowledge Management within the Enterprise

The MGKME, described hereafter (Ref. Fig. 3), supports our full meaning of KM as defined in paragraph 2.1. It is an empirical model based both on our experience within the industry, and on our research works. MGKME rests on a Sociotechnical approach. It focuses on people and value adding processes. Moreover, the MGKME presents an attempt to articulate the Deming's Cycle PDCA and the Single-Loop Learning and Double-Loop Learning defined in the Argyris & Schön's organizational learning theory. It suggests "*ad hoc* infrastructures" derived from the Nonaka and Takeuchi's SECI model and the Japanese concept of "*BA*". It highlights four generic KM processes [8].

MGKME is composed of two main categories of elements: (I) the underlying elements consist of sociotechnical environment and value adding processes; (II) the operating elements focus on the underlying elements. They consist of managerial guiding principles, *ad hoc* infrastructures, generic KM processes, organizational learning processes, and methods and supporting tools. Key Issues to address for every elements of each level are synthesized in Table 1 and Table 2.

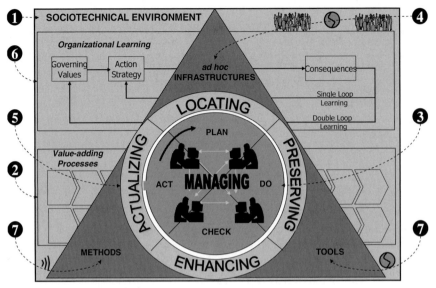

©Michel Grundstein

Fig. 3. Model for Global Knowledge Management within the Enterprise [8]

Table 1. MGKME's Underlying Elements

Model Level	Elements	Key Issues
I U N D E R L Y I N G LEVEL	❶ Sociotechnical Environment	Enterprise 's Activities (sector, key value-chain elements, geographical distribution, size, market, mass or batch manufacturing processes, product lifecycle, oral or written culture) Relations and Interactions between ICT, Structure, and People: their roles, their tasks Capability to learn and Innovate Social and Intellectual Capital Management Involvement
	❷ Value-adding Processes	Porter's Primary and Support Activities : Running Processes Business Processes Design and Development Processes Innovative Product and Services Processes

Table 2. MGKME's Operating Elements

Model Level	Elements	Key Issues
II O P E R A T I N G LEVEL	❸ Managerial Guiding Principles	Vision KM Governance Principles (strategic alignment, articulation between quality and organizational learning management) Main Development Axes Indicators
	❹ *ad hoc* Infrastructures	Content and Document Management Systems Collaborative Information Systems Organizational conditions encouraging interaction, communication, and knowledge sharing
	❺ Generic KM Processes	Locating Process Preserving Process Enhancing Process Actualizing Process
	❻ Organizational Learning Process	Team Learning Processes New Organizational Structures Experiments General Vision, and Systemic Approach Routines (defensive or constructive) Knowledge Dissemination Constant Evolution versus Change [13]
	❼ Methods and Supporting Tools	General Methods and Tools Knowledge Engineering, Artificial Intelligence (Semantic WEB and Ontology) CSCW -Computer Supported Cooperative Work (Multi-agents Systems) Social Networks (Identification, Visualization, and Informal Social Network Analysis Systems) Impact of Web 2.0

5 Assessing the Enterprise's KM Maturity Level

The Enterprise's KMS components materialize partial or total MGKME's elements. Thus, in a specific context, we can identify and analyze the Knowledge Management System Components implemented in the real field, and assess the maturity level by comparing these components with the MGKME elements.

Accordingly, when referring to MGKME, it is possible to measure the status of the Enterprise's KMS. This status combined with the characteristics of the IT Governance Maturity Model [3], enable to assess the Enterprise's KM Maturity level. You will find the characteristics of each level of maturity in Table 3.

Table 3. The Enterprise's KM Maturity levels

Maturity levels	Characteristics
Level 0 *Non-existent*	There is a total absence of recognizable Knowledge Management System. The company did not become aware that Knowledge Management must be studied and be considered.
Level 1 *Initial/Ad hoc*	The company became aware of the importance of Knowledge Management. However, she has no global vision. There are no standardized processes but approaches in this sense tend to be applied on an individual basis. The implementation of Knowledge Management System or one of its components is not organized.
Level 2 *Repeatable but intuitive*	Knowledge Management System is badly identified and is characterized by a partial implementation of the MGKME's elements. The processes are developed until the stage where different persons executing the same task use similar procedures. There is no formal training or no communication of standard procedures, and responsibility is left with the individual. One rests a lot on individual knowledge increasing so the probability to make errors.
Level 3 *Defined Process*	Knowledge Management System is well identified and is characterized by a partial implementation of the MGKME's elements. Procedures were standardized, informed and communicated by way of sessions of training. However, their use is left with the initiative of each, and it is likely that abnormalities will be noticed. Procedures are not sophisticated but formalize existing practices.
Level 4 *Managed and Measurable*	Knowledge Management System is well identified and is characterized by a partial implementation of the MGKME's elements. It is possible to control and to measure correspondence to procedures, and to act when processes seem not to work correctly. Processes are in constant improvement and correspond to a good practice. The automation and the use of tools are made in a limited or partial way.
Level 5 *Optimized*	Knowledge Management System is well identified and is characterized by a total implementation of the MGKME's elements. Processes reached the level of the best practices, further to a constant improvement and to a comparison with the other companies.

6   Future Trends

In the Knowledge Society, Enterprises are concerned with Knowledge Management (KM) as a key factor for improving their efficiency and competitiveness. In this article, we propose an Enterprise's KM maturity level analysis transposed from the IT Governance Maturity Model suggested in COBIT®, which rests on the MGKME, a Model for General Knowledge Management within the Enterprise. We expect that the MGKME will serve as an open model that allows everyone to take into account his own situation, to establish his own KM Empirical Model, to supply a KM vision to his company, and to be able to assess where the company's KMS is and where it has to go. Moreover, the MGKME can serves as a template for the design and the implementation of a KMS including individuals as users who are also components of the system.

In the future, we should complete the MGKME, by extending our study and developing appropriated methods, completing our set of qualitative indicators and specific tools to enable assessing the status of an Enterprise's KMS.

References

1. CEN-CWA 14924-1 : Knowledge Management Framework. In: European Guide to Good Practice in Knowledge Management (Part 1). Brussels: CEN, CWA 14924-1:2004 (E) (2004) (June 19, 2004), `ftp://cenftp1.cenorm.be/PUBLIC/CWAs/ e-Europe/ KM/CWA14924-01-2004-Mar.pdf`
2. Wiig, K.: People-Focused Knowledge Management. How Effective Decision Making Leads to Corporate Success. Elsevier Butterworth-Heinemann, Burlington (2004)
3. COBIT®: Control Objectives for Information and Related Technology. Control Objectives, Management Guidelines, Maturity Models, 4th edn. IT Governance Institute, Rolling Meadows Illinois (2005)
4. Coakes, E.: Knowledge Management: A Sociotechnical Perspective. In: Cokes, E., Willis, D., Clarke, S. (eds.) Knowledge Management in the Sociotechnical World ch. 2, pp. 4–14. Springer, London (2002)
5. Porter, M.E.: Competitive Advantage: Creating and Substaining Superior Performance. The Free Press, New York (1985)
6. Deming, W.E.: Out of the Crisis. MIT Press International, Cambridge (1982)
7. Argyris, C., Schön, D.A.: Organizational Learning II. Theory, Method, and Practice. Addison-Wesley Publishing Company, Readings (1996)
8. Grundstein, M.: Knowledge Workers as an Integral Component in Global Information System Design. In: Law, W. (ed.) Information Resources Management: Global Challenges ch. XI, pp. 236–261. Idea Group Inc., Hershey (2007)
9. Nonaka, I., Takeuchi, H.: The Knowledge Creating Company. Oxford University Press, New York (1995)
10. Nonaka, I., Konno, N.: The Concept of Ba: Building a Foundation for Knowledge Creation. California Management Review 40(3), 40–54 (Spring 1998)
11. Nonaka, I., Toyama, R., Konno, N.: SECI, Ba and Leadership: A Unified Model of Dynamic Knowledge Creation. Long Range Planning 33, 5–34 (2000)
12. Rosenthal-Sabroux, C., Grundstein, M.: A Global Vision of Information Management. In: Workshop MoDISE-EUS 2008 Model Driven Engineering: Enterprise, User ad System Models, CAISE 2008, Montpellier, France (2008)
13. Alter, N.: L'innovation ordinaire. Presses Universitaires de France, Paris (2000)

Grid Technologies to Support B2B Collaboration

Nicola Capuano[1,2], Matteo Gaeta[1], Sergio Miranda[1], Francesco Orciuoli[1,2],
and Pierluigi Ritrovato[1]

[1] University of Salerno, Department of Information Engineering and Applied Mathematics,
via Ponte don Melillo, 84084 Fisciano (SA), Italy
[2] CRMPA, Centro di Ricerca in Matematica Pura ed Applicata,
via Ponte don Melillo, 84084 Fisciano (SA), Italy
ncapuano@unisa.it, {gaeta,smiranda,orciuoli,
ritrovato}@diima.unisa.it

Abstract. In the context of the European Project BEinGRID (FP6), the authors
have defined a set of design patterns to develop software components based on
service oriented Grid technologies. Some of these patterns have been used to
improve software components of a Service Oriented Grid Middleware, named
GRASP, that the authors have defined, designed and implemented in the frame
of a former homonymous European Project (FP5). The main improvement of
GRASP due to the application of the BEinGRID design patterns is the support
for the creation of Virtual Organizations. This paper presents the authors experience and lessons learnt in adopting the GRASP middleware to set up a
business to business federated environment supporting collaborations among
enterprises. The concrete case study relates to the on line gaming applications
and the adoption of the Software as a Service business model to provide the
game applications.

Keywords: virtual organization management, SaaS, SOA, grid, design patterns.

1 Introduction

We present in this paper the improvement done to the GRASP middleware [12] in
order to allow the creation and management of a federated environment. GRASP
middleware is the main result of the homonymous FP5 EU project and represents
novel architecture supporting Grid-enabled collaboration for the purposes of Application Service Provision.

Leveraging the convergence of Grid and Web services technologies [1] [2], during
the GRASP project authors anticipated the emergence of new business and scientific
computing paradigms that are based on dynamic Virtual Organisations (VOs) [11].
These VOs span across organisational boundaries and enable the enactment of collaborative processes that integrate services, resources and knowledge in order to perform tasks that the VO partners could not undertake on their own.

In the context of the FP6 EU IP BEinGRID [10], authors have analysed a set of
concrete case of studies relating to the adoption of Grid technologies in business domains. During this analysis, some concrete requirements have been elicited and

M.D. Lytras et al. (Eds.): WSKS 2008, CCIS 19, pp. 388–397, 2008.

design patterns [13] to develop software components [14] based on service oriented Grid technologies have been produced.

In the definition of the design patterns, the authors have taken into consideration past experiences such as [3], [4], [5], [6] and [8]. Relying on these patterns and component, the GRASP middleware has been improved. This paper focuses mainly on the components and on their preliminary evaluation. For more information on the design patterns, interested readers can refer to [9].

The rest of the paper is organized in the following way. The section 2 briefly describe the GRASP middleware, its key and distinctive features with respect to other middleware. The section 3 presents the improvement of the GRASP middleware due to the application of the BEinGRID design patterns. The Section 4 presents the concrete case study, our preliminary results and the lessons learnt. The section 5 draws conclusions and presents future work.

2   The GRASP Middleware

The GRid based Application Service Provision (GRASP) project [12] have experimented the use Grid computing in order to support the operation and evaluate the sustainability of new models of ASP and thus contribute to the evolution from traditional ASP via IBSP to new paradigms.

Basically, two new ASP models have been investigated in GRASP:

– the "federated" ASP model, which can be described as the collaboration of many (ASP) GridService providers that provide services that can be combined to complex services addressing a customer need that each of them could not achieve themselves, and
– the "many-to-many" model, which is essentially an evolution of the classic "one-to-many" ASP model, achieved by evolving its foundation from the client-server to the service-oriented paradigm: the entity can take the role of either a consumer or a service provider in the context of the same application depending on the required interactions.

GRASP has explored the use of Web Services as a means of providing a timely and effective technological basis supporting the evolution of the ASP market towards a sustainable Utility Computing model.

The main results achieved in GRASP are an architectural framework for Grid-based Application Service Provision, a prototype realization of this framework in a GRASP platform and "proof-of-concept" implementations of "federated" and "many-to-many" ASP models in multiple domains.

In order to support the ASP models, the GRASP middleware presents the following services.

Orchestration – One of the most important aspects of the new Grid based ASP models is that no longer one single vendor controls the whole process. This means that a mechanism is needed that orchestrate the services offered by different vendors and ensure a controlled collaboration. The GRASP orchestration service is based on BPEL4WS and provide the possibility for a hybrid orchestration for Grid Services but also for Web Services.

SLA Monitoring – The Orchestrator can only fulfil its task in controlling the collaboration between the different services if enough information for the decision process is avail-able. The SLA monitoring services monitor, enforce and provide notifications in order to assist the Orchestrator in this task.

Accounting & Billing – Without Accounting & Billing no Application Service Provision can be performed. As the services are no longer controlled by one single entity but from many different service providers over time new ways on collecting provided services must be introduced. Especially for the "many-to-many" model new solutions must be identified.

The following picture present a graphical view of the three key pillars of GRASP.

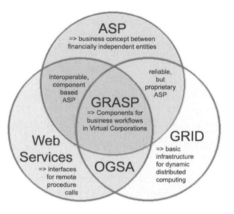

Fig. 1. GRASP Pillars

3   Evolution of GRASP towards Supporting B2B Collaboration

The GRASP middleware provides a solid foundation for Services-to-Services interactions but it lacks of capabilities to support the VO formation and lifecycle management. In the context of the BEinGRID project, two components have been designed and developed to fulfil this lack.

The following two sections present an overview of these components, namely the VO Set-up and the Application Virtualisation

3.1   VO Set-Up

This component is required to set up relevant information of a B2B collaboration allowing the finalization of the VO Creation process.

During the VO Creation process, in general, there is the need to perform operations like configuration of the infrastructure, instantiation and orchestration of the application service, assignment and set up of resources and activation of services, notification of the involved members, and manifestation of the new VO.

The high level architecture of this component is presented below:

- **VO Set-up:** This is in charge to finalise the VO Creation process. It is mainly a façade interacting with the other components
- **Registry:** This contains new members and service instances of the VO
- **Federation:** This is in charge to create a federation and to manage the identify of the federation members. This component can be designed according to the Secure Federation Design Patterns and other patterns proposed by the security area of the BEinGRID project [10].

The component is useful in several concrete scenarios where there is a low level of dynamicity in the VO creation process (meaning that the other steps of the creation process, such as agreement negotiations and policy definition, may be performed off-line). It is worth to mention that the Federation subcomponent of the VO Set-up is the most challenging one.

In contrast to the current state of the art, that is mainly based of results coming from the efforts of the eScience community (e.g. VOMS), the solutions proposed take into consideration the needs and requirements of the business world. This aspect has a deep impact in the design and implementation of the proposed software components.

While, in fact, most of the eScience solutions propose and implement coarse-grained models to address issues related to membership and management of resources in a Virtual Organisation (for instance, allowing the access to a whole resources for job submission) in our case we have requirements that foresees a fine-grained approach (for instance, allowing the access to specific capabilities offered by a Service Provider).

The main benefits, as evidenced at the end of the previous section, relates to the federation part of the component. These allow, on the one hand, managing the life-cycle of circles of trust between providers, and therefore the life-cycle management of federation of trust realms, and on the other hand, managing the life-cycled of identities and privileges of users and resources within such federations of trust realms.

The obvious benefits include:

- Facilitating the creation of communities of identity providers that enable identity brokerage and management by supporting open standards such as Liberty Alliance, SAML and WS-Federation, and therefore giving rise to new means of revenue generation.
- Enabling the customer to choose the identity provider that is more appropriate for a specific collaboration instead of being locked into what is incorporated in their SOA platform by some middleware vendor or instead of departing in expensive product integration projects that give them identity provision and federation, at a very high cost, for the specific application at hand.

3.2 Application Virtualisation

This component provides a way to integrate and expose application capabilities through a single access point that is configured to manage the execution of the exposed capabilities and forward requests to the application capabilities.

In a VO, in fact, there can be the need to expose application capabilities, for direct usage or for composition, as network hosted services in order to avoid direct and unmanaged access of VO members to VO resources.

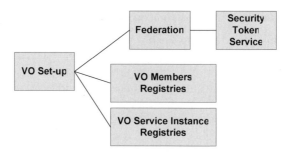

Fig. 2. VO Set-Up

It is appropr\iate to apply this component when there is the need to:

- decouple service access logic from the rest of the application
- hide the complexities of accessing a service from the application
- have a single point providing common management
- avoid direct access to resources

Figure 3 shows a high level diagram of the component. In the picture there are notes evidencing that some components relates to other patterns produced in the BE-inGRID project (of the VOM and/or other clusters). This means that, for instance, the Policy&Rules component can be designed according to the patterns proposed by the Security Cluster.

The Application Virtualization component follows the Façade pattern by Gamma et al [3] and it is in charge to invoke the other classes of the system in order to execute the virtualization process.

The Application Virtualization, the Runtime Monitor and the Management Service can iterate (in some way) the Observer pattern. Management Service Instances notify the Runtime monitor with the updates of some parameters and the Runtime Monitor can notify violation to the Application Virtualization.

If the Application Virtualization component is also the Gateway, when a request for accessing a service arrives, the Application Virtualization can operate according to the Chain of Responsibility [3] and pass the request along a chain of handlers. The building blocks are described below.

- **Application Virtualization:** This implements the virtualization process steps. It delegates requests to appropriate subsystem objects. It returns to client a reference to access the created application instance through the Gateway. It can be config-ured to be the Gateway and when a request for accessing a service arrives, it can pass the request along a chain of handlers.
- **End Point Reference Mapping:** This is in charge to map the End Point Reference (EPR) of the created application service instances to the EPR of the Gateway. It is also in charge to Activate and Deactivate the application service instances if, re-spectively, the process creation and termination of service instances succeed.
- **Policy & Rules:** This is in charge to apply the policies and rules associated to the application service instance. It can work according to the policy patterns identified by the General Security cluster of the BEinGRID project [10].

- **Runtime Monitor:** This is in charge to collect the management information of the application service instances. It evaluates the execution of the application service instances again the parameters of the contracts associated to it. It notifies eventual violations. It can work according to the patterns to monitor & evaluate the SLA identified by the SLA Management cluster of the BEinGRID project [10].
- **Registry:** A registry of the created application instances.
- **Management Service:** This notifies the Runtime Monitor of the change of the status of some parameters of the application service instance.

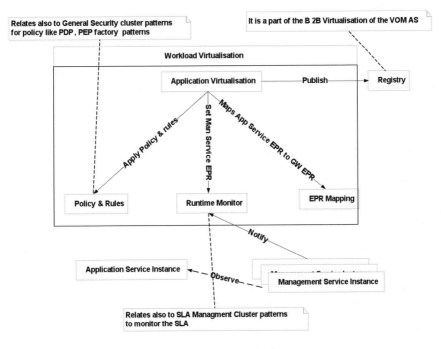

Fig. 3. Application Virtualization

The obvious benefits include cost-reduction, operational management risk mitigation through outsourcing, and reducing time-to-market timescales.

In addition the Application Virtualisation offers to the customer (i.e. the Application Service Provider), the ability to select among competing offerings of infrastructure services such as Identity providers, Access & Policy management service providers. Such a choice offers to the customer, on the one hand, the potential of avoiding to be locked into investing in proprietary SOA solutions that fit one market sector but are not good for another and on the other, hand, the prospect of getting better value for money by increasing the competition between vendors offering enabling enterprise solutions as a service in an ISV fashion though "pay-per-use" or "pay-as-you-grow" models.

4 Case Study: On Line Gaming Application

Within the context of the BEinGRID project, the evolution of the GRASP middleware has been adopted in the pilot focusing on the design and development of a Virtual Hosting Environment (VHE) for on-line gaming [15].

Virtualization of Hosting Environments refers to the federation of a set of distributed hosting environments for execution of an application and the possibility to provide a single access point (e.g. the VHE Gateway) to this set of federated hosting environments.

In a typical scenario, a number of host providers offer hosting resources to the Application Providers for deploying and running their applications, which are then "virtualized" with the use of middleware services for managing non-functional aspects of the application, and are transparently exposed to the end user via a single VHE.

Consider the case depicted in Figure 4 which is being addressed in the pilot, as an example of a business model enabled with the VHE.

In this scenario, the game application provider deploys its gaming application onto two different execution environments (gaming servers), owned by different host providers. The game platform provider, who wants to offer the game to an end user, discovers gaming servers and creates business relationships with them, and also with a separate service provider who offers a system for community management (of gaming clans, tournaments, advanced statistics). Through use of the VHE, these various services are offered transparently to an end user, including the game platform provider's ability to perform the load balancing and server selection based on the defined SLAs

The VHE developed in this business experiment consists of a network of B2B service gateways integrated with common capabilities for B2B trust federation, identity management, access control, SLA management, accounting and monitoring, as well as application service and resource virtualisation. The B2B gateway functionality is complemented by a federated messaging bus and community management services that facilitate the establishment of B2B collaborations (e.g. in the form of Virtual Organisations).

The scenario presented above is clearly a B2B collaborative scenario which foresee the federation of several Service and Game providers. Currently, we are finalising the development of this scenario but we have done preliminary tests in order to validate the capabilities of the VO set-up and Application Virtualisation components.

With respect to the VO Set-up, the purpose of our preliminary tests has been to assess the following functionalities required in the VO formation phase:

− Discovery of potential members on the basis of the capabilities they can offer to the VO,
− Invite potential member to join the VO,
− Start the federation process (Identity Mgm),
− Publish VO members, after their acceptance of the invitation,

Before doing the test, our scenario presumes that each potential member of the VO has advertised to the rest of the world its capabilities. This is done, in our scenario, off-line by the Game Pro\vider Administrator. The Game Provider presents a single point of access and a two level hierarchy of registries to publish its business capabilities. One on each hosts of the provider domain there is an Host Instance Registry. One on the provider gateway, there is a Gateway Instance Registry.

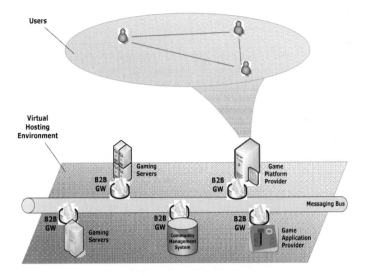

Fig. 4. VHE-enabled Gaming Scenario

The Game Provider has a business relationship with an entity providing a general catalogue and if it wants, the Game Provider advertises to the rest of the world its capabilities via the catalogue.

The following picture presents the situation. A part from the registry management part of the VO set-up component, that involves traditional publish / update operations, our tests have been mainly focused on the secure B2B federation of VO members.

From a methodological point of view, we have assessed the added-value of the proposed model for federation of administrative domains with respect to the current state of the art. The proposed model allows, for example, a single administrative domain to federate just a specific capability. This allows a more fine grained approach to resources and services federation more suitable for business applications with respect to the models proposed in the eScience community.

With respect to the Application Virtualisation component, the tests executed have had the purpose of assessing both the Virtualisation process and the graceful shutdown.

The virtualisation process is executed when there is the need to configure the VO underlying infrastructure. The process involves the creation of the business service that a member has promised to offer, the configuration of the management services (e.g. security services, SLA services, Accounting) and, eventually, the integration and exposition via Gateway of the created instances.

By the reverse, the graceful shutdown is executed in the VO dissolution phase when the resources have to be released and the bindings of the VO member need to be removed. The process involves invoking the VO Set-up to remove service instance entries from Service Instance Registry, clean up and destroy the management services, clean-up the Gateway (e.g. remove its internal mapping between virtual and real EPRs) and, eventually, destroy the business service instance.

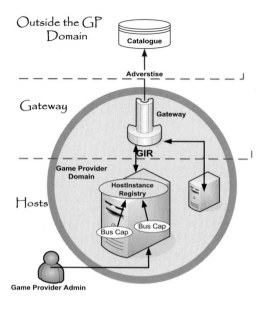

Fig. 5. Game advertising

5 Conclusions and Future Work

In this paper, we have presented the improvement of the GRASP middleware in order to allow B2B collaboration in the context of dynamic VOs. The software components presented can be reused in several common contexts where there is the need to federate different administrative domain and, as evidenced, can be composed in order to address complex issues, such as the creation and management of the VHE previously described.

As evidenced in the previous section, our preliminary results allows us to assess the benefits of virtualisation process and the graceful shutdown as well as of the federation model.

The full validation of these component is coming as part of other activities of the BEinGRID project. Currently, in fact, it is started a second wave of business experiment having the purpose of selecting some of the developed components and adopting them in their architecture for validation and evaluation purposes.

This document has been produced in the context of the BEinGRID Project http://www.beingrid.eu. The BEinGRID Project is part of the European Community's Sixth Framework Program for research and is as such co-funded by the European Commission. A sincere thank goes to all the organisations involved in the BEinGRID Business Experiment 09. The European Commission has no liability in respect of this document, which is merely representing the authors' views.

References

1. Foster, I., Kesselman, C., Nick, J.M., Tuecke, S.: The Physiology of the Grid: An Open Grid Services Architecture for Distributed Systems Integration. Globus Alliance Technical Report (2002)
2. Foster, I., Kesselman, C., Nick, J.M., Tuecke, S.: Grid Services for distributed systems. IEEE Computer (2002)
3. Gamma, E., Helm, R., Johnson, R., Vlissides, J.: Design Patterns: Elements of Reusable Object-Oriented Software. Addison-Wesley, Reading (1995) ISBN 0201633612
4. Easton et al.: Patterns: Emerging Patterns for Enterprise Grids, IBM Redbook, http://www.redbooks.ibm.com/abstracts/sg246682.html
5. Rana, O.F., Walker, D.W.: Service Design Patterns for Computational Grids. In: Rabhi, F.A., Gorlatch, S. (eds.) Patterns and Skeletons for Parallel and Distributed Computing. Springer, Heidelberg (2002)
6. Fowler, M.: Patterns of Enterprise Application Architecture. Addison-Wesley, Reading (2003)
7. Buschmann, F., et al.: Pattern-Oriented Software Architecture. John Wiley & Sons Ltd., Chichester (1996)
8. Alur, D., Crupi, J., Malks, D.: Core J2EE Patterns: Best Practices and Design Strategies. Prentice Hall, Englewood Cliffs (2001)
9. Gaeta, A., Gaeta, M., Smith, A., Djordjevic, I., Dimitrakos, T., Colombo, M., Miranda, S.: Design patterns for Secure Virtual Organization Management Architecture. In: Proceeding of the First International Workshop on Security, Trust and Privacy in Grid Systems, Nice, France, September 17 (2007)
10. BEinGRID project website, http://www.beingrid.eu
11. Foster, I., Kesselman, C., Tuecke, S.: The Anatomy of the Grid: Enabling Scalable Virtual Organizations. International Journal of Supercomputer Applications 15(3), 200–222 (2001)
12. GRASP Project, http://eu-grasp.net/english/default.htm
13. VO Management Design Patterns, http://www.gridipedia.eu/258.html
14. VO Management Software Components, http://www.gridipedia.eu/259.html
15. BEinGRID BE09, http://www.beingrid.eu/index.php?id=be9

Strategic and Managerial Ties for the New Product Development

Angelo Corallo, Nouha Taifi, and Giuseppina Passiante

eBusiness Management Section
Scuola Superiore ISUFI
University of Salento
Lecce, Italy 73100
{angelo.corallo,nouha.taifi,giuseppina.passiante}@ebms.unile.it

Abstract. The extended enterprise continuously creates partnerships with external partners for innovation. The structuring of these partners into networks and communities of practice is an efficient manner to manage their knowledge. In this paper, we show that strategic communities can emerge from managerial networks through a case study about a large manufacturing company, in the automotive industry, gathering its after sales services partners in a network, for the managerial collaboration, and the most strategic ones in a community. We use various data collection methods: interviews with the managers of the network and the strategic community, a survey dedicated to a sample from the network population, and a questionnaire to the strategic partners. We provide the mechanisms and dynamics of the managerial and strategic ties. The firsts are known-interdependencies, integrated IT-tools, trust and collaborative leadership. The successful collaboration contributes to the identification of the most strategic partners, thus the emergence of strategic ties. The strategic community uses a specific IT-tool to insert technical new knowledge that is filtered by strategic gatekeepers and benefits from a non-financial reward system to enhance knowledge sharing.

Keywords: Extended enterprise, new product development, networks and strategic communities.

1 Introduction

In the actual unstable environment, firms have to deal with complex technological and product development to acquire competitive advantage. They have to integrate external knowledge to accelerate the NPD process. The creation of inter-organizational collaboration with external actors is an efficient manner to gather new knowledge. Thus, it is important to structure them for the acceleration of the NPD process and to determine the relationship among them and the extended enterprise.

The paper is organized as follows. We first present the theoretical background concerning the importance of networks and strategic communities of practice for the new product development, then, the research framework and propositions, concerning the managerial and strategic ties, and structure of relationships. In the fourth section, we

M.D. Lytras et al. (Eds.): WSKS 2008, CCIS 19, pp. 398–405, 2008.

present the research method –case study- and the data collection method. In the fifth section, the results of the research are explained and in the sixth section, there is a discussion including theoretical and managerial implications for the creation of managerial and strategic ties for NPD.

2 Theoretical Backgrounds

Firms nowadays are aware of the importance of inter-organizational collaboration. This allows them to create value, sustain business performance and innovativeness [1, 2]. For example, in research, related to the automobile product development, collaboration among firms lead to knowledge exchange for exploratory products' problem-solving [2, 3-5].

[6] mention that networks are a type of collaboration leading to long-term relationships among firms that have different skills and competences that can be merged and integrated in the product development [7]. In the networks, informal linkages [8-9] among different firms are more important than formal ones for the innovation process [10-12] since they are not rigidly structured, thus facilitate communication of ideas. However, direct ties also provide resource-sharing and information-spillover benefits [7].

Whether direct or indirect, the relationships in networks are represented by face-to-face or IT-based interactions. Virtual linkages, using internetworking technologies lead to the creation of virtual networks –borderless- that are focused on the integration and exchange of value and knowledge [13]. Knowledge networks [14] focus on the mechanisms regarding the social context in which knowledge is created and shared. [15] argues that knowledge networks are communities of practice [9, 16] consisting of people sharing the same practice virtually –virtual community [17] with a focus on knowledge.

For the acceleration of the new product development, a further concept was established by [18-21] merging both networks and communities concepts. The strategic communities (SC) are communities of practice integrating the strategic members of different organizations and creating strong ties among them for the creation of new knowledge dedicated to the NPD process.

3 Research Framework and Propositions

The business environment is assisting to the emergence of a new form of extended enterprise (EE) [22-23] that is using integrated IT systems with partners in a collaborative environment where boundaries are overlapped [24]. The extended enterprise is indeed extending its collaboration with external actors for the purpose of innovation but if a clear map of these relationships and structure of relationships is not in place, the external actors' contribution to the EE will grow at a very low rate.

In this research, we analyze the relationships and structure of relationships of the extended enterprise and its external partners for the acceleration of the new product development.

Proposition 1: There are managerial and strategic ties connecting the extended enterprise with the external partners.

The managerial ties represent the relationship among the EE and the partners for the managerial purposes. Thus, a collaborative environment is created. The strategic ties represent the relationship among the firm and the strategic partners, thus, a strategic environment.

Proposition 2: The managerial ties the firm has with the partners contribute to the creation of strategic ties with strategic partners.

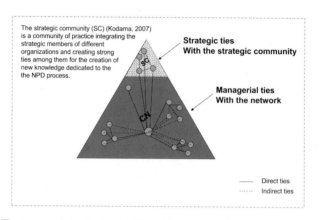

Fig. 1. The managerial and strategic ties with the network and strategic community

Through the collaborative environment, more strategic relationships can be created for the purpose of knowledge creation and sharing for the NPD process.

Proposition 3: Strategic communities can emerge from the members of the managerial network.

[18-21] mentioned the fact that networking the strategic communities of partners accelerates the new product development process. We also propose that the creation of strategic communities can be through the network of partners; the creation of strategic communities from the network for NPD acceleration.

4   Method

4.1   Case Study Research

Case study researches are preferred when the focus is on contemporary events and behaviour cannot be controlled. A case study analysis will allow us to identify and analyze the relationships and structure of relationships a firm and its network of external partners. The unit of analysis in this research is the relationship among a large manufacturing company in the automotive industry and partners –named dealers' network that provide the after sales services to the customers of the firm. And, there is a subunit of analysis which is the relationship among the firm and the strategic partners –expert dealers.

[25] research, in the automotive sector, mentions the importance of the integration of the after sales service in the idea generation step for accelerating the new product development process. The after sales services sector plays an important role in the innovation process; these organizations have new technical knowledge that can introduce new products [26-27] and are seen as a relevant resource of revenue and economic performance [28].

4.2 Data Collection Method

Following are the data collection methods used in a logical manner for the purpose of the research:

- Semi-structured interviews with the firm's managers responsible of the dealers' network to map and structure the relationships and categorize the mechanisms of the collaborative environment.
- Semi-structured interviews with the firm's managers responsible of the expert dealers to provide data about the relationships and processes involved in the strategic environment.
- Survey, dedicated to a significant sample from the population of the network of dealers to investigate on their satisfaction concerning the mechanisms of the collaborative environment. The questionnaire consisted of closed ended questions with a lickert scale from 1 to 10 where 1 is the lowest level and 10 the highest level of dealers' satisfaction.
- E-mail questionnaire dedicated to the expert dealers. We received 36 responses which represents 72% of the population -to investigate on their point of view concerning the mechanisms of the strategic environment.

5   Results

5.1   The Managerial Environment

The managerial structure and the mechanisms existing among the firm and the dealers' network are the basis for the collaboration among them. The analysis of the structure of the collaboration reveals that there are direct and indirect connections among the firm and the small and medium-sized dealers and that these latter are gathered in a network. Besides, the collaboration relationships among the firm and the dealers' network take place through IT-based, face to face-based and professional trainings mechanisms. These mechanisms are the pillars of the communication among the firm and the dealers

The survey dedicated to the dealers's network sample also provided significant insights about the collaborative environment. The dealers consider the managerial mechanisms as efficient and useful for the after sales services activities, however, a continuous reengineering and restructuring is necessary for the development and the adaptation of the collaborative environment to the after sales services activities needs and requirements.

5.2 The Strategic Environment

The relationship among the firm and the expert dealers have indeed led to the creation of a strategic community that is IT-based. In fact, the expert dealers use a specific IT-tool to insert new technical knowledge derived from their experience in the after sales services activities and they benefit from a reward system to enhance their motivation to share their knowledge with the firm. In order to initiate the SC, the firm approached some of the dynamic dealers in the network that have proved to be efficient and high performers. The firm, as the catalyst of the strategic community, grasps filters and integrates the technical knowledge in the NPD and after sales services development. The expert dealers provide information for problems-solving and quality level of the after sales services. From the questionnaire, we conclude that the expert dealers do have clear ideas about the purpose of the creation of the strategic community. The creation of this latter is for the integration of their technical knowledge in the NPD process.

6 Discussions

The managerial environment, the IT and face to face-based mechanisms are the pillars of the relationships among the firm and the dealers' network and the structure of the managerial ties –into direct and indirect connections among the firm and the dealers' network- are the results of the importance of the dealers for the after sales services activities. The firm collaborates with the dealers' network for managerial purposes – after sales services activities and strategic purposes -the development of the after sales services. Thus, the firm also has strategic relationships with the dealers' network.

The strategic environment created among the firm and the after sales services has the purpose of grasping the technical knowledge of the expert dealers for the NPD acceleration; the dealers are strategic to the development of the after sales services. For the strategic needs of the firm, this latter structured the expert dealers in the strategic community, provided them with the necessary IT-system for knowledge sharing, offered an incentive system for motivation and orchestrated the relationships with the support of catalysts representing the leadership of the firm.

6.1 Implications for Theory

The extended enterprise structures its external partners into networks to accelerate communication and knowledge sharing. The strategic communities of the partners contribute to the integration of new knowledge in the NPD process and this is more efficient through integrated information technologies.

There are managerial ties and strategic ties among the firm and the external partners and the strategic ties emerge from the managerial ties, that is, the firm creates strategic communities from its network of partners.

6.2 Implications for Practice

Concerning the managerial implications, the results of the study provide strategic guidelines dedicated to the creation of communities from the networks of partners for the purpose of accelerating the new product development process.

First, managers, having known interdependencies, with the network of partners, can use integrative IT-tools and systems to facilitate communication and knowledge sharing. And the success of these interactions depends on the collaborative leadership and trust-based relationships among the firm and the network of partners. Once these managerial mechanisms and dynamics are put in place, the collaborative environment among the firm and the partners' network can become strategic –not only managerial.

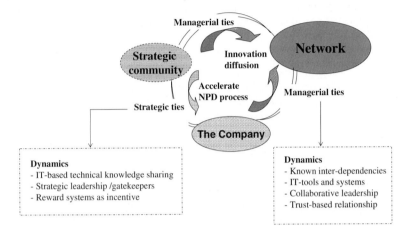

Fig. 2. The dynamics of the managerial and strategic ties for the NPD acceleration

The firm can gather strategic partners in strategic communities for new knowledge integration. In order to select the partners, the managers can investigate on the partner performance in the market and on its collaboration status with the firm.

And in order to support the knowledge sharing among the firm and the strategic community, management can base the interactions on the IT-systems already put in place for the managerial collaboration. However, a special IT-application dedicated to the strategic partners can be created, thus enhancing the sense of belonging of the partners to an expert community.

Finally, the management should be characterized by strategic leadership in order to develop the strategic ties among the firm and the expert partners and knowledge must be filtered by gatekeepers for the most relevant one to the NPD. Also, a reward system can be used in order to motivate the partners to collaborate more on sharing new knowledge.

6.3 Limitations and Future Research

In this study, we focused on the relationship among the firm and the after sales services organizations; these organizations are in fact external actors, thus, their integration in the NPD process is strategic, however, future research must be done about the relationships among the firm and other types of external actors –as the suppliers and research laboratories partners- to improve the research study.

The automotive industry is a dynamic environment where the use of ITs is necessary for the collaboration with partners, thus, the automotive industry reflects the needs of the research objectives. However, in order to develop more the research, it is possible to make case study researches in other industries –as the aerospace or the software industry- to compare cases and confirm the implications to management.

References

1. Dyer, J.H., Singh, H.: The Relational View: Cooperative Strategy and Sources of Inter-Organizational Competitive Advantage. Academy of Management Review A 23(4), 660–679 (1998)
2. Lorenzoni, G., Lipparini, A.: The leveraging of interfirm relationships as a distinctive organizational capability: a longitudinal study. Strategic Management Journal 20(4), 317–337 (1999)
3. Takeishi, A.: Knowledge Partitioning in the Inter-Firm division of labour: The Case of Automotive product development. Organization Science A 13(3), 321–338 (2002)
4. Clark, K.B., Fujimoto, T.: Product Development Performance. Strategy, Organization, and Management in the World Automobile Industry. Harvard Business School Press, Boston (1991)
5. Wasti, S.N., Liker, J.K.: Collaborating with Suppliers in Product Development: A U.S. and Japan Comparative Study. IEEE Transactions on Engineering Management A 46(4), 444–465 (1999)
6. Tidd, J., Bessant, J., Pavitt, K.: Managing Innovation: Integrating Technological, Market and Organizational change, 3rd edn. John Wiley & Sons, Ltd., Chichester (2005)
7. Ahuja, G.: Collaboration Networks, Structural Holes, and Innovation: A Longitudinal Study, Administrative Science Quarterly (2000)
8. Brown, J.S., Duguid, P.: Organizational learning and communities of practice: Toward a unified view of working, learning, and innovation. Organization Science 2(1), 40–57 (1991)
9. Wenger, E., Snyder, W.M.: Communities of Practice: The Organizational Frontier, pp. 139–145. Harvard Business Review (2000)
10. Weenig, M.W.H., Midden, C.J.H.: Communication network influences on information diffusion and persuasion. Journal of Personality and Social Psychology 61, 734–742 (1991)
11. Weenig, M.W.H.: The strength of weak and strong communication ties in a community information program. Journal of Applied Social Psychology 23, 1712–1731 (1993)
12. Weenig, M.W.H.: Communication networks in the diffusion of an innovation in an organization. Journal of Applied Social Psychology 29, 1072–1092 (1999)
13. Romano, A., Passiante, G.: Un modello per la gestione innovativa dei Sistemi Economici locali - Il Sistema Innovativo Virtuale. In: Valdani, E., Ancarani, F. (eds.) Strategie di marketing del territorio, Ed. EGEA, Milano, pp. 83–112 (2000)
14. Seufert, A., von Krogh, G., Bach, A.: Toward knowledge networking. Journal of Knowledge management 2(3), 180–190 (1999)
15. Magnusson, M.G.: Managing the knowledge landscape of an MNC: Knowledge networks at Ericsson. Knowledge and Processes Management 11(4), 261–272 (2004)
16. Wenger, E., McDermott, R., Snyder, W.: Cultivating communities of practice. McGraw-Hill, Europe (2002)
17. Lipnack, J., Stamps, J.: Virtual Teams: Reaching Across Space, Time, and Organizations with technology. John Wiley and Sons, Chichester (1997)
18. Kodama, M.: Strategic innovation at large companies through strategic community management: an NTT multimedia revolution case study. European Journal of Innovation Management 2, 95–108 (1999)

19. Kodama, M.: New business through strategic community management: case study of multimedia business field. International Journal of Human Resource Management 11, 1062–1084 (2001)
20. Kodama, M.: Strategic partnership with innovative customers: a Japanese case study. Information Systems Management 19(2), 31–52 (2002)
21. Kodama, M.: New knowledge creation through leadership-based strategic community—a case of new product development in IT and multimedia business fields. Technovation 25(8), 895–908 (2005)
22. Konsynski, B.R.: Strategic control in the extended enterprise. IBM systems journal 32(1) (1993)
23. Davis, E.W., Speckman, R.E.: The Extended Enterprise: Gaining Competitive Advantage through Collaborative Supply Chains. Prentice Hall, Englewood Cliffs (2007)
24. Passiante, G., Fayyoumi, A., Filieri, R., Taifi, N.: Modelling the Extended Enterprise in the digital economy: some empirical evidence. In: Proceedings of the 8th GITMA conference, Napoli, Italy (June 2007)
25. Wheelwright, S.C., Clark, K.B.: Revolutionizing Product Development. Free Press, New York (1992)
26. Goffin, K.: Customer support –A cross-industry study of distribution channels and strategies. International Journal of Physical Distribution and Logistics Management 29(6), 352–374 (1999)
27. Goffin, K., New, C.: Customer support and new product development - An exploratory study. International Journal of Operations & Production Management 21(3) (2001)
28. Saccania, N., Johanssonb, P., Peronaa, M.: Configuring the after-sales service supply chain: A multiple case study. Int. J. Production Economics 110, 52–69 (2007)

Semantic Web or Web 2.0? Socialization of the Semantic Web

Jorge Morato, Anabel Fraga, Yorgos Andreadakis, and Sonia Sánchez-Cuadrado

Carlos III of Madrid University, Computer Science Department,
Av. Universidad 30, Leganés,
28911 Madrid, Spain
{jorge,afraga,gand,ssanchec}@ie.inf.uc3m.es
http://www.uc3m.es

Abstract. Web 2.0 and the Semantic Web are approaches that target the improvement of the Web through the optimization of mechanisms for sharing information and resources. This document argues that Web 2.0 is not an immature stage of the Semantic Web but an orthogonal dimension of another Web aspect, the semantic. Unfortunately, both dimensions are not independent; the more developed a semantic representation of a system is, in order to be more useful for the Semantic Web, the more distant it is to the Web 2.0. A semantic system highly formalized is less intuitive and less usable by users. For that reason, with the intention of avoiding the inverse relation between both dimensions, eight proposals are positioned and discussed in order to enable a real Social Semantic Web.

Keywords: Information resource management, Intelligent Web Services and Semantic Web, User Interfaces, Web technologies.

1 Introduction

WEB 2.0 [10], [18] and Semantic Web (SW) 1 are technologies with a great potential for the network and ultimately, for the final user. Both, aim to improving the mechanisms for sharing information and resources. Frequently, Web 2.0 is presented as an intermediate stage to future Web 3.0 (called Semantic Web) [11], [5], [9]. We analyze and compare characteristics of both Webs. In our research, this perception of evolution comes as an apparent contradiction with the analysis of characteristics of one against the other, presenting thus, contradictory approaches between both of them. In this document, we argue that both points of view, each kinds of Web, responds in fact to diverse Web requirements.

The following sections demonstrate a light description of both Webs. The most relevant differentiating characteristics will be analyzed so that later, an integrated vision will be proposed. Finally, possible solutions are demonstrated and the principle conclusions are as future work.

1.1 The Web 2.0

Dale Dougherty from O'Reilly Media 10 was the person that invented the term Web 2.0 at a conference with Craig Cline from MediaLive. During the speech on the

M.D. Lytras et al. (Eds.): WSKS 2008, CCIS 19, pp. 406–415, 2008.
© Springer-Verlag Berlin Heidelberg 2008

evolution of the Internet they realized the numerous collaborative services that had emerged, as well as the will of the users to share resources. The term was affirmed in the 2004 Web 2.0 Conference, in a way that in one year the term Web 2.0 already had 10 millions references in Google, even though its significance remained vague. In contrast with Semantic Web, its appearance was not a response to a planned and co-ordinated effort, neither the assumption on behalf of the experts that the Web was evolving autonomously, was suggesting such a proposal.

Web 2.0 is a platform, where users are the principal centre of attention [10] [18], the user decides what to use and how to use it. Applications such as Flick or YouTube demonstrate the great acceptance and vitality of this proposal. This approach is based on the implication and the collaboration of users for the management of resources, which requires friendly and well designed user interfaces. The architecture of these applications permits to users to describe resources with tags. In contrast to Semantic Web, this Web lacks a central authority that organizes and standardizes the way that the Web is managed, which impedes a predetermined general progress on behalf of computer applications.

1.2 The Semantic Web

Tim Berners-Lee created this concept by proposing a network in which computers would be able to analyze all Web data: content, links, transactions between persons and computers. A Semantic Web that could be able to do this is now emerging, and this way, when this is possible there will be a qualitative leap in the interconnection between multiple repositories, electronic commerce, semantic queries and automatic question-answer systems, making thus possible the improvement of efficiency of intelligent agents [1].

Semantic Web already counts one decade of work on it and a great effort invested for its development by private and academic entities, but regretfully their results are currently scarce, because this forward-looking approach implicates a "technical con-struct of protocols, process, languages, and tools that make it all work" according to James Hendler in his viewpoint about to *"The dark side of the Semantic Web"* [9].

However, two factors present Semantic Web as an attractive solution; these are the interoperability and the creation of semantic resources with the common domain knowledge:

1. Interoperability: some authors consider the Semantic Web as a project for creating a universal mediator for information interchange. This is feasible through the crea-tion of interoperable documents with a non ambiguous semantic for the computer applications of the Word Wide Web. In other words, it's about converting the Web to a great database. The interoperability between the documents is sustained through the use of a common language based on RDF (Resource Description Framework) [20], a language which uses XML (Extensible Markup Language) [21]. Hence, this means that like XML, RDF can be interpreted by computers as it uses tags as part of a well structured language [13] for data interchange (XML) [21]. The advantages of obtaining this interoperability are obvious for querying multiple repositories, knowledge reuse, the conceptual navigation and the fusion of Knowledge Organization Systems (KOS) through multiple domains [22], [23].

There are still more advantages for the interaction with computer applications in a normalized way.

2. Semantic Resources: Semantic Web requires that the semantic knowledge should be expressed in documents written in a Web language oriented to knowledge modeling like RDF. These documents model KOS and its instances. KOS, e.g. the ontologies, have an important role in the Semantic Web because they support the semantic knowledge used in the document indexing giving as a result more relevant and noiseless information for the user. KOS, define the terms utilized for describing and representing an area of knowledge [3], [14]. These resources are used by persons, databases, and applications that need to share information on a specific domain, considering for every domain the specification of a knowledge area, such as medicine, real estate, commercial management, etc. At least, KOS contain lists of concepts and some type of relation between them, but their complexity can reach that of formal ontologies (heavyweight ontologies), that contain computer processable definitions as basic concepts of the domain, axioms and inference rules.

2   Analysis

2.1   Web 2.0 and Semantic Web Comparison

To respond to question about why a web 2.0 is actually being more used than semantic web, we analyze and compare some characteristics between both webs according to different criteria. Some of them make evident that they treat two concepts with different approaches. The following table (table 1) displays this analysis:

At first glance, it could be assumed that both Web 2.0 and Semantic Web could be contradictory. At the same time though, they could be suggested as two complementary aspects of the Web, which by operating synergicly, they can increase its potential.

2.2   Web 2.0 and Semantic Web Dimensions

As illustrated in the previous section, the differences between the two perspectives seem to suggest, that there is no common niche for their co-existence. Their incompatibility could be less apparent if they were considered as different perspectives for the management of the Web, which instead of antagonizing, they complement each other, thus incrementing its potential.

Web design principles deals with several items related with the user interaction as, usability, findability, comprehendability, readability, simplicity, accesibility, aesthetics, credibility and so on. Most of these concepts (e.g. usability, comprehendability, readability, or simplicity) represent the degree of easiness to interact with a Web, regardless of the user skills or background. In our study, we collect these aspects under the name of "user interaction dimension". This dimension represents the easiness to manage a KOS. Figure 1 shows how in the Spectrum of the ontologies [3] a higher degree in semantics implies a lower degree in most of these aspects.

Table 1. Differences between Web 2.0 and Semantic Web

	Semantic WebW	eb 2.0
Origin	Proposed by Tim Berners-Lee as an evolution of the Web	Discovery of the Web's natural evolution
Dissemination	Scarce [12]	Very High
Coordination	Centralized, mostly by W3CN	on Existent
Focus	Computer Applications	Persons
First Mentioned	1999 [2] (called Web 3.0 since 2006)	2003, first conference 2004
Expression	Controlled Language, using languages for expressing ontologies, KOS and metadata vocabularies	Free language, expressed using folksonomies (collection of keywords in natural language to tag web resources), keywords named tags, with problems of synonymy and polysemy
Some Characteristics	Use of a standardized language with uniform syntax and unambiguous semantic. Interoperability: Information interchange between any repository. Scarce usability	Description of resources for the improvement of its free distribution, it shares knowledge and development Collaborative Architecture High Usability The more use a resource has, the more useful it is.

Therefore we consider that we are at a space named the Web that has, at least two dimensions, one that measures the degree of contact with the user and the other displays the degree of used semantic for expressing and organizing the information in a specific system. Both dimensions are illustrated in figure 1 as the abscissas and the ordinates respectively.

The user implication in the creation and use of semantic documents is greater when the contact dimension is nearer the extreme positive, as in the case of Web 2.0. This is actually the extreme point of this dimension which is due to that the user expresses through the folksonomies [19], [15] the ultimate aim of the resource, whilst on the contrary, the nearer to the negative side, the smaller the user's implication. Thus it becomes evident that the Semantic Web will never be realized if the usability is not improved for expressing formally semantic documents with OWL. It must be noted that the contact dimension does not incorporate only the usability aspects and interfaces, but also other aspects such as the degree to which the user perceives as valuable effort for improving a resource, or the degree to which the collaboration with other systems is promoted.

The vertical dimension illustrates the proximity with the user. The horizontal dimension is necessary to guarantee interoperability and express common sense. Therefore both perspectives can survive together, and the ideal Web will be the integration of one into the other, an environment that we name Social Semantic Web.

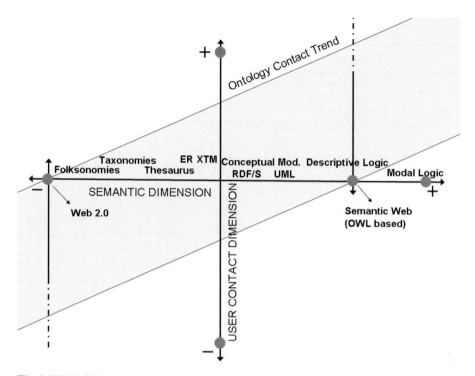

Fig. 1. Web 2.0 Dimension (contact with the user dimensions) and the Semantic Web (semantic dimension) based on the spectrum of ontologies [3]

The semantic dimension (the Semantic Web) could be moved to the vertical dimension, i.e., that of the contact with the user (Web 2.0), and this dimension could be moved along the horizontal axis that represents the semantic dimension. The cross-point of both dimensions will indicate the degree of semantic and user proximity, depending on the proximity to the extreme positive or negative.

This exposed formulation can be extended with more concepts that involve the Semantic Web and Web 2.0, in order to emphasize other relevant aspects. For example, questions such as: "which is the final functionality?", "what is the goal for developing a system?", or "how many modeling elements are necessary for creating the ontology under a predetermined paradigm?".

As it has been mentioned, these dimensions do not seem to be completely independent. With no doubt Knowledge Organization Systems (KOS) lightly formalized (Light weight ontologies), improve the usability, management and understanding on behalf of the user, which is obvious if we observe the Web 2.0 tags popularity (also called folksonomies) [15] for describing multimedia resources of the Invisible Web. Though, through the approach of strategies oriented to usability improvement, the reliability and the use of semantic resources on behalf of the users, it is possible to appreciate the orthogonality of the variables. Some of these measures are discussed in the following section.

3 Discussion

There are some pending considerations in order to achieve Social Semantic Web. Eight issues will be discussed which could improve the contact dimension respecting the semantic.

3.1 Analyze Which Are the Actual Social Semantic Web Documents

Possibly, in reality, the closest to the Social Semantic Web are the RSS[1] documents. These documents which can be found by millions over the Internet unify the contents syndication (which is a typical objective of Web 2.0) with the expression of RDF syndication (in the case of RSS 1.0) or XML (in the case of RSS 2.0). With no doubt, as in the case of Dublin Core 6 vocabulary, success has been based on two factors: the appearance of usable readers oriented to the final user and the simplicity of the used metadata vocabulary. Some RSS editor are available[2], these editors aids users in the intuitive creation of RSS by means of forms, exporting the results in XML files. As an extra feature some editors include a file transfer protocol.

HTML's metatags and Microformats[3] are two solutions with popular support, and even though they are not very promising for creating the Semantic Web, they demonstrate that the solution for implanting this Web has to be simple.

3.2 Analyze Which Are the Actual Social Semantic Web Documents

The creation of ontologies in a collaborative way is a complex matter, because the ontologies are based on the consensus for determining the concepts and relevant interrelations between them, and this consensus impedes the increase of the number of users. On the other hand, the more specific the domain is, the harder the identification of available experts to collaborate is.

A possible solution is that the public organizations could support and finance the creation of these resources. The option of private funding for their creation does not seem realistic, as the result should be a product free of charge and reusable by third parties.

3.3 Establish Mechanisms for Centralizing the Semantic Documents in a Common Repository and Eliminate Unnecessary Duplicates

There are actually at least four metadata vocabularies for expressing a thesaurus of type KOS. E.g. SKOS-Core[4] by W3C, PSI[5] by Topic Maps, Zthes[6] and MADS[7]. The

---

[1] RSS 2.0 (2.0.10) specification by the RSS Advisory Board http://www.rssboard.org/rss-specification.

[2] RSSeditor http://www.rss-info.com/en_rsseditor.html

[3] Microformats http://microformats.org/

[4] SKOS Core Guide http://www.w3.org/TR/2005/WD-swbp-skos-core-guide-20050510/.

[5] Published Subject Indicators For Modelling Thesaurii
http://www.techquila.com/psi/thesaurus/

[6] Zthes - specifications for thesaurus representation, access and navigation
http://zthes.z3950.org/

[7] Metadata Authority Description Schema (MADS) http://www.loc.gov/standards/mads/

duplicity for the uncontrolled creation of controlled vocabularies provokes distrust and confusion to the user that does not know which is the ideal vocabulary or the most generalized.

3.4 Improve the Contact Dimension in the Use of Documents RDF-OWL

The difficulty in the use of some languages such as OWL does not encourage some users to collaborate. Hence, according to Gómez-Pérez and her colleagues 8, the validation of the OWL ontology, on behalf of the domain experts, is one of the bottlenecks in ontologies creation.

The problem has been resolved in previous occasions with some propositions as in the case of Wikipedia in which the improvements are realized through different profiles for creating, editing or validating the new content, under a friendly user interface, or even the creation of news Wikis through tags that would be coded in RDF in a transparent way [7].

Some applications of Altova (SemanticWorks[8]) and of Microsoft (InfoPath[9]) or the forms already mentioned in section 2.1 for RSS editing, facilitate the instances incorporation in RDF.

Another relative problem at this point is the improvement of the interfaces for navigating through these documents, something which is intended to be tackled by the Tabulator[10] project.

3.5 Improve the Contact Dimension in the Use of Documents RDF-OWL

Some Web resources are being under analysis for their evolution to KOS complexes, e.g. the folkontologies [4], [17], which study evolution mechanisms starting from a folksonomy.

Another example, on this evolution is given in the Wikipedia [11] [12]. Without a doubt, the incorporation of the tag clouds with linguistic tools and statistics can help in this process. An example, on how it could be done is Piggy Bank [13], which is an application that captures locally the tags of the RDF visited, in order to organize them in a local ontology and share it in the Semantic Bank.

3.6 Conversion of the Folksonomies into More Complex KOS

It must be clear to the user that his collaboration for the improvement of the resource does not implicate the obligation of paying a charge for his future use of the improved

---

[8] Altova SemanticWorks - visual RDF and OWL editor that autogenerates RDF/XML and N-Triples http://www.altova.com/products/semanticworks/semantic_web_rdf_owl_editor.html

[9] Information about Infopath 2003 product
   http://www.microsoft.com/spain/office/products/infopath/default.mspx

[10] Tabulator: Async Javascript and Semantic Web
   http://dig.csail.mit.edu/2005/ajar/release/tabulator/0.8/tab.html

[11] Harvesting Wiki Consensus - Using Wikipedia Entries citeseer.ist.psu.edu/747700.html

[12] Ontoworld.org http://ontoworld.org/wiki/Main_Page

[13] SIMILE- My Piggy Bank http://simile.mit.edu/wiki/Piggy_Bank

resource. Moreover, the user has to be conscious of the benefits that the Semantic Web will entail in the short term.

3.7 Conversion of the Folksonomies into More Complex KOS

Semantic spam will be a reality when the transition towards Semantic Web commences. A great number of Web engines do not use HTML's metatags in the positioning, because of the frequent initial use of fraudulent techniques for optimization.

3.8 Conversion of the Folksonomies into More Complex KOS

If the repositories of all the companies of a domain were exporting their data under the same model and metadata vocabulary, this would increment the interoperability for consulting diverse repositories. Then this would facilitate the automatization in different degrees of the comparison of prices and services. This could provoke an initial mistrust of certain companies, although it has been foreseen that this tendency is reduced when a certain critical weight of the Semantic Web is reached, for that reason the likelihood to be demoted in the market is a great risk to be taken.

4 Conclusions

Web 2.0 and Semantic Web have both a great potential for creating a more powerful Web for the final users. Web 2.0 is frequently presented as an intermediate stage towards Web 3.0 or the Semantic Web, in which the first will disappear whilst the Web will be maturing. Surely, this gives the impression that the two Webs can not co-exist together due to their noticeable differences. Some of these differences are: Web 2.0 is oriented to persons, while the Semantic Web is oriented to applications; this is due to that the first employs a free language and latter a controlled language. Web 2.0 attempts to give the users a legible and usable semantic and the Semantic Web projects the correct interpretation of the semantic for computer applications against legibility.

Therefore, alter questioning the reason for their mutual existence and why Web 2.0 or Social Web have had such a success comparing with Semantic Web, it becomes evident that they treat two independent necessities equally indispensables.

In this article is presented as a novelty the interpretation of Web 2.0 and the Semantic Web as two independent dimensions but essential for the development of the Web, both far from being irreconcilables or successive stages. This way, is presented a visual medium for interpreting the degree in which both dimensions are reached for a specific system.

It is unlikely the existence of a great number of semantic documents without implicating the users in their creation and utilization. This implication can not be achieved without taking care aspects, such as legibility, usability and actual implication in the design of these documents, since the lack of these characteristics restrain their popularity. In other words, it is necessary to socialize the Semantic Web in order to achieve a Social Semantic Web. This has been indicated by various critical factors that can influence the solution of this problem.

As a future development two aspects can be analyzed, the decomposition of both dimensions into a single space which also includes other relevant aspects such as the system's goal and the creation of a metric that permits the measurement of the degree in which both dimensions are satisfactory for a specific system.

Acknowledgments. This work presented here was carried out within the framework of a research Project financed by the Spanish government (Ministerio de Educación y Ciencia Sec. de Estado de Universidades e Invest., TIN 2007-67153).

References

1. Berners-Lee, T., Fischetti, M.: Weaving the web, 1st edn. Harper, San Francisco (1999)
2. Berners-Lee, T., et al.: Weaving the Web: The Original design and Ultimate Destiny of the World Wide Web by its Inventor. Harper, San Francisco (1999)
3. Daconta, M., et al.: The Semantic Web. A guide to the future of XML, Web Services, and Knowledge Management, Indianapolis. Wiley, Chichester (2003)
4. Damme, C., Hepp, M., Siorpaes, K.: Ontology: An Integrated Approach for Turning Folk-sonomies into Ontologies (2007),
   `http://www.heppnetz.de/files/vandammeheppsiorpaes-`
   `folksontology-semnet2007-crc.pdf`
5. Davies, J., Lytras, M., Sheth Amit, P.: Semantic-Web-Based Knowledge Mangement. IEEE Computer Society, Los Alamitos (2007),
   `http://www.computer.org/internet`
6. DCMI, Dublin Core Metadata Initiative (2007), `http://es.dublincore.org/`
7. Fuentes, D.: CoolWikNews: More than meets the eye in the XXI century journalism. Emerging technologies form semantic work environments: techniques, methods, and applications (2007); In: Rech,J., Decker, B., Ras, E.(eds). Emerging technologies for seman-tic work enviroments: Techniques, methods, and applications, Universidad Carlos III de Madrid, Germany (submitted, 2007)
8. Gómez-Pérez, A., Fernández-López, M., Corcho, O.: Ontological Engineering. Springer, London (2003)
9. Hendler, J.: The Dark Side of the Semantic Web. IEEE Intelligent Systems 22(1), 2–4 (2007)
10. O'Reilly, T.: What Is Web 2.0. Design Patterns and Business Models for the Next Genera-tion of Software (2005),
    `http://www.oreillynet.com/pub/a/oreilly/tim/news/2005/09/30/`
    `what-is-web-20.html`
11. Lassila, O., Hendler, J.: Embracing Web 3.0. IEEE Internet Computing 11(3), 90–93 (2007)
12. Palacios, V., Morato, J., Llorens, J., Moreiro, J.A.: Indicadores Web sobre utilización de ontologies. In: CISTI 2006 (Conferência Ibérica de Sistemas e Tecnologias de Informa-ção). Actas da 1ª Conferência Ibérica de Sistemas e Tecnologias de Informação, Ofir (Por-tugal), 21-23 June 2006, vol. II, pp. 199–214 (2006)
13. Laurent, St.S.: Describing your Data: DTDs and XML Schemas, XML dot COM (1999),
    `http://www.xml.com/pub/a/1999/12/dtd/index.html`
14. Berners-Lee, T., Hendler, J., Lassila, O.: The Semantic Web, Scientific Am. (May 2001)
15. Gruber, T.: Ontology of Folksonomy: A Mash-Up of Apples and Oranges. Int'l J. Seman-tic Web and Information Systems 3(1), 1–11 (2005)

16. Treese, W.: Web 2.0: is it really different? NetWorker 10(2), 15–17 (2006),
    http://doi.acm.org/10.1145/1138096.1138106
17. Van Damme, C., Hepp, M., Siorpaes, K.: FolksOntology: An Integrated Approach for
    Turning Folksonomies into Ontologies. In: ESWC 2007. Proceedings of the Workshop
    Bridging the Gap between Semantic Web and Web 2.0, Innsbruck, Austria (2007)
18. Van Der Henst, C.:Qué es la Web 2.0? (2006),
    http://www.maestrosdelweb.com/editorial/web2/
19. Vander Wal, T.: Folksonomy (2004), http://vanderwal.net/folksonomy.html
20. W3C, Primer: Getting into RDF & Semantic Web using N3 (2005),
    http://www.w3.org/2000/10/swap/Primer
21. W3C, Extensible Markup Language (XML) (2006), http://www.w3.org/XML/
22. W3C, Ontologies (2007),
    http://www.w3c.es/Traducciones/es/SW/2005/owlfaq
23. Zeng, M.L., Chan, L.M.: Trends and issues in establishing interoperability among knowl-
    edge organization systems. J. Am. Soc. Inf. Sci. Technol. 55(5), 377–395 (2004),
    http://dx.doi.org/10.1002/asi.10387

A Critical Review of the Impact of Knowledge Management on Higher Education

Dionysia A. Alexandropoulou, Vasilis A. Angelis, and Maria Mavri

Department of Business Administration, University of the Aegean, 8 Michalon str.,
Chios Island, Greece
d.alexandropoulou@aegean.gr, v.angelis@aegean.gr,
m.mavri@ba.aegean.gr

Abstract. Universities have always been in the knowledge business per se. Even if they are acknowledged as having different missions, all are closely related to the management of knowledge. Nowadays, taken into account Lisbon Agenda and the Bologna process, European universities are at the forefront of changes. The challenges that they face urge them to incorporate knowledge management practices in order to help them enhance their functions and be more competitive and transparent. This paper reviews the impact of knowledge management on higher education institutions and it investigates aspects such as missions of universities and knowledge management, the benefits for universities when adopting knowledge management and examples of implementing KM practices by universities.

1 Introduction

The field of Knowledge Management has its roots in the late 70s when Peter Drucker [5] pointed out that management in the twenty-first century should focus on knowledge workers. However, the two most popular dimensions of knowledge, tacit and explicit, date back to 1967 [16]. Nowadays, the emergence of the knowledge economy has led management to consider the expertise and knowledge of employees as strategic resources that can be efficiently handled by knowledge management.

In search of higher education knowledge management's roots one could argue that it has long existed within higher education if we consider that *tacit* knowledge (know-how and learning embedded within the minds of the people in the university) has been converted into *explicit* (documented information that can facilitate action) for at least a century, through writing scientific articles and the setting up of libraries for preserving institute's literature [9]. Universities' most valuable resources are their researchers, managers and students within their organizational processes and networks. Despite this, it is difficult to find many examples of institutions that systematically develop initiatives aiming at sharing knowledge and achieving operational excellence [8].

The scope of this paper is to present a literature review concerning universities, Knowledge Management and how the two topics are related. Therefore, this paper first outlines the missions that universities fulfill. Then, it examines the challenges that universities face and the impact of KM on them, before exploring the way that

M.D. Lytras et al. (Eds.): WSKS 2008, CCIS 19, pp. 416–421, 2008.

Knowledge Management, or parts of it, have been applied in some universities. Finally, recommendations for future research directions are given.

2 Missions of the University

According to Slaughter and Leslie [22] "universities are the repositories for much of the more scarce and valuable human capital that nations possess, capital that is valuable because it is essential to the development of the high technology and technoscience necessary for competing successfully in the global economy". The main aims of the universities are reflected in their three missions.

First of all, there is the research mission. This corresponds with knowledge creation and aims at expanding the frontiers of human knowledge and promoting creativity. It includes the production of doctoral researchers along with codified knowledge.

Education/teaching constitutes the second mission which aims at knowledge dissemination. The knowledge created through research is transferred to university students not only through teaching in classes but also through skills training, attitude formation, etc.[14].

The third mission is service to society. This means that university knowledge is diffused to society at large and universities participate in activities that serve the local, national and international needs. The third mission incorporates mostly everything that involves transfer of knowledge to other than students and can include various tasks, from contract research to job creation through spin-offs [10].

3 Challenges Facing Universities and How Knowledge Management Can Contribute to Their Missions

In order to excel in the future, higher education institutions have to be managed in a comprehensive and systematic knowledge perspective [23]. They face challenges that range from the emergence of knowledge society, reduction of governmental support, governmental policy concerning the development of usable knowledge, demographic changes, to the internationalization of higher education and globalization, the creation of new and private universities or even "corporate universities", set up by companies in order to contribute to lifelong learning [17],[18],[2].

In an environment contingent on knowledge such as a university, knowledge assets are tangible (information, records, curriculums and research results) or intangible (individual expertise, organizational knowledge kept in human minds, interactions and knowledge – related processes [6]. It is, therefore, critical for universities to be involved in knowledge management practices since their main goals are the production and the diffusion of knowledge and their main investments are in human resources and research.

Research and Knowledge Management. The "knowledge creation" dimension of knowledge management lies heavily on this mission. The management of research usually depends on the university and it can be done "top down" or "bottom up". According to the "top down" approach, the research administrative authorities choose their preferred research areas while the "bottom- up" approach depends on the individual's research interests. Another way for managing research is to have "exogenous" (market – driven innovation) and "endogenous" (curiosity- driven invention) research [15].

Education - Teaching and Knowledge Management. It is argued that the main role of education is to confer credentials and prepare students to become life–long learners [10]. Thus, the focus shifts from just teaching to learning, whereby students are equipped with broader skills that will allow them to learn actively even when the teaching has stopped. The education component of universities coincides with the knowledge dissemination dimension of knowledge management. What do universities do in order to manage knowledge dissemination? Some institutes have incorporated processes of evaluation, both by the university staff as well as by students, and processes of quality controls carried out by groups of specialists in their fields [14].

Service to society. This third mission of a university encompasses the knowledge transfer to non-academic partners (i.e. industry, public authorities and the public generally) and the service that a university can offer society through different ways, (for example job creation through spin-off companies). Businesses often view universities as a source for novelties and technological breakthroughs in order to boost their innovative evolution. It also encompasses the accountability dimension. Public authorities and public in general are very interested in knowing what exactly people behind walls are doing, how the university can contribute to region's well being and economic improvement and finally where exactly public funds are given [7]. To respond to this challenge, universities can employ knowledge management practices in order to share their knowledge and make all their processes transparent. Cronin [4] suggests that by setting up publicly accessible repositories of scholarly expertise and interest, transparency and information exchange can be promoted. In this way, the university can disseminate information to stakeholders regarding the results derived from public funds [19], [17].

Knowledge management can act as a binder for the three missions of the university described above. It facilitates the transfer of existing knowledge and the creation of new knowledge through interdisciplinary collaborations. It can upgrade education by making available to all faculty members institutional knowledge that may reside within academics [23]. In addition, knowledge management can provide a framework in which new activities are managed (such as the offering of training courses and the use of laboratories facilities for industrial applications), therefore acting as common ground between the three missions of the university.

KM can withdraw the obstacle of unawareness of what the researcher next door is doing. As mentioned above, researchers tend to be solely or partly isolated in their research activities and might not be aware of the valuable expertise within the university that could contribute to their own work and this in turn often leads to reduced innovation and productivity [11].

Another issue that calls for new management and reporting systems is the increasingly provided autonomy of many higher education institutions regarding their organisation, management and budget allocation. Even from now, universities face increasing competition for students and resources. In order to attract students and obtain resources, an institution needs to be able to show the caliber of the faculty and quality of the research undertaken. Knowledge management can lead to better decision – making capabilities, reduced "product cycle" (for example curriculums), improved academic and administrative services and reduced costs [8]. It is often directly tied with strategic planning which needs data so as to make projections and forecasts of different academic issues in order to plan the future.

According to Reid [18] two are the main reasons why universities should be engaged in knowledge management. Firstly, the development of technology- based methods for the creation, storage and dissemination of knowledge along with the increasing emphasis in universities on business strategy (i.e. intellectual capital as a competitive advantage). Secondly, the "knowledge economy", a competitive economic environment that require graduates with information literacy skills.

Milam [12] adds that by implementing knowledge management, universities will be able to attract more students, increase graduation rates, retain employees, and enhance systems in order to provide information for decision- making and be competitive when students' needs are to be met.

However, it is striking to observe that although a university could be considered as the ultimate knowledge organization as argued above, many researchers are not aware of the research activities within their own universities [7]. This stems from the fact that there is a cultural challenge when talking about academia; researchers and academics tend to individualism, they consider knowledge to be their own intellectual capital, their property. In some cases, the perception is that any attempt to exploit this capital would be against their work ethic. That is encouraged even more if we consider that in many universities, academics are rewarded and promoted on the basis of their individual performance, rather than being part of a team. Therefore, knowledge creation appears to be more interesting than knowledge distribution and dissemination [11],[4]. It is crucial for the successful implementation of knowledge management in universities to be able to have an answer for all stakeholders to the question *"What's in for me?"*

4   Knowledge Management Initiatives at Institutions of Higher Education

Knowledge Management at Institutions of Higher Education constitutes a research field that is relatively recent and corresponding published work is rather limited. This results in having limited examples of cases where KM initiatives, fully or partially, have been applied to universities. In relation to the above, Reid [18] mentions that at the University of South Australia, they have incorporated technical solutions in order to manage the knowledge. A web-enabled database has been considered to be the key technology. Apart from the latter, the knowledge management strategies employed, include high bandwidth on campus network, standardized hardware and software platform, a single entry for all staff, students and education offerings etc. All these resulted in the development of online educational material that allowed academic control over content and allowed capacity for professional development.

Along the same philosophy, Oosterlinck [15] describes that at K.U. Leuven University, Holland, the managing of the university's portfolio has been done since 2000 through the structure of KU Leuven Research and Development, with the set up of an internal intellectual property liaison office. In addition, the transfer of knowledge is done through the creation of spin – off companies. The knowledge creation or research is managed by several committees that protect research quality, provide information and help relating to research programs. Most of this information is included on the university's web site.

Other research includes Knowledge Management audits. The objective is to measure the level of practice among the academicians and to formulate indicators by which knowledge management can be successfully incorporated in structure, facilities and culture [13],[2],[1].

5   Conclusions- Future Work

KM in universities has been applied most times by either taking the processes as they are implemented in the business sector without adjusting them to the specific characteristics of universities, or by focusing only on information technology applications.

It would be interesting for future research to record the different ways by which different universities manage knowledge creation, dissemination and transfer to academic and non-academic partners and develop a knowledge management framework that will take into account all stakeholders' needs concerning the managing of knowledge within the university in order for all to underpin a system approach to organisational knowledge management.

References

1. Basu, B., Sengupta, K.: Assessing Factors of knowledge management initiatives of academic institutions - a Case of an Indian Business School. The Electronic Journal of Knowledge Management 5(3), 273–282 (2007)
2. Biloslavo, R., Trnavčevič, A.: Knowledge Management Audit in a Higher Educational Insti-tution: A case study. Knowledge and Process Management 14(4), 275–286 (2007)
3. Cronin, B.: Knowledge management organisational culture and Anglo- American Higher Education. Journal of Information Science 27(3), 129–137 (2001)
4. Drucker, P.: The age of Discontinuity. HarperCollins, New York (1978)
5. Gilliland- Swetland, A.J.: Revaluing Records: From risk management to enterprise management. In: Bernbom, G. (ed.) Information Alchemy: The art and Science of Knowledge Management, pp. 81–98. Jossey- Bass, San Francisco (2001)
6. Jones, N.B., Provost, D., Pascale, D.: Developing a University Research Web- Based Knowledge Portal. International Journal of Knowledge and Learning 2(1/2), 106–118 (2006)
7. Kidwell, J.J., Vander Linde, K.M., Johnson, S.L.: Applying corporate Knowledge Management Practices in Higher Education. In: Bernbom, G. (ed.) Information Alchemy: The art and Science of Knowledge Management, pp. 1–24. Jossey- Bass, San Francisco (2001)
8. Lyman, P.: Knowledge Discovery in a Networked World. In: Bernbom, G. (ed.) Information Alchemy: The art and Science of Knowledge Management, pp. 43–66. Jossey- Bass, San Francisco (2001)

9. Metaxiotis, K., Psarras, J.: Applying Knowledge Management in Higher Education: The creation of a learning organisation. Journal of Information and Knowledge Management 2(4), 353–359 (2002)

10. McManus, D., Loughridge, B.: Corporate information, institutional culture and knowledge management: a UK university library perspective. New Library world 103(1180), 320–327 (2002)

11. Milam, J.: Knowledge Management for High Education. ERIC Clearinghouse on Higher Education, Washingthton (2001)

12. Mohayidin, M.G., Azirawani, N., Kamaruddin, M.N., Margono, M.I.: The Application of Knowledge Management in Enhancing the Performance of Malaysian Universities. The Electronic Journal of Knowledge Management 5(3), 301–312 (2007)

13. Oosterlinck, A.: Knowledge Management in post-secondary education: Universities (2002), http://www.oecd/dataoecd/46/21/2074921.pdf

14. Oosterlinck, A.: University/Industry Knowledge Management: A University perspective (2001), http://www.oecd/dataoecd/11/8/2668332.pdf

15. Polayni, M.: The Tacit Dimension. Routledge, New York (1967)

16. Ramirez, Y., Lorduy, C., Rojas, J.: Intellectual capital in management in Spanish Universities. Journal of Intellectual Capital 8(4), 732–748 (2007)

17. Reid, I.C.: The Web, Knowledge management and universities. In: Proceedings (AusWeb2k), The Sixth Australian World Wide Web Conference, Cairns (2000)

18. Sánchez, P., Elena, S., Castrillo, R.: The ICU Report: An Intellectual capital proposal for university strategic behaviour. In: IMHE What Works Conference, Paris (2007)

19. Slaughter, S., Lesley, L.: Academic capitalism: Politics, policies and entrepreneurial university. Johns Hopkins Press, Baltimore (1997)

20. Steyn, G.M.: Harnessing the Power of Knowledge in Higher Education. Education 123, 615–631 (2002)

On Growth of Network and Centrality's Change Analysis of Co-inventors Network in Enterprise

Satomi Takagi and Ryoko Toyama

[1] Japan Advanced Institute of Science and Technology
Nomishi Asahidai 1-1 Isikawaken Japan
s-takagi@jaist.ac.jp
[2] Chuo graduate school of strategic management
Kasuga1-13-27 Bunkyouku Toukyouto Japan
rtoyama@tamacc.chuo-u.ac.jp

Abstract. The theme of this research is to point out the influence of Growth of networks and organization change give co-inventors networks. Especially, change in central person's role and generation of weak ties. I did two investigations. The first method is Network analysis. I made networks from co-inventors relation based on patents for which one company applied by using patent database. And each actor's degree centrality and betweeness centrality in each fiscal year were examined. Second method is interview. As a result (1) When scale of the enterprise is small, only two inventors had relations with a lot of another inventors, and they were mediated between another inventors. (2) When scale of the enterprise grows, their relations of co-inventors has decrease, but they were playing role of mediation between another inventors by using networks that they established in old times.

Keywords: Knowledge management; Knowledge creation; Network analysis; Organization dynamics; co-inventors network.

1 Knowledge Creation and Network

I will begin by considering social capital. Putnam gave the most lucid definition about social capital in recent years. According to Putnam, Social capital is trust and network. [1][2] He pointed out that Network for trust and mutual aid increases the creativity of the community. In the knowledge creation in the enterprise, the network is one of the concepts paying attention. Ba and Network are the most important concepts for Knowledge Creation. The reason is necessary in the enterprise create knowledge as a whole, that share in-house knowledge by networks and unite knowledge made in each Ba by the networks. Researches on the engineer's networks in enterprise have been in innovation research. There are three stages, the first is in section, the second is inter section, the third is inter organization. There are two important concepts in the research on engineer's network. The first concept is centrality. Many of these analyses assumed that outside knowledge is transferred through a central person in network. [3] The second concept is strength of tie. In the network concerning the knowledge creation, the link is a transmission route of knowledge. The quality and the efficiency of the knowledge that can be transmitted are different according to strength of tie. [4]

M.D. Lytras et al. (Eds.): WSKS 2008, CCIS 19, pp. 422–427, 2008.

2   Centrality Measure

Many researchers are developing centrality measures for a variety of research purposes. Freeman systematized these, and brought them together in three typical measures. Degree centrality is decided by measuring degrees of the node. [5][6] Adjacent centrality is decided by reciprocal of sum total of distance of the node and other nodes. Betweeness centrality is decided by how much contribute to the median of other nodes. [6] As stated above, many of these analyses assumed that outside knowledge is transferred through a central person. Gatekeeper plays this role in research and development. [3] The features of the gatekeeper, as Allen points out, that they are excellent engineers, they are central people of internal communications networks, and they are belong to gatekeeper networks. [3]

3   Strength of Tie

Various measures are used to decide strength of tie, Such as close relatives or acquaintances [7] communications frequency [4], etc. Recently,Barabasi insisted that high betweeness and low degree centrality centrality means weakness of tie. [8] Hansen analyzed the influence of strength of tie on search and transfer of information between sections in the enterprise. A weak tie is suitable for searching for information, and transferring for explicit knowledge. But, a weak tie is unsuitable for transfer of tacit knowledge. A strong tie is unsuitable for searching for information and transferring explicit knowledge. But a strong tie is suitable of transfer for complex information and tacit knowledge.

4   Discussion

Many discussions about the communications networks in innovation research assume that central persons get information from his outside networks, There are (Thought to be weak ties) then he transfer information inside the organization. Many of these discussions are static analyses. These discussions assume neither growth nor change in the network. But, Human relationship and organization structure always change. Should not that central persons were in center position even if time passes, and had an outside network from the start. This drives us to two questions.

Question1: How does central persons, role change due to the growth of the network?

Question2: How did the central person make weak ties?

5   Method

I performed two investigations. The first is Network analysis. I made and analyzed the network of co-inventor's relation on patents for which the enterprise had applied. The second is interview. I interviewed inventors who appeared in the network.

5.1 Network Analysis

Patent application is one of the indices to measure Knowledge creation of the enterprise. Recently, Japan also has disclosed the patent database, and it is expected to be analyzed in various ways. However, the research to analyze relations of inventors is rare. Japanese law concerning patents doesn't have a clear answer to the problem of "Who is invent it?" But according to judicial precedent "the inventor" is interpreted to be the person who gave the idea for the invention. [10] I chose The Mayekawa Mfg.Co.,Ltd. as the subject of my investigation. This is a Japanese enterprise that does manufacturing sales of plants. I made co-inventors network maps in each one years by using information of Patent applied for by Mayekawa Mfg.,Co.,Ltd. with in each one year.(From 1973 to 2003)

5.2 Result

I assume that inventors are nodes, and relations of co-inventors are links. An identification number was applied to each inventor. The network was made visible by using UCINET, typical network analysis software. (Figure.1) And, I investigation betweeness centrality and degree centrality of appearing inventors in these graphs. I display 20 of the people who have highest betweeness centrality in each year. (Table.1).

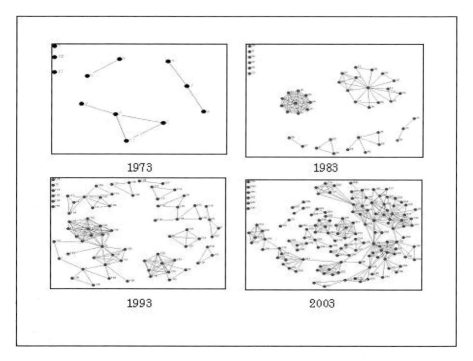

Fig. 1. These graph indicate relations of co-inventors of patents applied for in each one year (put one every ten years)

Table 1. This table shows 20 people that Bitowinessentorariti is the highest in each fiscal year

1973				1993			
Rank Betweenss	ID	Be-tweeness	De-gree	Rank Betweenss	ID	Be-tweeness	De-gree
1	0	30	6	1	248	45	10
2	2	20	4	2	78	32	10
3	5	0	1	3	249	20	5
4	11	0	1	4	0	12	5
5	12	0	1	5	150	12	8
6	13	0	1	6	332	8	4
7	14	0	1	7	131	65	4
8	15	0	1	8	2	5	2
9	16	0	1	9	10	3	4
10	17	0	1	10	347	1.935	10
11	18	0	2	11	196	1.935	10
12	19	0	2	12	24	1.935	10
13				13	346	1.935	10
14				14	348	1.935	10
15				15	345	1.935	10
16				16	231	1.5	3
17				17	350	1.143	9
18				18	199	0.125	9
19				19	344	0.125	9
20				20	7	0	0
1983				2003			
1	0	77.5	14	1	131	1194.139	24
2	2	5	4	2	52	994.428	24
3	28	1	2	3	150	800.689	19
4	76	0.5	3	4	78	695.564	29
5	27	0	9	5	225	560.077	20
6	21	0	1	6	489	544.199	17
7	51	0	0	7	383	500.922	17
8	17	0	3	8	334	489.043	18
9	55	0	4	9	449	463.289	17
10	58	0	2	10	608	453.525	6
11	61	0	2	11	554	418.922	16
12	67	0	9	12	552	415.614	9
13	68	0	9	13	576	394.504	23
14	68	0	9	14	88	393.335	21
15	70	0	9	15	570	376.204	14
16	71	0	9	16	451	340.211	16
17	75	0	2	17	180	269.333	11
18	54	0	2	18	82	263.606	14
19	79	0	1	19	230	262.152	17
20	80	0	1	20	28	244.828	11

5.3 Interview

Interviews ware done in the form of field interview and open-ended interview. Interviews ware ten hours or more. Interviewees ware seven inventors, from the people whom with high betweeness centrality. These are the main two question items. First, who was the center of the communications network? Second, what has been your career?

5.4 Result

What kind of people with a high betweeness centrality . Who has excellent talent, a person who accomplished great achievements in the past, a person who was managing patent information, in organization.

The most important addition to be made to what I have said about results of interviews, is the transition of human relationships. The research and development was done under the guidance of number0 and 2 (refer to figure1). These two inventors were superiors, in 1970's period. (At that time, only engineers ware inventing.) Some of their subordinates became project leaders and presidents of subsidiary companies, in the 1980's period. At that time, they relied on the network that they had before made. Moreover, not only engineers but also the people in charge of sales became inventors in the latter half of the 1980's.

6 Conclusion

Question1 How does a central persons, role change due to the growth of the network?

Answer: When the network and organization are small, only number 0 and 2 (they were superiors in laboratory) were related to a lot of another inventors.

When the scale of enterprise and network grows, (They were not superior in these days) their relations of co-inventors has decrease, but they were playing role of mediation between another inventors by using networks that they established in old times.

Question2 How did central persons make weak ties?

Answer: Many central people made weak ties by counting on relations to the people them had worked before. The degree of Person who was playing the center role in 1970's had decreased by the 1990's. (They were not superior in 1990's). But, they are playing the role of mediation between another inventors by networks that they built before.

In conclusion, change of network was caused by the enterprise growth. But, People who belong to the enterprise might still maintain their old network. There is a lot of research on communication network among knowledge creation are in innovation research. And, many of these discussions are static analyses. But, for this investigation, I insist necessity to refer to a past network of actor.

References

1. Putnum, R.D.: Making Democracy Work. Princeton University Press, Princeton (1993)
2. Putnum, R.D.: Bowling Alone: The Collapse and Revival of American Community. Touchstone Books (2001)
3. Allen, T.J.: Managing the flow of technology: Technology transfer and the dissemination of technological information within the R & D organization. MIT Press, Cambridge (1977)
4. Hansen, M.T.: The search-transfer problem: the role of weak ties in sharing knowledge across organization subunits. Administrative Science Quarrely 44(1), 82–111 (1998)
5. Nieminien, J.: On the centrality in a directed graph. Social science Research 2, 371–378 (1973)
6. Freeman, L.C.: Centrality in Social Networks Conceptual Clarification. Social Networks 1, 215–239 (1979)
7. Granovetter, M.S.: The Strength of Weak Ties. The American Journal of Sociology 78(6), 1360–1380 (1973)
8. Onela, J.P., Saramaki, J., Hyvonen, J., Szabo, G., Menezes, M., Kaski, K., Barabasi, A.L., Kertesz, J.: Analysis of a large-scale weighted network of one-to-one human communication. New Journal of Physics 9, 179–204 (2007)
9. Suzuki, M.: Kyoudoukennkyuu no seika no kennrika oyobi katuyou wo meguru houteki syomonndai: Tokkyo no keiei keizaibunseki. Yuhido, pp. 345–369 (2007)

Computer-Supported Interaction for Preparing Logically Organized Documents

Toyohide Watanabe and Kei Kato

Department of Systems and Social Informatics,
Graduate School of Information Science, Nagoya University
Furo-cho, Chikusa-ku, Nagoya 464-8603, Japan
watanabe@is.nagoya-u.ac.jp

Abstract. It is not always easy for many persons to prepare documents with constructive form and logical story. This is because the work of document preparation is one of creative activities of individual persons with their own knowledge, experiences, motivations, etc. The logically organized document is defined as one with story-like scenario. In this paper, we propose an experimental method for composing the logically organized documents. The main idea is to design and implement the composition process as the working procedure with query list and logic tree. The query list defines what should be discussed in the document, while the logic tree specifies how to write down topics. This paper makes these roles in the composition process clear and then reports our interaction through the interface on the prototype system.

Keywords: logically organized document, query list, logic tree, fitness, generality.

1 Introduction

To make up documents in the well structure and concise description is one of important works when we exchange our own intentions interactively, discuss effectively with other related persons and make our own considerations, ideas, opinions and so on explicit [1]. This work is always regarded as a necessary and un-avoidable task for all persons in order to participate into some meetings occasionally, make up plans successfully, organize events cooperatively and so on. However, it is not always easy for many persons to instantly prepare meaningful documents without any prerequisite skills, heuristics, know-how and experiences. Of course, many kinds of documents are available in accordance with the usage purposes of meetings, planning, managements, events, etc. Various documents are inherently designed under systematical composition styles, attended with their application-specific context structures [2, 3]. For example, the scientific papers are generally organized as the story construction of four main description viewpoints: "Introduction", "Development", "Turn" and "Conclusion". Namely, many of documents should be prepared with the constructive layout and story-like scenario so as to describe the key topic clearly: the scenario takes a very important role to express the key-subject of document definitely, and also its attended layout makes its descriptive procedure clear from viewpoints of understandability and effectiveness.

M.D. Lytras et al. (Eds.): WSKS 2008, CCIS 19, pp. 428–434, 2008.
© Springer-Verlag Berlin Heidelberg 2008

In this paper, we address a computer-supported function for composing documents logically: we call the document, which was composed logically on the basis of definitely specified scenario and constructively structured form, a logically organized document, hereafter. Our discussion points focus on how to compose this logically organized document.

2 Framework

The document should be organized so as to make the structure of story-like scenario, based on the main topic and its related sub-topics, stepwise and successive. Our logically organized document is composed of query list and logic trees definitely. This query list specifies what should be discussed in the document. For example, the query list consists of a set of several queries, related to the following discussion points: What is the background?, What is the objective?, What is the successful approach?, What is the result?, What is the current situation?, etc.

While, the logic tree specifies how to write down topics. Namely, this tree represents a hierarchical structure of topics to be discussed logically: the root node is the final result in the document; the child node linked directly to the root node is an intermediate sub-result which can support straightly the final result; and the same structure is repeatedly organized for the terminal nodes in the tree. The leaf node generally corresponds to a sub-title of each section or sub-section. Also, the brother-relationship between neighbor nodes in the same node depth is called MECE (Mutually Exclusive and Collectively Exhaustive), and also the parent-child relationship between upper node and lower node is called "So What?/Why So?". Our logically organized document is constructed as a forest for pairs of a query in the query list and a logic tree, as shown in Figure 1.

When we prepare our document by using the computer-supported functionality, the following requirements are necessary [2-4]:

1) to provide deterministic strategies to organize documents systematically and write down them logically;
2) to make up documents contextually by extracting the reusable knowledge from the already composed documents;
3) to support the effective functions and cooperative environment for users.

These requirements indicate the necessity for our computer-supported mechanism for promoting knowledge-creative work from a viewpoint of document preparation.

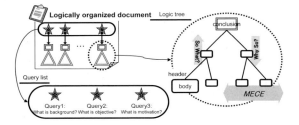

Fig. 1. Logically organized document

Next, we define objects to be manipulated in our computer-supported document preparation environment. The basic objects are queries in the query list or nodes in the logic tree. We call these objects *elements*, hereafter. Our *elements* are characterized as agents in the agent-oriented paradigm, and should also interact coordinately in well defined structure with the story-like scenario because they take individual different roles under the constructive and logical relationships as queries in the query list and nodes in the logic tree. The structure of *element* is illustrated in Figure 2.

(1) The sensor is a function to grasp the situation of environment collectively, assigned to each element: in this case, two kinds of data are collected:
   - An *element* or a set of *elements* which users edited or composed.   We call this *element*, which are focused directly by the user, the *focus element*;
   - Coordinative relationship to be established among *focus elements*.
   The *focus elements* are determined in accordance with the editing work of user, as follows:
   - *Element* editing phase: edited *element* or its related *elements*.   In this case, the related *elements* are queries in the query list or nodes in the logic tree, related directly to editing operations;
   - *Element* generation phase: newly generated *elements*;
   - Alternation phase of query list: *elements* included in the query list;
   - Construction phase of logic tree: a set of child nodes, whose parent node is modified.
(2) The judgment function takes a role to select the next action of agent-specific *element* on the basis of information, propagated from the sensor.
(3) The effecter takes a play to interact with its surrounding environment according to the instruction ordered from the judgment function.
(4) The inner information contains various types of data, assigned uniquely to the *element*: *ID*, *Type*, *Index*, *Content* and *Feature*.
   - *ID* is a unique identifier, assigned to each *element*;
   - *Type* is categorized into four classes:
      "Query": queries which are not contained in the query list;
      "Query list": queries in the query list;
      "Node": all nodes in the logic trees;
      "Node-MECE": some nodes in the logic trees which are specified by MECE between existing documents.

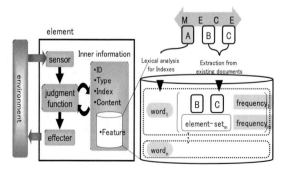

Fig. 2. Element structure and Feature

- *Index* is an entry for the corresponding *element*. In case that *Type* of *element* is "Node", this entry is a link to MECE;
- *Content* is a set of statements to be written in the logically organized document;
- *Feature* represents information about co-existence relationship MECE (*element* set), related appropriately to the *element*. *Feature* is a tuple list of co-existence relationship MECE, concerning to all words in *Index*, as illustrated in Figure 2, and is defined as follows:

Feature = { tuple of co-existence relationship MECE }* ,
    tuple of co-existence relationship MECE = (word, { a tuple list with MECE, co-existence frequency }*)

The co-existence frequency is an occurrence ratio that a set of *elements* has the co-existence relationship MECE for a certain word.

3 Processing Method

Fitness

It is necessary to judge whether the co-existence relationship to be useful in the editing environment is consistently adaptable to its own *Feature* when the *element* should be activated. For this purpose, we use the measurement of fitness. If the value of fitness is higher it is said that the *element* is more adaptable to the editing environment. The fitness $Fit(\mathbf{E}, \mathbf{F})$ of *element* (or *elements*) $\mathbf{E}$ with the co-existence relationship for *focus element* (or *focus elements*) $\mathbf{F}$ is computed on the basis of both the tuple list of co-existence relationships, contained in *Feature*, and the co-existence relationship, attended to the *focus element*. The flow-like procedure is shown in Figure 3. In this case, this processing can be performed only when the number of *element* sets for tuple list of co-existence relationships is equal to the number of *elements* in the *focus element*. The co-existence relationship in the *focus element* is looked upon as the weighted index vector $\mathbf{f}$. The weighted index vector can be composed by double weighted processing for these indexes, after the indexes have been extracted by the lexical analysis and un-used terms from the extracted indexes have been deleted. $Fit(\mathbf{E}, \mathbf{F})$ is defined as follows: here, " $\Sigma_{i=1, n} X_i$ " is a summation of n variables X_i from 1 to n, in this paper.

$$Fit(\mathbf{E}, \mathbf{F}) = \Sigma_{i=1, n} \{ totalSim(srt_i, \mathbf{f}) \}.$$

Where, srt_i ($1 \leq i \leq n$, n: number of tuples) is a tuple of co-existence relationship in *Feature* of *element* $\mathbf{E}$. $totalSim(srt_i, \mathbf{f})$ is a summation of the similarity between tuple list of co-existence relationship for the *element* set and that in the *focus element*.

The similarity is computed as the summation of weighted index vector for *cosine* function between *element* set and *focus element*. Thus, $totalSim(srt_i, \mathbf{f})$ is estimated as follows:

$$totalSim(srt_i, \mathbf{f}) = \Sigma_{j=1, m} \{ \cos(\mathbf{es}_{ij}, \mathbf{f}) \times w_j \}.$$

Where, $\mathbf{es}_{ij}$ ($1 \leq j \leq m$, m: number of *element* sets) is a weighted index vector in *element* sets of co-existence relationship srt_i, and w_j is the co-existence frequency for an *element* set.

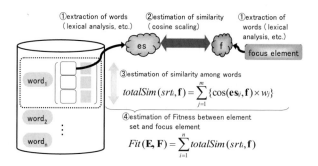

Fig. 3. Estimation of Fitness

Generality

The generality is a criterion to indicate how generic the logically established co-existence relationship keeps in the document preparation support environment. Namely, the co-existence relationship with high generality is looked upon as a successful relationship in our support environment. The generality $Gen(\mathbf{F})$ in *focus element* **F** is computed from both co-existence relationships in all support environments and these in the *focus element*. In this case, the generality is effective for the co-existence relationship when the number of *focus elements* is equal to the number of *element* sets. $Gen(\mathbf{F})$ is as follows:

$$Gen(\mathbf{F}) = \Sigma_{i=1,\,n} \{ \cos(\mathbf{f}, \mathbf{e}_{\mathrm{s}i}) \times c_i \}$$

Where, c_i ($1 \leqq i \leqq n$, n: number of co-existence relationships) is the co-existence frequency in the effective support environment. $\mathbf{e}_{\mathrm{s}i}$ is a weighted index vector for the *element* set in the co-existence relationship. **f** is a weighted index vector of *element* sets in the *focus element*.

Agent Behavior between Co-existence Relationships

Each *element* decides its own behavior on the basis of *focus elements* indicated from sensors. The judgment function, first of all, computes the fitness for *focus element* and the generality of *focus element*. After then, two decision making processes are selected, corresponding to the following cases:

Case 1: in *focus element*

In this case, the *element* judges whether it in itself should be deleted. The judgment is dependent on:

- Is the co-existence relationship in the *focus element* adaptable to self?
- Which is the co-existence relationship in the *focus element* more general in two situations such as self-existence or self-non-existence?

In order to estimate the above two terms the generality $Gen(\mathbf{F\text{-}E})$ is computed. When $Fit(\mathbf{E}, \mathbf{F}) <$ threshold and $Gen(\mathbf{F}) < Gen(\mathbf{F\text{-}E})$, the *element* itself proposes "deletion" operation to the user.

Case 2: not in *focus element*

In this case, the *element* judges whether it in itself must be moved from the *focus element*. The judgment term is:

- Is the co-existence relationship in the *focus element* adaptable to its own situation?

When threshold < *Fit*(**E**, **F**), the *element* can propose "addition" operation to the user.

4 Prototype System

The prototype system was implemented by JAVA (J2SE version 1.4) with a view to supporting the work of document preparation. This system provides the preparation functions for manipulating logically organized documents by looking upon the *elements*, such as sub-components in the query list and the logic tree, as basic operation units. The interface in our prototype system consists of four composite parts as shown in Figure 4.

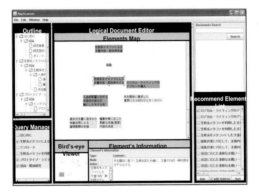

Fig. 4. Interaction window

5 Conclusion

In this paper, we proposed a framework for composing logically documents, and also implemented the prototype system. Our research viewpoint is how to compose the logically organized document. Our model and its prototype system were designed and implemented according to the following requirements:

- to compose logically documents by making use of existing knowledge;
- to provide cooperative environment for users;
- to support the logical implication.

Our prototype system can satisfy these requirements sufficiently, but must be practically evaluated through the trial use cases.

References

[1] Tansley, A.G.: The User and Abuse of Vegetational Concepts and Terms. Ecology 16(3), 284–307 (1935)
[2] Teruta, K., Okada, K.: Logical Thinking. Toyo Keizai Chinho-sha (2001) (in Japanese)
[3] Teruya, K.: Logical Writing. Toyo Keizai Chinho-sha (2006) (in Japanese)
[4] Nakakoji, N., Fischer, G.: Intertwining Knowledge Delivery, Construction and Elicitation: A Process Model for Human-Computer Collaboration in Design. Knowledge-Based Systems Journal: Special Issue on Human-Computer Collaboration 8(2-3), 94–104 (1995)

How Intranet Has Been Evolving in Banking: A Longitudinal Research

Mariano Corso[1], Antonella Martini[2], and Alessandro Piva[1]

[1] School of Management, Politecnico di Milano, 20133 Milano, Italy
[2] Faculty of Engineering, University of Pisa, 56122 PISA, Italy
{Mariano.Corso,Alessandro.Piva}@polimi.it,
Antonella.Martini@dsea.unipi.it

Abstract. This article aims to provide the state of the art of Intranet in Italian banking industry and its evolution since 2004. The research involves a panel of banks (which covers the 80% of the Italian banking industry in terms of employees) and is based on both longitudinal case studies and survey. Two evolution era have been identified and frameworks reported. Findings reveal that, although following different paths and approaches and often without a common vision, the banks are moving more and more towards networked management of core processes with levels of integration within a 'single virtual working environment': the workspace.

Keywords: Intranet; banking industry; Working environement; longitudinal case studies.

1 Introduction

The banking system is one of the business sectors which has shown the greatest interest in the adoption and use of Intranet. From the outset, banks appreciated that this technology offered an immediate and low-cost channel to distribute to branches a broad variety of information, ranging from company directives to forms, commercial documents and internal regulations.

The flexibility of the technology involved and the availability of development skills within organizations made the banks' first steps into Intranet years ago relatively easy and gave rise to the 'spontaneous' growth of this functionality, with an excellent ratio between results in terms of efficiency and services and generally very limited investment. In recent years, the Italian banking system has seen a rapid development in tools and working modes. The aim of this article is to analyse how Intranets have been evolving in the banking industry. Results are based on evidence from empirical research undertaken in Italy by the Observatory on Intranets from 2004 to 2007. Longitudinal case studies and surveys from the Italian banking industry were undertaken. The article is structured as follows: §2 describes the framework of the study (research topic and framework); § 3 the methodology, while §4 and §5 focuses on results and future trends.

M.D. Lytras et al. (Eds.): WSKS 2008, CCIS 19, pp. 435–442, 2008.

2 Investigation Framework

This § reports the detailed definitions of the topic of research - *what* we mean by Intranet and *how* we operationalised the definitions – and the framework adopted.

The Research Topic: the what and the how. There are many definitions of Intranets, ranging from a purely technological interpretation to a functional definition. In our analysis, Intranet will be interpreted as *all the applications/services supporting business processes (primary, secondary, and of knowledge management) based on web technologies that an organization makes available to its employees.*

We define '*Intranet model*' as the combination of the macro-processes (P) supported by a specific Intranet, the functionalities (F) and the services (S) delivered to workers.

- Processes: the value chain has been used to identify the following four macro-processes (ABI Lab, 2006): Managerial processes, Marketing, customer service and vendor processes, Operations, Support processes;
- Functionalities: we classified Intranet functionalities in six main macro-categories (Dias, 2001; Phifer, 2002):Publishing, Document Management, Community, Collaborative Work, Legacy Integration, Self Service;
- Services: the above mentioned functionalities are classified into specific services on the Intranet which can be divided into two groups: informational services and interactive services.

The Research Framework. The investigation framework presents a static and a dynamic dimension. The static dimension 'takes a picture' of Intranet in a specific moment, while the dynamic view shows the trend from the beginning up to now. To build the framework, we referred to the results gathered by the Permanent Observatory on Intranet in the period 2004-06.

The identification of Intranet requirements phase starts with the definition of a strategy and a development plan that will be then translated into services and associated user requirements.

Only after a careful analysis of the internal processes and the competitive differences firms want to obtain is it possible to define the action context of the Intranet as processes, people and objectives and, as a consequence, think about both the services to supply and the most suitable technological solution to implement them. Besides, one of the fundamental determinants at the basis of the success/failure of Intranet projects is the capacity to manage the organisational change process which is embedded in Intranet development, introduction and management.

The investigation framework should also be seen in a dynamic sense. Indeed, an Intranet initiative should not be interpreted as an isolated project, but within a longer evolutionary process which through follow-up initiatives and development phases brings Intranets to assume an increasingly relevant role in facilitating and sustaining organisational change.

3   Methodology

The methodological approach used is the longitudinal multiple-case study, which has proved the most suitable given the organizational complexity of the phenomenon and the need to understand the 'how and why'. The research started in 2004 with 20 banks participating, and almost the totality of them renewed their participation in the following years.

In addition, each year, a survey was performed in order to better analyse a particular topic; as reported in the table, the overall number of respondents per year cover more than 70% of the whole Italian banking sector (per number of employees).

Table 1. The Observatory panel

	N. OF CASES (% of the Italian banking sector in terms of employees; % in terms of branches)	N. OF RESPONDENT TO SURVEY (% of the Italian banking sector in terms of employees)	FOCUS
2004	20	---	- Intranet models
2005	15 (50%; 45%)	40 (77%)	- Evolution of models - Processes - Governance choices
2006	16 (67%; 58%)	50 (80%)	- Evolution of models - Web counter - Document Management - Community & Collaboration tools
2007	15 (50%; 45%)	38 (71%)	- Evolution of models - Managerial process - Professional families

The case studies were analysed using a retrospective logic, in order to verify the evolution of the observed variables. The majority (90%) are also longitudinal cases.

Data were collected in order to acquire as much information as possible about the individual Intranet and the external context. We have used multiple qualitative and quantitative data collection methods (Yin, 1994) in order to obtain the triangulation of the acquired information. In particular, data was gathered from the following sources: Documents regarding the analysed organisation, Questionnaires, Semi-structured interviews with Intranet managers and On-line analysis of the Intranet.

The comprehensibility and completeness of questionnaires were tested by pilot interviews. In order to ensure comparative results, the protocol was structured in three sections: *strategy*, *organization* and *technology*, with a total of 71 questions.

Furthermore, the questionnaire covers quantitative and qualitative information, open and closed questions, static and dynamic data (retrospective case studies). The interviews were carried out by telephone or face-to-face. Each interview was recorded and transcribed. The use of semi-structured interviews gives interviewers and interviewees considerable freedom, while ensuring that all the relevant subjects are discussed and all the required information is collected. Hence, a check list with the subjects to cover was prepared, but the order of the questions, the topics to discuss in depth, the level of detail, the words to use etc. were defined by the interviewer during the meeting. For each case study a report was written.

4   What It Has Changed from 2004 to 2006

In this § we report first the Intranet models in banking and then their evolution in the 2004-2006 period.

Models and their Evolutions. The analysis of the services offered by the Intranets examined in the present study reveals four models which differ in terms of the main services supported (Fig. 1):

- Institutional Intranet. Offers information services, often together with advanced transactional services supporting secondary processes;
- Informational Intranet. Aimed at facilitating the diffusion of information for both primary and secondary processes;
- Operational Intranet. Supports primary processes with advanced informational and transactional services;
- 'All Three' Intranet. Advanced support (informational and operational) of multiple processes (both primary and secondary).

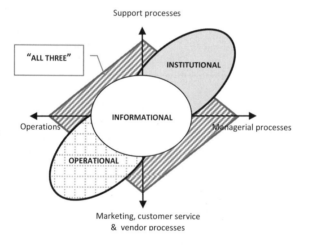

Fig. 1. Intranet models

   In the 2005 panel of 15 banks, there were 7 Informational Intranets, 3 Institutional Intranets and 5 Operational Intranets. The 2006 panel of 16 banks shows a reduction in the number of Informational and Institutional Intranets in favor of the Operational and Composite types (Table 2).

   The planned or expected development confirm this shift towards more complete models directed to core processes and not only providing support. In particular, there is a strong emphasis on marketing, customer service and vendor processes: 13 of the 16 banks declared their intention to introduce new transactional services, such as commercial desktops for managers and promoters, CRM systems, tools to manage marketing campaigns and questionnaires to collect feedback from the network.

Table 2. Intranet evolution

Year	Institutional	Informational	Operational	All three
2004	8		12	
2005	3	7	5	
2006	1	5	6	4

With regards the other macro-processes, 8 banks plan to raise the level of support to operations through, in some cases complex, projects, such as the web-counter, 7 institutions will increase support to managerial processes with the help of planning and control tools, and dash-board monitors for branch managers, while 10 banks intend to introduce new services for support processes with a particular focus on the management of human resources and self-service HR tools.

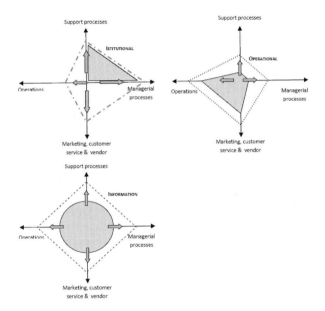

Fig. 2. Intranet model evolution

Discussion. Although the Italian banks are facing phenomena of organizational transformation, little attention is actually paid to Intranet. The great majority of the banks analyzed claims to consider the development of Intranet as 'one of a number of ICT projects', while for the remaining 34%, Intranet is one of the less important projects. The reasons cited are tied to a reductive and static vision of the Intranet, which is seen as a 'defined and consolidated project' that has already received enough investment, rather than a system to be developed incrementally through progressive enrichment of the functionality provided. Moreover, when we look in depth and assess the projects classified as important, we note a prejudice and a purely terminological distinction.

The more important projects often include web applications supporting core processes, such as the web-counter, the commercial desk, dedicated portals for product groups (finance, consumer credit, wealth management) or professional families (directors, managers, promoters), all of which could be fully part of an Intranet environment defined in broader terms. The analysis of the services and processes supported shows that although the strategic importance of Intranet is low, they are developing into environments supporting all company processes. Compared to observations in 2005, there is a progressive broadening of the Intranet environment in terms of level of process support and user-base reached. In particular, there is an increase in the coverage of marketing, customer service and vendor processes.

During 2006, Institutional Intranets have shown an increase in the level of transactional support of processes already covered (support and managerial), with a notable broadening to marketing, customer service and vendor processes. The Informational Intranets have invested in the creation of transactional services for various processes, so raising the quality of the support provided to the various company areas.

Finally, Operational Intranets, which have become the virtual working environment of some professional families, offer a natural integration of services providing information, support to people, and/or monitoring, control and planning.

The broadening of the Intranet environment has resulted in a complex model with less clearly defined boundaries (the Composite 'All Three' model) providing advanced support to multiple processes (primary and secondary).

Summary. The analyses reveal that, although following different paths and approaches and often without a common vision, the banks are moving more and more towards networked management of core processes with levels of integration within a 'single virtual working environment' that vary in function of the awareness of the strategic role of Intranet and the presence of integrated development plans for the bank's entire information system.

It has been identified a move towards the composite model ('All three') supporting multiple processes (primary and secondary) at both informational and transactional level (Fig. 2). The results revealed that advanced Intranets are going beyond the boundary of support and managerial processes to assist users across the board even in core activities typical of operational and commercial processes.

5   What It Has Been Changing Since 2006

For years Intranet was seen merely as an information channel of use in managing unidirectional communication towards. However, a new vision of Intranet it has been emerging: a tool centered and focused on people and their needs, but with a strategic objective to create a complete workspace to support employees' day-by-day operations, knowledge management, collaboration and communication processes. We named 'virtual workspace' this new working environment.

Signals for a New Intranet Era. The challenge emerging from the research seems to be that of creating integrated workspaces where people can find what they need to work, to know, to inform themselves and to integrate.

The evolution of the banking system is beginning to reveal forces pushing towards single and integrated working environments: the need to re-design the organization and its processes in the light of phenomena such as M&A and internationalization; the need to develop and manage new skills and geographically dispersed professional families; the need to control and improve processes within increasingly complex and geographically dispersed networks of competence..

A New Working Environment. In order to work effectively, each employee needs a series of supports and conditions that a company can design and provide via the virtual workspace. Four dimensions have been identified; each dimension represents a virtual personal 'space' where the worker can find what he needs to do his job, to learn, to interact with others (Fig. 3):

- *enterprise services*: as workers and citizens of their company, employees need those services (e.g. work time management, refund of expenses, job posting) and those resources (booking facilities, purchase requests, IT help desk, library system);
- *communication & socialization tools*: employees live in their working environment and try to find the answer to their socialization, sharing and membership needs there;
- *knowledge & collaboration tools*: in order to be effective, employees need access to the codified knowledge, to be connected to the professional and social network and to be able to share experience and information. These tools can be collaboration-oriented, or KM tools;
- *working tools*: to provide personal and integrated access to operative tools and information.

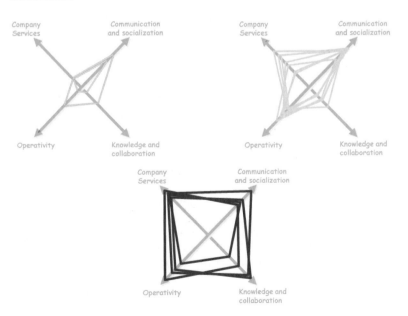

Fig. 3. The v-Workspace dimensions

It has been analysed the positioning of the Intranets of the panel on the virtual workspace framework and three evolution stages emerged: in the *focused stage* (2 cases) the workspace dimensions which are more emphasized are communication & socialisation and working tools; *composite stage* (7 cases) in which Intranet develops by combining communication & socialisation with working tools and enterprise services; *Advanced stage* (4 cases), the Intranet loses a specific focus and reaches a very high level of support of all dimensions, becoming an integrated workspace.

Compared to the multi-industry panel of 110 firms, the maturity level of Intranets in banking is higher: 31% of cases belong to advanced stage respect to 9% of the multi-industry panel.

If we analyse the single workspace dimensions, it results that Intranets of the banking panel have a higher support respect to the ones of the multi-industry panel (Table 3).

Table 3. Comparing banking to other sectors

Panel	Enterprise services	Communication & socialisation	Knowledge & collaboration	Working tools
Banking	31%	100%	25%	54%
Multi-industry	17%	73%	17%	34%

References

1. Abi Lab, Process Taxonomy, (2006) Available At: www.Abilab.It
2. Adams, J. D.: Managing Dispersed Work Effectively. Od Practitioner. vol. 33 No.1 (2001)
3. Burton B.: Best Practices For Delivering Business Value From Collaboration. Gartner Research (2005)
4. Corso M., Giacobbe A., Martini A.: Communities And Collaboration Tools In Italian Banking Industry. International Journal Of Electronic Banking. Issn 1753-5239. vol. 1, N. 1/2 (2008a)
5. Corso M., Giacobbe A., Martini A.: Rethinking Knowledge Management. The Role Of Ict And The Rise Of The Virtual Workspace. International Journal Learning And Intellectual Capital, vol. 5, No. 4 (2008b)
6. Dias C.: Corporate Portals: A Literature Review Of A New Concept In Information Management. International Journal Of Information Management. vol. 21, pp. 269--287 (2001)
7. Greer T.: Understanding Intranets. Microsoft Press (1998)
8. Harris K., Berg T.: Business-To-Employee: The Roadmap To Strategy. Gartner Group. (2002)
9. Phifer G.: A Vertical Look At Portals. Research Av-14-9816. Gartner Research, Inc (2002)
10. Tyndale P.: A Taxonomy Of Knowledge Management Software Tools: Origins And Applications, Evaluation And Program Planning. vol. 25, pp. 183--190, (Www.Elsevier.Com/Locate/Evalprogplan) (2002)
11. Yin R.: Case Study Research. Sage Publications. Beverly Hills, Ca, (1984)

Is the Digital Generation Ready for Web 2.0-Based Learning?

Vladlena Benson

Department of Informatics and Operations Management, Kingston University London,
Kingston Upon Thames KT2 7LB, UK
v.benson@kingston.ac.uk

Abstract. The growing popularity of web 2.0, particularly social networking tools, among young people makes it attractive for pedagogical use. Successful realization of web 2.0-based learning requires thorough understanding of the potential barriers influencing acceptance of web 2.0 by current and future students. This article presents the findings of a broader research into the use of web 2.0 by the digital generation, young people at the age of entering HE and current students. In conclusion, the article argues for the urgent need to educate current and future web 2.0 users about the relevant issues of privacy and information security.

Keywords: web 2.0, social networking, trust, cybertrust, web-based learning.

1 Introduction

Web 2.0 technologies represent a turning point in managing, organizing and repurposing of information and knowledge sharing [1], they promise to revolutionize education process and its established dependence on traditional Virtual Learning Environments (VLEs). Web 2.0 technologies, including social networking services, podcasts, blogging, wikis, have been driven and popularized by the younger generation [2]. Today's nineteen-twenty year olds are comfortable and agile users of web technology [3], driving the expansion of web 2.0 social applications outside informal socializing. Web 2.0 tools appear promising and valuable in educational settings, however, more careful consideration and evaluation studies are needed in order for "pedagogy 2.0" to emerge and establish itself. Focusing on the social networking services, this paper attempts to gain an insight into the social behavior and perceptions surrounding information sharing among young learner. The discussion presented in this paper is threefold. First we focus on establishing how young learners use the web and how it fits in their everyday life, employment, learning, etc. Next we explore characteristics of web 2.0 activity, learners' concerns and perceptions surrounding trust in social networking and information sharing. Finally, we discovered that being a comfortable user of technology does not necessarily include an in-depth understanding of the information security risks users of web 2.0 exposed themselves to. Threats to privacy and information security arising from social networking activity are hardly addressed in ICT education, including at HE level. This paper takes a broader look at what barriers, in addition to the perceptions of trust and privacy by learners, exist which need to be addressed for web 2.0 to become a truly popular educational tool.

M.D. Lytras et al. (Eds.): WSKS 2008, CCIS 19, pp. 443–447, 2008.
© Springer-Verlag Berlin Heidelberg 2008

2 Methodology

"Our students have changed radically. Today's students are no longer the people our educational system was designed to teach" [4].

In order to explore various aspects of web activity among representatives of the digital generation, concerns and perceptions surrounding pervasiveness of web 2.0 in their lives, an online survey was conducted. The questionnaire was administered via the SurveyMonkey facility to young individuals studying at a post 92 UK university. The questionnaire began by assessing patterns of web usage, which was examined here from three perspectives: (1) the rate of individuals' web usage (i.e. the duration of daily activities on the web), (2) the level of competency (i.e. Internet and computer proficiency), and (3) types of Internet activities (i.e. purpose of Internet usage). The rate of web usage was measured by asking respondents for how many hours a day they used the Internet. The level of competency was measured by asking respondents to rank whether they considered themselves confident users of the Internet and computers. One of the main aspects of interest to this research was the types of activities which younger students undertake on the web.

In order to investigate in more depth the issues associated with the social networking activity of students following set of questions were included in the survey. Concerns about privacy and security issues were also covered by a set of questions on perceptions of safety, information sharing and exposure of information to third parties.

The sample consisted of undergraduate and graduate students in full time higher education during 2007-2008 academic year. A total of 650 respondents completed the survey with reasonably equal participation of male (53.9%) and female (46.1%) students. Respondents' age was well representative of the digital generation as younger learners, having the mean of 20.04 (median 19) years old.

3 Social Web: An Innate Medium for Digital Learners

The use of web technology has become intrinsic to the daily lives of the digital generation of learners [3]. Recent studies [5] concur that young learners are very skilful in using technology.

3.1 Technology Aptitudes

Given that the sample of respondents came from a non-IT focused field of study, it was important to obtain an insight into their technology skill levels as a potential indicator of readiness for web 2.0 learning. The findings of this research confirm prior conclusions that younger students find themselves confident users of technology regardless of their field. Respondents reported very high levels of confidence using a computer and the Internet. Further statistical analysis of data revealed that there was no statistically significant difference between males and females in their confident use of either PC or the Internet. Also, females appear to be more likely than males to spend more than 8 hours on the Internet per day.

3.2 Patterns in Web Usage

Internet use data reported in [6] shows that students are more likely than other occupational groups to undertake communication activities online. They use web for interpersonal communication and social networking [5] forming connections and expanding their existing social circuits. Other studies established that the web has become the prevalent source of information among young individuals [7]. This study explored patterns of web usage by students, find out how the digital generation uses the web, which activities are now intrinsic to their routine lives. Respondents of the survey ranked their daily web activities in order of priority as follows:

1. As the source of information,
2. Social networking,
3. Communication,
4. Learning,
5. Entertainment,
6. Online shopping,
7. Online banking,
8. Entrepreneurship,
9. Employment.

Overall, the results helped paint a general picture of a current student with information search, communication and networking activities occupying most of their time on the web. The good news to educators is that our students are highly adapt-able to web-based learning and information gathering, and put these activities as the top of their priority list.

3.3 Perceptions of Trust and Privacy in Social Web

According to [8] those who learn more about the web, while becoming a user, might obtain a higher level of trust in technology. Dutton and Shepherd [9] argue that trust on the web and related information and communication technologies could be critical to the successful development of e-learning as well as other sectors of e-services. The findings of the survey revealed that current learners have been assimilated (or vise versa) by the social web. Respondents reported an astounding 96.7% of the sample as registered and using social networking websites. However, only 9.7% of them said that they strongly feel safe disclosing personal information through a social networking site. Furthermore, 72.1 % of the respondents never tried checking which personal information about themselves is available on the web as a result of social networking activity. According to [9] as people use the web more and gain more expertise they are likely to become less concerned over the risks of Internet use. Digital learners, as shown by the survey results, have mastered web tools and actively use them in their daily lives, the question of whether they become too trustful in the social web environment remains open for further exploration.

4 Discussion

4.1 Nature of Social Web: Student- vs. Instructor- Driven

Over the past decade we witnessed a number of important transformations in educational processes due to the emergence of the Internet, including development of e-learning in its own right. This development was driven by educators who saw it as a potential time and cost effective alternative. Learners embraced e-learning and successfully adapted to web-based educational modes. However, with the social technology being at a very early stage, wide spread and successful adoption of web 2.0-based learning are less obvious. From the data collected through the study it was revealed that social web 2.0 is driven by the digital learners, which are its intuitive and confident users. It is possible that the informal use of social networking by students may not translate into an effective formal learning environment.

4.2 Skill Gap: Students Are Better Than Teachers?

As shown by the survey findings students spend an incredible amount of time on the web with social networking occupying one of the top places among their most popular activities. It appears to be their social comfort zone, however the preceding generation, including current instructors, have not shown an enthusiastic involvement in social networking activity or mastering the new technology tools.

4.3 Trust and Information Sharing

Recent research [9] has argued that skill levels in using the Internet determine the perceptions about trust on the web. From the survey findings it is clear that although students deem themselves as web users with high expertise, they lack an adequate education about the threats they are exposed to, especially in the web 2.0 area. The fact that students tend to be intuitive users of social networks (has anyone read an instruction manual for the safe use of Facebook?) may tell HE institutions about the need to include information security and privacy into the formal curriculum thereby protecting the digital generation against web 2.0 threats.

4.4 Lack of Web 2.0-Based Educational Frameworks

At the beginning of e-learning developments a great deal of research has been done on advancement of various e-learning models. A viable pedagogical framework for web 2.0 is yet to materialize. Besides social networking, which has an incredible potential for collaborative work among students with or without instructor mediation, has a proven set of pedagogical constructs emerged in web 2.0? University context, design, planning, development of straightforward assessment strategies, staff development needs are yet to be taken into account as factors influencing acceptance of web 2.0 –based learning in HE.

5 Conclusion

The advent of web 2.0 has caused a significant change in the way the technology is used in all sectors of the knowledge economy, including education. A deep penetration of web 2.0 into the lives of students over the recent years has raised the question of whether it is the learning environment of learners' choice. Learners seem to have developed a social world that is parallel to their everyday work and study activities; and the results of the survey of over six hundred young learners have shown an incredible level of social networking activity in HEI. While web 2.0 tools offer definite pedagogical potential, wide acceptance of web 2.0 – based learning relies on factors ranging from skill levels to trust on the web. We argue that more research into the "pedagogy 2.0" is definitely needed. Finally, it is imperative for HE institutions to integrate safety and privacy aspects of web technology into their curriculum to foster secured, trusted and appropriate use of web 2.0 applications in learning and teaching.

References

1. Shadbolt, N., Berners-Lee, T., Hall, W.: The semantic web revisited. IEEE Intelligent Systems 21(3), 96–101 (2006)
2. Aroyo, L., Dicheva, D.: The new challenges for e-learning: The educational semantic web. Educational Technology and Society 7(4), 59–69 (2004)
3. Berners-Lee, T.: The fractal nature of the web (1998) (Retrieved 07/09, 2008), http://www.w3.org/DesignIssues/Fractal.html
4. Green, H., Hannon, C.: Their space: Education for a digital generation. Demos, London (2007)
5. Prensky, M.: Digital natives, digital immigrants. On the Horizon MCB University Press, 9(5) (2001), http://www.marcprensky.com/writing/Prensky%20-%20Digital%20Natives,%20Digital%20Immigrants%20-%20Part1.pdf
6. Conole, G., De Laat, M., Dillon, T., Darby, J.: JISC LXP: Student Experiences of Technologies Final Report (2006) (Retrieved 7 July, 2008), http://www.jisc.ac.uk/media/documents/programmes/elearning_pedagogy/lxp%20project%20final%20report%20dec%2006.pdf
7. Dutton, W.H., Helsper, E.: Oxford internet survey 2007 report: The internet in Britain. Oxford Internet Institute, Oxford (2007)
8. White, D.: Results and analysis of web 2.0 services survey. JISC, UK (2007), http://www.jisc.ac.uk/media/documents/programmes/digitalrepositories/spiresurvey.pdf
9. MacKenzie, D.: The certainty trough. In: Dutton, W.H. (ed.) Society on the Line, pp. 43–46. Oxford University Press, Oxford (1999)
10. Dutton, W.H., Shepherd, A.: Trust in the internet as an experience technology. Information, Communication & Society 9(4) (2007)
11. Devedzic, V.: Key issues in next-generation web-based education. IEEE Transactions on Systems, Man, and Cybernetics, Part C – Applications and Reviews 33(3) (2003)
12. Johnson, S.: Everything bad is good for you: How today's popular culture is actually making us smarter. Penguin Books, London (2005)
13. Kohut, A., Parker, K., Keeter, S., Doherty, C., Dimock, M.: A portrait of generation next, Washington DC, USA (2007), http://people-press.org/reports/pdf/300.pdf

Lean Six Sigma Applied to Supply Chains within a Services Organisation – A Practical Solution

Nuran Fraser[1] and John Fraser[2]

[1] MMU Business School
[2] GE Money

Abstract. Although there are differences between the Lean and Six Sigma approaches as well as the difference between a manufacturing and services environment, there were also some key learnings demonstrated. Certainly some of the key issues uncovered is that clear objectives combined with accurately set parameters and data gathering aligned with stakeholder buy-in is key to the success of a project of this nature. The implications and strategy adopted by the services company are borne out with the results as outlined in this study and further supports the deployment of a carefully thought through L6S programme within services supply chains.

1 Introduction

Lean Six Sigma has been around in business as a form of quality programme for more than two decades now. Established by Motorola in the mid-Eighties, it has since been adopted by a number of very high profile organisations including Boeing, Kodak and GE. What has sometimes been questioned by businesses is the tangible value that a programme such as L6S delivers. This is particularly true in services where there are many intangible processes and effects that require careful thought so that a true measure may be defined. Historically, the first firms to grasp L6S were mainly in the manufacturing sector. This was due to the fact that the core Six Sigma methodology revolved around the reduction of defects in a process. As with Aircraft Engines, this might be a defect in the width of a piece of steel for use in the manufacture of a turbo fan engine. This might typically lead to a catastrophic failure, so a solid quantitative methodology lends itself well to the prevention of problems in this type of scenario.

Services by its nature is very often bound by time in terms of the processes that are run and lead to the delivery of an outcome that then benefits a customer. This is where Lean comes in as a methodology that looks at how waste (in terms of time) may be taken out of process and allows that process to become more efficient and, in turn, builds capacity. This is where the focus of this paper will be, however to better outline the building blocks of Six Sigma we need to first look at the methodology.

M.D. Lytras et al. (Eds.): WSKS 2008, CCIS 19, pp. 448–460, 2008.

2   Research Methodology

2.1   Secondary Research

The authors have performed extensive reading on supply chain management and on the application of Lean 6 Sigma methodologies, in order to provide a good theoretical background on the subject being studied. This has included books, academic journals, Newspaper and magazine articles, and Internet sources.Illustrations to support the theories can be found along the text of this paper.A list of all the literature and sources of information used for the outcome of this work can be found in the reference section of this paper.

2.2   Primary Research

The main thrust of this paper revolves around a project run at GE within its customer services department with the objective of improving a process, eliminating waste and building capacity in the department.

3   A Case Study for Best Practice Deployment of L6S in a Services Environment

The case study that will be used for this paper centres around the National Grid, who as a client of GE Fleet Services, required renewal prompts for its vehicles to be issued to drivers in a timely and resource efficient manner. Please note that the case and the associated opinions as outlined in this paper in no way represents the opinions of either GE or the National Grid and are those of the authors of this paper only. Please note that the screen shots act as section headings throughout.

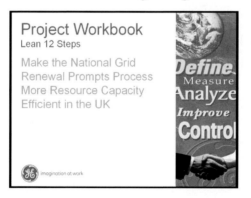

As discussed in the initial section of this paper, the first step in a L6S project is to define what is being undertaken and what represents success.

Identifying the CTQ or what is 'Critical To Quality' is the first step and is ultimately what the customer wishes to gain from this exercise. The Big Y is the Yield that is expected to result and the little y represents a measure of this Big Y. In this case, the

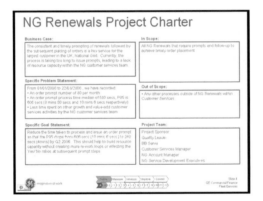

Voice of the Customer is expressed as:'Need to reduce the amount of time taken to issue and manage order prompts. From the point that drivers are identified for a prompt to the point that it is issued by email is using too much resource capacity in terms of time'. The Big Y is then defined as to 'Free up resource capacity when running renewal prompts' The measure associated with this or the little y is then defined as 'Time spent running prompts. This process of defining the CTQs is completed with the customer's approval and buy-in.

As a next step, the Project Charter is then drawn up and populated with relevant details covering the business case, objectives, scope, timelines and team involved in delivering on the customer's CTQs. The separate sections as outlined in the charter above are outlined below by way of an explanation of the steps involved:

3.1 Business Case (Reason to Run with This Project)

The consistent and timely prompting of renewals followed by the subsequent placing of orders is a key service for the largest customer in the UK, National Grid. Currently, the process is taking too long to issue prompts, leading to a lack of resource capacity within the NG customer services team.

3.2 Specific Problem Statement (Clearly Quantify What the Problem Is)

From 01/01/2006 to 22/03/2006 , we have recorded:

- An order prompt number of 80 per month
- An order prompt process time median of 530 secs; P95 is 606 secs (8 mins 50 secs and 10 mins 6 secs respectively)

This has resulted in less time spent on other growth and value-add customer services activities by the National Grid customer services team.

3.3 Specific Goal Statement

Reduce the time taken to process and issue an order prompt so that the P95 drops from 606 secs (10 mins 6 secs) to 240 secs (4mins) by Q2 2006. This should help to build resource capacity without creating more re-work loops or effecting the Yes/ No ratios at subsequent prompt steps. Note that the median is the mid-point of a set of data, not the mean or average. Whether to use the mean or the median is determined by the nature and spread of the data. So, for the numbers, 1, 20, 45, 100, 1000; the median is 45. The average would be all of the numbers added together and divided by 5.As for the P95 reference, this relates to the percentile of a group of numbers. The P95 relates to the 95th percentile and means that in this case 95% of all prompts are issued within the time specified. So, the target of 240 secs or 4 mins is what we would like 95% of prompts to be processed within.

3.3.1 In Scope (What Is the Focus of This Project)
All NG Renewals that require prompts and follow-up to achieve timely order placement.

3.3.2 Out of Scope (What Is Not Being Included in the Project)
Any other processes outside of NG Renewals within Customer Services.

3.3.3 Project Team (Who Are the Stakeholders Who Will Work on This Project)
- Project Sponsor
- Quality Leader
- BB Serve
- Customer Services Manager
- NG Account Manager
- NG Service Delivery Executives.

3.4 Define Process Map

A high level process map is drawn up to highlight the areas of focus for the project. In this case, those that are outlined in yellow on this page, as follows:

1. Filter invoked and renewals identified
2. Check driver details and validate
3. Mail-merge letter and prepare email for issue
4. Dispatch to driver

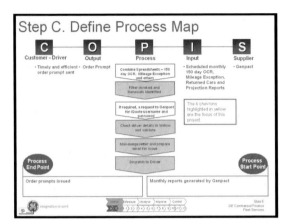

These are the areas that this project looked to improve that would in turn lead to the achievement of the specific goals as outlined.

3.5 Select CTQ (Critical to Quality) Characteristics

The CTQ characteristics are then outlined and this relates back to where the improvement is being made within the business.

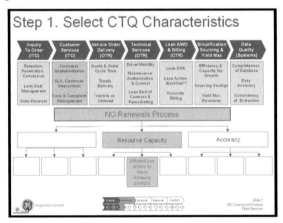

3.6 Define Performance Standards

This step is one of the most critical as it outlines very clearly what is being targeted for improvement and how the various processes may be defined to ensure that the desired performance is achieved. Starting with the left hand box and then working down the table to the right:

3.6.1 Voice of Customer (as Previously Stated)
Need to reduce the amount of time taken to issue and manage order prompts.

3.6.2 Unit Definition – Processed Order Prompt (What Unit Are We Measuring)

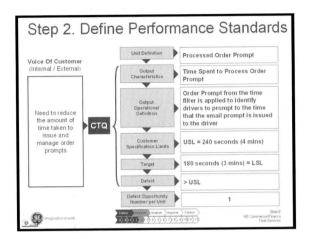

3.6.3 Output Characteristics - Time Spent to Process Order Prompt

3.6.4 Output Operational Definition
Order Prompt from the time filter is applied to identify drivers to prompt to the time that the email prompt is issued to the driver.

3.6.5 Customer Specification Limits
USL = 240 seconds (4 mins) – USL stand for the Upper Specification Limit and this,as you may recall, is with the P95 measure.

Target - 180 seconds (3 mins) = LSL – this is the ideal situation for the customer and is regarded as the Lower Specification Limit (LSL).

3.6.6 Defect
This is basically saying, what represents a defect in this process and the definition of a defect is if the time taken is greater than the Upper Spec Limit, > USL.

3.6.7 Defect Opportunity Number per Unit
This is asking how many opportunities per prompt are there for a defect to occur. As the defect is defined as total time taken for prompt to be identified and then issued this is 1.

3.7 Measurement System Analysis

This step looks to identify how a particular measuring system may or may not affect the recording of processes or parts under investigation. For example, using a digital stopwatch for a sprint race will record a very accurate time with little bias added from the stopwatch itself in terms of +/ - fractions of a second. However, if a wall clock was used with no second hand, then the only unit that could be measured would be minutes and for a sprint race this would not be sensitive enough. Indeed even with a second hand, the clock may still not have the accuracy required to record a faithful time.

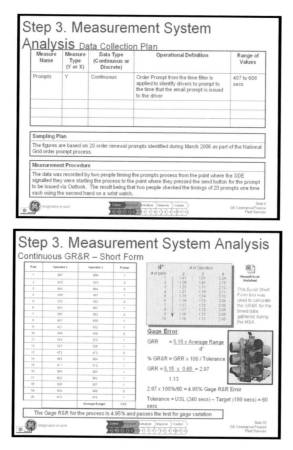

For this project, the following procedure was outlined and followed:

3.7.1 Operational Definition of the Measurement

Order Prompt from the time filter is applied to identify drivers to prompt to the time that the email prompt is issued to the driver.

3.7.2 Sampling Plan (What Is Measured to Determine the Bias of the Gage)

The figures are based on 20 order renewal prompts identified during March 2006 as part of the National Grid order prompt process.

3.7.3 Measurement Procedure

The data was recorded by two people timing the prompts process from the point where the SDE signalled they were starting the process to the point where they pressed the send button for the prompt to be issued via Outlook. The result being that two people checked the timings of 20 prompts one time each using the second hand on a wrist watch. A short form gauge R&R was then run on the 20 observations and it was found that the gage would not a bias beyond any reasonable level and that the project could be based around the measures as taken using the second hand of a watch.

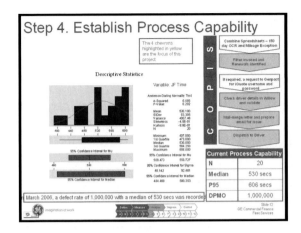

3.8   Establishing the Process Capability

This step essentially quantifies where the process sits today. This is achieved in this case using a statistical tool to provide a measure. Looking at the bottom right hand table outlines the capability as follows, based on 20 observations:

- N = 20 (observations)
- Median = 530 seconds
- P95 = 606 seconds
- DPMO = 1,000,000

The above basically demonstrated that the process was completely defective and that not one of the prompts issued met with the customers desired Upper Specification Limit as previously defined.The second slide illustrates in a graphic format a similar conclusion, that the USL = 240 seconds and the observations as measured are well above that time.

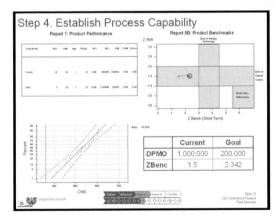

3.9 Value Added Goals

This step allows a summary of the value added tasks that are key to this process happening and also outlines the non value added tasks that can occur within this process. The aim being to maximise the value added tasks and reduce or eliminate the non value added tasks.

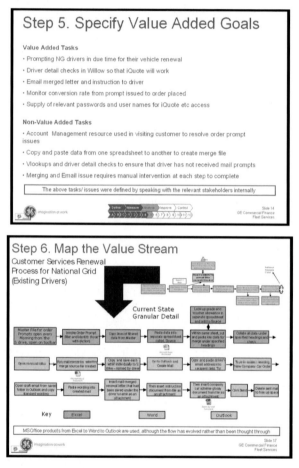

4 Mapping the Value Stream (VSM)

Moving into the Analyse phase, the objective here is to walk the process and ensure that it is fully representative of the process being measured. This involved sitting with the operator as they went through the process and recording each step with a description of the activity. The length of time that it took for each step was also measured as well as any waste in between those steps.Colour coding was used to differentiate between one application as used and another. In this case, all were MS office products but they had been used in a piecemeal manner and the process had evolved around these rather than being something that was carefully conceived and deployed.

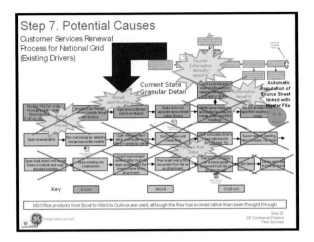

4.1 The Next Stage Is to Look at Potential Causes

This allows an objective view of the process and highlights and isolates causes of wasted time. In this instance, a lot of manual intervention, re-keying, verification and manual mail-merging being the main issues.

4.2 Establish a New Process Flow

Through workouts and drilldowns on the various steps along with the input of stake-holders including IT, a new flow was developed that allowed a large number of the non value added steps to be removed and a new process to be implemented that allows for a more streamlined and accountable output. The key to the new flow was in allowing the various applications to operate more effectively by both optimising their performance individually and also in heling them to talk more efficiently between each other.

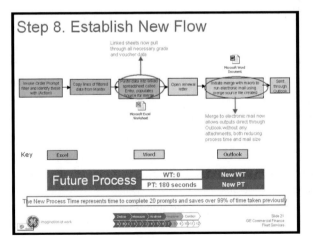

This was achieved by making the filtering process more automated within Excel, so that relevant data was pulled through to an appropriate template and also merging directly to a email message rather than merging to a word document to create a letter, then saving that letter and sending the combined as part of an email message.

The end result is that through all of this change and refinement, the process time for 20 prompts was reduced to 180 seconds combined, representing a time saving of 99% over what was achieved before.

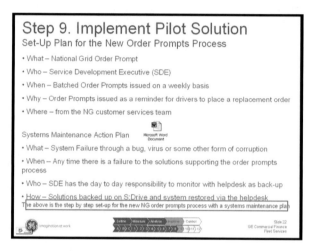

4.3 Implementing the Pilot Solution

This step basically outlines the various stages required to complete the new process and represents a workplan with roles and responsibilities for anyone looking at understanding how the new process will work from an operational perspective.

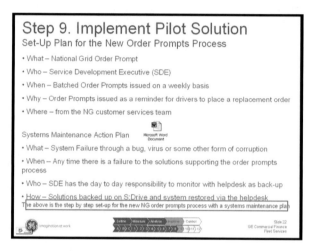

4.4 MSA at Step 10

The key at this step is to measure the 'X' rather than the 'Y'. So, where the Y is the main yield or output, then the X is the variable that affects the Y. For example, (X1 + X2 + X3 + X4) = Y. There may be many variables that affect the Y. In this instance, the inputs in terms of the refining of the applications used and the efficiencies in the manner in which they talk to each other means that in this case the measurement of the Xs are closely matched with the Y. So a measure of the time taken to issue the prompts and a record is what is shown here. This is where the 180 seconds for 20 prompts can be clearly seen and the reduced file size is illustrated.

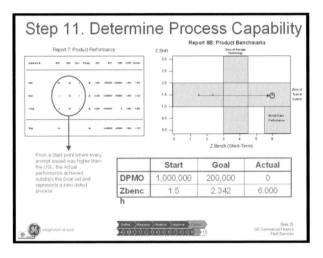

4.5 New Process Capability

Once the new process has been established, the capability of the process may be measured. Due to the prompts being issued at a rate of 20 in 180 seconds, this represents a capability of 6 sigma and a defect rate of 0.

4.6 Implement Process Control

The aim of this step is to ensure that the new process does not lapse back to a previous state and the benefits of the new method is lost. The tool used here was a Failure Modes and Effects Analysis (FMEA) that basically looks at the severity, occurrence and detectability of factors that may arise such as systems failure or different operators running the prompts that may then have an adverse affect on performance.These project conclusions more or less speak for themselves and can be read and understood as is. One of the key aspects here is that a project with a relatively short timeframe (6 weeks) was able to achieve such significant improvements and in turn both meet the needs of the external customer and the GE business. This project subsequently received recognition from the business sponsor and quality leader in the form of an award.

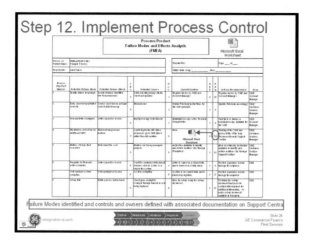

5 Conclusion

Lean Six Sigma has had a great deal of practitioner and academic coverage over the past year or two as organisations such as the NHS has embraced the methodologies to enhance and refine their processes. However, there has also been a great deal of scepticism shown by the industry at large as to the costs and timescales for delivery of such improvements. This GE project clearly demonstrates the value of a well applied L6S method to solve a process problem within a services environment in a timely manner and create capacity in an over-stretched customer services department. There are lessons that can be learned here to benefit the further work of the Knowledge Society. The society should look to champion the ease of application of Lean through the use of a simple and transparent methodology that may be widely accepted and understood across both the public and private sectors.

References

Bendell, T.: Qualityworld – What is Six Sigma? The Chartered Quality Institute, London (2000)

Brook, Q.: Six Sigma and Minitab – A Tool Box Guide for Managers. Black Belts and Green Belts QSB Consulting Ltd. (2004)

George, M.: The Six Sigma Way. McGraw-Hill, New York (2000)

Geroge, M.: Lean Six Sigma For Service. McGraw-Hill, New York (2003)

Christopher, M.: Logistics and Supply Chain Management – Strategies for Reducing Cost and Improving Service, 2nd edn. Financial Times Pitman, London (1998)

Porter, M.: Competitive Advantage: Creating and Sustaining Superior Performance. Free, London (1998)

Ross, D.F.: Distribution: Planning and Control. Chapman & Hall Materials Management/ Logistics Series, Boca Raton (1995)

Donnelly, T., Mellahi, K., Morris, D.: European Business Review. Bradford 14(1), 30 (10 pages) (2002)

Van Weele, A.: Purchasing and Supply Chain Management: Analysis, Planning and Practice, 3rd edn. Thomson Learning, London (2002)

Walters, D.: Operations Strategy. Palgrave Macmillan, Basingstoke (2002)

The Project Manager as Knowledge Creator and Communicator Analyzed with the Help of the Theatre Metaphor for Conscious Experience

Kaj U. Koskinen[1] and Pekka Pihlanto[2]

[1] Industrial Managenet and Engineering
Tampere University of Technology, Pori
Pohjoisranta 11, P.O.Box 300, FI-28101 Pori, Finland
kaj.koskinen@tut.fi
[2] TSE Business and Innovation Department
Turku School of Economics
Rehtorinpellonkatu 3, FI-20500 Turku, Finland
Pekka.Pihlanto@tse.fi

Abstract. This conceptual paper describes a project manager's knowledge creation and communication with the help of the theatre metaphor for conscious experience. At the beginning of the paper the concept of project manager is described. Then the notions of knowledge creation and communication are highlighted, followed by a detailed depiction of the theatre metaphor. And finally a project manager's knowledge creation and communication is described with the help of the theatre metaphor.

Keywords: project manager; knowledge creation and communication; theatre metaphor; human brain.

1 Introduction

Project management is the dynamic process of leading, co-ordinating, planning, and controlling a diverse and complex set of processes and people in the pursuit of achieving project objectives (Pinto and Kharbanda, 1995). That is, the successful management of projects is both a human and a technical challenge, requiring a far-sighted strategic outlook coupled with the flexibility to react to conflicts and problem areas as they arise on a daily basis. This means that a project manager participates continuously in ongoing processes of evaluating alternatives for meeting an objective, in which expectations about a particular course of action impel him or her to select that course of action most likely to result in attaining the objective. In other words, a project manager is a participant in uninterrupted situations where new knowledge is created.

However, in a project work context knowledge creation is often a complex task. This is due to the fact that the individuals involved in project planning and deliveries are often a set of diversely thinking people with different needs and opinions. Therefore, the personality of a project manager plays an important role in how the project is executed.

M.D. Lytras et al. (Eds.): WSKS 2008, CCIS 19, pp. 461–467, 2008.

It is obviously very important to know how a project manager's knowledge creation process is structured and how it functions. Therefore, the goal of this conceptual paper is to describe the project manager's knowledge creation process with the help of the theatre metaphor presented by Baars (1997). In the pursuit of this goal the following discussion first describes the concept of project manager. Then the discussion deals with the notion of the theatre metaphor. And then follows the main content of this paper – an analysis of the project manager's knowledge creation process.

2 Project Manager

Nowadays project managers must take a significant role in the change process by engaging in personal transformation, and become coaches and facilitators serving others. Sustainability and continuity of knowledge creation initiatives are much more prevalent in organisations where leaders who lead by learning are fully engaged in the process. However, project managers may be unaware that their behaviour is inconsistent with what they espouse. They cannot see themselves and they need others to help them to do this.

According to Pinto and Kharbanda (1995), a consensual leadership style is wasted, unless the members of the team have access to and are able to collect necessary knowledge. This means that the effective project manager must have good interaction relationships with four groups of people, namely interaction relationships with customers, subordinates, peers, and superiors, i.e. project stakeholders.

Fortunately, nowadays project management has begun to emphasise behavioural management over technical management, and situated leadership has also received more attention (e.g. Lytras and Pouloidi, 2003). Effective interpersonal relations have also become an important contributory factor in sharing knowledge between the project stakeholders. Project managers now need to be able to talk with many different people in many different functions and situations.

However, to be able to share useful knowledge, the project manager has to create it effectively. A basic condition for this is that he or she understands the conditions of mental processes by which knowledge creation is realised in a human mind. So next we concentrate on the nature and structure of these mental processes.

3 Knowledge Creation and Communication

The individual people – project managers in our case – use *meaning* as their basic form of knowledge creation. All kinds of knowledge a project manager acquires, understands and creates is represented in the form of meanings. As a means for forming meanings they use their *consciousness* i.e. their thinking processes or mind. (e.g. Luhmann, 1986; about meanings and consciousness in connection of the so-called holistic concept of man, HCM, see Rauhala 1986, 1988; Pihlanto, 2000, 2002).

The basic mode of knowledge creation, i.e. consciousness, is defined in the following way: psychical-mental activities constitute, in the form of recurring processes, the consciousness of a project manager. An object in a special situation, for example a task in a project, provides the consciousness with a meaningful content. A meaning emerges in the consciousness as this content becomes referred to the object located in the situation in such a manner that the project manager understands what the object implies (Pihlanto, 2000, 2002). This means that a project manager can understand an object only in terms of meanings. The network of all meanings accumulated in the consciousness is called the *worldview* of an individual (in psychological terms, worldview is about the same as "memory"). The worldview is recurrently redefined as new meanings emerge on the basis of new contents from one's situation.

Everything in this process occurs in terms of *understanding*, which means that a project manager interprets phenomena and objects located in his or her situation in terms of their 'being something'. Understanding is complete only after a meaning is generated.

Knowledge communication actually means transfer of knowledge between the worldviews of individuals, and to be transferred genuinely, knowledge must be understood in the consciousness of the receiving party (Pihlanto, 2000, 2002; Koskinen and Pihlanto, 2006). These personal worldviews are derived from the individuals' previous experiences, i.e. previous understanding, which is stored into their worldviews in the form of meanings.

4 The Theatre Metaphor

4.1 The Stage of the Theatre

The theatre metaphor describes the functioning and nature of certain brain modules and the consciousness (the mind), which are essential for an individual's thinking processes – knowledge creation included. The basic idea of this metaphor is that the human brain and consciousness work together like a *theatre*. A central feature of this metaphor is that the conscious experience of a person is strictly limited by capacity. According to the theatre metaphor, conscious experience is realized on the "stage of the theatre, in the spotlight of attention," while the rest of the stage corresponds to the immediate working memory (Baars 1997: 41-42).

4.2 The Players on the Stage

In the theatre metaphor, the *players or actors* appearing under the spotlight of the stage are defined as the contents of conscious experience. Conscious contents emerge when the spotlight of attention falls on a player. Keen competition and cooperation occur between the different players trying to reach the stage. The players are of three origins: *inner and outer senses,* and *ideas*. Inner senses introduce such players as visual imagery, inner speech, dreams and imagined feelings. Outer senses produce seeing, hearing, feeling, tasting and smelling sensations. Ideas consist of imagined and verbalized ideas as well as fringe consciousness and intuitions. (Baars 1997: 43-44, 62-93).

Applying the terms of the holistic concept of man, all these players are types of *meanings* appearing in the consciousness of a project manager. Outer sensations are meanings formed from objects located in the situation at hand. Inner speech and imagination correspond to meanings usually recalled from the worldview. Inner speech-type meanings are "heard" in speech form in the consciousness. Correspondingly, visual imagery represents meanings experienced in a visual form.

4.3 Context Operators

Behind the scene there are executive processes – *context operators* – such as *director*, *spotlight controller* and *local contexts*. They set the background against which the "brightly lit" players play their roles. Context is defined as any source of *knowledge* that shapes conscious experiences, without itself being conscious (Baars 1997: 115-118). Local contexts may be called the scenery of the stage.

Baars (1997) does not clearly separate *director* and *spotlight controller*. Therefore, we apply these concepts synonymously using the term *director*. The director performs executive functions and maintains long-term stability in a person's experiences (Baars 1997: 142).

In terms of the holistic concept of man, *context operators* refer to certain unconscious content in the project manager's worldview, which shapes and guides conscious experience.

4.4 The Audience of the Theatre

The players in the spotlight are the only ones capable of disseminating knowledge to the *audience* consisting of specialized expert organs in the brain, which represent the unconscious resources of memory, knowledge and automatic mechanisms (Baars 1997: 44-45). Members of the audience share a vast network connecting each to another, enabling them to carry out routine tasks without consciousness. The audience includes *memory systems, interpreting conscious contents, automatisms,* and *motivational systems*, which are triggered when their "calling conditions" appear: for instance, a visual experience may trigger a linguistic analysis or object recognition (Baars 1997: 44-46).

The spotlight selects the most important events on the stage, which are then distributed to the audience consisting of unconscious routines and knowledge sources (Baars 1997: 42, 46-47).

In terms of the holistic concept of man, the audience is located in the worldview – the cumulative inventory of previous understanding. Objects in the situation are understood in relation to this previous understanding, which is according to the theatre metaphor, stored in the "separate automatic units created in the past with the help of consciousness."

According to the theatre metaphor, the project manager's consciousness and brain function in the way described above, while he or she is creating new knowledge and communicating it to other people in the project work setting. In the following, we demonstrate in more detail the nature of the project manager's work by applying the theatre metaphor.

5 Knowledge Creation and Communication in the Theatre of Consciousness of the Project Manager

With the help of the theatre metaphor it is possible to understand the anatomy of knowledge creation and communication in quite an different way than applying, for instance, the common *Homo economicus* metaphor, according to which the project manager is a pure rational stimulus-response type individual.

According to the theatre metaphor, everything that a project manager can be aware of is called *players,* which appear in the spotlight of attention on the *stage* of working memory. The players are in a competitive relationship with each other while trying to reach the spotlight. As a project manager is creating knowledge, in principle, players of all three origins – inner and outer senses, and ideas – are struggling together to get in.

The starting point for a project manager's knowledge creating process may be a player called an *idea*, which the manager imagines in his or her consciousness (mind) – or in the spotlight of attention.

Into this process enter also such *inner sensations* concerning the task at hand in a project work: the project manager hears inner speech and imagines things with the "mind's eye". Inner speech may correspond to a real conversation, containing arguments and counterarguments.

Because project work is essentially a team activity enterprise, already at the beginning of the knowledge creation process players from outside – i.e. inputs by *outer senses* - enter on the stage. These include observations based on different kinds of written sources, but also comments, questions and answers by the project team members. These players may represent, for instance, facts, but also pure opinions. Anyway, all these represent inputs – meanings – to the project manager's knowledge creation process.

Players provided by inner and outer senses do not play their role among themselves only, but participants such as the *director* have their say. In a manager's mind there is a "control unit", which makes choices and presents objections as to the suggestions appearing as players on the stage. In addition, the *scenery* defines the contexts in which the "brightly lit" players appear and play their roles. The scenery represents the project manager's source of contextual knowledge. Even if more or less unconscious, it shapes the project manager's conscious experience in the knowledge creation process.

For instance, while reading a project cost report, a multitude of contextual factors frame the project manager's attitudes towards every new piece of knowledge, and this, in turn, reflects on his or her knowledge creation.

Further, an additional source of influence affecting the players on the stage – called *audience* – is present in a project manager's knowledge creation. It represents certain unconsciously functioning modules in the brain. The audience analogy comes from the fact that also in a real theatre, players give knowledge (the lines) to the audience, and the audience influences the players by its reactions.

In the theatre metaphor, the audience comprises memory systems, interpretations, automatisms and motivational systems, which all offer highly individual and as such also potentially surprising inputs to the process of creating knowledge, i.e. the players on the stage – all this controlled by the director and under the influence of contextual aspects called the scenery.

For instance, the project manager's visual experience (e.g. a report or a look on a project team member's face) in a project meeting may trigger a linguistic analysis, object recognition or emotional response in the manager's brain. The manager himself or herself does not have to be aware of these processes, only the resulting conscious reaction – a new player (meaning) appears in the spotlight. The team members may be surprised of the manager's reaction, because the reason for it resides deep in the manager's audience or worldview.

6 Conclusions

Our basic message through this paper is that without a proper understanding of the real nature of the human actor, it is hard for the project manager to understand the behaviour of the other project stakeholders and organisational actors, and cannot therefore succeed in the project implementation in the best possible way. The theatre metaphor provides a possibility to approach the project manager's knowledge creation and communication on a decisively deeper level than is common in management studies, because the former is based on the results of modern brain research.

Perhaps the most important individual finding produced by the theatre metaphor is the notion of the *spotlight* of conscious experience. It clearly demonstrates the limitations of human experience and consciousness. This means that a project manager and also other project stakeholders are aware of only a very limited amount of knowledge. It is important to notice that the people involved in a project task do not adopt all knowledge offered to them: when a project manager communicates with people, he or she tries to get a message to appear as meanings – i.e. players – into the spotlight of their attention. Therefore, only when this message is assessed well enough by the people, it enters into the spotlight, and, consequently, he or she understands it.

As all project stakeholders' brain and consciousness function in the way like in a theatre, it is easy to imagine how challenging tasks project management and knowledge creation are. In particular, the great relevance of unconscious – a kind of instinctive – processes represented by context operators and audience suggested in the theatre metaphor, testify that human activity has typically coincidental and subjective features. Consequently, the project manager and other people involved are by no means invariably conscious, easily anticipated and always rational actors.

Of course, the project manager has to some degree of free will to assess the "suggestions" of the hidden brain modules, but can never totally master his or her knowledge creation process. This, of course, applies also to the other people involved. Therefore, the manager in charge of the project must be constantly aware of this problem area and try to critically control his or her knowledge creation process, as well as try to understand and forecast other stakeholders' reactions.

Finally, it should be realised, however, that the coincidental nature of the human brain is not only a problem for the project manager, but it also means a potential for creativity, which is a key resource in project management.

References

1. Baars, B.J.: The Theater of Consciousness. The Workspace of the Mind. Oxford University Press, Oxford (1997)
2. Koskinen, K.U., Pihlanto, P.: Competence Transfer from Old Timers to Newcomers Analysed with the Help of the Holistic Concept of Man. Knowledge and Process Management 13(1), 3–12 (2006)
3. Luhmann, N.: The Autopoiesis of Social Systems. In: Geyer, F., van der Zouwen, J. (eds.) Sociocybernetic Paradoxes, pp. 172–192. SAGE, Beverly Hills (1986)

4. Lytras, M.D., Pouloudi, A.: Project Management as a Knowledge Management Primer: the Learning Infrastructure in Knowledge-intensive Organizations: Projects as Knowledge Transformations and Beyond. The Learning Organization 10(4), 237–250 (2003)
5. Pihlanto, P.: An Actor in an Individual Situation: The Holistic Individual Image and Perspectives on Accounting Research, Series Discussion and Working Papers 4:2000, Publications of the Turku School of Economics and Business Administration, Turku (2000)
6. Pihlanto, P.: Understanding Behaviour of the Decision-maker in an Accounting Context. The Theater Metaphor for Conscious Experience and the Holistic Individual Image, Publications of the Turku School of Economics and Business Administration. Series A-1: 2002, Turku (2002)
7. Pinto, J.K., Kharbanda, O.P.: Successful Project Managers: Leading Your Team to Success. Van Nostrand Reinhold, New York (1995)
8. Rauhala, L.: Ihmiskäsitys ihmistyössä (The Conception of Human Being in Helping People), 3rd edn. Helsinki, Gaudeamus (1986)
9. Rauhala, L.: Holistinen ihmiskäsitys (The Holistic Conception of Man). Journal of Social Medicine, 190–201 (1988)

Software Engineering 2.0: A Social Global Repository Based on Semantic Annotation and Social Web for Knowledge Management

Ricardo Colomo-Palacios[1], Juan Miguel Gómez-Berbís[1],
Ángel García-Crespo[1], and Inmaculada Puebla-Sánchez[2]

[1] Universidad Carlos III de Madrid, Computer Science Department
Av. Universidad 30, Leganés, 28911, Madrid, Spain
{ricardo.colomo,juanmiguel.gomez,angelgarcia}@uc3m.es
[2] Universidad Francisco de Vitoria, Computer Science Department,
Ctra. Pozuelo-Majadahonda Km. 1.8, 28223 Pozuelo de Alarcón, Madrid, Spain
i.puebla.prof@ufv.es

Abstract. The effective management of the software development process has become an essential for business survival in an ever more competitive industry. In order to gain business strengths from the development process, organizations need to carry out software development in the most efficient manner possible, avoiding redundancy and time losses. This paper presents an architecture which combines the strengths of two technologies, Web 2.0 and the Semantic Web, as a solution to reuse and extrapolate knowledge and software products across projects and organizations.

Keywords: Software Engineering, Web 2.0, Semantic Web, Reuse, Knowledge extrapolation.

1 Introduction

The spread of Information Systems in organizational environments in recent years has turned their development into a critical task for corporations. In this setting, the crucial development process, as well as the large volumes of information which support this process, have meant that the management of the process, in the context of reutilization, extrapolation and transferability of Software Engineering (SE) elements, has become an essential research field. Additionally, the globalization of technologies, such as the Internet, and its subsequent reinvention as the Web 2.0 [1] have lead to a scenario where the possibilities for reuse and transfer of SE products are multiplied, and transcend organizational boundaries. Globalization and participation have opened up infinite opportunities for exploiting the capacities which a network of users can contribute to the software development process.

The current research is set within this background, and represents the fusion of some of the most important topics in knowledge management and knowledge reuse: the application of semantics and the integration of Web 2.0 elements. The present work proposes Social Global Repository (SGR), a tool created for the exploitation of

M.D. Lytras et al. (Eds.): WSKS 2008, CCIS 19, pp. 468–475, 2008.

the collective knowledge generated by software processes. The use of this knowledge is realized by the benefits gained from the combination of various aspects: firstly, the semantic annotation of the different products which are generated during the software development process. The second benefit is gained from the transferability between the products generated, and the last factor which is exploited is the social interaction of the users of the platform, inspired by their experiences with the products and their use of the products in projects.

2 Background

The term "Semantic Web" was coined by [2] to describe the evolution from a document-based web towards a new paradigm that includes data and information for computers to manipulate. Ontologies [3] are the technological cornerstones of the Semantic Web, because they provide structured vocabularies that describe a formal specification of a shared conceptualization. The fundamental aim of the Semantic Web is to answer the ever-growing need for data integration on the Web. It is precisely the integration of data on the Web which is the foundation that provides the starting point for the current research. Semantic Web provides a complementary vision as a knowledge management environment [4] that, in many cases has expanded and replaced previous knowledge management archetypes [5]. In other hand, Web 2.0 is seen as a new deal for software management [6].Particularly, in the SE domain, the capacities of the Semantic Web to be used as a Corpora of Reusable Contents [7] have been identified, and its potential uses for reutilization and transfer of knowledge in various environments have been established including experience management [8].

A specific example of the application of such technology is in the field of Requirements Engineering, where semantics has been used for diverse aspects such as how to apply the use of Semantic Wikis for the determination of requirements [9] or the application of semantics for Aspect-Oriented Requirements Engineering [10]. However, the efforts to integrate the Semantic Web and Web 2.0 have now gone beyond Requirements Engineering, including aspects such as the modeling of ontologies for the CMMi maturity model [11] of the software process [12], [13] or software maintenance [14]. In this specific field, which is focused on information reuse, extrapolation, and integration, in the context of software development projects, a number of initiatives have been launched to benefit from the capabilities brought about by the advent of the Semantic Web.

Possibly the most relevant initiative is the proposal to facilitate Software Reuse by searching the knowledge repository and suggesting relevant knowledge for the current task the user is performing [15]. Without a doubt, the initiative described in the current work is an innovative proposal, and which opens up new horizons for the possibilities brought about by the reuse of knowledge generated in Software Development projects. The functionalities of the tool presented in this work combine the benefits of search and organization of information offered by the Semantic Web, the transferability of the products generated by the SE process, and extend the functionalities to users by incorporating their participation using Web 2.0 tools.

3 Social Global Repository (SGR)

In our particular case, the breakthrough of adding semantic metadata to a Software Repository is the ability to enable automatic or semi-automatic sharing and discovery of a number of features. This approach is at risk of the so-called chick-en-egg problem of metadata. The provider of the service would request for a good reason, a good application or benefit, of providing the metadata. However, if the metadata is not generated, no application or value-added functionality can be achieved. Metadata is provided through the tagging system, which certainly constitutes an interesting development, since emerging folksonomies (a set of tags, useful in learning and knowledge environments [16]) are organically appearing, because a number of people are interested in particular information and are encouraged to describe it, being it rather than a centralized form of classification, a free bottom-up attempt to classify information [17]. Users are moving towards the concept of shallow ontologies which comprise relatively few unchanging terms that organize very large amounts of data, by using a set of very common and always-showing-up terms and relations.

This issue has loomed over recent sharing-oriented software projects and it is of the utmost importance for our approach. The lack of motivation and accuracy of efficiency from the user perspective in providing the metadata could hamper the SGR's full potential. However, a twofold strategy has been developed which overcomes the problem in the SGR approach:

1 Stakeholders of the SGR are gaining in terms of productivity and efficiency from the very first moment they provide metadata and use another stakeholder's metadata. The sharing of knowledge about software project elements enables a quid pro quo benefit situation as described in ProLink [18]. Particularly, the ever-changing nature of IT is the perfect growing field for various experiences that can very much help the lack of knowledge, background and expertise, by distributing the knowledge gained from these experiences across different infrastructures and environments. This can be achieved by means of sharing resources. Harnessing the potential spread of knowledge through a Social environment is not new, but must be leveraged with a technology that allows the determination of expertise that are hidden somewhere around the world wide web.

2 Metadata is also clearly creating the boundaries of sharing in organizations. There is a critical tradeoff associated with the tension between user privacy requirements, and providing persistent and increasingly broad visibility of their activities. Identity tradeoffs in community networks are even greater - in exchange for our privacy, we expect to gain a sense of security and well-being. The significance of adding privacy-enhancing technologies (PET) in virtual community networks is overwhelming [19]. In the SGR both premises are addressed since sharing of requirements and knowledge gains visibility (and it is used by a broad base of software projects stakeholders), while also protecting their privacy.

Integration of Software Requirements in the SGR conceptual framework through semantics is a growing and recognized challenge that can revolutionize IT working environments as we know them today. Nevertheless, it must rely on a consistent architecture.

Software architectures are becoming increasingly intelligent and interactive. By replacing locally managed hardcoded software structures, with an intelligent on-demand information paradigm, this model changes how business applications are delivered, bringing new levels of ease, adoption and success to the challenging area of Information Systems. In this section, we will discuss and depict the main components of our software sharing knowledge intensive platform. Conventional application architectures, at least those of interactive software applications supporting end users, have at least seven architectural layers [20]:

- Graphical User Interfaces (GUIs) in Web browsers
- User interface logic drivers
- Business Processes
- Business logic implementations
- Business rules constraining valid operations
- A persistence layer
- Storage systems for storing and recalling data

These seven layers execute any successful user request on the GUI, and any response travels through them all on the way back to the GUI. That means fourteen layers back and forth. For our particular context, it is noteworthy that our platform will be using a "semantic" data representation as well as a data-interpretation model [20]. For the sake of simplicity, we have coupled and regrouped several of these seven layers as can be seen in Figure 1.

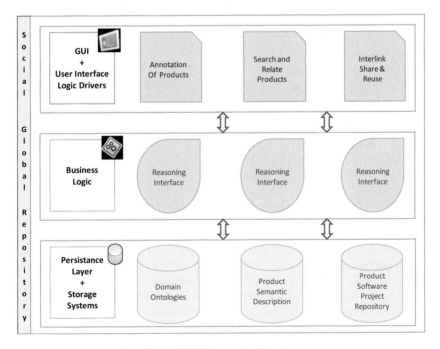

Fig. 1. SGR System Architecture

Particularly, we have grouped the first two into a presentation layer, which covers the annotation of software products, reuse, sharing and interlink, in addition to search, functionalities. Business processes and business logical implementations, together with business rules constraining valid operations are concentrated on the Business Logic layer. Finally, the persistence layer and storage systems for storing data are located in the last layer. Hence, we finally derive into the canonical three-tier architecture, due to the fact that we want to decouple the views, the business and the data access management. Each of these tiers will contain one or more subsystems.

In the following, we will present the different layers of the architecture, de-scribing the components belonging to each layer. Firstly, the User Interface and User Interface Driver layer is composed OF three components. The Annotation of Software Products component provides semantic annotation through visualization of the various semantic descriptions (and their underlying ontologies). Annotation is simply the adding of extra information asserted with a particular point in a document or other piece of information, in our case, semantic information. Secondly, the Search component, the core of the GUI provides extra functionality to find and relate software products from among the various software projects included in the SGR. The Search component is hence the entry-point to locate and retrieve software products from the whole platform. Finally, the Interlink, Share and Reuse component.

The Business Logic Layer is the added-value component of the platform. The Reasoner and Inference engine enables required reasoning capacities that would derive knowledge from the user queries and preferences related to the current semantic descriptions of a number of software products. Inference can intelligently match preferences of users and semantic descriptions for extracting new knowledge. The Business Rules engine validates if operations can be applied, and the Visibility Constraints refers to the tradeoff between public awareness and public concerns mentioned in the previous section, SGR, as discussed by [19].

The Persistence and Storage Systems layer enables data to perform the business process execution of the platform. There are three main components, namely: the Domain Ontologies, Semantic Descriptions and Software Project Repositories. Both the first and the second consist of a RDF (or another potential Semantic language, such as OWL, for that matter) semantic data store system that allows semantic querying, and offers a higher abstraction layer to enable fast storage and retrieval of large amounts of RDF while keeping a small footprint and a lightweight architecture approach. An example could be the OpenRDF Sesame RDF Storage system, which deal with data and legacy integration. Currently, we have focused for our implementation in RDF, given that the advantages of using RDF as a "lightweight" ontology language are supported by reliable implementations, software scalability and a mature base of developers and users.

In what follows, we focus on our proof-of-concept implementation, the SGR system which has been used for the management of a set of software projects, related to the European Software Agency (ESA) standard. SGR has been developed using Sun Microsystems' JEE (Java Enterprise Edition) technology. This technology has been designed to develop and run distributed and multi-layered Java applications.

In SGR, the classes that define the application's behavior implement Action interface. These classes contain a method named execute that carries out the operations needed for each kind of action and they are in charge of accessing application's model, making the appropriated modifications on it. Action classes are supported by other classes named ActionForm. These classes gather the information introduced by the user in the form, validate it and make it available for the corresponding Action class. The data layer in SGR is divided into two elements: the database that stores the control information of the application, such as login information, and the semantic repository where all the data of user's projects is stored. This semantic repository leans on a database instance to obtain persistence.

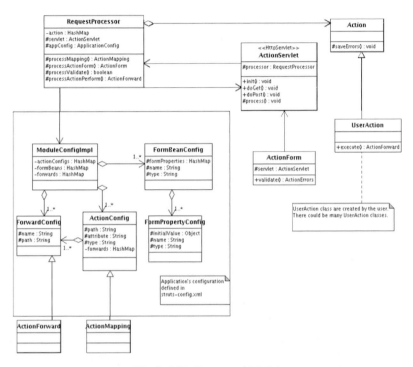

Fig. 2. SGR Conceptual Model

Jena has been used to provide semantics to SGR. Jena is a framework for Java that provides an API for writing and extracting data from RDF graphs. Jena has been chosen because, in contrast to other frameworks like Sesame, Jena provides OWL support. For improving SGR's performance, the data layer manager SDB has been chosen instead of RDB (the default database manager in Jena). It has been specifically designed to work with SPARQL, the query language developed by the W3C. The differences between them are taken from [21], the most important factor being that "RDB uses a denormalised database layout in order that all statement-level operations do not require additional joins. The SDB layout is normalized so that the triple table is narrower and uses integers for RDF nodes, then does do joins to get the node representation. In SPARQL queries, there is often a sufficiently complex graph pattern that the SDB design tradeoff provides significant advantages in query performance". The organizational aspect of SGR is arranged around projects. This means that the main unit with which the users will work is the software project. There is no possibility of working with the application without creating a project and developing it in terms of the ESA methodology for SE. Inside a software project, SGR allows the user to define any number of user requirements, software requirements, architectural components and detailed components, as well as all the relations established between them. This point gives an idea of the application's organizational model. SGR establishes that one user can work in one or more projects, each of these projects can be composed of one or more users and, as previously mentioned, the four main phases of the ESA methodology with their corresponding elements are developed in each project.

Concerning SGR's visual aspect, all the information is visually organized in the form of trees. In every page where it is necessary to show requirements (user or software requirements), components (architectural or detailed components), ontology terms, traceability matrices or search results, hierarchical trees are used.

The interaction between users and this kind of visual representation is realized as follows. If a tree node is selected, then all the information pertinent to that node is shown in the same web page, allowing the user to see all the information about an element without seeing the rest of the tree containing all the elements of the current phase.

4   Conclusions

Integration of SE products and artifacts through semantics is a growing and recognized challenge that can revolutionize the application development environment as we know it. With the rise of the Semantic Web, the ontology-based approach to social networks has gained momentum. In such a context, sharing and taking advantage of a number of information sources, tracing products and artifacts, knowledge, experience and expertise in different contexts can bridge the gap of knowledge integration and product extrapolation and reuse. In this work, we have presented a novel approach to achieve knowledge extrapolation and software lifecycle products reuse across projects and organizations through a semantics-based social network, providing an architecture and a proof-of-concept implementation.

Our future work in application areas of the framework presented will focus on the extension of the system constructed, incorporating semantic descriptions of web services, which can be developed as an additional component of the future platform. This generates an extra software product for the user, which can be reused and transferred in the same way as User Requirements, Software Requirements, and the other products which comprise the Software Development process. Therefore, this new research has the objective of offering to users of the architecture the ability to integrate web services previously disconnected to the platform, as well as benefiting from complete documentation for projects, which will be generated during a standardized development process. This characteristic, which extends the concept of free software towards new horizons, would permit users to incorporate disintegrated web services, not only at the application level, but also as a fundamental part of the corporate development process.

References

1. O'Reilly, T.: What is web 2.0? O'Reilly NetWork (June 20, 2008),
   http://www.oreillynet.com/pub/a/oreilly/tim/news/2005/09/30/what-is-web-20.html
2. Berners-Lee, T., Hendler, J., Lassila, O.: The Semantic Web. Scientific American (May 2001)

3. Fensel, D.: Ontologies: A Silver Bullet for Knowledge Management and Electronic Commerce. Springer, Berlin (2001)
4. Warren, P.: Knowledge Management and the Semantic Web: From Scenario to Technology. IEEE Intelligent Systems, 53–59 (January/February 2006)
5. Davies, J., Lytras, M., Sheth, A.P.: Semantic-Web-Based Knowledge Management. IEEE Internet Computing, 14–16 (September-October 2007)
6. Chatti, M.A., JArke, M., Frosch-Wilke, D.: The future of e-learning: a shift to knowledge networking and social software. International Journal of Knowledge and Learning 3(4/5), 404–420 (2007)
7. Tetlow, P., Pan, J.Z., Oberle, D., Wallace, E., Uschold, M., Kendall, E.: Ontology Driven Architectures and Potential Uses of the Semantic Web in Systems and Software Engineering. W3C Working Draft (2006)
8. Mohamed, A.H., Lee, S.P., Salim, S.S.: An Ontology-Based Knowledge Model for Software Experience Management. International Journal of the Computer, the Internet and Management 14(3), 79–88 (2006)
9. Decker, B., Ras, E., Rech, J., Jaubert, P., Rieth, M.: Wiki-Based Stakeholder Participation in Requirements Engineering. IEEE Software 24(2), 28–35 (2007)
10. Chitchyan, R., Rashid, A., Rayson, P., Waters, R.: Semantics-Based Composition for Aspect-Oriented Requirements Engineering. In: Proceedings of the 6th international conference on Aspect-oriented software development, Vancouver, British Columbia, Canada (2007)
11. Capability maturity model integration (CMMI), version 1.1 CMMI for software engineering (CMMI-SW, v1.1) staged representation. Technical Report CMU/SEI-2002-TR-029, ESC/TR-2002-029, Carnegie Mellon, Software Engineering Institute, Pittsburgh (2002)
12. Liao, L., Qu, Y., Leung, H.: A software process ontology and its application. In: ISWC 2005 Workshop on Semantic Web Enabled Software Engineering (2005)
13. Soydan, G.H., Kokar, M.M.: An OWL Ontology for Representing the CMMI-SW Model. In: 2nd International Workshop on Semantic Web Enabled Software Engineering (2006)
14. Hyland-Wood, D., Carrington, D., Kaplan, S.: Toward a software maintenance methodology using semantic web techniques. In: Proceedings of Second International IEEE Workshop on Software Evolvability (2006)
15. Antunes, B., Seco, N., Gomes, P.: A Software Reuse System based on the Semantic Web. In: Proc. of the 3rd International Workshop on Semantic Web Enabled Software Engineering of the European Semantic Web Conference, Innsbruck, Austria (2007)
16. Lux, M., Dosinger, G.: From folksonomies to ontologies: employing wisdom of the crowds to serve learning purposes. International Journal of Knowledge and Learning 3(4/5), 515–528 (2007)
17. Shadbolt, N., Hall, W., Berners-Lee, T.: The Semantic Web revisited. IEEE Intelligent Systems 21(3), 96–101 (2006)
18. Gómez-Berbís, J.M., Colomo-Palacios, R., Ruiz-Mezcua, B., García-Crespo, A.: ProLink: A Semantics-based Social Network for Software Project. International Journal of Information Technology and Management 7(4), 392–405 (2008)
19. Chewar, C.M., McCrickard, D.S., Carroll, J.M.: Persistent virtual identity in community networks: Impact to social capital value chains. Technical Report TR-03-01 of Computer Science Dept. at Virginia Tech.,
http://eprints.cs.vt.edu/archive/00000650/01/hcic-cmc.pdf
20. Bussler, C.: Is Semantic Web Technology Taking the Wrong Turn? IEEE Internet Computing 12(1), 75–79 (2008)
21. Jena Project, http://jena.hpl.hp.com/wiki/SDB/Query_performance

Tools for the Information System Function Management: A Roadmap

António Trigo[1], João Varajão[2], and João Barroso[3]

[1] Escola Superior de Tecnologia e Gestão de Mirandela, Instituto Politécnico de Bragança, Rua João Maria Sarmento Pimentel, Apartado 128, 5370-326 Mirandela, Portugal
trigo@ipb.pt
[2] Departamento de Engenharias, Universidade de Trás-os-Montes e Alto Douro, Apartado 1013, 5001-801 Vila Real, Portugal
jvarajao@utad.pt
[3] Grupo de Investigação em Engenharia do Conhecimento e Apoio à Decisão, Instituto Superior de Engenharia do Porto, Rua Dr. António Bernardino de Almeida, 431, 4200-072 Porto, Portugal
jbarroso@utad.pt

Abstract. Information technology and information systems have evolved dramatically over the last half-century, playing an absolutely central and crucial role in the success of today's organizations. Therefore, the complexity of the information systems function has also increased significantly, which requires the use of more evolved software tools to support the information system function activities. In this paper we present a matrix of the main tools available for the information system function, which can help Chief Information Officers to identify the right tools to use in their departments.

1 Introduction

The Information Technologies and Information Systems (IT/IS) play an absolutely central and crucial role in today's modern organizations. As time goes by it becomes clearer that without an efficient use of IT/IS, companies cannot be competitive or generate revenue and in the great majority of the cases their own survival depends on that capacity [1].

Organizations currently use multiple IT/IS solutions to support their activities at all management levels and few of them try to conduct their businesses without seeking to exploit the advantages of IT/IS solutions [2]. In order to ensure the proper operation of IT/IS, companies require an Information System Function (ISF) that is well structured and skillful, and able to provide all services that are required [2]. Commonly found services in the ISF are thus, e.g., project management, application development and maintenance, IT management, help desk, network management, and many others.

This paper presents a research work conducted on ISF activities and supporting tools. Firstly, we present and characterize the ISF and its activities. Then we

M.D. Lytras et al. (Eds.): WSKS 2008, CCIS 19, pp. 476–483, 2008.

present the different tools we found that support the ISF activities. Finally, we present a matrix, of activities versus tools, which results from the comparison of the different tools functionalities and ISF activities.

2   Information System Function Activities

In what is essentially a dynamic environment, under constant change, Information Systems (IS) play a role that is absolutely central to organizational activities, by simplifying or determining almost all organizational initiatives. As such, they must be carefully planned, designed, developed, used, and managed, in order to provide the necessary support to information needs of organizations, at their several levels and scopes [3].

Information Systems Function (ISF) is composed by the set of organizational activities aiming to optimize the organization's IS, under three main views, which provide a complete perspective [2,3]: activities (planning, development, exploitation, and management), resources (human, financial, technological, and informational), and influencing factors (structural, environmental, social, cultural, psychological, and time-related).

It's useful to conceptualize the ISF by the means of four main groups of activities [2]: Information Systems Planning (ISP), Information Systems Development (ISD), Information Systems Exploitation (ISE), and Information Systems Management (ISM), as we can see in the Fig. 1.

ISP is responsible for identifying the systems that are needed in an organization, thus preceding ISD, in charge of developing the systems identified during ISP. Afterwards, ISE is responsible for ensuring the proper usage of the IS, in the best interests of the organization. The ISM is required to provide structure and control to all these activities. ISP is a necessary precursor to ISD, since it provides a long-term vision, by identifying the potential systems and defining a full set of management policies and approaches. It is assumed that ISP is integrated and aligned with the business planning, being therefore a planning strength for

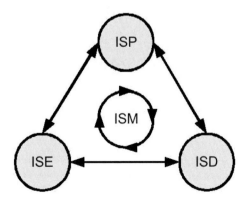

Fig. 1. ISF main group of activities. Source: [2].

organizational change, provided by ISD, since a new system frequently implies a new form of organization.

In order to support the needs of the organization as time elapses, IS must adapt to the naturally occurring changes. In this sense, it is possible to consider a cyclical and continuous sequence of ISF activities: the several activities feed each other in each system generation, and possess strong interlinks. It is possible to consider a logical sequence of activities, under which an IS is thought-over (in the scope of ISP), produced (in the scope of ISD), and then used (in the scope of ISE). However, in practice these activities take place concurrently, with significant inter-relationships and interdependences; and these relationships are strongly interactive. The several activities cannot be approached in isolation; they must be taken in account and integrated together.

There are multiple propositions for ISP, ISD, ISE, and ISM, each involving several activities [4] and denominations [5]. It is somewhat hard to come across two authors agreeing in detail over the same proposition [6]. However, in spite of all variations, their nature is mostly similar. Table 1 presents those activities that met major dissemination and are most commonly accepted for the ISF.

Table 1. ISF activities. Source: [2].

Groups of activities	Activities
Information Systems Planning	IS Strategy analysis
	IS Strategy definition
	IS Strategy implementation
Information Systems Development	IS Strategy analysis
	IS Strategy definition
	IS Strategy implementation
Information Systems Exploitation	IS Strategy analysis
	IS Strategy definition
	IS Strategy implementation
Information Systems Management	Organization and control

ISM activity is, therefore, at the ISF core, beeing responsible for [7]: the strategic alignment of the IT/IS strategy with the organization strategy, measuring the performance of the IT/IS solutions in use, risk management and accountability.

3   ISF Support Tools

Among other tools available to support the ISF, we can find frameworks, methods, techniques, models and applications. Some of the most popular tools are presented in Table 2 and described in the next paragraphs.

One kind of the tools we identified as important are the laws to which the organization must comply. Although these cannot be considered tools in a pure

Table 2. ISF main support tools

Usage	Tools
Law conformity	SOX, Basel II, HIPAA
IT strategy	IT BSC, ROI, TCO, EVA
Risk management	COSO
IT Governance	CobiT
Project management	PMBoK, PRINCE2
Systems development	CMMI, Spice
Quality management	Six Sigma, ISO 9000, TickIT
Security management	BS 17799, ISO 27000
IT services, operations and infrastructure	ITIL, ISO 20000, eTOM, BPM

way, the ISF and IS manager, must be aware of them, as being part of the requisites of the IT/IS of the organization, which are: the Sarbannes-Oxley Act [8], Basel II [9] and Health Insurance Portability and Accountability Act (HIPAA) [10], among others, depending on the field of actuation of the organization.

The IT Balanced Scored Card (BSC) is a method inspired on the BSC, a methodology of enterprise management developed by professors Robert Kaplan and David Norton at the Harvard Business School [11]. The IT BSC is derived from the organization BSC in order to translate to ISF the vision and strategy of the organization providing metrics to IT and aligning the IT strategy with the business strategy. Other tools such as the metrics Return on Investment (ROI), Total Cost of Ownership (TCO) and Earned Value Analysis (EVA) can, and should be, together with IT BSC, to evaluate IT/IS investments and strategies [12,13,14].

The "Internal Control - Integrated Framework"[15], from the Committee of Sponsoring Organizations of the Treadway Commission (COSO), presents a common definition of internal control and provides a framework against which internal control systems can be assessed and improved. This framework aims to help risk management activities within an organization [15].

The Control Objectives for Information and related Technology (CobiT) is a framework that consists of a guide for the IT/IS management. It helps to understand and manage the risk and benefits of IT/IS use. It is divided in four domains: Planning and organization, acquisition and implementation, deliver and support, and monitoring [16].

For project management we identified the PMBoK and Prince2 methodologies. The PMBoK guide recognizes five basic process groups and nine knowledge areas typical of almost all projects. The five basic process groups are: Initiating, Planning, Executing, Controlling and Monitoring, and Closing [17]. Regarding PMBoK, we have several products, such as [18]: Method123, CA Clarity, HP PPM, Primavera Systems, Microsoft Project, Planview and Compuware. Prince2 is a process-based approach for project management describing procedures to coordinate people and activities in a project, such as how to design and supervise the project, what to do if the project has to be adjusted or if it does not develop as planned. [19].

With regard to the development of software solutions we identified the Capability Maturity Model® Integration (CMMI) [20], which consists of 22 to 25 process areas with capability or maturity levels, and Software Process Improvement and Capability dEtermination (Spice) [21], a framework for the assessment of software processes.

Regarding quality management in IT/IS our literature review conducted us to ISO 9000, Six Sigma and TickIT. ISO 9000 is the most well-known quality management framework [22], TickIT [23] is a quality-management certification program for software, which in addition to a general objective of improving software quality seeks to improve and regulate the behavior of auditors working in the IT/IS sector through training, and subsequent certification. Six Sigma [24] is a method for the development of IT/IS solutions focused on the quality of the solutions developed, defining service level agreements and metrics to evaluate those service levels agreements.

Security management is covered by the ISO 27000 standard [25,26], derived from the previous BS 17799 standard [27] and provides best practice recommendations on information security management for use by those who are responsible for initiating, implementing or maintaining Information Security Management Systems.

The Information Technology Infrastructure Library (ITIL) is a framework more focused on the ISD and ISE activities, concretely in the management of IS services. It consist of several books of best practices. Regarding ITIL we identified three software suppliers: Microsoft with the packages Microsoft Operations Manager [28], Microsoft System Management Server [30] and more recently the System Center [30]; HP with the HP OpenView platform [31]; and IBM with Tivoli platform [32].

Business Process Management (BPM) tools are another groups of tools use to implement business operations derived from the analysis conducted to the business processes. In this group of tools, called Business Process Management Systems (BPMS), we have some vendor propositions, such as, Savvion Business-Manager, Intalio|BPMS, BEA Aqualogic, IBM Webshpere BPM, etc.

4   ISF Support Tools Roadmap

Based on other studies [33,34,35] that map diferent tools functionalities, and on the ISF activities caracterization, in table 1, we propose the following matrix of tools for the four major groups of ISF activities. In this table we decided to classify the different tools accordingly to the activities in which they may be used. So, we propose the following classification:

T – Total, in the situation where a given tool covers almost all the aspects of the group of activities;

P – Partial, in the situation where a given tool covers some of the aspects of the group of ISF activities;

Table 3. ISF support tools matrix

Tools/ISF activities	ISP	ISD	ISE	ISM
SOX, Basel II, HIPAA	P	B	B	P
IT BSC	T	B	B	T
ROI	P	P	B	P
TCO	P	P	B	P
EVA	P	B	B	P
COSO	T	T	B	B
CobiT	T	P	T	T
PMBoK	B	B	P	B
Prince2	B	P	P	P
CMMI	B	T	P	B
Spice	B	T	P	B
Six Sigma	B	T	B	P
ISO 9000	B	T	B	P
TickIT	B	T	B	P
ISO 27000	B	T	T	B
ITIL	B	P	T	P
ISO 20000	B	P	T	P
eTOM	B	P	T	P
BPM	B	P	T	P

B – Basic, in the situation where a given tool covers few or none of the aspects of the ISF activities.

As we can see in table 3, the CobiT framework is the only tool that covers all the activities of the ISF. However, it does not describe how certain processes should be implemented. That is why it was given a "P" in the assessement regarding the ISD. Although table 3 can, and should be used, by the IS manager as a roadmap of the tools to use in the ISF activities, some of the tools, in particular cases, might be used in other ISF activities, beyond those presented in the table.

5   Advanced Systems for the Knowledge Society

Economic productivity in 21st century will depend on enhanced application of information and knowledge to economic activity [37]. In this new emerging society, knowledge society, organizations are becoming increasingly dependent on their IT/IS. This study offers to IS manager, responsible for the organization's IT/IS, a framework that allows him/her to choose the most appropriate and up to date tools for the management of the IT/IS in order to improve the maturity and effectiveness of the organization IT/IS.

6   Conclusions

While there is no single right way for all organizations to approach improvements in ISM, this paper proposes a comprehensive and integrated framework and roadmap, which identifies the appropriate tools for each of the major ISF activities group.

In a previous study conducted by us [36] we discover that the majority of Portuguese CIOs were not aware of some of the tools presented here, using the spreadsheet calculator as the support tool for almost all of ISF activities. So, beyond presenting a roadmap of tools for ISF management, which can also be used for IT governance, this paper contributes to promote and encourage CIOs to use the presented tools that can give them competitive advantage in today's knowledge society.

References

1. Varajão, J.: Gestão da função de sistemas de informação. Dirigir - Revista para chefias e quadros. IEFP, 3–9 (2006)
2. Varajão, J.E.Q.: Contributos para a melhoria do sucesso da adopção de tecnologias de informação e desenvolvimento de sistemas de informação nas organizações. Departamento de Sistemas de Informação, Phd. Thesis. Universidade do Minho, Guimarães, 439 (2002)
3. Varajão, J.E.Q.: A Arquitectura da Gestão de Sistemas de Informação. FCA - Editora de Informática, Lisboa (2005)
4. Kendall, K.E., Kendall, J.E.: Systems Analysis and Design. Prentice Hall, Englewood Cliffs (1992)
5. Martin, E.W., DeHayes, D.W., Hoffer, J.A., Perkins, W.C.: Managing Information Technology: What Managers Need to Know. MacMillan, Basingstoke (1994)
6. Sager, M.: Managing Advanced Information Systems. Prentice Hall, Englewood Cliffs (1990)
7. Symons, C.: IT Governance Framework. Forrester (2005)
8. Damianides, M.: Sarbanes-Oxley and it Governance: New Guidance on it Control and Compliance. Information Systems Management 22, 77–85 (2005)
9. BIS: Basel II: International Convergence of Capital Measurement and Capital Standards: a Revised Framework. Bank For International Settlements (2004)
10. OCR: Summary of the HIPAA privacy rule. Office for Civil Rights (2005)
11. Kaplan, R.S., Norton, D.P.: The Balanced Scorecard - Measures that drive performance. Harvard Business Review 70, 71–79 (1992)
12. Redman, B., Kirwin, B., Berg, T.: TCO: A Critical Tool for Managing IT. Research Note (R-06-1697). Gartner Group (1998)
13. Symons, C., Orlov, L.M., Bright, S.: Add EVA to IT Investment Analysis. Forrester (2005)
14. Pisello, T., Strassmann, P.: IT Value Chain Management - Maximizing the ROI from IT Investments. The Information Economics Press (2003)
15. COSO: Executive Summary. Enterprise Risk Management - Integrated Framework. Committee of Sponsoring Organizations of the Treadway Commission, 16 (2004)
16. ITGI: CobiT 4.1 - Executive Summary. ITGI, Rolling Meadows (2007)

17. PMI: A Guide to the Project Management Body of Knowledge (PMBOK® Guide), 3rd edn. Project Management Institute (2004)
18. Light, M., Stang, D.B.: Magic Quadrant for IT Project and Portfolio Management, vol. 2008. Gartner Inc. (2007)
19. OGC: Managing Successful Projects with PRINCE2 Manual 2005. The Stationery Office. Office of Government of Commerce (2005)
20. CMMI®, S.E.I.: For Development, Version 1.2 Software Engineering Institute, Carnegie Mellon University, Pittsburgh (2006)
21. Loon, H.: Process Assessment and ISO/IEC 15504: A reference book. Springer Science, New York (2004)
22. ISO: ISO 9000 and ISO 14000. International Organization for Standard (2007)
23. BSI: Issue 5.0 of the TickIT Guide. British Standards Institution, London (2001)
24. Fry, M., Bott, M.: Combining ITIL® and Six Sigma to Improve Information Technology Service Management at General Electric. BMC Software (2004)
25. ISO/IEC: ISO/IEC 27001:2005. International Organization for Standardization / International Electrotechnical Commission, Geneva (2005)
26. ISO/IEC: ISO/IEC 27002:2005. International Organization for Standardization / International Electrotechnical Commission, Geneva (2005)
27. ISO/IEC: ISO/IEC 17799. International Organization for Standardization / International Electrotechnical Commission, Geneva (2005)
28. Microsoft: Microsoft Operations Manager 2005 Product Overview (2004)
29. Microsoft: Systems Management Server 2003 Product Overview (2003)
30. Chappell, D.: Introducing Microsoft System Center. Chappell & Associates (2007)
31. HP: The HP IT Service Management (ITSM) Reference Model - A model for successfully providing and managing IT services. HP (2007)
32. IBM: Tivoli Software: Use product solutions from IBM Tivoli software to align with the best practices of the ITIL. IBM Corporation (2006)
33. ITGI: Aligning COBIT®, ITIL® and ISO 17799 for Business Benefit. IT Governance Institute, Rolling Meadows (2005)
34. Huang, J.: eTOM and ITIL: Should you be Bi-lingual as an IT Outsourcing Service Provider?: BPTrends (2005)
35. ITGI: CobiT Mapping: Overview of International IT Guidance. IT Governance Institute, Rolling Meadows (2006)
36. Trigo, A., Varajao, J., Figueiredo, N., Barroso, J.: Software tools used by the CIO in large Portuguese companies. In: Soliman, K.S. (ed.) Information Management in the Modern Organizations: Trends & Solutions, vol. 1(2), pp. 372–378 (2008)
37. Information Society Comission.: Building the Knowledge Society. Dublin 2 (2002)

A Teleological Perspective Towards the Definition and Measurement of Intellectual Capital

Gloria H.W. Liu[1] and Eric T.G. Wang[2]

[1] Graduate Institute of Human Resource Management, National Central University, Taiwan
glorialiu@mgt.ncu.edu.tw
[2] Department of Information Management, National Central University, Taiwan
ewang@mgt.ncu.edu.tw

Abstract. The employee-centered thinking bears the hallmark of a post-industrialization era, which culminates in the attempt to manage and measure intangible assets. Nevertheless, invisibility of the IC construct per se generates insurmountable divisions ontologically and methodologically. We adopt a teleological perspective to classify and simplify extant IC metrics so as to single out the fundamental issues concerning its measurement. Moral considerations are stressed to materialize the faithful marriage between the human focus and the efficiency focus of business conducts related to IC reporting. In the conclusion, we articulate theoretical and practical opportunities implied by the teleological perspective, which encompasses both utilitarian and moral considerations, in improving operationalization and measurement of IC.

Keywords: Intellectual Capital, Definition, Measurement, Ontological assumptions, Teleology.

1 Introduction

Edvinsson [1] estimates the ratio between intangibles and physical assets as between 5:1 and 16:1. In fact, the ratio is getting larger. Many firms have developed their own measurements (e.g. Skandia Navigator). Recognizing the societal implications of intellectual capital (IC), some national or supranational institutions also dedicated to develop disclosure guidelines [2,3]. Since 1990s, IC studies have been initiated by or targeted the audience of practitioners. Absence of theoretical deliberation is obvious. In regard to IC measurement, although empirical evidence yields some robust and consistent indicators [4,5], given the complexity and lack of inherent meanings of the statistics, clarification of methodological assumptions is required to assist the interpretation of indicators. A derived question then is whether the traditional accounting criteria are applicable. This paper reveals different ontological and methodological assumptions of IC and its measures and find out new relationships between incompatible conceptualizations and measurement practices from an extended teleological perspective.

2 Definitions and Some Ontological Considerations

Initially conceived by Galbraith in 1969 as 'pure intellect' and the 'intellectual action', Stewart [6] endows a strategic value by defining IC as 'packaged useful knowledge' that

M.D. Lytras et al. (Eds.): WSKS 2008, CCIS 19, pp. 484–491, 2008.

'can be put to use to create wealth'. Nahapiet and Goshal [7] define IC as knowledge and knowing capabilities. These definitions link IC to strategic activities of knowledge creation, leverage or organizational learning. Despite the conceptual denotation that 'pure intellect' or 'packaged useful knowledge' refers to somewhat stable attributes, IC alludes to a transformation process.

Classification implies definition and expresses certain ontological assumptions. To date a consensus concerning IC elements emerges. That is, IC comprises the human capital, the organizational capital and the relational capital. First, the human capital generally refers to employees' capabilities to think, create, adapt and network as well as their experiences, skills, motivation etc. The human capital mainly exists at the individual level, and only through interventions or activation mechanisms can it be mobilized and become usable for an organization. Second, the organizational capital ranges from databases, IT systems to intellectual property assets, and to abstract concepts of business models, corporate culture and routines. The organizational capital belongs to or is embedded in an organization. Third, the relational capital comprises the relations with stakeholders, and an organization's reputation and image that accumulate from the interaction with stakeholders. We discover early researchers adopt a content perspective by revealing ingredients and attributes of IC elements [1]. Following the same classification schema, researches from a process perspective concern how the phenomenon of interest happens. Empirical findings [5,8] support the mediation effect of relational capital and organizational capital on the relationship between human capital and firm performance. In addition to the underdeveloped processual perspective, a contextual perspective is missing. Contextual factors may regulate, activate or coordinate actions and behaviors, and accordingly trigger a transformation process. Relevant contextual factors may include psychological contracts, social structures, supplier satisfaction and other factors beyond the organizational boundaries.

2.1 Ontological Division

IC research is observed adopting an inverse development path, from the applied research to the basic research. Many measures are developed before ontological assumptions are articulated. In the following, we adopt a relative approach to investigate the ontological assumptions of IC concepts. It is essential to recognize that every point on the continuum is a mixture since concepts of the social science are, more or less, socially constructed. From the perspective of objective reality, social reality is the reality in its own right. An impersonal social form of 'universalism' and 'affective neutrality' is stressed [9]. On the other hand, social constructionists stress the constructive nature of artifacts. Déjean et al. [10] regard measurement as a constructive framework, a screen to bring something into existence. With a focus on the creation and construction of social reality, we may be better able to see multiple possibilities and the potential reciprocal relations.

Building on the preceding discussion, we examine divergent attributes, value orientations, logics and methodological consequences of IC emanating from different ontological assumptions. On the one hand, ontological assumptions of 'IC as an objective reality' are essentially vestiges from financial accounting, which contends elements have relatively stable attributes, and can be linked with firm performance in a static causal map. Existence of IC is always of a positive value regardless of its context, and its absence means the value of zero. The combination logic thus is always additive and complementary. On the other hand, 'IC as a social construct' assumes that relations among IC elements are dialectical and multiple, dependent on the contexts and the enactment of agents. In this sense, IC can be assets or liabilities dependent on the context [11]. The combination logic is thus contingent. Imposition of general rules will always involve incomplete specification and missing value. As such, one methodological consequence of this ontological distinction is that the former tends to de-contextualize IC and find out universal relationships among elements, whereas the latter is apt to stress constitutive processes of IC against specific contexts. Among the extant definitions, viewing IC as an objective reality with a content focus predominates. Appeal of this assumption is that IC can be simplified into a single formula by positing relationships under parsimonious conditions. Nevertheless, it limits the possibilities IC promises. Although researchers start looking closely at interactions of IC elements and contextual factors by case studies [12,13,14], transformation processes of IC elements and the effect of contextual moderation and mediation are usually ignored.

In summary, the ontological distinction orthogonal to the three foci of content, process and context permits us to cross-classify different means by which we can apply to define the notion of IC. A process-focus definition of IC, which describes how intellectual inputs are dynamically transformed by behaviors or actions, will significantly complement the content-focus definitions; and by considering contextual factors, notions of IC will be interpretable in an increasingly complex social system.

3   Measurement and Some Methodological Considerations

There is no shortage of IC measurement tools. Using classification as an analytical tool, we adopt Fincham and Roslender's [15] classification scheme to organize extant tools into three categories: the scorecard approach, the hard valuation approach and the narrative approach. To further elaborate the framework, we discuss the focus, dominant ontological assumptions, and methodological strengths and weaknesses of each approach. If accuracy is not a desideratum, then what other criteria should IC measurement be subject to? Inspired by ethnostatistics [16] and evaluation criteria of ethnographic texts [17], we propose three preliminary criteria in the end of this section.

First, the scorecard approach emphasizes a flexible set of indicators to reflect the unique strategy of an organization. This approach conceptualizes IC as an objective reality whose stable attributes are suitable for an additive logic. Examples include Skandia's value scheme [1] and the balanced scorecard [18]. This approach produces a relevant and modestly idiosyncratic representation of a firm's IC. Relations of indicators are assumed to be complementary and additive. However, the scorecard approach, essentially a balance sheet approach, has been criticized for its failure to present the dynamic relationships and interactions between IC elements [19]. Second, the hard valuation approach emphasizes orthodox measurement and treatment of indicators. Examples include the market-to-book ratio, Tobin's Q and Calculated Intangible Value. A more complex example is the Value Creation Index that statistically derives nine value drivers. This approach employs accurate numbers to represent IC, usually ratio scales which can be linearly transformed to generate a composite.

Comparability and reliability are ensured. Nevertheless, it can be superficial to translate everything into numbers which makes no qualitative difference in a decision. This approach merely uses financial figures as the data source so it might be argued that they are not, in essence, IC measures. In most cases, value of IC is regarded as residual or excess returns gained on hard assets. Third, the narrative approach attends to the interaction and transformation among IC elements, sometimes with the aid of a visual representation. IC is conceived as a socially constructed concept, and measurement tools are one of the instruments in shaping and disciplining behaviors and decisions. Agreement overrides correspondence [20], and an authentic and persuasive narration of IC elements outweighs reliable and comparable measures. Narration of IC is contingent on contexts. Measurements of this approach can produce a convincing story and be translated into actionable management plans. However, its idiosyncratic nature at the cost of numerical accuracy limits the comparability and reliability.

3.1 Methodological Division

Measuring and counting express an attitude to a phenomenon, which is usually materialized in the operational definitions. Accordingly, methodological distinction is a corollary of the ontological division. First, measurement will be perceived differently. For the objective reality camp, measurement should be a realistic representation of the one absolute truth, whereas for social constructionists, measurement is a tool to construct or legitimize the reality. The second issue is about the data source. What constitutes the valid proxy? How many indicators will be enough? The hard valuation approach usually uses annual reports as a source. Mouritsen et al. [13] indicate the number of indicators ranges from 5-6 to over 50. No consensus is reached, and most suggestions are mainly arbitrary. Third, evaluation criteria have to be aligned. Drawn from mathematics and the measurement theory, Pike and Roos [21] conceive five criteria—complete measures, distinct measures to prevent double counting, independence of the entities being measured, agreeability of the mapping from the empirical to the numerical system, and commensurability to enable subsequent aggregation. This is a stern test and none of the eight IC measurement tools analyzed are completely compliant. It is obvious that Pike and Roos have conceived IC as an objective reality. For social constructionists, multiple and dialectical relationships of IC might require different criteria. Here we propose three criteria, namely authenticity, consistency and criticality.

First, authenticity can be achieved by incorporating multiple perspectives and interests. IC features various ownerships. The human capital is 'owned' by the employee. The relational capital resides in networks, and from the perspective of social capital [22], it cannot be appropriated by those outside the networks. The organizational capital is embedded within an organization. Many theories, such as stakeholder theory [23], psychological contracts [24] and social contracts [25], can lend themselves to distinguish the primary stakeholders and understand stakeholders' expectations and reactions when contracts are violated. Second, to be consistent, measurement results are expected to evolve along a main theme. The theme may be a rationale or a theoretical perspective to assist the interpretation. Guthrie et al. [26] propose stakeholder theory as a way to explain stakeholders' power or to argue that stakeholders have a right to fair treatment. Third, a critical report has to be 'provoca-tive' and challenges the current patterns. To sum up, various ownerships, dynamic transformation of IC elements and contextual complexity make contradictions an inherent part of IC. We need to think out of box, and critically evaluate current con-ceptualizations of IC.

4   Search for Causes

Andriessen [27] envisages the standardization of the most promising IC metrics. We doubt such a possibility and suggest IC measurements be adapted to users' motives. This does not imply the irrelevance of functional and causal explanations. We contend that at the budding stage of radical social institutions, such as IC measuring, inten-tional explanations is more relevant given the ambiguous functions and causality of IC measurement. However, human intentions and ethics are inseparable. Later, a higher-order cause of IC measurement will be discussed.

Clarification of measuring motives has several advantages. First, it prevents the management from being led by fashion. Second, the teleological perspective has a heuristic value to improve extant definitions and measures. Many researchers suggest possible purposes of measurement [26,27], including strategy formation, making trade-off decisions, knowledge management, capital attraction, transactional require-ment, legal compliance etc. Andriessen [27] summarizes these into three categories, namely improving internal management, improving external reporting, and statutory and transactional issues. However, difference of disclosure requirements between the last two categories is more of a degree. Accordingly, we treat 'statutory and transac-tional issues' as a special case of 'improving external reporting'. Examples, major concerns, suitable measurement approaches and methodological issues of each motive will be examined respectively.

Mouritsen and Larsen [29] regard IC information as part of an internal manage-ment control system. The information then sometimes should go beyond an objective representation to allow managers to craft strategies that benefit the aspirations or visions of an organization. The major issue is whether IC information can be inter-preted into unique and workable plans. A systemic viewpoint is required since the management of IC information comprises only a subsystem of the management con-trol system. Within the subsystem of IC management, attention to the interaction and transformation of IC elements, so-called 'inter-capital flow' [19], will enhance sys-temic unity, in turn contributing to the sustainability of the whole organization. Applicable measurement approaches will include the scorecard approach and the narrative approach.

External reporting motive is even more complex and requires an analytical level beyond the organization. Examples may include capital attraction, communication with stakeholders, reputation management, transactional requirements, and statutory requirements etc. The major issue is whether IC report is accountable. Viewing the intellectual capital as competitive advantage, the management may be reluctant to reveal crucial information, giving rise to the dilemma of confidentiality vs. account-ability. It is even worse that false information is fabricated. To improve the account-ability and transparency of external reporting, IC information is expected to be reliable and comparable by use of standardized treatment. As such, the hard valuation and the scorecard approaches are suitable. Another relevant issue is the bureaucratization of external IC reporting by legislation as with the case of Danish Financial Statement Act. Gröjer and Johanson [30] have warned of its ceremonial acceptance. In the future, this issue warrants attentions since interventions of political institutions are increasing.

4.1 A Higher-Order Cause

The concept of IC reinforces the employee-centered thinking. Other than profit maximization, more internal and external pressures demand business organizations to fulfill broader responsibilities. In fact, financial performance does not necessarily conflict with the fulfillment of these responsibilities as shown by the meta-analysis of Orlitzky et al. [31]. In addition to the proactive initiatives and prescriptive arguments of corporate social responsibilities, publicity of many business scandals also imparts an ugly truth, urging contemplation on the higher-order cause of business conducts, particularly the measuring practices. To avoid the potential short-termism of a teleological perspective, we defend our arguments by adding a moral leg as a higher-order cause. The utilitarian leg suggests utility of IC be determined by the analysis of overall cost and benefit. The challenge is where to demarcate the boundaries of stakeholders and calculate the overall utility and meanwhile stay moral. It is suggested to encompass multiple stakeholders, in particularly, the primary stakeholders and their interests. Hence, instead of satisfying the desire for more subtle control of people, the concept of IC and its measurement can be a powerful weapon for firms to fulfill broader responsibilities. It is our responsibilities to remind firms of careful and moral use of it.

5   Implications and Conclusions

We found ourselves in a paradoxical position of trying to materialize our intellectual capital so that we can manage and control it better, but we also know that it is in our own interest that IC stays intangible so our competitors will not be able to replicate it. Problems with conceptualizing and measuring IC thus are not only technical, but also intentional. Contrary to Andrissen's [27] optimistic anticipation, we reveal the insurmountable ontological and methodological distinctions. This article proposes an overarching teleological perspective to classify and simplify these problems so that subsequent research can focus on solving the most fundamental issues in accordance with measuring motives.

This paper contributes to a better understanding of IC in three ways. First, clarification of ontological assumptions reveals the possibility of a new research agenda. Other than viewing IC as an objective reality with a content focus, alternative assumptions and foci are possible. The dominant research agenda, viewing IC as an objective reality with a content focus, may contribute to the discovery of what are typical of IC, whereas assumptions of subjective construction, stressing the constructive nature of IC, are inherently more in line with the process and context foci and may contribute to our understanding of IC in use. Second, identification of the underlying ontological assumptions of each measurement approach not only allows us to capture the major methodological issue, but also has implications for the choice of evaluation criteria. Third, our argument illustrates the importance of motives to improve understanding and measuring of IC. No measurement approach is inherently superior. It is human intentions that decide how we define and process IC information and in turn it influences how we perceive the world which gradually shifts to the control by numbers [16]. The extended teleological perspective also has some practical implications. First, the teleological perspective portrays the problem-solving or improvement paths of IC definition and measurement by first setting up a future status to be pursued. Second, we contend the moral branch of the teleological perspective should be embraced as a higher-order cause. By embracing morality as a higher-order cause, the measuring practices will be of internal good so that organizations can possibly further achieve pragmatic good of efficiency or profits [32]. Or, it is going to be an unfaithful marriage between the human focus and the efficiency focus, if organizations do not have a higher-order cause to guide their conducts.

References

1. Edvinsson, L.: Developing Intellectual Capital at Skandia. Long Range Planning 30, 366–373 (1997)
2. Danish Financial Statement Act (Danish Act no. 448 of 7 June 2001), http://www.eogs.dk/graphics/Regnskab/Regnskabslov_en.html
3. Meritum: Guidelines for Managing and Reporting on Intangibles, Fundacion Airtel Movil, Madrid (2002)
4. OrdÑez de Pablos, P.: Measuring and Reporting Structural Capital: Lessons from European Learning Firms. Journal of Intellectual Capital 5, 629–647 (2004)
5. Wang, W.Y., Chang, C.: Intellectual Capital and Performance in Causal Models: Evidence from the Information Technology Industry in Taiwan. Journal of Intellectual Capital 6, 222–236 (2005)
6. Steward, T.: Intellectual Capital: The New Wealth of Organizations. Doubleday, NY (1997)
7. Nahapiet, J., Ghoshal, S.: Social Capital, Intellectual Capital and the Organizational Advantage. Academy of Management Review 23, 242–266 (1998)
8. Bontis, N.: Intellectual Capital: an Exploratory Study that Develops Measure and Models. Management Decision 36, 63–76 (1998)
9. Parsons, T.: The Social System. Free Press, NY (1951)
10. Déjean, F., Gond, J.P., Leca, B.: Measuring the Unmeasured: an Institutional Entrepreneur Strategy in an Emerging Industry. Human Relations 57, 741–764 (2004)
11. Dzinkowski, R.: The Measurement and Management of Intellectual Capital: an Introduction. Management Accounting 78, 32–36 (2000)
12. Larsen, H.T., Bukh, P.N.D., Mouritsen, J.: Intellectual Capital Statements and Knowledge Management: Measuring, Reporting, Acting. Australian Accounting Review 9, 15–26 (1999)
13. Mouritsen, J., Larsen, H.T., Bukh, P.N.D.: Intellectual Capital and the Capable Firm: Narrating, Visualizing and Numbering for Managing Knowledge. Accounting, Organizations and Society 26, 735–762 (2001)

14. Johanson, U., Mårtensson, M., Skoog, M.: Mobilizing Cthrough the Management Control of Intangibles. Accounting, Organizations and Society 26, 715–733 (2001)
15. Fincham, R., Roslender, R.: Intellectual Capital Accounting as Management Fashion: a Review and Critique. European Accounting Review 12, 781–795 (2003)
16. Gephart, R.P.: Ethnostatistics and Organizational Research Methodologies: an Introduction. Organizational Research Methods 9, 417–431 (2006)
17. Golden-Biddle, K., Locke, K.: Appealing Work: an Investigations of How Ethnographic Texts Convince. Organization Science 4, 595–616 (1993)
18. Kaplan, R., Norton, D.: The Balanced Scorecard: Measures that Drive Performance, 71–79 (January-Febuary 1992)
19. Roos, G., Roos, J.: Measuring your Company's Intellectual Performance. Long Range Planning 30, 413–426 (1997)
20. Catasus, B., Gröjer, J.-E.: Indicators: on Visualizing, Classifying and Dramatizing. Journal of Intellectual Capital 7, 187–203 (2006)
21. Pike, S., Roos, G.: Mathematics and Modern Business Management. Journal of Intellectual Capital 5, 243–256 (2004)
22. Coleman, J.S.: Social Capital in the Creation of Human Capital. American Journal of Sociology 94, 95–120 (1988)
23. Freeman, R.E.: Strategic Management: a Stakeholder Approach. Pitman, Boston
24. Rousseau, D.M.: The Idiosyncratic Deal: Flexibility versus Fairness. Organizational Dynamics 29, 260–273 (1984)
25. Donaldson, T., Dunfee, T.W.: Ties that Bind: a Social Contracts Approach to Business Ethics. Harvard Business School Press, Boston (1999)
26. Guthrie, J., Petty, R., Yongvanich, K., Ricceri, F.: Using Content Analysis as a Research Method to Inquire into Intellectual Capital Reporting. Journal of Intellectual Capital 5, 282–293 (2004)
27. Andriessen, D.: IC Valuation and Measurement: Classifying the State of the Art. Journal of Intellectual Capital 5, 230–242 (2004)
28. Marr, B., Gray, D., Neely, A.: Why do Firms Measure Their Intellectual Capital? Journal of Intellectual Capital 4, 441–464 (2003)
29. Mouritsen, J., Larsen, H.T.: The 2nd Wave of Knowledge Management: the Management Control of Knowledge Resources through Intellectual Capital Information. Management Accounting Research 16, 371–394 (2005)
30. Gröjer, J.-E., Johanson, U.: Current Development in Human Resource Costing and Accounting: Reality Present, Researchers Absent? Accounting, Auditing and Accountability Journal 11, 495–505 (1998)
31. Orlitzky, M., Schmidt, F.L., Rynes, S.L.: Corporate Social and Financial Performance: a Meta-Analysis. Organization Studies 24, 403–441 (2003)
32. Collier, J.: Theorising the Ethical Organization. Business Ethics Quarterly 8, 621–654 (1998)

A Decision Analytic Tool for Assessing Decision Making Performance

K. Nadia Papamichail[1], Nikolas Hadjiprocopiou[2], Procopis Hadjiprocopiou[2],
Vidya Rajaram[1], and Stephen J. Brewis[3]

[1] Manchester Business School, University of Manchester, Booth Street East, Manchester,
M15 6PB, U.K.
{nadia.papamichail,vidya.rajaram}@mbs.ac.uk
[2] School of Computer Science, University of Manchester, Oxford Road, Manchester,
M13 9PL, U.K.
{hadjiprn,hadjiprp}@cs.man.ac.uk
[3] BT Wholesale, UK
steve.brewis@bt.com

Abstract. Nowadays managers have to take increasingly complex decisions. This is due to several factors including aggressive market competition, information overload and a trend to move operations abroad. In their effort to overcome ill-defined problems, managers often use ICTs such as decision support systems and intelligent systems to identify patterns and make predictions. Such technologies can potentially improve the quality of the decisions taken. This paper presents a decision-analytic tool that assesses decision making processes within decision lifecycles. The setting is the telecom industry but the tool can be applied in a variety of sectors such as banking and consultancy. Results of comparative and subjective evaluations are presented to highlight the benefits and limitations of the system.

1 Introduction

Because of increased complexity and uncertainty in highly competitive markets, commercial organisations strive nowadays to exceed expectations and devise strategies so as to gain a competitive advantage. Achieving this objective depends to a large extent to the decisions that executives, middle managers and employees take. As many analysts suggest (see for example Forrester [4]), a decision taken at the strategic level can make or break an organisation. Equally, a large number of wrong decisions at the operational and tactical levels (e.g. sales tactics, dealing with customer complaints etc) can have a major financial impact.

Most companies lack strategic policies for decision making and as a result half of all organisational decisions fail [11]. Managers are often unaware how vital and crucial the process of decision making is [10]. Decisions that appear to be accurate, consistent and successful at first, may lead to negative outcomes that were difficult to predict [14].

M.D. Lytras et al. (Eds.): WSKS 2008, CCIS 19, pp. 492–496, 2008.
© Springer-Verlag Berlin Heidelberg 2008

Over the years, many researchers focused on techniques and ways to support and improve decision making and address uncertainty and complexity issues. Decision Support Systems (DSS) have been introduced to assist in that respect. As French et al [6] point out a decision support system (DSS) "is a computer-based system which supports the decision making process, helping decision makers to understand the problem before them and to form and explore the implications of their judgements and hence to make a decision based upon understanding". DSS are used to enhance decision making capabilities by helping decision makers to learn about a decision domain in a structured and systematic way [3][13]. They help decision makers to explore complex options [15] and alternatives [9].

This work introduces a DSS for assessing decision making capabilities within organisations. We use the term 'decision analytic tool' to describe the system because it places an emphasis on the analysis of the problem (i.e. how well decision makers take decisions). We apply our research within decision lifecycles or projects that start with a strategic decision (e.g. to invest in an initiative) and it is followed by decisions at the tactical and operational levels. In the telecom sector for example, a high level decision is to design a new product. This is usually followed by decisions at the tactical level (e.g. middle managers have to decide when to launch the product and devise a marketing campaign) and decisions at the operational level (e.g. dealing with customers' concerns and complaints). In the banking sector, a strategic decision is to close down a number of branches to reduce operational costs. This is followed by tactical decisions (e.g. which branches to close down, whether to lay-off staff, sell-off property) and operational decisions (e.g. move customer accounts to minimise disruption to customers). An overview of decision making practices in the telecom sector is given in Brewis et al. [2].

The structure of the paper is as follows. A brief literature review is given next. This is followed by the description of the tool and a brief presentation of the evaluation results. Finally, the significance of our research is discussed in the conclusions section.

2   Background

Decision making is a central organisational activity [5]. As Garvin and Roberto [7] point out decision making is not an instantaneous event but it is rather a process which might take days, weeks, months, or even years to complete. As the decision making process unfolds, it requires support at all organisational levels. The difference between successful and unsuccessful decision makers is that the former design and manage decisions as processes, whereas the later view decisions as events.

The most commonly discussed distinction between decisions is their classification into strategic, tactical and operational [6]. This categorisation is often referred to as strategy pyramid. Operational decisions are the day-to-day decisions that line managers and employees take. These are usually highly structured (also called programmed) and repetitive decisions whose time span of discretion is short. Tactical decisions are typically taken by middle managers so as to ensure the successful implementation of the decisions taken at the top. Finally, strategic decisions are usually taken by senior managers who decide high-level objectives and set the direction of their firm. They are highly unstructured and are typically called as non-programmed.

Papamichail and Rajaram [12] propose a framework for assessing decision making processes within decision lifecycles. As these processes unfold, strategic, tactical and operational decisions can be taken at different points. A decision taken often triggers other decisions at the same or at another level. The main elements of the framework include management structures (i.e. how easy it is to implement a decision, whether there is a trusting environment within the organisation, a clear vision in place etc), efficiency (i.e. time, resources), people & skills (i.e. staff with decision making skills) and information (i.e. ability to collect and disseminate timely and accurate information). Whilst stakeholders e.g. customers, business partners and employees can shape decision making policies, environmental factors cal also influence decision making performance.

3   A Decision Analytic Tool

A decision analytic tool for assessing decision making and organisational performance has been developed. The setting is the telecommunications industry. The system assists a user in appraising the decision making capabilities of a telecom company and make performance comparisons with competitors. The framework can easily be adapted to other settings.

The decision analytic tool measures the views of stakeholders (i.e. customers, employees, investors, business partners) on the performance of an organisation. It also measures organisational decision making capability by applying the framework developed by Papamichail and Rajaram [12]. The main criteria/attributes are customers, employees, investors, organisational decision making, and suppliers. All these factors contribute to the 'eudemonic index' that measures the well-being of an organisation.

All the measures/criteria/attributes are structured into an attribute tree (see Fig. 1). EI is the abbreviation of the eudemonic index and reflects the performance of the organisation with respect to the main criteria. The main component of the interface is called the Tree Pane (Fig. 1) where the user formulates the problem by identifying criteria and potential alternatives. The Tree Pane facilitates understanding of the dependencies among the criteria.

Each node on the main Tree Pane depicts a measure/criterion/attribute relating to stakeholder related performance or overall organisational decision making performance. Each node is further decomposed into sub-criteria. For example, the customer-related criterion can be decomposed into the following sub-criteria: loyalty, satisfaction, perceived value and expectations. The sub-trees of the nodes of the second level (i.e. customers, employees, etc.) are presented in different panes to avoid busy screens, whilst the main tree and sub-trees are plotted from the left to right with the overall attributes leftmost. Fig. 1 illustrates the first and second level attributes.

The importance of a criterion may vary depending on an organisation's priority and focus on various aspects of organisational performance. Different criteria may carry a different weight. The decision analytic tool provides a functionality where the decision maker can assign weights to criteria and scores to a company. The scores reflect how well a company performs on the criteria provided. The results are aggregated using a multi-attribute value function [1]. A company can be assessed against one or more competitors to establish how well it performs. In our example, we consider two companies (Company X and Company Y).

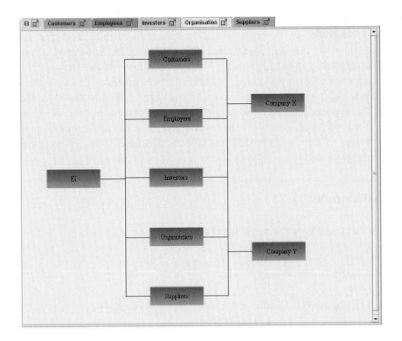

Fig. 1. The main attribute tree

The system generates a range of graphs including a bar chart for the weights and a spider-net plot and a histogram chart for the ranking results. The graphs help users establish which criteria contribute more to the differentiation of the alternatives. Other features include sensitivity analysis graphs, pareto plots and explanation reports.

The decision analytic tool has been evaluated at two levels: Its technical capabilities have been compared against other commercial multi-attribute decision analytic tools. The tool shares several features and functionalities with other software packages. It displays an attribute tree and allows the user to add/delete attributes/alternatives and set weights/scores. Unlike other tools, it can manage large attribute trees. Additionally, in order to prevent busy screens, the attribute tree is decomposed into sub-trees that are depicted in different panels.

Usability criteria such as completeness, understanding, flexibility, user performance and ease of use have been used to establish the attitudes of users towards the tool. The system was presented to users and a questionnaire that included open-ended questions was administered. The results indicate that the system is easy to use. The subjects also found that the help facility of the tool was very useful providing advice about the navigation of the system.

4 Conclusions

This paper presents a decision analytic tool for measuring decision making performance in relation to internal capabilities and stakeholder views. The system presents a framework that is structured in the form of an attribute tree. The main functionalities of the input interface are the creation and modification of the initial tree, the assignment of attribute weights and alternative values, as well as their presentation. The results are visualised in various graphs.

The evaluation of the system suggests that the tool provides functional capabilities comparable to those provided by commercial packages. The developed tool appears to help users assess decision making capabilities and make comparisons. Even though the tool was found to be easy to use, we believe that we can improve it further by adding a range of intelligent features to help novice users who are not familiar with decision analysis concepts.

Acknowledgment

This work was funded by the EPSRC (EP/D015391/1).

References

1. Belton, V., Stewart, T.J.: Multiple Criteria Decision Analysis An Integrated Approach (2001)
2. Brewis, S.J., Papamichail, N., Rajaram, V.: Decision Making Practices in Commercial Enterprises: A Cybernetic Intervention into a Business Model. Journal Organizational Transformation and Social Change (in press, 2008)
3. Finlay, P.N.: A Classification of Success Factors for Decision Support Systems. The Journal of Strategic Information Systems 7(1), 53–70 (1998)
4. Forrester: Enterprise Visibility Makes Decisions Profitable. Consultancy Report (2003)
5. French, S., Xu, D.L.: Comparison Study of Multi-Attribute Decision Analytic Software. Journal of Multi-Criteria Decision Analysis 13(2-3), 65–80 (2005)
6. French, S., Maule, J., Papamichail, K.N.: Decision Behaviour, Analysis and Support. Cambridge University Press, Cambridge (2009)
7. Garvin, D.A., Roberto, M.A.: What You Don't Know About Making Decisions. Harvard Business Review 79(8), 108–116 (2001)
8. Neely, A.D.: Business Performance Measurement: Theory and Practice. Cambridge University Press, Cambridge (2002)
9. Nissen, M.E.: Knowledge-Based Knowledge Management in the Reengineering Domain. Decision Support Systems 27(1), 47–65 (1999)
10. Nutt, P.: Better Decision-Making: a Field Study. Business strategy review, 45 (1997)
11. Nutt, P.C.: Surprising But True: Half the Decisions in Organizations Fail. Academy of Management Executive 13(4), 75–90 (1999)
12. Papamichail, K.N., Rajaram, V.: A Framework for Assessing Decision Making Practices Management Decision (submitted, 2008)
13. Parikh, M., Fazlollahi, B., Verma, S.: The Effectiveness of Decisional Guidance: An Empirical Evaluation. Decision Sciences 32(2), 303–331 (2001)
14. Reiter-Palmon, R., Illies, J.J.: Leadership and Creativity: Understanding Leadership from a Creative Problem-Solving Perspective. Leadership Quart. 15, 55–77 (2004)
15. Sharda, R., Barr, S.H., McDonnell, J.C.: Decision Support System Effectiveness: A Review and an Empirical Test. Management Science 34(2), 139–159 (1988)

Studying Research on E-Markets during 1995-2005

Nikos Manouselis[1,2] and Constantina Costopoulou[1]

[1] Greek Research & Technology Network (GRNET) S.A.,
56 Mesogion Av., 115 27, Athens, Greece
nikosm@ieee.org
[2] Informatics Laboratory, Div. of Informatics, Mathematics & Statistics, Dept. of Science,
Agricultural University of Athens, 75 Iera Odos Str., 11855, Athens, Greece
tina@aua.gr

Abstract. The field of electronic markets (e-markets) is an active research field that attracts growing international attention, and the volume of related publications is increasing every year. The aim of this paper is to provide an overview of the developments in this research field during the decade 1995-2005. This paper uses a two-level approach for the analysis and categorization of e-market literature according to research topics and characteristics. It classifies 248 e-market research papers published in scientific journals. The results presented in this paper illustrate the distribution of research interest among the various e-market topics, assess the maturity of this field, and provide insights useful for current and future research.

Keywords: e-commerce, e-markets, literature review.

1 Introduction

Electronic commerce (e-commerce) has been now established as a research field that attracts contributions from different disciplines (such as Computer Science, Information Systems, Economics, etc.). Electronic markets (e-markets) have early emerged as an important topic inside e-commerce research. An e-market can be defined as a multi-party e-commerce platform intermediating between buyers and suppliers [9]. E-markets are therefore information systems intended to provide their users (that is, market participants) with online services that will facilitate information exchange and transactions. In the past years, e-markets began to stand out as a distinct research field with multiple organizational, economic, technical and other dimensions [10]. In turn, e-market research papers have flourished in the past years.

Within this context, the scope of this paper is to provide a classification and assessment of published research paper pertaining to e-markets. This attempt may be an interesting and useful contribution to researchers, managers, and practitioners/implementers. It can also provide answers to questions such as the following: which topics attract more research attention after more than ten years of active research? What type of research is being conducted and which research methods are engaged? How credible are the research claims? To whom is e-market research addressed and who publishes it?

M.D. Lytras et al. (Eds.): WSKS 2008, CCIS 19, pp. 497–506, 2008.

To our knowledge, the first related review and assessment of the area of e-markets has been the study of Smith et al. [14]. Its perspective was rather economic and explored three aspects of business-to-consumer (B2C) e-markets: efficiency in online markets, price dispersion in online markets, and important developments to watch. The paper also referred to an extensive bibliography of related research. Moreover, a short review of representative e-market papers has been included in the larger study of e-commerce literature [8]. It examined e-commerce research from an economic perspective, as well as a number of issues related with e-markets. A very comprehensive literature review in the area of e-markets has been the one of Grieger [5]. The author focused on the supply chain dimension of e-markets, carried out a literature review that contributed to the e-market discussion, and called for more supply chain management research in the e-markets research area. Furthermore, Anandalingam et al. [1] presented an introductory survey of essential literature on e-markets. Although several market mechanisms and settings have been reviewed, the authors' focus seemed to be more on auctions.

Previous studies have either adopted a specific perspective when analyzing e-market literature (such as [14]) or have focused on a particular type of e-markets (such as [5]. Furthermore, to our knowledge, there has not been so far an overall classification of e-market literature according to research topics. Additionally, the type and maturity of e-market research has not been yet assessed. To this direction, this paper applies a two-level analysis approach to classify e-market literature according to research topics and characteristics. The results of this study illustrate the increasing interest in organizational, economic, technical and other topics related with e-markets, assess the maturity of this field, and provide insights useful for current and future research.

2 Methodology

This section focuses on the methodology of this work. We have developed and used a classification framework with both e-market research topics (first-level of our analysis), and research characteristics (second-level of our analysis). For these two levels, we have adopted and appropriately adapted existing classification frameworks, which have already been proven in similar studies (e.g. [8],[16],[12],[15],[13],[11],[3]). It has been concluded that the framework proposed by Urbaczewski et al. [16] covers the generic e-market topics with its organizational, economic, technical and other topic areas. In this light, its topic areas have been appropriately elaborated, and used for the first-level analysis of this paper.

To define the second-level, we have been based on an existing framework. It has been proposed by Groenlund [6], and it has provided good results when applied to assess the state-of-the-art in e-government research. This level identifies two categories of research characteristics: the maturity of the field (for example, the balance among methods used, changing over time from simple arguments, philosophical discussions and case stories to more methodologically sound methods such as experiments or ethnological observation); and the focus of the field (for example, disciplines which this research involves and its target groups).

Then, we analyzed the papers that have been collected throughout an extensive e-market literature review. This review was based on a study of publications in scientific journals with a long tradition as well as journals specifically focusing on e-commerce (that have appeared during the late '90s) [2]. It covered eighteen journals that were considered as well-accepted publication outlets for e-commerce research. Year 1995 was chosen as a starting date for our review, since our study revealed that e-market papers started appearing systematically in these journals from that year and forth. Overall, a total of 248 papers have been finally classified.

3 Results

The sample of papers that have been studied and classified following the proposed framework can be found at http://e-services.aua.gr/emarkets_literature.htm. It is interesting to study their distribution according to their year of publication, during the decade 1995-2005. By doing so, we noted that after 1999 the number of e-market papers published every year gets close to 30, and after 2001 it reaches almost 40 per year. This observation can be possibly explained by the dot.com explosion of 1999 which led many researchers focus on the e-market phenomenon. Despite the slight drops in 2000 and 2003, the number of e-market publications generally remained high, reaching the number of 45 in 2004. The number of published e-market papers for 2005 was also high.

From our point of view, the main reason for this increase in e-market research is the great interest that this area attracted after 1999. The increased number of new scientific journals specializing in e-commerce (5 out of the 18 examined journals were launched after 1999) might also account for a part of this increase, since it allowed to specialized e-market research find its way to the research community.

The first step of our study (*first-level analysis*) examined the distribution of the 248 e-market papers in four topic areas, namely Organizational, Economic, Technical and Other. The highest percentage of publications belongs to the Economic and the Technical topic areas (35% and 30% of the total, respectively). Organizational topics also attract important research interest, since 23% of the published papers cover this area. Furthermore, an important number of papers cover Other topics as well (about 14% of the total). In general, we note that e-market research is covering all four topic areas of the first-level of the framework, with more focus (as probably expected) in Economic, Technical and Organizational topics.

A more focused analysis of the Organizational topic area papers indicated how they are distributed in the various Organizational topics. Thus, it has been observed that most papers cover topics related with Forms and Structures of e-markets (20.4% of the total Organizational topic area) as well as their Adoption (25.5%). Other topics with significant coverage include Strategic (17.3%), Overview (14.3%), and e-market Business Models (14.3%). Papers covering the Diffusion and Use of e-markets are a small proportion of the total Organizational-related publications (about 8.2%).

In the Economic topic area, papers are mostly published on topics around the design and study of Value Distribution Mechanisms (34.5% of total Economic Research papers), as well as around Intermediaries (44.8%). Papers around Pricing topics (with 15.2%), and Transaction Cost topics (with 5.5%) cover only a small part of this topic area.

Regarding the papers of the Technical topic area, it was impressive to note how Architectures (with 39% of total Technical topic area papers) and Protocols/Algorithms (with 32.2%) monopolize this area. In the journals examined, Interoperability (which is identified as a key issue from e-commerce experts, as discovered by [4]) has been addressed by only 4.2% of the published papers. Moreover, Technological topics are not often encountered in the examined publications. Nevertheless, this can be due to the fact that research about such technical issues usually covers all e-commerce areas rather than e-markets in particular. Therefore, it is probably published in more general papers or more technically specialized journals. Services seem to be also attracting an important degree of attention: about 16.1% of Technical papers are about e-markets' Services.

Finally, the distribution of e-market papers that are related with Other topics shows that most of these papers (35% of the ones related with this topic area) deal with Behavior topics (such as consumer and seller behaviors). Trust is another topic attracting attention, since 30% of papers in this area are addressing it. Evaluation-related papers cover about 17% of Other topics, whereas Social-related papers (such as ones addressing reputation and communities-related research) about 12%. Legal topics are addressed by only 5% of the papers published in this area. Only one paper (1.7%) proposed a new methodology for carrying out e-market research.

The next step of our study (*second-level analysis*) focused on the assessment of published papers. The results of the e-market papers' classification among the second-level dimensions demonstrate that all Research Types are being carried out in the e-market area. Additionally, the field seems to be a rather mature one: 28% of the published papers test a proposed theory (i.e. Theory Testing), and 22% of the papers apply a theory for the needs of a specific implementation (i.e. Applied). These two types add up to a total of 50% of all e-market papers. A reservation exists for some papers which are characterized as Applied and are classified in this category, but which are not testing some particular theory. In many cases, such papers simply present a prototype implementation and cannot be considered a complete contribution. Nevertheless, the percentage of Applied research indicates the practical focus that e-market research has.

Figure 1 examines how Research Type changes according to each topic area. Papers contributing to Organizational topics, conduct Philosophical, Descriptive and Theory Testing research. On the other hand, Economic contributions are in their majority Theory Testing and Applied research. Technical contributions, as expected, are mostly Applied. Other contributions are in their larger parts Theory Testing and Theory Generation ones. In the future, it would be also interesting to examine how the Research Type is changing over time, in order to assess if theoretical and descriptive papers were published in the early years, whereas the practical applications and theory testing papers more recently.

In terms of the Research Method used, the results have demonstrated that the methods applied more often are Product description (in 23% of the papers) and Case Story (19%). Experiments also have an important share of the Research Methods used, either being real Experiments (11%) or simulated ones (9%). On the other hand, very few papers review e-market literature: although there are several Surveys of e-market cases (8%), there is a small percentage that concerns Literature studies (1%). This indicates there is a shortage of comprehensive literature studies in the area of e-markets. These results also indicate that about one third of e-market research is not based on actual data (Argument and Case Story papers together reach a percentage of 29.5%). This might be an indication that data from existing e-market applications have to be furthermore collected and researched. Such work is already underway in some popular public e-markets such as e-Bay. See for example the work of Ward and Clark [17] or Hayne et al. [7], who are researching data collected from e-Bay's operation.

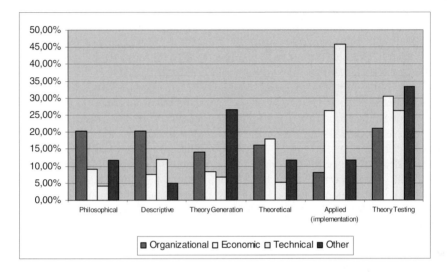

Fig. 1. Publications per Research Type and per Topic Area

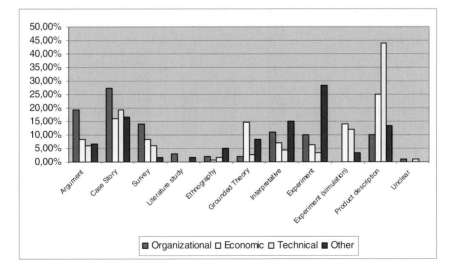

Fig. 2. Publications per Research Method and per topic area

As demonstrated in Figure 2, papers contributing to Organizational topics use mostly Case Story as well as Argument, as their method. Economic papers are largely using Product Description, but they are also the papers most engaging Grounded Theory methods. Technical papers mostly engage Product Description, and in a smaller percentage, Case Story methods. Finally, Other contributions are mostly using experimentation methods (real or simulated). Again, an analysis of how Research Methods change with time is an interesting issue to examine in the future. We would expect more data-oriented methods to appear as time goes by.

The analysis of papers according to their Claims provides an interesting observation concerning the current status of e-market research. Above it has been indicated that about half of the e-market papers (50%) seem to be generally testing some proposed theory (Theory Testing) or to be implementing it (Applied). Nevertheless, only 16.9% of the e-market papers claim generality (Normative ones) of their results. Additionally, only another 27.4% claims validity for the specific case described (Descriptive ones). That is, 55.6% of the e-market literature published in the examined journals does not claim either generality or at least validity of its results for the specific case examined. Focusing on the claims that the papers from each topic area make, it can be noted (Figure 3) that Organizational papers mostly report Lessons learned. Economic contributions have high percentages of Lessons learned papers, as well as of Descriptive ones. Technical contributions have also high percentage of papers reporting Lessons learned and Descriptive results, but many of them also report Ongoing Research. Finally, Other contributions are mostly presenting Descriptive and Normative results.

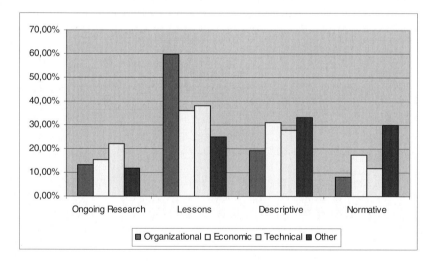

Fig. 3. Publications per Claim and per topic area

Classifying papers according to their Focus Unit, it is observed that e-market literature mostly focuses on the product or method it describes or proposes. More than 53% of the papers focus on their Method. Smaller percentages of papers also focus on Organizations (12%) or a specific Sector (18%). There is only a small percentage of papers that focus on the Individuals' or the Groups' perspectives (3% and 7% respectively). Finally, the small percentage of papers focusing on the Society (7%) might be an indication that e-market research has not yet studied the effects of e-markets on a societal level, e.g. examining how they are changing the way e-commerce is or will be carried out. These could be a reason for performing more research to this direction, both from the e-market participants' perspective, as well as from the the societal perspective. On the other hand, the fact that this review has not included journals from more sociological, psychological or cultural disciplines could be a reason for our observation. Figure 4 demonstrates the change of Focus Unit per topic area. Economic, Technical and Other papers focus on the presented Method. Other papers are the ones belonging to the most Individual- and Group-oriented contributions. On the other hand, Organizational papers are the contributions mostly focusing on Sector-, Organization-, and Society-oriented topics.

The distribution of the e-market papers according to their Target Audience demonstrates that in the examined set of journals, most e-market papers aim to Researchers (72.2%). Small percentages of papers were identified as aiming to Practitioners (13.3%) or Managers (12.5%). This might occur because the examined journals mostly publish scientific research papers. Nevertheless, some of the covered journals have a wider audience. Thus, this could be a serious indication that e-market research has not yet been connected to the market. Figure 5 illustrates how Organizational papers target mostly on Researchers and Managers. Economic papers mostly target to Researchers and not to Practitioners/Implementers. Technical papers target mostly on Researchers and Practitioners/Implementers rather than Managers. Finally, Other papers are generally addressing the audience of Researchers.

Judging from the affiliation of their authors (based on Institution Type), it has been possible to identify that the majority of published papers come from Universities (about 88% of published papers). A small percentage also comes from authors affiliated with Companies and Research Institutes (5.6% in both cases). One explanation might be the fact that university staff is required to regularly publish their research in order to advance its career. Nevertheless, these results may be providing another indication that e-market research has not yet found its way towards the market, despite the high number of currently operating e-markets. Figure 6 illustrates these results, also showing that papers coming from Companies are usually addressing Technical issues, whereas papers from Research Institutes usually address Economic and Technical ones.

In terms of Disciplines where the authors belong, results indicate that, in general, e-market research is published from people with Computer Science (about 32%), Information Systems (29%) and Management or Marketing (26.6%) backgrounds. This classification cannot be considered tentative, since the disciplines' definition and categorization may vary, affecting so the classification results. In general, the subjective impression that we have from our study is that e-market research is mostly coming from technology-oriented disciplines. A small percentage of e-market papers come from authors that belong to an Economic discipline (9.7%). A possible explanation could be the fact that the set of examined journals did not include ones with a clear economic focus. Figure 7 presents the disciplines of the primary author(s) per topic area. It demonstrates how Technical papers mostly come from authors with a Computer Science background, whereas Organizational papers from authors with an

Information Systems or Management background. Other papers usually come from authors with an Information Systems or Management background as well. Finally, it is interesting to note that many of the Economic papers are contributed from authors with a primarily Computer Science background. We also examined the Geographical origin of e-market papers' authors. As it has been probably expected, more than half of the papers (about 56%) come from the United States. Other countries which demonstrate high activity of e-market research according to our study, are Germany (about 7% of the papers had German authors), as well as Netherlands, UK and Switzerland (each publishing around 3% of overall e-market research).

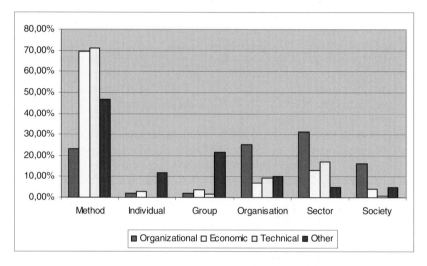

Fig. 4. Publications per Focus Unit and per topic area

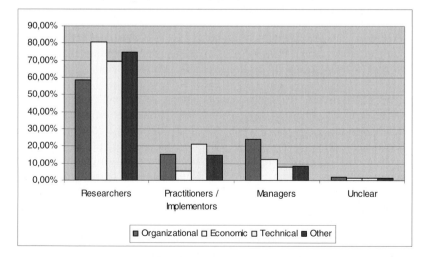

Fig. 5. Publications per Target Audience and per topic area

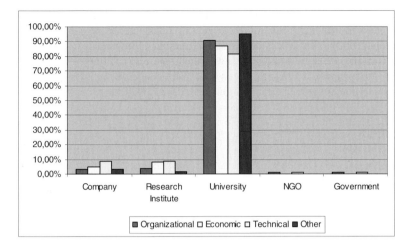

Fig. 6. Publications per Institution and per topic area

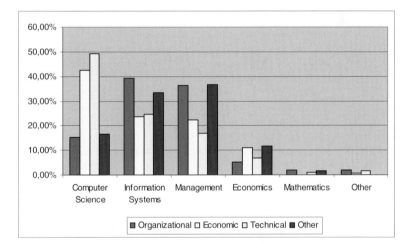

Fig. 7. Publications per Discipline and per topic area

Finally, authors from the South Korea and Finland follow, each publishing about 2.5% of the examined e-market papers. It is encouraging that there are authors from over 31 countries who have contributed to the e-market research so far. Nevertheless, Europe and Asia seem to be still under-represented.

4 Conclusions

This paper aims to provide a structure to the numerous research papers pertaining to e-markets. It integrates existing and proven frameworks into a two-level framework for the classification of e-market literature. This has been used to classify 248 e-market papers published in a representative sample of scientific journals that are considered well-known publication outlets for e-commerce research (Bharati and Tarasewich, 2002). The results illustrate the increasing interest in the various topics related with-markets, assess the maturity of this field, and provide insights which may be useful for current and future research. The full version of this study is available at: http://infolab-dev.aua.gr/files/publications/en/1170237144.pdf

References

1. Anandalingam, G., Day, R.W., Raghavan, S.: The Landscape of Electronic Market Design. Management Science 51(3), 316–327 (2005)
2. Bharati, P., Tarasewich, P.: Global Perceptions of Journals Publishing E-Commerce Research. Communications of the ACM 45(5) (2002)
3. CEN: Summaries of some Frameworks, Architectures and Models for Electronic Commerce, European Committee for Standardization, CWA 14228:2001E (2001)
4. Dai, Q., Kauffman, R.J.: B2B E-Commerce Revisited: Leading Perspectives on the Key Issues and Research Directions. Electronic Markets 12(2), 67–83 (2002)
5. Grieger, M.: Electronic Marketplaces: A Literature Review and a Call for Supply Chain Management Research. European Journal of Operational Research 144, 280–294 (2003)
6. Groenlund, A.: State of the Art in e-Gov Research – A Survey. In: Traunmüller, R. (ed.) EGOV 2004. LNCS, vol. 3183, pp. 178–185. Springer, Heidelberg (2004)
7. Hayne, S.C., Smith, C.A.P., Vijayasarathey, L.R.: Who Wins on eBay: An Analysis of Bidders and Their Bid Behaviours. Electronic Markets 13(4), 282–293 (2003)
8. Kauffman, R.J., Walden, E.A.: Economics and Electronic Commerce: Survey and Directions for Research. International Journal of Electronic Commerce 5(4), 5–116 (2001)
9. Le, T.T.: Pathways to Leadership for Business-to-Business Electronic Marketplaces. Electronic Markets 12(2), 112–119 (2002)
10. Lee, T.-R., Li, J.-M.: Key factors in forming an e-marketplace: An empirical analysis. Electronic Commerce Research and Applications 5(2), 105–116 (2006)
11. Liang, T.P., Chen, D.-N.: Evolution of Information Systems Research. In: Pacific Asian Conference on Information Systems, Adelaide, Australia (2003)
12. Ngai, E.W.T., Wat, F.K.T.: A Literature Review and Classification of Electronic Commerce Research. Information and Management 39, 415–429 (2002)
13. Orlikowski, W.J., Iacono, S.: Research Commentary: Desperately Seeking the IT in IT Research – A Call to Theorizing the IT Artifact. Information Systems Research 12(2), 121–134 (2001)
14. Smith, M.D., Bailey, J., Brynjolfsson, E.: Understanding Digital Markets: Review and Assessment. In: Brynjolfsson, E., Kahin, B. (eds.) Understanding the Digital Economy. MIT Press, Cambridge (1999)
15. Turban, E., King, D., Lee, J.K., Viehland, D.: Electronic Commerce 2004: A Managerial Perspective. Prentice Hall, Englewood Cliffs (2004)
16. Urbaczewski, A., Jessup, L.M., Wheeler, B.: Electronic Commerce Research: A Taxonomy and a Synthesis. Journal of Organisational Computing and Electronic Commerce 12(4), 263–305 (2002)
17. Ward, S.G., Clark, J.M.: Bidding Behavior in On-line Auctions: An Examination of the eBay Pokemon Card Market. International Journal of Electronic Commerce 6(4) (2002)

Knowledge Agent Theory and Its Autopoietic Characteristics for Authentic Knowledge Management

Chee Kooi Chan, Yan Yu Chan, and W.H. Ip

Institute of Textiles and Clothing, The Hong Kong Polytechnic University,
Hong Kong
tcchanck@inet.polyu.edu.hk, tcrachan@inet.polyu.edu.hk,
mfwhip@inet.polyu.edu.hk

Abstract. Knowledge management is a relatively new academic discipline. Currently, the major studies are in the areas of knowledge transformation and taxonomy. Although many researchers stress that knowledge activists play an essential role in activating the knowledge process, the study of individual behaviour in organisations is neglected. In this paper, we conceptualise knowledge agent theory as a living system and explain its autopoietic characteristics. An empirical study of the organisations that supply stochastic demand products shows that their open work environment and free-thinking atmosphere enable knowledge agents to widen their self-referential and self-observing capacities, which encourages them to activate the knowledge process.

Keywords: autopoietic living system, knowledge agent theory, self-referential, self-observing.

1 Introduction

Knowledge is generally described as a factor which improves the performance of productivity. Management gurus, therefore, pay attention to the application of knowledge in the aspect of improving product, service or production process (Argyris 1977, Drucker 1993, Imai 1997). Von Krogh, Ichijo and Nonaka (2000), argue that "knowledge is justified true beliefs". They consider knowledge as a dynamic human process of justifying personal belief toward the truth. They narrow down knowledge as a sense of a construction of reality, where an individual justifies the truthfulness of their beliefs based on their observations of the world.

From pragmatic view, knowledge is aimed at solving a problem (Styhre, 2003). All of human knowledge consists of actions and the products of acts. Consequently, all knowledge is subject to further inquiry, examination, review, and revision. The action research school (Argyris & Schon 1996) is based on this philosophy and developed a theory for organisation learning. From an epistemological aspect, when beliefs are justified as true, they generate a capacity to act, particularly to make a decision (Davenport & Prusak, 1998; Manjula & Mustapha 2006).

M.D. Lytras et al. (Eds.): WSKS 2008, CCIS 19, pp. 507–512, 2008.

2   The Nature of Knowledge

Popular descriptions of knowledge conceptualise it into two poles, namely explicit and tacit knowledge (Nonaka and Takeuchi 1995, Polanyi 1966, Styhre 2003). Firestone and McElroy (2003) argue that there should be another type of knowledge: implicit knowledge. They define implicit knowledge as that held in the form of one's conceptual framework, as expressed in one's language that can be transformed into explicit knowledge. In this process, we need a knowledge agent who plays a vital role in learning and activating the learned knowledge.

From a life cycle perspective (Birkinshaw & Sheehan 2002, Bukowitz W & Williams R 2000, McElroy M 2003, Wiig 1993), knowledge is alive when it is applied in work. The knowledge, however, can be activated only if there is a 'knowledge agent' who is willing to learn the explicit knowledge and apply it in his/her work. Extending the life cycle nature of knowledge concept, we consider knowledge may be contained in two forms, namely in organic and inorganic forms. In an organic form, knowledge may grow via refinement, by a transfer to other members and/or be reproduced by learning. It may hibernate in an inactive state, either to be used later or to enter another stage of life, by being forgotten or lost temporary. In inorganic form, knowledge is transformed into an explicit form and stored. It would subsequently either be activated via a knowledge agent to become organic again, or be forgotten, decay, be damaged or lost. So, keeping knowledge in an organic status avoids it becoming dead stock. This status needs to satisfy two conditions: the knowledge is being activated and there is a knowledge agent to activate it.

The potential achievement of acquiring knowledge in an organisation is to develop a sense to receive the signal of changes in the environment and respond to them in order to make better decisions or solutions. There is an issue as to whether it is the organisation or the individual that establishes such a sense. As we mentioned earlier, knowledge is in an individual's mind and in organisational routines, processes, practices and norms. To manage an organisation's knowledge, by only considering the system's side is insufficient to cover the other key factor: individuals. Knowledge agent refers to an individual, function or organisation as the energy sources of the actions for the process. So, it is important to find out the ontology of the knowledge agent by which management may learn the way to motivate people for knowledge processes in the knowledge emphasis era.

3   Knowledge Agent Theory (KAT)

Knowledge in nature is not a living thing. It must be stored in containers. In order to activate organisation knowledge, organisation needs knowledge agents, who have organic and autopoietic nature, to act the role. Maturana and Varela (1980) define an autopoietic entity as a unified network of the processes of the production of components which: (i) through their interactions and transformation continuously regenerate and realise the network of processes that produced them, and (ii) constitute it as a concrete unity in the space in which they exist by specifying the topological domain of its realisation as such a network. Von Krogh (1995) summarised the concepts of an autopoietic system into four basic properties: autonomous, able to operate in an open and closed system, self-referential and self-observing. A knowledge agent must keep his own components at a survival level by self-producing, because knowledge in nature cannot be transferred to any entity that does not take part in the cognitive process. The property, however, is not necessarily linked with the components that an organisation requires for survival, so unless the entity opens its system to take some inputs from an external environment and interacts with these external components it will not survive.

In the case where a knowledge agent finds his knowledge stock cannot support his existence, he would self-produce the component he thinks is important through interactions with other knowledge components. The external environment, however, will trigger him for change only if the environment perturbs its existence. Then the self-observing property helps the knowledge agent increase his awareness of the activating knowledge process. The concept of self-reference is another important explanation of the interaction of components within the boundary of knowledge agents. The self-reference of a knowledge agent means that the knowledge of the individual is recursively accumulated by the entity from his previous knowledge. It is preparation for life. An autopoietic system may be self-referential in regards to a specific space-time combination, but it can also be self-referential in regards to its own evolution. This property is similar to the pragmatic approach of knowledge generation. The implication of this property is that an entity learns through self-reference, which is a feature all living systems have in regards to previous knowledge.

To understand the behaviours of an organisation as a whole, we need to consider the epistemology of organisations for knowledge agent theory development. The KAT aims at explaining the behaviour of an entity, which is willing to contribute to knowledge process in an organisation, for the life of the entity. The source of willingness is viewed from the entity's standpoint and it needs compensation for perturbations. So the KAT is trying to answer the question: Why individuals within an organisation come to know.

The constructs of KAT embrace two beliefs: (1) A Knowledge Agent is a living system with autopoietic properties who originally interacts with his components aiming at the self-production of his own components: knowledge for coping with problems; (2) A Knowledge Agent is an enabler, who consciously and unconsciously contributes, depending on the tempo and spatial situation, in vitalising an organisation to become a quasi-living system.

4 Empirical Study

The aims of the empirical study are to explore and compare the knowledge management approach of successful companies in the same product supply chain so that to identify conditions to remain the autopoietic characteristics towards knowledge agents. In this paper, we will limit our discussion with the findings to examine about the KAT and organisation condition to maintain autopoietic characteristics of being a knowledge agent via knowledge creation and transference. We selected three companies in the U.S., Hong Kong, and Spain respectively with stochastic demand from the highly competitive fashion industry, for our study.

4.1 Findings

Company I is an American multi-national private company supplying raw materials for the apparel market. With a strong cultural principle of freedom, the company encourages, helps, and allows its associates to grow in knowledge. There are no hierarchical levels in the organization. The company emphasises that knowledge management should allow for knowledge flow within the organization and always tries to establish a physical environment that encourages associates to share knowledge. Its Hong Kong branch adopted the concept of a public library layout where individuals do not occupy any work table permanently. This physical layout provides an environment for people to change places when they need to work with others. All associates are free to contact any others they believe they may obtain knowledge from others, individuals are also willing to share what they know.

Company II is an international Original Equipment Manufacturer (OEM) with over 30,000 employees. Employees, either individual or in team, can propose improvement plans to management. When a plan is accepted, it gains resource support from management. Each year, all managerial-level staff participates at a corporate conference in order to contribute new knowledge to other production plants. The group uses knowledge sharing as a platform to encourage employees to create and organise new knowledge from their existing knowledge. Employees who contribute knowledge to colleagues receive recognition. The practice of sharing knowledge in the company is not only for transferring knowledge within the corporation quickly. The power of sharing knowledge is twofold. Firstly, it helps employees to internalise their tacit knowledge for transference (Ordonez de Pablos 2006). Employees continuously self-reference their own experience and rationalise the experience into knowledge. Secondly, through the sharing knowledge practice, employees are motivated to create and to learn new knowledge, because this process enables individuals to examine the response from outside. As we discussed earlier, a knowledge agent has self-observing characteristics. Through the knowledge sharing process individuals can arouse their awareness of changes in their external environment.

Company III is a Spanish-based, global fashion manufacturer and retailer owns 3,836 retail shops in 70 countries. Market knowledge, which embraces customers' preferences and trends, is a crucial factor for fast fashion (Gereffi 1994, Gereffi & Memedovic 2003, Christopher & Towill 2001, Dove 1999, Goldman & Nagel 1995, Naylor et al 1999, Sarkis 2001,). The company has a core belief: "timeliness", which is the solution of their business. They emphasise that the retail shop is a restart point of their business because they can collect much information from customers. Individuals are the knowledge units for learning about changes in the market and solving business problems. The company has identified smooth communication as the key to eliminate unnecessary delays during production so that the total lead time can be minimised. There is neither a hierarchical boundary nor any physical fixture restricting employees' communication. Employees have their job responsibilities and therefore, they have to make their own judgments and decisions concerning the handling of their daily tasks. Therefore, individuals have the drive to learn new knowledge for coping with their new challenges every moment. The openness of the company leads employees to build up their autonomy to create new things and/or to establish different ways to do things.

4.2 Discussion

In our Knowledge Agent Theory, we explained that knowledge agents must be living systems with autopoietic characteristics in order to become organic containers, which retain the knowledge necessary for helping an organisation achieve something through innovation or solution. Knowledge agents, therefore, should have the capacity to activate knowledge processes, be willing to make an effort, and have a plan to realise the knowledge processes. In our study, the findings indicate there are several common elements among the organisations we visited. In each, the knowledge agent holds the conditions needed to perform the tasks to activate the knowledge processes underpinned with autopoietic characteristics.

Firstly, none of the three organisations aim at transferring tacit or implicit knowledge into explicit knowledge. Instead, they encourage individuals to generate and share knowledge in order to solve their business issues. Solving problems is the destination, and knowledge creation is the means. Given these aims the organisations provide a physical working environment and a non-physical status, in which the office layout is open and free, and there is no hierarchy. This environment nurtures company employees so that they are capable of getting the skills for acquiring and implementing knowledge. This environment also arouses an employee's self-observance of the need for change, and a self-reference of past experience and future expansion of knowledge boundaries. The openness of communication encourages employees to communicate with each other. The companies also create an atmosphere where employees continuously learn through multi-dimensions: from colleagues, customers and business partners. With the principle of respect for other people's views and knowledge, the employees are also willing to open their learning system to expand their knowledge boundary.

Secondly, all there organisations emphasised that they are willing to share the risk of employees' initiatives in pursuing new methods whether they are for solving operational problems or dealing with new requirements in the market. The main characteristic of autopoiesis is its self-producing component for survival. It is an individual's ability to interpret survival components via their self-observing process. So past experience is an essential reference for employees. It helps them decide to choose an action: whether they will act, or stand still, or choose to be conservative in a changing environment. The role of an organisation is to minimise the chance that an individual will refuse to learn new things (Gueldenberg 2004).

References

Argyris, C.: Double Loop learning in organizations. Harvard Business Review, 115–125 (September-October 1977)

Argyris, C., Schön, D.A.: Organizational Learning II: theory, method, and practice. Addison-Wesley Pub. Co., Reading (1996)

Birkinshaw, J., Sheehan, T.: Managing the Knowledge Life Cycle, pp. 75–83. MIT Sloan Management Review, Cambridge (2002)

Bukowitz, W., Williams, R.: The knowledge management fieldbook. Prentice Hall, London (2002)

Christopher, M., Towill, D.: An integrated model for the design of agile supply chains. Int. J. of Physical Distribution & Logistics Management 3(4) (2001)

Davenport, T.H., Prusak, L.: Working Knowledge. Harvard Business School Press, Boston (1998)

Dove, R.: Knowledge management, response ability, and the agile enterprise. J. of Knowledge Management 3(1), 18–35 (1999)

Drucker, P.F.: Post-Capitalist Society. Butterworth-Heinemann, Oxford (1993)

Firestone, J.M., Mcelroy, M.W.: Key Issues in the New Knowledge management. Butterworth Heinemann, Boston (2003)

Gereffi, G.: The organization of buyer-driven global commodity chains: How US retailers shape overseas production networks. In: Gereffi, G., Korzeniewiez, M. (eds.) Commodity Chains and Global Capitalism, Praeger, Westport, CT (1994)

Gereffi, G., Memedovic, O.: The Global Apparel Value Chain: What Prospects for Upgrading by Developing countries, UNIDO, Vienna (2003)

Goldman, S.L., Nagel, R.N., Preiss, K.: Agile Competitors and Virtual Organizations: Strategies for enriching the customer, Van Nostrand Reinhold, New York (1995)

Gueldenberg, S.: Leadership requirements in learning organisations and methods to impact. Int. J. Learning and Intellectual Capital 1(4) (2004)

Imai, M.: Gemba kaizen: a commonsense low-cost approach to management. McGraw-Hill, New York (1997)

von Krough, G., Roos, J.: Organizational Epistemology. St Martin's Press, New York (1995)

von Krough, G., Nonaka, I.K.: Enabling Knowledge Creation. Oxford University Press, New York (2000)

Manjula, J., Mustapha, S.M.: Issue on Knowledge Management in organisations Today. In: Knowledge Management International Conference and Exhibition (2006)

Maturana, H.R., Varela, F.J.: Autopoiesis and Cognition. D. Reidel Publishing Co., Dordrecht (1980)

McElroy, M.: The new knowledge management: complexity, learning and sustainable innovation. Butterworth-Heinemann, Boston (2003)

Naylor, J.B., Naim, M.M., Berry, D.: Leagility: Integrating the lean and agile manufacturing paradigms in the total supply chain. Int. J. of Production Economics 62, 107–118 (1999)

Nonaka, I., Takeuchi, H.: The knowledge-creating company. Oxford University Press, New York (1995)

Ordonez de Pablos, P.: Knowledge flows and learning at interorganisational level. Int. J. Knowledge and Learning 2(1/2) (2006)

Sarkis, J.: Benchmarking for agility. Benchmarking: An Int. J. 8(2), 88–107 (2001)

Sveiby, K.E.: The New Organizational Wealth. Berret-Koehler, San Francisco (1997)

Snowden, D.: Complex acts of knowing: paradox and descriptive self-awareness. J. of Knowledge Management 6(2), 100–111 (2002)

Wiig, K.M.: Knowledge Management Foundations. Schema Press, Texas (1993)

The Effect of Organizational Learning Tools in Business Results

Inocencia Mª Martínez León[1], Josefa Ruiz Mercader[2],
and Juan Antonio Martínez León[3]

[1] Technical University of Cartagena, Business Economy Department, Faculty of Business,
Paseo Alfonso XIII, 50. C.P.: 30203, Cartagena Murcia
ino.martinez@upct.es
[2] University of Murcia, Organization & Finance Department, Facultad de Economía y
Empresa Campus de Espinardo. C.P.: 30100, Espinardo Murcia
peparuiz@um.es
[3] Technical University of Cartagena, Information Technology and Communications
Department. Escuela Técnica Superior de Ingeniería de Telecomunicación
Campus de la Muralla del Mar. C.P.: 30203, Cartagena Murcia
juanleonxxi@hotmail.com

Abstract. The importance of the tools that facilitate organizational learning has traditionally been outlined in the literature. Information Technologies (ITs) are considered as common facilitating tools for all learning agents by researches and practitioners. Our study focuses on the question what ITs are essential for organizational learning and how they actively contribute to the business results (operative and financial). The results exhibit that the use of databases generates larger sales volumes and better operative results. Companies with low profits tend to use Internet more often and this use improves operative results. Also the use of the electronic mail increases the sales volume.

Keywords: Organizational learning; tools; information technologies; internet; intranet; database; financial and operative results; competitive advantage.

1 Introduction

Today we live in what is clearly manifesting as an ever increasing knowledge society. Learning is the key factor that distinguishes the knowledge society from the information society. In this emerging global, multicultural and networked world, information technologies will become natural extensions to people cognition.

Organizational learning is "the capacity to drive a process that transforms the information in knowledge. This process is generated by different agents: organization, groups and individuals. It is affected by a set of factors related to the agents and the organizational context, and facilitated by series of tools". It improves the managerial activity, its performance, and therefore its source of competitive advantages.

The direct result of organizational leaning is knowledge, which is "information combined with experience, context, interpretation, and reflection". Knowledge is an intangible resource, one of the most important strategic assets in organizations and a

M.D. Lytras et al. (Eds.): WSKS 2008, CCIS 19, pp. 513–520, 2008.
© Springer-Verlag Berlin Heidelberg 2008

vital source of competitive advantage (Spender and Grant, 1996). Consequently, an extensive body of research in organizational learning has focused on identifying the facilitating tools that create knowledge and enhance business performance.

In this context, our paper identifies the main organizational learning tools (OLT), empirically exploring actual OLT use and analysis the significant influence of OLT on financial and operative results of the firms.

2 Conceptual Background

The facilitating learning tools help to appropriately develop the learning process in the company, independently of their agents (individual, group and organization). ITs are considered as the most important common tools used by the firms in the organizational learning process and knowledge management (Nonaka et al., 2001).

2.1 The Information Technologies

IT is the capability to electronically input, process, store, output, transmit, and receive data and information, including text, graphics, sound, and video, as well as the ability to control machines of all kinds electronically. Consequently, IT allows: a) the efficient generation, accumulation, dissemination, utilization, and protection of information (Davenport et al., 1998; Ruggles, 1998; Nonaka et al., 2001); b) the improvement and easiness to code, to assimilate and to store information; c) the efficiently and effectively management of knowledge (Nonaka et al., 2001); d) the enhancement of the communication and collaboration (McCampbell *et al.*, 1999); e) the encouragement to share the best practices between departments and employees (Frappaolo and Capshaw, 1999) and f) the reinforcement of organizational memory (Croasdell, 2001).

There are multiple technological tools related to information appropriating and knowledge management, which facilitate the organizational learning. They are:

Internet allows the search and the exchange of data and information (Croasdell, 2001), and general and specific knowledge. These skills streamline learning processes because: a) to make easy the access to information, b) to increase the amount of information on individuals by automatically connecting different data, c) to facilitate the learning process, and d) to construct knowledge networks, because it has a high potential of the reciprocity.

The *corporate Intranet* is an intra-organizational network based on Internet technology (Harvey et al., 1998). If it is well structured, it supports the appropriating, connecting, disseminating, utilizing and protecting information (Ruggles, 1998; Nonaka et al., 2001). Accordingly, this tool sustains the creation of knowledge, facilitates exchange, distribution and deposit of the available organizational knowledge.

The *databases* are deposits of past data, information and knowledge, which permit the creation and maintenance of an organizational shared intelligence and memory (Ruggles, 1998; Croasdell, 2001). They also permit that organizations detect similar pattern from previous contexts (Croasdell, 2001), adapt quickly to the changing opportunities and improve their organizational learning process. The use of database reporting has evolved from the defined reports done by the IT's department throught the use of Business Intelligence applications.

The *electronic mail* facilitates the exchange of information between individuals or groups by off-line messages, which can contain documents, programs and texts. It allows the users to process and filter more information, which improve their professionalism and efficiency (Huber, 1991; Day, 1999). Also, it permits the learning among groups and organizations.

The *videoconference* permits the simultaneous dialogue through a virtual interaction among people (De Geus, 1997; Davenport et al., 1998), and the exchange of documents, files and shows. Their use facilitates the frequent exchange of information and the creation, diffusion and transfer of knowledge.

One step further, we can find the *groupware*. This software facilitates the remote communication, which make easy the work in dispersed work teams, and conducive to knowledge generation and transfer (Ruggles, 1998; Nonaka et al., 2001).

Finally, the *simuworld* develops techniques to anticipate what will happen in a future, starting from an initial situation. It improves the decision-making learning.

2.2 Variables of Business Performance

Literature exhibits different opinions on what is understood by business performance.

This multidimensional variable is reflected through financial and non financial assets.

The organizational learning produces changes in organizational behaviour which are not reflected directly in business performance. Consequently, a simple measure doesn't reflect their main results. For this reason, financial and operative results have been considered in this research.

The financial results have been measured using two variables, net profits and sales volume (Tippins and Sohi, 2003). The operative results are based on nonfinancial indicators, coming from Kaplan and Norton (1996) orientations and agrarian sector report recomendations, using a Likert scale type of 7 points.

2.3 Information Technologies as Organizational Learning Tools and Its Influence on Business Results

2.3.1 Information Technology and Its Influence on Business Results

Theoretically, the use of ITs is a source of competitive advantages (Kettinger et al., 1994), but there are not any empirical evidence of ITs provides differential performance (value) over competitors (Carr, 2003 & 2004; Real et al., 2006). However, it is possible to confirm the indirect effect of ITs on performance, mediated by organizational learning (Real et al., 2006). Therefore, ITs have been considered as OLT.

This evidence requires a detailed analysis of the main ITs in the companies: Internet, database and electronic mail, and their contribution to organizational learning.

2.3.2 Organizational Learning as a Determinant of Business Results

Researchers tend to agree that organizational learning has a positive effect on performance and business results. In this sense, there is enough evidence to support a positive link between organizational learning and financial results (Slater and Narver, 1995; Tippins & Sohi, 2003; Pérez et al., 2004; Jimenez and Cegarra, 2007). So, authors, such as Bontis et al. (2002) and Real et al. (2006), declare organizational learning has a positive effect on operative results.

2.3.3 The Influence of Organizational Learning Tools on Financial and Operative Results

This study considers ITs as OLT, because they capture, access, storage, revise and retrieve structured data, diagrams, models, text, and images. Consequently, OLT help to develop a set of competences and support organizational learning, which on generate a real value for financial (net profit and sales volume) and operative results.

However, the scientific concept of OLT and their influence on business results has not yet evolved, and there are not any confirmation of this relation. In contrast, we have verified that organizational learning has a positive effect on business results and ITs are not in themselves able to improve business results, but they has a indirect effect, mediated by organizational learning (Real et al., 2006). In agreement with the above, the following working hypotheses can be drawn up:

> H1: organizational learning tools positively affect the net profit.
> H2: organizational learning tools positively affect the sales volume.
> H3: organizational learning tools positively affect operative results.

3   Methods

3.1 Sample and Procedures

An empirical study was carried out on large Spanish agriculture firms, because large size is associated with mayor learning process. We chose companies with 1 Meuro of sales volume, which gave us an objective population of 173 firms. The data were collected via a personal survey to the general manager. One hundred and thirteen questionnaires were returned, of which all were considered valid, which represents a response rate of 65.3% and 5.56% sampling error for a confidence interval of 95%.

3.2 Scale Development and Validation

Our scale development and refinement is based upon a Malhotra (1999) methodology, facilitated by a Delphi Methodology. The preliminary test was developed interviewing other managers from the same sector. Table 1 shows the definitive component of the OLT. This scale exhibits excellent reliability with estimate of .81.

Table 1. Definitive components of organizational learning' technological tools

Technological Tool	Uses
Is there Internet link?	It is used to obtain current clients' information.
	It is used to obtain potential clients' information.
	It is used to obtain suppliers' information.
	It is used to obtain information of sector associations.
Have the firm databases?	To plan of production
	To stock and storehouse management
	To commercial management
Has the firm electronic mail?	It is used to obtain current clients' information.
	It is used to obtain potential clients' information.
	It is used to obtain suppliers' information.
	It is used to obtain information of sector associations.

3.3 Formative Measure of Organizational Learning Tools

In the literature revised, a measurement of the OLT has not been detected. In our opinion, it is necessary the creation of a formative measurement that allows to measure clearly and simply the level of use of such instruments.

Use a formative model is justified because a OLT construct is composed by three proposed tools, which do not necessarily have to be correlated. So, companies can have different use' level of databases, but they not employ e-mail or internet for those purposes. It is also true that companies with high scores on the three tools will have learnt more than companies with high scores on only some of them. This is a logical statement, but it is not compatible with the reflective view because we can expect that if there are organizational learning differences between companies, this will be reflected in all the dimensions, not only in some of them. Finally, the dimensions of OLT are not interchangeable because if we disregard one of them, the meaning of the construct is clearly altered.

4 Contrasting the Theoretical Model

In order to test the proposed hypotheses, we have estimated a formative measure of use of the OLT. Next, a one-factor ANOVA (Analysis of Variance) has been carried out for each one of the components and the different dependent variables (net profits, sales volume and operative results). Some applied ANOVA techniques on averaged data, drawing (mean) performance comparisons over firms at different levels or ranges of OLT.

To test the homogeneity of variances in the groups, the test of Levene was used. Since the variances are not equal, the test of Tamhane and Bonferroni were selected to see which mean values differ statistically from each other (SPSS, 1996, 1994). The results of these tests are shown in Table 3.

5 Results

Table 2 shows the descriptive information of use of OLT and its components. The agricultural firms use an average of 7.5 instruments of 11 uses considered. These results show us that the electronic mail is the tool less used (mean is of 2.5 on 4 included practices) compare to Internet (2.7 on 4) and database (2.3 on 3).

Table 2. Descriptive information about organizational learning tools and their components

	Index of organizational learning tools' use	Subindex of Internet' use	Subindex of database' use	Subindex of e-mail' use
Items number	11	4	3	4
Arithmetic mean	7.5	2.7	2.3	2.5
Medium	7.6	2.9	2.4	2.4

Overall ANOVA results are reported in Table 3, which shows the proportion of variance of each independent variables (each subindex) explained by factor Net profit. The results of ANOVA analyses show that the use of Internet has a significantly influence in this factor, while the others not.

Table 3. ANOVA results to Factor Net Profit, Sales Volume and Operative Result

	Internet' use			Database' use			E-mail' use		
Net Profit	Mean	N	Anova Test	Mean	N	Anova Test	Mean	N	Anova Test
1. High	2.04	25							
2. Intermediate	1.85	64	(1)						
3. Losses	2.32	19	(2)						
Inter-group Significant Results	0.016[b]			[c] NS			[c] NS		
	Internet' use			**Database' use**			**E-mail' use**		
Sales Volume	Mean	N	Anova Test	Mean	N	Anova Test	Mean	N	Anova Test
1. High				2.14	22	(3)	2.65	32	(3)
2. Medium				2.53	53	(3)	2.34	38	(3)
3. Small				1.80	31	(1,2)	1.75	36	(1,2)
Inter-group Significant Results	[c] NS			0.009 [a]			0.001 [b]		
	Internet' use			**Database' use**			**E-mail' use**		
Operative Results	Mean	N	Anova Test	Mean	N	Anova Test	Mean	N	Anova Test
1. High	3.12	24	(2)	3.21	24	(3)			
2. Medium	2.56	62	(1)	2.69	55	(3)			
3. Small	2.39	18		2.14	28	(1,2)			
Inter-group Significant Results	0.058 [a]			0.002 [b]			[c] NS		

[a] Variance analysis using statistical Bonferroni; [b] Variance analysis using statistical Tamhane test. [c]NS: no significant.

Table 3 exhibits the existent relation between OLT and performance variables:

a) Net profit: the ANOVA analysis confirms significant differences among companies with intermediate benefits (1.85) compare to firms which get losses (2.32). Databases and electronic mail has not significant relationship with net profit. This shows the general hypothesis is partially accepted.

b) Sales volume: the hypothesis 2 is partially accepted, because the databases and the electronic mail have a positive influence in the sales volume while the Internet use has not a significant relationship with the financial result. So, we can conclude that those organizations with high databases and electronic mail uses get great sales volumes.

c) Operative results: the hypothesis 3 is partially accepted, because the Internet and databases use have a positive influence in the firms' operative results. The electronic mail use has not any significant relationship in this variable. Thus, we can conclude that those organizations with high Internet and databases uses get better operative results.

6 Discussion

The essential purpose of this study is to test empirically the relationship between OLT and their effect on business performance. The findings in this study indicate that the grade of use of the OLT is close to 68% of the considered ITs. Database is broadly used in the firm's. Internet is not so important in our study, due to a) the construction and design of a Web site is a big step for these agricultural companies, b) the production companies are less interesting in image projection than commercial firms (Berranger et al., 2001); and c) production centres' (farms) are dispersed geographically, where internet access and other technological infrastructure could be expensive. However, electronic mail is proportionally less used, due to middle field manager are not technical skilled.

This study tries to find support for the association of OLT and business results (financial and operative) in the companies. Surprisingly, we have obtained empirical evidence that the organizations with larger use of Internet get fewer net profits. We identify larger companies as firm profile that uses Internet, because a) they have an important area of influence; b) its production centres are dispersed geographically, c) the increasing customer requirements' force to use this tool, and d) its has sufficient human and economic resources to efficiently implant and use this tool.

Internet has not got any significant influence on sales volume. However, this tool has a significant influence on operative result, as we proposed in the hypothesis.

The companies with higher use of databases obtain great sales volumes and operative results. As we explained before, databases provide information and knowledge about the product, market and customers' necessities, which allow improving the product design and adapting continuously the company to the turbulent environment.

Finally, the study states that the use of the electronic mail has a more positive impact on the sales volume. Contrary to expectation, electronic mail has not got any significant impact on net profit and operative results. This situation is inconsistent with our predictions and even opposite to the literature.

References

1. Berranger, P., Tucker, D., Jones, L.: Internet Diffusion in Creative Micro-Businesses: Identifying Change Agent Characteristics As Critical Success Factors. Journal of Organizational Computing and Electronic Commerce 11(3), 197–214 (2001)
2. Bontis, N., Crossan, M.M., Hulland, J.: Managing an Organizational Learning System by Aligning Stocks and Flows. Journal of Management Studies 39(4), 43–469 (2002)
3. Carr, N.G.: IT doesn't matter. Harvard Business Review 41, 9 (2003)
4. Carr, N.G.: Does it matter? Information Technology and Corrosion of Competitive Advantage. Harvard Business School Press (2004)
5. Croasdell, D.T.: It´s Role in Organizational Memory and Learning. Information Systems Management 18(1), 8–11 (2001)
6. Crossan, M.M., Lane, H.W., White, R.E., Djurfeldt, L.: Organizational learning: Dimensions for a theory. International Journal of Organizational Analysis 3(4), 337–360 (1995)

7. Davenport, T.H., DeLong, D.W., Beers, M.C.: Successful knowledge management projects. Sloan Management Review 39(2), 43–57 (1998)
8. Day, R.: Learning Organizations: the Future. NZ Business 13(1), 55–56 (1999)
9. De Geus, A.P.: The Living Company. Harvard Business Review 75(2), 51–59 (1997)
10. Frappaolo, C., Capshaw, C.: Knowledge management software: capturing the essence of know-how and innovation. Information Management Journal 33(3), 44–48 (1999)
11. Harvey, M., Palmer, J., Speier, C.: Implementing Intra-Organizational Learning: A Phased-Model Approach Supported by Intranet Technology. European Management Journal 16(3), 341–354 (1998)
12. Huber, G.P.: Organizational Learning. The Contributing Processes and the Literatures. Organization Science 2(1), 88–115 (1991)
13. Jimenez-Jimenez, D., Cegarra-Navarro, J.G.: The Performance Effect of Organizational Learning and Market Orientation. Industrial Marketing Management 36, 694–708 (2007)
14. Kettinger, W.J., Grover, V., Guha, S., Segars, A.H.: Strategic Information Systems Revisited: A Study in Sustainability and Performance. MIS Quarterly 18(1), 33–51 (1994)
15. Leonard Barton, D.: Wellsprings of Knowledge: Building and Sustaining the Sources of Innovation. Harvard Business School Press, Boston (1995)
16. Marsick, V.J., Watkins, K.E.: Facilitating Learning Organizations: Making Learning Count. Gower, Aldershot (1999)
17. McCampbell, A.S., Clare, L.M., Gitters, S.H.: Knowledge Management: The New Challenge for the 21st Century. Journal of Management Journal 40(6), 172–179 (1999)
18. Nonaka, I., Reinmöller, P., Toyama, R.: Integrated information technology systems for knowledge creation. In: Dierkes, M., Berthoin-Antal, A., Child, J., Nonaka, I. (eds.) Handbook of Organizational Learning and Knowledge. Oxford University Press, Nueva York (2001)
19. Pérez, S., Montes, J.M., Vazquez, C.J.: Managing knowledge: the link between culture and organizational learning. Journal of Knowledge Management 8(6), 93–104 (2004)
20. Real, J.C., Leal, A., Roldán, J.L.: Information technology as a determinant of organizational learning and technological distinctive competencies. Industrial Marketing Management 35, 505–521 (2006)
21. Ruggles, R.: The State of the Notion: Knowledge Management in Practice. California Management Review 40(3), 80–89 (1998)
22. Slater, S.F., Narver, J.C.: Market Orientation and the Learning Organization. Journal of Marketing 59(3), 63–74 (1995)
23. Spender, J.C., Grant, R.: Knowledge and the Firm: Overview. Strategic Management Journal 17, 5–9 (1996)
24. Tippins, M.J., Sohi, R.S.: It Competency and Firm Performance: Is Organizational Learning a Missing Link. Strategic Management Journal 24(8), 745–761 (2003)

Classification of Satellite Images Using the Cellular Automata Approach

Moisés Espínola[1], Rosa Ayala[1], Saturnino Leguizamón[2], and Massimo Menenti[3]

[1] Department of Computer Science, University of Almeria, Spain
[2] DICT, University of Mendoza, Argentina
[3] CNR, Institute for Mediterranean Agriculture and Forest Systems (ISaFoM), Italy

Abstract. Nowadays, remote sensing allows us the acquisition of information using techniques that do not require be in contact with the object or area being observed. This science can be used in many environmental applications, helping to solve and improve the social problems derived from them. Examples of remotely sensed applications are in soil quality, water resources, environmental management and protection or meteorology, among others. The classification algorithms are one of the most important techniques used in remote sensing that help developers to interpret the information contained in the satellite images. At present, there are several classification processes, i.e., maximum likelihood, paralelepiped or minimum distance classifier, among others. In this paper, we investigate a new Classification Algorithm based on Cellular Automata (*ACA*): a technique usually used by researchers on Complex Systems. This kind of classifier will be validated and experimented in the SOLERES framework.

Keywords: Remote sensing, Cellular Automata, Classification, Satellite Image.

1 Introduction

Remote Sensing is the most relevant science that permits us to obtain information about the surface of the land and environmental information values, without having actual contact with the area [8]. This science has reached a great advance in the last years. The analysts use the classification algorithms to interpret the information contained in the satellite images. In the literature, there are different procedures to classify images.

In this paper we propose a new procedure for the classification of satellite images. The new algorithm of classification uses the Cellular Automata for the assignment of the pixels to the different classes. Cellular Automata have been applied in many fields related to simulation processes [6] or ecosystem modelling in complex systems. In remote sensing, Cellular Automata have been used in image enhancement or edges detection [7]. The application of Cellular Automata to classification process is a new field of investigation.

This new classification process is incorporated into an environmental Information System. This kind of Information System is designed to solve environmental problems, facilitate risk analysis and improve environmental stewardship.

M.D. Lytras et al. (Eds.): WSKS 2008, CCIS 19, pp. 521–526, 2008.

In this paper, we focus on describing *ACA*, the new algorithm of classification based on cellular automata.

The rest of the paper is structured as follows. Section 2 and 3 briefly describes some of the more common techniques used in classification of satellite images and simulation using cellular automata, respectively. In Section 4, we focus in the use of cellular automata to classify satellite images. Finally, in Section 5, we finish the paper explaining some conclusions and future work.

2   Classification of Satellite Images

The aim of satellite images classification is to divide image pixels into discrete classes (spectral classes). The resulting classified image is essentially a thematic map of the original image [9]. Figure 1 shows the classification process.

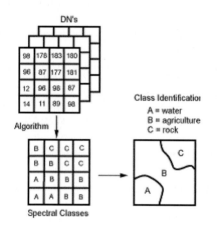

Fig. 1. Classification process

Common classification procedures can be broken down into two divisions based on the method used: *supervised classification* and *unsupervised classification*. In a supervised classification, the analyst selects samples of the different elements to identify in the image.

In this method the analyst knowledge of the study area determines the quality of the training set. Then, the computer uses an algorithm to compare each pixel in the image to these signatures. The pixels are labelled as the class most closely resembles digitally [2].

There are several types of statistics-based supervised classification algorithms. Some of the more popular ones are *parallelepiped, minimum distance, maximum likelihood, fuzzy supervised, neural model* and *Mahalanobis distance*, among others. The difference among the types of supervised classification is how they determine similarity between pixels. In an unsupervised classification, the analyst only specifies the number of classes, and the algorithm groups the classes, based solely on the numerical information in the data. In these algorithms, the analyst has not to know the zone to study. There are many algorithms of classification unsupervised. The Isodata algorithm is the most known unsupervised classification tool. Others unsupervised classifiers are *k-means*, *Leader*, *neural model unsupervised* or *MaxiMin*. The use of supervised or unsupervised procedures depends of the analyst knowledge about the study zone [1]. Figure 2 shows a satellite image classified using an unsupervised classifier and Figure 3 shows a supervised classifier.

In spite of the great number of classifiers that exist, there are several researchers studying new classification methods. We have invested a new classification algorithm based on cellular automata.

3   Application of Cellular Automata

In recent years Cellular Automata have become a powerful tool applied in satellite images especially to simulate processes. A cellular automaton consists of a grid of cells that are normally distributed in a matrix form. When we work with satellite images, we consider each pixel of the image as a cell of the cellular automaton.

Cellular automata have the following basic features:

- *States*: each cell can take an integer value that corresponds to the current state of that cell. There is a finite set of states.
- *Neighbourhood*: is a collection of cells that interact with the current one. To perform simulations on a satellite image we normally take the 8 around pixels as neighbourhood.
- *Transition function (f)*: takes as input arguments the cell and neighbourhood values, and returns the new state of the current cell.

The transition function is applied to each cell of the grid across several iterations. Therefore Cellular Automata have an evolution process because some cells are changing their states across the different iterations. From this point of view, Cellular Automata can be used in simulation applications that experiment a time evolution like fire diseases, snow-cover process [4] or land features dynamics [5].

4   Cellular Automata for Classifying Satellite Images

So far Cellular Automata have been applied on satellite images mainly to simulate processes. In this paper we propose an important alternative: the use of cellular automata to classify satellite images.

We must accomodate the following correspondences between Cellular Automata and the elements of a generic process of image classification before implementing the *ACA* algorithm (shown in Table 1):

- Each cell of the grid corresponds to a pixel of the image.
- Each state of cellular automaton will represent a different class of the final classification.
- The neighbourhood of each cell will consist of the 8 nearest cells.
- The transition function (*f*) must correctly classify each pixel of the image based on the features of the current cell and its neighborhood.

Fig. 2. Satellite image classified using an unsupervised classifier

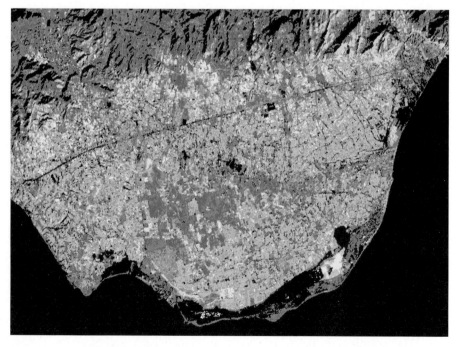

Fig. 3. Satellite image classified using a supervised classifier

Table 1. Classification Algorithm based on Cellular Automata (ACA)

1. *We must determine the number k of states of the cellular automaton.*
2. *The transition function (f) is applied to each cell in lonely mode, without having into account the neighbourhood of each cell. The result obtained is a provisional and not optimal pre-classification of the image into the k classes established in the step 1. In the following steps, the classification algorithm will improve this initial classification.*
3. *The transition function (f) is applied to each cell having into account its neighbourhood, so that some cells change their state and the current classification is improved.*
4. *If there are some cells that have changed their state in the last step, return to the step 3.*

ACA improves the results obtained by another unsupervised classification algorithms, because in the classification process of each image pixel we use the around pixels as neighbourhood in the transition function *f*, and this relationship among the image pixels offers an optimal final classification.

The reader will find more information about the ACA proposal and the SOLERES project at http://www.ual.es/acg/soleres.

5 Conclusions and Future Work

Remote Sensing techniques improve human life offering a lot of useful applications that can be used in several areas of knowledge. In this study we have analyzed the quality of image classification outputs using many classification algorithms. We have used an approach from the measurements of signature *separability* and *thresholding* analysis [3]. This approach, that defines relationships between spectral reflectances and physical attributes, shows that the Classification Algorithm based on Cellular Automata *(ACA)* offers good results comparing others unsupervised algorithms.

As a future work, we are designing a new performance indicator to evaluate the image classifiers. This performance indicator evaluates different aspects related to the classification process. The new indicator and the new classifier based on cellular automata will be validated and experimented in the SOLERES framework.

Acknowledgments. This work has been partially supported by the EU (FEDER) and the Spanish MEC under grant of the project I+D TIN2007-61497 *"SOLERES. A Spatio-Temporal Environmental Management System based on Neural-Networks, Agents and Soft. Components"*.

References

1. Ayala, R.M., Menenti, M., Girolana, D.: Evaluation methodology for classification process of digital images Igarss 2002. In: IEEE Int. Geoscience and Remote Sensing Symposium and the 24th Canadian Symposium on Remote Sensing. VI, Toronto, Canada, pp. 3363–3365 (2002)

2. Ayala, R., Becerra, A., Flores, I.M., Bienvenido, J.F., Díaz, J.R.: Evaluation of Greenhouse Covered Extensions and Required Resources with Satellite Images and GIS. Almería's Case. In: Second European Conference of the European Federation for Information Technology in Agriculture, Food and the Environment, Bonn, Germany, September 27-30 (1999)
3. D'Urso, G., Menenti, M.: Performance indicators for the statistical evaluation of digital image classification. ISPR Journal of Photogrammetry & Remote Sensig 51, 78–90 (1996)
4. Leguizamón, S.: Modeling land features dynamics by using cellular automata techniques. In: Proceedings of the ISPR Technical Comision 7 Mid-Term Synmposium From pixels to Processess. Organized by ITC, Enschede, The Netherlands (2006)
5. Leguizamón, S.: Simulation of snow-cover dynamics using the cellular automata approach. In: Proceedings of the 8th International Symposium on High-Mountain Remote Sensing Cartography, La Paz, Bolivia (2005)
6. Muzy, A., Innocenti, E., Hill, D., Aiello, A., Santucci, J.F., Santonio, P.A., Hill, D.: Dynamic structure cellular automata in a fire spreading application. In: First Int. Conference on Informatics in Control, Automation and Robotics, Setubal, Portugal, pp. 143–151 (2004)
7. Popovici, A., Popovici, D.: Cellular Automata in Image Processing. In: Proceedings of the 15th International Symposium on the Mathematical Theory of Networks and Systems (2002)
8. Rees, W.G.: Physical Principles of Remote Sensing, 2nd edn. Cambridge University Press, Cambridge (2001)
9. Schowengerdt, R.A.: Techniques for Image Processing and Classification in Remote Sensing. Academic Press, London (1985)

Preliminary Study of the Expected Performance of MAUT Collaborative Filtering Algorithms

Nikos Manouselis[1,2] and Constantina Costopoulou[1]

[1] Greek Research & Technology Network (GRNET) S.A.,
56 Mesogion Av., 115 27, Athens, Greece
nikosm@ieee.org
[2] Informatics Laboratory, Div. of Informatics, Mathematics & Statistics, Dept. of Science,
Agricultural University of Athens, 75 Iera Odos Str., 11855, Athens, Greece
tina@aua.gr

Abstract. This paper presents the results of an initial study on how a set of multi-attribute utility collaborative filtering algorithms are expected to perform, under various experimental conditions. An online simulator has been used to produce a large number of synthetic data sets with varying properties. Then, the examined algorithms have been executed and evaluated upon all data sets, using different performance metrics. A statistical analysis of the results has followed, trying to make initial conclusions about the expected performance of the studied algorithms under different operational conditions.

Keywords: collaborative filtering, simulation, multi-attribute utility.

1 Introduction

The problem of recommendation has been identified as the way to help individuals in a community to find information or products that are most likely to be interesting to them or to be relevant to their needs [11]. In a recommender system, the items of interest and the user preferences are represented in various forms, which may involve one or more variables. Particularly in systems where recommendations are based on the opinion of others, the incorporation of the multiple criteria that can affect the users' opinions into the recommendation problem, can potentially lead to more realistic recommendations [1]. To this direction, several recommender systems have already been engaging multiple criteria for the production of recommendations. Such systems, referred to as multi-criteria recommenders, early demonstrated the potential of applying multi-criteria decision making (MCDM) methods to facilitate recommendation in numerous application domains [2].

Evaluation studies of recommender systems indicate that careful testing and parameterization has to be carried out, before a recommender system is finally deployed in a real setting [3,5,7,8]. On the other hand, most current multi-criteria recommenders usually remain at a design or prototyping stage of development [13]. Testing methods and tools that may support their systematic implementation and evaluation in the context of real-life applications are limited [15]. Experimental testing for multi-criteria recommenders could be greatly facilitated by testing tools that

M.D. Lytras et al. (Eds.): WSKS 2008, CCIS 19, pp. 527–536, 2008.

would allow the simulated execution of multi-criteria recommendation algorithms, similar to tools proposed for single-criterion recommenders (e.g. [4,6,15]).

In this paper we present a preliminary study that introduces the use of such a testing tool in order to carry out a simulated study of a particular class of multi-criteria recommenders, namely multi-attribute utility collaborative filtering systems. The tool is used (i) to create a large variety of synthetic data sets with item evaluations, and (ii) to execute a previously proposed family of algorithms (which are not presented here for brevity reasons) upon these data sets [12]. The results are then statistically analysed, aiming to reach some first conclusions about how the performance of the algorithms is expected to change, as the properties of the data set vary. A number of relevant hypotheses are formed, and their validity is discussed.

2   Multi-attribute Collaborative Filtering

In collaborative filtering, the recommendation problem can be formulated as it follows [2,12]: let C be the set of all users and S the set of all possible items that can be recommended. We define $U^c(s)$ as a utility function $U^c(s) : C \times S \rightarrow \Re^+$ that measures the appropriateness of recommending an item s to user c. It is assumed that this function is not known for the whole C x S space but only on some subset of it. Therefore, in the context of recommendation, we want to use the evaluations that users in C have provided about items in S, in order to be able for each user $c \in C$:

(i) to estimate (or approach) the utility function $U^c(s)$ for an item s of the space S for which $U^c(s)$ is not yet known; or,

(ii) choose a set of N items $S' \subseteq S$ that will maximize $U^c(s)$:

$$\forall c \in C, s = \max_{s \in S} U^c(s) \tag{1}$$

The goal of collaborative filtering system is then to provide to an interested user (called the *active user*) $a \in C$ either an estimation of the utility for a particular target item s that he has not previously evaluated, or a ranking of a subset of items $S'' \subseteq S$. For the items in S'' that the active user a has not evaluated yet, this corresponds again to the prediction of the utility $U^a(s)$ for each item $s \in S''$ that this user has not evaluated. Thus, we may address both goals in a similar manner, by calculating the prediction of $U^a(s)$. In most recommender systems, the utility function $U^c(s)$ usually considers one attribute of an item, referred to as its overall evaluation or *rating*. Nevertheless, utility may also involve more than one item attributes. The recommendation problem therefore becomes a multi-criteria one.

Engaging Multi-Attribute Utility Theory (MAUT) [9], the recommendation problem in collaborative filtering systems may be defined in of the simplest forms of multi-criteria decision modeling. In this case, the multiple attributes describing an item s can be defined as a set of criteria upon which a user evaluates the item. The utility function $U^c(s)$ is then referred to as the *total utility* of an item s, which is calculated by synthesizing the *partial utilities* of item s on each one of the criteria. Due to the modelling of this recommendation problem using MAUT principles, we refer to it using the term *multi-attribute utility (MAUT) collaborative filtering.*

3   Collaborative Filtering Simulator (CollaFiS)

CollaFiS is a Web-based testing tool that aims to support people interested in parameterizing and evaluating collaborative filtering algorithms under various experimental conditions [11]. The rationale for developing CollaFiS has been that similar tools already exist for single-criterion recommenders [4,6,14]. An important difference is that for their experimental testing, single-criterion systems mainly use publicly available data sets from real operation (e.g. the MovieLens, EachMovie and Jester data sets) [8]. Such data sets are made freely available to recommender systems' researchers, in order to test new features or algorithms in a simulated environment, before their actual deployment. In a similar manner, the systematic evaluation of multi-criteria recommenders would require their experimental investigation using data sets with multi-criteria evaluations. Unfortunately, multi-criteria evaluation data sets from real-life applications are not publicly available until today [1,13], therefore only experimental data sets that have been collected through pilot user studies or synthetic (simulated) data sets can be used for this purpose [15]. In this direction, CollaFiS has been designed to support the creation of synthesized data sets (with either single-criterion or multi-criteria evaluations), allowing also the manual definition of some of their properties. For example, it allows for the manipulation of: the total number of items that may be recommended; the number and scales of the criteria upon which items may be evaluated; the total number of users that provide an evaluation of items; and the total number of multi-criteria evaluations that users have already provided over items.

Then, one or more multi-attribute utility collaborative filtering algorithms may then be selected and parameterized, before their execution upon the synthetic data sets. Their performance is measured according to different metrics, such as accuracy of predictions, coverage of predictions, as well as execution time. CollaFiS has been developed using MySQL and PHP technologies in order to be easily accessed and used online [11].

At the current version of CollaFiS, apart from some basic single-criterion algorithms that have been long proposed and tested in the literature [7], a family of previously proposed multi-criteria algorithms has also been implemented. These are neighborhood-based MAUT algorithms for collaborative filtering. That is, they create a 'neighborhood' $D \subseteq C$ of users that have similar preferences with the active user and who have previously evaluated a target item s, and calculate the prediction of $U^a(s)$ according to how the users in the neighborhood D have evaluated s. Several design options can be considered for the parameterization of the proposed algorithms [12], leading to a large number of variations for each algorithm in the proposed family. In our previous work [12], CollaFiS has been used to experimentally investigate the performance of the proposed algorithms upon a particular data set. In the experiment presented in this paper, a different approach has been followed.

4   Evaluation Scenario and Experimental Setting

A typical evaluation scenario for testing collaborative filtering algorithms is the simulated execution of examined algorithms upon a data set with actual evaluations, and the selection/parameterization of the algorithm that seems to be performing better in the particular context. In this study, we adopted a slightly different approach, which carried out a simulated investigation of how the examined algorithms were expected to perform under a variety of operating conditions. More specifically, the aim of our experiment has been to experimentally evaluate the performance of the previously proposed family of MAUT algorithms, upon a variety of data sets with different characteristics, and, in this way, to try to make some initial conclusions about their expected behavior.

The rationale behind the particular evaluation scenario is based on some observations that were made during our previous experiments using CollaFiS. It has been noted that the performance of examined algorithms was changing, depending on the properties of the data set. Considering the fact that different application domains lead to data sets with completely different properties [13], it may be assumed that an algorithm performing well in a particular domain may not perform similarly well in another. For instance, an algorithm that has proven to be performing very good upon the MovieLens data set, may prove to perform poorly when used to support recommendation in a Greek site of movie lovers, which contains less movies, is used by fewer users, and where the number of movies rated by users is much higher than MovieLens. Such a wrong estimation can lead a system developer to choosing an algorithm inappropriate for the needs of the application domain, leading in turn to wasted development effort and possible user disappointment.

Having a prior view of how a particular algorithm is expected to perform in the case of various data sets, may offer a number of practical advantages. For instance, it may help the recommender system developer to chose the algorithm that seems to be performing better upon the evaluations' data set of a particular application domain, change to a more efficient recommendation algorithm when the data set grows with time, or even to build a recommender system that will dynamically select an algorithm according to the current properties of the data set.

The experimental process followed in the examined evaluation scenario, has been the following:

1. The CollaFiS simulator has been used to create a variety of synthetic data sets. The properties of these data sets have been different, e.g. ranging from single-criterion to multi-criteria data sets, or from very sparse to very dense ones.
2. The examined set of MAUT algorithms has been executed upon all data sets, and their performance has been measured using a variety of metrics.
3. Results have been statistically analyzed in order to see if any conclusions can be made about the change of the algorithm performance according to the different data set properties.

In total, 243 synthetic data sets have been produced. The data set characteristics have been ranged as it is illustrated in Table 1. For each one of the data set properties that we examined (i.e. number of criteria used for rating an item, number of scales

Table 1. Range of properties of synthetic data sets used in the experiment

	Min	Max
Criteria	1 criterion	10 criteria
Evaluation scales	2-scale (binary)	10-scale
Items	100 items	1,000 items
Users	50 users	250 users
Evaluations/Ratings	5 evaluations	2,500 evaluations

used for rating upon each criterion, total number of items in the system, total number of users in the system, total number of evaluations/ratings in the system), a variety of values have been tested. In this way, data sets with very different properties occurred: e.g. one extreme case was a very sparse data set that had 250 users and 500 items, but only 5 ratings (because very few users rated some item).

An overall number of 369 algorithm variations belonging to the same family have been examined [12]. The simulation took place in a PC with a Pentium 4 (2.5GhZ, 256 MB RAM) running Microsoft Windows XP, Apache server 1.3.33, PHP 5.0.3, and MySQL Server 4.1. For our experimental testing, three particular performance evaluation metrics have been used:

- *Accuracy*: predictive accuracy of the algorithms has been measured through the mean-absolute error (MAE) of the predicted utility against the actual utility of an item.
- *Coverage*: coverage of the algorithms has been measured as the percentage of items for which an algorithm could produce a prediction.
- *Time*: prediction speed has been measured as the mean time required per item for an algorithm to calculate a prediction and present it to the user.

The goal of the experiment has been to investigate how the properties of the data sets affected the performance of the family of algorithms. Thus, for each metric, a number of hypotheses have been formed:

- **A1:** The higher the number of criteria that a data set involves, the lowest the mean MAE of the produced predictions.
- **A2:** The higher the number of evaluation scales that the criteria use, the lower the mean MAE.
- **A3:** The highest the number of the items candidate for recommendation, the lower the mean MAE.
- **A4:** The highest the number of users using the system, the lower the mean MAE.
- **A5:** The highest the number of evaluations that users have provided, the lower the mean MAE.
- **B1:** There is no relation between the number of criteria that a data set involves and the coverage of the produced predictions.
- **B2:** There is no relation between the number of the criteria evaluation scales and the coverage of the produced predictions.
- **B3:** The higher the number of the items in the system (i.e. the more sparse the data set), the lower the coverage of the algorithm.

- **B4:** The higher the number of users involved, the higher the coverage of the algorithm.
- **B5:** The higher the number of evaluations available (i.e. the denser the data set), the higher the coverage of the algorithm.
- **C1:** A higher number of criteria requires more time for processing, and eventually leads to higher execution time.
- **C2:** A higher number of evaluation scales requires higher execution time.
- **C3:** A higher number of items requires higher execution time.
- **C4:** A higher number of users requires higher execution time.
- **C5:** A higher number of evaluations requires higher execution time.

Next, the validity of these hypotheses is explored by statistically analyzing the simulation results (using the SPSS package).

Table 2. Pearson correlation coefficients for each pair of examined variables

No.	Data Set Property	Metric	Pearson	Sign. (2-tailed)
A1	# of criteria	MAE	-0.139(**)	0.000
A2	# of scales	MAE	0.289(**)	0.000
A3	# of items	MAE	-0.043(**)	0.000
A4	# of users	MAE	0.041(**)	0.000
A5	# of evaluations	MAE	0.344(**)	0.000
B1	# of criteria	Coverage	-0.017	0.127
B2	# of scales	Coverage	0.009	0.424
B3	# of items	Coverage	-0.237(**)	0.000
B4	# of users	Coverage	0.127(**)	0.000
B5	# of evaluations	Coverage	0.430(**)	0.000
C1	# of criteria	Time	0.067(**)	0.000
C2	# of scales	Time	0.000	0.990
C3	# of items	Time	-0.171(**)	0.000
C4	# of users	Time	0.238(**)	0.000
C5	# of evaluations	Time	0.498(**)	0.000

** Correlation is significant at the 0.01 level (2-tailed)

5 Results

Initially, to examine the relation between each data set property and each evaluation metric, we first created the scatterplots of the metric values for each property. To reach conclusions that can be considered statistically significant (and thus may be more safely generalized), further analysis has taken place. More specifically, we have proceeded to the calculation of the Pearson correlation between each data set property and each evaluation metric. The results are presented in Table 2.

From these results, a number of conclusions could be drawn for each of the examined hypotheses. More specifically, for the MAE-related hypotheses the statistical analysis has demonstrated the following:

- *Hypothesis A1*. A weak negative correlation has been identified between the number of criteria that a data set involves and the MAE of the algorithms. The correlation has been found significant at the 0.01 level (2-tailed). This means that the higher the number of criteria used, the lowest the mean MAE of the produced predictions. Thus, Hypothesis A1 can be considered to be confirmed.
- *Hypothesis A2*. A weak positive correlation has been identified between the number of evaluation scales that the criteria use and the MAE of the algorithms. The correlation has been found significant at the 0.01 level (2-tailed). This means that the higher the number of evaluation scales, the higher the mean MAE of the produced predictions. Thus, Hypothesis A2 cannot be considered to be confirmed.
- *Hypothesis A3*. A weak negative correlation has been identified between the number of items available in the system and the MAE of the algorithms. The correlation has been found significant at the 0.01 level (2-tailed). This means that the highest the number of the items involved, the lowest the mean MAE. Thus, Hypothesis A3 can be considered to be confirmed.
- *Hypothesis A4*. A weak positive correlation has been identified between if the number of users using the system and the MAE of the algorithms. The correlation has been found significant at the 0.01 level (2-tailed). This means that the highest the number of users involved, the lowest the mean MAE. Thus, Hypothesis A4 can be considered to be confirmed.
- *Hypothesis A5*. A positive correlation has been identified between the number of evaluations that users have provided and the MAE of the algorithms. The correlation has been found significant at the 0.01 level (2-tailed). This means that the highest the number of evaluations available, the highest the mean MAE. Thus, Hypothesis A5 can not be considered confirmed.

In addition, for the coverage-related hypotheses the statistical analysis has demonstrated the following:

- *Hypothesis B1*. A weak negative correlation has been identified between the number of criteria that a data set involves and the coverage of the algorithms. The correlation has been found non-significant. This means that the number of criteria used does not seriously affect the coverage of the algorithm. Thus, Hypothesis B1 can be considered to be confirmed.
- *Hypothesis B2*. A very weak, positive, and not significant correlation has been identified between the number of evaluation scales that the criteria use and the coverage. This means that a relation cannot be identified between these two parameters. Thus, Hypothesis B2 can be considered confirmed.
- *Hypothesis B3*. A weak negative correlation has been identified between the number of items available in the system and the coverage of the algorithms. The correlation has been found significant at the 0.01 level (2-tailed). This means that the highest the number of the items involved, the lowest the coverage. Thus, Hypothesis B3 can not be considered confirmed.
- *Hypothesis B4*. A weak positive correlation has been identified between the number of users using the system and the coverage of the algorithms. The correlation has been found significant at the 0.01 level (2-tailed). This means that the highest the number of users involved, the highest the coverage. Thus, Hypothesis B4 can be considered to be confirmed.

- *Hypothesis B5.* A positive correlation has been identified between the number of evaluations that users have provided and the coverage of the algorithms. The correlation has been found significant at the 0.01 level (2-tailed). This means that the highest the number of evaluations available, the highest the coverage. Thus, Hypothesis B5 can be considered to be confirmed.

Finally, the following have been demonstrated for the time-related hypotheses:

- *Hypothesis C1.* A weak positive correlation has been identified between the number of criteria that a data set involves and the execution time of the algorithms. The correlation has been found significant at the 0.01 level (2-tailed). This means that the higher the number of criteria, the higher the required execution time. Thus, Hypothesis C1 can be considered to be confirmed.
- *Hypothesis C2.* A very weak, positive, and not significant correlation has been identified between the number of evaluation scales that the criteria use and the execution time. This means that a relation cannot be identified between these two parameters. Thus, Hypothesis C2 cannot be considered confirmed.
- *Hypothesis C3.* A weak negative correlation has been identified between the number of items available in the system and the execution time. The correlation has been found significant at the 0.01 level (2-tailed). This means that the higher the number of items, the lower the required execution time. Thus, Hypothesis C3 cannot be considered confirmed.
- *Hypothesis C4.* A positive correlation has been identified between the number of users using the system and the execution time. The correlation has been found significant at the 0.01 level (2-tailed). This means that the higher the number of users, the higher the required execution time. Thus, Hypothesis C4 can be considered to be confirmed.
- *Hypothesis C5.* A strong positive correlation has been identified between the number of evaluations that users have provided and the execution time. The correlation has been found significant at the 0.01 level (2-tailed). This means that the higher the number of evaluations, the higher the required execution time. Thus, Hypothesis C5 can be considered to be confirmed.

Although we have tried to make some conclusions about the hypotheses based on the correlations, they are still too weak in order to assume that these results can be generalized. Therefore we can make some very initial observations that may serve as directions to explore in future experiments. To start with, the predictive accuracy of the studied family of multi-attribute utility algorithms seems to be affected by:

- the number of criteria used to evaluate the items in the data set,
- the number of items candidate for recommendation,
- and the number of users providing evaluations.

It appears that as the number of criteria or the number of items grows, the accuracy of the examined MAUT algorithms increases. On the other hand, it was strange to observe that in our experiment the accuracy of the examined algorithms decreased as the number of users increased. An explanation could be that an increase in the number of users does not necessary mean that there is an increase in the number of evaluations/ratings as well, and a sparse data set where lots of users have provided few, dispersed ratings could be a case where inaccurate recommendations appear. Another observation that contradicted with our initial expectations has been that prediction accuracy did not seem to be affected by the number of evaluation scales or the number of evaluations available in the system. Again, the reason could be the variety of data sets that have been employed. In the case of a more focused analysis (e.g. with data sets of a particular expected density), the results would be probably more easily explainable.

Similarly, the coverage of the studied MAUT algorithms seems to be affected by the number of items, the number of users, and the number of evaluations. It was expected to observe that an increase to the the number of evaluations/ratings, or an increase to the number of users, would lead to an increase of the coverage as well. It was also partially expected to observe that as the number of items increases, the coverage becomes lower. The multi-criteria nature of the recommendation problem (i.e. the number of criteria) didn't appear to affect the coverage. Neither did the number of evaluation scales that the users engage for rating, as it would have been expected.

Along the same lines, it was logical to observe the prediction speed of the algorithms decreases as the number of criteria, users or evaluations increases. On the other hand, it has been also observed that as the number of items grows, the execution time becomes less. This could be an indication that for the examined neighborhood-based algorithms, the number of items is not adding complexity to their execution. Nevertheless, this is an issue that can be further explored through a formal complexity analysis of the algorithms.

6   Conclusions

This paper presents the results from a preliminary simulation analysis of a family of previously proposed MAUT algorithms for neighborhood-based collaborative filtering, under various experimental conditions. CollaFiS, a Web-based simulation environment for the creation of synthetic data sets and the simulated execution of collaborative filtering algorithms has been used. Such experiments could support recommender system implementers to choose an algorithm that will perform better under several expected operational scenarios. In addition, such experiments may help recommendation algorithm developers to explore the expected behavior of new algorithms under various conditions, e.g. demonstrating how sensitive they are to changes in data set properties.

The preliminary study presented in this paper is this paper is only a small step towards the goal of understanding how can a recommender system be matched to the properties of the data set. One of the aspects to be carefully approached in future work is the detailed representation of meaningful data set properties, that can be also appropriately manipulated during their synthetic (simulated) creation. In addition, the variety of the produced data sets to be studied in a future experiment should be of a greater magnitude, since 243 sets that are limiting items from 100 to 1,000 and users from 50 to 250) cannot be considered an accurate representation of the actual properties of an expected application domain.

References

1. Adomavicius, G., Kwon, Y.: New Recommendation Techniques for Multi-Criteria Rating Systems. IEEE Intelligent Systems 22(3), 48–55 (2007)
2. Adomavicius, G., Tuzhilin, A.: Towards the Next Generation of Recommender Systems: A Survey of the State-of-the-Art and Possible Extensions. IEEE Transactions on Data & Knowledge Engineering 17(6) (2005)
3. Breese, J.S., Heckerman, D., Kadie, C.: Empirical Analysis of Predictive Algorithms for Collaborative Filtering. In: 14th UAI, Madison WI, USA (1998)
4. Cosley, D., Lawrence, S., Pennock, D.M.: REFEREE: An open framework for practical testing of recommender systems using ResearchIndex. In: 28th VLDB Conference, Hong Kong, China (2002)
5. Deshpande, M., Karypis, G.: Item-based Top-N Recommendation Algorithms. ACM Transactions on Information Systems 22(1), 143–177 (2004)
6. Fisher, D., Hildrum, K., Hong, J., Newman, M., Thomas, M., Vuduc, R.: SWAMI: A Framework for Collaborative Filtering Algorithm Development and Evaluation. In: 23rd ACM SIGIR Conference, Athens, Greece (2000)
7. Herlocker, J., Konstan, J.A., Riedl, J.: An Empirical Analysis of Design Choices in Neighborhood-Based Collaborative Filtering Algorithms. Information Retrieval 5 (2002)
8. Herlocker, J.L., Konstan, J.A., Terveen, L.G., Riedl, J.T.: Evaluating Collaborative Filtering Recommender Systems. ACM Transactions on Information Systems 22(1), 5–53 (2004)
9. Keeney, R.L.: Value-focused Thinking: A Path to Creative Decisionmaking. Harvard University Press, Cambridge (1992)
10. Konstan, J.A.: Introduction To Recommender Systems: Algorithms and Evaluation. ACM Transactions on Information Systems 22(1) (2004)
11. Manouselis, N., Costopoulou, C.: Designing a Web-based testing tool for multi-criteria recommender systems. Engineering Letters, on Web Engineering (2006) (special issue)
12. Manouselis, N., Costopoulou, C.: Experimental Analysis of Design Choices in a Multi-Criteria Recommender System. International Journal of Pattern Recognition and AI, Sp. Issue on Personalization Techniques for Recommender Systems & IUI 20(7) (2007)
13. Manouselis, N., Costopoulou, C.: Analysis and Classification of Multi-Criteria Recommender Systems. World Wide Web: Internet and Web Information Systems, Special Issue on Multi-channel Adaptive Information Systems on the World Wide Web 10(4), 415–441 (2007)
14. Montaner, M., Lopez, B., de la Rosa, J.L.: Evaluation of Recommender Systems through Simulated Users. In: 6th ICEIS, International Conference on Enterprise Information Systems, Porto, Portugal (2004)
15. Tso, K.H.L., Schmidt-Thieme, L.: Evaluation of Attribute-aware Recommender System Algorithms on Data with Varying Characteristics. In: 10th PAKDD Conference, Singapore (2006)

Distributed Dependable Enterprise Business System – DDEBS

Kiran Ijaz, Umar Manzoor, and Arshad Ali Shahid

Department of Computer Science, National University of Computer & Emerging Sciences,
H-11/4, Islamabad, Pakistan
kiran.ijaz@nu.edu.pk, umarmanzoor@gmail.com,
arshad.ali@nu.edu.pk

Abstract. The inherent qualities of agent technology make it a perfect choice for many real world applications. However this usefulness can be undermined due to problems incurred by the lack of fault tolerance and security in Multi Agent Based Applications. In this paper we have proposed an infrastructure which provides fault tolerance (at both agent and system level) and security. An algorithm similar to the sliding window model ensures the agent level fault tolerance, while the system level fault tolerance has been provided by dynamic discovery of alternate paths. The proposed framework is envisaged to be used in critical financial applications like Banking applications, E-commerce, Stock exchange etc. Therefore security is provided by means of Triple DES Algorithm for encryption / decryption and MD5 Algorithm for the integrity of the message.

Keywords: Fault Tolerance, Distributed Transactions, Dependable Systems, fault tolerant behavior, FTIMA Architecture, Multi-agent System.

1 Introduction

Multi Agent System (MAS) is a promising paradigm for developing distributed Applications. MAS is a society of autonomous agents, working together to perform a task, by dividing it into subtasks and assigning each agent a specific task in the social dimensions of the problem domain [5]. These agents plan, coordinate, schedule, learn from the environment, and communicate in a multi-agent system.

Online transactions for business systems and e-commerce have become a common phenomenon in the current era of IT development. The use of transactions is a very popular concept for the management of larger data collections. A user who performs an online transaction wants a guaranteed operation and that too within a certain time limit. A characteristic of distributed systems that distinguishes them from single machine systems is the notion of partial failure [1]. A partial failure may happen when one component e.g. a node, link etc. fails. This failure may affect the proper operation of other components, while at the same time leaving other components totally unaffected.

We propose the use of multi-agent system where mobile agents guarantee transactions. The proposed system will provide an acceptable fault tolerant behavior in case of failures. The system or components are designed in such a way that, in the event of

M.D. Lytras et al. (Eds.): WSKS 2008, CCIS 19, pp. 537–542, 2008.
© Springer-Verlag Berlin Heidelberg 2008

a component failure, a backup component or procedure can immediately takes its place with no loss of service. The mobile agents play a central role for guaranteed fault tolerant behavior in this distributed environment. This architecture is envisaged to be used in critical financial applications like banking, E-commerce, stock exchange etc, therefore information security being an important concern has also been catered for. [1, 2, 3].We has developed a simulated environment having multiple ATM's with distributed transactions. This test bed was evaluated with three major concerns, 1) fault tolerance provided in this distributed environment, 2) path optimization provided on network, and 3) security.

2   Related Work

MAS's have been used in a large number of applications because of their tremendous inherent capabilities. However issues related to fault tolerance and security make these agents unsuitable for real world systems. In distributed applications an agent can be lost due to the errors of the networks or the host. Fault-tolerance in mobile agents prevents a partial or complete loss of the agent and enables it to reach to its destination [4]. Some of the fault tolerance mechanisms have already been discussed in the literature. One way to achieve fault tolerance given in [6] is to detect the crash of an agent and resolve the issue through cloning. This method does not cater for the ex-actly-one property where as Strasser et al [7, 8] offers the same by defining the explicit stages of computation and gather results in similar constrained step manner of execution. Secondly improve the reliability using a flexible itinerary with the possibility to defer un-available hosts.

The k shortest paths problem is to list the k paths connecting a given source-destination pair in the graph with minimum total length. Multiple path computation algorithm in [9] introduces routing paths with minimum overlapping of paths on each other. Grover's algorithm [10] calculates the k-shortest link-disjoint paths in a distributed manner and used Dijkstra for path calculation [11].

In [12] Authors discusses the techniques for designing and analyzing distributed security transactions by introducing a security layer. Practical techniques for securing distributed computing systems have been discussed in [13] and presents Cryptography, the Kerberos authentication model and DCE security.

3   System Architecture

The system architecture of DDEBS is composed of the following three main modules *(1)* Fault Tolerance Provider Module (FTP) *(2)* Path Optimization Module (POM) *(3)* Encryption Module (EM). These three modules make a layer between transaction management agent and Java Agent Development Environment (JADE).

3.1   Fault Tolerance Provider Module (FTP)

While lots of work has already been done on fault tolerance, what distinguishes our proposed architecture is a number of features unique to it. First of all it provides both system level and agent level fault tolerance. System level fault tolerance has been provided by the discovery of alternate paths while agent accounted cloning serves the purpose of agent level fault tolerance. Secondly, lacked by the current systems, our proposed system provides what is called continuous monitoring. The actual mechanism for overall system behavior is the result of collaborative efforts done by five types of agents which are 1) Transaction Manager Agent 2) Observer Agent 3) Ping Agent 4) Transaction Agent 5) Statistical Agent

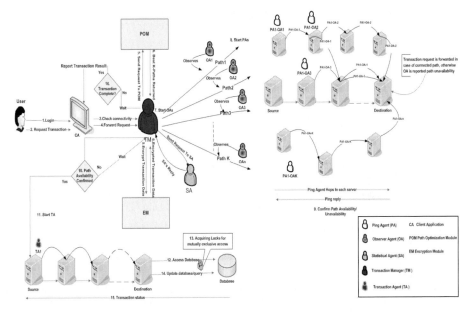

Fig. 1. Architecture Diagram of Distributed Dependable Enterprise Business System

The application starts up as an agent, the Transaction Manager (TM). This agent, by reading a configuration file written in XML starts doing the configuration settings. The next step in the process is optimal path determination [2]. The TM sends a request to the path optimization module with source and destination machines as request parameters. After this, a GUI, customized for financial transaction on an ATM machine, is shown. When the transaction is started, TM starts another type of agents called Observer Agents - OAs. These OAs sit at the path edges and monitor the transactions. An OA is started for each alternate path. To ensure fault tolerance from the first step path availability is checked before routing the transaction using Ping Agents (PAs) whose sole purpose to confirm path availability or unavailability.

To harness the power of parallel processing the OAs are started at the same time. The ping agents started by these OAs hop from machine to machine in the assigned path. On reaching their destination, these PAs report availability to their corresponding OAs. In the case when some path is unavailable, the PAs inform the OAs about it and stop their execution. In this way, the TM gets to know about the best available path. TM starts the transaction agent (TA) which performs the transaction by moving to the final destination. On reaching their destination the TAs report success to the TM and also periodically updates the TM about the transaction status. The system also incorporates a mechanism to ensure whether an agent is lost or whether its execution has only been delayed due to slow processors or communication links [1]. Another important entity in the system is the statistical agent. It collects the statistics about the transactions performed, the paths taken, unavailable paths etc.

3.2 Path Optimization Module (POM)

The POM reads two files containing network configuration. Based on this information, a total of K (provided in the configuration file) alternate paths are discovered. The POM returns to the TM a list of K alternate paths for the transaction. The provided list of available paths is then sorted on the basis of path weights [2].

3.3 Encryption Module (EM)

Since these agents carrying the transaction parameters roam on uncertain networks and their messages travel on insecure transmission channels a very important concern is that of security. This concern is aggravated by the fact that most business transactions involve money matters, with account numbers, personal identification numbers etc as transaction information. Access to this information by any unwanted third party can be a serious issue. To ensure that no intruder can get access to this information, the system's encryption module encrypts all information and messages using Triple DES [3].

4 Performance Analysis

The performance and efficiency of the Distributed Dependable Enterprise System – DDEBS was observed with different configuration. Some of the performance analysis is presented in this section. The results described in this section are simulated on a network (in the form of graph) containing 50 machines with edge density of 0.50. Machine 1 was the source while machine 50 was set as the agent destination. The fault tolerance window size was set to 3. We have observed through the simulated experiments that the proposed approach yields improved transaction time and minimize the delays in transaction because of faults in the network link or any other failure. Table 1 shows the average time of different activities of DDEBS. In initialization Transaction Manager – TM loads the GUI and reads the network file. TM takes 1.56 seconds for initialization.

After initialization TM creates Observer agents – OA, number of OA depends on the K-shortest paths given in the configuration, this activity takes 0.10 seconds. Observer agent creates Ping Agent – PA and this activity takes 0.07 seconds. Transaction Agent – TA takes 3.97 seconds to complete the one transaction. Path Optimization Module – POM takes 2.76 to extract K-Shortest paths from the network. Encryption / Decryption of single message take 1.54 seconds.

Figure 2 (a) shows the comparison of K-Shortest Paths (dynamic path) and single path with reference to the transaction time. If any failure during the transaction in case of single path, the whole transaction has to be restarted and it takes double time where as in dynamic path selection, the transaction is re-routed dynamically on some other path. For single failure in one transaction dynamic routing takes 2.76 seconds extra where as single path takes 3.99 seconds.

Table 1. Average Time in Seconds of Different Operations

	Operation Description	Time(Sec)
1	Transaction Manager Initialization	1.56
2	Observer Agent Creation & Initialization	0.10
3	Ping Agent Creation & Initialization	0.07
4	Transaction Agent Creation & Initialization	0.09
5	Transaction Time	3.97
6	Path Optimization Module Time	2.76
7	Encryption Time	1.54

Figure 2 (b) shows the comparison of transaction time with and with out encryption. For encrypting / decrypting one transaction in takes 1.54 seconds and for 100 transactions the difference is only 154 seconds which is very minimal. In financial application a minor change in the transaction can cause a great loss to the user / company. As the proposed framework is planned to be used in critical financial applications (like Banking applications and E-commerce) therefore encryption overhead should be ignored and in DDEBS the overhead is very minimal 1.54 seconds per transaction.

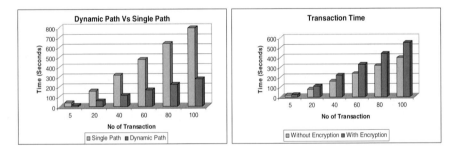

Fig. 2 (a). Dynamic Vs Single Path **(b)** Comparison of Transaction Time With & Without Encryption

5   Conclusion

Multi Agent Systems usefulness can be undermined due to problems incurred by the lack of fault tolerance and security in these Applications. In this paper we have proposed an infrastructure which provides fault tolerance and security. We have developed a simulated environment having multiple ATM's with distributed transactions. This test bed was evaluated with three major concerns, 1) fault tolerance provided in this distributed environment, 2) path optimization provided on network, and 3) security. We have observed through the simulated experiments that the proposed approach yields improved transaction time and minimize the delays in transaction because of faults in the network link or any other failure.

Acknowledgments. The Implementation of the concept was done as Final Year Project carried out by Ms. Summiya, Ms Hina Saleem and Ms. Wajiha Shammim. We appreciate their contribution.

References

1. Summiya, K.I., Manzoor, U., Shahid, A.A.: A Fault Tolerant Infrastructure for Mobile Agents. In: proceeding of International Conference on Intelligent Agents, Web Technologies and Internet Commerce (IAWTIC 2006), Sydney, Australia (December 2006)
2. Ijaz, K., Manzoor, U., Shahid, A.A.: Routing Framework for FTIMA – A Fault Tolerance Infrastructure for Mobile Agents. In: proceeding of "International Conference on Artificial Intelligence, Knowledge Engineering and Data Bases (AIKED 2008), Cambridge, UK, 20-22 Febuary (2008)
3. Manzoor, U., Ijaz, K., Shammim, W., Shahid, A.A.: Ensuring Data Security & Consistency in FTIMA - A Fault Tolerant Infrastructure for Mobile Agents. In: proceeding of International Conference on Parallel and Distributed Computing Systems (PDCS 2007), Vienna, Austria,
4. Vogler, H., Kunkelmann, T., Moschgath, M.-L.: Distributed Transaction Processing as a Reliability Concept for Mobile Agents. In: proceeding of 6th IEEE Workshop on Future Trends of Distributed Computing Systems (FTDCS 1997), pp. 59–64 (1997)
5. Weiss, G.: Multiagent Systems A Modern Approach to Distributed Artificial Intelligence, ch. 1-4. MIT Press, Cambridge (1999)
6. Pleisch, S., Schiper, A.: A fault-tolerant mobile agent system based on the agent-dependent approach. In: Proceedings of the IEEE International Conference on Dependable Systems and Networks, Göteborg, Sweden, pp. 215–224 (July 2001)
7. Strasser, M., Rothermel, K.: Reliability Concepts for Mobile Agents. International Journal of Cooperative Information Systems 7(4) (1998)
8. Strasser, M., Rothermel, K., Maihofer, C.: Providing Reliable Agents for Electronic Commerce. IEEE, Los Alamitos (1998)
9. Lee, S.S., Gerla, M.: Fault Tolerance and Load Balancing in QoS Provisioning with Multiple MPLS Paths, Research Paper. In: proceedings of the ninth Ninth International Workshop on Quality of Service (IWQoS), Karlsuhe, Germany (June 2001)
10. Grover, W.D.: Selfhealing networks—a distributed algorithm for k-shortest link-disjoint paths in a multi-graph with applications in real time network restoration, Ph.D. Thesis, University of Alberta, Department of Electrical Engineering (1989)
11. Macgregor, M.H., Grover, W.D.: Optimized k-shortest-paths Algorithm for Facility Restoration, Research Paper, Canada. John Wiley & Sons, Ltd, Chichester (1994)
12. Broadfoot, P., Lowe, G.: On Distributed Security Transactions that Use Secure Transport Protocols CSFW. In: 16th IEEE Computer Security Foundations Workshop (CSFW 2003) (2003)
13. Stallings, W.: Book, Cryptography and Network Security, Principles and Practices, 3rd edn. Prentice Hall Press, Englewood Cliffs

An Ontology Crystallization Approach to Designing Performance-Based Testing Scenario

Jui-Feng Weng, Shian-Shyong Tseng[*], and Jun-Ming Su

Department of Computer Science, National Chiao Tung University, ROC
1001 University Road, Hsinchu, Taiwan 300, ROC
roy@cis.nctu.edu.tw, sstseng@cs.nctu.edu.tw,
jmsu@csie.nctu.edu.tw

Abstract. The design of Performance-Based Testing is an interesting and important issue for the assessment of the students' problem solving or inquiry process capabilities. In this paper, we aim to design a wiki-like authoring environment based upon the Performance Assessment Ontology to support the collaborative design. However, the ontology inconsistency and incompleteness issues become more serious when constructing the ontology collaboratively. Therefore, the Ontology Crystallization scheme is proposed to support the scenario design with collaborative brainstorming and social agreement evaluation. There are three phases which are concept boundary extension phase, ontology integration phase, and conflict resolution phase. The collaborative brainstorming is based on the sharing of designed ontology, and the conflict resolution is based on the modified Delphi Method with questionnaire based voting. To demonstrate our scheme, it is applied to the designing of the "Banana Farm" assessment scenario. Finally, the experiment and evaluation shows the effectiveness of the designed result.

Keywords: Collaborative design, modified Delphi Method, ontology crystallization, wiki.

1 Introduction

Traditionally, the assessment of the students' problem solving or inquiry process capabilities in nature science learning domain is an interesting and important issue. With the growth of testing and assessment technology, the developing of Performance-Based Testing (PBT) in which students are asked to perform some actions to solve the predefined tasks in the assessment scenario becomes a feasible solution to solve the above problem. For each stage in the scenario, the activities should be designed properly in order to evaluate the effectiveness of the students' learning performance. However, the design of assessment activities is difficult because the cause and effect criteria of the actions, the learners' portfolio, the connectivity of simulated reality scenario, etc. should be taken into consideration.

In this paper, we aim to design a role playing learning game called "Banana Farm" using banana planting as background story. The related learning capabilities of nature

---

[*] Corresponding author.

M.D. Lytras et al. (Eds.): WSKS 2008, CCIS 19, pp. 543–548, 2008.
© Springer-Verlag Berlin Heidelberg 2008

science such as *"learner can be aware of the reason of status change and inquiry from performing actions"*, *"learner can identify and interpret the attributes and physical meaning of information"*, *"learner can learn inquiry for problem solving, explanation from variable and dependent variable"*, etc. should be assessed. Since the assessment is based on observation of students' inquiry processes, the simulated environment together with the accessible actions should be realistic and meaningful.

To support the design of assessment scenario, our idea is to develop a wiki-like authoring environment for the community based upon the Performance Assessment Ontology (PAO), where concept nodes represent the actions and affected environmental status and the assertions represent the causal links between stages. However, the ontology inconsistency and incompleteness issues become more serious when constructing the ontology collaboratively. It is still difficult and time consuming to rely on the system administrator to solve the problem, so how to facilitate the ontology construction with convergence process is our concern. It raises the technical issue of "how to enhance the creativity of community and resolve conflict opinions to achieve the social agreement".

To solve the issue above, the **Ontology Crystallization scheme** is proposed to support the scenario design with collaborative brainstorming and social agreement evaluation. Accordingly, there are three phases in the ontology crystallization scheme. The first is ***concept boundary extension phase***; the community members are asked to contribute their concepts for assessment activity. The difference of users' contributed designs can be detected and the feedback can be sent to each other to extend their *concept boundaries*. The second is ***ontology integration phase***; different designs can be integrated based on the predefined knowledge structure and the constructed folksonomy. The third is ***conflict resolution phase***; if the user's opinion against to each other; then the modified Delphi Method is proposed to converge their opinions iteratively. In each iteration, the questionnaire is generated based on different predefined conflict conditions and corresponding template items to collect the opinions from community members. Therefore, the conflict can be resolved based on the voting results to achieve the social agreement.

To demonstrate our scheme, the "Banana Farm" assessment scenario including several stages such as fruit sowing, planting, harvesting, transportation, marketing, etc. is proposed, where several alternative inquiry processes for planting strategy are provided such as "mass production may affect the fertility of soil", "the usage of pesticides may affect if the banana is sweet or not", etc. Besides, the marketing scenario is also provided to simulate the feedback of customers for different banana status. The prototype system based upon the designed scenario has also been implemented and evaluated by 48 junior high school students. Finally, the result shows that the designed scenario is acceptable to support the assessment of required learning capabilities.

2   Paper Preparation

In traditional RPL, student takes the role of a person and experiences the impacts of the role with predefined situations. It is helpful for learning [3]. With the growth of learning technology, e-RPL becomes popular gradually [1][5][6][7]. Also, the interest surrounding gaming in education has waxed and waned several times over recent years [1][4]. It is reasonable for student playing role in interactive game environment.

[6] is a web-based role-playing simulation generator. It generates web-based role-playing scenario for student to use. In designers' point of view, they don't know students' intention when they see the web page. Otherwise, the student could link to other web pages without any intervention. [1] have mentioned that it is possible to use different web-based Interface for students with different cognitive style having their own learning preferences. In the RPL, how to analyze the learning portfolio to provide intension assessment is still an important and cchallenging issue.

In the researches of game to learning [7], a simulation game called "Farmtasia" was implemented with knowledge of geography, biology, chemistry, technology and economics. It provided the statistic information of players' behaviors that allows teacher to observe players' learning progress. In [8], the other simulation game called "Fish Tank System" was proposed to model the nitrogen cycle in an aquarium. The multi-agents approach was used to build the environment.

In summary, the surveyed systems of game to learning were focused on applying existing game to the learning subject but are lack of how to design the assessment scenario for performance-based testing requirements.

3   The Collaborative Design for PBT

The game design for PBT is difficult because the issues of cause and effect criteria of the actions, the simulated reality scenario, learners' portfolio analysis, etc. should be concerned. Traditionally PBT design, a group of senior designers are required to have lots of meetings and discussions, so that it is costly and time consuming. Therefore, to support the collaborative design process, we aim to construct a wiki-like collaborative design platform to facilitate the design with collective intelligence. There are two issues of the collaborative design that should be solved. The first is vocabulary issue of how to share the designs of designers since they usually use different vocabulary. The second is the knowledge integration issue of how to resolve the conflicts of design mismatches among designers to achieve the social agreement.

To solve the issues above, our idea is constructing the collaborative design environment based upon the Ontology-based approach. Thus, we firstly define the Performance Assessment Ontology (PAO) to manage the learning capabilities and corresponding actions of game design.

Definition 1. Performance Assessment Ontology: O=(C, R), where
- Concept: The internal node represents the categorized learning capability, and the leaf nodes represent the designed actions in the game.
- Relations: the "a_part_of" relation represents the hierarchical classification structure; the "is_a" relation represents reference relation of internal node and leaf node, the "PR" relation represents the prerequisite sequence of the game scenario.

As shown in Fig. 1, with the defined PAO, the knowledge integration of collaborative design can be reduced to the collaborative ontology construction issue. However, the ontology inconsistency and incompleteness issues become more serious when constructing the ontology collaboratively. It raises the technical issue of "how to enhance the creativity of community and resolve conflict opinions to achieve the social agreement".

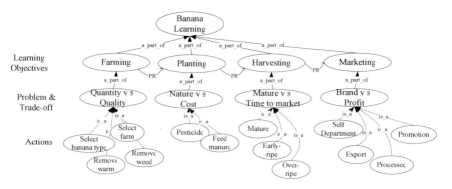

Fig. 1. The Performance Assessment Ontology of banana learning

To solve the technical issue, the Ontology Crystallization scheme is proposed. In the knowledge society of ontology crystallization scheme, there are two roles: one is community organizer who should setup the initial learning objectives in the ontology structure; the other is the community member who should design the gaming actions for each stages of the learning objectives. As shown in Fig. 2, there are three phases in the Ontology Crystallization scheme which are concept boundary extension phase, ontology integration phase, and conflict resolution phase.

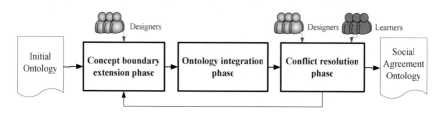

Fig. 2. The Ontology Crystallization scheme

In the **concept boundary extension phase**, the wiki-like collaborative ontology design platform is proposed. To support the knowledge sharing in the collaborative design, the ontology alignment can be done by the predefined stages of learning objectives as shown in the first layer of Fig. 1. Thus, for the same stage, the designers can break their concept boundary to inspire more creativity by sharing their designs with other community members. Besides, the vocabulary issue can be eliminated in this phase by constructing the folksonomy in the wiki-like design platform. Thus, the designers can have the same terminology. In the **ontology integration phase**, the designed game scene and game actions are integrated based on the learning objectives and trade-off attributes. If actions are designed to affect the same attributes, these actions are integrated in the same scene. Next, in the **conflict resolution phase**, it can provide some recommendation for designers to enrich the actions or hold a voting by questionnaires if there is inconsistency.

4   Conflict Resolution with Ontology Crystallizer

During the collaborative design, there are three criteria for the PBT design:

- Completeness: there should be multiple actions in the same learning objective to support trade-offs of game actions. Thus, the selection of different game actions for learners can represent different inquiry process.
- Consistency: since the provided actions should support different inquiry for the learners, the designed actions cannot be redundant or conflict with respect to the same trade-off. Thus, the designed scenario can make sense to the learners.
- Satisfaction: the designed results should be evaluated by designers of the community and evaluation result should achieve the social agreement.

Accordingly, the *Modified Delphi-method* [2] is proposed to iteratively apply integration and conflict resolution process to converge the designs. In the Modified Delphi Method, designers are participated as domain experts to evaluate or resolve the conflicts by the questionnaire. Therefore, the questionnaire for different situations should be predefined to support the community organizer collects the opinions or voting results of community members. The predefined questionnaire items are as follows.

- Insufficient: lack of trade-off actions in one stage. To resolve this design mismatch, the questionnaire should ask *"Would you please provide more actions that have trade-offs to current designed actions?"*.
- Mismatch: actions of different trade-offs in the same stage. *"Do you agree that the related actions of trade-off A are better than related actions of trade-off B?"*
- Conflicts: the same action but different result. *"Do you agree that the action A is more reasonable than the action B?"*
- Redundant: different actions but the same result. *"Do you agree that the action A the same with the action B? If so, please select which one is better."*

With the predefined questionnaire items, the design conflicts or mismatch can be resolved by the designer community with majority of the voting.

5   Implementation and Experiment

To show the idea of Ontology Crystallization scheme, the assessment of banana planting is designed for nature science course of junior high school. Several designers including junior high school teacher, programmer, e-learning expert etc. were involved in the design community. After 3 months of design process and around 15 iterations of discussion, finally the 7 stages assessment scenario is designed including actions of "Banana Types Selection", "Field Sowing", "Disaster Problem Solving", "Harvest Timing Selection", "Product Selection", "Marketing Strategy", and "Target Marketing".

To evaluate the effectiveness of the designed PBT, 48 junior high school students with 4 types of group are involved to test the designed scenario. The questionnaire with 9 questions for learning satisfaction was asked to evaluate the designed game scenario in Fig. 5. In the evaluation of assisting of learning achievement, most of students think that it is useful for their learning of nature science.

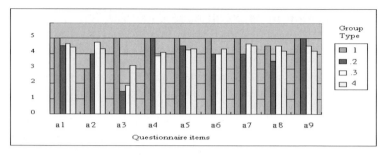

Fig. 5. Satisfaction of game scenario design

6 Conclusion

In this paper, we proposed the Wiki-like collaborative design approach to stimulate the creativity of designers by sharing their design concepts. To resolve the design mismatch issues, the Ontology crystallization scheme was proposed to detect the conflicts or redundancies by the predefined ontology patterns. Next, the Modified Delphi-Method was applied to converge the designers' opinions iteratively to achieve the social agreement. Finally, the design platform is implemented the content and evaluate the effectiveness of the design.

Acknowledgments. This research was partially supported by National Science Council of Republic of China under the number of NSC95-2520-S009-007-MY3, NSC95-2520-S009-008-MY3, and NSC96-2522-S -009-002.

References

1. Chuang, T.Y., Chen, W.F.: Effect of Computer-Based Video Games on Children: An Experimental Study. In: The First IEEE International Workshop on Digital Game and Intelligent Toy Enhanced Learning (2007)
2. Dalkey, N., Helmer, O.: An experimental application of the Delphi method to the use of experts. Management Science 9(3) (1963)
3. Duveen, J., Solomon, J.: The Great Evolution Trial: Use of Role-Play in the Classroom. Journal of Research in Science Teaching 31(5), 575–582 (1994)
4. Gee, P.: Learning by Design: Games as Learning Machines. Interactive Educational Multimedia 8 (2004)
5. Ho, P.C., Chung, S.M., Tsai, M.H.: A Case Study of Game Design for E-Learning, Edutainment (2006)
6. Naidu, S., Ip, A., Linser, R.: Dynamic Goal-Based Role-Play Simulation on the Web: A Case Study. Educational Technology & Society 3(3) (2000)
7. Shang, J., Jong, S.Y., Lee, F.L., Lee, H.M.: A Pilot Study on Virtual Interactive Student-Oriented Learning Environment. In: The First IEEE International Workshop on Digital Game and Intelligent Toy Enhanced Learning (2007)
8. Tan, J., Biswas, G.: Simulation-Based Game Learning Environments: Building and Sustaining a Fish Tank. In: The First IEEE International Workshop on Digital Game and Intelligent Toy Enhanced Learning (2007)

The Art and Impact of Physical and Virtual Enterprise Incubators: The Greek Paradigm

Spyros Tzafestas

Intelligent Automation Systems Group, Institute of Communication and Computer Systems,
National Technical University of Athens,
Zografou 15773, Athens, Greece
tzafesta@softlab.ntua.gr
http://www.ece.ntua.gr/images/pages/ias

Abstract. This article presents a compilation of the basic concepts and issues involved in the art of designing and operating enterprise/business incubators (BINCs). These include the definition, the models, the starting process, the good practices, the assessment, the impacts, and the business sectors of BINCs. Then, the current status of the BINC activity in Greece is discussed and a virtual/electronic BINC developed for Greek social economy enterprises within the framework of the DYEKO EQUAL project is briefly outlined. The article concludes with some empirical observations concerning the Greek BINCs, and some suggestions for their further expansion and improvement.

Keywords: Business incubator, virtual incubator, good practice, incubator assessment, incubator impact, Greek incubators. MAIN TRACK: IV.

1 Introduction

Formally, the concept of *business incubation was* firstly introduced by Joseph Mancuso in 1959 when establishing a warehouse at the Batavia Industrial Center (Batavia, New York) [1]. The incubation process has been expanded quickly in the U.S.A., Europe and Worldwide and in the 1980s was turned to a "real art" with strong positive results in the economic development and the sustainability of enterprises and companies [2-6]. In the Helsinki Summit of 1998, the European Union (EU) defined *a business incubator* (**BINC**) as *"the place where start-up enterprises are concentrated in a restricted space"*. Incubation activity does not take place only in developed countries. An increasing number of incubator environments are established and operated in developing countries and raise the need and interest for financial support from national and worldwide sponsors (World Bank, European Union, etc.)

Actually there does not exist a globally accepted definition of a *business incubator*. This is due to that **BINCs** provide several types and mixes of support, which include *place* (office, factory, and so on), *business support* and *networking*. According to the free encyclopedia (Wikipedia): *"***BINCs*** are programs designed to accelerate the successful development of entrepreneurial companies through an array of business support resources and services, developed and orchestrated by incubator management and offered both in the incubator and through its network of contacts"*. Of course,

M.D. Lytras et al. (Eds.): WSKS 2008, CCIS 19, pp. 549–559, 2008.

BINCs differ in the way they offer their services, in the kind of their organization, and in the types of their customers. **BINCs** are distinguished from *science and technology parks* because they are dedicated to start-up and young enterprises. Science and technology parks are large-scale facilities that include and serve everything from very small enterprises to corporated companies, governmental bodies or university laboratories. Most of the science and technology parks do not include assistance for business operations which is the basic characteristic of a **BINC** program.

In general, an incubator must provide management guidance, technical help, and consulting suitable for early stage growing companies. Incubator clients have access to proper rental space and flexible leases, shared fundamental business services and hardware/software equipment, technology support, and advice/assistance to get the economic support necessary for the client enterprises to grow.

2 Business Incubator Models

The operational model a **BINC** determines its organization and operation style, i.e. the structure, the purpose of services, the possibilities of finance, and the external cooperation. The three principal incubator models found in the literature are:

1. The **physical incubator model,** where the incubation process and the services offered are concentrated in a building. This has the advantage that the interaction, the partnership creation and the solution of common problems are stimulated by the proximity of incubator's clients [2-8].
2. The **virtual (or electronic) incubator model,** also referred to as "portal model", where the incubation process (support and services) are offered through the Internet [9-12].
3. The **mixed incubator model**, where the incubation process is performed "in house" for some enterprises and via the Internet for some others.

The physical incubator model, which is the most "natural" one, is extensively employed in the classical incubators. The electronic incubator model also called the *"model without walls"* has been used to support the start-up and development of enterprises over the Internet. The current trend of widely using the World Wide Web in the economic, enterprise and production activities has as a result the increasing adoption of the virtual and mixed models. The incubator operational model of a particular incubator is designed and developed by the team of the project, which must include representatives of all enterprises/organizations participating in the project, in order to take into account the points of view and interests of all of them.

The three basic constituents that are involved in the incubation process are:

- Services
- Network of relations
- Financing

The physical incubators provide a restricted repertory of services, since the services are offered within the incubator's building. Virtual incubators do not have this type of restriction, since their services are offered through the Web. The physical incubators limit their networks of relationships to their own physical space of activity, which may result in reduced quality of the relationship's network. On the contrary electronic incubators can assure relationships' networks of higher quality. Physical incubators have restricted capability to offer financial support to incubated enterprises from their own funds and resources, whereas electronic incubators have the possibility to seek and secure more financial alternatives [9, 10].

3 Starting a Binc

Business incubators are now recognized to be an effective tool for stimulating entrepreneurship and generating sustainable business growth. The decision, however, whether or not an incubator is the best business development tool in each case, should be based on careful feasibility analysis and proper planning. Actually, a good understanding of the target enterprise clients and of the market conditions existing in the surrounding environment is needed before deciding to start or not a BINC. Decisions should also be made about the services to be offered, the financing of the start-up, the incubators' governing structure, the human resources needed "in house" vs. "contract out", and so on. The feasibility study should give well justified answers to critical questions, such as whether the proposed incubator project has a solid market, a strong societal support, sufficient financial resources and true champions. The BINC developers should correctly identify the obstacles that are predicted to be faced and the ways to surmount them.

The development of the BINC must assure that will be "in-line" with and promote the community's broader economic development goals. To ensure that a starting BINC will be successful, the "*good practices*" attained from previous BINC projects should be adopted, and adapted to the particular situation at hand. Although there are various types of BINC, they all share many good practices and common features. Finally, the legal status of the BINC is a strategic decision, because the flexibility and efficiency of the BINC will be influenced by this decision. Efficient incubation is not easy and needs a long-term commitment from stakeholders who will have to face many challenges through the life of the BINC. BINCs have substantial differences in their:

- **Sponsors** (state, business, university, venture capital, etc).
- **Objectives** (from empowerment to technology commercialization).
- **Location** (urban, suburban, rural, international).
- **Sectoral focus** (technology and mixed, including arts and catering incubators).
- **Business model** (not for-profit, for-profit).

In developed countries these include a large repertory of business. In the developing countries the main focus is on technology incubators aiming at commercializing technological innovations. The following list illustrates how the primary sponsors influence the BINC goals [3]:

Sponsor	Desired goals
Research Institute	*Commercialization of research results*
Technical University	*Innovations, facility/graduate student participation*

Public/private partnership	*Investment, development, equity*
Private sector	*Profit, patents, spin-offs*
Venture capital-based	*Winning enterprises, high portfolio returns*

A starting incubator must itself possess the dynamism of entrepreneurial ventures and become self reliant within a reasonable time (say after 4-5 years of operation). A BINC should offer value-adding counseling, training, networking services, etc. Of course, it should be mentioned that most of the existing BINCs (both in developed and developing countries) are *non-profit organizations* operated with income mainly from rentals and services, supplemented by subsidies.

4 Binc Good Practices

Not all BINCs operate following *"good or best practices"*. At the one end, there are incubators that operate in a weak business environment and are characterized by a low quality selection procedure for client enterprises, not well organized support services, non professional persons acting as managers, and low rental as an attraction policy. At the other end of the spectrum we have BINCs with well-designed facilities and professional management in a good knowledge environment, that charge near market rents and provide high-level innovative and value –adding services. These BINCs follow *"best practices"* and their performance is the outcome of proper preparation, sufficient funding, entrepreneurial quality and an incubation process that matches well the location and time of the specific environment.

The poor BINCs have to search to find the best practices worldwide and adapt them to their own conditions, constraints, and environment. In this way the image of the overall incubation industry will be improved at the benefit of the society. In [3] *R. Lalkaka* presents a wide repertory of worldwide BINC programs focusing on their best practices. Countries considered include USA, China, Brazil, Japan, India, Republic of Korea, Uzbekistan, South Africa, Malaysia, Indonesia, Egypt and Poland.

The sources of BINC success can be expressed by five interlinked rings as shown in Fig.1.

In developing countries the interactions are usually weak and unstructured, and typically the universities and private sector have the weakest interactions (links).

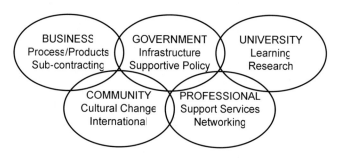

Fig. 1. Interactions of BINC stakeholders [3]

- The public/government policy facilitates venture creation and offers the business infrastructure.
- The universities provide the knowledge base for learning, research and decision making.
- The private sector encourages and provides partnerships for mentoring and marketing.
- The professional sector provides the support services and the local/global networking.
- The community/society participates by promoting and extending entrepreneurism.

Some key success factors or best practices drawn from the experience of Brazil and China are the following:

- Identify strong sponsors and a clear mission.
- Find a committed champion.
- Select a good location for the functional buildings and their organization.
- Form a well trained and dedicated management team.
- Select good entrepreneurial tenants (clients).
- Mobilize investment and working capital for incubator and its tenants.
- Develop creative ways of raising revenues.
- Secure added value via quality services to tenants and their affiliates.
- Promote the participation of women.
- Monitor the BINC's performance and assess its impact.
- Create fruitful cooperation with universities and research institutes.
- Strengthen industry associations and international relationships.

The above key success factors are also applicable to other countries, of course with variations of importance and influence.

5 Assessment of Incubators

Most of the incubation programs all over the world are actually *"public-private partnership"* in which the initial funding comes from the governmental side. The private sector enters if it sees that the program will lead to more business opportunities or create spin-offs. Naturally, the funding bodies select for funding BINC programs that after an initial period of development can become financially viable. However, only a few BINCs have built into their management systems proper tools for accurately estimating their impact, effectiveness and sustainability. The evaluation process is complex and multiparametric, needing step-by-step analysis of the factors that influence the BINC operation internally and externally. It is noted that it is not always possible to quantify in economic terms the performance of a BINC. Measures of performance are the *medium – term benefits* for the clients/tenants, sponsors, local community, region and nation.

Some criteria that can be measured are:

- The number of enterprises generated.
- The employment created.

- The growth in the company's assets, sales and exports.
- The corporate and personal taxes generated.
- The survival rates of the ventures incubated.
- The technologies commercialized.
- The revenues earned by patents and licensing.
- The number of graduating firms.
- The added value offered to incubating clients in comparison with those of the open marketspace.

Other criteria not so easily measured are:

- The benefits for the society.
- The enhancement of skills.
- The attitudinal changes.
- The improved self-esteem and optimism for the future.

The measure of the performance of a given incubator can be assigned to professional auditors who must assess the outcomes with reference to the expectations of the sponsors and donors. The audit must include internal as well as external auditing. A generic diagram showing typical loops of inputs and outputs expected from a BINC is given Fig.2.

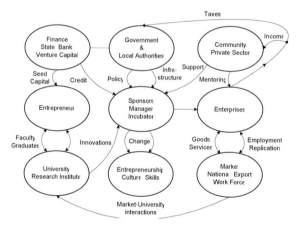

Fig. 2. General structure of assessment of BINC impact, effectiveness and sustainability

6   Impact of Incubators

The impact of a BINC to different stakeholders is as follows [3]:

- **For clients:** BINCs increase the possibilities of success, improve credibility, help in the enhancement of skills, promote the synergy among the client enterprises, facilitate the cooperation with mentors, and assure access to information, knowledge and initial funds.

- **For governments:** BINCs assist to overcome market failures, promote regional development, create jobs, generate incomes and taxes, and become a tool of the commitment of the government to aid small business.
- **For universities and research centers:** BINCs contribute to the establishment of cooperative interactions between university-research-private sector, promote research commercialization, and enhance the opportunities to staff/students to better utilize their knowledge.
- **For business:** BINCs provide additional chances for acquiring innovations, offer chain management and spin-offs, and help the client enterprises to meet their responsibilities for the society.
- **For the local community:** BINCs create self-esteem and entrepreneurial culture, along with local incomes from the graduating business that stay within the area.
- **For the international society:** BINCs produce opportunities of trade and technology transfer between client enterprises and their host incubators, and facilitate the exchange of experiences via associations and alliances.

The above benefits are not always achieved due to poor management and other weaknesses. However, there is an increasing evidence that in most BINCs some or all of the above benefits are realizable and out-weight the net public subsidy. The BINCs nurture entrepreneurs, who create enterprises that after graduating generate direct and indirect employment with incomes and assets that help to secure the sustainability of the economic growth. Usually the start-up entrepreneurs create jobs for themselves and conserve their funds, but when they leave the BINC some of them grow exponentially and create jobs, incomes and taxes.

7 Business Incubators in Greece

7.1 General Issues

The business incubation activity in Greece began about one and a half decades ago. Today there exist six independent autonomously operating BINCs in Greece [13]. Most of them were created with the help of national and EU funding within the framework of the European -Greek development program **ELEFTHO (ΕΛΕΥΘΩ)** [15]. Generally, the Greek BINCs follow the traditional operation model(s) described in Section 2, but their approach to the implementation is usually different than that of other countries. The differences are mainly due to the way and the level of economic support that offer to their client enterprises. Some of them have their own funds to assist the incubates, while the majority of them are mediators and bring into contact the incubators with possible *"Venture Capital"* sponsors. Those which are embedded in the activity of VCs, are accepted as members in the *Hellenic Venture Association* and have the benefits of the relevant legislation. Actually, their activity presents peculiarities that cannot be faced by the legislation of stockholder companies. Some other efforts that are made in Greece in the private or public sector, do not actually arrive at the true incubator level, mainly because they do not provide funding support to their clients, and so they do not possess part of their capital.

7.2 Presentation of Three Greek Incubators

Here we will briefly present three Greek BINCs in order to show the level and impact of their activity. These are the following:

- **i4G :** Incubation for Growth
- **I-CUBE :** Intelligent Ideas Incubator
- **THERMI:** Business Incubator

I4G: This is one of the most successful incubators of Greece and constitutes one of the *EUROCONSULTANS S.A.* main tools for implementing its entrepreneurial goal to establish links among research and business [16]. Its operation is based on three fundamental issues, namely:

- Housing and operating support
- Effective management consulting services
- Provision of capital

The long-term vision of **i4G** is to maximize its workforce and expertise acquired within the incubator's everyday operation, in order to promote its operational model and make it identifiable within an international incubator network extending over European Middle East and North Africa countries.

Based on the 15 enterprises currently incubated in i4G (*Actus, CellMedical S.A., Digital Innovations, Entersoft S.A., Exper Team, ICTV Hellas S.A., Medical Technology S.A.,* e.t.c.), whose activities cover informatics, communication, digital economy, industrial applications, environmental protection, medical applications and wireless communications, we can say that i4G achieves its goals to contribute to the local and regional economic and sustainable development.

I-CUBE A.E.: This incubator operates since December 2000 and invests in new business schemes, providing integrated support at strategic, management and technical level [17]. **i-cube** provides services in informatics, specializing particularly in network and Internet problems. Among the applications of interest to **i-cube** a dominating position is kept by renewal energy resources and the environment (photovoltaic and wind electric energy production, etc). The stockholder capital of   **i-cube** is about €300.000 (ranging from 100 k€ to 800 k€). Part of this investment is financed by the Ministry of Development (GSRT) through the **ELEFTHO** Program. The **i-Cube BINC** lowers the investment risk for the investor, the incubator and the inventor, and offers integrated services, synergetic actions (sales channels, suppliers, etc) and joint ventures. **i-Cube** has a network of sponsors/investors and cooperators.

According to the data published by **i-Cube**, 14 enterprises have been incubated till now. Thirteen of them are commercial companies and five have successfully graduated (taking a stockholding part of **i-Cube A.E.**). These companies are: *SYMPER A.E., SPIRIT, INNOVIS, THERON, Click Home.gr, Travel Zone, Oration, Future Reality, Regate, Imagics, R.E. Net, MindWell and Your Partner.* From the above it follows that **i-Cube A.E.** plays well its role towards the improvement of local and regional sustainable development.

THERMI A.E.: This incubator is relatively new (2004) and has a supermodern building of 6.000 square meters (the largest in Southeast Europe) with an impressive infrastructure [18]. **THERMI's** total investment is 14,5 Mega euro. By the end of

2006 this BINC had 31 new high technology incubated companies coming mainly from the following branches:

- Medicine, biomedicine and biotechnology
- Software research and production
- Computer hardware and digital equipment
- Intelligent mechanisms and systems
- Telemetry, telematics and wireless data transmission
- Development of environment protection systems
- Energy systems production and distribution
- Implementation and utilization of Internet systems
- Agro technology

Stockholders of *THERMI A.E.* are the following companies: *KOUBAS* and *SYM-METOCHES A.E., PROTON BANK A.E.* and *IBG A.E.* (a daughter company of *MARFIN FINANCIAL GROUP).* Through the company *INI – NOVATION GREECE A.E.,* THERMI A.E. BINC is participating in the international network *INI – Graphics Net* which has created BINCs and other bodies of technology development and transfer in Europe, U.S.A. and many Asian countries *INI-NOVATION GREECE A.E.,* a consultancy company, is the basic cooperator of *INI-Graphics Net* for innovative technology transfer in the Southeastern Europe with its center in Thessaloniki. THERMI A.E. has developed an integrated enterprise support system, called *"THERMI DEVELOPMENT"* with a competent group of professional advisors as its basic constituent.

7.3 The Virtual Incubator DYEKO

This electronic incubator was developed within the framework of the **EQUAL project DYEKO:** *"Support Network for Social Economy and Enterprises"* co –financed by the EU (*EQUAL Europe*)[19] and the Greek Ministry of Employment and Social Care (*EQUAL Greece*)[20]. Coordinator of the consortium was the *21 OTA Coalition* (21 Municipalities of Attica) and partners: The Institute of Communication and Computer Systems (ICCS) of NTU Athens, Asset Tech., Holargos Municipality KEK, Panhellenic Women Society "Panathinaiki" and KPEE (Political Research and Communication Center).

The main goal of DYEKO was to promote womens' entrepreneurship in social economy, directing it toward the real needs of the women in North and East Athens. This has been accomplished through the creation of four pilot small size social economy enterprises owned exclusively by women entrepreneurs. The actual implementation of the project was based on the *VIRTUAL BINC* which provided the proper mentoring and support services to the starting social enterprises. In addition, Holargos KEK has runned a number of seminars for selected groups of unemployed women (supported by the E & SC Ministry). The pilot enterprises were given an initial capital by the E & SC Ministry to start their business. An important component of the DYEKO project was the European cooperation which was realized through the creation of the European Consortium **"Terra di Projetti"** (Italy, France, Czech Rep., Greece). This consortium has performed several joint actions, namely educational visits, common workshops, working groups, and exchange of experience and good practices on the operation of social economy enterprises.

Among the support services offered by the DYEKO virtual BINC are the following: advice and help in marketing, accounting, taxation, insurance, banking/finance, and legislation actions. Also, fundamental educational material on social economy, informatics and related topics is offered in the incubator. The current virtual incubator of DYEKO (in Greek) can be found at the site:

http://argo.cs.unipi.gr/e-thermokoitida.gr/index.php.

This will be moved soon to the server of a public Internet provider.

8 Conclusions and Suggestions

A study of the Greek BINCs was conducted by the interdepartmental MBA of *Athens Economic University* using a set of questionnaires and personal interviews [14]. The final distribution of the people that provided answers is: 24% BINC staff members, 43% incubees' staff members, and 33% other specialists (from government, sponsoring bodies, academic institutions, advisors, auditors, etc). Three different types of questionnaires were provided dealing, respectively, with economic figures, specialized issues, and evaluation of the *ELEFTHO* program.

Very broadly the following results were drawn:

- The contribution of the government to the development of incubators is poor, and must be strengthened.
- The cooperation of universities with the incubators is very week. More involvement of universities is needed in the effort to create a culture that reinforces entrepreneurship.
- The two weakest points of the Greek incubator activity are: (i) the
- More attention is given by the incubators to internal services (accounting and legislation services, personnel recruitment) and external services (market search, sales, etc), than to pre-incubating services and access to potential sponsors.
- The survival index of the "graduates" is low (12.56 %).
- The ratio: "Incubator personnel/incubating companies" is 1:1.5. The corresponding figure in the EU is 1:14.

On the basis of the above empirical observations, the following minimal set of additional suggestions for improving the Greek business incubation efficiency and impact is the following:

- The government must offer a better environment for entrepreneurship and venture creation (better corruption fighting, bureaucracy simplification, legislation improvement, etc).
- The incubators and their clients must strengthen their cooperation with universities.
- The incubating enterprises must increase their links with sponsors.
- Better coordination of all the players involved in the incubation game is needed for improved efficiency.
- The relevant university and state research teams must cooperate with the proper private sector bodies towards identifying the key factors and developing a valid and sustainable Greek incubator model.
- More virtual incubators should be developed (virtual incubators either within the framework of the existing incubators or as separate entities).

References

1. Wikipedia: Virtual Business Incubator,
   `http://en.wikipedia.org/wiki/Virtual_Business_Incubator`
2. Knopp, L.: State of the Business Incubation Industry, National Business Incubation Association (NBIA), Athens, Ohio, U.S.A (2007)
3. Lalkala, R.: Best Practices in Business Incubation: Lessons (yet to be) Learned, 2001 Urban Enterprise Conf., Brussels (November 2001),
   `http://www.urban-enterprise2001.be-RustamLALKALA`
4. Lalkala, R.: Technology Business Incubators to Help Build an Innovation-Based Economy. Journal of Change Management 3(2), 167–176 (2002)
5. Costa-David, J., Malan, J., Lalkala, R.: Improving Business Incubator Performance through Benchmarking and Evaluation, NBIA Intl. Business Incubation Conf., Toronto, Canada (2002)
6. EU Centre for Strategy and Evaluation Services: Benchmarking of Business Incubators, Final Report, EC Enterprise DG, Brussels (2002)
7. Lalkala, R.: Technology Business Incubators: Critical Determinants of Success, NYAS Annals,New York, vol. 798 (1996)
8. Wolfe, C., Adkins, D., Sherman, H.: Best Practices in Action: Guidelines for Incubating First Class Incubation Programs, NBIA, Athens, Ohio, U.S.A (2001)
9. Dahl, D.: A New Generation of "Virtual" Business Incubators is Jump-Starting Start-Ups Nationwide, Goliath-Business Knowledge on Demand, Publication time (February 1 2005), `http://goliath.ecnext.com/coms2/gi_0199-3842334/A-new-generation-of-virtual.html`
10. Holst, M.: Developing the Concept of a Virtual Incubator, Report of Project Entrepreneurial Knowledge Community (April 2007), `http://www.cdt.ltu.se/main.php/reportVirtualincubator.pdf?fileitem=1419321`
11. Nowak, M.J., Grantham, C.E.: The Virtual Incubator: Managing Human Capital in the Software Industry. Research Policy (Science Direct) 29(2), 125–134 (2000), `http://www.sciencedirect.com`
12. Hausner, U., Hussla, I., Thiemann, A.: Virtual Business Incubator, ITZE HOE. In: Proc. e-2002-eBusiness and eWork Conf., Prague, Czech Republic, October 16-18 (2002) e-mail: hussla@izet.de
13. ESEE: Greek Business Incubators-Technology Parks, `http://www.esee.gr`
14. Pappas, A.: Critical Success Factors of Business Incubators: Evaluation of their Efficiency in Greece, M.B.A. Thesis, Economic Univ. of Athens (A. Ioannidis, Supervisor) (2006)
15. ELEFTHO (ΕΛΕΥΘΩ): Enterprise Incubator Program, E.P.AN-Action 4.2.1, General Secretariat for Research and Technology, Athens, Greece, `http://www.gsrt.gr`, `http://www.gsrt.gr`
16. Incubation for Growth (i4G), `http://www.i4G.gr`
17. Tsalkitzi, E.: From the Technological Idea to the Entrepreneurial Entity: The Example of I-CUBE A.E. In: Two-Day Workshop of Athens T.E.I. Interconnection Bureau, Thematic Unit: Education and Entrepreneurship, April 3-4 (2008)
18. THERMI Business Incubator, `http://www.thermokoitida.gr`
19. Equal Europe,
   `http://ec.europa.eu/employment_social/equal/index_en.cfm`
20. Equal Greece, `http://www.equal-greece.gr`

Designing IT Systems for NGOs: Issues and Directions

Saqib Saeed, Markus Rohde, and Volker Wulf

Department of Information Systems and New Media,
University of Siegen, Hölderlinstr. 3,
57076 Siegen, Germany
{Saqib.Saeed,Markus.Rohde,Volker.Wulf}@uni-siegen.de

Abstract. IT support in voulantary organizations is an interesting emergent field of research. Recent literature has highlighted that many NGOs are still in early stage of IT adoption, in their organizational settings. In this paper we analyze types and organizational structures of voulantary organizations to find out the factors which differentiate IT support in these organizations as compared to other organizations. The paper reviews the state of the art and discusses important issues which are worth investigating for the improvement of IT support in voulantary organizations.

Keywords: Community computing, IT support, NGOs.

1 Introduction

The civil society organizations form an important constituent of any society along with business and governmental organizations. Civil society organizations are quite diverse in their compositions and operations. NGOs are the most widely known fraction of civil society organizations to which we will focus our discussion in this paper. With the evolution of North-South cooperation, NGOs gained more prominence. In the wake of this North-South collaboration some NGOs established operations in remote continents while others preferred to collaborate with local partners [1]. This geographical diversity requires efficient communication methodologies to optimize the operations. Despite the tremendous trend of embedding information technology in organizational processes, use of ICT in NGO sector is slimmer. The research efforts have highlighted that most non-governmental organizations lack appropriation of information technologies [2]. There is awareness among community organizations to use technology in their activities but the complexity of technologies and lack of technological knowledge are big obstacles [3]. A study by the Association of Progressive Communication (APC) revealed that most of transnational civil society organizations are strong in the areas of internet access and e-mail use and rather weak in areas such as holding online meetings and running internet advocacy campaigns [4]. Goatman and Lewis in 2007 surveyed 1000 UK charities and found that non profit institutions are positive about use of websites and are interested in improving use of internet technologies in future. They also found out that currently websites are only used to present information about their activities rather finding new collaborators, fund raising and community interaction [5]. Kellogg Foundation's ePilanthropy 2001 report

M.D. Lytras et al. (Eds.): WSKS 2008, CCIS 19, pp. 560–565, 2008.

describes that technology and internet services are far from being integrated into organizational process of voulantary organizations [6]. Another study by TBC Research UK in 2001 found that 62% of voluntary organizations have indicated a poor relationship between their mission and information technology strategy [2]. In 2004 Cogburn empirically evaluated computer mediated communication among civil society representatives at United Nations World Summit on Information Society (WSIS) and its preparation phase meetings. He described that the majority of computer mediated communication took place using e-mail lists while other complex tools such as document repositories, wikis, blogs, and Web conferencing, have not been used effectively [7]. In this context the appropriation of ICT in the organizational settings of NGOs seems to be an important research area.

2 Structure of NGOs

The appropriation of technology can be achieved when the technologies are designed keeping in mind the structure and practices of an application area. For this reason it is important to understand the types and structures of NGOs, which will help finding differences in the needs of NGOs. With respect to their work focus NGOs can be categorized into two groups: operational and advocacy NGOs [8]. Normally, operational NGOs focus on small scale change by carrying out projects at grass root levels whereas advocacy NGOs aim at large scale change by influencing the political system. So the support of ICT facilities for communication process in NGOs could be among office settings, office-government, field-government, office-public, field-public, office-donor and office- other NGOs. Operational NGOs have strong presence of staff at headquarters for planning and on the field staff for implementation whereas advocacy NGOs will focus on awareness, opinion and policy making resulting in absence of field activities. The geographical distances among field, office and headquarter locations add further complexity in designing ICT systems for NGOs. This involvement at different state and local levels introduces problems like different governmental partners, differences in languages being spoken, difference in working habits and cultural differences among the staff of NGOs. Some NGOs may have centralized control at headquarter level while others have independent offices in the distributed locations [8]. The management of ICT infrastructures at centrally controlled NGOs is simpler as compared to NGOs who have distributed autonomous offices. The requirements of NGOs in office settings will be further different from each other depending upon their operational area e.g. a child care NGO and an emergency relief organization have rather different needs.

Organizational structure of NGOs and level of professionalism of staff are other important dimensions. Small NGOs normally don't have a stable defined organizational structure. This results in lack of organizational knowledge and inconsistency in decision making, posing difficulty in establishing ICT infrastructures in the NGO sector. Secondly, NGOs normally do not have formal requirements of a specific profile to become a member. So, volunteer will not possess any specific skill set or profile. This typically results in low emphasis on developing ICT infrastructures and using IT capabilities to perform their tasks. Whereas big transnational NGOs have large number of dedicated staff, so they have specialized IT staff to help them in establishing IT infrastructure and using computing capabilities. So the usability issues should also be considered while designing the ICT systems. The NGOs normally lack funding as donors are normally interested in supporting NGOs in their core activities but it is hard to find a donor who is interested in financing these NGOs to establish and maintain ICT infrastructures so open source development can reduce the financial issues to a large extent.

3   State of the Art

The work to appropriate technology in the non-profit sector has its precedents. There have been examples of appropriating technology in non-profit organizations by different researchers. Benston has described that how participatory design method can be used to help non-profit sector organizations [9]. CAVEAT is an example of involving a Canadian non-profit organization to establish a prototype of an organization information system. McPhail et al. established this prototype using participatory design methodology and employing off the shelf database components [10]. There has been an effort by Trigg to involve a local non-profit organization for a database design activity [11]. Another effort to empower NGOs with computing capabilities is carried out in the "Civic Nexus" project [3], [12]. The objective of the project was to empower regional volunteer organizations in the Centre County Pennsylvania by involving volunteers not just in simple tool development but in the whole technological process [13]. Participatory design and end user development concepts are applied to the regional non-governmental organizations [14]. Based on experiences with community groups in Centre County, Pennsylvania, and Montgomery County, Virginia they have also developed design patterns to improve learning of basic use of ICT among NGO staff [15]. The main focus of this work is on technological sustainability within community organizations [16]. Rohde has investigated how Iranian NGOs can benefit from social capital fostered by introduction of a Communities of Practice concept. In this case methods of participatory design are applied to electronically network an Iranian NGO community to gain advantages of social capital [17]. Shamail et al. have advocated the idea of development of web portal for better capacity building in social organizations in Pakistan [18]. The 'Sahana' is another instance of computerization effort in NGOs. It is an open source disaster management system which is developed by Lanka Software Foundation, an NGO in Sri Lanka. The software was developed by a group of volunteers from Sri Lankan ICT industry. The software was used in the 2004 Tsunami in Sri Lanka, 2005 Pakistan earthquake, 2006 Philippines mudslides and 2006 Yogayakarta earthquake in Indonesia. The system is in place in Sri lanka's largest NGO "Sarvodaya" to combat with future disasters [19]. Klein et al. have presented a computer supported cooperative learning environment for NGOs, which are engaged in Africa promoting children rights by using art work. The system enables NGOs to share their ideas and best practices [20].

There has also been related work to investigate ICT usage in NGOs working in transnational context. Mclever focused on transnational NGOs after his experiences on drafting legislation for civil society's agenda on World Summit on International Society (WSIS). He has worked on transnational, multi lingual collaborative legislative work among NGOs. He analyzed that a number of systems have been developed that support various aspects of versioning and collaborative work but are not specifically designed to support legislative drafting [21]. Saeed et al. described how knowledge management and expertise recommending systems can help NGOs and Donor organizations in establishing successful collaborations [1]. In 2003 Interagency Working Group (IWG) on Emergency Capacity was formed by a consortium of seven NGOs to analyze collaborative capacity-building effort. Currion published his findings and recommendations on the use of ICTs by the IWG NGOs, based on his headquarter visit of participating NGOs and field visits in Pakistan and Sudan [22].

4 Conclusion

The objective of this paper is to highlight the importance of ICT support for NGOs and stress the need for further research to empower this important sector with modern computing technologies. This discussion highlights sporadic efforts to embed information technology in NGOs. One central research question which needs to be answered is how information technology services and applications can be effectively embedded in organizational settings of transnational NGOs to achieve technological appropriation.

The structure and working methodology of NGOs show some similarities with business/governmental organizations but considerable differences too. So it needs to be investigated how the organizational structure and application area affect the IT requirements of transnational NGOs. As the volunteers are the core of many NGOs and since these NGOs are highly dynamic organizations, it is also worth investigating how knowledge management technologies can overcome existing shortcomings and help in establishing organizational knowledge. Furthermore, transnational NGOs have different technological levels of staff, different cultural values and diversity in technological infrastructure, which make technological appropriation much more complex. There is need for developing effective applications to enhance the internal and external communication among transnational NGOs. In this context there is need for more ethnographic studies and participatory development efforts to enable NGOs' staff with technologies helping effective communication among stakeholders (Donors, NGOs, Public, Staff and Government representatives.) Another interesting question is how new forms of media are being used for advocacy and mobilization purposes in North and South.

The technological support by advanced ICT systems like web 2.0 can help NGOs in improving their operations and reach. New web based media can support communication among stakeholders [23]. The importance of effective knowledge management methodologies is proven [24], [25]. So these advanced systems can help for the effective management of knowledge in organizational settings of NGOs. This could also prove to be a step forward towards transformation into knowledge society as these could support existing efforts for open access, freedom of speech and reduction of the digital divide.

References

1. Saeed, S., Reichling, T., Wulf, V.: Applying Knowledge Management to Support Networking among NGOs and Donors. In: IADIS International Conference on E-Society, Algarve, Portugal, pp. 626–628 (2008)
2. Surman, M., Reilly, K.: Appropriating the Internet for Social Change: Towards the Strategic use of Networked Technologies by Transnational Civil Society Organizations. Social Science Research Council (2003), http://programs.ssrc.org/itic/publications/knowledge_report/final_entire_surman_reilly.pdf
3. Farooq, U., Merkel, C.B., Xiao, L., Nash, H., Rosson, M.B., Carroll, J.M.: Participatory Design as a Learning Process: Enhancing Community-based Watershed Management through Technology. In: Depoe, S.P. (ed.) The Environmental Communication Yearbook, vol. 3, pp. 243–267 (2006)
4. APC. Unpublished findings from interviews with civil society technology practitioners. APC Learners and Practitioners Network Program (2002)
5. Goatman, A.K., Lewis, B.R.: Charity e-volution? An Evaluation of the attitudes of UK Charities towards Website Adoption and use. International Journal of Nonprofit and Voluntary Sector Marketing 12(1), 33–46 (2007)
6. Clohesy, S.: e-Philantropy v.2.001 - From Entrepreneurial Adventure to Online Community. Kellogg Foundation (2001),
   http://www.actknowledgeworks.net/ephil/
7. Cogburn, D.L.: Diversity Matters, Even at a Distance: Evaluating the Impact of Computer-Mediated Communication on Civil Society Participation in the World Summit on the Information Society. Information Technologies and International Development 1(3-4), 15–40 (2004)
8. Mostashari, A.: An Introduction to Non Governmental Organizations Management Iranian Study Group MIT (2005), http://web.mit.edu/isg/NGOManagement.pdf
9. Benston, M.: Participatory Designs by Non-profit Groups. In: Participatory Design Conference, pp. 107–113. Palo Alto, CA (1990)
10. McPhail, B., Costantino, T., Bruckmann, D., Barclay, R., Clement, A.: CAVEAT Exemplar: Participatory Design in a Non-Profit Volunteer Organisation. Computer Supported Cooperative Work 7(3), 223–241 (1998)
11. Trigg, R.H.: From sand box to fund box: Weaving Participatory Design into the Fabric of a Busy Non-profit. In: Participatory Design Conference, pp. 174–183. Palo Alto, CA (2000)
12. Farooq, U., Merkel, C.B., Nash, H., Rosson, M.B., Carroll, J.M., Xiao, L.: Participatory Design as Apprenticeship: Sustainable Watershed Management as a Community Computing Application. In: 38th Annual Hawaii International Conference on System Sciences, Hawaii (2005)
13. Merkel, C.B., Xiao, L., Farooq, U., Ganoe, C.H., Lee, R., Carroll, J.M., Rosson, M.B.: Participatory Design in Community Computing Contexts: Tales from the Field. In: Participatory Design Conference, Toronto, Canada, pp. 1–10 (2004)
14. Farooq, U.: Conceptual and Technical Scaffolds for End User Development: Using scenarios and wikis in community computing. In: IEEE Symposium on Visual Languages and Human-Centric Computing: Graduate Student Consortium on Toward Diversity in Information Access and Manipulation, Los Alamitos, California, pp. 329–330 (2005)
15. Carroll, J.M., Farooq, U.: Patterns as a Paradigm for Theory in Community-based Learning. International Journal of Computer-Supported Collaborative Learning 2, 41–59 (2007)

16. Merkel, C., Clitherow, M., Farooq, U., Xiao, L., Carroll, J.M., Rosson, M.B.: Sustaining Computer Use and Learning in Community Computing Contexts: Making Technology Part of 'Who They Are and What They Do. The Journal of Community Informatics 1(2), 158–174 (2005)
17. Rohde, M.: Find what binds. Building Social Capital in an Iranian NGO Community System. In: Huysman, M., Wulf, V. (eds.) Social Capital and Information Technology, pp. 75–112. MIT Press, Cambridge (2004)
18. Shamail, S., Awais, M.M., Masud, S., Shams, S.: Web Based Portal for Capacity Building of Development Sector Enterprises in Pakistan. In: 2nd WSEAS Conference on E-Activities, Singapore (2003)
19. Currion, P., Silva, C., Van de Walle, B.: Open Source Software for Disaster Management. Communications of the ACM 50(3), 61–65 (2007)
20. Klein, R.R., Letaief, R., Carter, S., Chabert, G., Lasonen, J., Lubart, T.: CSCL for NGO's Cross Cultural Virtual Teams in Africa: an Ethiopian Children Advocacy Case Study against Exclusion and Toward Facilitation of Expression, Innovation and Creativity. In: 5th IEEE International Conference on Advanced Learning Technologies, pp. 1037–1041. IEEE Press, Los Alamitos (2005)
21. McIver, J.W.: Tools for Collaboration between Trans-national NGOs: Multilingual, Legislative Drafting. In: International Colloquium Communication and Democracy: Technology and Citizen Engagement, Fredericton, New Brunswick, Canada (2004)
22. Currion, P.: NGO Information Technology and Requirements Assessment Report, Emergency Capacity Building Project (2006),
http://www.ecbproject.org/publications
23. Fuchs, C.: Towards a dynamic Theory of Virtual Communities. International Journal of Knowledge and Learning 3(4/5), 372–403 (2007)
24. Stehr, N.: Societal Transformations, Globalization and the Knowledge Society. International Journal of Knowledge and Learning 3(2/3), 139–153 (2007)
25. Joia, A.L.: Knowledge Management Strategies: Creating and Testing a Measurement Scale. International Journal of Learning and Intellectual Capital 4(3), 203–221 (2007)

Developing Ontology Based Applications of Semantic Web Using UML to OWL Conversion

Moein Mehrolhassani[1] and Atilla ELÇİ[2]

[1] Department of Computer Engineering and Internet Technologies Research Center-Eastern Mediterranean UniversityGazimagusa, TRNC via Merisn 10 Turkey
moein.mehrolhassani@emu.edu.tr
[2] Department of Computer Engineering and Internet Technologies Research Center-Eastern Mediterranean UniversityGazimagusa, TRNC via Merisn 10 Turkey
atilla.elci@emu.edu.tr

Abstract. The aim of this paper is to present an approach to develop ontology based applications for semantic web using OWL [9] ontologies derived UML [19]. Description logic based ontology languages such as OWL are usually defined in terms of an abstract (text-based) syntax and most care is spent on the formal semantics. The absence of a visual syntax has lead to propose a particular visual notation for the classic description logic. Conversion from UML to OWL should be done in a very precise way because it is not as straightforward as it seems. It is quite likely that there are multiple alternatives in OWL for representing of elements of the same UML construct and we would probably need best practices for the same. The study will devise a straightforward standard approach for converting UML diagrams to OWL to be used by developing tools to produce an ontology based application.

1 Introduction

Nowadays websites and web services are everywhere, realizing complex business applications and combining them in order to develop a better application has lead to reuse the existing web services instead of redesign and developing them. UML is the standard for modeling object-oriented software for large number of web services and web applications, and has been accepted by societies and system developers throughout the world, also so many tools support software and business modeling using UML. On the other hand there is a new proposal to increase the capability of the existing web, this new proposal is "Semantic Web" which is not something distinct from the existing one but which enables people and machines to understand and work together by giving well-defined meaning to information. To provide expressiveness and to support inferencing, many languages are proposed which OWL in one of them. OWL provides more advanced semantic concepts than other languages [9].

The popularity, flexibility and ease of use of UML in one hand, and OWL which is developed to satisfy the requirements for a language to support the Semantic Web on the other hand has lead to several proposals to reuse current web applications, which are designed by UML, for future web, the SW (Semantic Web).bSome other

M.D. Lytras et al. (Eds.): WSKS 2008, CCIS 19, pp. 566–577, 2008.

investigations are done in order to reach to a standard and straightforward conversion rules from UML models to OWL, some proceed in the inverse way from OWL to UML, some used intermediate tools in order to reach the goal, and some attempted to graphically visualize OWL into UML models.

Among studies that have been done before, however none of them found a perfect solution, there is something missing in between, and brings us to this question, "what about DIAGRAMS?[19]" , and its due to the fact that no one before took UML diagrams kind into consideration in conversion from UML to OWL. UML consists of thirteen different kinds of diagrams, and each has its own functionality and is provided to accomplish specific task(s) in the design phase of any application. Therefore we decided to go over all thirteen UML diagrams and inspect for possible mapping, and if so the conversion will be done by considering all detail elements of the diagram.

The application description generated by converting UML design is going to be used as basis for an OWL ontology and diagram for visualization of the ontology, classes, properties, relations, etc. Protégé as an ontology engineering tool will be used in this process. Queries and inferring are to be done using inference tools, such as Algernon API that is a plug-in for Protégé 3..3.1.[16][7] For Graphical representation of ontology plug-ins of Protégé and other visualization tools may be used in this study. The rest of the paper is organized as follow: Section2: Mapping UML diagrams to OWL. Section 3: Case study. Section 4: Conclusion. Section 5: References.

2   Mapping UML Diagrams into OWL

In this section we will take all thirteen UML diagrams one by one into considerations for mapping to OWL.

3   Use Case Diagram

Use Case diagram is one of the behavioral diagrams defined by the Unified Modeling Language (UML)[18][19] and OWL is just to represent static information therefore it could be used to add some annotations to our ontology describing the ability, functionality and the usage of the ontology for users that are modeled as actors in Use Case Diagram.. For example the use case in Figure 1 could be used to add some notes and comments to the BuyCafé   ontology using   owl:AnnotationProperty, rdfs:comment and rdfs:lable[9].

Fig. 1. Use Case Diagram

The mapping of "Customer" and its use case in Figure 1 to OWL is shown below:

```
<owl:Annotationproperty rdf:about=":"&BuyCafé">
<rdfs:lable>Customer</rdfs:lable>
<rdfs:comment> Customer- Buy Café </rdfs:comment>
</owl:Annotationproperty>
```

3.1 Package Diagram

As each package[18] can contain any number of diagrams of any UML type and will provide a special functionality therefore the package name in UML could be considered as namespace and ontology name. For example the package name"Good_Order" in Figure 2 could be used for both namespace and ontology name as follow:

```
    xmlns=
"http://www.owl-ontologies.com/Good_Order.owl#"
    xml:base=
"http://www.owl-ontologies.com/ Good_Order.owl"
```

Both Access and Merge relations in package diagram could be demonstrated in OWL using owl:imports property. The owl:imports property shows dependencies because the importing ontology is dependent on the imported ontology.The owl:import is a property for ontology to define the URI of the imported ontology whose assertions apply to the ontology that is importing the ontology.To illustrate dependency in Figure 2 in OWL having two different URIs related to Product Orders and Human_Resourses ontologies (packages in UML) the following code is generated:

```
    <rdf:RDF xmlns=
"http://www.owl-ontologies.com/ Good_Order #"
    xml:base=
"http://www.owl-ontologies.com/ Good_Order "
    ns#">
```

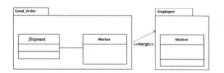

Fig. 2. Package Diagram

```
    <owl:Ontology rdf:about="">
<owl:imports rdf:resource=
 http://www.owl-ontologies.com/Employee/>
    </owl:Ontology>
```

3.2 Class Diagram

Classe[19]s are exists in Both UML and OWL. A class in OWL is consists of zero or more instances. A class in UML is a more general construct, but one of its uses is as a set of objects (instances). The set of instances associated at a particular time with a class is called the class' extent. . Instances in UML could be mapped to Individuals in OWL as follow:

<**ClassName** rdf:ID = "*InstanceNameInUML*"/>

In owl we are permitted to create instances which are not belong to any class and it's due to the fact that the universal class thing extents all individuals in a given OWL model, and all classes are subclasses of owl:thing. Implementation, but such definition is not allowed in UML and each instance must belong to a class.

Attributes within each class have unique names, but the same attribute with same name may exist in another class, therefore we'll have two attributes in two different classes with same name WHEREAS property name must be unique within the ontology. One solution to this issue is to use a combined name for property in OWL. This could be done by using attributes class name after its name with a underline symbol in between. As a result well have a unique attribute name in our ontology. The following is converted attribute to OWL property:

```
<owl:DatatypeProperty rdf:
      ID="AttributeNme_ClassName">
 <rdfs:domain rdf:resource="className"/>
 <rdfs:range rdf:resource="attributeType"/>
<owl:DatatypeProperty>
```

Most of the data types defined in UML are supported in OWL therefore translation from UML to OWL is straight forward as we'll define the data type as the range of the owl:DatatypeProperty.

```
        Event
-name: String
-start_date: Calendar
-/end_date: Calendar
-duration_in_days: int
-nbr_of_shows_allowed: int
```

Fig. 3. Class Diagram

The conversion of first attribute in Figure 3 will be as follow which has String data type:

```
<owl:DatatypeProperty rdf:ID="eventName">
   koja<rdfs:domain rdf:resource="event"/>
      <rdfs:range rdf:resource=" http://www.w3.org/2001/XMLSchema#string"/>
</owl:DatatypeProperty>
```

Mapping multiplicity on attributes to OWL will be done using owl:Restriction and owl:Cardinality on data type definition of the attribute. The default value in UML is demonstrated in OWL using owl:hasValue to assign the specific value to the attribute.

```
        Venue
-capacity[1] : int = 25
```

Fig. 4. Multiplicity, Default Value in Class diagram

Visibilities which are defined in UML have no equivalent in OWL because there is no information hiding and encapsulation in OWL, as result all visibilities in UML are considered as public in OWL. Property Strings in UML are expressed in OCL[20]. The corresponding mapping of Figure 4 to OWL will be as below:

```
<owl:Restriction>
<owl:onProperty rdf:resource="venueCapacity"/>
            <owl:cardinality rdf:datatype="&xsd;String">1</owl:cardinality>
<owl:hasValue rdf:datatype="&xsd;int">25</owl:
    hasValue >
</owl:Restriction>
```

The nature of OWL is to demonstrate static information and prepare them in such a way that is readable for machines so they can do computation on information provided to them by OWL. As result OWL generally is not able to express operations defined in UML therefore we propose to place a reference in OWL to refer to the algorithm, procedure, and etc. used in the program as operation. The alternative approach is to treat them as annotations of the ontology or that specific class. mAs responsibilities are not exactly elements of UML class and are extra description about that class, just like Attached Notes, we can keep this information as annotations to our ontology. Such conversion could be done using six predefined annotation properties (owl:versionInfo, owl:annotationProperty, rdfs:label, rdfs:comment, rdfs:seeAlso and rdfs:isDefinedBy) of OWL[9]. The class responsibility in Figure 5 would be mapped to the following OWL code:

Fig. 5. Class Responsibility

```
<owl:Class rdf:ID="washingmachine">
        <rdfs:lable>Responsibility</rdfs:lable>
        <rdfs:comment>Cleans the dirty clothes </rdfs:comment>
</owl:Class>
```

But for constraint the situation is slightly different. The UML works with still another – and much more formal – way of adding constraints that make definitions more explicit, it's an entire language called Object Constraint Language (OCL). An OCL has its own set of rules, terms, and operators. Relation is between two classes we have to be mapped into owl:ObjectProperty[9]. As we know each property in OWL has a domain and a range which both would be classes.

Fig. 6. Relations in Class diagram

Consider Figure 6, to map this relation to OWL we have to define an object property whose name is venueHosts (as we agreed before to use combine name for uniqueness). Roles in UML that are placed near each end of the associations are to be converted to some annotation or comments in OWL because they are not name of the associations. In some cases roles are replaced with association name, in such a case roles could be considered as association name. The conversion of Figure 6 is to be done using rdfs:comment, after declaration of range and domain of the association as below:

```
<owl:ObjectProperty rdf:ID = "venueHosts"/>
    <rdfs:domain rdf:resource="venue"/>
        <rdfs:comment>host</rdfs:comment>
    <rdfs:range rdf:resource="event "/>
        <rdfs:comment>hosted</rdfs:comment>
    </owl:ObjectProperty>
```

Just like Operations, Interfaces are also parts of the behavioral features of the UML and could not be converted into OWL. Same applies to the visibility rules and all will be considered as public in OWL. When an association is established between two classes it is considered as bi-directional association in UML. In mapping to OWL if we don't consider this default the conversion will not be fully correct because an object property will be created whose domain is Venue and range is Event according to Figure 7 and this is just half of all, and in addition another object property should be created with of course different name whose range is the domain of first object property and its domain is the range of that object property and the second (or first) object property should be defined as inverse of the other in order to demonstrate the full relation between two classes. To demonstrate multiplicities defined on association ends of Figure 7, OWL Cardinality and Restriction are used. OWL uses Restrictions to represent Cardinality. So in addition to map Class to OWL Class, some OWL Restrictions will be generated based on multiplicity definitions of the association ends and corresponding RDFSsubClassOf[5] relationships between OWLClass, and OWL Restriction will also be created. The following is the OWL description of Figure 7, the inverse part could be generated in same fashion .

```
<owl:ObjectProperty rdf:ID="venueHosts">
    <rdfs:domain rdf:resource="#venue"/>
    <rdfs:range rdf:resource="#event"/>
    <owl:inverseOf rdf:resource="#eventHosted"/>
</owl:ObjectProperty>
<owl:Class rdf:ID="venue ">
    <rdfs:subClassOf rdf:resource="&owl;Thing"/>
    <rdfs:subClassOf>
    <owl:Restriction>
    <owl:onProperty rdf:resource="# venueHosts "/>
    <owl:minCardinality rdf:datatype="&xsd;int">0</owl:minCardinality>
    </owl:Restriction>
    </rdfs:subClassOf>
</owl:Class>
```

Fig. 7. Associations and Multiplicity

OWL cannot adequately express some qualifiers that are used to define constraints on properties like 'key' qualifier which is used to indicate that the value of a property must be unique for all instances of a particular class. To shows logical constraints like "OR", "AND" and "NOT" in OWL three properties are used. These three are "owl:IntersectionOf" for "AND", "owl:unionOf" for "OR" and "owl:complementOf" for "NOT".

Fig. 8. Association Class

Mapping of Association class in Figure 8 to OWL could be done by defining a class named Contract and two functional properties that demonstrate associations between Contract-Player and Contract-Team. The functional property between Contract and Player will have domain as Contract class and range as Player class. The functional property between contract and team will have same domain and range as Player Team class. The N-ary association would be translated as a Class whose instances are instances of links in the association, and properties whose domains are the association class and ranges are the classes attached to the member ends of the associations. Since one instance of a link includes only one instance of the class at each member end, all the properties are functional (owl:FunctionalProperty)[9].

The mapping of UML generalization to OWL is straightforward. Both languages support the subclass relationship. Both also support subproperties. Subclass relationship in UML is defined by generalization and in OWL by rdfs:subClassOf. Sunbproperty in UML is generalization of association and in OWL is shows by rdfs:subPropertyOf. There are a number of subclasses of dependency, including abstraction, usage, permission, realization and substitution. OWL does not have a comparable feature except as annotations. Same applies to Aggregation, Composition and Context and could not be mapped into OWL.

3.3 Object Diagram

In UML the extent of a class is an object consisting of instances. An instance consists of a set of slots each of which contains a value drawn from the type of the property of the slot. The instance is associated with one or more classifiers. Instances in UML are represented by Object diagram. In OWL, the extent of a class is a set of individuals, which are represented by names. Individual is defined independently of classes. There is a universal class Thing whose extent is all individuals in a given OWL model, and all classes are subclasses of Thing. The main difference between UML and OWL in respect of instances is that in OWL an individual may be an instance of Thing and not necessarily any other class, so could be outside the system in a UML model. The conversion in Object to Individual in OWL is straightforward.

3.4 Timing Diagram

In order to map Timing diagram in Figure 9 to OWL we can define a class with the name of "TimingClass" which the timing diagram name will be added to the beginning of this name that, for Fig. 9 it would be "washingMachineTimingClass". This class well keeps the timing information related to the timing diagram in UML such as total time, each state's duration, and etc. We proposed two different approaches. First one is to create a timing class (for Figure 9) which contains five data properties totalTime, soaking, washing, rising and spinning each keeping their own duration and totalTime keeps the total time of the diagram.

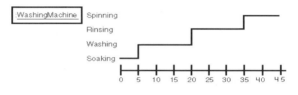

Fig. 9. Timing Class

Second approach is to create the same class with just one totalTime data property and take each state (Soaking, Washing, Rising, And Spinning) as a class and makes them subclass of "washingMachineTimingClass".

3.5 Sequence Diagram

Sequence diagram [19] is a time-oriented view of the interaction between objects to accomplish a behavioral goal of the system. An interaction may be modeled at any level of abstraction within the system design, from subsystem interactions to instance-level interaction for a single operation or activity. As there is no direct mapping from sequence diagram to OWL we decided to propose a new approach to model sequence diagram into OWL. To do so we have to break down the sequence diagram into portions of time which only two objects are interacting. Now at this moment we have only two objects and a relation between them. Figure 10 which is broke down section of a complete Sequence diagram demonstrates a transaction between objects of two classes Patron and Waiter and an association between them.

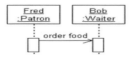

Fig. 10. Sequence diagram

The main idea of doing this breakdown is to enable querying and representing processes of sequence diagram using ontology. To do this we have to create a temporary ontology for a specific portion of sequence diagram as mentioned before and perform queries on that ontology and when done destroy the ontology. This generation and destruction should be done in automatic manner and could not be done by human like ontologies we have today because it is needed to be created in a short time, used and destroyed[1],[3]. The creation of the temporal ontology has to be done in several steps therefore it is Boot strap ontology. Steps of generating this temporal ontology are showed as bellow:

- **Step 0:** the generator must go over all thirteen diagrams of UML and all possible mappings to OWL which are provided before as in our study then load them into cash memory in order to make the generation as fast as possible.
- **Step 1:** go back to the broke down portion of the sequence diagram and check what diagram out of those thirteen UML diagrams is used in this portion (interaction). For example here Class diagram (Patron and Waiter) is participating in this transaction. If no more new diagram go to step 3
- **Step 2:** gather information for conversion of that diagram to OWL that is mentioned in Step 1 in order to generate the Temporary ontology. Go back to step and check for any other diagram like for this example Object diagram (Fred and Bob) is also participating.
- **Step 3:** create the temporal ontology based on diagrams in step 1 and 2.
- **Step 4:** perform query(s) on the generated temporal ontology and get the result(s).
- **Step 5:** destroy the temporal ontology.

The generation of temporal ontologies for each portion of the sequence diagram must be done in parallel because creating, querying and destroying one may last longer that the other.

3.6 Interaction Overview and Collaboration Diagrams

Collaboration diagram (Communication in UML 2.0) is like the Sequence diagram the only difference is that it shows the sequence of messages by numbering them. For mapping to OWL same technique (Temporal ontology[3],[2]) as for Sequence diagram could be used. Interaction Overview diagram is not a new diagram proposed in UML 2.0 but actually it's an activity diagram which have sequence diagram as its activities. For the activity part of the diagram there in no mapping to OWL and as for the part related to sequence diagram the Temporal Ontology approach could be used.

3.7 Component Diagram

Components are similar in practice to package diagrams, as they define boundaries and are used to group elements into logical structures. The difference between package diagrams and component diagrams is that Component Diagrams offer a more semantically rich grouping mechanism. With component diagrams all of the model elements are private, whereas package diagrams only display public items. As Component diagrams are to show a particular task or functionality like packages and are contained classes as well, therefore we can treat them as ontology. Component name will be the name of the ontology and dependencies between them could be shown using import property of OWL. In mapping Component diagram to OWL we have to be aware of the key capability of Component diagram which is encapsulation. Unfortunately OWL is unable to provide information hiding and encapsulation. The rest of the UML diagrams have no equivalent in OWL, therefore the conversion is not possible. These diagrams are Composite Structure, Deployment, Activity and Machine State.

4   Case Study

The aim of our study was to convert UML to OWL. In previous sections we went through all UML diagrams one by one and checked for possible mapping to OWL in detail. Now it's time to bring our study to real world and see how much our conversion is reliable? It is important to note that not all the diagrams must appear in every UML model. Most UML models, in fact, contain a subset of the diagrams.

We decided to covert a web based application [21] which is designed by UML. The application is developed based on five UML diagrams, Use Case, Class, Object, Sequence, and State Machine and is designed to centralize course materials such as Announcements, Lecture Notes, Grades and etc. and   make it easier for students to find course materials for their courses. Here we've just showed class diagram of the application which is the most important diagram in conversion of UML to OWL, and demonstrated in Figure 11, the class diagram includes 10 classes. Mapping of class elements to OWL are done as we explained before. Figure 12 show the graphical view of converted ontology classes and their individuals which is created by Jambalaya plug-in [16] of protégé 3.3.1.   As it's clear from the Figure 12, same number of classes is presented in our ontology as we had in our UML class diagram. Individuals are created based on Object diagram. Case diagram is mapped to some annotations to our ontology.

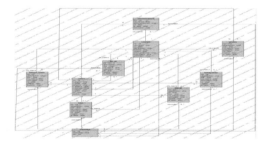

Fig. 11. Case study - Class diagram

Use The Machine State and Sequence diagrams are used in development phase of the application. To check the accuracy of our conversion we decided to perform a query to get the announcement for course code "ECON_315" which is taught by a lecturer whose name is "caner_barin" to see whether we get the same result, and if so, our conversion is accurate. This query is done in three different way, First: from the actual application, Second: from Algernon tab of Protégé, and third: from our ontology based application (Figure 13 from top to down). Queries on our developed application are performed using RDQL [8]. We can see that all results are same therefore we can conclude that our conversion is accurate.

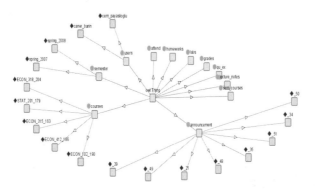

Fig. 12. Protégé classes

5   Conclusion and Future Work

In this study we took all UML diagrams into consideration and figured out some transformation rules from UML to OWL. Among UML diagrams the Class diagrams plays an important role and it's because ontologies are based on classes and the relations between them. We proposed new approaches to map Sequence, Collaboration, Use Case, Package and Timing diagrams into OWL. To check the accuracy of our conversion we brought our conversion rules into real world and applied to a working web based application, then performed some queries in different environments and got same result from all which shows the accuracy of our conversion.

Go To Top

Announcement	Date
Quiz 2 will be held on Friday, 2 May 2008 at lecture hour 11.30. Chapter 10, 11,12	30 April 2008

?Announcement	?Result	?date
Quiz 2 will be held on Friday, 2 May 2008 at lecture hour 11.30. Chapter 10, 11,12	http://protege.stanford.edu/kb#_35	30 April 2008

Results		
Index	Announecement	CourseCode
1	"Quiz 2 will be held on Friday, 2 May 2008 at lecture hour 11.30. Chapter 10,11,12 "	ECON_315_163 _35

Fig. 13. Query samples

All UML diagrams should be prepared as detail as possible to get a rich ontology bases information systems out of them, which could provide us with reasoning and inference ability and makes the searches much more meaning full facilitates to find the exact information in order to reply a query which is not doable with RDBMS. In addition this conversion rules could be used for creating advanced systems for the knowledge society. In future works we are focusing on conversion of those diagrams which had no mapping to OWL, specially the new approach which introduced the use of Temporal Ontology [2] in Sequence diagram. In addition we will try bringing security issues like information hiding and encapsulation into OWL.

References

[1] Raubal, M., Kuhn, W.: Ontology-Based Task Simulation. Spatial Cognition & Computation 4(1), 15–37 (2004)

[2] Kuhn, W., Raubal, M., Peter, G.: Cognitive Semantics and Spatio-Temporal Ontologies. Spatial Cognition & Computation 7(1), 3–12 (2007)

[3] Ying, X., Fu-yuan, X.: Researching on The Method and Technology of Creating Temporal Categories for an Ontology of Time, Agents, Web Technologies and Internet Commerce. In: International Conference on Computational Intelligence for Modelling, Control and Automation, 2006 and International Conference on Intelligent, November 2006, p. 264 (2006)

[4] Noy, N.F., Sintek, M., Decker, S., Crubezy, M., Fergerson, R.W., Musen, M.A.: Creating Semantic Web contents with Protege-2000. Intelligent Systems. IEEE Intelligent Systems and Their Applications 16(2) (2001); 10.1109/5254.920601

[5] Decker, S., Melnik, S., van Harmelen, F., Fensel, D., Klein, M., Broekstra, J., Erdmann, M., Horrocks, I.: The Semantic Web: the roles of XML and RDF. 1089-7801 CODEN: IICOFX INSPEC Accession Number:6730135 Digital Object Identifier: 10.1109/4236.877487 Posted online: 2002-08-06 23:22:12.0 4(5) (2000)

[6] Maedche, A., Staab, S.: Ontology learning for the Semantic Web. Intelligent Systems, IEEE [IEEE Intelligent Systems and Their Applications]. 16(2), 72–79 (2001); ISSN: 1541-1672 INSPEC, Accession Number:6941091, Digital Object Identifier: 10.1109/5254.920602, Posted online: 2005-04-04 09:37:49.0

[7] Alani, H.: TGVizTab: An Ontology Visualisation Extension for Protégé. In: Proceedings of Knowledge Capture (K-Cap 2003), Workshop on Visualization Information in Knowledge Engineering, Sanibel Island, Florida, USA (2003)

[8] Tun, M.T., Thein, N.L.: Informative Query Answering by using RDQL for E-Commerce. In: APSITT 2005 Proceedings. 6th Asia-Pacific Symposium on Information and Telecommunication Technologies, 09-10 November 2005, pp. 142–147 (2005); 2006-02-13 09:03:04.0

[9] Lee, W.: OWL: Representing Information Using the Web Ontology Language. Trafford Publishing (2005) ISBN:1412034485,2005

[10] Algernon : Algernon Tutorial 1.bPaths, Clauses and Relations (Accessed 11 September 2007), http://www.algernon-j.sourceforge.net/tutorial/1b.html

[11] RDQL - A Query Language for RDF (Accessed 17 August 2007), http://www.w3.org/Submission/RDQL

[12] Protégé: An integrated tool for ontology and knowledge-base editing (Accessed 6 June 2007), http://www.protege.stanford.edu

[13] Schmuller, J.: Sams Teach Yourself UML in 24 Hours, 2nd edn. SAMS publishing ISBN: 0-672-32238-2

[14] UML (Accessed July 2, 2008), http://www.omg.org/gettingstarted/what_is_uml.htm

[15] OCL (Accessed June 29, 2008), http://www.omg.org/technology/documents/formal/ocl.htm

[16] Department on Economics-Eastern Mediterranean University (Accessed June 25, 2008), http://economics.emu.edu.tr

Studying Students' Conceptual Grasp of OOP Concepts in Two Interactive Programming Environments

Stelios Xinogalos

Department of Applied Informatics, University of Macedonia
Egnatia 156, P.O. Box 1591, 54006 Thessaloniki, Greece
stelios@uom.gr

Abstract. Teaching Object Oriented Programming (OOP) to novices is widely known to be quite problematic. Students might be able to write a piece of code in an OOP language, usually Java, but their conceptual grasp of object-oriented concepts seems to be limited. This leads to poor implementation of object-oriented concepts and inability to take advantage of the strengths of OOP. Various teaching approaches and specially designed programming environments have been proposed for supporting the teaching and learning of OOP. In this paper, we present our findings regarding students' conceptual grasp of OOP concepts in two distinct educational programming environments: *BlueJ* and *objectKarel*. Their special feature in comparison with similar environments is that they are highly interactive.

Keywords: Interactive Programming Environments, Object-Oriented Programming, Educational Software, Computer Science Education Research.

1 Introduction

Teaching Object Oriented Programming (OOP) to novices is widely known to be quite problematic. Students might be able to write a piece of code in an OOP language, usually Java, but their conceptual grasp of OO concepts seems to be limited. This is confirmed by the various misconceptions, erroneous student-constructed rules and errors recorded in the literature ([3], [4], [5], [6], [7], [11]). This leads to poor implementation of object-oriented concepts and inability to take advantage of the strengths of OOP. Various teaching approaches and advanced educational tools have been proposed in the era of knowledge society for making the teaching and learning of OOP concepts easier and more effective.

In this paper we present the results of teaching fundamental OOP concepts with the educational programming environment of *BlueJ* [8] and the programming microworld *objectKarel* [14]. First, the main features of both the environments are presented. This presentation is followed by a description of the empirical study, including the main features of the teachings, as well as the goals and the design of the empirical study. Then the results that refer to the students' conceptual grasp of OOP concepts in both environments are presented in conjunction. Finally, some conclusions are drawn regarding the goals and the hypotheses of the study.

M.D. Lytras et al. (Eds.): WSKS 2008, CCIS 19, pp. 578–585, 2008.

2   The Programming Environments BlueJ and objectKarel

Both *BlueJ* and *objectKarel* are highly interactive OOP environments. They provide the ability of creating objects and interacting with them without having to write source code.

Students can use the interactive interface of *BlueJ* [8] for creating objects and invoking their methods. An object is created by right-clicking on a class from the class diagram of a project presented in the main window of the environment. Then a method of the object is invoked by right-clicking on its visual depiction and selecting the method name from the pop-up menu that appears. Students can also inspect the state of the objects that they have created. *BlueJ* also provides a visual debugger that allows step-by-step execution.

objectKarel ([12], [14]) is based on Karel++ [2] and uses a programming language closely related to C++ and Java. The actors of the microworld are robots that live in a world consisting of horizontal streets and vertical avenues, wall sections and beepers, which are small plastic cones that emit a "beep" noise. *objectKarel* incorporates a series of lessons and interactive activities for familiarizing students with OOP concepts before they are asked to implement them [13]. Students use a structure editor for developing programs, so as to avoid focusing on the syntactic details of the programming language. The structure editor has the form of a menu that is automatically updated when changes are made to classes, and dialog boxes. Object construction, method calling, definition of new classes and editing is accomplished through this interactive structure editor. The errors that can arise are very few and are presented at the bottom of the main window, while there is the ability of interaction between error messages and the corresponding lines of source code. Students can run a program, trace through it with a speed defined by them or execute it step by step. Also, *objectKarel* incorporates the technology of explanatory visualization, that is the presentation of explanatory messages in natural language about the semantics of the current statement.

3   The Empirical Study

BlueJ and *objectKarel* were used for teaching OOP concepts to undergraduate students. Both teachings were organized by the same research team with a focus on OOP concepts and were entirely taught by the same instructor. Next, we describe briefly the main characteristics of the two teachings.

BlueJ and the series of lessons suggested by Barnes and Kölling at their book "Objects First with Java: A practical introduction using BlueJ" [1] were used for teaching the 3rd semester compulsory course "Object-oriented Design and Programming" at the department of Technology Management, University of Macedonia. Students are taught the main concepts of programming in the 2nd semester with C as a programming language. In the final exams of the 2nd semester course a high failure rate was recorded for the specific group of students. The 3rd semester course consisted of a weekly two-hour theory session and a weekly two-hour laboratory session. Eleven theory lessons and eleven laboratory lessons were given. Approximately 45 students attended the lessons.

objectKarel was used for teaching the main concepts of OOP to undergraduate students at the department of Applied Informatics, University of Macedonia. The students that participated in the empirical study had attended the 1st semester compulsory course "Programming", which is based on the procedural programming paradigm and uses Pascal as the programming language, and they had all failed in the exams. In the *objectKarel* seminar five two-hour lessons were given to nineteen students. All the lessons were carried out at the laboratory, and the programming environment was used as the medium of instruction.

Both teachings, although different, shared the same goal: introducing students to the main concepts of OOP. In order to study students' conceptual grasp of OOP concepts the two groups of students took a common test especially designed for this purpose.

The empirical study described had two *goals*:

- The first one was to study to what degree difficulties and misconceptions regarding the teaching of OOP that have been recorded in the literature appear in the context of teachings based on educational programming environments, such as *BlueJ* and *objectKarel*.
- The second one was to study if there is significant difference in students' conceptual grasp of OOP concepts when taught with *BlueJ* and *objectKarel*. In other words, our goal was to compare the didactic effectiveness of two interactive environments that are typical representatives of an educational programming environment based on Java and a programming microworld based on Karel the robot.

In order to achieve the goals of the empirical study we used a test that was answered by both groups at the end of the lessons. Students answered the test without having made any special preparation, revision or study – as is usually the case in periods of exams, since it was given in the context of an activity and not in the context of the final exams. 34 students of the BlueJ group and 19 students of the objectKarel group took this test.

The test consisted of six open type questions specially designed to test students' conceptual grasp of basic OOP concepts – objects, classes, multilevel inheritance, polymorphism and overriding – and not their code cutting prowess. The last two questions tested students' ability to extract information regarding these basic concepts from excerpts of code. Due to the fact that the last two questions referred to the metaphor used on the microworld of Karel++, the BlueJ group was given - besides the source code in Java – a description of the microworld. Furthermore, the *BlueJ* group was given twice the time of the *objectKarel* group (2 hours instead of 1) for answering the questionnaire. In addition, they had the chance to ask for help regarding the metaphor, although it is quite clear and easy to understand.

More information regarding the two teachings can be found in [15], where the results of the study related to the concepts of objects and classes are described.

4   The Results

Next, we present the results of the study. For each question that is examined comparatively in the two environments, we remind some basic findings recorded in the literature and present the relevant results from our study.

Question 1: Are the concepts "class" and "object" identical? Justify your answer.

Literature review. Experience has shown that students often confuse the concepts class and object. However, the results of studies reported in the literature are not consistent. Holland et al. [6], in contrast with Carter & Fowler [3], state that some students confuse the two concepts and cannot differentiate between classes and their instances. The problem is more intense when the teacher uses examples that use just one instance of each class.

Study review. The results of the teachings based on *objectKarel* and *BlueJ* were not the same. Specifically, the misconception recorded by Holland et al. [6] was not confirmed for the *objectKarel* group, since 95% of the students differentiated between classes and their instances and gave a correct explanation for their answer. On the other hand, 47% of the *BlueJ* group seems to face difficulties, since 18% did not answer at all and 29% of them gave a wrong or insufficient explanation.

Question 2: Is it possible for the way that an object responds to a message (or in other words the way that an object executes a method) to alter depending on the state of the object; Justify your answer.

Literature review. Holland et al. [6] state that "students may fail to realize that the behavior of some objects may alter substantially depending on their state" (pp. 132), if the examples that are used "overemphasize the data aspects of objects at the expense of the behavioral aspect". Of course, our hypothesis was that the misconception that "objects are simple records" would not be recorded in our studies, since: (i) both the language and the environment of objectKarel emphasize the behavioral aspect of objects; (ii) the projects used in the BlueJ study, that is the projects described in the book "Objects First with Java: A practical introduction using BlueJ", are well-designed and do not treat objects as database records.

Study review. As expected, due to the assignments and the programming environment of *objectKarel*, the misconception that "objects are simple records" and as a consequence they respond to a message always in the same way independently of their state [6], was not confirmed. However, our hypothesis was not confirmed for the *BlueJ* group too. Specifically, the misconception mentioned above was recorded in the answers of many students. Only 24% of the students gave a full answer and 12% answered correctly but gave wrong explanation.

Question 3: Can we send more messages to an object through a single message; Give an example.

Literature review. The third and fourth question were motivated by the misconception that *"work in methods is exclusively done by assignment (and not by message passing)"* (pp. 132), recorded by Holland et al. [6]. Of course, this misconception suggests that students comprehend that the state of an object can change when it executes a method, but they have the impression that this is accomplished with assignment rather than method passing. However, besides checking if this misconception is confirmed we also wanted to test to what degree students comprehend that the execution of a method may alter the state of an object (question 4).

Study review. The misconception that *"work in methods is exclusively done by assignment (and not by message passing)"* [6] was not confirmed for the *objectKarel* group. This result was expected, since with the specific programming language and the visual step-by-step execution of programs, it would be very difficult for students not to comprehend that work in messages/methods is accomplished with method passing. As for the *BlueJ* group 47% of the students gave a correct answer, but from these students only 26% gave a full answer (including a correct example). However, we cannot claim that half the students of the *BlueJ* group have acquired the specific misconception, since 41% did not answer at all.

Question 4: Can a method change the state of the object that executes it? Give an example.
Literature review. See above the sub-section "Literature review" of Question 3.

Study review. Although this question seems simple enough and one would expect that all, or at least nearly all, the students would answer it correctly this was not the case for the *BlueJ* group. The fact that the majority of students (59%) in the *BlueJ* group did not answer this question at all – even without justification – clearly shows that students face difficulties. On the other hand, the *objectKarel* group seems to have fully comprehended the relation between an object's state and method execution.

Question 5: In the context of the 5th question students were asked to study a piece of code containing the interface of three classes that made use of inheritance and a test class where three objects were constructed (one of each class), and then define: (1) the names of the objects; (2) the initial values of the properties/fields of each object; and (3) the names of the messages that each robot can respond to (or in other words the methods that it can execute).

Literature review. Our aim with this question was to test whether students confuse the concepts "class" and "object" as stated by Holland et al. [6] or not (Carter & Fowler [3]). This was explicitly asked to students in the first question, but in the 5th question students had to extract the corresponding information from a piece of code. Furthermore, we wanted to investigate whether students can extract correct information from a piece of code that implements multilevel inheritance, since we were not able to track down any relevant results in the literature.
Study review. The results of the answers that were given by the two groups of students were different, as was the case for the previous questions too.

For the *objectKarel* group the students' answers on this question combined with the answers on the first question make clear that: (1) All the students comprehended the concept of class, object and object's properties; (2) Half the students (53%) seem to have comprehended the concept of multilevel inheritance.

For the *BlueJ* group it became clear that: (1) Many students face difficulties with the concepts class, object and object's properties, while several students seem to confuse the name of an object with the name of its class; (2) Students' difficulties related to multilevel inheritance are clearly much more severe. It is surprising that none of the students recognized that the source code presented to them – in fact just the interface of 3 classes – implements a 3-level inheritance.

Question 6: In the context of the last question students were asked to study two different versions (called cases A and B) of two classes implementing a polymorphic method. The difference in the 2nd class of case B was that the polymorphic method was overridden, and the overriding method used duplicate code instead of making a super call to the overridden method. Students had to answer the following questions: (1) Is it possible for methods of different classes to have the same name? If yes, which is the difference in cases A and B? (2) In case B could the method be implemented in a different way? If yes, write the new definition of the method. (3) Could we have one instead of two classes? If yes, write the new program.

Literature review. The concepts of polymorphism and overriding, as known, cause many difficulties to students. Of course, this is not surprising if we take into account that students, as shown from the answers to the previous question too, face difficulties with multilevel inheritance. Fleury [5], for example, has found that one third of students believe that *"the Java compiler can distinguish between same-named methods only if they have differences in their parameter lists"* (pp. 198). In other words, one third of the students believe that we cannot have methods with the same name in different classes. One of the aims of this question was to check if this misconception is confirmed in the teaching of OOP with *objectKarel* and *BlueJ*. Furthermore, we wanted to study whether the students can differentiate between polymorphism and overriding. We also wanted to study if students understand the concept of class reuse, or they find duplicate code easier, as Fleury [4] and Topor [11] have stated.

Study review. Fleury's result that one third of the students believe that we cannot have methods with the same name in different classes was not confirmed for the *objectKarel* group, but it was confirmed for the *BlueJ* group. It is not easy to give with certainty the percentage of students that has this conception, since 70% of the students of the *BlueJ* group did not answer the corresponding question at all, but it is clear that these students face difficulties. 95% of the students of the *objectKarel* group, and just 18% of the *BlueJ* group recognized the difference between cases A and B, which lies in the super/parent class of the 2nd class. However, only 16% of the students of the *objectKarel* group (and no one of the *BlueJ* group) made a reference to polymorphism and overriding and explained their meaning. Of course, we could not expect more from the *objectKarel* group, since only a 2-hour lesson was devoted to polymorphism and overriding.

The fact that students face difficulties with the concepts of polymorphism and overriding was confirmed in our study. In the second part of the question 37% of the students of the *objectKarel* group recognized the use of duplicate code in case B and used a super call to the overridden method in the method of the subclass. For the *BlueJ* group this percentage was just 3%.

5   Conclusions

Teaching OOP with Educational Programming Environments is thought to have more positive results than teaching with conventional environments. In this paper we attempted to examine students' conceptual grasp of OOP concepts in *BlueJ* and *objectKarel*. The most important finding of our study was that the students taught with *objectKarel* were found to have a significantly better conceptual grasp of basic OOP concepts than the students taught with *BlueJ*. Specifically, the students taught with *objectKarel* answered with greater frequency, gave more correct answers and provided better justifications. Furthermore, significant deviations were recorded in comparison with the results recorded in the literature (see Table 1).

Table 1. Difficulties recorded in the literature that were also recorded in a significant number of students in the teachings based on *BlueJ* and *objectKarel*

Difficulty/misconception	BlueJ	objectKarel
"Object – class conflation" [6]	✓	✗
"Objects are simple records: students fail to realize that the behavior of some objects may alter substantially depending on their state" [6]	✓	✗
"Work in methods is exclusively done by assignment and not by message passing" [6]	✓	✗
"We cannot have methods with the same name in different classes" [5]	✓	✗
"Students find duplicate code easier than class reuse" ([4], [11])	✓	✓
Difficulty in extracting information about the properties fields of an object from a piece of code	✓	✗
Difficulty in extracting correct information from a piece of code that implements multilevel inheritance	✓	✓
Difficulties in extinguishing between polymorphism and overriding	✓	✓

These differences may be attributed to the obvious simplicity of the microworld and the nature of the programming language that *objectKarel* uses. In our opinion, these differences are equally attributed to the way the two environments function. *objectKarel* aims mainly at a "basic" understanding of concepts, a comprehension of how each concept is defined and used, while *BlueJ* aims more at an understanding of the object-oriented design of a solution to a problem, that is a "functional" comprehension of the basic OOP tools.

In addition, *objectKarel* offers a clearer depiction of the OOP concepts examined, which makes it easier for students to comprehend them and be more confident about their knowledge. In *objectKarel* the objects are robots that are constantly depicted on the screen along with the source code. Step by step execution is the standard way of executing programs and there is no need to set breakpoints, as is the case in BlueJ. When a method is executed: (1) *objectKarel* students see on their screen that the object's state changes and furthermore they are presented with a message in natural language explaining what has happened; (2) *BlueJ* students have to use the inspect function and keep track of the changes in the object's state that is usually not depicted.

The results of our empirical study have showed that *objectKarel* seems to be a better choice when the goal is teaching basic OOP concepts. However, *objectKarel* cannot support standalone the teaching of more advanced OOP concepts or a conventional OOP language. *BlueJ* is an ideal environment for such teachings, and is used for this purpose in many Universities. Although, this is the common case our empirical study implies that the combined use of *objectKarel* and *BlueJ* could have even more positive results. We believe that the use of *objectKarel* for presenting the basic OOP concepts at the very first lessons of a course, followed by a conventional teaching based on *BlueJ* would provide the maximum support to students struggling with understanding the essence of OOP concepts and learning the language's syntax.

References

1. Barnes, D., Kölling, M.: Objects First with Java: A practical introduction using BlueJ. Prentice Hall, Englewood Cliffs (2004)
2. Bergin, J., Stehlik, M., Roberts, J., Pattis, R.: Karel++ - A Gentle Introduction to the Art of Object-Oriented Programming. John Wiley & Sons, Chichester (1997)
3. Carter, J., Fowler, A.: Object Oriented Students? SIGCSE Bulletin 28(3), 271 (1998)
4. Fleury, A.: Encapsulation and reuse as viewed by java students. ACM SIGCSE Bulletin 33(1), 189–193 (2001)
5. Fleury, A.: Programming in Java: student-constructed rules. ACM SIGCSE Bulletin 32(1), 197–201 (2000)
6. Holland, S., Griffiths, R., Woodman, M.: Avoiding object misconceptions. ACM SIGCSE Bulletin 29(1), 131–134 (1997)
7. Hristova, M., Misra, A., Rutter, M., Mercuri, R.: Identifying and Correcting Java Programming Errors for Introductory Computer Science Students. ACM SIGCSE Bulletin 35(1), 153–156 (2003)
8. Kölling, M., Quig, B., Patterson, A., Rosenberg, J.: The BlueJ system and its pedagogy. Journal of Computer Science Education 13(4), 249–268 (2003)
9. objectKarel, http://www.csis.pace.edu/~bergin/temp/findkarel.html
10. Pattis, R.E., Roberts, J., Stehlik, M.: Karel the Robot: A Gentle Introduction to the Art of Programming, 2nd edn. John Wiley & Sons, Chichester (1995)
11. Topor, R.: Common (Java) programming errors (last access May 2006), http://www.cit.gu.edu.au/~rwt/p2.02.1/errors.html
12. Xinogalos, S.: Educational Technology: a Didactic Microworld for an Introduction to OOP. Ph.D. Thesis, University of Macedonia, Thessaloniki, Greece (2002)
13. Xinogalos, S., Satratzemi, M.: Using Hands-on Activities for Motivating Students with OOP Concepts Before They Are Asked to Implement. Them ACM SIGCSE Bulletin 37(3), 380 (2005)
14. Xinogalos, S., Satratzemi, M., Dagdilelis, V.: An introduction to object-oriented programming with a didactic microworld: objectKarel. Computers & Education 47(2), 148–171 (2006)
15. Xinogalos, S., Satratzemi, M., Dagdilelis, V.: A Comparison of Two Object-Oriented Programming Environments for Novices. In: Proceedings of IASTED CATE 2007, pp. 49–54 (2007)

Interview-Based Photo Tagging for Expressing Course Concepts in Ubiquitous Chinese Poetry Learning

Wen-Chung Shih[2], Shian-Shyong Tseng[1,2,*], Che-Ching Yang[1], Jui-Feng Weng[1], and Tyne Liang[1]

[1] Department of Computer Science
National Chiao Tung University, Hsinchu, 30010, Taiwan (R.O.C.)
{sstseng,jerome,roy,tliang}@cis.nctu.edu.tw
[2] Department of Information Science and Applications
Asia University, Taichung, 41354, Taiwan (R.O.C.)
wjshih1@gmail.com, sstseng@asia.edu.tw

Abstract. Traditional Chinese poetry instruction mainly focuses on vocabulary explanation and recitation, through which it is not easy for students to catch the embedded meaning of the poems. Ubiquitous learning, emerging as a promising learning paradigm, can provide an adaptive environment according to the learner's context. When the learner is situated in an environment similar to what the poem describes, it will be easier for the learner to understand what the poet meant, thus enhancing the learning performance. To support the poetry appreciation in U-Learning environments, our idea is to provide an interview-based tool which can assist students to clearly express their intended concepts for a Chinese poem. We reduce the Course Concept Expression Problem to the interview-based tagging problem. The interview-based methodology consists of several iterations to find the user's intended concept for a poem. A prototype has been implemented, which will be used to evaluate the effectiveness of the proposed approach in the near future.

Keywords: Ubiquitous learning, Chinese poetry learning, Intention finding, Tag mapping, Interview-based approach, Ontology.

1 Introduction

Chinese language learning has attracted a lot of attention all over the world in the recent decade. However, the flexible expression of Chinese makes it difficult to learn advanced features of Chinese, such as the poetry of the Tang Dynasty, which is characterized by a lot of information embedded in the limited number of Chinese characters. Therefore, how to assist learners in understanding of the embedded meanings of a poem is a challenging issue. As the rapid development of wireless sensor technologies, Ubiquitous Learning (U-Learning) has emerged as promising learning paradigm [1, 2, 3]. In U-learning, the context information of learning environment such as location, profile, time, etc. can be considered to provide the suitable learning services for learners. The main advantage of U-Learning is its context-awareness, which can

---

* Corresponding author.

M.D. Lytras et al. (Eds.): WSKS 2008, CCIS 19, pp. 586–592, 2008.
© Springer-Verlag Berlin Heidelberg 2008

support adaptive learning strategies. When U-Learning is applied to Chinese poetry learning, the abstract embedded meaning of a poem can be expressed by concrete scenery, photograph, text, etc., thus enhancing the learning performance.

For example, Immersive Poetry Learning has been proposed to support the poetry appreciation learning, which is a multiple-stimulation learning environment with three properties: the Vision such as scenic spot, the Reading with occasional poetry, and the Emotional Reinforcement such as background music. One scenario in this environment can be that while learner goes traveling with GPS-enabled handheld device, s/he can request the Immersive Poetry Learning service to suggest and introduce a poetry which is related to scenes around the learner. Besides, based on the emotional property of the poetry, auxiliary tools such as the background music can be generated and played to reinforce the emotional feeling of the poem.

In this paper, to support the poetry appreciation in U-Learning environments, our idea is to provide an interview-based tool which can assist students to clearly express their intended concepts for a Chinese poem. We reduce the Course Concept Expression Problem to the interview-based tagging problem. In essence, the course concepts are modeled by the pre-defined complete domain ontology. The learners can express the intended concepts learned from the poems by giving text tags or/and taking photographs. In this way, finding the user's intended concept for a tag is reduced to finding a mapping from a tag to an intended concept.

The interview-based methodology consists of several iterations to find the user's intended concept for a poem. In each iteration, content-based text search is used to find candidate concepts for the user to verify the intended concept. According to the learners' feedback, the ontology is traversed to approach the learner's intention. The iterative process continues to provide the next candidate concept for the learner to verify until the intended concept is found with sufficient user satisfaction. The issues of interview convergence, domain ontology construction and maintenance have also been discussed in this work. A prototype has been implemented, and experiments will be conducted in the near future to show that this approach can effectively improve learning performance for Chinese poetry learning. The proposed approach can also be applied to a number of Tang Poetry learning activities, including poetry learning, assessment of learning performance and poetry recommendation.

2   Problem Definition

Poets usually expressed everything in his/her poem such as what they saw and what they felt; therefore the writing style of Chinese classical poetry can be concluded as five aspects: narration, scenery description, object description, chant history and lyric [4]. Fewer vocabularies in a poem contain profound implied meaning. Hence, the learning objectives of Chinese classical poems can be divided to four items: concepts (people, events, time, place, and objects), poet's affection, poet's embedded meaning, and vocabularies in the poem. These items can be further generalized as follows:

General Conception

Explicit Meaning (EM): the concepts of Chinese classical poetry

Vocabulary mapping (VM): the vocabularies in the poem which can be mapped to the previous concepts

Artistic Conception

Implicit meaning (IM): the embedded meaning of a poem

Affective meaning (AM): poet's affection in the poem

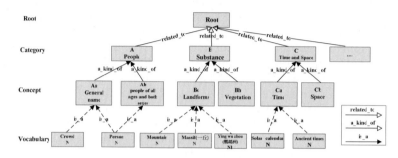

Fig. 1. Concept Hierarchy of Tang Poetry

Therefore, the assessment to learn Chinese classical poetry is that students are asked to restate their thoughts (*EM, VM, IM, and AM*) about Chinese classical poetry. Owing to the fact that the structure of course concepts should be designed in advance and its structure is hierarchical, the knowledge structure of ontology particularly fits this purpose. One of the technical issues raised by this problem is: how to represent the domain knowledge of Chinese poetry in terms of ontology? To cope with this issue, *Intention Ontology (IO)* is defined and designed to be a guiding principle for students to restate *4Ms*. *IO* has the following purposes: **General ontology**, **Interaction guidance** and **Semantic interpretation**. General ontology is that *IO* is a general ontology and students can choose dissimilar tags on the same poem based on the ontology. *IO* is also an interaction guidance to guide/assist students to find out the answers or express their intended concepts. Otherwise, students are hard to express their intention toward the cognition and perception of poem; therefore, *IO* is used to assist students finding their intension step by step which is semantic interpretation. *IO* includes three ontologies: *Concept Ontology, Implicit Ontology* and *Affective Ontology*. Concept ontology is *Concept Hierarchy of Tang Poetry (CHTP)* [5, 6], which have four levels, three kind of relationships, twelve categories and 94 concepts as Figure 1. *Implicit Ontology* and *Affective Ontology* are built by the process of knowledge acquisition from domain experts.

The problem definition of this paper is that given a photo and its tag *t* produced by a user which represents one of *4Ms*, the problem is to interactively find an entity *e* in *IO* from a rough concept to an exact concept by an interview process, such that $USL_u(t, e)$ is greater than a pre-defined threshold.

$$0 \leq USL_u(t, e) \leq 1$$

$USL_u(t, e)$: the satisfaction degree of a user *u* for using an entity *e* to represent the meaning of a tag *t*.

3   Intention Finding

The process of intention finding includes two steps: **Interview Process** and **Observational Learning**.

3.1 Interview Process

Chinese poetry learning is an advanced Chinese learning and the learning objectives of Chinese classical poetry contain two aspects: General Conception and Artistic conception. Because of the insufficient expressing ability, it is hard for students to express their thinking precisely. Therefore, the **Interview Process Algorithm (IPA)** is used to assist students to find their intention. IPA includes three iterations: **Poetry recommendation iteration**, **General conception tagging iteration**, and **Artistic conception tagging iteration**. These iterations will be described as follows.

There is a heuristic that students get their favorite course to learn; they will have the best learning effect. Otherwise, it will be better for students to learn Chinese classical poems in outdoor environment. Therefore, we proposed poetry recommendation iteration to interact with students and recommend student's favorite poem in the environment of U-learning. In the environment of U-learning, sensors are deployed to detect learner's context information and learner uses personal digital assistant or mobile phone through wireless communication accessing system to learn without the restriction of time and place. During poetry recommendation iteration, students input *Learner's Information (LI)* which includes people, events, time, place, and objects to the system. This system will calculate the similarity degree between LI and the vocabularies of each poem in the *Chinese classical poetry database (CCPDB)*. Poems whose similarity values are greater than the pre-defined threshold will be recommended to students. The similarity function adopts Jaccard coefficient as follows.

$$sim(LI, poem_i) = \frac{Z}{X + Y - Z}$$

X: the number of LI
Y: the EM number of $poem_i$
Z: the number of overlapped vocabularies in LI and the EM of $poem_i$

Once students choose their favorite poem, they can express their thinking about General conception and Artistic conception. The system is just like an agent to guide students to find their intentions and the process is similar to Problem Posing approach [7]. General conception tagging contains two iterations: EM tagging and VM tagging. Students choose appropriate tags for expressing the concepts of poems to indicate their intention during EM tagging. Hence the system will produce suitable questions by traversing the CHTP and interact with students. There are many concepts in the same level of CHTP; therefore **Conception Selection Algorithm (CSA)** is used to calculate the similarity values between the tags of recommended poems and concepts of the same level in the CHTP. After using the CSA, only the concepts with similarity values greater than the pre-defined threshold will be presented to the students. Then, students choose one tag and the system will prompt concepts of lower levels in CHTP to students. Otherwise, **Remained Concepts Computation Algorithm** is also used to remind students of the number of concepts they need to tag. After EM tagging iteration, students try to find vocabularies from poem which corresponds to previously chosen concepts during VM iteration.

Artistic conception tagging is a higher level appreciation process which contains two iterations: IM tagging and AM tagging. IM tagging iteration is used for student to tag poet's embedded meaning in the poem. The system will use the Ontology to produce suitable questions and interact with students. AM tagging iteration is used for student to tag his/her affection about this poem. The system will interact with Affective Ontology to produce adequate questions and prompts to students.

Interview Process Algorithm
Input: Intention Ontology, Learner's Information, CCPDB
Output: Learner's tags
Step 1: **Poetry recommendation**
      System recommends poems based on LI.
Step 2: **General conception tagging**
    2.1 **EM tagging**
        Learner interacts with system to choose appropriate concepts to express concepts of poem.
    2.2 **VM tagging**
        Learner tries to find out vocabularies, which correspond to previous chosen concepts, from poems.
Step 3: **Artistic conception tagging**
    3.1 **IM tagging**
        Learner interacts with system to find out the embedded meaning from poem.
    3.2 **AM tagging**
        Learner interacts with system to express his/her feeling about this poem.

Conception Selection Algorithm
Input: Intention Ontology, the tags of recommendation poem, Learner's tags

Output: Adequate related tags
Step 1: computing the similarity between the lower level tags and adequate tags
Step 2: representing higher similarity degree of tags to learner

Remained Concepts Computation Algorithm:
Input: the tags of recommendation poem, Learner's tags
Output: the amount of remained concepts
Step 1: computing the amount of remained concepts and representing to learner

IPA is a learning guidance tool which can assist students to find out his/her intention. The example of learning flow is described as follows. The system acquires the location information {Lalu hotel} by GPS and the student, Jack, inputs keywords {太陽(sun), 山(mountain)} to the system. The system recommends several poems to Jack and he picks one {Deng Guanquelou (登鸛雀樓)}. Then system tries to guide Jack to describe his cognition and perception precisely about *4Ms* Through IPA, the student's learning ability can be greatly fostered.

Example
    Role: teacher and thirty second-grade junior high school students
    Background: outdoor teaching in the Lalu hotel
    Poetry recommendation:

《Deng Guanquelou》
白日依山盡，黃河入海流。
欲窮千里目，更上一層樓。

The process to describe cognition and perception:

System: What kind of cognition and perception do you want to describe first? 1)
    EM, 2) **IM**, 3) **AM**

Jack: EM

System: What kind of EM do you want to express in this poem? 1) Heavenly body,
    2) Landform, 3) meteorology, 4) Natural object

Jack: Heavenly body

System: What kind of heavenly body do you want to express in this poem? 1) Sun,
2) Moon, 3) Comet

Jack: Sun

System: Which **vocabulary** in the poem can be mapped to the previous concept?

Jack: 白日(sun)

3.2 Observational Learning

Observational learning [8] is a vicarious learning. Students don't need to learn by
themselves and they can foster their learning ability by watching other student's
learning. Therefore, students observe other's tag and it may arouse the student's potential and exhibit ability. Students can go back to Interview Process to alter their tags
and the tags about the poem will be complete.

After the iteration between Interview Process and Observation learning, students
evaluate whether this system can express his/her intension which means students will
have satisfaction scoring toward this system. In the end, the tags of each student are
sent to the system as feedback and all of the tags are shared with each other. In other
words, this system accumulates everybody's knowledge and the learning process is a
collaborative Knowledge Construction.

4 Prototype

The learning process is described as follows. First, student's context information is
extracted from detected environmental information and student can input some keywords to system such as people, events, time, place, and objects. System calculates
the similarity between LI and vocabularies of each poem in the CCPDB. Afterward
the recommendation poems are shown in Figure 2 and student can pick his/her favorite

Fig. 2. Recommendation poem

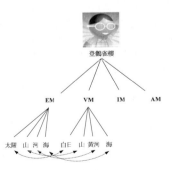

Fig. 3. Jack's concept map

one. After that, student interacts with system to annotate what he/she thought (*4Ms*) about this poem and the interview process is described as previous example. Student Jack just annotated 2Ms (EM and VM) and his concept map is shown in Figure 3. The result shows that students think that this system can accurately find out their intention.

5 Conclusion

To foster students' learning ability, an interview-based approach for expressing course concepts in ubiquitous Chinese poetry learning is proposed. Students interact with system to find their intentions with the aid of interview-based approach. Through the proposed methodology, student's intention can be found and his/her learning ability can be greatly promoted. To support the poetry appreciation in U-Learning environments, our idea is to provide an interview-based tool which can assist students to clearly express their intended concepts for a Chinese poem. We reduce the Course Concept Expression Problem to the interview-based tagging problem. The interview-based methodology consists of several iterations to find the user's intended concept for a poem. A prototype has been implemented to conduct further experiments.

In the near future, a knowledge-based system including the knowledge such as meter and rhyme will be proposed to construct and maintain a Tang Poetry Knowledge base for ubiquitous poetry learning. Thus, the structure of knowledge could be added, searched and managed; moreover, the referable information of writing poetry could also be provided at the same time.

Acknowledgements

This research was partially supported by National Science Council of Republic of China under the number of NSC95-2520-S009-007-MY3 and NSC95-2520-S009-008-MY3.

References

[1] Abowd, G.D., Atkeson, C.G.: CyberGuide: A Mobile Context-Aware Tour Guide. Wireless Networks 3(5) (1997)
[2] Yang, S.J.H.: Context Aware Ubiquitous Learning Environments for Peer-to-Peer Collaborative Learning. Educational Technology & Society 9(1) (2006)
[3] Yin, C., Ogata, H.: Ubiquitous-Learning System for the Japanese Polite Expressions (2005)
[4] Luo, F.Z., Zhang, R.Y., Lin, J.W., Tseng, Y.Y., Chen, Y.R.: The multimedia teach-ing system for 300 Tang Poems. In: The Proceedings of first International conference on internet Chinese education (1999)
[5] Mei, J.J., Zhu, Y.M., Gao, Y.Q., Yin, H.X.: Tongyici cilin Thesaurus. Commercial Press, Shanghai (1984)
[6] Weng, J.F., Tseng, S.S., Su, J.M., Wang, Y.J.: Constructing an Immersive Poetry Learning Multimedia Environment Using Ontology-based Approach. In: The First IEEE International Conference on Ubi-media Computing and Workshops (2008)
[7] Problem posing approach,
    http://www.angelfire.com/or/sociologyshop/appa.html
[8] Observational learning,
    http://en.wikipedia.org/wiki/Observational_learning

Travel Navigator

Michele Angelaccio, Berta Buttarazzi, and Arianna Nori

University of Rome Tor Vergata, Engineering Faculty
00133 Rome, Italy
{angelaccio,buttarazzi}@disp.uniroma2.it

Abstract. In recent decades, the phenomenon of tourism has taken a major importance, both economic development. Indeed, for several years, it has noticed a gradual increase of services offered to tourists starting from the traditional tourist guides, to web portals devoted to this sector and community formed to share travel, photos, videos, etc.. What, however, in recent years is spreading and especially evolving is a new angle: instead consult tourist guides during the trip or websites before departure, why not have a united solution? That is a device that has the main functions of a tourist guide and the power of the Web to get updated information as soon as possible and especially at any timeformat.

Keywords: Tourism, navigator, smartphone, web, GPS.

1 Introduction

Phenomenon of tourism in recent years, has taken a major importance, both economic development. Indeed, for several years, has noticed a gradual increase of services offered to tourists starting from the traditional tourist guides, to web portals devoted to the sector and the community formed to share experiences about travel, photos, videos, etc.. What, however, in recent years is evolving is a new point of view: instead consult tourist guides during the trip or websites before departure, why not have a united solution? That is a device that has the main functions of a tourist guide and function of Web to get updated information as soon as possible and especially at any time.

1.1 Function

Prototype developed has the function of:

- **navigation system:** as it referencing the current position where the user is located, seek an address and calculate the path to achieve it, choose points of interest and view them on a map, create thematic itineraries;
- **tourist guide:** in fact selecting a monument, a museum or simply looking for a work you can view a brief description, pictures and video about it;
- **emergency telephone:** in this software there is a section that allows you to send emergency request with a text message (SMS) with the geographical coordinates of the point where the user.

M.D. Lytras et al. (Eds.): WSKS 2008, CCIS 19, pp. 593–597, 2008.

1.2 Architecture

Architecture consists of three levels:

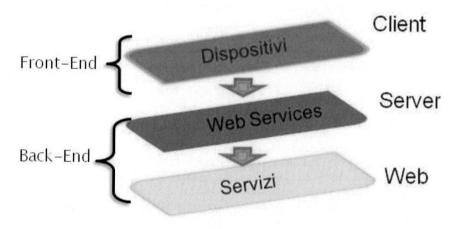

Fig. 1. Levels of architecture user to develop device

Client Side. This layer is represented by all devices based on any platform, which use the features made available to the software created, accessing Web services.

Server Side. In this level access those entities, in collaboration with the project, providing content such as tourist information, cultural and other.

Web Side. This layer is made up of all services made available by outside companies that can be accessed through the API. Examples are the Google Maps API and Microsoft Maps API live, used in this project.

1.3 Back End Area

Back End consists of a Server which have some Web Services and a database based on SQL Server 2005. The actors involved in this system are of two types:

• **content providers:** outside companies that offer their content such descriptions, pictures, video monuments, works, etc., manually entering this information into a web portal;

• **service providers:** are those companies that are already found on the web, who developed the Web Services that can be accessed through the API (such as Google Maps API or Microsoft Live Maps) which they issued.

Main actor of this architecture is the Web Service.

A Web Service is a service to invoke with http protocol: series of functions that are exposed through a server connected to a network, and which may be recalled remotely on a number of conventions clearly defined: the protocol.

In this way, different applications, different operating system, programming language, type and location of the server where they are executed, are able to automatically work together, exchange data, make queries on databases, complete calculations.

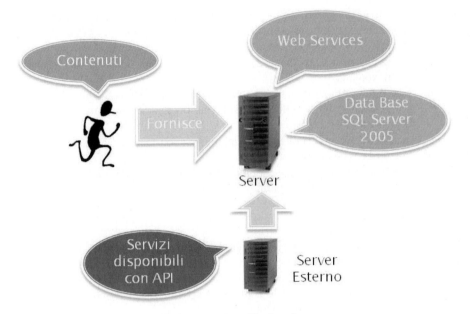

Fig. 2. Operation of back end area

Then in architecture developed, companies can insert their own content by accessing the web portal made available, contents are stored in the database; whenever the server receives a request for information processes the data in the database of content, access the Web Services using external APIs and releases the information through the html pages viewable on the browser.

In this case, were used two external Web Services in particular:

Google Maps: to use the maps that Google provides, and all those functions necessary to draw a path, make a point of interest, etc..

Microsoft Live Maps: to search for businesses by reference on the map.

1.4 Front End Area

In this architecture, Front End Area is the software developed for the client side. This software, which we built with Visual Studio 2008, reality could be developed in any other programming language that interface with Web Services to access the functions it needs. It is known that the main characteristic of Web Services is interoperability, namely the possibility of using the functions already implemented to create new services regardless of platform development.

The main functions that this software must have are as follows:

- established a point of departure (according to its current location or by entering an address) and a destination point, view a map on the path to be carried out;

- create a personalized itinerary based on the story of the monuments (itinerary Roman history, itinerary Etruscan history, etc..) or specialities of the place (for example wine and food itinerary, etc..), or even to the events of the day;
- see points of interest along a route, a path created, or simply according to where you are;
- search for display on the map a point of interest such as monuments, museums, castles, villages and each displaying images or videos to it to learn the history and characteristics;
- make an emergency request by sending the coordinates and possible description of the type of relief requested.
- The functions listed represent only a part of the functions implemented in architecture under consideration.

1.5 Operating Principle

Tourists request information it needs; server processes this request using the functions available on the web service and creates a html page containing JavaScript code needed to display the map; software appears, via web browsers, content of html page.

From the map created you can add points of interest, or displaying images, video and description of a specific monument.

Technique which you can merge into a single container, in this case the html page, multiple sources of different format (images, video, text) from different servers and spread, called Mash-ups.

Fig. 3. Operation of front end area

In architecture is realized Mash-up on three levels:

- content: content, inserted by the actors who work on the project and stored in a database SQL Server 2005, are read through xml and incorporated within the map, on the basis of location, contained in a webpage;
- Google Maps API: Google Maps to display the information available, such maps, routes, driving directions and enter it in a different web page with other information;
- Maps API Live: in particular API made available by Microsoft were used on those in search of business.

1.6 Future Development

Future development of architecture created are possible in both functions of client software, and actors who interact with the system:

- development of client software in languages Open Source;
- use of additional APIs to add new features to software;
- involvement of other actors content providers;

Using the new player made available in Microsoft (Silverlight), for the moment only in the desktop version but also short-mobile, to see maps and interactive content.

Obviously list above is just a small part of possible developments with the architecture in question, given the continuous development of platforms and technologies, and given also the strong interest in the tourism sector.

References

1. Ballinger, K.: Net Web Service: Architecture and Implementation. Addison Wesley Professional, Reading (2003)
2. Zhang, Q., Xie, X., Wang, L., Yue, L., Ma, W.-Y.: Detecting geographical serving area of web resources. In: Proc. of the 3th ACM workshop on Geographical information retrieval (2006)
3. Zhang, V.W., Rey, B., Stipp, E., Jones, R.: Geomodification in query rewriting. In: Proc. of the 3th ACM workshop on Geographical information retrieval (2006)
4. Borges, K.A.V., Laender, A.H.F., Medeiros, C.B., Clodoveu, J., Davis, A.: Discovering geographic locations in web pages using urban addresses. In: Proc. of the 4th ACM workshop on Geographical information retrieval, pp. 31–36 (2007)
5. APIs Google Maps, http://code.google.com/apis/maps/documentation
6. APIs Maps Live, http://dev.live.com/virtualearth/default.aspx
7. MSDN, http://msdn.microsoft.com/it-it/library

Moving Assistive Technology on the Web: The Farfalla Experience

Andrea Mangiatordi[1], Riccardo Dondi[2], and Walter Fornasa[2]

[1] Università degli Studi di Milano Bicocca
`a.mangiatordi@campus.unimib.it`
[2] Università degli Studi di Bergamo
`{riccardo.dondi,walter.fornasa}@unibg.it`

Abstract. In this paper we present Farfalla, a web tool designed to support people with various limitations, ranging between mobility problems and visual impairments. The main goal of Farfalla is to integrate typical Assistive Technology functionalities into a web-based platform in order to enable users with disabilities to browse web pages and to fill forms using different input and output methods. The project is still in progress: the user interface and one of the possible input methods have already been prototyped, while some other functionalities have still to be developed.

Keywords: accessibility, disability, assistive technology, web applications.

1 Introduction

Technology, and in particular computers, can play a fundamental role in helping disabled people in their integration in the information society [10,11,12]. Assistive technologies are defined by the Individuals with Disabilities Education Act of 2004 as "any item, piece of equipment, or product system, whether acquired commercially off the shelf, modified, or customized, that is used to increase, maintain, or improve functional capabilities of a child with a disability" [10]. In their generalist and technology-independent approach, they have inspired the development of many software or ad-hoc hardware interfaces with this goal [1]. Assistive technology are also good instruments for enhancing the ability to communicate: for example they can help people with physical problems in writing, but they can also be useful to children with cognitive disabilities [3].

The aim of this project is to integrate typical Assistive Technology functionalities inside a web application, in order to give to disabled people a completely independent hardware instrument to browse the web and to access its contents. In the rest of the paper we give an overview of the project features and its architecture, and we present the already implemented writing interface.

2 Farfalla: Project Overview

The main objective of the project is to create a flexible instrument, a web based platform for different Assistive Technology solutions.

M.D. Lytras et al. (Eds.): WSKS 2008, CCIS 19, pp. 598–602, 2008.

The original idea was to develop an interface allowing the users to write text documents and to save them using only a restricted number of keys. Then this system turned out to be effective also for browsing web pages. This could improve the ability to retrieve information and to communicate, allowing the user to access the multitude of services and applications that the web makes available.

The earliest functionality developed for the Farfalla project was a writing interface which enables users to write text documents using only a restricted region of the keyboard. This, combined with the browsing functionality, allows also to browse the content of a web page, moving a sort of cursor between the links and the other active elements (e.g. buttons, or text areas), and to fill forms, using only 5 keys.

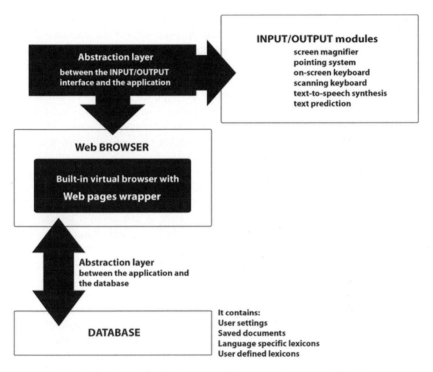

Fig. 1. A scheme illustrating the multi-layer architecture of Farfalla

The architecture of Farfalla consists of a database repository and of a virtual browser which acts inside an ordinary browser. This browser is composed of different layers: at the bottom level there is a web pages wrapper, while an abstraction layer determines how input and output signals can be transmitted between the browser and the user. On an upper level there is a modular input/output interface. In the database repository, all the information about the environment of a specific user is stored. The application layer consists of a collection of scripts written in PHP and Javascript, executed by an Apache Web Server. The main function of the wrapper is to read web pages from remote servers and to optimize their contents automatically to display them inside a web browser frame.

3   Farfalla as a Writing and Browsing Tool for Disabled People

Farfalla aims to build a number of new input methods and output channels to interact with web pages. Some software exists to help people with physical limitations, including Gestele [7], which has been successfully applied to assist disabled people in telephone communication. It allows the user to compose text using a scanning system and to send it vocally through the phone with the help of a Text-to-Speech synthesis engine.

3.1   Browsing and Writing Using Five Keys

The first input method we have developed so far allows the user to interact with the PC using just a small region of the keyboard. In what follows we consider the arrow keys of a standard keyboard, but these keys can be customized. Using keys that are in a limited region of the keyboard is considered fundamental to minimize the hand movements, since a user could move its hands in a limited way.

The same set of keys can be used to move between the elements of a web page or to fill in web forms. The integrated writing system is based on a scanning interface, where the user simply moves a cursor over a set of characters. A text-prediction system has been developed which can lower the number of required keystrokes (see [5] for a survey on different text prediction systems).

The text entry interface of Farfalla consists of two main regions. The higher one, highlighted in blue, shows in white color the text already inserted by the user. On the lower part there is a plain sequence of alphabetical characters. The user can move a cursor on this line from left to right and backwards. A character is selected for the insertion simply by pressing the down arrow control key, and characters can be deleted pressing the up arrow control key. Furthermore, as the user inserts a word, Farfalla also suggests a possible completion of the word, shown in a different color (grey) in the same region.

The interface has been designed in order to be simple and easy to use. The alphabet is maintained as a plain sequence (and not, for example, as an image of the PC keyboard), following the ideas in [13], since it is a simple and natural representation.

Two main relevant aspects of our software are the character arrangement and the cursor mode (that is the behaviour of the cursor once a character has been inserted). Following the ideas and the experimental results presented in [13], the characters are arranged in alphabetical order, with the space in first position. For the cursor a "snap-to-home" mode is adopted: after a character is inserted, the cursor jumps to the space character.

3.2   Text Prediction for Assisted Writing

Text prediction is one of the key issues to support users in many different fields, for example in the use of mobile phones. Several text prediction algorithms have been proposed in the literature (see [5] for a survey on different text prediction systems). Since one of our goals is to minimize the number of movements of the hands and fingers of the user (hence, the number of key strokes of the users), offering an effective text prediction system is one of the main focuses of the software. On the other hand, another goal is to maintain the system as fast and easy to use as possible, avoiding that the prediction system slows down the insertion of characters by the user or it becomes too intrusive for the user herself (for example, suggesting too many words and hence generating confusion in the user and slowing the insertion process).

The text-prediction module uses two dictionaries stored in the database: a standard dictionary, containing a list of words with the frequency of each of them in a certain language, and a second archive, called personal dictionary, containing the words inserted in previous sessions by the specific user, with their frequency and recency. Recency is represented by the date and hour of their last occurrence, expressed as an integer.

The personal archive is particularly useful because it contains the words inserted by each user. When the user is inserting text, the system looks for the word to be suggested searching at first in the personal archive, then in the standard archive. The candidate words are those words which contain the partially inserted text as a prefix. Next the system selects the word with the highest score from the candidate words pool. This score of each possible suggestion is calculated for each word in real time, as each character is inserted.

The score is calculated as the percentage which the frequency value of each word represents in relation to the sum of all frequency values of every eligible word. To this percentage another value is added, given again by the percentage of the recency value of one single word against the sum of all selected values. For this score to be computed, we need a method to express time values in the form of an integer, so the UNIX time stamp of the last insertion of every word was adopted. If the user's insertion is not recognized as a word in the personal archive, the suggestion algorithm switches to the standard archive, simply suggesting the most frequent word and adding the new word with frequency set to 1.

4   Conclusions and Future Work

One of the most relevant features of Farfalla is its simple and intuitive interface. Thus, although the tool is going to be enriched, one of the primary goals is to maintain the software as simple and as flexible as possible, in order to allow other software developers to extend its functionalities, writing plugins for it.

The future objectives and priorities will be the following:

- compatibility with the most popular and visited websites, in order to grant the users the possibility to access the most famous research engines and web services;
- adherence of the program modules to the WHO International Classification of Functioning, Disability and Health;
- testing with groups of disabled users.

The project is also supported by a website illustrating its development: see *http://www.farfalla-project.org* for more details.

Acknowledgments

Andrea Mangiatordi and Riccardo Dondi are partially supported by FAR 2007 - Università degli Studi di Bergamo grant "Strumenti per l'organizzazione efficiente dell'informazione digitale".

References

1. Alliance for Technology Access, Computer Resources for People with Disabilities, Hunter House, Alameda (2004)
2. Bellman, T., MacKenzie, I.S.: A Probabilistic Character Layout Strategy for Mobile Text Entry. In: Proceedings of the Nordic Conference on Computer Human Interaction (Nordi-CHI 1998), pp. 168–176 (1998)
3. Chatti, M.A., Jarke, M., Frosch-Wilke, D.: The future of e-learning: a shift to knowledge networking and social software. International Journal of Knowledge and Learning 3(4/5), 404–420 (2007)
4. Dell, G., Newton, D.A., Petroff, J.G.: Assistive Technology in the Classroom - Enhancing the School Experiences of Students with Disabilities. Pearson Education Inc. (2007)
5. Fuchs, C.: Towards a dynamic theory of virtual communities. International Journal of Knowledge and Learning 3(4/5), 372–403 (2007)
6. Garay-Vitoria, N., Abascal, J.: Text Prediction Systems: a Survey. Universal Access in the Information Society 4(3), 188–203 (2006)
7. Garay-Vitoria, N., Cerraeta, I., Lòpez, J.M., Fajardo, I.: Assistive Technology and Affective Mediation. Human Technology 2(1), 55–83 (2006)
8. Hill, J.R.: Reflections on resource-based learning environments: continuing the exploration of opportunities and obstacles. International Journal of Knowledge and Learning 3(1), 12–29 (2007)
9. Hunnicutt, S.: Using Syntactic and Semantic Information in a Word Prediction Aid. In: Proceedings of the European Conference on Speech Communication and Technology 1, Paris, pp. 191–193 (1989)
10. Individuals with Disabilities Education Act of 2004, 20 U.S.C, 1401–1481 (2004)
11. Johansen, S., Hansen, J.P.: Augmentative and Alternative Communication: the Future of Text on the Move. Universal Access in the Information Society 5(2), 125–149 (2006)
12. Lee, A.: Learning Disabilities and Assistive Technology, McGowan (1999)
13. MacKenzie, I.S.: Mobile Text Entry Using Three Keys. In: Proceedings of the Nordic Conference on Computer Human Interaction (NordiCHI 2002), pp. 19–23 (2002)
14. Nisbet, P., Spooner, R., Arthur, E., Whittaker, P.: Supportive Writing Technology, CALL Centre, University of Edinburgh (1999)
15. Stehr, N.: Societal transformations, globalisation and the knowledge society. International Journal of Knowledge and Learning 3(2/3), 139–153 (2007)
16. Swiffin, A.L., Arnott, J.L., Newell, A.F.: The Use of Syntax in a Predictive Communication Aid for the Physically Handicapped. In: RESNA 10th Annual Conference, San Jose, California, pp. 124–126 (1987)

Evaluation of Mobile Tourist Guides

Michael Kenteris, Damianos Gavalas, and Daphne Economou

University of the Aegean, Department of Cultural Technology and Communication, Greece
m.kenteris@ct.aegean.gr, dgavalas@aegean.gr,
d.economou@ct.aegean.gr

Abstract. Mobile guides have been in the spot light for the past decade or so they are becoming excessively available to tourists visiting places around the world. Most of which are to be used via a network connection on a browser based device and others as such as proprietary mobile applications, installed on-device. As such, some guides are used as navigational assistants in large cities solely for exploratory services and others can be used indoors as museum guides. This paper researches past and present mobile guide applications using a detailed set of evaluation criteria to extract design principles which can be used by an application-designer or an application-developer.

Keywords: mobile tourism, map guides, guide architecture, evaluation.

1 Introduction

The convergence of information technology, the internet and telecommunications have generated radical changes to tourism industry. In parallel, mobile phones are transcending from a traditional voice communication devices to instruments facilitating an interaction of the three major sectors noted above [1]. The mobile phone sector increasingly supports personal navigational systems and the usage of the mobile web platform [2]. However, by nature, mobile phones will always have differences in comparison to the desktop computer; let it be screen size, input methods, or just capabilities. Given current technology constraints of the mobile web platform on mobile devices, a number of traditional web applications are still turning up as robust mobile applications running in conjunction to mobile browsers. These applications are compensating on constraints which have arisen due to the lack of compliance to static web standards [3].

This paper focuses on the evaluation of research and commercial applications which are used by tourists (and not only) to get information, navigation, guidance or just cultural information using a mobile device. In this evaluation we envisaged design guidelines of a tourist platform which could be used by tourists on and off the web in a static or in a mobile environment. The remainder of this article is organized as follows: Section 2 introduces the design criteria which were used in this evaluation, Section 3 discusses the included projects with relevance to the design criteria stated in section 2. Section 3 concludes with an evaluation table portraying major design principles for mobile tourism guides.

M.D. Lytras et al. (Eds.): WSKS 2008, CCIS 19, pp. 603–610, 2008.

2 Design Criteria

The main goal of this paper is to extract design principles which can be applied to the technology infrastructure with respect to services offered to tourists via web or mobile applications, on/offline. wanting to see what architectural solutions are given to such a desired mixed mode (static or mobile) user experience. The extracted design criteria are expected to aid application designers and developers in the development of a mobile tourist application. To meet this objective a large number of websites, web applications, and mobile guide applications have been evaluated. We considered including not only milestone research mobile guide applications but also commercial navigational assistants and web-to-mobile applications readily available to all tourists via the web. Indeed, focus is given to mobile tourist guides systems running on any hardware architecture using or not a connection medium.

Most research on evaluation of mobile guides has been presented by scope of issue [4][5]. Kray et al [4] studied map-based navigational guides evaluating guides based upon 5 issues: basic features offered, situational factors, adaptation capabilities, user interaction and architecture. Chen and Kotz [5] considered the issue of context-aware to evaluate mobile guides. Our work additionally tries to answer two questions: what design principles can be used by application-designers for the design of mobile tourist guides; what technological choices do developers have while embarking on this specific area. Those basic questions brought forward a new sub-set of evaluation criteria which took into consideration our vision of the creation of a nomadic tourist information platform [9] running on readily available mobile technology.

The main categories of design principles found in reviewing literature can be summarized in the following:

- What *architecture* was used; which technology platform was chosen to implement the applications in stake; could these be used in today's mass mobile technology devices?
- What *information models* were adapted for mobile guides; do they make use of personal profiling and or collaborative filtering techniques to offer personalized information and services; could the information model be updated easily?
- What type of *network infrastructure* was needed to support the project on hand (e.g. WiFi, BT, and 3G); could the application adapt to changing networking environments? What was the cost of usage of such systems to the users?
- What type of *positioning technologies* and *map technologies* were used to support indoor and outdoor use; Were maps used to support the user? Could they be used to support route finding, dynamic itinerary support to users? What types of location-based services were offered? How did navigational technology support the user context with respect to information provided to them?
- What types of *input/output modalities* were used? Did the projects offer various types of information using multimodality techniques such as 3D graphics or speech? Could it support different languages?
- What *unique services* were designed and how were they implemented (e.g. using web agents, web services); were these services accepted by tourist users? Did the projects integrate any existing standards-based frameworks or initiatives to support tourist users or were all services propriety based?

3 The Evaluation

Many projects related to mobile tourism have been carried out so far. In our survey we focused to research projects listed as being milestone and also m-guide applications which have investigated specific design issues of interest to this paper.

3.1 Architecture / Development Platforms Used

The architecture of a mobile system depicts the way a system is designed and reveals the mobile devices targeted. While researching the types of architecture and platforms used in implementing mobile tourism guides it became clear that most systems used some sort of connection to an external source, but how this connection was used varied in different ways. In specific, in the Cyberguide project [6], its technological infrastructure alternated due to the release of different prototypes. The GUIDE system [7] used specific mobile devices namely Fujitsu TeamPad 7600 portable PC with 2 hours of autonomy and a transflective monitor. Also, the LoL@ project [8] was based on conventional Internet Software technology and user interface paradigms, extended by concepts to improve usability for the mobile domain. In the HIPPIE/HIPS project [9] clients were PDAs which used a thin client (web browser) application with client-server architecture requiring a stable network connection to operate.

The SmartKom [15] used a distributed component architecture using an agent based multi-blackboard system. SmartKom includes more than 40 asynchronously running modules coded in four different programming languages: C, C++, Java, and Prolog.

3.2 Information Model

The information model of each system varies in the type of information provided to the user. It was noted that the more detailed information given to a tourist, the more complex the information model was. The knowledge of the user's location and usage context resulted to context-aware information systems offering personalized information to each tourist. Some systems were noted as using an adapting personal profile and others used collaborative filtering techniques to offer a more personalized information system.

As of the Cyberguide information model, it was divided into four independent components named as: the Cartographer which had knowledge of the physical surroundings, the Librarian providing access to information of sights, the Navigator which was aware of the tourist's location and surroundings and the Messenger which offered communication services to tourist to communicate with sights (University staff) and for the system to communicate with visitors or groups of visitors. Whereas, the LoL@ implemented a hierarchical approach to model information using a browser metaphor of hypertext links, linking to text and multimedia information. The Hippie project was based on context sensitive models which apart from location, positioning and direction-detection also used an adaptable personal profile, acquired from the user explicitly and implicitly, logging the users' preferences which resulted to a context aware system; the system knew of its surrounds by having access to the organizations information system. The HIPS project was based on an Adaptive Hypermedia information model having a web-based infrastructure.

The Deep Map information model was quite complex as it was connected to the spatial and the other databases. Apart from the use of text, audio, video, 3D and VR as output using a dynamic multilingual information model. It also used '4D' techniques to portray representations in 3D of original buildings which no longer existed. In the CRUMPET project, the adaptation of services resided on the notion of filtering based on a user profile which was gathered by getting information of user interests, abilities and characteristics. If the user frequently requested information of a particular category, this particular category of information was known to be preferred by the user thus allowing the system to offer more personalized information.

3.3 Network Infrastructure

Regarding the network infrastructure, apart from which type of connection was used to link the mobile device to a central information management system, the way the system handled network outages was a key issue in the paper.

The Cyberguide used a Wireless network to implement a messaging service; it was designed to cater for communication between tourists and the system. The system could not adapt to changing networking environments or predict networking shortages. The Guide system was based on a city installation of a wireless LAN infrastructure. This wireless LAN was used as a location finding source and also a source of a centralized information service which a user could pull information from or be pushed information directly to the mobile device according to its position. In cases of network failures a caching mechanism was implemented to counter for such an outage. The LoL@ implemented a network-centric 3-tier application architecture using UMTS (3G) or GPRS network via a mobile phone.

3.4 Positioning/Map Technologies

The use of maps and positioning technology was thought as being key issues of most mobile tourist applications. Most systems used a map of some sort and were stated as using GPS for outdoor positioning and IrDA for indoor positioning as appropriate. The Cyberguide system included mapping, information retrieval, positioning and communication services. All maps and information was stored locally on the devices. All outdoor maps were vector-based allowing for scaling and path generation whereas indoor maps were raster-based. The user could access information via the map interface which also showed icons of Points of Interest (POI). By clicking on these POI's the user could access information about that sight. The map showed the position of the user and the POI's in vicinity. The outdoor CyberGuide system used GPS for positioning; as for indoor, IrDA sensors were used, yet no adaptation techniques were implemented in the case of failure of these positioning techniques.

The Guide system was one of the first installations to confirm the use of a map for electronic tourist guides. These maps were raster-based and were presented to tourists on demand to show the area of issue. Wireless hotspots were strategically setup in a way as to offer broad location positioning services. This type of technology was mainly chosen because the infrastructure was already in place but also argued that in specific built up areas of the Lancaster city a GPS system would not be adequate to get positioning information. As of the LoL@ project a central feature was its navigational and routing.

3.5 Input/Output Modalities

Some projects implemented a standard input modality using some sort of input device, whereas other projects offer various types of information using hi technology multimodality techniques such as 3D graphics or speech. All I/O modalities are reviewed in this section also noting the type of multilingual support implemented.

The CyberGuide system gave textual information via a user interface of buttons, the system was considered as having a unimodal user interface and there was no reference to bilingual support. The content of the Guide system was multilingual and based on a distributed and dynamic information model. The LoL@ project was implemented for 3 languages (including speech input support) and had the ability to detect visitors selected language via the SIM card of the device or by manually choosing localization language; support for input based on voice commands was also implemented. Speech recognition was implemented using the Nuance Speech toolkit. This toolkit has heavy hardware resource requirements, as such a dedicated server was used to host the speech recognition software and all voice commands were transmitted from the mobile device via Voice-over-IP solution based on Session Initiation Protocol (SIP) and the GSM voice codec for server processing.

3.6 Unique Services

Most mobile tourist applications offer services of some sort. These services are seen as an essential part of a mobile tourist guide, regardless of users' appreciation. Nevertheless, each system offering a unique service is evaluated herein.

The Cyberguide system could document user visits which at a later stage could be sent via email to the visitor. The Guide system gave enough flexibility to visitors to use upon request, providing them an intelligent tour guide builder that developed customized tour guides based on time constraints and dynamic changes to the user's environment (stopped, for coffee, slow walker). The Guide system also offered support for Interactive Services; a communication tool for visitors to contact the local Tourist Information Center, messaging tool amongst visitors. It also had a built-in ticketing service where visitors could book accommodation and buy tickets avoiding queues. The LoL@ system implemented a tourist diary service offered upon confirmation of arrival to a sight or by accessing the My Data menu item to enter information. This was later uploaded to the server and enabled viewing the log of visited sights.

Table 1 summarizes all systems stated in this paper against the evaluation criteria used to focus on the six areas of interest. It is evident that with respect to the information model most systems implemented proprietary applications using explicit and implicit means to offer adaptable information of a personalized nature customize.

This evaluation presented in this paper revealed the design principles which need to be taken into account at the analysis and design stage of mobile tourist guide. Key issues which were brought out of this evaluation fall into 5 categories.

The *architecture* which can be used, the *information model*, the map and *positioning technologies* which can be used to implement location-based services, the *modalities* which can be used to cater for input and output methods and the *unique services* that should be accounted for inclusion in mobile tourism applications. In general,

Table 1. Features of the reviewed mobile guides, navigational assistants and city guides

	Information Model	Position/MAP Technologies	Input/Output Modalities	Architecture/ Network Infrastructue	Unique Services
Cyberguide	On-device storage. Proprietary application Distributed Dynamic Information. Context Aware..	Map based IrDA and GPS. Automatic logging system	Pen / Screen Not Multilingual	Visual basic-Run time system – PDA WLAN Non cognitive resource adaptable	Guided tours. Messaging. Broadcasting. Post visit logging.
GUIDE	Centralized Hypermedia personal profile. Push & pull information.	Map - Guidance WLAN positioning. No adaptation	Pen / Screen Multilingual	JAVA – Portable PC WLAN Adaptable to failing resource	Communication Ticketing service tour generation
LoL@	Centralized Hypermedia model	Map - Guidance/Route Cell-id and GPS. User adaptable positioning. Manual logging system.	Pen / Key Pad 3 language Multilingual	JAVA APLET enabled VoIP Speech input UMTS Adaptable to failing resource	Pre-visit Post -visit Commenting diary service
Hippie/HIPS	Centralized Hypermedia model Personal Profile. Push & Pull Context aware	Guidance Electronic Compass IrDA sensors – object level and room level	Pen / Screen Not Multilingual	Microsoft. Net PDA - Subnotebooks Client -Server browser WLAN	Pre-visit Messaging. Broadcasting. Post visit logging
TellMaris	Proprietary application, not context aware	Map - Route finding. GPS	Pen/Screen 3D graphics Modality	Windows CE PDA Nokia S60 platform WLAN GPRS; UMTS	Exploratory
Deep Map	User context and context aware	Guidance Vector maps Route finding. User adaptable positioning.	Pen/Screen Multilingual support	Standards-compliant open source agent framework WLAN GPRS, UMTS	Agent based services
CRUMPET	Explicit and Implicit personal profile. User-aware unobtrusive proactive tips Context aware	Itinerary planning. Guidance Vector maps Route finding. location-based services	Pen/Screen Multilingual support	Client -Server Standards-compliant open source framework WLAN, GPRS, UMTS Cognitive resource adaptation	Guided tours Group meeting scheduler
SmartKom	Centralized Hypermedia model Personal presentation model	Guidance Maps Route finding GPS adaptable	Pen/Screen, speech Multimodality input / output. Multilingual	Agent Architecture. Multi-blackboard system. GSM, GPRS; UMTS	Communication Localized information
REAL	Localized information. User-aware. unobtrusive proactive tips. Proprietary application	Active location sensitivity Passive location sensitivity	3D-pointing device. 3D graphics Modality Speech input	PalmOS/Pocket PC GPS + Electronic compass (outdoor) IrDA indoor WLAN,GPRS, UMTS	Exploratory
Mytilene e-guide	Hierarchical information presentation Explicit personal profile Proprietary application	Raster based map Orientation	Keypad	J2ME application based system BlueTooth	Exploratory Push model

most architectures were based upon the 3-tier model, yet it was seen for modularity purpose the use of compliant agents would bring about an open modularity for ease of expansion.

The information models which can be used directly reflect the amount of information a user can receive and how this information is relevant to the user and the users' context. Regarding positioning technologies, most systems used a map as a central feature which in turn offered navigational and routing capabilities. Referring to I/O modalities, the systems implementing speech modalities for input or output were said to be resource-constrained, requiring large chunks of bandwidth to function. Lastly, the unique services offered to users should be designed and implemented in a user-centric fashion, making such services useful and user friendly.

References

[1] Mobile Phones - Convergence, Mobile Phones - Convergence (last visited May 2008)
[2] Press release June 5 2007 (last visited May 2008),
    http://bango.com/news/pressreleases/143_mobilewebgrowth.aspx
[3] Mobile google maps (last visited May 2008), http://www.google.com/gmm/
[4] Kray, C., Baus, J., Cheverst, K.: A survey of map-based mobile Guides. In: Zipf, A. (ed.) Map-based mobile services – Theories, Methods and Implementations, pp. 197–216. Springer-Verlag, Berlin (2005)
[5] Chen, G., Kotz, D.: A Survey of Context-Aware Mobile Computing Research, Dartmouth Computer Science Technical Report TR2000-381 (2001)
[6] Abowd, D.A., Atkeson, C.G., Hong, J., Long, S., Pinkerton, M.: Cyperguide: A Mobile Context-Aware Tour Guide. Wireless Networks 3(5), 421–433 (1996)
[7] Cheverst, K., Davies, N., Mitchell, K., Friday, A.: Experiences of developing and deploying a context-aware tourist guide: The GUIDE project. In: MOBICOM 2000, pp. 20–31 (2000)
[8] Umlauft, M., Pospischil, G., Niklfeld, G., Michlmayr, E.: LoL@, a Mobile Tourist Guide for UMTS. Journal on Information Technology & Toursim 5(3), 151–164 (2003); In: Werthner, H., Veit, E. (ed.) Congnizant
[9] Oppermann, R., Specht, M.: A Nomadic Information System for Adaptive Exhibition Guidance. In: Proceedings of the International Conference on Hypermedia and Interactivity in Museums (ichim 1999), pp. 103–109 (1999)
[10] Kray, C., Laakso, K., Elting, C., Coors, V.: Presenting Route Instructions on Mobile Devices. In: Proceedings of the 2003 International Conference on Intelligent User Interfaces, IUI 2003, pp. 117–124 (2003)
[11] Economou, D., Gavalas, D., Kenteris, M., Tsekouras, G.E.: Cultural Applications for Mobile Devices: Issues and Requirements for Authoring Tools and Development Platforms. In: ACM Mobile Computing & Communications Review (in press)
[12] Przybilski, M., Campadello, S., Saridakis, T.: Mobile, on Demand Access of Service-Annotated 3D Maps. In: Proceedings of the 22nd IASTED International Conference on Software Engineering (SE 2004), pp. 719–725 (2004)
[13] Malaka, R., Zipf, A.: DEEP MAP - Challenging IT Research in the Framework of a Tourist Information System. In: Proceedings of the 7th International Congress on Tourism and Communications Technologies in Tourism (ENTER 2000), pp. 15–27 (2000)

[14] Schmidt-Belz, B., Laamanen, H., Poslad, S., Zipf, A.: Location-based mobile tourist ser-
     vices first user, Information and Communication Technologies in Tourism (ENTER
     2003). In: Proceedings of the International Conference in Helsinki, Finland (2003)
[15] Wahlster, W.: SmartKom: Symmetric Multimodality in an Adaptive and Reusable Dia-
     logue Shell. In: Krahl, R., Günther, D. (eds.) Proceedings of the Human Computer Inter-
     action Status Conference 2003, June, pp. 47–62. DLR, Berlin (2003)
[16] Baus, J., Kruger, A., Wahlster, W.: A resource-adaptive mobile navigation system, Inter-
     national Conference on Intelligent User Interfaces archive. In: Proceedings of the 7th in-
     ternational conference on Intelligent user interfaces table of contents, USA, pp. 15–22.
     ACM, New York (2002)
[17] Rudström, A.: Co-construction of hybrid spaces. In: Doctoral Thesis, Department of
     Computer and Systems Sciences, University of Stockholm and SICS (2005)
[18] Luyten, K., Coninx, K., Houben, G., Winters, F.: Blended maps and layered semantics for
     a tourist mobile guide. In: Proceedings of HCI International 2005 (2005)
[19] Kenteris, M., Gavalas, D., Economou, D.: An Innovative Mobile Electronic Tourist Guide
     Application, Personal and Ubiquitous Computing. Springer, Heidelberg (in press)

Airlines Websites Evaluation Around the World

George Apostolou and Anastasios A. Economides

Information Systems Department, University of Macedonia,
156 Egnatia Avenue, Thessaloniki, 54006 Greece
economid@uom.gr

Abstract. This paper focuses on the airline industry on the Web and develops a customer-oriented airline site evaluation framework (ASEF). ASEF is specific-oriented towards the airline sites. It may be useful not only to users that purchase airline services via Internet but also to designers and developers of airline websites. It may be used as a guide in order to improve their services considering all quality criteria. Furthermore, the paper evaluates the sites of thirty major airlines across all over the world. Guidelines and proposals for sites' improvement are given.

Keywords: airline, e-booking, e-commerce, e-services, e-ticketing, e-tourism, evaluation, knowledge society, usability, portal, quality.

1 Introduction

Recently, we become witnesses to a major transformation of our lives into a global community which is based on the Internet. In a Knowledge Society, everyone would have access to knowledge and learning [1]. Not only the society but also the economy will be based on knowledge. Specifically, the airline industry is one of the most transformed in the web marketplace [2]. Airline customers are coming back to purchase online tickets primarily because of the satisfaction of the online booking process and a positive attitude towards using the online booking system [3]. Airline website attributes would be organized into the following factors: value-aided service, targeted information, advanced booking features, basic look and book features, trust and interaction, in-flight options, and frequent flyer programs [4]. Of these, basic "look and book" features were considered as most important by customers. Internet apprehension and customer satisfaction regarding airline websites are also important [5].

Knowledge accessibility, dissemination and exploitation are essential in the Knowledge Society. Managers need recommendations on effective website design. The past few years, we witnessed an increase in the number of academic studies concerning general website evaluation [6-12]. However, there are significant differences in the design of websites across different industry groups [13]. Several evaluation instruments with domain-specific quality criteria have been developed. Examples include the evaluation of bookstores [11, 14], university knowledge portals [15], job sites [16], and museum sites [17]. Regarding the airline industry, an evaluation instrument was the Perceived Airline Website Quality Instrument (PAWQI) [12]. However, it did not provide specific airline industry-oriented criteria

M.D. Lytras et al. (Eds.): WSKS 2008, CCIS 19, pp. 611–617, 2008.

and the analyzed case was only for New Zealand. In this paper, we attempt to address the need for a customer-oriented Airline Site Evaluation Framework (ASEF) which combines criteria derived from evaluation methods and instruments developed in the past [18] but with a specific airline industry oriented way. Furthermore, we apply ASEF to evaluate 30 major airlines' sites from all around the world.

2   Airline Site Evaluation Framework (ASEF)

Driven by the need for a specific airline industry oriented evaluation framework we develop the Airline Site Evaluation Framework (ASEF). It consists of five categories: Finding, Interface, Navigation, Content, Reliability, and Technical aspects. Each category consists of several sub-categories, and each sub-category consists of several criteria:

1. **Site Finding**
   1.1. **URL intuitive, easy to remember and type**
   1.2. **Easy to find site using search engines**

2. **Interface**
   2.1. **Visually attractive site** (Effective use of White space, Effective & consistent use of Colors, Effective & consistent use of Background, Effective & consistent use of Buttons which are appropriately situated, Consistent Style of pages)
   2.2. **Flexibility** (Printable version of certain pages is available, Multilingual content, Customization of site content depending on user's country/continent, Special needs person accommodation/ non-discrimination)
   2.3. **Multimedia** (Multimedia usage takes into consideration user's hardware constraints, Widely available multimedia format, Multimedia help to the understanding of the site, Adequate media richness)
   2.4. **Text** (Consistent and easy to read Fonts, Easy to change the Size of fonts, Correct Spelling and Grammar)

3. **Navigation**
   3.1. **Structure** (Intuitive Organization & Structure, Easy Navigation, Help-Bar shows the steps of the transaction, Facilities (e.g. Icons) help Navigation, Friendly Orientation shows the progress of the transaction, Logical Site Map or Table of Contents)
   3.2. **Internet Booking Engine** (Easy to use Internet Booking Engine, Many search options are available to help user find preferable flight, Ability to search and book other services (car hire, hotel, etc.), Many search options are available to help user find preferable other services, No errors, In case of not finding flight (or other services), proposals of related flights (or other services), Findings of the Internet Booking Engine are accurate and well described)
   3.3. **Search Engine** (Internal site search engine is available and appropriate situated, Findings of the Internal Search Engine are accurate and well described)

3.4. **Navigational Necessities** (No broken links, No "Under-Construction" and "Non-Updated Content" pages, Hyperlinks clearly described, well labeled and defined, Pages sized to fit in browser window, Easy to Return to Main page from every page, No pop-up pages, Easy access to Help from every page)

4. **Content**

    4.1. **Services Information** (Full Itineraries information, Full Fare and Refund policy information, Full On-Flight Services information, Full Fleet and Airports information, Full Services for Special Passenger Categories and Pets information, Full Fare Rules, Contact information, Website Terms and Conditions, Carriage Conditions information, Full information regarding other services e.g. car hire, hotel)

    4.2. **Special Offers & Frequent Flyer Program** (Newsletter free subscription, Special online Prices for Flight services, Special online Prices for Other services e.g. car hire, hotel, Online free subscription to Frequent Flyer Program, Privileges for online buying tickets or other services, Personal Information and Services for a Frequent Flyer Passenger, Frequent Flyer Privileges and Rewards are valid for a network of airlines and other companies e.g. car hire, hotel.)

    4.3. **Company Information** (Complete and appropriately situated company information, Complete list and contact information of around the world offices)

    4.4. **Advertisement** (Advertisement of company's products and services, Advertisement of other companies, Pleasant and appropriately situated advertisements)

    4.5. **Support of Website Users** (Feedback forms, Telephone numbers -Help Desk, E-mail addresses, Tool-free tele-assistance, Round the clock Help Desk)

    4.6. **Services for Website Users** (Current flight status information, Boarding-pass printing and quick check-in capability, VIP services)

    4.7. **Competency of the Provided Assistance** (FAQ and detailed Help explain every procedure, Help for any kind of users)

5. **Reliability**

    5.1. **Registration** (Registration is Optional, Easy to register, Easy to Login, Easy to modify registered profile, Offers to registered users)

    5.2. **Transaction Procedure** (Full Current and Next transaction step information, Easy to Go Back or Exit from the transaction procedure, Procedure for purchasing other services e.g. car hire, hotel, is completed in the airline's website)

    5.3. **E-Ticketing** (Various alternative methods of payment, Acknowledgment of transaction can be printed and sent to customer via e-mail, SMS, etc.)

    5.4. **Paper Ticket** (Various alternative methods of payment, Various alternative methods of ticket delivery, Acknowledgment of transaction can be printed and sent to customer via e-mail, SMS, fax, or mail, No extra delivery charges and no extra charges for paper ticket)

    5.5. **Privacy Policy** (Full privacy policy statement available, No personal information is forwarded to third parties without user's agreement)

6. **Technical aspects**
   6.1. **Loading Speed** (Fast Main page loading, Fast page loading, Consideration of non-broadband users)
   6.2. **Security** (Security protocols are used during the transaction, Well known security protocols used during the transaction, Security protocols are used during the user registration, Well known security protocols used during the user registration, Security systems accredited by authorization organizations)
   6.3. **Browser** (Cross-browser compatibility, Appropriate resolution and screen fitting)

3 Evaluation Results and Discussion

We evaluated the websites of 10 European airlines, 10 Asian airlines and 10 American and Oceania airlines. The evaluator is called to answer if and to what degree the evaluated website meets the "ideal" situation regarding each criterion. So, for each criterion, the evaluator gives three points if the reality fits in with the "ideal" situation; two points if the reality is close to the "ideal"; one point if the reality is far from the "ideal"; zero points if the reality has no relation with the "ideal". Regarding some criteria, the evaluator can give either three or zero points.

Starting, it was easy to find the sites. The average score for Finding was 5.67 (out of 6). Regarding the Interface, the European sites scored higher than the rest. BritishAirways.com achieved the highest score (46 out of 48). All sites scored low regarding Flexibility. Only 9 sites (BritishAirways.com, Lufthansa.com, KLM.com, AuA.com, Emirates.com, RegionalExpress.com.au, AmericanAirlines.com, AirCanada.com, and United.com) provided some accommodation for persons with special needs. So, further accessibility improvements should be offered by all sites in order to facilitate the access to the sites by people with disabilities and special needs. Some steps towards this direction would be the following: 1) the maintenance of a simple, consistent page layout throughout the site; 2) a simple background with enough contrast; 3) inclusion of text descriptions for graphical elements on the site; 4) resizable fonts; 5) provision of audio description and captions or transcripts of video; 6) inclusion of a guide about accessibility. Vision and speech as communication channels would be also exploited [19]. Users prefer simple and playful interaction [20].

Regarding Navigation, the American & Oceania sites outperformed in all the subcategories except in the Structure subcategory where the European sites achieved the highest average. The major drawbacks were the Internet Booking Engines, and the lack of internal search engine on their main page. United.com achieved the highest score (61 out of 63). CathayPacific.com was the only one to score perfectly regarding Navigational Necessities

Regarding the Content, there were not large differences among the geographical segments' averages. However, many sites did not take serious attention on the Special Offers & Frequent Flyer Program subcategory. More specifically, half of the sites did not considered special offers for online customers, and most of the Frequent Flyer Programs were not organized well. However, Lufthansa.com, Iberia.com, AuA.com, Ana.co.jp, Emirates.com, AirCanada.com and United.com achieved the best score in this sub-category. Regarding the Services for Web Site Users subcategory, all European sites scored high by offering Boarding Pass Printing and Quick Check-In Capability for the site users. Finally, regarding the Support for Web Site Users and the Competency of the Provided Assistance subcategories, only seven sites (Lufthansa.com, KoreanAir.com, Cathaypacific.com, AirNewZealand.com, Delta.com, AirCanada.com and United.com.) achieved the perfect score in this sub-category. Regarding the Services for Website Users sub-category, European sites scored higher than the rest mainly because they offered Boarding Pass Printing and Quick Check-In. Only seven sites (Lufthansa.com, KoreanAir.com, Cathaypacific.com, AirNewZealand.com, Delta.com, AirCanada.com and United.com) achieved the perfect score in the Support of Website Users and the Competence of the Provided Assistance sub-categories. This fact is alarming because the provided help to the site users is of vital importance. If an online customer does not get support and help from a site whenever he wants it and the way he wants it, then he will just click to another site. AirCanada.com was the only site that achieved the perfect score (87 points) regarding Content. It would be considered as a reference guide for Content.

Regarding Reliability, the Asian sites achieved the highest average score by gaining extra points especially in the Transaction Procedure and the Privacy Policy subcategories. Most sites did not achieve good scores in the Transaction Procedure subcategory with the exception of Lufthansa.com and Emirates.com. Most sites did not offer alternative methods of payment except from credit cards. Moreover, almost all sites did not offer both forms of ticketing (paper ticket and e-ticket). These insufficiencies should be resolved and the sites should provide more alternative methods of payments like prepaid cards, electronic writ, electronic money, cash on delivery etc. Furthermore, they should consider that some customers value both forms of ticketing as important. In the Reliability category, only Lufthansa.com, CathayPacific.com, Emirates.com and Ans.co.jp succeeded in getting more than 45 points (out of 51).

Regarding the Technical Aspects, Asian sites achieved the highest average (26.5 out of 30). The best sites were: AuA.com, Qantas.com and AirNewZealand.com. As expected, almost all sites achieved high scores in the Security subcategory. However, there were some problems in the Loading Speed and Browser subcategories especially for the European sites. Finally, the sites should support all major browsers (e.g. Internet Explore, Mozilla Firefox, Netscape Navigator and Opera).

Overall, American & Oceania sites (average score= 227.5) as well as European sites (average score=227.2) scored higher than the Asian sites (average score= 218). The United.com (264 points), AuA.com (258 points) and Emirates.com (257 points) were the best sites as they approached the maximum possible score (285 points). They would be considered as best practice cases by web developers and airline managers who want to build a reliable, customer-oriented and easy-to-use site.

4   Conclusions

This paper contributes to the literature on the evaluation of airlines sites by providing an airline site evaluation framework. Designers and developers of airline sites would use this framework to evaluate the current status of their sites and take appropriate actions in areas where they face inefficiencies.

In addition, 30 airlines sites were evaluated using this framework. Although there were not significant differences among geographical regions, some sites outperformed. These sites would be considered as guides for improved site design. However, most airlines sites should take into serious consideration the persons with special needs. Also, flexibility in various ways (e.g. method of payment, ticket type, ticket delivery, seat selection, meal selection) should be supported. Specifically for booking, a user would be able to declare a time span of several days and times in order to find the cheapest flight. Governments would require airlines to develop websites with various capabilities (e.g. fonts' enlargement, text to speech conversion, voice commands) for people with special needs. Governments should also ensure that personal data would not be used by anyone without the person's authorization.

Future research could examine the improvements made over time. Also, a single airline site would be evaluated by many users of various ages, educational and social levels in order to discover any differences in their preferences. Finally, the concepts presented in this framework could be extended to other market domains.

References

1. Lytras, M.D., Sicilia, M.A.: The knowledge society: A manifesto for knowledge and learning. International Journal of Knowledge and Learning 1(1/2), 1–11 (2005)
2. Dutta, S., Segev, A.: Business transformation on the Internet. In: Barnes, S., Hunt, B. (eds.) E-Commerce and V-Business, pp. 5–22. Butterworth – Heinemann, Oxford (2001)
3. Koppius, O., Speelman, W., Stulp, O., Verhoef, B., van Heck, E.: Why are customers coming back to buy their airline tickets online? In: ICEC 2005, pp. 319–326. ACM, New York (2005)
4. Benckendorff, P.: An exploratory analysis of traveller preferences for airline website content. Information Technology & Tourism 8, 149–159 (2006)
5. Lubbe, B.: The effect of Internet apprehension and website satisfaction on air travelers adoption of an airline's website. Journal of Air Transport Management 13, 75–80 (2007)
6. Schubert, P., Selz, D.: Measuring the effectiveness of electronic commerce websites with the Web Assessment Method. In: Hunt, B. (ed.) E-Commerce and V-Business. Imperial College, London (2001)
7. Schubert, P., Dettling, W.: Extended Web Assessment Method (EWAM) – Evaluation of e-commerce applications from the customer's viewpoint. In: Proceedings of the 35th Hawaii International Conference on System Sciences, IEEE, Los Alamitos (2002)
8. Liu, C., Arnett, K.P., Litecky, C.: Design quality of web sites for electronic commerce: Fortune 1000 webmasters evaluations. Electronic Markets 10(2), 120–129 (2000)
9. Olsina, L., Rossi, G.: Towards web site quantitative evaluation: Defining quality characteristics and attributes. In: Proceedings of IV International WebNet Conference, World Conference on the WWW and Internet, Hawaii, USA, pp. 834–839 (1999)
10. Barnes, S.J., Vidgen, R.T.: Assessing the quality of auction web sites. In: Proceedings of the 34th Hawaii International Conference on System Sciences. IEEE, Los Alamitos (2001)
11. Barnes, S.J., Vidgen, R.T.: An integrative approach to the assessment of e-commerce quality. Journal of Electronic Commerce Research 3(3), 114–127 (2002)
12. Shchiglik, C., Barnes, S.J.: Evaluating website quality in the airline industry. The Journal of Computer Information Systems 44(3), 17–25 (2004)
13. Kim, S.E., Shaw, T., Schneider, H.: Web site design benchmarking within industry groups. Internet Research: Electronic Networking Applications and Policy 13(1), 17–26 (2003)

14. Heijden, H., Verhagen, T.: Measuring and assessing online store image: a study of two online bookshops in Benelux. In: Proceedings of the 35th Hawaii International Conference on System Sciences. IEEE, Los Alamitos (2002)
15. Jones, N.B., Provost, D.M., Pascale, D.S.: Developing a university research web-based knowledge portal. International Journal of Knowledge and Learning 2(1/2), 106–118 (2006)
16. Terzis, V., Economides, A.A.: Job site evaluation framework (JSEF) and comparison among Greek and foreign job sites. Human Systems Management 24(3), 223–237 (2005)
17. Pallas, J., Economides, A.A.: Evaluation of art museums web sites worldwide. Information Services & Use 28(1), 45–57 (2008)
18. Merwe, V.D., Bekker, J.: A framework and methodology for evaluating ecommerce web sites. Internet Research: Electronic Networking Applications and Policy 13(5), 330–341 (2003)
19. Porta, M.: E-learning and machine perception: In pursuit of human-line interaction in computer-based teaching systems. International Journal of Knowledge and Learning 3(2/3), 281–298 (2007)
20. Groth, K., Bogdan, C., Lindqvist, S., Sundblad, Y.: Simple and playful interaction for informal communication and learning. International Journal of Knowledge and Learning 3(2/3), 191–208 (2007)

Framing Knowledge: Global Youth Culture as Knowledge Society (Research in Progress)

Maureen H. Donovan

Ohio State University Libraries, 1858 Neil Avenue Mall, Columbus OH 43210-1286 USA
donovan.1@osu.edu
http://library.osu.edu/blogs/japanese

Abstract. Widespread distribution of Japanese comics (manga) is part of a global youth culture that can be viewed as a knowledge society. The paper presents research in progress about how knowledge is being "framed" by young people through established forms or structures, through discipline associated with active learning and participation, and through thoughtful reflection and discussion with peers. Historical and qualitative methodologies are emphasized.

Keywords: global youth culture, manga, comics, books, Japan, Japanese culture, knowledge society, social networking, contemplation, ethnography.

1 Introduction

Changes in creating, accessing, and using information happen within a global context and are driving forces in societies around the world. An emerging "commons" of globally distributed information and knowledge is having an impact on the work and leisure activities of people everywhere. Although information and communication technologies (ICTs) are implemented in different societies in varying ways, and significant "divides" affect individuals' and societies' access to technology and information, some widespread trends are emerging that seem "new." One of them has been the development of a global youth culture. What is different about today's global youth culture? Can studying global youth culture help us to understand broader topics, such as: how individuals navigate in the increasing (over)abundance of information, relationships among producers and users in the Knowledge Society, transborder flows of information and knowledge, the parts various stakeholders play in the production, dissemination, and management of information in the Knowledge Society?

As Japanese Studies Librarian, I collect resources in Japanese and other languages for the Ohio State University Libraries to support teaching, learning, research and service related to Japan at the university. Supporting the activities of Ohio State's Cartoon Research Library, I have been collecting Japanese cartoons and comics (manga and anime) over the past 25 years, as I watched their popularity develop from the obsession of a fringe subculture to the underpinnings of a global youth culture. Gradually some specific questions began to interest me, including:

M.D. Lytras et al. (Eds.): WSKS 2008, CCIS 19, pp. 618–623, 2008.

- What can analysis of the spread of interest in Japanese manga and anime around the world tell us about changing meanings of culture in the Knowledge Society?
- To what extent does communication in popular culture domains mirror and/or differ from trends in academic/scientific communication in today's interconnected world?
- What is it about manga and anime, as well as other artistic or cultural forms emerging from Japanese culture (martial arts, bonsai gardening, haiku poetry composition, etc), that makes them so attractive in a global context?
- Although apparently a fan-driven phenomenon, to what extent is this growing popularity pushed by commercial publishers that control intellectual property rights? How does commodification of culture facilitate/impede accessibility?
- What is the relation of global youth culture to local culture? How do local cultures fare within the context of a globalized Knowledge Society? How widely has global youth culture spread? Are there "divides" that exclude some youth from participation/awareness of global youth culture?

These and other related questions have interested me now for several years, as I struggle to identify appropriate methodologies with which to pursue them. Three years ago I began teaching a 1-credit freshman seminar, "Analyzing the Appeal of Manga," primarily as a way of immersing myself in this and getting closer to understanding what drives undergraduates who have a passion for manga. As I have been teaching this course the broad range of interconnected issues, trends, theories, and empirical concerns related to those questions is gradually becoming clearer to me and I am increasingly convinced of its relevance to wider issues regarding the Knowledge Society.

This paper presents initial ideas about my plans to proceed with this research. Although the research is still at an exploratory stage, I am developing working hypotheses that: 1) Young people are attracted, at least in part, to the discipline associated with established forms or structures (manga, martial arts, haiku, etc) when they choose to participate in global youth society. 2) Active learning and participation through training or copying is another commonality, closely related to the social networking through which discovery and access take place. 3) Contrary to what might be portrayed in mainstream media, at least some young people find opportunities for thoughtful reflection and discussion with peers of broad issues confronting society through engagement in this global youth culture. These three aspects of my working hypothesis amount to a kind of "framing" of knowledge on the part of young people, so I have chosen to use that term to describe this project, especially since it helps me to focus my attention within this complex subject.

2   Progress Thus Far

My early research was related to the nature of manga itself, including its genres and other characteristics and was primarily related to my activities at the library. [1].

In 2006 in a paper I presented at the International Congress on Asian Digital Libraries I began exploring broader issues, specifically related to access resources, often created by fans and/or scholars themselves, which assist in identifying and using manga and anime. My conclusion to that paper includes the following statement that reflects my awareness of this is as a user-driven phenomenon with interesting characteristics:

".... although copyright restrictions appear to have created insurmountable impediments to digital library growth for manga studies, neither fans nor scholars have been deterred by the limitations and have constructed useful access resources even in the absence of true digital libraries. The trend to make fee-based access to online manga available is emerging with a robust support structure already in place that will continue to facilitate access." [2].

3 Theoretical Background

3.1 Framing Knowledge through *Established Forms* or *Structures*

Selective investigation of key works on the forms of Japanese art and literature is essential to this project. Eiko Ikegami's *Bonds of Civility: Aesthetic Networks and the Political Origins of Japanese Culture* [3] is particularly relevant, since its focus is on how aesthetic patterns of socializing and the use of particular aesthetic forms became intertwined with political and associational life in pre-modern Japan. Other works on Japanese literary forms, such as Alexander Allard's study of *bunraku* [4], are also relevant, especially those related to the spread of those art forms abroad, such as Earl Miner's classic study of literary inter-relations between Japanese, French and English literature in the nineteenth and early twentieth centuries [5].

Characteristics of comics as a medium. A great amount of research is currently underway regarding "graphic novels," as manga are known in the United States to distinguish them from comics which are meant primarily for children. [6] In my teaching I use Scott McCloud's work, which draws attention to how this communication form engages readers, specifically through: iconic characters with whom a reader can identify, environments that pull the reader in, creation of a sense of refuge and silence by using successive panels to survey a whole scene, subjective motion, real world anchors, use of archetypes, and, especially, through sophisticated storytelling focused on issues of universal concern.[7] [8]

Relation to postmodern art. Postmodern approaches in art, architecture and literature arose as reactions to established modernist forms, which themselves arose in subversion to earlier styles. Recent studies of the Dada and Futurist movements (global) [9] and the MAVO movement (Japan) provide context for understanding the emergence of manga as a global phenomenon.[10]

3.2 Framing Knowledge through *Discipline* Associated with *Active Learning* and *Participation*

Reading manga requires an active participation on the part of the reader since parts of the story are omitted between the panels. Fans construct their own "story arcs" about what happened "behind the scenes." Many manga readers go further and compose their own manga, either as online comics or for sale/distribution through comic conventions. In Japan these are huge events where publishers scout out promising talent for future publication, while the vast majority of participants simply enjoy the opportunity to share their work with other fans. Increasingly this kind of sharing happens online as well.

There is a growing literature about the participatory aspects of global youth culture, especially in anthropology. A "do-it-yourself" (DIY) movement is associated with the spread of manga and anime as reflected at anime conventions and elsewhere, including within the world of fashion. A growing literature on social networking is relevant in this context. In particular, I am interested in the process of resource discovery through social networks and Web 2.0 recommender systems of various kinds (commercially developed; fan/researcher developed).

In this regard I am also exploring the related topic of sports, globalization, and the role of the media in the consumption and delivery of sport, especially martial arts. [11]

3.3 Framing Knowledge through *Thoughtful Reflection* and *Discussion with Peers*

Gabriel Zaid reminds us in *So Many Books* that writing a book is a form of communication between an author and an audience. [12] Zaid notes that these days the number of books being written is increasing faster than the number of readers. At the same time he reminds us that to write a book is to open up a conversation with readers and to provide an opportunity for readers to gather and discuss the book as well. This is very descriptive of what is happening in global youth society.

David M. Levy's research on the lack of time for thoughtful reflection and contemplation in today's "more-faster-better" society is also relevant. [13] Drawing attention to earlier research of Josef Pieper on the practice of "leisure" as essential to culture, Levy points to the central importance of the expression of the human spirit, and "of an openness to the world, to things as they are, rather than as we wish them to be." [14]

One hypothesis that I have developed is that manga are a kind of refuge for young people in today's accelerated lifestyle. Scott McCloud identifies "the sense of reader participation, a feeling of being part of the story, rather than simply observing from afar" [15] as the quality of manga that fuels its global success. Often there is a crystallizing moment in a manga that captures the essence of a feeling or experience which stands out in the storyline and provides a focus of attention and reflection, an opportunity for readers to reflect in a kind of meditative way on "things as they are." Of course, young people are also attracted to sex, action, and violence found in manga, but my work with undergraduate students over the past three years has shown me that it would be simplistic to see these popular culture materials only in that light.

4   Methodological Outline

Research conducted thus far has been exploratory and I am still deciding on the most appropriate methodologies to pursue. Emphasis will be on historical and qualitative research methods.

4.1 Historical Research

I am conducting historical research on manga as books with the aim of understanding what aspects have led to their success in Japan and catapulted them onto the world stage. This study uses research resources in Ohio State's Cartoon Research Library and explores what Pierre Bourdieu described as "power relationships in the field of production." [16] Current research focuses on 1) the evolution of guides to manga over the decades in Japan and new guides developed specifically for a global context, and 2) manga instruction manuals and the evolution of technical terminologies, as well as how those have changed in transnational settings.

4.2 Ethnographical Study

I am preparing to conduct a study of manga fans among Ohio State University students and local anime convention participants. American college students who read manga will be the focus of planned interviews aimed at refining the hypotheses outlined above. Do the three aspects show up when students are interviewed about how they read manga or do I need to revise them? This part of the study can be seen as dealing with the reception and acclimatization of manga within an American context. Depending on how it goes, I may want to replicate it in other contexts, perhaps with cooperation of researchers elsewhere. I will use techniques of focused ethnography for this aspect of the study. In designing my study I have been influenced by user studies conducted by Susan Gibbons and Nancy Fried Foster as part of the Extensible Catalog project at the University of Rochester. [17][18]

4.3 Action Research

As a librarian I am interested in supporting people in their information life. Therefore I am also drawn to use what is called "action research" (AR) for another aspect of this study. My reason for choosing AR as a methodology is that I have a hunch, articulated above, that some aspects of the "framing" that take pace within global youth society can be extended beyond that context and may have wider application beyond the social networking of youth. As a starting point, I plan to include the following in forming a critical reference group of people who would participate in the research and benefit from its results. This are likely to include non-participants in global youth culture (among young people), representatives of their parents' generation, people who feel overwhelmed with information over-abundance, people who shake their heads at a youth's absorption in global youth culture and so on. The "action" that I will seek as a follow up to this research is related to improving their information lives.

4.4 Content Analysis

Another approach that I am taking is analysis of writings about global youth culture, manga, etc in blogs and other online sources as well as publications in print. To what extent do young people have self-awareness of their participation in a global youth culture and what do they say about it themselves? Is there validation of my hypotheses in their writings? Also, I am collecting publication and circulation data regarding the global distribution of manga.

References

1. Donovan, M.H.: Problems and Perspectives from a University Library Manga Collection. Manga Kenkyu 6, 156–165 (2004) (in Japanese)
2. Donovan, M.H.: Accessing Japanese Digital Libraries: Three Case Studies. In: Sugimoto, S., Hunter, J., Rauber, A., Morishima, A. (eds.) ICADL 2006. LNCS, vol. 4312, pp. 410–418. Springer, Heidelberg (2006)
3. Ikegami, E.: Bonds of Civility: Aesthetic Networks and the Political Origins of Japanese Culture. Cambridge University Press, Cambridge (2005)
4. Alland, A.: The Construction of Reality and Unreality in Japanese Theatre. The Drama Review 23(2), 3–10 (1979)
5. Miner, E.: The Japanese Tradition in British and American Literature. Princeton UP, Princeton (1966)
6. Comics research bibliography, `http://www.rpi.edu/~bulloj/comxbib.html`
7. McCloud, S.: Understanding Comics. Harper, New York (1994)
8. McCloud, S.: Making comics. Harper, New York (2006)
9. Dickerman, L.: The Dada Seminars. Library of Congress, Washington (2005)
10. Weisenfeld, G.: Mavo. University of California Press, Berkeley (2002)
11. Jarvie, G.: Sport, Culture and Society. Routledge, New York (2006)
12. Zaid, G.: So Many Books. Paul Dry Books, Philadelphia (2003)
13. Levy, D.M.: No Time to Think: Reflections on Information Technology and Contemplative Scholarship. Ethics and Information Technology 9, 237–249 (2007)
14. Pieper, J.: Leisure: The Basis of Culture. Faber, London (1952)
15. McCloud, S.: Making comics. Harper, New York (2006)
16. Bourdieu, P.: The Field of Cultural Production. Polity, Cambridge (1993)
17. Foster, N.F., Gibbons, S.: Studying Students: The Undergraduate Research Project at the University of Rochester. ACRL, Chicago (2007)
18. Extensible Catalog, `http://www.extensiblecatalog.info/`

New Technology
in Modern Museum Policy

Ioannis Tallis[1] and Sofia Mytilinaiou[2]

[1] Phd Candidate, Scholar of the Propontis foundation,
University of the Aegean, Lesvos, Greece
ctm04014@ct.aegean.gr
[2] Phd Candidate, Scholar of the Greek Scholarship Foundation,
University of the Aegean, Lesvos, Greece
ctm04012@ct.aegean.gr

Abstract. The wide technological development influences comprehensively all levels of culture by altering the configuration criteria and finally the character of modern patterns of culture. The contribution of the digital media in creation and management of cultural content is related both to the field of art and display conveyor, including the museum. Initially, representation concerns the detachment of the artifacts from specific spatiotemporal facts, where they belonged, and their replacement within a physical or virtual exhibitional space. The creation of semantical digital substitutes of the artifacts result in the creation of a new artifact that refers to the without being a copy of it. Representation is a reality interpretation, an intermediation. What exactly do we choose to show in a digital work and with what criteria? We promote one aspect within the framework of an external objective model-or a palimpsest perspective of an older trace? It is exactly this procedure that raises management issues nowadays more than ever.

Keywords: Museum, Digital Media, Interactivity, Digital Culture, Communication ,Representation, Documentation.

1 Introduction

In the age of new cultural forms generation, when change and subversion are seeked in social and political level, technological achievements make their presence felt in almost every aspect of life. They basically conduce to communication among groups and communities at global level. Initially, new ways of access and transmission of data is attainable, for example through the Internet and namely the connection to digital libraries and research engines. Furthermore, technologically advanced systems are supporting data management by taking into account the benefits of technical software, like databases. The constant and exponential growth of the volume of data results in the demand of information management. The exponential technological development along with the globalization innovate a mutation of the criteria concerning data management that is also related to the field of museum exhibitions. Particularly, this process involves archive documentation and filing, following the display of available

M.D. Lytras et al. (Eds.): WSKS 2008, CCIS 19, pp. 624–634, 2008.
© Springer-Verlag Berlin Heidelberg 2008

artifacts at exhibitions in physical or virtual environment.The integration and contribution of technological achievements in case of museum policy is intent nowadays. Modern theories and specific requirements, especially at communication level, have defined the philosophy and strategy of exhibition planning, by supporting the educational and entertaining aspect of display aiming at fathom knowledge and broadening of the perception range. Representation and exposition, and eventually the message, of museum collections are moulded in consonance with specific perceptive frameworks. At the same time, conception is moulded by culture, which is formed by social groups with common interests and activities. More specifically, the generation of digital culture has been born out to be evolving much differently than in the past.

2   Digital Culture within the Framework of Modern Society

Culture is defined as the life attitude and activity originated by a definite social group within the framework of specific historical and social concurrences. Determined characteristics, weaved out of a common objective, induce relevant activities. It is a broad concept concerning multiple culture patterns that express the values and philosophy of a certain social group[1]. In the past, cultures consisted of concrete cores, no matter what their topic was (politics, art, philosophy, etc.). The fields of differentiation were explicit, contrary to nowadays, when they appear as new behavioral forms with hybrid characteristics. Their limits are indiscernible resulting in their constant amplification.The development of digital culture is verified, considering the broad application of electronic media. Virtual reality and derivative products play an assertive role, as digital offspring appear in almost every aspect of social life, especially in matters of communication and management like public instrumentalities, museums etc. New technologies provide advanced organization systems to administrate an enormous amount of data. Through the Internet, the access to information resources is possible, while encouraging active participation in communities of knowledge exchange. Taking into account modern trend, polymorphous forms of digital culture are ascertained to be constantly developing.

Digital culture is a phenomenon of particular dynamic, an "open" communication schema where everyone is able to participate. In its present form, the lack of assemblage and contexture out of a cohesive matter comprises the basic feature that generates consecutive reassignment and evolution in terms of structure and activity. It forms a dynamic that is inclined to assimilate an increasing amount of new patterns and characteristics. The bounds diffusion between physical and virtual reality is an essential attribute of postmodern experience. The coexistence and communication between them has evolved to such an extent that has actuated an expansion of stimuli beyond the dimensions of reality. The creation of virtual environments mainly aims at personal association and interaction. It lays emphasis on the sense of presence in a field with structural elements and stimuli adequate to evoke social association on the occasion of approach and processing of content. An opportunity is offered to constitute communities of common features that surpass physical dimensions of time and space.Within the framework of digital culture, the application of virtual media is also focused on the creation and

---

[1] Williams, R., *The Long Revolution,* Chatto and Windus, London, 1961.

promotion of artifacts. New forms of art are shaped in an alternative configuration, like installations, multimedia applications, digital photography, design of virtual and physical worlds etc. In the meanwhile, the contribution of digital evolution affects the policy of modern museums, in matters of management. By providing the production and interpretation of collections with a multidimensional medium, both ordinary objects and artworks are assembled to virtual or hybrid exhibitional unities.The whirl of technological evolution has induced lack of mechanisms to control and administrate consequent applications that tend to be consolidated in variable sections of communication, as their use is altering communication scale and dimension.

3   The Museum as a Storage Area

The notion of the Museum as a cultural organization appeared for the first time in the 17th century, and its identity has been constantly modified throughout the years. Museums of the past, having as their primary objective the safekeeping of the artifacts could be described as storage areas of various objects. For almost 350 years museums have been a static showcase of exhibits with a projective character. However, showing the artifacts and placing them in semantic unities by classifying them within the space is just one way of communicating. This approach is asking the public to accept and assimilate an objective truth throughout the viewpoints and beliefs of a certain Authority- the museum, i.e. the scientific community, a rule. Until the twentieth century museums were regarded as places where the traces of heritage were collected within the framework of safekeeping and maintaining a historical past.

Museums, in their contemporary object-oriented form, are a modern cultural fabrication made by an organized and well-structured society. When the first museum was created in 1652, it was thought to be an institution that compiled many collections of "great significance". In the early stages of the operation of museums, organizing an exhibition gave birth to special territorial and semantic schemes by accumulating or removing objects: exhibitions or parts of them that form narrations through correlations among the exhibits. This procedure depends solely on the availability of the artifacts and the museum commissaries' judgment refusing to take into consideration the visitors' needs and the impact that the exhibition is having on them.

3.1   The Evolution of the Organization – New Museum Policies

The evolution phases of cultural institutions are expressions of a specific historical and social framework reflecting the needs of a respective era. Museum organizations are having the tendency to develop an alternative character that mostly focuses on cultural management and communicating with the public. According to the modern cultural facts that include patterns of both the past and the future, projects of safekeeping, promoting and diffusing information are being organized everyday. In other words, we are experiencing the transition of the museum as a safekeeping organization to the museum as an educational and management organization.

In modern times, the museum uses objects as a historic reference. Traces, as a whole, form a representation of the cultural scenery under a certain umbrella no matter if this concerns the past, the present, or the future. In a modern industrial history museum one can find information concerning labor conditions of the past generations, whereas in a science and technology museum we come across contemporary technological advances along with future suggestions. In this way, organizations are suggesting an alternative interpretation of the reality that works as a new cultural product.

The museum as a conveyor of a social and cultural coincidence expresses the scientific and philosophic ideas within the framework of specific time-and-place data. In the post-modern period, the tendency is to focus more on the actual use of objects and the development of a new dimension concerning the communication with the public. Unlike museums of the past that used to be identified by their building infrastructure, contemporary museums are not exclusively restricted within their premises but they also include a sequence of procedures that take place in a combination of actual and virtual areas. The goal of this new communicational museum policy is to convert the passive message- receiver visitor into an active conveyor of knowledge and experience, surpassing in this way the old one-dimension visiting model[2]. Exhibitions are formed according to the active participation of the public offering to it the chance to have a closer contact and interact with the exhibits.

The educational dimension of museum visits is reinvented as the addition of more ideas and perspectives, concerning both the management and the message analysis of the exhibits, is reinforced[3]. The juxtaposition of various points of view is influencing the formation of a holistic viewpoint regarding the facts behind the traces of the present. Through dialogue, interaction with the artifacts and activities that include them, spectators participate actively in a training procedure on which they form their personal opinion. The analysis of respective perspectives contributes to the broadening or their cognitional fields, according to their interests and beliefs.

In this way visiting a museum becomes a multidimensional experience through a series of actions like workshops, discussions, and more collaborative actions. At the same time, shops and coffee shops are created within the framework of a wider social policy, and they offer privileges to special social groups (reduced admission fees, free admission cards etc).

3.2 Communicational and Educational Issues

Digital patterns of the 21st century include the notion of communication. The respective needs shape the primary criterion of formation and use of the digital media, and, hence, of information management. In the case of museums, these needs focus, on one hand, on spare time activities and, thus, on visitors' entertainment, and on the other side, on the educational procedure which is addressed to specific age groups every time. Within the framework of modern communicational policy, the combination of recreational and educational character of the visit is the privilege on which the training procedure is based. The conducted tour to the contents of the museum by the aid of specialized personnel along with the interaction with the educational applications

---

[2] Adams, M., Moussouri, Th., "The interactive experience: Linking research and practice", Institute for Learning Innovation, Annapolis, MD, Research Center for Museums and Galleries, University of Leicester, Interactive Learning in Museums of Art and Design, 2002, in: http://www.vam.ac.uk/files/file_upload/5748_file.pdf, accessed on: 2-06-2008

[3] Hooper-Greenhill, E., *Museums and the Interpretation of Visual Culture*, New York, Routledge, 2000, p. 151-162

both in real and digital level enriches the museum experience. The combination of analysing and communicating ideas within an environment that varies in many ways from the typical school experience makes this experience a substantial educational one[4]. Being in touch with the exhibits and locating them within their social and cultural environment of origin provides visitors with the chance to travel in an intelligible way and become familiar with places far away from their own reality. The artifacts that compose the various collections convey meanings, suggest human presence, and they also have a symbolic character as well. They are narrating stories about worlds with different philosophies and cultures originating from places far away in time and space, in other words, they offer visitors an alternative approach that resembles to a discovery of a world related to the existent one, or even a perspective through which, according to Socrates 'we discover things not by their names but by themselves[5].Using as a starting point a fact or an object the visitors are asked to start an intellectual procedure, to form their own opinion. Their perception focuses on the elements that relate to their interests and beliefs. Consequently, they shape a subjective version, which they are asked to communicate through the dialogue that evolves either within conducted tours or within an interactive framework throughout educational applications.

Every object has its own story. Through physical contact and 'narrations' visitors can come across a different reality. At the same time every person has their own past, and throughout our personal experiences we all have developed a different character and a personal way of interpreting things. Understanding the values and cultural data that an artifact represents has to do with the visitor's personal perception. The ideas and emotions that were born thanks to this procedure help spectators to shape their own unique experience; an interpretation based mostly on the subjective intellectual procedure conditioned by the crystallization of personal thoughts[6].

3.3 Matters of Representation

One of the primary issues that concern the fields of culture preservation, management, and promotion - while at the same time affected by technological advances - is the representation issue: meaning the reproduction procedure of cultural elements aiming at their promotion to specific categories of visitors-spectators[7]. The basic requirement is the existence of a commonly accepted communicational code that would correspond to a specific cultural and interpretative framework. Speculation about the objective of the representation concerns the question whether this identifies with the notion of emulating the real thing or it is the conversion of reality into a symbolic level[8]. While expressing the culture philosophy and aesthetics throughout the years issues have been raised concerning the way in which every individual experiences and

---

[4] Hein, H. S., *The Museum in Transition, A Philosophical Perspective,* Smithsonian Books, Washington, 2000, p. 108-126

[5] Plato, *Dialogues, Kratylos,* Papyros, Athens, 1966, p. 160-180

[6] Roberts, L., *From knowledge to narrative: Educators and the changing museum*, Smithsonian Press, London, 1997

[7] Papageorgiou, D., "Cultural Representation: problems and perspectives", in: Papageorgiou, D., Boubaris, N., Myrivili, E. (ed.), *Cultural Representation,* Kritike, Athens, 2006, p. 17-55

[8] Mouriki, A., *Transformations of the Aesthetics* (greek edition), Nefeli, Athens, 2003, p. 40-53

communicates the world, as this is perceived. Nowadays the idea that representation is a way of emulating reality has been rejected. Every effort to emulate the world is considered to be pointless, whereas the notion of reality is thought to be a subjective thing. On the contrary, a special attention has been paid to the interpretation that is rendered through artistic, social, or better put cultural practice. In this way a cultural institution that undertakes the representation and exhibition of a particular theme, is actually expressing the perception of a specific intellectual and cultural system of time and space. Representation is a reality interpretation, intermediation[9]. It 'modifies the content as it promotes just one aspect of the situation and not an objective total view. What exactly do we choose to show in a digital work and with what criteria? We promote one aspect within the framework of an external objective model or a palimpsest perspective of an older trace? It is exactly this procedure that raises management issues nowadays more than ever.

4   The Contribution of Technology to the Museums

Within the framework of technology evolution, the integration of advanced technological systems in museum policy holds a substantial role in the sophistication of the institution. New media afford enhanced possibilities that contribute to the exposition of the exhibits in two ways: firstly to the institution archives organization, and secondly, to the communication of the museum with the public. As far as the first case concerns, electronic systems implement administrative processes, by meeting particular requirements, like among others, by passing of the time-consuming and arduous hand-written registration. Digital applications that support the enhancement of established registration templates and center to the documentation, conservation and displacement of artifacts, due to lending procedure among various museums. In more details, such applications include valid, digital databases for information search, documentation software (filling, authoring, design etc.) and systems considering acquisition and loan of artifacts[10]. Practically, in 1960 relevant programs were organized like the Museum Computer Network (MCN) and the Information Retrieval Group of the Museums Association (IRGMA), while in 1970 leading programs of national heritage documentation were effectuating in France (Inventaire Général: IG) and Canada (National Inventory Program: NIP). More recent research is accomplished, among others, by: Museum Documentation Association (MDA- United Kingdom), Museums Computer Network (MCN-USA), Canadian Heritage Information Network (CHIN-Canada)[11] and mainly CIDOC (International Committee of Museum Documentation) and ICOM (International Council of Museums) both constituted in France. Regarding the second case, technology contributes to the collection management and display by laying emphasis on the active participation of the public. Multimedia implementations are assigned to enhance the interactive and

---

[9] Williams, R., *Marxism and Literature, Marxist Introductions Series*, Oxford University Press, London and New York, 1977

[10] ICOM, CIDOC, *Handbook of the Documentation of the Folkloric Collections 1998* (greek edition), Ethno Museum-net, Athens, 1998, p. 9

[11] Oikonomou, M., *Museum: Warehouse or Live Organization? Museological Questions and Issues*, (greek edition), Kritike, 2003, p. 124

educational aspect of the visit in a museum. Additionally, the existence of supplementary and elucidatory information concerning the exhibits advances education and communication with experiential elements, imparting knowledge through experience. Within a specific framework of action, visitor's public association with the exhibits indicates his/her interests and concepts. A characteristic example is the interaction of the spectator with the collections by using devices that detect every movement of his, through sensors, without having to carry any electronic device. He/she may freely walk around to activate actions on specific interfaces (like narrations, video projection, etc.) and collect pieces of information. Accordingly, manifold stimulus is provided that excite the association of the visitors with the collections, aspiring the cultivation of their abilities and the amplification of their cognitive field.Multimedia applications accompany the content of collections, on one hand integrated in the physical environment of display, and on the other hand, formed as autonomous educational unities. They form applications that accomplish to surpass the limits of space-time and include collections out of objects that only in virtual sphere may be encountered, correlated and comprise exhibitions that interact with the public. An environment enriched with potentials beyond the feasible association that is adapted, to a certain extent, to the particular needs and interests of the visitor. Ultimately, new technologic systems contribute to the development of applications that appeal to the disabled people. Special studies are brought into effect, which particularize in the approach of this target group. The new media provide an exhibition with prerequisites according to certain requirements for the transmission and interchange of knowledge, intending to an equal treatment of a secluded public.

Due to digital achievements, a visit to a museum is converted into an integral experience. On the occasion of the approach and editing of the exhibition content, the sense of presence is emphasized in recreational and educational aspects, in a physical or hybrid environment. Stimuli are disposed aiming at social association and the enhancement of the visit at a cognitive and emotional level.

5   Speculation on the Use of New Technologies in Museums

New technologies and the use of the applications deriving from them in museums have raised a series of questions concerning both practical choices and theoretical issues as well. Technological products relate on one hand with exhibition monitoring and, on the hand with museum organization and management. Our objective is to create an "open" communicational procedure between the public and the cultural institution, that is to say a dialogue based on the objects and the ideas that are born and exchanged within the framework of an exhibition. The above-mentioned speculation has to do with the alteration of the information within the framework of representation, the use of technology as an end in itself, the information loss in cases of errors and the large cost.

Digital technology support representation and image promotion by shaping structure that relates to phenomenology. The final product is always a version, a personal perspective and it does not express an overall objective aspect. Every artifact disposes its own different features that concern its material substance, while on the same time are also indicative of its creation environment and use. Its register in digital form and its integration into a virtual exhibition takes places according to the conditions imposed by respective expressive medium every time. The use of the medium, especially in its digital form requires the appropriate designing in order to highlight the object itself and keep the role of technology at an absolutely supportive level.

5.1   Representation of the Real

The content of the collections is represented and promoted by setting the relationship between artwork and material at a speculation basis of conflictive opinions[12]. One opinion claims that the represented elements are a proof of the existence of the objects meaning the space and time within which the latter was created and where it belongs. On the other side lays the viewpoint that supports the idea that representation elements have an emulative role. In this case, the representation of the artifact identifies semantically with the original, since the aesthetics and qualities of the representation medium identifies with the properties and dynamics of the exhibits.

Cultural works cannot be reproduced. The use of signifiers, in digital or analogical form, as a mere proof of existence of the objects, is an inadequate element to the analysis of the messages they convey. The exhibition planning (in physical and virtual environment) creates a cultural, ideological and perceptive scheme, that is to say a reality that varies from the one of the artifacts, within which we are asked to observe and interpret collections.   The issue of representation as far as authenticity is concerned raises the speculation regarding the bounds between real and virtual exhibits.   If the significance received by the exhibit through its historical properties is considered to be a criterion of authenticity, then its representation is creating a new cultural pattern13. The repositioning of the artifacts and their integration into the new exhibition environment, through their digitalisation and organization in a multimedia application, generates a new digital artwork; an artwork that represents the real without being its copy.   The analysis of the properties and messages of the digital artwork offer a more integrated approach to the exhibits. The applications may be used both independently and in combination with the actual artifact offering a deepening into knowledge based on the objects. In this way, a more overall aspect about the evolution of philosophy and human conception throughout the years is rendered.

5.2   The Media as en End-in-Itself

Including interactive applications in museum exhibitions demands proportion at aesthetic and semantic level, between the display of the contained artifacts and the attendance of medium that is used. The main target is to bring into focus the qualities and values that the artifacts convey other than the technological achievement itself. The usage of elements of impressiveness based on digital media denotes lack of educational orientation that undermines the actual participation and activation of the visitor at cognitive and emotional level.

---

[12] Tsatsoulis, D., *Image language. Surrealistic plays and social-semiotic readings* (greek edition), Ellinika Grammata, Athens, 2000, p.154-155.

[13] Umberto, E., *Osservazioni sulla nozione di giacimento culturale*, (greek translation), Thessalonica, 1992, p. 55.

The exposition of artifacts aims at the accentuation of the messages and aesthetics of an exhibition. For this reason the artifact is highlighted by maintaining the necessary transparency of the media[14], so as the latter receives less significance. Aiming at the overall harmony, it is substantial to lay emphasis on the content of the exhibition instead of the digital medium used.Philosophy and aesthetics of postmodern times are opposed to this view and come forward with the shift of interest on impressions related basically on the medium. McLuhan[15] alleged that the seeking of truth of things remains on their form and particularly on the codes of the medium applied. "The medium is the message" briefs his position, focusing on the latter's influence at psychological and social level and degrading, in that way, the value of the content.

Technology applied as an end-in-itself in the development and organization of a cultural institution may make an impact on the visitor over the messages of the exhibition[16]. Abuse of the media proves the inefficiency of museum policies to support educational and communicative relation with the public[17]. René Magritte avoided confusing the signified with the signifier, an aspect that the usage of technological systems should assert in the development of museum applications[18].

5.3 Practical Issues

The use of digital media by cultural organizations require attentive consideration and planning in order to cope with practical issues, like the cost of incorporation and preservation of technological systems of management archive, the time-consuming training programs needed to specialize the concerned employees and the conservation of digital data throughout time.

The implementation of management systems in museums entails the expenditure of resources at multiple levels. These recourses involve financial costs, as well as matters of time and effort needed to organize the museum archives, which comprises the content of current and possible exhibitions. The systems in question require a lot of money both for their preservation, and their upgrade when necessary. The implementation of adequate software programs requires training and adaptation to new methodologies of documentation, whereas certain security risks exist for the museum archive. Given that respective funds along with manpower could be invested in various fields of museum evolution, amendable planning is necessary considering the implementation of management and documentation systems

6 Conclusions

Technological evolution has affected almost every aspect of social life, especially the fields of communication and administration. Apparently, digital culture has been evolved, setting

---

[14] Mouriki, A., *Transformations of the Aesthetics* (greek edition), Nefeli, Athens, 2003, p. 58-59.

[15] McLuhan, M., *The medium is the message: an inventory of effects*, Hardwired, San Fransisco, 1996, p. 159.

[16] Umberto, 1992, p. 38.

[17] Burcaw, G. E., *Introduction to Museum Work*, American Association for State and Local History (AASLH) Press, Tennessee, 1983, p. 26-27.

[18] Nakou E., *Museums: We, the objects and the culture* (greek edition), Nisos, 1995, p. 74.

new forms of social association. Contemporary media contribute to the enhancement of information interchange and raises subjects that refer, initially, to the need of managing data of such volume in variable sections of communication, focusing on museums archives. Moreover, new forms of media are essential for the exhibition organization, as they conduce to the representation and integration of artifacts into virtual environments, enriched with interactive potentials.

Culture development stages are substantial to be followed up and analyzed. Which are the characteristics and how they were moulded during time? Which are the hubs that altered and shaped contemporary identity of culture? Culture development is grounded on relevant considerations that expound self-knowledge, for the sense of collective identity is strengthened and is rallied around the constant culture evolution.

Museums are systems of artifacts documentation and exposition in the context of cultural conservation and display. Representations of the present and the past ascribe messages within specified cultural and interpretive framework. Museum exhibition bears a twofold character, both recreational and educational. Visitors' interaction is evoked through various stimuli to fathom to knowledge that derive from association with the artifacts. In this way, the configuration of exhibitions targets at interactivity at social, cognitive and emotional level.

References

Adams, M., Moussouri, Th.: The interactive experience: Linking research and practice", Institute for Learning Innovation, Annapolis, MD, Research Center for Museums and Galleries, University of Leicester, Interactive Learning in Museums of Art and Design (2002) (accessed on: 2-06-2008),
http://www.vam.ac.uk/files/file_upload/5748_file.pdf
Arnheim, R.: Art and Visual Perception. A psychology of the creative eye (greek translation), Themelio, Athens (2004)
Burcaw, G.E.: Introduction to Museum Work, American Association for State and Local History. AASLH Press, Tennessee (1983)
Baudrillard, J.: Simulances et simulation, Galilee, Paris (1995)
Edson, G., Dean, D.: The Handbook for Museums, Routledge, London, New York (2007)
Hall, S., Held, D., McGrew, A.: Modernity and its Futures: Understanding Modern Societies, Book IV (greek translation), Savvalas, Athens (2003)
Hein, H.S.: The Museum in Transition, A Philosophical Perspective. Smithsonian Books, Washington (2000)
Hooper-Greenhill, E.: Museums and the Interpretation of Visual Culture, New York, Routledge (2000)
ICOM, CIDOC, Handbook of the Documentation of the Folkloric Collections 1998 (greek edition), Ethno Museum-net, Athens (1998)
McLuhan, M.: The medium is the message: an inventory of effects, Hardwired, San Fransisco (1996)
Mouriki, A.: Transformations of the Aesthetics (greek edition), Nefeli, Athens (2003)
Nakou, E.: Museums: We, the objects and the culture (greek edition), Nisos (1995)
Oikonomou, M.: Museum: Warehouse or Live Organization? Museological Questions and Issues (greek edition), Kritike (2003)
Plato, Dialogues, Kratylos (greek edition), Papyros, Athens (1966)

Papageorgiou, D.: Cultural Representation: problems and perspectives. In: Papageorgiou, D., Boubaris, N., Myrivili, E. (eds.) Cultural Representation (greek edition), Kritike, Athens (2006)

Roberts, L.: From knowledge to narrative: Educators and the changing museum. Smithsonian Press, London (1997)

Rush, M.: New Media in Art. Thames & Hudson Ltd., London (2005)

Tsatsoulis, D.: Image language. Surrealistic plays and social-semiotic readings (greek edition), Ellinika Grammata, Athens (2000)

Umberto, E.: Osservazioni sulla nozione di giacimento culturale (greek translation) Paratiritis, Thessalonica (1992)

Williams, R.: The Long Revolution, Chatto and Windus, London (1961)

Williams, R.: Marxism and Literature, Marxist Introductions Series. Oxford University Press, London (1977)

Deploying Thick Mobile Clients Using Thin Client Architecture: A Case in Mobile Tourist Guides

Michael Kenteris, Daphne Economou, Damianos Gavalas, and Dionysios Zamplaras

University of the Aegean, Department of Cultural Technology and Communication, Greece
m.kenteris@ct.aegean.gr, d.economou@ct.aegean.gr,
dgavalas@aegean.gr, ctm04004@ct.aegean.gr

Abstract. This paper introduces an approach of enhancing tourism web sites, giving the ability for such sites to be used as a tool to allow tourists to tag content of choice for downloading and viewing on their own mobile device whilst on visit. Tourists, upon installation to their mobile device, can view content material and a map of Mytilene (Lesvos, Greece) without the need to "connect" to any mobile operator network, thereby saving high roaming charges. Our case-study has been the design and implementation of a Multi-Platform Mobile Tourist Guide system for the Municipality of Mytilene (Greece), which uses a thin PC client via Internet to present tourist content giving the user the opportunity to select content of choice and the ability to dynamically build a thick client mobile tourist application or use the PDA Installation available at the Municipal tourist office.

Keywords: mobile tourism, web platforms, PDA guides, Java ME mobile clients, mobile porting.

1 Introduction

Mobile tourist guides enhance tourism experience and offer a more appreciative experience [3], even more so by incorporating features like maps and location-based services [18][14]. However, there are issues which still hinder the penetration and market success of such technology. Not only are there usability issues when designing for mobile devices, like device capabilities, screen size and input methods [1]; one must take into account the compatibility issues of web platforms in comparison to mobile web platforms [16] and the cost of use of such technology for tourists [10]. The convergence of traditional web technology to mobile web technology is becoming an international reality [5]. It has been argued, the main reason behind the low impact of mobile web technology applications was the high cost which users bear when connecting to the mobile web [10].

Admittedly, due to high roaming charges, tourists have been one of the last target groups that accessed data via mobile devices while traveling. Recently, the European commission has set the pace to lower roaming charges by someway forcing network operators to decrease prices of roaming [4]; tourists are amongst the user groups that will benefit from use of mobile web services.

M.D. Lytras et al. (Eds.): WSKS 2008, CCIS 19, pp. 635–640, 2008.

Nevertheless, it is argued that even if prices drop to an affordable level, 65% of the mobile phone users will not be keen on paying for these extra services and would use them only if they were free of charge [11]. So the question is: can a tourist benefit from the use of mobile technology enough so as to be motivated to use the mobile web and incur the corresponding costs? This question in part has been answered by research [1], [2], [10], [18], [19] in the past 10 years: dynamic live data, location-based services, dynamic maps, multimodality, and ubiquity are all benefits of use of mobile web devices. While traveling though, roaming charges are not a negligible parameter for most tourists. Given the fact that the cost of an online experience abroad can reach 17 € per MB [17] and that the average size of our mobile tourist application can reach and exceed the 5 MB mark, it can be argued that cost of data roaming are unacceptable. Thus, allowing for the tourists to 'build' unique tourist guides before or whilst on their visit, which runs on any mobile device without incurring any costs of connection, is believed to represent a rather promising mobile business paradigm.

In the past decade a growing body of commercial and research initiatives that incorporate electronic tourist guide functionality into mobile devices have been reported [18]. Many navigational assistants either in-car systems or pedestrian navigational assistants used as a way finding or route planning system have in built city guide information. These technologies in general have had a limited success; this is mainly due to the lack of study of the special characteristics of tourism [19], yet also due to the vast technology based problems that arise trying to port mobile applications to readily available mobile devices.

This paper conveys the experiences gained from designing and developing a complete e-tourist framework for the Mytilene Municipal council for both web and mobile device users.

2   Design Issues

The multi-platform application has been designed taking into account several usability guidelines associated to three main characteristics of mobile applications, namely, small screens, limited input and mobility, as well as requirements results performed in past experiments [3]. In the design of the e-guide system, e-commerce concepts were used. The user has the ability to tag the content of choice just like an "add to shopping cart" function, upon going to the "download now" section just like the "checkout" area of an e-commerce site. The user is given the choice to download a customized tourist mobile application to his PC and then to his mobile phone, as suggested in [10]. In the actual implementation of this overall project the Municipal of Mytilene has anticipated situations were visitors have already arrived to the island and have no access to the internet/PC. An info kiosk will be installed at the airport of Mytilene and at the local tourist office both with Bluetooth capabilities which upon completion of download section the PC application will push the mobile guide directly to the users mobile phone via a Bluetooth connection. The PDA installation has been installed at the municipals local tourist office, where upon tourists can freely loan a PDA which has been loaded with content of the city and with predefined tours incorporating text images and video narrations.

3 Development of a Multi-platform Mobile Tourist Guide

In the course of designing and implementing the tourist guide, the project team was confronted with ubiquity platform problems, i.e. the adaptation of the developed online PC web application to a mobile web application for mobile devices (PDAs and mobile phones) which can be used in an offline environment. The traditional PC web client platforms are not fully compatible with mobile web client platforms [7]. This means that mobile web applications are not able to provide rich user interfaces or allow applications to run offline or more so, to run online whenever there is data to retrieve [13]. Additionally, for the mobile application there was a need to access device capabilities, i.e. access to GPS, camera which could not be achieved by using a web application through a mobile web client. This meant that the web application needed to be re-designed and re-implemented to be used on a mobile device with a rich user interface, to be able to run offline and have access to device capabilities.

A solution which best fits this case is the use of thin clients (i.e web browser) technology for PC web and the use of thick clients (i.e. applications ported to various mobile handsets) technology for mobile devices An example of this approach is Google maps [6]. Google maps are based on a technology called AJAX [7], a client-side technology not completely supported by mini web browsers [15]. A user can view Google maps via a PC web browser; however, Gmaps Java ME application should be installed to view Google maps via a mobile device [16]. Gmaps can be downloaded to a PC and the installed via cable, IR or Bluetooth to the phone or can be installed via WAP [5].

The tourist web site was implemented using JSP [9] / MySQL [12] web technologies and follows a 3-tier model, i.e. presentation - logic - database. Figure 1a, shows the website main screen page in the center there is a Ajax based map which show location markers of tourist content. The content was categorized with respect to content type (Figure 1b). The "download now" button selection (check out) initiates the process of downloading and customizing the content to the user's device. This is a 4-step process where the user is asked to login/register, to specify the device desired for the application to be ported on, to choose to include memory consuming images, videos, and workable map files, to dynamically generate the e-guide that can be download on to their personal device (mobile phone or PDA).

The actual mobile application has been developed on the top of Java ME Platform [8], (previously known as Java 2 Platform, Micro Edition or J2ME), essentially comprising a certified collection of Java APIs for the development of software for small, resource-constrained devices such as cell phones, PDAs and set-top boxes.

The mobile tourist application allows for dual navigation, from the text menu or directly from the map where the content is shown via markers which can be displayed by category of by municipal region. The Java ME application has been designed in such a way as to dynamically build the content pages accordingly. This application also handles multiple video and audio files used as narrations for tourists whilst on location.

The PDA application has been implemented using the NaviPocket v. 2.4 by OPHRYS SYSTEMS (founded in 1992 is a company specializing in audio-guides and information systems for museums and cultural sites). The application has been designed for mobility by providing an interface with simple menus (see Figure 3) and concise information so that interaction with the application requires minimal effort and does not distract the user's attention from other activities (walking, talking etc.).

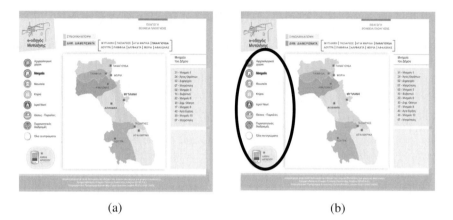

(a)   (b)

Fig. 1. Screenshots taken from the *Mytilene e-guide web application*

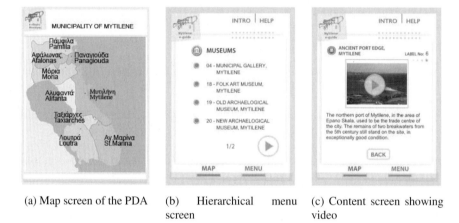

(a) Map screen of the PDA   (b)   Hierarchical   menu   (c) Content screen showing
                                screen   video

Fig. 2. Screenshots of the PDA application which tourist can freely loan from the local tourist office

The user can navigate through the content by choosing manually the sections of interest with a PDA stylus. Alternatively, the content can be automatically selected by the software, since it makes use of GPS technology which determines the visitors' position in the city. The user can choose to switch between manual and auto guidance at any time while using the system. In addition, in order to avoid user distraction and to address the stakeholders' request for incorporating multimedia techniques to effectively provide information about a sight, videos made of narration and animated pictures were included in the application

4   Evaluation and Future Work

Both experimental and field studies were performed revealing a high degree of satisfaction among participants although. However, useful feedback was received on how to improve the application's content and on types of new services to be added Participants' feedback was gathered for improving the application's content and introducing new services to be added [10]. A compilation of these suggestions follows and will be taken into account in future releases of the electronic guide:

- exchange of tourist reviews/impressions/suggestions with other tourists, especially with those that share similar tourist interests
- inclusion of emergency contacts in the city map (pharmacies, hospitals, police stations, port & tourist police authorities, etc) and search facilities to locate the shortest contacts, depending on the current location of the user
- inclusion of 3D city maps to ease the recognition of the surrounding environment
- enhancement of digitized maps so as to provide three zoom levels (instead of two), target highlighting, street names and clickable objects, like city attractions, to provide quick access to important tourist information
- provision of daily/weakly weather forecast reports
- provision of multimodal orientation and navigation features (e.g. synthetic speech in addition to textual and graphical information)
- suggestion of daily, personalized tourist itineraries that will dynamically adapt on current weather conditions.

5   Conclusions

In this paper we presented three case studies which have been developed, which focused on the use of the web, mobile phones and PDAs for providing cultural and tourist information and promoting cultural content and tourist facilities. The prototypes implementation contributed to the evaluation of the main advantages and shortcomings of such development technologies.

In the context of the Municipal Council of Mytilene project, a three part system was implemented. A website tool was built to offer tourist to build a customized mobile application for there visit. A thick client application platform was used to build the mobile web application which does not need constant connection to the internet and a PDA installation which tourist can manually view tourist content or use in automatic mode where depending on Position the user is pushed information. of the municipal whilst having multimedia content on hand. Lastly a PDA system was implemented using a Hierarchical menu system which can easily be used by tourist in a roaming environment.

References

[1] Brown, B., Perry, M.: Of maps and guidebooks: designing geographical technologies. SIGGROUP Bull. 22(3), 28–32 (2001)
[2] Jones, M., Marsden, G.: Mobile Interaction Design. J. Wiley and sons, Chichester (2005)
[3] Economou, D., Gavalas, D., Kenteris, M.: Cultural Applications for Mobile Devices: Issues and Requirements for Authoring Tools and Development Platforms. In: ACM Mobile Computing & Communications Review, ACM SIGMOBILE (in press)

[4] Europa - Information Society, International roaming tariffs (last visited October 10th 2007),
http://ec.europa.eu/information_society/activities/roaming/index_en.htm

[5] Gavalas, D., Economou, D.: The Technology Landscape of Wireless Web. International Journal of Mobile Communications 5(5), 508–527 (2007)

[6] Google maps (last visited January 8th 2007), http://maps.google.com/

[7] Holzner, S.: Ajax Bible. Wiley, Chichester (2007)

[8] Java ME Platform (last visited January 8th 2007),
http://java.sun.com/javame/index.jsp

[9] JavaServer Pages Technology (last visited January 8th 2007),
http://java.sun.com/products/jsp/

[10] Kenteris, D.G., Economou, D.: An Innovative Mobile Electronic Tourist Guide Application. In: Personal and Ubiquitous Computing. Springer, Heidelberg (in press)

[11] Mobile Opportunity, The shape of the smartphone and mobile data markets (last visited January 8th 2007),
http://mobileopportunity.blogspot.com/2007/01/shape-of-smartphone-and-mobile-data.html

[12] MySQL (last visited January 8th 2007), http://www.mysql.com/

[13] Steinbock, D.: The Mobile Revolution: The Making of Mobile Services Worldwide. Kogan Page (2007)

[14] Techworld.com article about vodafone's flat rate for data roaming (last visited January 4th 2008),
http://www.techworld.com/mobility/news/index.cfm?newsid=8265

[15] Open Ajax Alliance on mobile Ajax (last visited December 28th 2007),
http://www.w3.org/2007/06/mobile-ajax/papers/

[16] Mobile Google map site (last visited December 28th 2007) ,
http://www.google.com/gmm/index.html

[17] Vodafone Greece data roaming charges (last visited January 10th, 2008),
http://www.vodafone.gr/live1/page.jsp?pid=0005070600&vars=0000000000

[18] Kray, C., Baus, J.: A survey of mobile guides. In Proceedings of HCI in Mobile Guides. In: Conjunction with Fifth International Symposium on Human computer Interaction with Mobile Devices and Services, pp. 1–5 (2003)

[19] Brown, B., Chalmers, M.: Tourism and Mobile Technology. In: Proceedings of the 8th European Conference on Computer Supported Cooperative Work (CSCW 2003), pp. 335–354 (2003)

An E-Culture Environment for Common Citizens and Visually Impaired Individuals

Athanasios Drigas, Leyteris Koukianakis, and John Glentzes

NCSR 'Demokritos',
Institute of Informatics and Telecommunications,
Net Media Lab,
Agia Paraskevi, 153 10, Athens, Greece
{dr,kouk,jglen}@imm.demokritos.gr

Abstract. The integration of modern Information and Communication Technologies (ICTs) within the cultural domain creates what is commonly known as e-culture. The need to create an e-culture environment arose from the undeniable fact that the cultural heritage of a nation defines a nation and therefore should be disseminated to all, regardless of their location and their disability. This article discusses an e-culture portal, which presents to any interested users, information regarding a significant number of Greek and Cypriot museums and galleries as well as their exhibits. The e-culture environment offers user friendly navigation techniques and contemporary multimedia tools and services for the better presentation of the e-material to the users-visitors, paying particular attention to common citizens and especially to visually impaired individuals, in order to offer them equal access to cultural heritage information. This environment is an inter-disciplinary application, combining the ICTs, cultural and e-inclusion domains (electronic support for disabled people).

Keywords: e-culture, cultural heritage, ICT, digitization.

1 Introduction

The digitization of arts and culture has to do with the relationship between ICTs and the production and consumption of art and culture. By merging the above, the term e-culture arises. In theory, e-culture comprises all processes of expression and reflection in the digital domain. That also includes, for instance, communities that share a certain lifestyle, interests or ideas [1], [2].

The term e-culture implied the need for a new type of policy. In fact, when it comes to cultural policy, developments surrounding ICT and digital media must be considered within a broad and integral perspective [3], [4], [5]. For this reason, the EU has already funded several projects. This program states that work will focus on "intelligent systems for dynamic access to and preservation of tangible and intangible cultural and scientific resources" [6].

New museums and galleries place a high value on accessibility and also on aesthetics issues. They are moving away from rows and rows of objects each fronted by a label containing limited and specific information. Strange then, that when these new

M.D. Lytras et al. (Eds.): WSKS 2008, CCIS 19, pp. 641–648, 2008.

museums start to digitize their collections they produce huge databases with modern agent-oriented methodologies [7], [8], [9], [10].

Moreover, the past years have seen the exploitation of multimedia techniques and lately the introduction of virtual reality methods to create new forms of presentation for museums' exhibitions. Virtual Reality can offer a number of advantages to museums, offering a way to overcome some common problems like the lack of space or the need of the visitors to interact with the exhibits [11], [12], [13], [14].

2   Abstract Level Description

The structure of the system content consists of the following five steps (Fig. 1):

- In the first step, a list of the existing museums and galleries categories in Greece and Cyprus appears. As a result of this categorization, the visitor can easily access the museum of his choice.
- The second step includes the listing and placing of museums/galleries, according to the corresponding categories. The total number of museums/galleries belonging to each category is satisfactory (having a mean term of 30) so that the user-visitor has a spherical and objective informing about every category
- During the third step, a study of every institutions' cultural content takes place, in order to show and present it in such a way that a user-visitor will not only obtain an integrated and representative view of a specific museum, but also he will ease his navigation, simultaneously making it more interesting
- Moving on, the cultural content which emerged from the previous step, is written and embedded into the whole system
- Finally, there is a thorough study of the system standards and outlines. The goal is to choose the appropriate techniques and technologies which will be used, so as to constitute the final product user-centered, user-friendly, and more importantly, to live up to the needs of disabled people and especially to those with visual disabilities in accord with the information and knowledge society strategies.

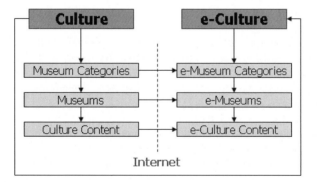

Fig. 1. System Structure

3   System Analysis

This portal's opening page (Fig. 2) starts with a graphic and art visual application with the harmonious arrangement of lines and shapes, influenced by ancient Greece, in order to introduce the visitor from the beginning to its ambience. It has a simple but functional structure so that the visitor can easily navigate throughout the various categories of museums and galleries.

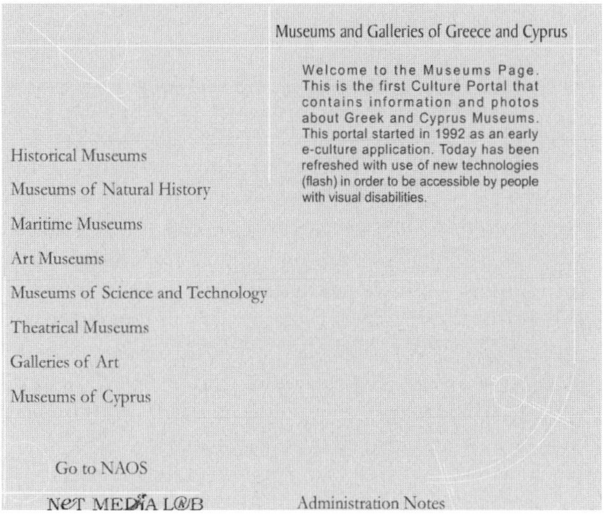

Museums and Galleries of Greece and Cyprus

Welcome to the Museums Page. This is the first Culture Portal that contains information and photos about Greek and Cyprus Museums. This portal started in 1992 as an early e-culture application. Today has been refreshed with use of new technologies (flash) in order to be accessible by people with visual disabilities.

Historical Museums

Museums of Natural History

Maritime Museums

Art Museums

Museums of Science and Technology

Theatrical Museums

Galleries of Art

Museums of Cyprus

Go to NAOS

NET MEDIA L@B   Administration Notes

Fig. 2. Main page with graphic arts

After the search of the various museums/galleries categories in Greece and Cyprus, the following basic list was made:

- Historical Museums
- Museums of Natural History
- Maritime Museums
- Art Museums
- Museums of Science and Technology
- Theatrical Museums
- Galleries of Art
- Museums of Cyprus

The above categories are representative because they reflect the Hellenic cultural activities over the centuries and their aspects, such as history, tradition and customs.

At this point, the user-visitor has the option to choose one of the above categories in order to navigate through the corresponding museums/galleries. The choice of these institutions was made with the criterion to cover as much geographical space as possible in the Greek and Cypriot territories. The reason is because every region has its own cultural roots and uniqueness and consequently, a user-visitor can be informed about the whole of a region's culture even if this region is remote.

In Fig. 3, part of the historical museums catalog is depicted. These museums exhibit the Greek history over the centuries, from the ancient years to the 20th century. For example, for the ancient Greek civilization some of them are: the museum of Atlantis, the Hippocratic museum of Kos etc, whereas for the modern era there are: the National Historical Museum, the Therissos Museum etc.

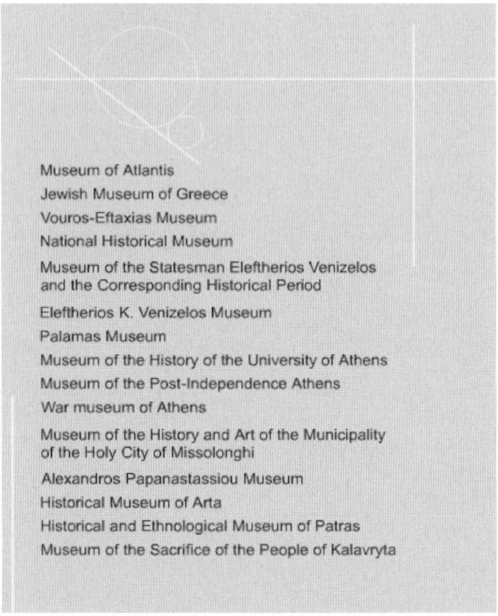

Museum of Atlantis
Jewish Museum of Greece
Vouros-Eftaxias Museum
National Historical Museum
Museum of the Statesman Eleftherios Venizelos and the Corresponding Historical Period
Eleftherios K. Venizelos Museum
Palamas Museum
Museum of the History of the University of Athens
Museum of the Post-Independence Athens
War museum of Athens
Museum of the History and Art of the Municipality of the Holy City of Missolonghi
Alexandros Papanastassiou Museum
Historical Museum of Arta
Historical and Ethnological Museum of Patras
Museum of the Sacrifice of the People of Kalavryta

Fig. 3. List of Historical Museums

The final step of the navigation through the portal is the projection and presentation of a specific institutions' cultural content. This presentation consists of the following parameters, which emerged after a thorough study showing their connection to the rest of the system (Fig. 4). These are:

- Museum Address
- Museum Information
- Museum Photos
- Exhibits Images

With these elements of cultural content, the following can be achieved: the user-visitor can easily and quickly find the address and other data (telephone numbers, fax numbers etc.) of the institution, brief information about the institution itself (foundation, inauguration, founder, and exhibit pieces), a brief set of photographs showing the indoor and outdoor areas of the institution and finally representative images of the most important exhibits.

When a user has chosen a specific category, he can proceed to the next, which is the choice of appearance of the cultural content of a particular institution (Fig. 5).

With the use of Flash technology within the system, a user-visitor can enlarge the parameters Museum Address and Museum Information aiming at the cultural content to be legible for individuals with visual disabilities (Fig. 6).

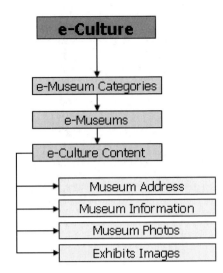

Fig. 4. E-culture content

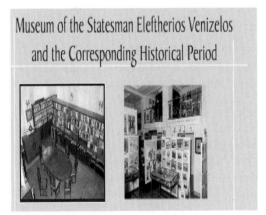

Fig. 5. Museum Photos

Choosing an image from the parameters Museum Photos and Exhibits Images, the visitor can view them in real size so as to have a clear picture of the exhibit or the institution areas.

To sum up, it can be said that the user-visitor has an integrated point of view of a museum and its exhibits as they are presented within the system. Of course, one cannot omit the fact that the knowledge-information presented within the environment is also available to people with visual disabilities, through the use of Flash technology, which is the backbone of the system, as it was previously mentioned. In this way, the system follows the «Information for All» logic and scheme as well as knowledge society strategies for user-centered systems [15].

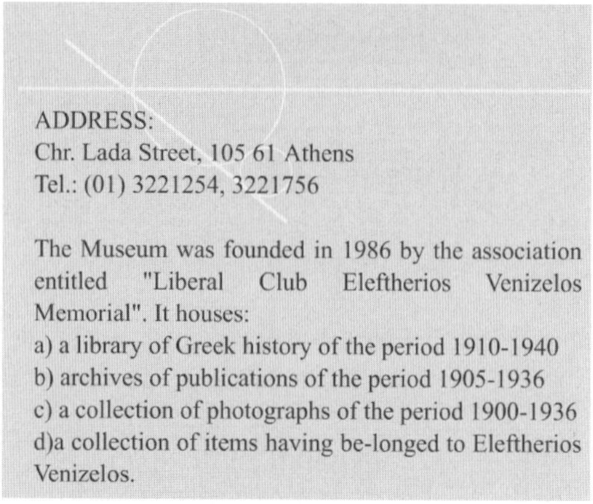

ADDRESS:
Chr. Lada Street, 105 61 Athens
Tel.: (01) 3221254, 3221756

The Museum was founded in 1986 by the association
entitled   "Liberal   Club   Eleftherios   Venizelos
Memorial". It houses:
a) a library of Greek history of the period 1910-1940
b) archives of publications of the period 1905-1936
c) a collection of photographs of the period 1900-1936
d) a collection of items having be-longed to Eleftherios
Venizelos.

Fig. 6. Zoom of Museum Address & Information

4   Benefits

The benefits of an e-culture system like the one described in this article and its importance to the information - knowledge society can be focused on the following:

- The diffusion of Greek civilization and generally of the Greek cultural heritage in a universal level. Additionally, this form of cultural heritage is at the disposal of every Greek citizen, that is, to the Greeks abroad and finally to foreign people who are eager to learn about Greek culture
- The cultural information is accessible from anyone, anywhere (even in remote places), at any time and with minimum cost [16]
- Saving and creating digital cultural content can lead to the preservation of cultural information during the course of time due to the constant physical degradation of monuments, statues etc. [15]
- Easy access to cultural information for disabled people complying with the user-centered strategy and the «equal access and knowledge for all» logic
- The projection of a country's cultural heritage can yield immediate results to the social sector of a country like the development of tourism, and in a wider sense the development of its economy [17], [18]
- The electronic projection of a country's cultural heritage is also a tool for education, study and research from scientists and students
- Finding new information out of existing information from other resources
- Creating new arts with the help of ICT tools, like graphic design, digital photography etc. As a result, new modern artists appear and simultaneously new professions and job vacancies are created [5],[19]

5   Future Work

The system presented is the first creative stage of an integrated e-culture system for navigation through Greek and Cypriot museums. The environment described in this article was created with the HTML programming language embedding at the same time the FLASH technology in order to achieve better visualization. The aforementioned technologies are compatible with every operational system as well as every Internet Browser. A future goal of the presented environment is the creation of an up-to-date integrated e-culture system using modern techniques and technologies. Great importance will be given to the promotion and presentation of cultural information, due to the fact that there are new techniques and tools in the area of informatics such as:

- 3-tier architecture system
- Database systems
- Virtual Reality
- Digital Photography
- DVB Technology
- 3D games
- Learning environments
- Agents and avatars
- Mobile access to heritage information
- Location-based services
- New displays and human interfaces
- Virtual communities

All the above play an important role towards the creation of a user friendly e-culture system, especially to children and the elderly who are not familiar with the use of a computer and its features [20].

6 Conclusions

From the detailed analysis carried out throughout this paper, the numerous advantages of the system that supports e-culture services became clear. Its main advantage is none other than the fact that it offers the pioneering experience for either a simple user-visitor or a scientist-researcher to combine two completely different worlds, the physical and online worlds, simultaneously.

This new e-culture challenge will drastically change the structures and relations that existed up to nowadays. Museum staff, volunteers and a wider public will require new skills to create, manage and maintain participatory and truly interactive digital applications. Museum people will need to understand experimental learning and the techniques of information management and multimedia creation. They will also need to draw on inputs from a wide range of disciplines, in the arts, sciences and humanities [5].

Culture is dynamic and creativity is at its core. Museums and galleries are centers for creativity. Their collections embody the accumulated cultural energy of contemporary and other times. They can be powerful catalysts for innovation. By making museums more accessible, a more creative society can be built.

References

1. Netherlands Council for Culture: From ICT to E-Culture, Netherlands State Secretary for Education. Advisory Report on the Digitalization of Culture and the Implications for Cultural Policy, Culture and Science (2003)
2. Van der Ploeg, F.: Culture as Confrontation - Basic Assumptions on Culture Policy over the Period 2001-2004. The State Secretary for Education, Culture and Science of Netherlands (2002)
3. Wahler, A.: What's next for the e-Culture Community. In: International Workshop on European Cultural Heritage: RTD Challenges Ahead (2004)
4. Veltman, K.: Forecast of Application of IT in Cultural Heritage in the Next Decade. In: JRES, pp. 13–37 (2003)
5. A Netful Of Jewels - New Museums in the Learning Age. In: National Museum Directors' Conference (1999)
6. Digital Culture - Access to and Preservation of Cultural Heritage. European Commission (2004)
7. Durbin, G.: Where Lies the Added Value in Digital Cultural Heritage? In: Salzburg Research Symposium (2004)
8. Giunchiglia, F., Mylopoulos, J., Perini, A.: The Tropos Software Development Methodology: Processes, Models and Diagrams. In: Giunchiglia, F., Odell, J.J., Weiss, G. (eds.) AOSE 2002. LNCS, vol. 2585. Springer, Heidelberg (2003)
9. Trant, J., Bearman, D.: Educational Use of Museum Multimedia, the AMICO Library. The Art Libraries Journal 27 (2002)
10. Loran, M.: Use of Websites to Increase Access and Develop Audiences in Museums: Experiences in British National Museums. E-Journal of the Humanities and Philology Studies of the UOC 7 (2005)
11. Carreras, C.: Narrowcasting of Virtual Cultural Portals: The Cases of Barcelona's Botanic Gardens and the Boí Valley. E-Journal of the Humanities and Philology Studies of the UOC 7 (2005)
12. Charitos, D., Lepouras, G., Bourdakis, V., et al.: An Approach to Designing and Implementing Virtual Museums. In: Seventh UK VR-SIG Conference (2000)
13. Lepouras, G., Charitos, D., Vassilakis, K., Charissi, A., Halatsi, L.: Building a VR-Museum in a Museum. In: Virtual Reality International Conference (VRIC) (2001)
14. Almeida, P., Yokoi, S.: Interactive Character as a Virtual Tour Guide to an Online Museum Exhibition. In: Museums and the Web: An International Conference (2003)
15. Cultural and Linguistic Diversity in the Information Society. UNESCO, WSIS Publication Series (2003)
16. Mayer, H.: Knowledge and Presentation. In: International Workshop on European Cultural Heritage: RTD Challenges Ahead (2004)
17. Veltman, K.: Challenges for ICT/UCT Applications in Cultural Heritage. E-Journal of the Humanities and Philology Studies of the UOC 7 (2005)
18. Go, F., Lee, R., Russo, A.: E-Heritage in the Globalizing Society: Enabling Cross-Cultural Engagement through ICT. In: Information Technology and Tourism, pp. 55–68 (2003)
19. Drigas, A.: Electronic - Digital Culture (E-Culture). In: Information Society and Culture (2005)
20. Geser, G., Mulrenin, A.: Are Small Heritage Institutions Ready for E-Culture? In: ICHIM-Digital Culture and Heritage (2004)

Arguments That Support Decisions in *E-Cognocracy:* A Quantitative Approach Based on Priorities Intensity

José Mª Moreno-Jiménez, Mª Teresa Escobar, Adrián Toncovich, and Alberto Turón

Zaragoza Multicriteria Decision Making Group
Faculty of Economics, University of Zaragoza, Spain
{moreno,mescobar,toncovic,turon}@unizar.es
(http://gdmz.unizar.es)

Abstract. This paper deals with the identification of the arguments that support the decisions made within the context of e-cognocracy. To this end, on the basis of a discussion carried out through communication media, more specifically a forum, we present different decisional tools oriented to the identification of the outstanding comments from the quantitative values corresponding to the decision makers' preferences. The arguments that support the decisions made by the different actors involved in the resolution process will be obtained from these comments by using text-mining techniques.

Keywords: e-cognocracy, e-democracy, e-participation, multicriteria decision-making, knowledge extraction, priority.

1 Introduction

E-cognocracy [1-5] is a new democratic system that, along with the direct involvement of citizens in the decision making processes, allows the extraction and diffusion of knowledge related with the scientific resolution of public decision making problems associated with the governance of the society.

This cognitive democracy combines representative or legal democracy with participative or direct democracy. The former is carried out by the citizens' representatives and the latter by the citizens themselves. Both democracies are aggregated by using different weights that depend of the type of problem.

Taking into account the main idea of e-cognocracy, that is to say, the democratization of knowledge, this paper deals with the identification of the arguments that support the decisions made within this context. To this end, we use a quantitative approach based on the priorities of the elements being compared. These priorities have been obtained using the Analytic Hierarchy Process [6], AHP, one of the multicriteria decision making methodologies that allows the incorporation of intangible and emotional aspects in the decision making process and best captures the holistic vision of reality.

By combining these priorities and the quantitative information included in the messages and comments raised in the discussion stage, we identify the relevant comments or opinions that support the selection of the different alternatives considered in the resolution process.

M.D. Lytras et al. (Eds.): WSKS 2008, CCIS 19, pp. 649–658, 2008.

Finally, from these messages, the arguments that support the decisions made will be obtained by using text-mining techniques.

This work has been structured as follows: Section 2 briefly presents e-cognocracy and its stages; Section 3 explains how priorities are used in order to identify the comments that support alternatives; Section 4 includes a case study related to the construction of a leisure complex near the city of Zaragoza, Spain and finally, Section 5 highlights the most important conclusions.

2   E-Cognocracy and Stages in Its Methodology

E-cognocracy [7] is a new democratic model that tries to make more ambitious use of democracy than the mere election of political representatives. In this regard, based on the evolution of living systems (only species that learn and adapt to the context are able to survive), e-cognocracy focuses on the extraction and social diffusion of the knowledge derived from the scientific resolution of highly complex problems associated with public decision making related with the governance of society. This is a new democratic system that combines representative democracy with participative democracy to address the limitations of both, particularly, the lack of transparency, control and participation of representative democracy and the populism and lack of global perspective in participative democracy.

This cognitive democracy (e-cognocracy) seeks to convince citizens and not to defeat them (e-democracy), by aggregating the results obtained from political parties (representative democracy) and citizens (participative democracy) by assigning different weights (w_1 and w_2) depending on the context of the problem (local, regional, national or supranational) and the objectives of the system. Its characteristics can be seen in [5], [7].

The key idea of e-cognocracy is to educate people (intelligence and learning), promote relations with others (communication and coexistence), improve society (quality of life and cohesion) and construct the future (evolution) in a world of increasing complexity [5].

The stages followed in the e-cognocracy process are:

Stage 1: *Problem Establishment*. Using the web, this stage identifies the relevant aspects of the problem: context, actors and factors (mission, criteria, subcriteria, attributes and alternatives), as well as their interdependencies and relationships.

Stage 2: *Problem Resolution*. This stage provides the priorities of the alternatives been compared. We do this end we employ AHP. The steps of its methodology are: (i) modelling, where a hierarchical representation of the problem (which should include all the relevant aspects of the decision problem) is established; (ii) Valuation, in which the actors incorporate their judgements through pairwise comparisons between the elements considered in the problem. A positive, reciprocal pairwise matrix is provided for each node of the hierarchy; (iii) Prioritization, where the local and global priorities are obtained by using any of the existing prioritization procedures and the

Hierarchical Composition Principle and (iv) Synthesis, in which the individual total priorities are derived by applying additive or multiplicative procedures. One of the main characteristics of AHP is the existence of a measure to evaluate the inconsistency of the decision maker when eliciting their judgements. Finally, the social priorities of the alternatives are obtained by aggregating the individual preferences or judgments [8].

Stage 3: *Model Exploitation*. This stage of the resolution process derives the patterns of behaviour of the actors involved in the resolution process. This is done by considering the incorporation of uncertainty through interval judgments and the identification of the opinion groups and the critical points of the problem by using analytical and graphical visualization tools.

Stage 4: *Discussion*. Using any media or collaborative tool (forum in our case), the citizens' representatives (through their respective political parties) and the citizens themselves (through the network) give their motives and justify the decisions. From these comments and messages, the arguments that support the alternatives, as well the attributes that are more relevant in the resolution process are identified. This new knowledge about the problem, explicit knowledge, is put into the network. In this way, the actors involved in the resolution process would learn about the problem and its resolution before beginning a new round in preference elicitation.

Stage 5: *Second round in problem resolution*. After updating the individual preferences with the explicit knowledge derived in the previous resolution stage, the priorities of the alternatives in a second round are obtained.

Stage 6: *Knowledge Extraction and Democratisation*. Using the information on the preferences of the two rounds and the quantitative information included in the comments elicited in the discussion stage, the comments that support each pattern of behaviour and each preference structure are identified. From these comments, and by using text-mining techniques, we will determine the motives of preference changes between the two rounds. This final step of e-cognocracy will be the subject of a different paper where we will present the qualitative (text-mining) approach followed in this case. In this context, and after measuring the changes in preferences, we also identify the social leaders, that is to say, the actors whose opinions provoke these preference changes and whose arguments are followed by the majority.

3 A Quantitative Approach in Searching for Arguments

This Section identifies the comments and messages included in the discussion stage of e-cognocracy that support the different patterns of behaviour that appeared in the problem resolution stage. By exclusively taking into account the quantitative information existing in the resolution process (the priorities of the alternatives in the two rounds and the information on comment importance), we propose a quantitative approach for identifying the arguments.

This approach deals with the individual priorities of alternatives obtained by using AHP and classifies decision makers into categories around the alternatives of the problem. In our case, we consider three alternatives A1, A2 and A3 and, associated with them, six different categories or regions: three where there is clear evidences in favour of the respective alternatives "A1", "A2" and "A3" and another three regions where there are some doubts about preferences: "A1_A2", "A1_A3" and "A2_A3".

For a better understanding of the procedure we have elaborated two graphical visualisation tools [9]: the *ternary diagram* and the *"Euclidean" bi-plot diagram*. The ternary diagram (Figure 1) represents in the simplex ($\sum_{j=1}^{n=3} w_j = 1$) the priority vector ($w^{[k]} = (w_1^{[k]}, w_2^{[k]}, w_3^{[k]})$), $k=1,\dots,r$ for the r decision makers ($D^{[k]}$, $k=1,\dots,r$) involved in the resolution process. The priorities are compositional data as they sum up to one. Their graphical representation in the simplex (Figure 1) may drive us to misinterpretation because the distance between different pair of points does not represent the same magnitude. In order to overcome this difficulty we employ a graphical representation of these compositional data based on the centred logratio transformation ($x_i = \log(w_i/g(w))$, where $g(w)$ is the geometric mean). The new values are obtained according to:

$$X = \frac{\sqrt{6}}{6}\left(2\log w_1 - \log w_2 - \log w_3\right)$$

$$Y = \frac{\sqrt{2}}{2}\left(\log w_2 - \log w_3\right) \tag{1}$$

$$Z = 0$$

Using these values we construct the Euclidean bi-plot (Figure 2) in which we can use the Euclidean distance in order to measure the magnitude of the distance between any pair of points. This distance corresponds to the Aitchison distance [10] between the respective points in the simplex.

In this graphic we consider six different sector regions of 60°: "A1", "A2", "A3", "A1_A2", "A1_A3" and "A2_A3". We also include two concentric circles that reflect the preference intensities. These circles are constructed depending of two preference thresholds: weak (q) and strong (p), fixed by the super decision in charge of solving the problem ($D^{[0]}$), which determine three intensity areas for each of the six regions previously established. We have also plotted how these concentric circles and sectors are represented in the simplex (Figure 1) using the inverse transformation.

Taking into account the sectors (width) and areas (weak and strong preferences), in a first step, we assign decision makers to each one of the 18 existing modalities. Next, we construct a table where the messages and their comments submitted to the forum are included as columns and the decision makers as rows. Each non- null entry of this table sets the category associated with the actor's priorities that comments the message. Finally, from the values included in each column we establish the categories for the comments and messages. If for a given column (message) all the decision-makers which have commented on it belong to a given sector (for example A1) we can deduce indirectly that the topic of this message favours this alternative.

This process allows the identification of the comments and messages that support the different patterns of behaviour or areas considered in the bi-plot graphic.

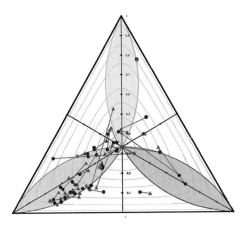

Fig. 1. *Ternary diagram.* The priority vector of each decision maker is represented by a blue circle (round 1) and a red triangle (round 2). The orange (bottom left), light blue (bottom right) and green (top) areas are the decision makers in favour of the alternatives A1, A2 and A3, respectively. The closer is the point to the vertex, the greater is the preference in favour of the respective alternative. The white areas outside the coloured lobes include those decision makers whose preferences are not so clearly defined in favour of a single alternative, and can be interpreted as (starting from the bottom left and following the counter clockwise direction): A1 but near A2, A2 but near A1, A2 but near A3, A3 but near A2, A3 but near A1, A1 but near A3.

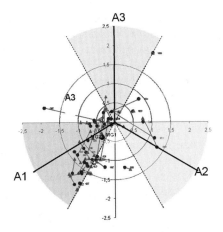

Fig. 2. *Bi-plot diagram.* The priority vector of each decision maker is represented in the same way as in Figure 1, but now the proximity to one alternative is indicated by the distance from the origin and the angle that the priority vector forms with the corresponding alternative axis. The distances between two different points can be interpreted in the "euclidean" sense.

4 Case Study

Gran Scala will be the largest leisure complex ever built in Europe. The project statistics are staggering: 17,000 million Euros in investment; 1,000 million in State and 677 million Euros in Aragon Regional Government revenues through taxation. Gran Scala is expected to receive 25 million visitors per year, create 65,000 direct and indirect jobs at its 70 hotels, 32 casinos, five theme parks, museums, golf courses and race-tracks. In other words, the project would transform the area into a town with a population of 100,000.

Since its inception, the project has caused much debate and controversy in Aragonese society. For these reasons, the project was selected for an electronic voting experiment with students from the Multicriteria Decision Making course of the 4th year of the Bachelor of Science in Business Administration at the University of Zaragoza. The experiment was intended to elicit the opinion and preferences of the students regarding the implementation of the Gran Scala Project in the "Los Monegros" district.

The stages of the experiment are the following:

1. Modelling, assessment and prioritization. This stage is based on the Analytic Hierarchy Process (AHP) methodology and the outcomes of it are the initial priorities for all the decision-makers.
2. Discussion, argumentation and feedback. In this stage a debate is implemented to improve the quantity and quality of the information available.
3. Final prioritization and conclusions. In this stage, a new assessment is made and the final priorities for the decision makers are obtained.

4.1 First Stage: Modelling

In this case, the hierarchy was directly introduced to the students and its design was not part of the decision making process. The hierarchy is composed by the goal (G), four criteria and three alternatives, as can be seen in Figure 3. The goal consists of determining the best course of action concerning the implementation of the Gran Scala project. The alternatives are evaluated with respect to four criteria in terms of their contribution to the goal: Benefits (B), Costs (C), Opportunities (O) and Risks (R). The alternatives considered in the process are: Implementation of the project (A1), Support for the majority's position (A2), and Rejection of the project (A3). The second alternative was introduced to provide an intermediate option and to serve as the recipient of potentially indifferent or undecided decision-makers. In theory, if the debate and discussion stage is carried out in a proper manner, part of those uncommitted or indifferent decision-makers will adopt a clear position as a result of a better understanding of the problem.

The factors that affect the decision are grouped in four main criteria (B, C, O, R). This general scheme was further detailed in order to facilitate a clear comprehension of the problem. We provided some economic, social and environmental ideas for benefits and costs (positive and negative short term effects), and opportunities and risks (positive and negative long term effects). The previous information was only used only to initiate the decision making process and accelerate the global comprehension of the situation under consideration. Students were completely free to make their own decisions and form their own opinions

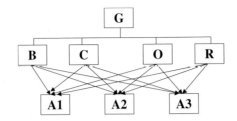

Fig. 3. Hierarchy considered in the *Gran Scala* problem. Three criteria have been introduced: B (benefits), C (costs), O (opportunities) and R (risks), in order to select one out of three alternatives: A1 (implementation of the project), A2 (support to the majority's position) and A3 (rejection of the project).

Once the hierarchy has been presented, it is possible to start the assessment process that will provide the priorities for the alternatives. This process was implemented using a web platform that allowed the full participation of the students. The data is then synthesized to obtain the priorities for the alternatives. This process is carried out by means of specific software that performs the calculations required by the AHP methodology.

4.2 Second Stage: Discussion

In this stage a debate session was initiated after the end of the first round of voting. The implementation of the process was performed through a web interface in the form of a discussion forum (Figures 4a,b,c,d). The students posted messages grouped in four categories associated to the criteria of the problem. Different threads of discussion were created and, in general, several comments related to the initial messages of the threads were also posted. When a message is posted on the forum the author of a message posts it on the forum he/she is required to express his/her appreciation concerning the importance of the message using a scale of 1 to 10 (1 is minimum, 10 is maximum importance). Furthermore, when a user of the forum reads a message they can make an evaluation by means of two numbers: the first number indicates on a scale of 1 to 10 the relevance of the message from the reader's viewpoint (1 is minimum, 10 is maximum importance) and the second number specifies, on a scale of 1 to 5, the position with respect to the message (where 5 means the reader is strongly in favour of the message, 1 means the reader is totally against it). With respect to the discussion through the forum, there were 77 messages (19 for benefits, 13 for costs, 22 for opportunities and 23 for risks), 257 comments (68+50+59+80) to the messages and 186 valuations. These numbers were then used to assign comments to categories. The discussion process was prolonged during ten days (24th February until 4th March 2008) in order to facilitate the sharing of viewpoints, information and feedback necessary to achieve an appropriate level of maturity in the participants' judgments.

4.3 Third Stage: Final Prioritization

In this stage a second round of voting is performed. The process follows the same pattern as the first round. A new assessment process is performed so the final priorities for the alternatives are obtained.

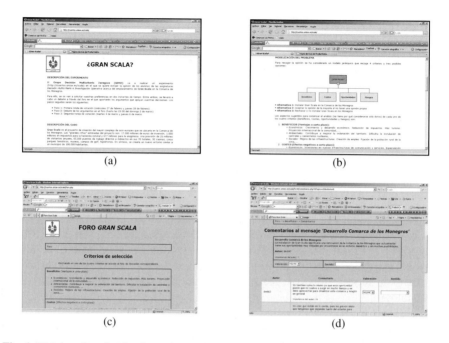

(a)   (b)

(c)   (d)

Fig. 4. Web interface for the discussion and prioritization. The decision makers can incorporate their judgements through pairwise comparisons between the elements of the hierarchy, as well as participate in the forum posting their own messages or comments to the previous posts, and evaluating either their own opinions or the others decision makers' messages.

4.4 Results

The results of the two rounds of voting are summarised in Tables 1 and 2. The values in each cell are the aggregate figures calculated by means of the geometric mean of the individual values. From the analysis of this data it is clear that positive criteria have a greater influence in the decision (around 60% in both rounds). Alternative 1 prevails in both rounds, but Alternatives 1 and 2 increase their priority values. This fact supports to a certain extent the benefits of the cognocratic approach because the

Table 1. Local priorities for the criteria of the problem in both rounds of voting

Round\Criterion	Benefits	Costs	Opportunities	Risks
Round 1	0,2645	0,1758	0,3467	0,2130
Round 2	0,2668	0,1718	0,3412	0,2202

Table 2. Alternatives' priorities in both rounds of voting

Round\Alternative	A1	A2	A3
Round 1	0,4793	0,2911	0,2296
Round 2	0,4829	0,2792	0,2379

priority value associated with the Alternative 2, linked to undecided or uncommitted decision makers, has decreased from the first to the second round of voting.

The quantitative analysis of the comments supports overwhelmingly the maintenance of the Alternative 1 as the leading option, although there are some threads of discussion that can be linked to the Alternative 2 and to a lesser extent to the Alternative 3.

5 Conclusions

This paper presents a method for identifying the messages that lead to the change of opinion of the decision makers that participate in a decision process in the context of e-cognocracy. For the case of n=3, the decision makers can be classified into 18 groups around the *3* alternatives considered, according to the strength and sense of the decision maker's preferences. With the help of the quantitative information included in the messages posted during the discussion stage, these messages can be associated with the alternatives they favour, identifying in this way those of them that support each pattern of behaviour and each preference structure. Two graphical representations are used for helping in the analysis of the results and in the identification of patterns of behaviour.

The application was tested by means of a website set up to this purpose, through which the decision makers could express their preferences, as well as participate in the discussion stage giving their opinion and evaluating the messages and comments.

These results will be complemented with another study being carried on the Zaragoza Multiciteria Decision Making Group in which text-mining techniques are used for finding out the reasons of preference changes between the two rounds. By using these techniques the outstanding ideas and opinions contained into the messages can be detected and relates with the changes observed in the preferences, so the actors whose arguments provoke those changes can be identified.

References

1. Moreno-Jiménez, J.M.: Las Nuevas Tecnologías y la Representación Democrática del Inmigrante. IV Jornadas Jurídicas de Albarracín. Consejo General del Poder Judicial (2003)
2. Moreno-Jiménez, J.M.: E-cognocracia y Representación Democrática del Inmigrante. Anales de Economía Aplicada (2004)
3. Moreno-Jiménez, J.M.: E-cognocracia: Nueva Sociedad, Nueva Democracia. Estudios de Economía Aplicada 24(1-2), 559–581 (2006)
4. Moreno-Jiménez, J.M., Polasek, W.: E-democracy and Knowledge. A Multicriteria Framework for the New Democratic Era. Journal Multicriteria Decision Analysis 12, 163–176 (2003)
5. Moreno-Jiménez, J.M., Polasek, W.: E-cognocracy and the participation of immigrants in e-governance. In: Böhlen, et al. (eds.) TED Conference on e-government 2005. Electronic democracy: The challenge ahead, vol. 13, pp. 18–26. University Rudolf Trauner-Verlag, Schriftenreihe Informatik (2005)
6. Saaty, T.: The Analytic Hierarchy Process. McGraw-Hill, New York (1980)

7. Moreno-Jiménez, J.M., Piles, J., Ruiz, J., Salazar, J.L., Sanz, A.: Some Notes on e-voting and e-cognocracy. In: Proceedings E-Government Interoperability Conference 2007, Paris, France (2007)
8. Escobar, M.T., Moreno-Jiménez, J.M.: Aggregation of Individual Preference Structures. Group Decision and Negotiation 16(4), 287–301 (2007)
9. Moreno-Jiménez, J.M., Salvador, M., Turón, A.: Group Preference Structures in AHP group decision making. In: Proceedings 2nd Compositional Data Analysis CODAWORK 2005, Gerona (2005)
10. Aitchison, J.: The Statistical Analysis of Compositional Data. Chapman and Hall, Boca Raton (1986)

The Impact of a Service Oriented Approach as an Enabler for E-Government Educational Services for All Citizens

Konstantinos Votis[1,2], Christos Alexakos[1], and Spiridon Likothanassis[1]

[1] Pattern Recognition Laboratory, Computer Engineering and Informatics,
University of Patras
{botis, alexakos, likothan}@ceid.upatras.gr
[2] Informatics and Telematics Institute, Centre for Research and Technology Hellas
Kvotis@iti.gr

Abstract. This paper presents an ontological modeling framework for the integration of networked educational environments in order to provide functionalities that enable (1) staff users to perform administrative activities online and to provide them with intelligent decisions about educational procedures in public administrations and (2) all citizens (with activity limitations or not) to access public educational buildings or schools, even for example, those who move about in a wheelchair. Thus, this framework provides an ontological knowledge model of infrastructures, school buildings, accessible patterns and any other relevant information that are important to improve the effectiveness and coherence of educational e-Government services for all citizens. Based on this framework, we have expressed the implicit model of current educational procedures in Greek educational system and developed a very promising experimental study to be adapted for all citizens' support.

Keywords: SoA, E-government, ontologies, education.

1 Introduction

To ensure continued competitiveness, public administration organisations need to constantly increase its agility and versatility [1]. Thus, e-Government services aim to relax the citizens interface with over-complicated and slow processes of local and regional governmental organizations [2]. The advent of easy to use and cost effective technologies such as the web has ease the way towards user friendly systems, however, these technologies are not adequate to handle the complexity of such systems. E-government processes are complicated and complex information systems with monolithic architectures are currently handling them [3]. This complexity is transferred to the users each time he/she transacts electronically with such a system. Users of such systems are both citizens and employees of governmental bodies.

In order to meet increased expectation, administrations need to deploy a variety of channels for their service delivery - channels that allow users to consume their services anytime, anywhere and anyhow [4]. New developments in IT allow the public

M.D. Lytras et al. (Eds.): WSKS 2008, CCIS 19, pp. 659–668, 2008.

sector to meet these challenges by adapting their front and back office: new ways of interaction through a variety of channels, restructured services that accommodate their users' needs, and re-organized business processes within and between separate administrative bodies. However, complexity needs to be handled first. Complexity can be handled initially by decomposing complex processes into simpler ones. Service-oriented computing (SOC) and artificial intelligence (AI) technologies permits the design of such architectures [5]. This paradigm was not available a few years ago but the advent of web services changed all this.

This work discusses the implementation of adaptivity and intelligent Educational Ontological Modeling Framework (EOMF) for the management of distributed educational departments (primary and secondary educational directorates) for the prefecture of Achaia in Greece. The solution incorporates powerful adaptivity for the management, authoring, delivery and monitoring of services. The enabling technology is based on SOC and results in significant reduction of the difficulty to access distributed resources within the prefecture. Dominant technologies are used such as Web Services and ontologies. The system increases the opportunities for the management board of the prefecture to take concrete strategically decisions regarding the educational departments (public primary and secondary schools) of the whole area as well as to depict their regional status. Administrators can use the proposed framework to make critical decisions in a variety of administrative areas, including forecast budget needs and educational trends, enrolment management to achieve an appropriate mix of students, improve or construct new educational facilities. They can have the ability to use data from multiple sources in order to gain useful insights. It's associated with a methodology for the classification of management and monitoring processes and with the integration and interoperability of heterogeneous systems and applications that are required, independently of the level that they reside in.

In addition a challenge of the proposed framework is also the integration of much possible accessible guidance for all citizens. So even if our living environment, not only technology, has normally been designed for the "average" user and then adapted to the needs of people who are more or less far from "average", based on our approach, each citizen (students, teachers, individuals) with activity limitation or not, can receive useful guidance route instructions for accessing, with safety, all public educational building and schools within the specific area, even for example those who move about in a wheelchair.

2 Proposed Service Oriented Architecture

A network of Educational Service Centres (ESC), one for the directorate of the primary education and another for the secondary education, constitute the proposed infrastructure as depicted in the following fig 1. Each ESC has a Portal for user access and it can supply the whole set of available services or a part of them. Moreover, some services can reside locally to the ESC and other remotely. In general a service may reside also out of an ESC, to local subsystems that contain useful data about the educational infrastructure. A unique point of access redirects the user to the preferred

ESC Portal but, in general, the user must be able to access the services he/she is sub-scribed to and his own profile from every Portal. From the point of view of the man-agement of Portals, each Portal has it own user management capability, based on a local database. This made necessary the development of opportune procedures of synchronization between the Portals. Each ESC integrates a Portal and a local script-ing module consisting of the corresponding mapping scheme referring to the User Ontology. The user can connect to any Portal in order to receive the same services as it was connected to the central one. An Educational Ontological Modeling Framework (EOMF) has been implemented as described in following section, integrating all source schemas, which acts as a mediator between the different source schemas (vari-ous data sources). When the mappings between the source schemas and the Educa-tional Model have been created, the user can browse the global schema and discover what information is present in the system and where the information is located.

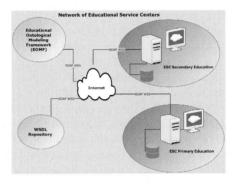

Fig. 1. Network of Educational Service Centres (ESC)

Collaboration among ESC portals is performed in terms of SOAP [6] messaging. Each portal implement one or more web services for accessing the corresponding stored data, and the descriptions associated with these services are gathered into a Central WSDL Repository (CWR). WSDL [7] provides an XML–based [8, 9] gram-mar for describing a web service interface. Portals wishing to provide services will publish on the CWR their WSDLs, and portals seeking services will retrieve the WSDLs out. To maintain that confidentiality and integrity of data exchanged among portals, Web Service Security (WS-S) [10] provided by OASIS organization is used. WS-S standard set of SOAP extensions that can be used when building secure Web services to implement message level integrity and confidentiality.

3   The Educational Ontological Modeling Framework (EOMF)

The main goal of the proposed framework is to provide support for the formal and unambiguous definitions of educational e-government domains, as well as the possi-ble semantic interactions between them. We have specified our framework to be inte-grated into the Educational Service Centers as described in the previous section. This will establish a common vocabulary for exchanging and describing the complex information that is related to administrative processes and intelligent decisions of educational foreseen issues. The EOMF aims to formalize conceptual information about: (a) The general characteristics of the educational system (school buildings, location, number of students, teachers and other aspects that should be taken into account when describing the Greek educational environment); (b) Student characteristics, encompasses intrinsic student diversity characteristics (e.g. students with impairments); (c) Characteristics of road networks (highway, street, foot road) and road accessibility standards with associated checkpoints (e.g. roads with safe pavements, appropriate wheel-chair bars, etc.); (d) Semantic verification rules to help describing requirements and constraints of users. In order to cope with these goals, the EOMF must comply with the following requirements: (1) To be as formal as possible, in order to provide all the necessary definitions in a concise, unambiguous, and unified form; (2) Provide information that can be easily processed by relevant users or citizens and integrated into educational processes;

One of the main issues in designing and developing the proposed framework was to make it maintainable and extensible, while assuring model consistency within the framework. Therefore, we have separated EOMF into two distinct dimensions: Educational Descriptions dimension, and Educational Mapping and rules dimension. Thus the first dimension provides constructs to describe different educational concepts and cuts the concept space into a Generic ontology and a set of Domain Specific ontologies, as detailed next. The second one aims to cover the establishment of mapping relationships between the ontologies of the first dimension, and the source schemas of the educational service centers to validate the semantics of these relationships. These relationships can be used, e.g., for efficient navigation and searching inside the ontologies, as well as to afford the creation of semantic rules-based accessibility verification. Also, it utilizes a lexical ontology that comprises a set of lexical and

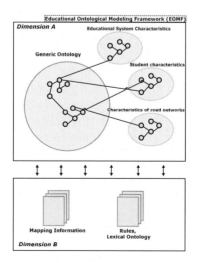

Fig. 2. Educational Ontological Modeling Framework (EOMF)

notational synonyms reinforcing the searching among the various ontology instances of the educational content. The overall of the EOMF is depicted in Figure 2.

The generic ontology of the first dimension is comprised of a single generic ontology describing the main knowledge domains that represent the contents of the educational centers (e.g educational system, class, student, teacher, etc.). This ontology is primarily used as a "catalogue" for the type of contents and the domain of knowledge that are integrated. Thus this ontology provides more abstract and generic knowledge derived by the educational environment. Domains are specified in classes and sub-classes providing a hierarchical model presenting all the knowledge fields that are included in the educational source schemas of the distributed servers (centres). A part of the Generic Ontology is depicted in Fig. 3.

We devised different domain specific ontologies to cope with the specific individual domains of the offering e-government educational services. Each domain ontology uses the basic entities of the Generic Ontology. This way, each ontology is able to represent a more detailed description of its corresponding domain, thus allowing the extension of EOMF into other domains.

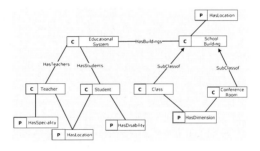

Fig. 3. Part of Generic Ontology

The most important domain ontologies which have been implemented within the EOMF are: *Educational System Characteristics:* This domain ontology covers the main and general characteristics which are of greater significance for the definition of the educational environment. Thus we have defined the main features that are present on different educational environments (e.g. primary or secondary), based on categorizations defined by the Greek Ministry of national education and religious affairs. Hence, we have defined a device domain that encompasses these specific issues. Modalities might be present on this educational system characteristics domain ontology as school buildings (e.g., classes, stadium, conference room, and laboratory), capacity of schools (e.g., number of students and teachers, location, dimension of places), educational equipment (computers, internet, books) and other appropriate aspects that should be taken into account when describing the Greek educational environment. An insight on the Educational System Characteristics domain is presented on Figure 4.

Student Characteristics: Regarding the description of student characteristics, comprise on the one hand the user's disabilities and individual's preferences and on the

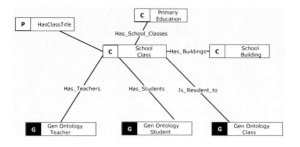

Fig. 4. Partial Educational System Characteristics domain

other hand personal information data (e.g. name, age, location of home, etc.). So, different categories of disabilities, based on the International Classification of Functioning, Disability and Health (ICF) approach [11] have been incorporated within the student characteristics domain ontology, amongst others visual and hearing impairments, learning impairments (e.g. disorders manifested by significant difficulties in the acquisition and use of listening, speaking, writing, reading, reasoning, or mathematical abilities), mobility disabilities, etc. Thus it is of great importance to consider the users personal capabilities determined by her/his impairments. The degree of the users' disabilities determines the extent of adaptations necessary to support the selection of the most accessible school location for them. In addition to considering the students personal capabilities it is important to respect their personal preferences. Thus, each student may have individual preferences of which school to select use and how to find out the most appropriate accessible road for moving to there. Figure 5 presents some of the concepts extracted from the Student Characteristics domain.

```
Student
  StudentName
  StudentLocation
  StudentAge
  StudentCharacteristics
  StudentAbility
    AbilityCognitive
    AbilityPhysical
  StudentDisability
    DisabilityCognitive
      CognitiveMemory
      CognitiveReading
    DisabilityPhysical
      PhysicalBlind
  PhysicalMotor
```

Fig. 5. Partial Student domain characteristics ontology

Road Network Characteristics: The Road Network domain ontology covers the main and general characteristics which are of greater significance for the definition of road networks and appropriate accessibility standards for students with disabilities. So, we have defined the main terms that are necessary for guidance route of students in order

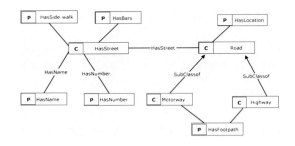

Fig. 6. Partial Road Network Characteristics domain ontology

to access the location of their school departments. These elements contain information about highway, streets, footpaths, etc., and road accessibility standards with associated checkpoints (e.g. roads with safe pavements, appropriate wheel-chair bars, etc.). The following figure 6 presents some of the concepts extracted from this domain ontology.

4 Mapping Methodology and Architectural Issues of the Proposed Framework

A methodology is required to address the mapping needs between the different implemented ontological frameworks providing the aforementioned semantic information and the source schemas of the ESCs. The first step in this methodology concerns the mapping of the domain ontologies to the Generic Ontology. This mapping is possible by affiliating the main classes of domain ontologies to the corresponding classes of the Generic Ontology. In the previous examples (figure 4), the mapping can be utilized by associating the class "Class" of the Generic Ontology to the class "SchoolClass" of the Educational System Characteristics domain ontology. The second step in our methodology regards the need for mapping between different domain ontologies. This mapping is necessary, since each domain ontology represents semantics of different knowledge domains which is important for the successfully delivering of the educational e-government services to the citizens. Since integration needs require that information is seamlessly passed among the different ontological layers or domains, domain ontology mapping is absolutely necessary.

The final step in our methodology introduces the mapping of the Generic and domain ontologies to the semantic information related with the actual description of database schemas in the different Educational Service Center systems. This mapping is related to the description, in ontology terms, of the ESC content (e.g. which server provides what). This semantic information stems from the semantic metadata description of the educational e-government content and has to be mapped to the corresponding classes and properties of the relevant domain description ontology. This methodology leads to the desirable unification of the Generic Ontology with the domain ontologies and the semantically described educational contents, and thus contributes to the creation of a flexible and reusable ontology metadata scheme.

The proposed dimensioned scheme provides the necessary supporting mechanism to a specific search engine to navigate through the ontology terms and instances faster and efficiently. The basic concept is the separation of the search process in three steps. In the first step, the engine searches in the Generic Ontology assisted by the synonyms and rules extracted by the lexical ontology aiming to find the proper domains where the results may be included. In the second step, using the mapping information between the Generic and Domain ontologies, the engine seeks the appropriate domain description ontologies to find the appropriate structural ontology terms that describe the corresponding semantic metadata structure. The linguistic information from the lexical ontology is also reinforcing the search process in the second step. In the final step of the search process, the search engine has extracted from step two the basic structural elements of the semantic metadata that will be used in the educational data searching within the ESCs. Utilizing the mapping information between the ontologies, the engine constructs the appropriate query for each of the distributed ESC servers.

The general representation of educational knowledge that is provided by the proposed EOMF empowers the search engine to search in each ESC which the educational content belongs to. Thus, the capability of adding new domains and new ESCs does not restrict the search process in certain domains. The enforcement of the above presented EOMF requires a specific architecture that makes it possible to integrate the different semantically annotated data schemas residing in different centers in a flexible and interoperable way. Our approach introduces a framework for the integration of networked educational environments and managing the search queries from users (administrative staff and citizens). The associated architecture of this framework (Fig. 7), involves the following functional elements: (a) The Educational Ontological Modeling Framework (EOMF) where the ontologies contained in the two dimensioned scheme; (b) The Scheme Integration Tool that provides the mechanism and the graphical interface for composing the mapping information between the ontologies of the EOMF; (c) The Query Graphical Interface providing the appropriate search forms to the user of the integrated system; (d) The Scheme Search Engine is the platform which accepts the queries from the Query Graphical Interface and initiates the ontology-based search process.

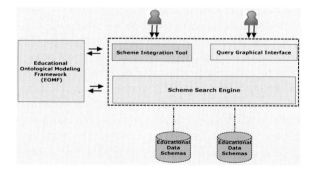

Fig. 7. Architecture of the proposed Framework

5 Conclusions

Semantic interoperability is a major objective and a necessary ingredient in e-government solutions. Although increasing efforts have been devoted to enabling ontologies-related and service oriented technologies, in Greek public administrations the level of supported public services have not yet penetrated the public administration to a satisfactory level. In this work, we discussed the role of ontologies in particular as a means to achieve semantic interoperability between educations service centers. The technology developed will reduce the difficulty to access distributed and more valuable and resources within the prefecture of Achaia, which has the responsibility for all the educational departments of the primary and secondary education. Given the nature of the domain knowledge embedded in e-government systems, administrators will increase the opportunities to take concrete strategically decisions regarding the educational departments (public primary and secondary schools) of the whole area as well as to depict the regional status of them. So from our point of view, the proposed architecture is quite unique for the Greek educational e-government services with the respect to other similar works.

Acknowledgement

This work was partially supported by the Prefecture of Achaia, Western Greece. The authors would like to thank Mr. Aggelopoulos Georgios, Educatonal co-prefect for the prefecture of Achaia.

References

1. van Overeem, A., Witters, J., Peristeras, V.: An Interoperability Framework for Pan-European E-Government Services (PEGS). In: International Conference on System Sciences (HICSS), Hawaii (2007)
2. Martin, B.: Information society revisited: from vision to reality. Journal of Information Science 31(1), 4–12 (2005)
3. Ramnath, R., Landsbergen, D.: IT-enabled sense-and-respond strategies in complex public organizations. Communications of the ACM 48(5), 58–64 (2005)
4. Stoltzfus, K.: Motivations for implementing e-government: an investigation of the global phenomenon. In: Proc. of the national conference on Digital government research, pp. 333–381 (2005)
5. Singh, P.M., Huhns, M.N.: Service Oriented Computing, Semantics, Processes, Agents. Wiley Press, Chichester (2005)
6. Box, D., Ehnebuske, D., Kakivaya, G., Layman, A., Mendelsohn, N., Nielsen, H.F., Thatte, S., Winer, D.: Simple Object Access Protocol (SOAP) Version 1.1 (2000), http://www.w3.org/
7. Christensen, E., Curbera, F., Meredith, G., Weerawarana, S.: Web Service Description Language (WSDL) 1.1 (2001), http://www.w3c.org/

8. Kreger, H.: Web Services Conceptual Architecture (2001), `http://www.ibm.com/`
9. Curbera, F., Nagy, W.A., Weerawana, S.: Web Service: Why and How? In: Proceedings of the OOPSLA 2001 Workshop on Object-Oriented Services, Tampa, Florida (2001)
10. OASIS Web Services Security (WSS) TC, `http://www.oasis-open.org/`
11. International Classification of Functioning, Disability and Health, `http://www.who.int/classifications/icf/site/index.cfm`

An Adapted Evaluation Method for Rural SMEs Oriented e-Learning Services/Projects

Ioannis Theotokas, Nikolaos Marianos, and Maria Lambrou

Department of Shipping Trade and Transport, University of the Aegean, Greece
n.marianos@chios.aegean.gr, gthetokas@aegean.gr,
mlambrou@aegean.gr

Abstract. Information and Communication Technologies (ICT) are becoming more widely used and are benefiting more people, making public services better, more cost effective, and more accessible. However, the SMEs in rural areas do not reap their benefits in full or are effectively cut off from them. The Rural-eGov project aims to bridge an existing gap in national and European training systems and practices. Advanced online services are constantly being developed around Europe. SMEs have to become aware of such services, and to get trained on how they can take advantage of them. Moreover, it will propose innovative training scenarios and content so that professionals of rural areas can get familiarized with e-government services, understand how they can benefit from using them in their business practices. The goal of this paper is to present an adapted evaluation method for rural SME's oriented e-learning services/projects, based on the experience of Rural-eGov Project.

Keywords: Rural SMEs, E-learning, Evaluation.

1 Introduction

A recent policy document from the EC ("i2010 – A European Information Society for growth and employment", EC, June 2005) outlines the importance of Information and Communication Technologies (ICT) in making public services better, more cost effective, and more accessible. ICT are becoming more widely used and are benefiting more people. On the other hand, according to this policy document, today over half of the EU population either does not reap these benefits in full or is effectively cut off from them. Reinforcing social, economic, and territorial cohesion by making ICT products and services more accessible from regions that are lagging behind, is an economic, social, ethical and political imperative for the Commission.

Experience from training SMEs in rural areas (through initiatives such as the 'Go-Online Training Support' in Greece and the 'Opportunity Wales' in UK) has demonstrated that ICT training activities have to develop (i) a specially designed training curriculum that can convince SMEs about the benefits they will reap from introducing ICT in their business, (ii) innovative training models that can combine traditional forms of learning with e-learning forms (such as blended learning models), and (iii) an online point of reference which SMEs can continuously access for information and content. These three aspects are all important when aiming to train rural SMEs on the use of e-government.

M.D. Lytras et al. (Eds.): WSKS 2008, CCIS 19, pp. 669–677, 2008.
© Springer-Verlag Berlin Heidelberg 2008

The Rural-eGov project aims to bridge an existing gap in national and European training systems and practices. Advanced online services are constantly being developed around Europe. Professionals have to (i) become aware of such services, and (ii) to get trained on how they can take advantage of them. The proposed approach will study, collect and categorize such services that can be of particular interest for rural SMEs in the Rural-eGov Observatory. Moreover, it will propose innovative training scenarios and e learning content so that professionals of rural areas can get familiarized with e-government services, understand how they can benefit from using them in their business practices, and thus become members of the Information Society. The countries participating to Rural-eGov project are Germany, Greece, Poland, Slovenia and Wales.

Evaluation is considered an integral part of the project that focuses on its development and result. It aims at monitoring the project's development, at assessing its effectiveness and at contributing to the continuous improvement of its quality. Thus, evaluation focuses on the project's overall development, on educational/ training methodology development and implementation. The goal of this paper is to present an adapted evaluation method for e-learning services/projects in the case of e-government environments.

The Rural-eGov project is aligned with the general strategies of the Knowledge Society. According to the editors of "Open Research Journal on Learning Technologies", Learning Technologies is a key pillar for the realization of the Knowledge Society. The Rural-eGov project promotes technology enhanced learning, developing innovative training scenarios and learning content, with the use of online/ interactive technologies. With the shift towards the knowledge society, the change of working conditions and the high-speed evolution of information and communication technologies, peoples' knowledge and skills need continuous updating (www.open-knowledge-society.org/journals/learn.htm). One of the projects main goals is to find and promote new ways for knowledge and learning diffusion. The focus of this goal is on applications of technologies for user-centered learning, building on the concept of human learning with some of the main objectives to be:

- To increase the efficiency of learning for individuals and groups
- To contribute to a deeper understanding of the learning process by exploring links between human learning, cognition and technologies.

Section 1 provides a description of the Rural-eGov Initiative, an overview of this paper, providing its scope and its linkage with the general knowledge society strategies. Section 2 provides an overview of the evaluation methodology and describes the evaluation methods and tools which are used in the project. Sections 3 and 4 describe the formative and the summative evaluation. Section 5 presents the results of the ongoing evaluation procedure and section 6 provides the conclusions of the paper.

2   Evaluation Approach, Methods and Tools

The evaluation methodology adopts a stakeholder approach. The stakeholder approach incorporates an evaluation process that involves a representative group of those people who manage, receive services, or otherwise have an interest in a project (www.michigan.gov, 2002). This is an involvement of those people who have a stake in the evaluation findings and the success of the project. Project partners, economic chambers, agriculture organizations, SMEs, instructors and trainees are all potential stakeholders.

The evaluation stakeholders in Rural-eGov project are the project educational experts, the trainers, the trainees (rural SMEs' employees/owners) and other online users. The project educational experts are associated with methodological partners and they participated in the formative evaluation. The trainers who participated in the pilot sessions also participate in the evaluation procedure. Trainers participated in questionnaire based survey, after the completion of a training session. The trainees, who are employees or owners of rural SMEs, participated in the evaluation procedures by filling questionnaires before and after the training sessions. Finally, various other online users, mostly associated with the methodological partners, such as experts and university students, will evaluate the observatory.

The evaluation methodology adopts a hybrid approach that combines qualitative and quantitative methods. The evaluation is considered as an internal-collaborative process that engages project's partners and trainees-SMEs aiming at the mutual understanding of the training objectives. At the same time, aims at the evaluation of the technical performance of the project with regards both the training process and the usability of the Rural-eGov Observatory. Based on the need to increase the validity and reliability of evaluation data, the methodology uses a variety of tools for data gathering. The evaluation methods and the relevant tools and their advantages and disadvantages for the scope of the project are presented in the following sections.

In general, quantitative methods claim to be objective and to support generalisable conclusions, while qualitative methods lay claim to flexibility, sensitivity and meaningful conclusions about specific problems (Oliver, 2000). Qualitative methods may lack in reliability, sample validity and subjectivity, whilst quantitative methods have issues concerning relevance, reductionism and the neglect of alternative world views. Several authors have advocated using qualitative and quantitative methodologies in order to triangulate results (Jones et al, 1996), thus enhancing the credibility of evaluation findings (Breen et al, 1998). Such models have been described as hybrid approaches (Oliver & Conole, 1998). Hybrid or eclectic models enable the evaluator to determine appropriate methods and match them to specific questions (Mandinach, 2005). Qualitative and quantitative methods are employed in combination to assure depth, scope, and dependability of findings.

USINACTS project's Usability Evaluation Guideline provides a list of the existing evaluation and testing methods, presenting their advantages and disadvantages (USINACTS, 1999). Evaluation methods include the experiments, interviews, surveys, observations, focus groups etc. The Rural-eGov evaluation is based on structured interviews, heuristic evaluation and input logging, which support the aims of the evaluation methodology, with regard to training context, training scenarios and usability evaluation. According to the Usability Evaluation Guideline, interviews, which are used successfully for user requirements and task analysis, are flexible, in-depth attitude and experience probing. Heuristic Evaluation it's used in early design stages and can find out individual usability problems and address expert user issues. Input logging is usually used for final testing and follow-up studies and it's main advantage is that it can find highly used (or unused) features and it can run continuously.

The methodology developed for the scope of the Rural-eGov evaluation is conducted it two main phases: Formative Evaluation and Summative Evaluation. Formative Evaluation focuses on the processes that are inputs for the development of the training scenarios and content. This approach minimizes the risk of delivering products that will not support properly the pilot sessions and the materialization of the Rural-eGov aims. Summative Evaluation focuses on the outcome of the project and its success, which includes the evaluation of the training sessions and content, as well as of the Rural-eGov observatory.

3   Formative Evaluation

Formative evaluation is typically conducted during the development or improvement of a program or product and it is conducted, often more than once, for in-house staff of the program with the intent to improve (Scriven, 1991).

Formative evaluation is an assessment of efforts prior to their completion for the purpose of improving the efforts. Formative evaluation focuses on implementation of the project. In training related projects, such as the Rural-eGov, formative evaluation concerns the content and the environment that this content will be offered and aims at drawing information used for the improvement of the design and development of the training. The following paragraphs describe the responsibilities, processes and tools that apply for content and training scenarios evaluation.

3.1   Training Scenarios Evaluation

Training scenarios evaluation were conducted by experts of the project partners' teams. Given that the scenarios are context specific in order to adjust to the needs of the identified users, evaluation was conducted by experts of both methodological and user partners. The questionnaire which was used as evaluation tool assess three dimensions using several performance criteria. The dimensions are a)suitability to user learning needs, b)diversity and c)stakeholders representation /user requirements.

3.2   Content Evaluation

Content evaluation was conducted by experts of the project partners' teams. The content evaluation tool is a questionnaire which is originally based on the Learning Object Review Instrument (LORI), an established, validated and widely used tool (Nesbit et al., 2003). The derived, specialized version produced for the Rural-eGov training resources includes five relevant dimensions: 1)Content quality, 2)Learning Goal Alignment, 3)Motivation, 4)Presentation Design and 5)Reusability.

4   Summative Evaluation

Summative Evaluation focuses on the outcomes of the project and their impact on the stakeholders (SMEs, Governmental agencies, public authorities, EU) aiming to prove the added value of the Rural-eGov. As benchmarks for the evaluation are considered the main and the specific aims of the project, which are mentioned in the technical annex. Summative Evaluation includes two separate phases that focus on the evaluation of the pilot sessions and the observatory respectively.

4.1 Pilot Sessions' Evaluation

The pilot evaluation taking place during summative evaluation was conducted during and after the pilot implementation of the Rural-eGov. During Pilot implementation the training scenarios were implemented and training sessions based on the content were organized. Pilot evaluation focuses on assessing the effectiveness and success of the training procedure as well as the users' satisfaction. Effectiveness and success are measured in regards to the various aspects of the training process.

The model that was used to evaluate the training scenarios is based on the one proposed by Kirkpatrick (Kirkpatrick, 1959). It is one of the most widely used models for evaluating training programs. According to Kirkpatrick there are four levels (to measure the quality or effectiveness of a training course. Each level has its own use and its advantages and disadvantages. Level 1 measures the learners' reaction to the training scenario. It records their impression of the content and the training scenario. It's the most primitive and widely used method of evaluation. Level 2 measures learning that has occurred. It records the knowledge elements the trainees believe they obtained from the content and training scenarios. Level 2 evaluation techniques are most reliable when pre- and post- evaluations are utilized.

Level 3 measures changes in behaviour on the job as a result of the training program. Level 3 records their personal opinion regarding their capability of using the knowledge they obtained to their regular business functions. It fulfils the managers' need to show concrete evidence that training is achieving its goals of changing behaviour on the job. It is difficult to run. The most commonly used tool is a follow-up questionnaire after training class has occurred. Level 4 measures the results of the training program as it affects the company's bottom line. Level 1 involves the trainee groups who will participate to the pilot phase. Level 2 involves the trainees and the tutors/ instructors.

Pilot sessions' evaluation includes pre-training evaluation, process evaluation and post training (outcome) evaluation. This means that data collection concerns the implementation of the pilot sessions as well as the results of the training process to the trainees which came out of a comparative approach (pre and post training situation).

Pilot sessions were implemented according to training scenario applied for each country. User partners are responsible for the organization of pilot sessions in their countries. They set up testing sample groups of users and were responsible for the implementation of the training scenario.

Based on the above, pilot evaluation includes as participating stakeholders the tutors and the trainees-users. The trainees filled questionnaires before and after the training sessions, while the tutors filled only one questionnaire after the training sessions. The questionnaires evaluate the training sessions according to the following main dimensions: 1)content, 2)form, 3)technical, 4)suitability to user learning needs, 5)diversity and 6)stakeholders representation / User requirements.

4.2 Observatory Evaluation

One of the deliverables of the Rural-eGov project is to design and develop a web-based observatory, which includes a collection and categorization of e-government services that can support SMEs from rural areas (termed as the Rural-eGov Observatory). Trough the Rural e-Gov Observatory, rural SMEs are able to access the digital training content and the collection of useful e-government services.

The evaluation of the Rural-eGov Observatory aims to provide feedback to the development team about the overall perception of the users about the quality of the Observatory, as well as the services and resources that they prefer. In this direction, two evaluation activities will take place: (a) a user-based evaluation of the Observatory using an online questionnaire; and (b) a log files analysis of the Observatory using the log files of the server and an appropriate log file analyzer.

The Rural-eGov Observatory evaluation effort is focused on three dimensions, Usability, Information Quality and Interaction Quality. The questionnaire to be used by Students, Instructors and Observatory Users for the online evaluation is based on the WebQual questionnaire (http://www.webqual.co.uk/index.htm). It is based on Version 4.0 of the questionnaire, which has been used in several evaluation studies of web sites and portals (http://www.webqual.co.uk/papers.htm). In addition, the WebTrends analyzer is expected to be used (http://www.webtrends.com/) for the analysis of the Observatory's server log files.

5   Evaluation Results

During the formative evaluation phase the project partners' experts evaluated the national training scenarios/content. Apart from some minor suggestions, the project experts agreed that the training scenarios were suitable to the user learning needs identified in a previous phase of the project and that their diversity was sufficient. All the experts strongly agreed that the training scenarios correspond to realistic business activities. The evaluation of the training content presented a similar success in the development procedure. The content quality was rated good and after the implementation of the suggested changes/additions, the quality was rated as very good. The alignment with the learning goal was very good and so was the reusability of the content. The motivation and the presentation design were rated as good and some changes were necessary.

The summative phase's pilot training sessions were conducted in the project partners' countries using the national training content developed for each country. The German training session had 18 participants with an average age of 32,5, the Greek 11 participants with an average age of 39, the Polish 18 participants with an average age of 37, the Slovenian 16 participants with an average age of 37 and the Welsh 10 participants with an average age of 52. Most of the participants of the German, Greek and Welsh pilot training sessions were farmers, while most of the participants of the Polish and the Slovenian pilot training sessions were involved in the Business and Commerce sector.

Almost 90% of the participants from all five countries knew some e-government services at a national level but only 55% had used them before. Almost 60% of the participants who used e-government services found them neither easy or difficult, while most of the rest 40% found them fairly easy to use. Most of the participants stated that before attending to the training sessions their level of experience in using e-government services was good or fair, while after attending to the training seminar their level of experience increased to very good or good.

Regarding the training content and its form all the trainees stated that the training session's objectives were clear to them and that the training session included useful instructional material. They also stated that this material was directly linked to topics' learning goals/objectives. All the trainees found the training session's material well organized. Regarding their technical suitability of the training sessions, almost all of the trainees agreed that the activities/training material stimulated their learning and that they were interested in more interactive material/ lessons, instead of traditional training methods. This vindicates on of the main goals of the Rural-eGov project, to develop interactive training scenarios/content. Almost everyone found the training session to be a success and that the training session/ material was responsive to their learning needs. Most of them requested even more interactive and hands-on training regarding the pc and internet access.

The majority of the trainees found the training scenarios content diverse enough.. The also stated their need for more training. While the duration of the training was enough, they requested more training. One four hour training session is not enough to cover their needs. It should be noted that the more interactive and training session is, the more time it needs to cover the same topics. Regarding the stakeholders represen-tation/ user requirements dimension, almost every trainee stated that the e-government services presented during training proved useful for the daily business operations of his SME and that the training session/ material was responsive to his learning needs.

The tutors' evaluation of the training sessions agrees with the trainees' evaluation. They agree that there is a need for more interactive training sessions/ material an more training sessions to coven the SMEs needs. They think that there should be follow up online interactive activities involving the tutor and the trainees, to assist the trainees to get accustomed to the e-government services use.

6 Conclusions

This paper analyses the methodology and the plan for the evaluation of the Rural-eGov project. Evaluation is considered an integral part of the project that focuses on its development and result. It aims at monitoring the project's development, at assess-ing its effectiveness and at contributing to the continuous improvement of its quality. At the same time it aims at assessing its overall outcome and impact as well as its strengths and weaknesses in relation to opportunities and threats. Thus, evaluation focuses on the project's overall development, on educational/ training methodology development and implementation. The overall development of the project is evaluated while it is implemented, but also at the end of the project, using various dimensions, performance criteria and evaluation questions.

The methodology presented in this paper includes formative and summative evaluation, the latter including pilot test. Formative Evaluation monitors the project's implementation and assures timely feedback and coordination in meeting the overall project objectives. The Pilot Test evaluates the integrated methodology to a target audience during and after the pilot application. Summative Evaluation focuses on the project's outcome objectives and of its success in attaining its expectations for participants

The evaluation methodology uses a mixed method approach that combines quantitative and qualitative elements. This approach supports better the objectives of the evaluation as it allows evaluation of both technical performance and human attitudes and increases the validity and reliability of evaluation data.

The results of the evaluation show that the project assumptions regarding the user needs of the rural SMEs are correct and indicate that the project is reaching its goals. There is indeed a need for more interactive and hands on training and the training scenarios seem to be adequate to cover this need. The evaluation procedure will continue with the evaluation of the online follow up sessions and the observatory. After the last phase is complete, then we will have the final results to support the findings of the project.

References

Bradbeer, J.: Evaluation, FDTL Technical Report no. 8, University of Portsmouth (1999)

Breen, R., Jenkins, A., Lindsay, R., Smith, P.: Insights Through Triangulation: Combining Research Methods to Enhance the Evaluation of IT Based Learning Methods. In: Oliver, M. (ed.) Innovation in the Evaluation of Learning Technology, pp. 151–168. University of North London Press, London (1998)

European Commission, COMMISSION RECOMMENDATION of 6 May 2003 concerning the definition of micro, small and medium-sized enterprises. Date Issued May 20,2003 (2003), http://europa.eu/
eur-lex/pri/en/oj/dat/2003/l_124/l_12420030520en00360041.pdf

Jones, A., Scanlon, E., Tosunoglu, C., Ross, S., Butcher, P., Murphy, P., Greenberg, J.: Evaluating CAL at the Open University: 15 Years On. Computers in Education 26(1-3), 5–15 (1996)

Kirkpatrick, D.L.: Techniques for Evaluating Training Programs - Part 2: Learning. Journal of the American Society of Training Directors, 21–26 (1959)

Mandinach, E.B.: The Development of Effective Evaluation Methods for E-Learning: A Concept Paper and Action Plan. Teachers College Record 107(8), 1814–1835 (2005)

Nesbit, J.C., Belfer, K., Leacock, T.: Learning Object Review Instrument (LORI). E-Learning Research and Assessment Network (2003), http://www.elera.net/eLera/Home/Articles/LORI%201.5.pdf

OECD, Creating Rural Indicators for Shaping Territorial Policy(Paris: OECD) (1994)

Oliver, M.: An introduction to the Evaluation of Learning Technology. Educational Technology & Society 3(4) (2000) ISSN 1436–4522

Oliver, M., Conole, G.: The Evaluation of Learning Technology – an overview. In: Oliver, M. (ed.) Innovation in the Evaluation of Learning Technology, pp. 5–22. University of North London Press, London (1998)

Scriven, M.: Beyond Formative and Summative Evaluation. In: McLaughlin, M.W., Phillips, E.C. (eds.) Evaluation and Education: A Quarter Century. University of Chicago Press, Chicago (1991)

USINACTS, Deliverable 7: ACTS Usability Evaluation Guideline, European Commission Brussels, 20-24 (1999)

Web Sources

http://www.michigan.gov (2002) "A Focus on Evaluation: A Stakeholder Evaluation Handbook",
    Library of Michigan.
http://www.open-knowledge-society.org/journals/learn.htm

A Practical Approach to a Semantic-Based eGovernment Platform: The PLEDGE project

Luis Álvarez Sabucedo, Luis Anido Rifón, and Ruben Míguez Pérez

Telematics Engineering Department, Universidade de Vigo, Spain
{Luis.Sabucedo,Luis.Anido,Ruben.Miguez}@det.uvigo.es

Abstract. In the current state of art for eGovernment solutions, there are several proposals that address the provision of services for citizens. This paper presents a citizen centered approach that takes advantage of current semantic technologies available. This approach is implemented in the so-called PLEDGE (Platform for LifeEvent Development in eGovernment Environments) project. In the frame of the former, the provision of an interoperable support for services from different public administrations is tackled. Semantic-based mechanism for the discovery, orchestration and composition of services from independent public administrations is described. To make that possible, it was required to make use of several semantic technologies. At last, some conclusions are presented.

1 Introduction

From the huge quantity and quality of new services in the domain, it is clear that eGovernment is becoming more and more popular. Information and Communication Technologies (ICTs) are providing a complete new support to deliver services to citizen in the scope of Public Administrations. The eGovernment domain is a promising eTechnology with a lot of future. It seems important to bear in mind that eGovernment is not solely a simple replacement of technology to provide a 24/7 service. Indeed, provision of eGovernment solutions involves a huge effort in re-engineering all processes involved in the public service to place the citizen at the center of the process. As a matter of fact, this technology forces PAs to re-orient and improve services by positioning the citizen at the center of all provided operations. These services should be, whenever possible, an end-to-end transaction in order to achieve a one-stop digital administration.

Upon the review of already developed solutions, we find out limitations in deployed eGovernment web portals and identify some concrete problems to overcome (see section 2). To deal with these ones, the PLEDGE project was developed. In particular, this project addresses problems related to the discovery and accessibility (in terms of software architecture) for services in the domain.

Bearing these concepts in mind, the use of a modeling tool called LifeEvent (LE hereafter) is proposed. This artifact models services from the point of view of the citizen in terms of their need. These LEs implies the use of Administrative Services (AS hereafter) to actually carry out services. The main goal of this

M.D. Lytras et al. (Eds.): WSKS 2008, CCIS 19, pp. 678–683, 2008.

proposal is to support in an simple manner from the point of view of the citizen searches and invocations on domain services, as shown on section 3.

In order to increase the possibilities of the system regarding automatization and interoperability issues, semantics is bring into scene. Nowadays, among the scientific community, semantics is usually considered the enabler technology to develop this sort of solutions. This technology offers us a new set of tools and capacities which have not been completely explored yet (see section 4). Therefore, its application to LEs and ASs lead us to the development of the PLEDGE project (see section 5). Finally, some conclusions are presented to the reader in section 6.

2   Analysis of the Problem and Motivation

A common feature in most solutions is the use of the Web support to deliver contents. Acting as a front-end solution for citizen, these Web pages offer an access to services. Nevertheless, as shown below there is still a long road ahead in order to achieve the desired quality level.

The vast majority of eGovernment solutions are presented to citizens by means of Web portals. The highest functioning Web portals show a complete system integration across agencies, whereas portals with the lowest level of functionality provide little more than access to forms and static pieces of information. High-functioning portals create a true one-stop service for citizens. In particular, usability, customization, openness and transparency represent key aspects of portal functionalities. Regretfully, upon the review of web portals[1], several drawbacks can be outlined. In our case, we are going to focus on problems related to locating services. This is not a simple task. When looking for a particular service in the web site of a PA, it is not a trivial task to find the proper place where the service is held. This is due to the wide variety of classifications for services, mechanisms for its invocations, visual interfaces and even problems such as finding out beforehand if the administration is responsible for the wished service.

By means of the review of several already deployed eGovernment platforms, notable difficulties for citizens have been unveiled. Two main shortcomings are present in current-fashion solutions from the point of view of the citizen: (i) It is not a simple task to discover which is the right service for a particular situation in the life of a citizen; and (ii) Administrations have not foreseen mechanisms to orchestrate services.

3   LifeEvents to Model Services

Taking into account the above mentioned considerations, a LE-based approach is proposed to deliver advanced tools in locating services. The very first goal is to model services from the point of view of the citizen and no longer from the perspective of the PA and its internal procedures.

Therefore, LEs can be defined in the scope of this proposal as "any particular situation in the life of a citizen that must be dealt with and requires assistance, support or license from PAs". We can consider as LEs, in the frame of this proposal, situations such as paying a fine, getting married, moving, losing one's wallet, . . .

Taking the analysis of the domain, already existing tools and the first evolution of the developed prototype as a basis, we are in a position to identify some relevant fields in the definition of LE: Task, Description, Input documents, Output documents, Scope, Area, Security Conditions, and Version among others.

Note that no PA is attached to a LE as the latter may involve several PAs and the citizen may not be aware of this situation.

If we take the definition of LE as a basis, a single LE can –and normally does– involve different operations in different administrations. For our proposal it is quite important to model these situations also. As already mentioned, LEs just model the need but for an eventual invocation, it is necessary to know which administrative services are required to really have a service. In order to model those interactions, another accessory artifact is introduced in the system: the Administrative Services. PAs can, and normally do, provide support to perform simple operations held directly by them. These operations may involve a more or less complex back-office mechanism but, in any case, they are invoked and fulfilled in a certain PA. Therefore, the fulfillment of a LE could involve several ASs in different PAs. ASs include the following information: Title, Description, Deadline, Public Administration, Law, Input and Output documents, Internal operations, and Related ASs among others.

4   Semantics in Use

The main goal of semantics is to make machines capable of understanding the information within the web. This feature will allow them to make more complex interactions without the need of human support. To accomplish this ambitious goal, a long evolution on the technological side has taken place during these last years. In this context, ontologies are a key element. By means of the former, we are addressing an ontology as a support to present abstract information about a certain domain in a concrete way by means of a machine-understandable data format.

To express an ontology in a formal manner, different languages[2] are at our disposal. OWL (Ontology Web Language)[3] is the W3C Recommendation intended to provide a fully functional way to express ontologies. Therefore, that is the option chosen for this platform.

The resulting ontology includes the definition of all the meaningful data in the system. Therefore, this ontology must be known and shared by all agents in the system. It is mainly made of some basic classes that characterize the system:

– Citizens. As the system final users, they are expected to be able to invoke all services available and interact with information in the system.

- Documents. They provide the legal support for all operations in the system. Security concerns must be deployed in their management, since they compel agents to respect the contents of the documents.
- LifeEvents. These elements model the need of citizens and they are the drivers towards the service completion provided by the Digital Lawyers. Certainly, their definition includes already mentioned fields.
- AdministrativeServices. This class holds the properties to express all the knowledge about ASs as they are defined in previous sections.

5   PLEDGE in Use

To deal with the fulfillment of services wihtin this framework, several agents with particular roles were identified. As show on Fig. 1, these agents are: citizen, the main character in the system; BPS, the Blue Page Server is responsible for locating services; PA, the Public Administrations (PAs) are responsible for executing ASs/LEs; and the cPortfolio. The latter is a sort of portfolio that is in charge for managing the citizen's documents.

As middleware technology, the use of Web Services was the chosen option. Taking advantage of the presented artifacts and the semantic support available, it is possible to provide support for advanced searching services. Taking into account the profile of the citizen, i.e., areas assigned, documents owned or desired, current location, and so on, it is possible to personalize the possible LEs the citizen may be interested at. Also, it is possible to discover which are the best ASs that may be invoked to fulfill a particular LE.

There are several high-level functions defined to support these: searchLEby-InputDocument, searchLEbyArea, searchASbyOutputDocument, . . . These functions deal with the task of locating those LEs/ASs that fit on the citizen's needs. These are implemented by mean of SPARQL[4] queries using Jena[5]. This library was the chosen option due to the large community of programmers currently working on its development and the support for required semantic operations such as executing queries or merging new instances.

These searches will be conducted on a shared pool where LEs and ASs from different PAs will be included. Of course, all of them will be described by means of the proposed ontology. This would allow the federation of contents from several PAs making possible the access to different services from a single service point. These features will be implemented by high-level functions such as ManageLE or ManageAS.

It is important to bear in mind that these searches will be conducted on a shared pool where LEs and ASs from different PAs will be included. Of course, all of them will be described by means of the proposed ontology. Once the citizen is aware of the proper LE to fulfill its needs, he/she needs to invoke it. This operation requires several steps:

1. Discover the information required to actually invoke the Web Service that implements the wished LE. This information is provided by means of a SAWSDL[6] file. This W3C technology uses semantic annotations on WSDL

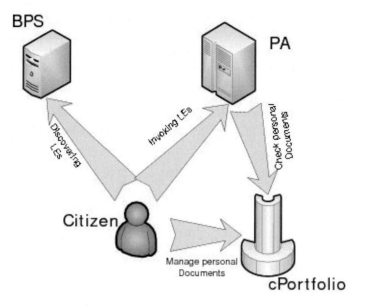

Fig. 1. Components of the system

files. Within this project, this feature is used to inform about the required data fields to invoke the service. The user must download this file as it referred in a particular property on the ontology for LEs/ASs.

2. Find out the data required to compose the call. This data is included in the above mentioned SAWSDL file. This information is gathered by the system using the support of the SAWSDL4J[7] library.
3. Make the final call to the Web Service. As the information to invoke the service is already available at the client, this one must compose the invocation using an API to actually call the Web Service, JWSD[8] in our case.
4. Track the operation. As response to this invocation, the PA (the agent that implements the AS) returns a code that allow the citizen to track the operation during its entire lifecycle.

All these operation are undertaken in a complete automatic manner by the developed system. Of course, further details about the conformance to local or national laws regarding documentation and legal procedures are not considered at this point and further implementations of the system should take care of them.

6   Conclusions

The main goal of this paper is the introduction of an ontology-based support to facilitate tasks related to services locating. These features implemented in the PLEDGE project. The use of LEs and ASs brought us several advances: services are defined in a more user-friendly manner, a uniform mechanism to characterize them is available, and their localization becomes easier as the semantic annotation provides new tools. In the literature, we can also find some interesting initiatives that make use, at different levels, of semantics applied to LE-based concepts in some manner: the Finnish Web site Suomi.fi[9], the EIP.AT project[10], the SemanticGov project[11], and the Access-eGov project[12].

Regarding these projects, the presented proposal goes a step further and suggests features not provided in these platforms such as the provision of a LEs pool from different PAs, semantic mechanisms to discover the proper LE, a new and flexible mechanism to compose new services from already existing operations, etc.

The provision of this platform has further implications than the technical ones. As a result of this project, as well as many others, citizen will enjoy a better service from their agencies. This enhancement on the quality of services is not just referred to a greater availability or the interoperability among different PAs but also to transparency in procedures, easier access to services, improvements in the level of democracy, etcetera.

Acknowledgment

This work has been funded by the Ministerio de Educación y Ciencia through the project (TIN2007-68125-C02-02) and Xunta de Galicia, Consellería de Innovación e Industria, project (PGIDIT06PXIB322285PR).

References

1. Papadomichelaki, X., Magoutas, B., Halaris, C., Apostolou, D., Mentzas, G.: A review of quality dimensions in e-government services (2007)
2. Gómez-Pérez, A., Fernández-López, M., Corcho, O.: Ontological Engineering. Springer, Heidelberg (2003)
3. W3C: Web ontology language (2004), http://www.w3.org/2004/OWL/
4. W3C: SPARQL Query Language for RDF (2006),
   http://www.w3.org/TR/rdf-sparql-query/
5. Hewlett-Packard: Jena (2005), http://www.hpl.hp.com/semweb/
6. Semantic Annotations for WSDL and XML Schema (2007),
   http://www.w3.org/TR/sawsdl/
7. Gomadam, K., Brewer, D., Wu, Z., Ranabahu, A.: SAWSDL4J Home (2008),
   http://knoesis.wright.edu/opensource/sawsdl4j/
8. SUN: Java Web Service Download (2008),
   http://java.sun.com/webservices/downloads/previous/index.jsp
9. SW-Suomi.fi - Semanttinen informaatioportaali (2007),
   http://www.museosuomi.fi/suomifi
10. EIP.AT (2006), http://eip.at
11. The SemanticGov Project (2006), http://www.semantic-gov.org
12. Access-eGov (2006), http://www.accessegov.org/

Pilot Evaluation of an Online Observatory of Agricultural Electronic Markets

Nikos Manouselis[1,2] and Constantina Costopoulou[1]

[1] Greek Research & Technology Network (GRNET) S.A.,
56 Mesogion Av., 115 27, Athens, Greece
nikosm@ieee.org
[2] Informatics Laboratory, Div. of Informatics, Mathematics & Statistics, Dept. of Science,
Agricultural University of Athens, 75 Iera Odos Str., 11855, Athens, Greece
tina@aua.gr

Abstract. The growing number of electronic markets (e-markets) that offer agricultural products and supplies and that are currently operating online, may create confusion to a typical Internet user that is searching for interesting e-markets online. To overcome this information overload, appropriate Internet-based services can be introduced. To this direction, this paper presents the development and pilot evaluation of an online observatory of Greek agricultural e-markets. This observatory aims to help users that search for agricultural e-markets online, according to characteristics such as their products, their services, or their geographical coverage.

Keywords: E-markets, agriculture, evaluation.

1 Introduction

Electronic markets (e-markets), which are also referred to as e-marketplaces or electronic trade systems [2], can be defined as information systems that intend to provide their users with online services that will facilitate information exchange for commercial transactions. E-markets are characterized by the very low-cost flow of information between market participants (e.g. producers and consumers), and they have been long expected to create economic value for buyers, sellers, market intermediaries, and for society as a whole [3]. In the agricultural sector, a plethora of e-markets have already started their operation [5]. These e-markets mainly provide products, supplies and services to the stakeholders of the agricultural sector and can be generally termed as agricultural e-markets.

Agricultural e-markets can be distinguished in three major categories [5]: (a) e-markets for the outputs of farms, which are usually operated by producers or retailers, and which sell agricultural products to consumers; (b) e-markets for the production factors and inputs of farms, which are usually operated by agribusinesses and sell products (e.g. machinery parts, seed, chemicals) to the producers; and (c) e-markets of services by third parties, which offer specialised support services to producers such as logistic, transport, banking, insurance and legal services. It is important to note that agricultural e-markets demonstrate different degrees of e-commerce adoption. For

M.D. Lytras et al. (Eds.): WSKS 2008, CCIS 19, pp. 684–693, 2008.

instance, there are e-markets that provide only product catalogue information, e-markets that also provide transaction settlement, and more sophisticated e-markets that support online negotiations as well.

However, from the online user's perspective (being it a consumer interested in agricultural products or a producer looking for farm supplies), tasks such as searching, locating, comparing and selecting an appropriate agricultural e-market can be difficult and time-consuming. The large amount of information from the variety of existing agricultural e-markets, as well as the complicated transactions offered by advanced e-markets, can become complex for a typical Internet user. To overcome such problems, Internet-based services may be introduced to help users find agricultural e-markets according to their specific needs and preferences. In this direction, this paper introduces an online observatory of agricultural e-markets, called the AgreMaM (Agricultural e-Markets Metadata) observatory.

2   AgreMaM Development

Software development involves a number of steps to be carried out, so that a software system is properly modelled, analysed, designed, specified and implemented. The Rational Unified Process (RUP) has been followed [1] to design and develop the prototype version of AgreMaM. RUP is an iterative software development process that is especially well suited to UML (http://www.uml.org), which is the de-facto software industry standard modelling language for visualizing, specifying, constructing and documenting the elements of systems in general, and software systems in particular. RUP is especially well suited to UML. It development starts with four process workflows (business modelling, requirements or system use case modelling, analysis and design, and implementation) that adopt the various UML views, and continues with five more process workflows (test, deployment, configuration management, project management and environment).

In previous work [7], we have presented the first four process workflows for AgreMaM. In this paper, we take the next step, by presenting the pilot testing (evaluation) of the system. The scope of building a Web-based access point (namely, an observatory) of agricultural e-markets is to provide an online environment that allows users to search, locate and select appropriate e-markets with agricultural products and supplies. The proposed AgreMaM observatory allows for searching of e-markets characteristics, as they are stored in the elements of a metadata model that is called Dublin Core for e-Markets (DC-EM) [4]. It is built upon a database of metadata descriptions, termed as a metadata repository. This section provides an overview of the RUP workflows that led to the implementation of the AgreMaM Observatory

Business modelling concentrates on the business activities that will be generally supported by the system (referred to here as the AgreMaM business), while the rest of process workflows focus on the system that will be built. It concerns the identification of business actors (anyone or anything that is external to the AgreMaM business but interacts with it), business workers (roles within the AgreMaM business), and business use cases (a group of related workflows within the AgreMaM business that provide value to the business actors). A Business Use Case Diagram illustrates business use cases, business actors, and business workers for business activities, as well as the interactions between them. Activity Diagrams can also be used to model the workflow through a particular business use case.

The AgreMaM business is the observatory that aims to facilitate online users when searching for agricultural e-markets that match their needs. We have identified two main business actors that will take advantage of the AgreMaM business, which are the following:

- *Consumer*, who is interested in finding agricultural e-markets to buy products or services (including all types of agricultural stakeholders that will perform as consumers/buyers).
- *Producer*, who is interested in finding agricultural e-markets to sell products or services, as well as making available his own e-market through AgreMaM (including all types of agricultural stakeholders that will perform as producers/sellers).

For simplicity reasons, we can accept that these two roles are interested in buying or selling products and/or services, they can be both considered as Customers of AgreMaM (Fig. 1). Furthermore, the business workers of AgreMaM are the following:

- *E-market researcher*, who is an actor internally concerned with searching, locating, and describing e-markets for AgreMaM.
- *Quality inspector*, who is an actor internally concerned with reviewing and approving the publication and modification of services (e.g. users' registration) and content (e.g. description of e-markets) in AgreMaM.

Figure 1 presents the Business Use Case Diagram for AgreMaM. The workflow of each business use case can be furthermore analyzed using Activity Diagrams.

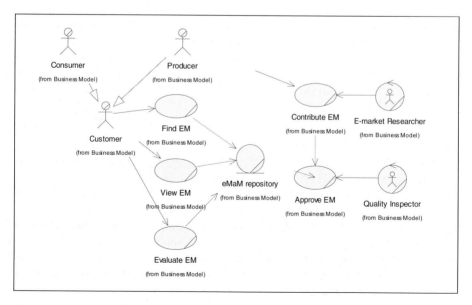

Fig. 1. Business Use Case Diagram for AgreMaM

Use cases and actors define the scope of the system built (Boggs & Boggs, 2002). Use cases include anything that is inside the system. Actors include anything that is external, interacting with the system. Reconsidering the AgreMaM business actors, we identified the following AgreMaM actors, from the system's perspective:

- *Customer*, a consumer or producer (referring to agricultural professionals or enterprises) that uses AgreMaM to find an appropriate e-market.
- *Author*, a producer describing his own e-market or an AgreMaM e-market researcher.
- *Reviewer*, the quality inspector responsible for approving the publication or modification of e-market descriptions in the repository of AgreMaM.
- *System administrator*, the quality inspector responsible for the proper functioning of the AgreMaM system and for the creation/approval of user registrations in AgreMaM.

The above actors are engaged in a number of AgreMaM system use cases, which are:

- *Make User Profile*, concerns submitting a registration request to the AgreMaM system so that a user profile is created.
- *Approve User Profile*, concerns checking and approving (or not) a user registration request.
- *Login*, concerns the logging into AgreMaM. It aims to allow only registered users to perform certain operations in the system.
- *Contribute EM*, concerns the description of an e-market according to the DC-EM model, and the submission of this description to AgreMaM for publication.
- *Approve EM*, concerns checking and approval (or not) of a submitted description of an e-market.
- *Modify EM*, concerns the modification of some elements of an e-market description and the submission of the modifications to AgreMaM for publication.
- *Evaluate EM*, concerns the submission of an evaluation (assessment of users' satisfaction) of an e-market whose description is in AgreMaM.
- *Delete EM*, concerns the request for deletion of an e-market description from AgreMaM.
- *Approve EM Modification*, concerns checking and approval (or not) of a modification or deletion of an e-market description.
- *Simple Search*, concerns the initiation of a simple keyword-based search for e-markets in AgreMaM and viewing a list of matching results
- *Advanced Search*, concerns the initiation of a search of combined keywords and viewing results.
- *Browse*, concerns browsing descriptions according to e-market characteristics and viewing results.
- *Recommend*, concerns the request for a recommendation of an appropriate e-market description, according to the stored e-market evaluations, and viewing a list of recommended results.
- *View EM*, concerns viewing the description and characteristics of an e-market as stored in AgreMaM's metadata repository.

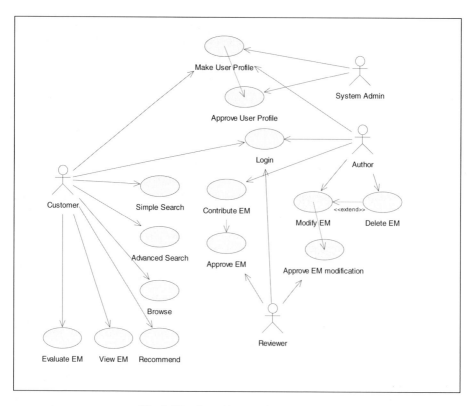

Fig. 2. Use Case Diagram for AgreMaM

Figure 2 illustrates the AgreMaM Use Case Diagram that provides an overview of the identified actors and use cases, as well as the associations between them.

In the AgreMaM system, use cases are supported by a set of corresponding sub-systems. The following AgreMaM sub-systems have been identified:

- *Interface sub-system*, responsible for the interaction with the users, passing information to and from the users to AgreMaM.
- *Search sub-system*, responsible for transforming user search interactions to queries that are understandable from AgreMaM, as well as for returning the results to the interface sub-system.
- *Repository sub-system*, responsible for storing the descriptions of e-markets, providing data to the AgreMaM interface according to the users' requests.

During the AgreMaM analysis, the interactions between the involved actors and the AgreMaM sub-systems are illustrated using a variety of other UML diagrams, such as Sequence Diagrams. This analysis is not presented in this paper due to space restrictions. The final result of the AgreMaM design is the Deployment Diagram. A Deployment Diagram is concerned with the physical deployment of the system, including issues such as the network layout and the location of components in the network. It illustrates all nodes of the system network, the connections between them, and the processes that will run on each one. Figure 3 presents the AgrMaM Diagram.

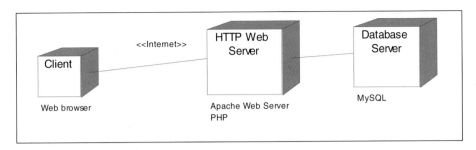

Fig. 3. Deployment Diagram for AgreMaM

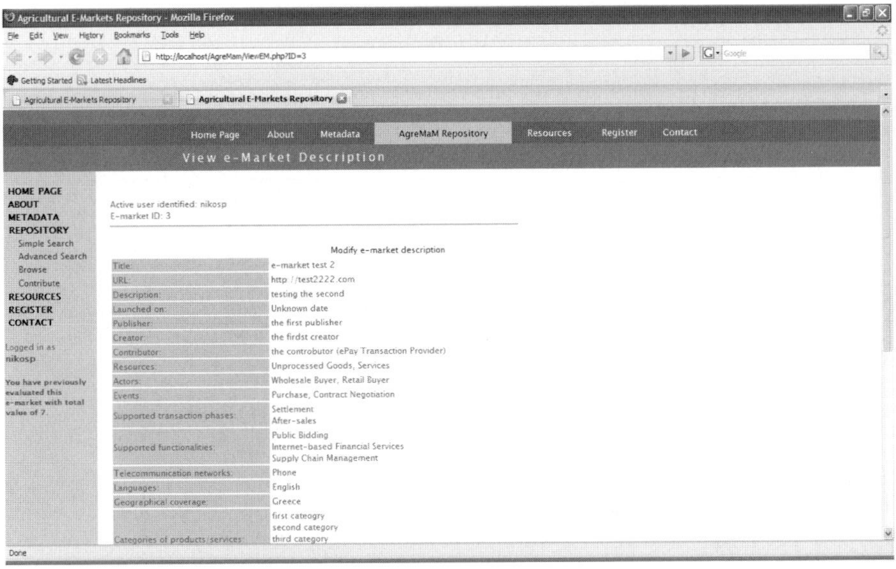

Fig. 4. Deployment Diagram for AgreMaM

The implementation process workflow has led to the deployment of the first version of the system. More specifically, the first public version of AgreMaM has been made available at: http://agremam.aua.gr/. Figure 4 presents a characteristic screenshot of the AgreMaM system: the interface for viewing an e-market description.

4   Pilot Evaluation

The first version of AgreMam has been made public since April 2007, and more than 200 Greek agricultural e-markets have been described and stored in its repository. In the context of the Computer Courses of the Agricultural University of Athens (http://infolab-dev.aua.gr), AgreMaM has been used during several Internet lab lectures to illustrate to young agricultural students the way new technologies can be used to promote agricultural products and supplies through e-markets. In this light, a pilot

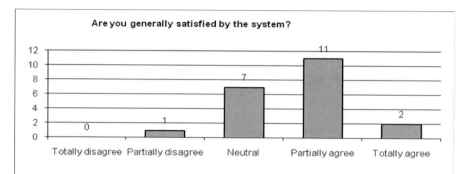

Fig. 5. Overall satisfaction from AgreMaM

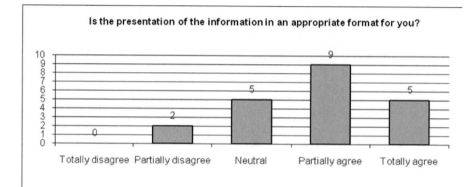

Fig. 6. Presentation of information in AgreMaM

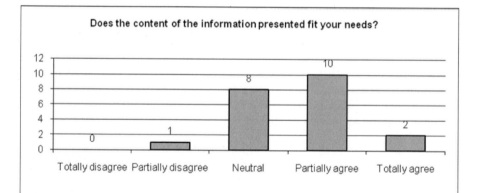

Fig. 7. Content of information in AgreMaM fitting user needs.

evaluation trial has also taken place with a selected group of agricultural students, inorder to collect useful feedback regarding the design and operation of the system, as well as of the information it stores about e-markets.

The evaluation trial was organized during December 2007, with a selection of users that were attending the lab lectures of the course "Introduction to Computers" for the 1st-year students of the Agricultural University of Athens. In total, twenty one people (n=21) have used the AgreMaM Observatory for about two hours, trying its functionalities and browsing through information about Greek e-markets. After the end of this period, the participants have been asked to complete a short questionnaire assessing their satisfaction from various system dimensions. The questionnaire questions and the collected results are presented in the following paragraphs.

The first question concerned the overall satisfaction of the participants from the AgreMaM system. As it is depicted in Figure 5, most of the participants are generally satisfied with AgreMaM (more than 60%). But there are also several participants (about 33%) who are neutrally positioned towards it.

As far as the presentation of information is concerned (Figure 6), a large percentage of the users (about 66%) have found that it is appropriate for them. Again, several people (about 24%) where neutrally positioned, and some (less than 1%) expressed a negative opinion.

In terms of content, Figure 7 illustrates how relevant the participants found the content of the information stored in AgreMaM (i.e. the description of agricultural e-markets). More than half (about 57%) replied that they felt that this content fit their needs, whereas several (38%) did not express some particular preference.

On the other hand, the majority (71%) found that the information is presented in a simple and understandable way (Figure 8). About 23% where neutrally positioned, and one person totally disagreed with this opinion.

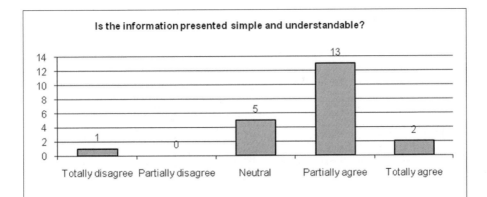

Fig. 8. Simple and understandable information in AgreMaM

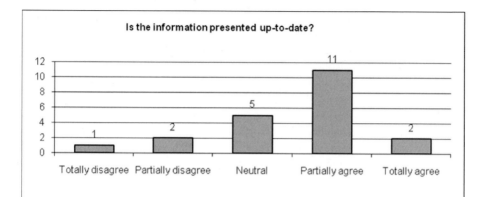

Fig. 9. Currency of information in AgreMaM

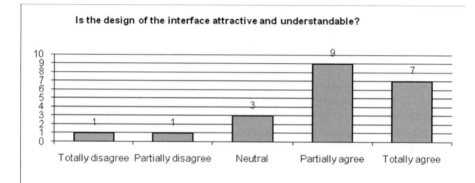

Fig. 10. AgreMaM interface attractive and understandable

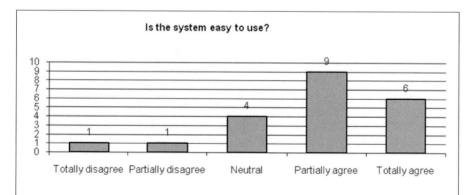

Fig. 11. AgreMaM easiness to use

Another attribute of the information about e-markets in AgreMaM that has been assessed is its currency. As Figure 9 shows, many (62%) felt that this information is up-to-date, but there where also a few respondents (about 14%) that had a more negative opinion.

In terms of interface design, most users (76%) found that it is attractive and understandable (Figure 10). Only two people (9%) disagreed totally or partially with this opinion.

Along the same line, the majority (76%) generally found the system easy to use, as Figure 11 illustrates. Again, two people (9%) disagree with this, whereas a few others (19%) are neutrally positioned.

4 Conclusions

This paper describes the development and pilot evaluation of AgreMaM, an online observatory for Greek agricultural e-markets. AgreMaM can support users who are searching for agricultural e-markets, based on characteristics such as their product types or their geographical coverage. In the paper, the analysis and design of Agre-MaM took place using the RUP software development process, based on a series of appropriate UML diagrams. The prototype version of AgreMaM has been populated with descriptions of e-markets, and an evaluation experiment with human users who have accessed and used AgreMaM in order to discover agricultural e-markets took place.

References

1. Boggs, W., Boggs, M.: Mastering UML with Rational Rose. SYBEX Inc. (2002)
2. Fritz, M., Hausen, T., Schiefer, G.: Electronic Trade Platforms in US and European Agri-Food Markets: An Analysis of Development and Development Directions. In: Schmitz, T.G., et al. (eds.) E-Commerce in Agribusiness. Florida, Longboat Key (2005)
3. Grieger, M.: Electronic Marketplaces: A Literature Review and a Call for Supply Chain Management Research. European Journal of Operational Research 144, 280–294 (2003)
4. Manouselis, N., Costopoulou, C.: A Metadata Model for E-Markets. International Journal of Metadata, Semantics & Ontologies 1 (2006)
5. Manouselis, N., Costopoulou, C., Patrikakis, C., Sideridis, A.: Using metadata to bring consumers closer to agricultural e-markets. In: EFITA/WCCA Joint Congress on IT in Agriculture, Villa Real, Portugal (2005)
6. Manouselis, N., Costopoulou, C.: Deploying an Observatory of Agricultural e-Markets. In: EFITA/WCCA 2007 Conference on Environmental and rural sustainability through ICT, Glaskow, UK (2007)

On Linking Cultural Spaces and e-Tourism: An Ontology-Based Approach

Elena García-Barriocanal and Miguel-Angel Sicilia

Information Engineering Research Unit
Computer Science Dept., University of Alcalá
Ctra. Barcelona km. 33.6 – 28871 Alcalá de Henares (Madrid), Spain
{elena.garciab,msicilia}@uah.es

Abstract. Cultural tourism is linked to the art, social practices or particularities of concrete geographical areas. Cultural tourism offerings require thus considering both the cultural aspects but also a variety of operational constraints mainly related to the availability of services for the tourist. The design of this kind of offerings or the provision to users with tools to personalize them can be supported by computer tools equipped with the required knowledge representation. Ontologies representing cultural spaces can be used for that purpose. This paper describes a partial ontological model for cultural spaces and the approach to link that model to services useful for devising touristic offerings. It also reports on a prototype for recommending short itineraries in the centre of the city of Alcalá de Henares.

Keywords: Cultural tourism, ontologies, Semantic Web, tourism, art and architecture, service ontology.

1 Introduction

Cultural tourism is a kind of tourism concerned with a country or region's culture. It usually focuses on concrete geographical areas of special interest or on communities who have diverse customs, unique forms of art and distinct social practices, which distinguish them from other types/forms of culture. Cultural tourism includes tourism in urban areas, but also tourism in rural areas showcasing the traditions of indigenous cultural communities and their differentiating values and lifestyle. The localization of this kind of tourism lead to a concept of "cultural space" that puts boundaries to the area and/or cultural aspects addressed. The value of cultural tourism offerings is associated with the degree in which the offering fits the preferences of the visitors, and creativity is considered as a key element in the design of cultural tourism experiences (Richards and Wilson, 2006). In competing for cultural tourists, it is important for destinations to understand the cultural motivations of visitors and non-visitors (or potential visitors). Preference for cultural tourism is defined as a selection of an activity that takes place on the mosaic of places, traditions, art forms, and experiences deserving separate study (Tran and Ralston, 2006). The inherent complexity of considering the mosaic of cultural aspects in a concrete area combines with the

M.D. Lytras et al. (Eds.): WSKS 2008, CCIS 19, pp. 694–701, 2008.

operational view on constraints, accessibility and availability of services of a various kind, including means of transport, hotels and restaurants, but also information services. Measures for the visitor-friendliness have been proposed that account for these kinds of aspects (Russo and van der Borg, 2002). Computer tools can be use for supporting preference gathering in cultural tourism. Gathering cultural preferences is challenging since it entails considering a wide number of aspects. A pragmatic approach can be that of recording a number of cultural aspects in some kind of knowledge representation and then provide tools to users that exploit them, eventually using the preferences recorded to recommend activities. Ontologies can be used as the knowledge representation formalism and they have already been applied to applications of e-tourism (Kanellopoulos and Panagopoulos, 2008). However, an ontological schema flexible enough for different aspects of cultural spaces integrated with a service view is still not available.

This paper describes a partial ontological model for cultural spaces and the approach to link that model to services. The model can be re-used and extended for any other cultural space. It also reports on a prototype for recommending short itineraries in the centre of the city of Alcalá de Henares (Spain). The rest of this paper is structured as follows. Section 2 describes the approach for the modeling of the main aspects of the ontology. The links of that ontology to services is provided in section 3. Then, section 4 reports on a prototype related to cultural objects in a concrete cultural space. Finally, conclusions and outlook are provided in Section 5.

2 Representing Cultural Spaces

Cultural spaces are determined by *tangible, material objects*. These objects are the base material for the design of the cultural tourism experiences. The representation of these material objects require representing geographical things, but also geopolitical entities or regions that are not determined solely by geography. Figure 1 depicts an excerpt of the a cultural space ontology and some instances particular to the municipality of Tineo in Asturias, Spain. In the left upper side, geographical things of some particular kinds are depicted. A significant amount of reuse in terminological structures and tools can be achieved by building KM systems on top of existing large terminological bases like OpenCyc. OpenCyc is the open source version of the Cyc Knowledge Base (Lenat, 1995). Cyc attempts to provide a comprehensive upper ontology of "commonsense" knowledge. Ontology elements prefixed by "oc_" are borrowed from OpenCyc. As an example, `Palace` is a concrete kind of building.

Schemas as the CIDOC CRM[1] can be used also for the description of these kinds of tangible objects. Geographical things can be either regions or concrete material elements, and in both cases there are of course part-of relationships describing the structure. Every geographical thing can be geocoded, e.g. by codes or geographic coordinates expressed as latitude-longitude. This can be combined with knowledge on traveling distance as that available in GPS car navigators to compute distances and times to destinations with reasonable degrees of reliability.

---

[1] http://cidoc.ics.forth.gr/

Aspects related to culture are depicted in the right upper part of Figure 1. In the example, art styles and historic figures are used as examples of the many facets that can be represented. Regarding historic figures, the `Events` in their lives are explicitly modeled, including the geographical places in which they took place. The relations from individuals to places as depicted in Figure 1 can then be inferred as it will be explained later.

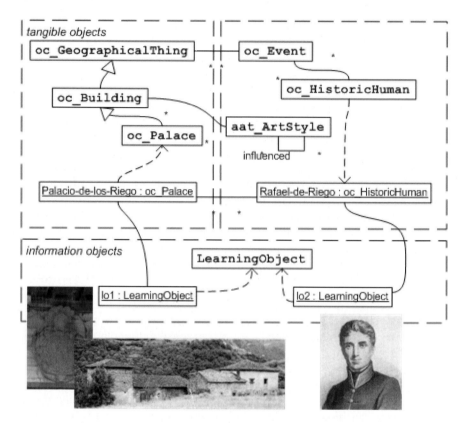

Fig. 1. Fragment of a basic ontology for cultural spaces

Regarding art styles, the basic conceptualization is borrowed from the *Art & Architecture Thesaurus* ® (AAT), an structured, controlled vocabulary that can be used to improve access to information about art, architecture, and material culture. It represents a knowledge base that includes semantic networks that show links and paths between concepts; these relationships can make retrieval more successful by themselves. It contains *terms* but no instances, and it is updated annually with the additions coming from diverse institutions. The translation of the AAT schema is straightforward, e.g. `aat_ArtStyle` represents the styles recorded in the AAT, which are related to the category of geographical things made by humans by a `hasStyle` predicate. Relations as `influenced` can be used to represent their relations. This enables a first form of preference refinement, since the relationships between styles can be used for a first selection of places to visit.

The bottom part of Figure 1 depicts the third concern of the ontology, the existence of learning or information objects that somewhat describe the elements in the other two aspects. These can be annotated following metadata standards as IEEE LOM, for which ontological versions yet exist (Sánchez-Alonso, Sicilia and Pareja, 2007). The three aspects sketched so far provide the basic model for describing a cultural space with the degree of detail or focus required, including information resources that can be used as on-line surrogates of the actual tangible objects. This enables a form of preparation and configuration of the touristic path on-line, as a pre-design for the experience.

3 Linking Cultural Spaces to e-Tourism Services

Richards and Raymond (2000) considered creative tourism as "tourism which offers visitors the opportunity to develop their creative potential through active participation in courses and learning experiences which are characteristic of the holiday destination where they are undertaken". This definition is similar to previous definitions of educational tourism, so the link to information or learning objects enables the connection of the educational and the purely touristic. Anyway, there is a need to connect the preferences expressed in the cultural space to concrete service needs. Not every cultural tourism path that comes from combining cultural preferences is feasible in practice for some users. Services are key elements in making a path possible for some users. Here we sketch the main modeling elements for such complex task. There exist various tourism ontologies and research efforts related to semantic metadata models applied to the tourism industry, collectively managed by the research community (OTA[2], IFITT[3], WTO[4] and other bodies and institutions). The e-tourism ontology[5] also provides a basic schema for accommodations, activities, events or locations, and there are other ontologies reported elsewhere (Cardoso, 2006). However, *services* are not integrated with cultural spaces in existing schemas. The EU Project OBELIX described a RDF service ontology in its deliverable D6.1. "*Service ontology specification*". That model divided the ontology in three viewpoints: service value (the customer perspective), service offering (the supplier perspective) and service process (how the service is actually performed), which has been adopted here.

The concept of `ServiceEvent` in OpenCyc represents the actual service interactions, and `ServiceProduct` the subset of those events that are done for payment. Also, `ServiceEstablishment` represents restaurants and other typical facilities in tourism. However we are interested in a detailed representation of `ServiceOfferings`, i.e. single or compound services offered that fulfill some types of needs. This way, the services can be classified by the tourist needs they address. For example, a `TransportNeed` from and to some concrete locations may be fulfilled

---

[2] OTA (open travel alliance) http://www.opentravel.org/
[3] IFIT (International Federation for IT and Travel & Tourism) http://www.ifitt.org
[4] The World Tourism Organization, http://www.world-tourism.org/
[5] http://e-tourism.deri.at/ont/

by a variety of offerings differing in price, quality and many other attributes. Two important aspects of this formulation are the following:

— Some of the attributes of service offerings, as `price` and `dura-tion` can then be used to adjust global constraints, e.g. the total price for fulfilling a set of needs should not exceed some given amount.

— Many service offerings are also geographically constrained, since they are provided in physical establishments, so the search for service offerings is driven by the geographical path to be followed.

A consequence of the above is that many different algorithms can be devised for automating the task of suggesting itineraries. For a given cultural space represented in ontological form, there is an associated collection of services, concretely those offered to tourists in that particular area. Then, an algorithm that attempts to devise a path for some preferences should take into account also the services available.

4 Case Study

The architecture of a cultural tourism itinerary generator for a geographically bounded location has been prototyped for the city of Alcalá de Henares. The center of the city is one of UNESCO's World Heritage Sites, and contains several historic buildings and places in which many events of the life of historical figures have taken place.

Fig. 2. Main user interface allowing the selection of cultural preferences

Figure 2 shows the main interface, in which the user is able to select either persons and/or architectural styles related to the city, along with a departure point for the visit under design.The architecture of the application uses the semantic learning object repository developed in the EU project LUISA[6], which uses the WSML[7] ontology language for describing the cultural space.The application provides two kinds of services: providing touristic itineraries and providing learning objects to learn more about the user's interests (in order to obtain information or prepare for a future visit, for example). In both cases users have to select the historical figures who are related to Alcalá de Henares or/and the architectural styles they would like to include in their visit or take information.In the case of taking a visit suggestion the user obtains a tourist route in which different buildings/places are involved, taken as departure point the place he or she selects. In the case that the user selects personalities exclusively, the route includes those places in which events related to selected personalities took place (rule 2 below). If the user only selects architectural styles, the route includes buildings/places of these styles or styles related to those selected, i.e. *influenced by* the selected styles or a *kind of* the selected styles (rule 1 below). If both personalities and styles are selected, then a visit which includes places related with personalities according to the selected styles is shown. WSML rules involved in this case are the following:

$$?styleA[relatedTo\ ?styleB]\ impliedBy \qquad ?styleA[aboutStyle\ ?styleB]\ or$$
$$?styeA[typeOf\ ?styleB]\ or \qquad ?styleA[influencedBy\ ?styleB] \tag{1}$$

$$?person[relatedTo\ ?monument]\ impliedBy$$
$$?event[doneBy\ ?person]\ and\ ?event[locatedAt\ ?monument] \tag{2}$$

In all cases, results are ordered by closeness to the initial place of the route and if two places are very close (distance between them is less or equal to 0.1 km.) and events related with the same personality took place in them then they are chronologically sorted. See figure 3 to take an example of the result in the case different literary Spanish personalities are selected (Cervantes, Lope de Vega, Calderon de la Barca, etc). As Cervantes birthplace and Antezana Hospital are very near, they are show in chronological order, for example.

The process can be viewed as a heuristic process of filtering and sorting that considers several aspects.The "*Learn more*" option provides the user with learning objects about the places in which events related to select personalities took place, places according to the selected styles (or related to the selected style) or places of the selected styles (or related to the selected styles) in which events related to select personalities took place. If some styles are selected, results are sorted as following (the higher the first):

1st) Learning objects about monuments that belong exactly to some of the selected styles.
2nd) Learning objects about monuments that belong to styles related with some of the selected styles.
3rd) Learning objects about monuments influenced by several selected styles.
4th) Learning objects about monuments influenced by some of selected styles.

---

[6] http://luisa.atosorigin.es/www/
[7] http://www.wsmo.org/wsml/

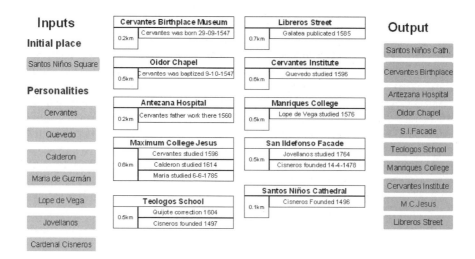

Fig. 3. Outputs for "take visit suggestions" option

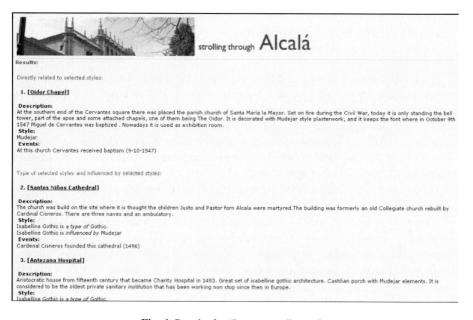

Fig. 4. Results for "Learn more" search

See figure 4 to see an example of results of learning objects about Mudejar or Gothic styles and related to Miguel de Cervantes or Cardenal Cisneros.

The algorithms described are only some straightforward options, but many other approaches can be devised, including more complex relationships or additional cultural aspects that indicate preference. Also, collaborative filtering approaches could be combined with algorithms as the above.

5 Conclusions and Outlook

The design of cultural tourism requires personalization to complex and varied preferences. Ontologies can be used for the purpose to represent geographically-bounded cultural spaces, and they can be used for the development of applications as itinerary generators or recommenders. Then, such ontologies can be combined with a model of service offerings so that the paths found to be closer to the user's preferences are constrained by the availability of the required and desired service offerings available.

The cultural aspects that may be considered in these kinds of support systems can be widely diverse and complex. Also, many different strategies and algorithms can be used to shape the recommended strategies and to compose the right mix of services for the given preferences. Both areas require extensive work and contrast before useful cultural tourism recommenders can be widespread.

Acknowledgements

This work has been supported by project LUISA (Learning Content Management System Using Innovative Semantic Web Services Architecture), code FP6–2004–IST–4 027149.

References

Cardoso, J.: Developing an OWL Ontology for E-Tourism. In: Semantic Web Services, Processes and Applications. Springer, Heidelberg (2006) ISBN:0-38730239-5

Lenat, D.: Cyc: A Large-Scale Investment in Knowledge Infrastructure. Communications of the ACM 38(11), 33–38 (1995)

Kanellopoulos, D., Panagopoulos, A.: Exploiting tourism destinations' knowledge in an RDF-based P2P network. Journal of Network and Computer Applications 31(2), 179–200 (2008)

Richards, G., Raymond, C.: Creative tourism. ATLAS news 2000(23), 16–20 (2000)

Richards, G., Wilson, J.: Developing creativity in tourist experiences: A solution to the serial reproduction of culture? Tourism Management 27(6), 1209–1223 (2006)

Russo, A., van der Borg, J.: Planning considerations for cultural tourism: a case study of four European cities. Tourism Management 23(6), 631–637 (2002)

Sánchez-Alonso, S., Sicilia, M.A., Pareja, M.: Mapping IEEE LOM to WSML: an ontology of learning objects. In: Proceedings of the ITA 2007 - 2nd International on Internet Technologies and Applications, pp. 92–101 (2007)

Tran, X., Ralston, L.: Tourist preferences influence of unconscious needs. Annals of Tourism Research 33(2), 424–441 (2006)

A Co-evolutionary Interaction Design of Digital TV Applications Based on Verbal Decision Analysis of User Experiences

Marilia Mendes, Ana Lisse Carvalho, Elizabeth Furtado, and Plácido Pinheiro

University of Fortaleza (UNIFOR), Graduate in Applied Computer Science (MIA), Av.
Washington Soares, 1321 - Fortaleza, Ce, Brazil
{marilia,ana.lisse}@edu.unifor.br, {elizabet,placido}@unifor.br

Abstract. Since mobile TV represents a new paradigm for interaction design,
many different candidate solutions of interaction can be possible. Following this
concept, a study was accomplished under the objective of finding a better interaction solution for an application of mobile TV. Three executable applications
of mobile TV prototypes were built. A Verbal Decision Analysis model was
applied on the investigations for the favorite characteristics in each prototype
based on the user's experience and their intentions of use. This model led a performance of a qualitative analysis which objectified the design of a new
prototype.

1 Introduction

In domains (as digital TV, smart home, and tangible interfaces) that represent a new
paradigm of interactivity, is challenging to decide which the most appropriate interaction design solution is. HCI researchers have promoted in their works the validation
of the design to the alternative solutions with users before producing the final result.
Taking into account the users preferences is an action that has also gained ground in
these works when designers are analyzing the better fitting solution(s).

Recent research reveals that the understanding of subjective user satisfaction is an
efficient parameter for evaluating interface [1]. In domain of interaction design for
digital TV, we claim that it is necessary to consider digital contents for supporting a
holistic evaluation (content and user interface) of the TV applications that show a
content through their user interfaces as soon as to provide users with interactive experiences of using all the possibilities of this integrated system.

In user interface projects it is very important to consider the users´ opinion of the
future system. Participants of a project must accomplish changes in functionalities
from users' contributions for improving the final version of the system. However, the
traditional processes of evaluation are quite strict and not flexible to the emergence of
new project alternatives and new ways of considering these alternatives. For example,
it is typical to find the following scenario: designers evaluate two or three interface
solutions applying usability tests, and choose one to implement. At traditional means,
usability tests are applied to all alternatives. This work goes beyond the evaluation of

M.D. Lytras et al. (Eds.): WSKS 2008, CCIS 19, pp. 702–711, 2008.
© Springer-Verlag Berlin Heidelberg 2008

this traditional view, by allowing designers to focus on only some criteria of the presented alternatives and by giving them the possibility to think about a new option.

In our approach, the evaluation process is conducted in three steps: first, the designers project high fidelity prototypes with characteristics that want to assess; second, designers carry out the usability tests and analyze the interaction users-TV content shown through each alternative of user's interfaces under the light of user's experience criteria (as users´ preference, their familiarity with technology) and; third, they organize their subjective questions by applying verbal decision analysis and in order to define the best characteristics selected by the users during the test process. As a result of this procedure a new alternative of Prototype for Mobile Television Applications can be produced.

We have chosen to apply the Verbal Decision Analysis strategy on the purpose of organizing the usability tests results with sophisticated interactive applications. The reason was that applying to problems which have qualitative nature and difficulty to be formalized, called unstructured [2], may help designers to understand and organize their subjective questions.

The main challenge of this paper is to demonstrate the odds of the construction of a new prototype (a design alternative) starting with the users' opinions, collected through usability tests and classified through a computational method like multicriteria model.

We do this, by integrating two different areas (HCI and OR - Operational Research) when we describe an approach for evaluating the Interaction design in a subjective perspective of OR. This approach is co-evolutionary because the evaluation process can restart (as many times as the designers want) being all the design alternatives used again by the same or similar sets of users by feeding the design of a final version.

In this paper, we first present the definition of the prototypes of a Mobile Digital Television Application we developed and implemented. Then we discuss about Verbal Decision Analysis. In the fourth Section, we show a new interaction project. Lastly, some conclusions and indications for future works are provided.

2   Definition of the Prototypes of a Mobile Digital Television Application

During the definition of the prototypes, several ways to implement a navigation solution (like to navigate among the existent options in a screen and among screens) appeared. We decided to investigate if a solution that was already known by the user would influence their preference for this said solution. Specifically, we desire to authenticate if a user's preference was influenced by your existent technologies experiences, as digital TV, mobile devices and desktops. Therefore, three mobile TVD prototypes were elaborated.

The proposals for the three versions of Digital Mobile Television were the following: The first proposal was based on applications for digital TV, the second proposal was based on applications for mobile devices, similar to palm applications. The third proposal was based on applications computers' desktops.

The first prototype was developed in an analogous way to the Portal TV application in digital television [3]. The prototype doesn't possess scrolling. It possesses arrows both for changing the screens with slower transition, like the TiVo [4] and for navigating resembling the Portal TV. We think it would be a favorite application for those who already saw or have some experience with digital TV. (See figure 1)

Fig. 1. Prototype 1. Similar to TVD applications.

For the development of the second prototype, we studied several applications for mobile devices. We also studied the main operating systems of mobile devices, such as "Palm OS", for instance. The operating system "Palm OS", used for almost 80% of the market of PDAs, was properly adapted for the touchscreen access and for considering the possibility of using the device with just one hand. The prototype possesses vertical scrolling, icons and texts. The passage of screens is accomplished through the click and the navigation happens in a fast way through the scrolling. (See figure 2)

Fig.2. Prototype 2. Similar to Palm applications.

The third prototype was developed in a way comparable to applications of computers (desktop applications). It was implemented brims for navigation and buttons to close the screen. The "x", for example, closes the current screen and returns to the previous screen in that the user was. (See figure 3)

Fig. 3. Prototype 3. Similar to Desktop applications.

Usability tests were applied with younger users who were wide experienced with palms, Digital TV (DTV) or desktop computing devices. The evaluated users were 12 university students and the length of the test for each user was between 20 and 30 minutes. The experiment took place in two different locations: the usability laboratory (called LUQS) and a natural environment (field study). Usability Specialists (authors of this paper) were present during the process. For each user, specialists informed how the test would be conducted. The test began with the explanation of a sample portal application for digital TV [3]. The next step concerned the interaction of the user with the mobile DTV applications.

Throughout the use of the applications, the users were observed and monitored with cameras. The users should execute four scenarios that were chosen according to the subjective aspects of each user. For example, if the user was a soccer fan who had a lot of experience with desktop applications, one example of scenario could be the following: execute sports programs in each one of the three prototypes. The observations were completed with semi-structured interviews about the context of each tested scenario, centered mainly on subjective reactions from users and their experience to handle the application. Questions concern the user general satisfaction, particular aspects of the user interface that are judged problematic (e.g. difficulties to discover, learn or remember some features of the interface) and suggestions for changes.

The scenarios and the questions applied were defined from some hypotheses, that were previously elaborated taking into account the interaction user-applications and the context of use (as the environment, the TV content shown through the user interfaces, the users experience, their emotions, etc.).

The hypotheses were the following:

- Hypothesis 1: The evidence of the of the interface functions facilitates the use and influences in the effort spent by the user to localize himself/herself in the application. We consider here the design decisions that resulted in functions are easily found by the users;
- Hypothesis 2: The user experience with applications which have similar ways of navigation will influence the choice of an interface. Aspects such as facility of use and, accuracy of an interface and user familiarity are included in this hypothesis;
- Hypothesis 3: The locomotion of the user while manipulating the device will influence in the choice of the interface. This hypothesis refers to design

decisions that result in less precision to navigate between the options and screens facilitate the navigation of a person while manipulating the application;

- Hypothesis 4: The involvement with the content influences in the user's choice, so that, if the content is interesting, it may be decisive for the user to choose the interface. This hypothesis refers to the holistic evaluation view: when the user uses an interface that has a content which attracts him, s/he will prefer this interface;
- Hypothesis 5: The emotion felt by the user when using the interface exercises a considerable influence in the choice. Aspect such as the user feeling states as pleasure in interactive experiences is considered in this hypothesis.

The hypotheses helped to identify what criteria could bring implication for choosing one specific solution or for choosing just some attributes belonging to the existing solutions. The investigation of this implication was made from the results of the tests [5] that are entered as data for the multi-criteria model used in this paper. Next we present a summary of the ZAPROS III method in order to get a better understanding on its implementation. After we will present how this investigation takes part.

3   Verbal Decision Analysis

The ZAPROS III method belongs to the Verbal Decision Analysis – VDA framework. It combines a group of methods that are essentially based on a verbal description of decision making problems. It was developed with the aim of ranking given multicriteria alternatives, which makes it different from other verbal decision making, such as ORCLASS [6], and PACOM mainly due to its applicability. The Verbal Decision Analysis supports the decision making process by verbal representation of the problem [7]. It can be applied to problems with the following characteristics [8]: the decision rule must be developed before the definition of alternatives; there are a large number of alternatives; criteria evaluations can only be established by human; the graduations of quality inherent to the criteria are verbal definitions that represent the subjective values of the decision maker.

The decision maker is the key element of multicriteria problems and all necessary attention should be given in order to have well formed rules and consistent and correctly evaluated alternatives. Thus, the categorization of preference will be adequately obtained according to the principle of good ordering established by Zorn's lemma [9].

The application of the method ZAPROS III to modeling problem can be applied following this three-step procedure:

- Elicitation of Criteria and their Values: Once the problem is defined, the criteria related to the decision making problem are elicited. Quality Variations (QV) of criteria are established through interviews and conversations with specialists in the area and decision makers;
- Organization of the Ordinal Scales of Preference: An ordinal scale of preference for quality variations for two criteria is established based on pair wise comparisons. The preference between these two criteria is chosen according to the decision maker and the obtained scales of preferences are denominated Joint Scale of Quality Variation (JSQV) for two criteria;

- Comparisons of Alternatives: The ranking of the alternatives is constructed by comparisons between pairs of alternatives.

By going through these phases, a problem modeled on the ZAPROS III method results in a display of alternatives [10]. The display gives us a quantitative notion of the order of preference, in an absolute form (in relation to all possible alternatives) and also a relative form (in relation to a restricted group of alternatives). The following is the modeled case study.

4   Evaluation of Alternatives by Applying the ZAPROS III Method

The specialists urged to analyze the aspects that had the greatest influence in the choice of a determined interface project. Then they established verbally some criteria for the implemented prototypes of mobile TVD applications as soon as the possible values for each criterion.

Table 1. Criteria and associated values

Represen-tation	Criteria	Values
A	Functions Evidence	A1. There was no difficulty on identifying the system functionalities; A2. There were some difficulties on the system functionalities' identification; A3. It was hard to identify the system functionalities.
B	User's familiarity with a determined technology	B1. No acquaintance was required with similar applications of a determined technology; B2. It was required little user's acquaintance with applications of a given technology; B3. The manipulation of the prototype was fairly easy when the user was proverbial with similar applications.
C	User's locomotion while manipulating the device	C1. The user was not hindered in any way when manipulating the prototype while moving; C2. The user was occasionally confused when manipulating the prototype while moving; C3. The spatial orientation of the application was hindered when the user was moving.
D	Content Influence	D1. There was no influence of content on choosing the interface; D2. The content exerted some influence on choosing the interface; D3. The content was decisive on choosing the interface.
E	User's feeling states	E1. The user felt fine (safe, modern, comfortable, etc.) when using the interface; E2. The user felt indifferent when using the interface; E3. The user felt bad (uncomfortable, unsafe, frustrated) when using the interface;

In table 1, the values are shown for the criteria directed to the aspects on which the definition of the influence among the standards is based. For instance, for functions evidence criterion there are three possible values related to the difficulty of the user for identifying the system functionalities.

The order of preference among the criteria values was established from the results of the tests (observation, questionnaires). For example, it was observed that when the users were moving and trying to execute a task in a determined prototype, they complained that it was difficult to move and manipulate the device at the same time. After the tests, the responses to the questionnaires were gathered and evaluated. Questions like "What prototype did you prefer? And Why?" indicated the order of preference among the project alternatives and also which criteria values were decisive for the choice. The JSQV was gradually elaborated and validated with information from the tests, and resulted in the following sentence:

$$A1 \prec A2 \prec B1 \prec B2 \prec C1 \prec E1 \prec D1 \prec E2 \prec D2 \prec B3 \prec D3 \prec C2 \prec C3 \prec A3 \prec E3$$

In a simplified way we read the sentence above from A1 to E3 in this way: A1 (No difficulty was found on identifying the system functionalities) is the preferable criteria value, and E3 (The user felt bad (uncomfortable, unsafe, frustrated) when using the interface) is the least desirable because it was not perceived.

The next step of the method was to carry out the comparison of the alternative standards. Each alternative was studied in order to define which criteria value the materialized prototypes. The usability tests also supplied important information on how the users described the alternative standards (for example, the majority of users said that access to content using prototype 3 (three) was quite easy. Three alternatives the most preferred of all were established from this information (presented by preference order):

- Prototype 1 - A2 B1 C2 D1 E2 (Alternative 1);
- Prototype 2 - A2 B3 C1 D1 E1 (Alternative 2);
- Prototype 3 - A2 B1 C1 D1 E2 (Alternative 3).

In a simplify way, the majority of users said for the second prototype that the interaction with the application was not damaged while moving (C1) and that they had fun using it (E1). The applied model was useful for the choice of the most favorite prototypes (details of this multicriteria model application can be obtained in previous works of the authors of this paper [5], [11] and [12]). However it is not enough to choose a single option among the presented three, instead we want to identify the best characteristics (represented by the criteria values) existing in the analyzed prototypes. Next we aim at showing how it is possible to elaborate a new prototype based on the identified characteristics.

5   Elaboration of a New Interaction Project

This section we will have two sub-sections. In the first one, we will analyze the values of criteria of each prototype that will be useful to develop a new proposal (project). In the second one, we will design this new project. For the creation of the new project it was considered JSQV and the selection of the best characteristic of each prototype with base on the values of criteria presented by them. To sketch the new interface, a tool was used called SketchiXML. SketchiXML is a multi-platform multi-agent interactive application that enables designers and end users to sketch user's interfaces with different levels of details and support for different contexts of use [13].

5.1 Analysis of the Values of Criteria of Each Prototype

In Figure 4, we can visualize in prominence the values of better rank in the scale JSQV of each prototype. They will be the base for analysis and subsequent elaboration of the new prototype.

Prototype 1 - A2 (B1) C2 D1 E2 (Alternative 1);

Prototype 2 - A2 B3 (C1) D1 (E1) (Alternative 2);

Prototype 3 - A2 (B1) (C1) D1 E2 (Alternative 3).

Fig. 4. Selection of the values in agreement with the scale

When a value is repeated in the three prototypes, as the value A2 (that means, the users had some difficulty on identifying the system functionalities), we make use of the same value for the three prototypes.

In the second column, we obtained two different values: B1 and B3. In agreement with the rank, B1 is preferred in relation to B3, for that reason we will consider the value B1 that was identified in the prototypes 1 and 3 with the characteristic: no acquaintance is required with similar applications of a determined technology (B1), meaning that it is not necessary to have experiences with a given technology for a good use of the two prototypes.

In the third column, we obtained two different values: C1 and C2. In agreement with the rank, C1 is preferred in relation to C2, for that reason we will consider the value C1 that was identified in the prototypes 2 and 3 with the characteristic: the user was not hindered in any way when manipulating the prototype while moving (C1), therefore we can consider in the new prototype, similar navigation ways of the prototypes 2 and 3, like scrolling and tabs. In the fourth column, the value D1 is repeated for the three prototypes. The value says that there was not influence of content on choosing the interface (D1). In the last column, we obtained two different values: E2 and E1. In agreement with the rank, the value E1 is preferred in relation to E2, for that reason we will consider the value E1 that was identified in the prototype 2 with the characteristic: the user felt fine (safe, modern, comfortable, etc.) when using the interface, therefore we should consider some of the characteristics of the prototype 2 that turned its comfortable use for the tested users.

5.2 The New Interaction Project

The new prototype (see figure 5) was projected based on analyzes explained in the previous item.

The prototype 1 contains criterion value B1 that is with rank 3 in the final scale, this means that it is very important that the new prototype does not demand any user experience with technology. Hence, we selected the arrow with explanatory label for symbol of the navigation: lateral (returning the previous screen) and of lower or of top (with passage of pages down and upward, respectively).

The third prototype presents besides the value B1, the value C1, because it makes the manipulation of the prototype easier, when the user is in movement. Therefore, it was necessary also to select some characteristic of this prototype. The selected characteristic was the one that possesses a larger area of contact through the tabs, then a junction of B1 was accomplished with C1, resulting in an arrow of such adult for navigation. Another selected characteristic of the prototype 3 was the located menu in the superior part of the screen.

The second prototype contains the value E1 as differential, and also contains the characteristic that was taken as advantage in the new prototype: the scrolling bar that was used for navigation interns through the widgets combox for list of title of the news and listbox for the content of the selected news.

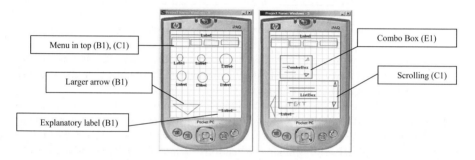

Fig. 5. New interaction project

We expect this proposal to be more adequate according to the following reasons: the use of bigger arrows makes possible the change of screens especially when the users are moving; the use of explanatory labels help the users about the context of the application; the menu located at the superior part of the screen was favored by the user because it makes easy the visualization of the options.

6 Conclusions and Future Works

In this work we showed ways of choosing a new project starting from tests with users and along with the analysis of these tests through the ZAPROS III multicriteria method.

The multicrieria method was useful in the elaboration of another design alternative, because it showed a structured model focused on users' preferences and by defining a rank with the best distinct characteristics by the own users in usability tests. This new e final prototype contemplated these best criteria. In our approach, it is not imperative to build a new design alternative or a final prototype. From a more general point of view, some useful lessons about the utility and the usability of similar systems (e.g. user interface guidelines) can be learned and further applied in future projects.

The idea of using sketchiXML for visualization of the this new prototype was considered useful because it is a fast way to obtain an initial sketch. In addition, this tool generates the interface specifications in a standard format, as the UsiXML. This format is widely interpreted by interface generation tools that are freely available for use. These tools allow the automatic generation of the final user interface. In our approach, executable prototypes need to be easily obtained and quickly tested by the users in order to support its evolutionary characteristic.

As future works and next steps, we intend to validate this new prototype with the users by performing a second test in order to verify if the prototype is really in agreement with the best suggested characteristics. Using the ZAPROS III multicriteria method, we will include the new developed prototype as another alternative in order to be sure that it is really the best of the fourth alternatives. This iterative feature characterizes the co-evolutionary process of the project

References

1. Chorianopoulos, K., Spinellis, D.: User interface evaluation of interactive TV: a media studies perspective. Univ. Access. Inf. Soc. 5, 209–210 (2006)
2. Simon, H., Newell, A.: Heuristic Problem Solving: The Next Advance in Operations Research. Oper. Res. 6, 4–10 (1958)
3. Furtado, E., Carvalho, F., Schilling, A., Falcão, D., Sousa, K., Fava, F.: Projeto de Interfaces de Usuário para a Televisão Digital Brasileira. In: SIBGRAPI 2005 – Simpósio Brasileiro de Computação Gráfica e Processamento de Imagens, Natal (2005)
4. TiVo, http://www.tivo.com/0.0.asp
5. Tamanini, I., Mendes, M., Carvalho, A., Furtado, E., Pinheiro, P.: A model for mobile television applications based on verbal decision analysis. In: Sobh, T.M. (ed.) International Joint Conferences on Computer, Information, and Systems Sciences, and Engineering (to appear, 2008)
6. Larichev, O.: Cognitive validity in design of decision-aiding techniques. Journal of Multi-Criteria Decision Analysis 1(3), 127–138 (1992)
7. Larichev, O., Moshkovich, H.: Verbal Decision Analysis For Unstructured Problems. Kluwer Academic Publishers, Boston (1997)
8. Larichev, O.: Ranking Multicriteria Alternatives: The Method ZAPROS III. European Journal of Operational Research 131 (2001)
9. Halmos, P.R.: Naive Set Theory, p. 116. Springer, Heidelberg (1974)
10. Figueira, J., Greco, S., Ehrgott, M. (eds.): Multiple Criteria Decision Analysis: State of the Art Surveys Series: International Series in Operations Research & Management Science, vol. 78, XXXVI, p. 1045 (2005)
11. Carvalho, A., Mendes, M., Pinheiro, P., Furtado, E.: Analysis of the Interaction Design for Mobile TV Applications based on Multi-Criteria. In: International Conference on Research and Practical Issues of Enterprise Information Systems (CONFENIS 2007), Beijing, China, October 14-17, (2007)
12. Carvalho, A., Mendes, M., Furtado, E., Pinheiro, P.: Avaliação de Projetos de Interação para Aplicações de TVD Móvel utilizando Multicritério. In: XXXIX Symposium of the Brazilian Operational Research Society (XXXIX SBPO), 2007, Fortaleza. XXXIX Symposium of the Brazilian Operational Research Society (2007)
13. Coyette, A., Vanderdonckt, J.: A Sketching Tool for Designing Anyuser, Anyplatform, Anywhere User Interfaces. In: Proc. of Interact. 2005 (2005)

Looking at the Knowledge Economy: Some Issues on Theory and Evidence

George M. Korres[1] and Constantinos Tsamadias[2]

[1] Associate Prof. Dr. George M. Korres, Department of Geography,
University of the Aegean, 17 Rizou Neroulou Street, Athens: 11141, Greece
Tel.: (+30)-6972188897
gkorres@hol.gr ,gkorres@geo.aegean.gr
[2.]Harokopio University, Athens, Greece

Abstract. Innovation activities contribute essentially to the regional dimension and growth. The technological infrastructure and innovation capabilities affect not only the regional growth, but also the whole periphery and economy as well. In the last decades, OECD /introduced some measures and indexes, concerning the Research and Development Expenditures, patents etc., that measuring the innovation activities. However, there are a lot of problems and questions regarding the measurement of innovation activities at a regional level. This paper attempts to analyze the whole framework of innovation statistics and in particular to examine the measurement and also the statistical estimation of innovation activities. On this context, it's also aiming to emphasize and to review the appropriate techniques, the most common methods and the particular problems.

Keywords: Innovation Activities, Knowledge Economy, Growth.

1 Introduction

The growing importance of technological change in world production and employment is one of the characteristics of the last four decades. Technological change is not only a determinant of growth but also affect the international competition and the modernisation of a country. The term "innovation" is somewhat ambiguous in common parlance it denotes both a process and its result. According to the definition proposed by the OECD in its "Frascati Manual", it involves the transformation of an idea into a marketable product or service, a new or improved manufacturing or distribution process, or a new method of social service. The term thus refers to the process. On the other hand, when the word "innovation" is used to refer to the new or improved product, equipment or service which is successful on the market, the emphasis is on the result of the process. This ambiguity can lead to confusion: when referring to the dissemination of innovation, does one mean the dissemination of the process, i.e. the methods and practices which make the innovation possible, or to the dissemination of the results, i.e. the new products? The distinction is important.

In the first sense of the term (innovation process), the emphasis is on the manner in which the innovation is designed and produced at the different stages leading up to it

M.D. Lytras et al. (Eds.): WSKS 2008, CCIS 19, pp. 712–719, 2008.

(creativity, marketing, research and development, design, production and distribution) and on their breakdown. This is not a linear process, with clearly-delimited sequences and automatic follow-on, but rather a system of interactions, of comings and goings between different functions and different players whose experience, knowledge and know-how are mutually reinforcing and cumulative. This why more and more importance is attached in practice to mechanisms for interaction within the firm (collaboration between the different units and participation of employees in organisational innovation), as well as to the networks linking the firm to its environment (other firms, support services, centres of expertise, research laboratories, etc.). Relations with the users, taking account of demand expressed, and anticipating the needs of the market and society are just as important - if not more so - than a mastery of the technology.

In the second sense (result of the innovation), the emphasis is on the new product, process or service. A distinction is made between radical innovation or breakthrough (for instance the launch of a new vaccine, the compact disk) and progressive innovation, which modifies the products, processes or services through successive improvements (e.g. the introduction of 32-bit chips to replace the 16-bit ones in electronic equipment, or the introduction of airbags in cars). New products, processes or services can appear in all sectors of activity, whether traditional or high-tech, public or market, industrial, agricultural or tertiary. Innovation may also concern services of general interest, such as public health, administrative procedures, the organisation of postal services or public education.

2 Knowledge-Based Economy

The increasing recognition by policy makers and academics of the importance of the emerting "knowledge-based economy" for future output and employment growth has yet to be reflected in any policy action. Of course. these positive employment outcomes achieved with a "painful" process of structural adjustment. Thus, the simple comparison, popular in many policy circles in the 1980s, of the United States' impressive and Europe's poor, experience in employment creation in the 1970s and l980s, is now being complemented by trends in employment growth by educational category and accompanying earnings. However, different countries appear to have responded in different ways. In the U.S.A. labour market adjustment- has led to a substantial decline in real wages for the least-educated and least-skilled workers: in Europe it has led to much higher levels of unemployment in the unskilled labour force. The overall long-term tendency towards a more strongly knowledge-based economy, in terms of both input proportions and the nature of the output, is accelerating. At the firm level, this is reflected in the fact that the shift in the demand for skills is strongest in firms introducing information technology. The dramatic decrease in the cost of obtaining data and information produces a shock effect, while the decline in the price or information is at the core of a new wave of productivity growth. This is especially true for organisations and institutions strongly involved in the production, use and distribution of knowledge (education, research, development, but also firms as learning organisations). The measurement problem is probably as pervasive as information and communication technologies. Even individual firms' accounts are becoming increasingly unreliable. Not surprisingly the debate on trends in aggregate productivity is strongly influenced by questions about measurement, not least because the decline in aggregate total factor productivity seems to be concentrated in the service sector and in conventionally measured capital productivity.

3   The Knowledge Economy: Knowledge Producers and Knowledge Users

There are two important types of knowledge industries to consider: First, there are those industries whose major product is knowledge itself; then there are industries that manage or convey information. The increased importance of knowledge means that the net stock of intangible capital (e.g., education and research and development) has grown faster than tangible capital (e.g., buildings, transportation, roads, and machinery).

In the New Economy, intangible capital has become at least as important as tangible capital, and a greater share of the value of tangible capital is based on intangible inputs. As we have become richer, we have increasingly consumed services and goods with higher value-added content. This trend is demonstrated by the fact that the economic output of the U.S. economy, as measured in tons, is roughly the same as it was a century ago, yet its real economic value is 20 times greater. In other words, we have added intangible attributes to goods and services, the most important being knowledge. One example is anti-lock brakes, which are the product of a generation of research and development, and are loaded with electronics. They don't weigh any more than conventional brakes, but they certainly provide a great deal more value to drivers. The Knowledge Innovation Assessment is an integrated design of ten diverse competencies essential in an innovation system:

Table 1. Knowledge Innovation Assessment

Collaborative Process	Products/Services
Performance Measures	Strategic Alliances
Education/Development	Market Image/Interaction
Learning Network	Leadership/Leverage
Market Positioning	Computer/Communications

It is a lack of investment in human capital, not a lack of investment in physical capital that prevents poor countries from catching up with rich ones. Educational attainment and public spending on education are correlated positively to economic growth. School quality measured, for example, by teacher pay, student-teacher ratio, and teacher education is positively correlated to future earnings of the students. Education is important in explaining the growth of national income. Life-long learning is also crucial. People with human capital migrate from places where it is scarce to places where it is abundant. "Human capital flight" or "brain drain" can lead to a permanent reduction in income and growth of the country of emigration relative to the country of immigration. We need more technical graduates. Research and Development ability to innovate a key competitive advantage.

4   Technological Framework and National System of Innovations

The analysis of system of innovations helps us to understand and to explain, why the development of technology is necessary in a certain direction and at a certain rate. We should be very careful in the definition of the "national systems" according to which sub-systems should be included and which process should be studied in the different countries. The government engages itself towards innovation policy because it has been considered that innovation is a key point for the national economic growth. In order to decide how the governments should decide to promote the innovations, it is useful to know the specific context in which the national government interfears. There is the concept of "national innovation system" itself. Each of the terms can be interpreted in a variety of ways and there is a question of whether in which technology and business are transnational increased the concept as a whole makes more sense.

Freeman first and Nelson after were the persons who had introduced and explained the use, the concept of national systems of innovations. Freeman in his book for Japan refers to the nation-specific organization of sub-systems and to the interaction between sub-systems. Freeman base in the interaction between the production system and the process of innovation. Nelson's work was based upon the production of knowledge and innovation and upon the innovation system in the narrow sense. Finally, the recent book of M. Porter was based in the following determinants of Firm strategy, factor conditions, demand conditions, and supporting industries that affecting the competitiveness of a national industry. The national systems of innovation presumes that nation states exist and this phenomenon has two dimensions:(a).the national-cultural (where all individuals belong to a nation which is defined by cultural, ethnical and linguistic characteristics), and (b).the etatist-political (where there is one geographical space controlled by one central state authority without foreign nationalities). In some cases, it is not even clear where locating the borders of a "national system of innovations". The first approach and definition of "system of innovations" is that, it's a social system that is constructed by a number of elements, while there is a close-relationship between these elements. These elements are "interacting" in the production, diffusion, and economic cycles. We can define "the system of innovations" from a "narrow" view. According to "the narrow definition" it includes organisations and institutions that of involved in searching and exploring the new technologies (such as technological institutes, and research departments). From the other side, the "broad" definition follows the theoretical perspective and includes the different parts of economic structure (such as the production system, and the marketing system). On international scene, when the large countries change the orientation of research activities, this is affects the small countries.

Figure 1 shows a simple model of national systems of innovations; in particular, we can see the information, communication, legal structures and congitive frameworks which influence all activities in the above diagram.

The "mechanisms" of technology and competition policies are usually complementary and both are aiming to increase the entrepreneur's creativity and to attribute the industrial and economic growth. It is important to harmonise the technology "mechanisms" with the competition policy. The competition policy that are related to research and technological activities have also an important impact in the market structure. If there is a healthy competitive environment in the market for goods.

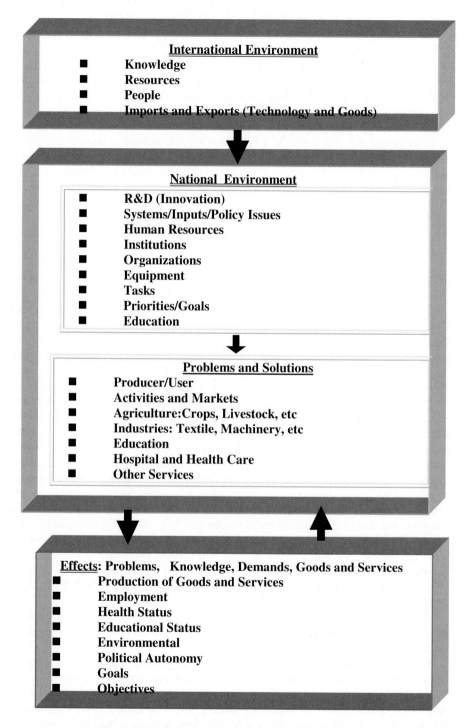

Fig. 1. A simple model of national systems of innovation

and services then the entrepreneurs have a greater incentive to develop new products and to invest in technologies and in research activities.

5   Knowledge, Innovation and Growth

The new theories of growth (known as "endogenous") stress that development of know-how and technological change - rather than the mere accumulation of capital - are the driving force behind lasting growth.

Table 2. Factors explaining the American and Japanese successes

Some of the factors explaining the American and Japanese successes	
United States	**Japan**
• A more important research effort	• idem
• A larger proportion of engineers and scientists in the active population	• idem
• Research efforts better coordinated, in particular with regard to civilian and defence research (in particular in the aeronautic, electronic and space sectors).	• A strong ability to adapt technological information, wherever it comes from. A strong tradition of cooperation between firms in the field of R&D
• A close University - Industry relationship allowing the blossoming of a large number of high technology firms.	• An improving cooperation University / Industry, especially via the secondment of industrial researchers in Universities
• A capital risk industry better developped which invests in high technology. NASDAQ, a stock exchange for dynamic SMEs.	• Stable and strong relationships between finance and industry fostering long term benefits and strategies.
• A cultural tradition favourable to risk taking and to enterprise spirit, a strong social acceptation of innovation.	• A culture favourable to the application of techniques and on going improvement.
• A lower cost for filing licenses, a single legal protection system favourable to the commercial exploitation of innovations	• A current practice of concerted strategies between companies, Universities and public authorities
• Reduced lead time for firms creation and limited red tape	• A strong mobility of staff within companies.

The meaning and scope of Innovation are defined in that Green Paper (COM(95)688. The Green Paper on Innovation opened up a number of pathways. For the sake of efficiency, this *"First Action Plan"* refers to a limited number of priority initiatives to be launched very soon at Community level and includes a number of schemes put into action or announced since the launch of the Green Paper, identified as essential to the innovation process.

On 20 November 1996, the Commission adopted the First Action Plan for Innovation in Europe following the wide ranging public debate stimulated by the Green Paper on Innovation. The Action Plan provides a general framework for action at the European and Member State level to support the innovation process. A limited number of priority measures, to be launched immediately by the Community, are identified. The plan also sets out those measures which are already underway or which have been announced since the launch of the Green Paper. Three main areas for action have been identified:

- *Fostering an innovation culture:* education and training, easier mobility for researchers and engineers, demonstration of effective approaches to innovation in the economy and in society, propagation of best management and organizational methods amongst businesses, and stimulation of innovation in the public sector and in government;
- *Establishing a framework conducive to innovation:* adaptation and simplification of the legal and regulatory environment, especially with respect to Intellectual Property Rights, and providing easier access to finance for innovative enterprises;

6 Conclusions

In knowledge-based economies, the efficient systems are those which combine the ability to produce knowledge, the mechanisms for disseminating it as widely as possible and the aptitude of the individuals, companies and organisations concerned to absorb and use it. The crucial factor for innovation is thus the link between research (the production of knowledge), training, mobility, interaction (the dissemination of knowledge) and the ability of firms, particularly SMEs, to absorb new technologies and know-how. The attractivity stems from three basic characteristics of the approach that deserve to be summarized here:

- *First*, it places innovations and knowledge creation at the very centre of focus, and goes beyond a narrow view of innovation to emphasize the interactive and dynamic nature of innovation.
- *Second*, it represents a considerable advance over the network school of innovation by a decisive shift in focus from firm to territory, from the knowledge creating firm to the knowledge-creating territory.
- *Third*, it views innovation as a social process that is institutionally embedded, and, thus, puts special emphasis on the institutional context and forms [i.e. formal and informal institutions] through which the processes of knowledge creation and dissemination occur.

References

1. Chenery, H., Srinivasan.: Handbook of development economics, ch. 30, vol. 2. North-Holland, Amsterdam (1989)
2. Cohen, W.M., Levinthal, D.A.: Innovation and Learning: The Two Faces of R&D. Economic Journal 99, 569–596 (1989)

3. Davenport, T., Prusak, L.: Working Knowledge. Harvard Business School Press, Boston (1998)
4. Dosi, G., Freeman, C., Nelson, R., Silverberg, G., Soete, L.: Technical change and economic theory. Pinter Publishers, London (1988)
5. Dosi, G., Pavitt, K., Soete, L.: The economics of technical change and international trade, London, Harvester, Wheatsheaf (1990)
6. Edquist, C.: Systems of Innovation. Technologies, Institutions and Organizations. Pinter, London (1997a)
7. Freeman, C.: Technology and Economic Performance: Lessons from Japan. Pinter, London (1987)
8. Freeman, C.: The economics of innovation. Elgar, Aldershot (1990)
9. Freeman, C.: Networks of Innovators: A Synthesis of Research Issues. Research Policy 20, 499–514 (1991)
10. Grossman, G., Helpman, E.: Innovation and growth in the global economy. MIT Press, Cambridge (1991)
11. Håkansson, H.: Industrial Technological Development: A Network Approach. Croom Helm, London (1987)
12. Hudson, R.: The Learning Economy, the Learning Firm and the Learning Region: A Sympathetic Critique of the Limits to Learning. European Urban and Regional Studies 6(1), 59–72 (1999)
13. Korres, G.: Technical change and economic growth: an empirical analysis of EEC countries. Avebury Press, London (1996)
14. Lundvall, B.-Å.: Innovation as an Interactive Process: From User-producer Interaction to the National System of Innovations. In: Dosi, G., Freeman, C., Nelson, R., Silverberg, G., Soete, L. (eds.) Technical Change and Economic Theory, pp. 349–369. Pinter, London (1988)
15. Lundvall, B.-Å. (ed.): National Systems of Innovation: Towards a Theory of Innovation and Interactive Learning. Pinter, London (1992)
16. Malecki, E.J., Oinas, P. (eds.): Making Connections. Technological Learning and Regional Economic Change. Ashgate, Aldershot (1999)
17. Perez, C., Soete, L.: Catching-up in technology: entry barriers and windows of opportunity. In: Dosi, et al. (eds.) Technical change and economic theory. Pinter (1988)
18. Petit, P., Tahar, G.: Dynamics of technological change and schemes of diffsuion, The Manchester School (December 1989)
19. Rosenberg, N.: Inside the Black Box. Cambridge University, Cambridge (1982)
20. Rosenberg, N., Landau, R., Mowery, D.C.: Technology and the wealth of nations. Stanford University Press, Stanford (1992)
21. Sharp, M.: The Community and the new technologies. In: Lodge, J. (ed.) The European Community and the challenge of the future. Pinter, pp. 202–220 (1993)
22. Stiglitz, J.E.: Learning to Learn, Localized Learning and Technological Progress. In: Dasgupta, P., Stoneman (eds.) Economic Policy and Technological Performance, pp. 125–153. Cambridge University Press, Cambridge (1987)
23. Stiglitz, J.E.: Knowledge as a Global Public Good Paper written as chapter in upcoming UNDP book Global Public Goods (1998a)
24. Watanabe, H.: A note on the classification of technical inventions, Economic Studies Quarterly, pp. 68–72 (September 1961)

The New Oil Pipeline from Bourgas to Alexandroupoli: Critical Analysis of Simulation Methods for the Protection of the Aegean Sea

Ioanna Genikomsidou and Nikolaos P. Ventikos

School of Naval Architecture and Marine Engineering, National Technical University of Athens, 9 Iroon Politehneiou st, 15773 Zografou, Greece
elidimioa@hotmail.com, niven@deslab.ntua.gr

Abstract. Simulation of models, based on multi-agent systems (Multi Agent models, MAS) is applied in various scientific fields in the last few years. In each simulation effort some basic elements are determined, like the problems that are going to be examined, the number of the interacting agents and their geometry, the network topology, the time calibration and other issues that concern the application of this methodology. In this paper we describe an agent-based model, which aims to designate an optimal solution for the confrontation of a likely oil slick in the marine region of Thrace, ensuring the effective implementation of the National Contingency Plan. As the construction of the pipeline from Bourgas to Alexandroupolis is aproaching, a possible increase in the number of tankers and in the corresponding transported quantity of oil through the Aegean Sea is expected. Therefore the posibility for the occurrence of an oil slick is considerably growing. The right strategic planning for relative incidents acquires national importance and becomes a significant part for the development of the wider area.

Keywords: oil pollution, maritime transport, environment, multi-agent systems, simulation.

1 Introduction

The construction of the oil pipeline from Bourgas to Alexandroupolis is a national issue which among other things is going to support a big part of the development of the area of Thrace. The aim of this development is to transport Russian oil (and probably oil from Kazakstan) through the Black Sea, Bulgaria, Greece and the Aegean Sea to the worldwide market, reinforcing the geopolitical role of the involved actors in the area and the world energy map.

A possible result of this construction will be the reduce of the transported volume of oil by tankers through the narrows of Bosphorus and the avoidance of accidents and possible pollution. On the other hand, if we focus in the area of Hellenic seas, the possibility of a new oil slick to be created is considerably increased, as the number of tankers and the transported quantity will may multiply through the Aegean Sea. A significant possibility of an accident to happen exists in the spaces of charge and discharge of oil.

M.D. Lytras et al. (Eds.): WSKS 2008, CCIS 19, pp. 720–726, 2008.

More specifically in this paper we present the simulation of a model that represents a possible accident in the wider marine region of Thrace (included the prefecture of Kavala), the results of which should converge in the most optimal choice for the confrontation of the oil slick, aiming at the maximisation of the utility of all involved members. The paper comprises of the following sections: Section 2 covers the theoretical background of agent-based models, section 3 introduces the structure and rational of the proposed model and the paper concludes with interesting insides of the above tasks.

2   Agent-Based Models

Agent-based models have been used since the mid-1990s to solve a variety of business and technology problems. Examples of applications include supply chain optimization and logistics (Tomas B. Klos and Bart Nooteboom,2001), modeling of consumer behavior (Leigh Tesfatsion, 2005), including word of mouth, social network effects (Nigel Gilbert and Pietro Terna, 1999), distributed computing, workforce management, and portfolio management. They have also been used to analyze traffic congestion (Bryan Raney and Kai Nagel, 2004). In these and other applications, the system of interest is simulated by capturing the behavior of individual agents and their interconnections. Agent-based modeling tools can be used to test how changes in individual behaviors will affect the system's emerging overall behavior. Other models have analyzed the spread of epidemics, the water management (Adamatti, et al, 2005), the threat of biowarfare (Carlos Castillo-Chavez and Fred S. Roberts, 2002), the growth and decline of ancient civilizations, and the human immune system (V. Baldazzi, F. Castiglione, M. Bernaschi, 2006).

2.1   Socio-Technical Systems in an ABM

In an ABM, a clear distinction between the social and technical aspects of a system can be made. Infrastructures can be considered from both the technical and social perspectives. The technical perspective includes the physical components of the infrastructure, harbours, polluted areas, ground shaping and areas for the placement of the equipment. The social perspective contains the body of human actors, governments, local residents, companies and environmental organizations. So, we can create two layers of networks. Physical links can exist only between physical parts of the network and never directly between actors. On the other hand, social links (such as a contract) can exist only between two actors. Relationships like the ownership relation connect the two layers of the model. Making this clear distinction is important because it allows experiments in which the physical context of decision making can be changed while keeping the model of decision making the same, or, on the other hand, changing decision making of actors given a certain physical network.

2.2   Applicability to the Case Study

Agent based modeling is a suitable approach for the case study discussed in this paper. By describing both the physical and the social networks, various experiments can be undertaken that can support the problem of the evaluation of the decision for the location of the equipment in order to achieve an adequate confrontation of an oil slick. Moreover, the same framework, as well as parts of the model, can be re-used to execute different experiments. For example, actors or parts of the physical network that were not present in a set of experiments can be included later.

2.3 Conceptual Design for the Model

In this Section we present the procedure that is followed in our model for the successful transaction of results. Six steps can be identified in the path towards the formulation of an optimal solution for the confrontation of oil slicks:

- Make a choice of the physical parameters, regarding the National Contingency Plan;
- Creation of different scenarios, containing all the parameters
- Identification of the available equipment
- Presenting the possible locations for the deployment of equipment
- Evaluating these locations through an agent-based program and choose the one that satisfies the criteria set for all the agents;
- Implementing the most desirable solution

First of all, we select all the physical parameters that have an important effect on the oil slick, considering the National Contingency Plan. The area that is included to our model starts from the geographic prefecture of Evros, and concludes to the geografic prefecture of Kavala. In this area we should take into consideration the sensitivity of given areas due to their rare flora and fauna and also due to the overall geomorphology of the region (Delta of Evros, Delta of Nestos) (figure 1). The physical parameters we need to know are changeable and will help us find the slick's

Fig. 1. Map of the geographical prefectures of Thrace and Kavala

Table 1. In this table are appeared the parameters that can affect the shape of the oil slick, as long as we have determined the type of oil and the season of the year, and are represented two examples of possible scenarios: scenario 1, ●   scenario 2 ▲

Distance to vulnerable areas (nm)	Season of year	Total amount of oil (m³)	Total amount of oil in case of an accident in the pipeline (m³)	Ship condition	Leakage rate (m³/h)	On-shore wind direction (North= 360°)	Wind speed (m/s)	Wave height (m)
Short ▲ (0-2)	Winter	0-5000 (Bunkers)	0-7	Not sinking ▲	Low ▲ (0-50)	165-194 ●	Breeze (0-10) ●	Low (0-0.5) ●
Medium (3-9) ●	Spring ●	5000-50000 (Small ● Tanker)	7-700	Sinking within days	Medium (50-100)	195-224	Gale (10-20)	Medim (0.5-2.5)
Large (>10) ●	Summer ▲	50000-150000 (Medium Tanker) ▲	>700 ▲	Sinking within hours ●	High (100-500) ●	225-254 ▲	Storm (>20) ▲	Medium-High ▲ (2.5-6.0)
	Autumn	>150000 (Large Tanker)			Very high (>500)	255-284 ▲		High (>6)
						285-314		
						315-344		

destination, and accordingly the most suitable places to deploy the equipment. Information about wind speed, height of the wave, wind direction, leakage rate, ship condition, type of oil, total amount of oil, season of the year and distance from vulnerable areas are indicatively what we need to know so as to configure some scenarios (table 1).

3   Definition of the Locations for the Deployment of Equipment

In this section, the case study is introduced in more detail. Section 3.1 presents the different players and the decisions that they have to make (table 2) and then Section 3.2 introduces the implemented model.

3.1   The Players and Their Decisions

The influencing factors, as we can see in table 2, are classified as direct and indirect factors. The former refer to players that have direct links with the abatement of an oil slick, while the latter addresses to the actors that do not present an immediate relation to this procedure. Once the influencing factors are identified, then the players and their decisions or objectives need to be clearly defined since these will be used to develop individual objective and constraint functions in the next stage. The influencing factors and decisions of each player are presented in Table 2.

Table 2. Influencing factors, decisions of the players and constraints

Influencing factors	Players	Examples	Decisions or objectives	Constraints/parameters
Direct	P1: Hellenic coastguard	Coordinates and monitors all necessary activities for the adequate confrontation of an oil slick	Maximize the rapidity of procedures and take the final decision	1. Total amount of oil 2. Distance to vulnerable area
Indirect	P2: environmental organizations	Stop all the actions that have irreversible effects on the environment	Minimize the environmental pollution and protect the vulnerable areas(ex. Delta of Evros)	3. Ship condition
Direct	P3: antipollution companies – contractors	Confrontation of a possible oil slick in every way	Use the less equipment they can to the best results, minimize the cost and maximize the efficiency	4. Leakage rate 5. Wind speed
Indirect	P4: local residents (tourist enterprises and fishermen)	Access in the marine regions: for the growth of fishery and tourist enterprises (mainly the summer period)	Maximize the production and their profits	6. On-shore wind direction
Direct	P5: ship's company/ insurance	Definition of the ship's problems and its condition	Choose the best solution regarding the ship's condition, minimizing the costs	7. Type of oil
Direct	P6: salvage companies	Towing of the ship under the necessary study and proximity of safe refuges	Maximize the profits, after a deal with the ship's company	8. Season of year
Indirect	P7: media	Influence the public opinion		9. Activities of the local residents that differentiates between the seasons of the year
Direct	P8: Merchant Marine Ministry		Sets the necessary procedures	

3.2   Introduction to the Model

The concept of a multi-objective evaluation model is illustrated in Fig. 2. Multi-objective evaluation model for the equipment location for the confrontation of a possible oil slick is an integration of two main models, one for the configuration of possible scenarios and a multi-objective evaluation model. The modelling process begins with an analysis of the physical parameters that comes up from the National Contingency Plan. The total amount of oil, distance to vulnerable area, ship condition, leakage rate, wind speed, on-shore wind direction, type of oil and the season of year that the accident happened are some of these parameters. We also have to take under consideration the activities of the local residents during the year. For example tourist enterprises have profits mainly on summer time. So we can categorize such activities in each season of year. The combination of these parameters gives different scenarios each time, which are presented in table 1. The result is a number of candidate scenarios to be used in the next process. It is screened to remove unlikely options according to specific criteria such as the overall capacity of the diffused oil. The next level is to identify the available equipment. After the determination of the equipment the model designate it's possible locations, based on the scenario parameters, the formation of the coasts, if they are rocky or sandy, approachable or not, and the depth of the sea This output data is then fed into individual stakeholders' objective function in the multi-objective evaluation model. The team of the interacting players (table 2) consists of salvage companies, antipollution companies, ship's company, local residents, environmental organizations, and Hellenic coastguard. The model is classified into three levels, namely operational, tactical, and strategic levels. The first level deals with the evaluation of individual objective functions, the second level deals with the interaction and negotiation among the players, and the third level deals with the global objective function and policy maker. The model determines if the solution is mutually satisfactory for every player by taking the results of every individual objective function into account. If so, the location choices become a final outcome. Otherwise the feedback will occur to re-select a new set of screened location options for the application of equipment. The process is repeated iteratively until the final solution is achieved.

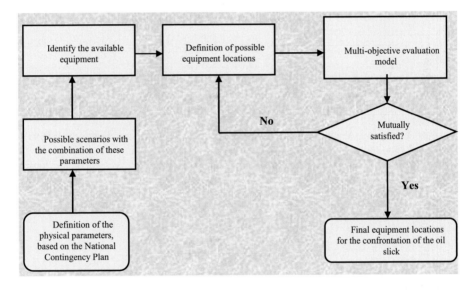

Fig. 2. Concept of multi-objective evaluation model for equipment location

4 Conclusions - Future Research

The study presented in this paper is currently ongoing. The network model is under construction so the results could be drafted and thereby assessed in short time. Behavioural model of decision analysis in group decision making is described. This model is described as a group disutility function, based on the property of convex dependence among multiple agents. The application of this approach to public sectors is shown in modelling environmental assessment with public participation. It is shown that by using this group disutility model we could model flexible decision makers who could change their attitude on the preference depending upon the disutility level of the other conflicting decision makers. As a result the ethical consensus formation process could be modelled. The results are useful for policy makers, on scene commanders, port authorities looking for new ways to evaluate different locations and more insight in the decision making process and negotiations between the actors.

References

1. Ackchail, S., Koen, V.D., Luis, F., Zofia, L.: Optimizing the Location of Intermodal Freight Hubs: An Overview of the Agent Based Modelling Approach. Journal of Transportation Systems Engineering and information Technology 7(4) (August 2007)
2. Baldazzi, V., Castiglione, F., Bernaschi, M.: An enhanced agent based model of the immune system response. Cellular Immunology 244, 77–79 (2006)
3. Castillo-Chavez, C., Roberts, F.S.: Mathematical Sciences Methods for the Study of Deliberate Releases of Biological Agents and their Consequences, Report on DIMACS Working Group Meeting, May 17 (2002)
4. Adamatti, D.F., Sichman, J.S., Rabak, C., Bommel, P., Ducrot, R., Camargo, M.E.S.A.: Jogoman: A Prototype Using Multi-Agent-Based Simulation and Role-Playing Games in Water Management (2005),
http://www.lti.pcs.usp.br/Pergamus/pubs/Adamatti-etal05-SMAGET.pdf
5. Raney, B., Nagel, K.: Iterative route planning for large-scale modular transportation simulations. Future Generation Computer Systems 20, 1101–1118 (2004)
6. Gilbert, N., Terna, P.: How to build and use agent-based models in social science, May 18 (1999)
7. Leigh Tesfatsion: Agent-based computational modeling and macroeconomics, ISU Economic Report 05023 (July 2005)
8. Klos, T.B., Nooteboom, B.: Agent-based computational transaction cost economics. Journal of Economics Dynamics and Control 25, 503–526 (2001)

Resources, Activities and Competitive Advantage: Application to Outsourcing

Anton Wiesmann[1] and Tatiana Zalan[2]

[1] International Graduate School of Business
University of South Australia
Adelaide, Australia
Anton.Wiesmann@postgrads.unisa.edu.au
[2] International Graduate School of Business
University of South Australia
Adelaide, Australia
tatiana.zalan@unisa.edu.au

Abstract. In this article we present an alternative approach to assessing competitive advantages of a firm and operationalizing the resource-based view (RBV) of the firm in the context of strategic outsourcing. When resource bundles are viewed in the form of activities, they become easier to observe, identify, understand and measure, thus activities can be used to operationalize bundles of resources and capabilities when empirically testing the RBV. We propose a conceptual model and present several propositions for subsequent empirical testing of the RBV.

Keywords: Resource Based View of the Firm, Outsourcing, Activity, Transaction Cost Economics, Resources, Capabilities.

1 Introduction

One of the key issues in strategic management has been to understand sustained competitive advantage (SCA) and unravel the way it can be systematically created (Meyer, 1991; Porter, 1980; Rumelt, 1984). The resource-based view of the firm (RBV) has become one of the most widely accepted theoretical perspectives on understanding the origins of competitive advantage and superior firm performance (Powell, 2001; Priem and Butler, 2001a; Rouse and Daellenbach, 2002; Bingham and Eisenhardt, 2007). However, the usefulness of the RBV as a theoretical framework has remained a subject of debate (Barney, 2001; Hoopes, Madsen and Walker, 2003; Priem and Butler, 2001a, 2001b; Williamson, 1999). Despite being conceptually strong, the RBV has little value as an analytical tool to solve practical business problems. Further, its empirical support has been weak: for example, a review of 55 empirical tests of the RBV suggests that little more than half (53%) of tests support the RBV and that the degree of support varies considerably with the independent variable used (Newbert, 2007). Moreover, when the independent variable is operationalized as a specific resource, empirical support is found for only 37%, (Newbert, 2007) The

M.D. Lytras et al. (Eds.): WSKS 2008, CCIS 19, pp. 727–740, 2008.

key reason for these inconclusive results has been the inherent difficulties of operationalzing the variables of the RBV and a clear logical treatment of its key propositions.

Resources and capabilities do not occur in static isolation, rather in bundles, which are difficult to observe, define and measure, thus very little empirical work using resource combination or bundles has been attempted. Further, intangible and hard-to-observe resources are, by definition `inimitable', thus measuring inimitable resources is an inherent difficulty in RBV research (Godfrey & Hill, 1995; Zander & Kogut, 1995). Godfrey and Hill (1995) hold that resources and capabilities are 'unobservable', because firm-specific capabilities are characterized by high levels of tacit knowledge and causal ambiguity. The less observable the resource and the more difficult it is to understand, the greater the likelihood that it is also an important source of SCA (Newbert, 2007). Thus, the 'best' resources can never be identified: as Collis (1994) argues, the strategy field may never find the ultimate source of SCA.

In this article we present an alternative approach to assessing competitive advantages of a firm and operationalizing the RBV within the context of strategic outsourcing. First, we examine the notion of firms as bundles of resources, capabilities and their relationship to organizational routines or activities. We then briefly discuss the theoretical foundations of strategic outsourcing and justify the choice of strategic outsourcing as a relevant background to test the RBV. We then propose a formalized conceptual model, where resources and capabilities can be viewed as bundles of activities (aka organizational routines), which can then be analyzed using Barney's (1991) VRIO framework to establish their competitive position. Finally, we present several propositions and suggestions for operationalization to empirically test the RBV.

2   Firms as Bundles of Resources

One of the primary critiques of Barney's (1991) expression of the RBV over time has been its rather static nature. Most notably, Priem and Butler (2001a, 2001b) argue that in 'although the RBV began as a dynamic approach ... much of the subsequent literature has been static in concept' (Priem and Butler, 2001: 33). They continue by noting that in Barney's interpretation of the RBV, 'the processes through which particular resources provide competitive advantage remain in a black box' (Barney, 2001: 33). Indeed, years later Barney admits adopting the assumption in 1991 that 'once a firm understands how to use its resources ... implementation follows, almost automatically' as if the 'actions the firm should take to exploit these resources will be self-evident' (Barney, 2001: 53).

Wernerfelt (1984) has introduced the notion that firms should be analyzed from the resource side (factor market) at the level of the firm, not just from the product side at the level of the industry. Elaborating on this idea, Barney (1986, 1991) argues that a firm has the potential to generate sustained competitive advantage from firm resources that are valuable, rare, inimitable, and non-substitutable. The fundamental principle of the RBV is that the basis for a competitive advantage of a firm lies primarily in the application of the bundles of valuable resources at the firm's disposal (Wernerfelt, 1984, p172; Rumelt, 1984, p557-558).

The components of these bundles can be either tangible or intangible, although there appears to be confusion in definition as to whether a specific intangible resource is in fact a resource or a capability (Galbreath, 2005). Certain intangible resources, such as knowledge, relationships, brand equity or culture could be considered as both capabilities and intangible resources. Tangible resources can be purchased or replicated, and tend to depreciate in value when used. In contrast intangible resources such as knowledge grow when used and depreciate when not used. Grant (1993) and Sobal and Lei (1994) assert that knowledge, and notably tacit knowledge, can lie at the base of sustainable competitive advantage (Ambrossini and Bowman,2001; Nonaka ,1991; Grant 1993; Spender 1993). This is so because tacit knowledge can be a resource that allows a firm to perform better than its competitors, it is a 'differential ability' (Conner, 1994), it is heterogeneously distributed across firms, unique, imperfectly immobile and imperfectly imitable. This argument, though, has remained largely theoretical, due to a lack of empirical evidence One of the reasons for the lack of field research is that the concept of tacit knowledge is difficult to operationalize (Ambrossini and Bowman, 2001:825).

Acknowledging the lack of standardized nomenclature, we define resources and capabilities as all factors that have the potential to contribute to the economic benefit of the firm. For the purpose of this article, bundles of resources and capabilities are described as in Figure 1 and comprise of 3 types: (1) tangible resources, (2) intangible resources and (3) capabilities. This categorization is based on definitions derived from the literature.

Given the inherent difficulty of operationalizing bundles of resources, firm activities may offer a better basis for analysis (Ghemawat, 2002). Activities can be viewed as the business processes, routines or procedures a firm develops to get something done (Nelson and Winter, 1982; Porter, 1991). To gain competitive advantage over competitors, a firm must either perform these activities at a lower cost or by means of differentiation that can justify premium pricing, or do both (Porter 1980; Ghemawat, 2002). Activities can be considered as the organizational exploitation of bundles of resources (Barney and Clarke, 2007), hence the firm can be viewed as a nexus of activities, where each activity employs a distinct set (i.e., bundle) of resources and capabilities to achieve a predefined business goal or outcome. We argue that a firm's overall competitive position is manifested by the aggregate competitive positioning of all of its activities.

Because an individual resource can be used in multiple activities, it can provide strategic value when utilized in one activity and be of little value in another. Thus, using individual resources as an independent variable may produce misleading results. Viewing bundles of resources as organizational processes (i.e. activities) can help to describe what a firm can do better (i.e. more effectively or efficiently) than its competitors (Barney and Clarke, 2007).

Although VRIO framework, implicitly acknowledges the importance of a resource combination (i.e bundles), it evaluates resources from a standalone viewpoint, thus ignores how resources are interdependent and configured with one another and the nature of relationships between them.

Thus while Barney talks about bundles of resources, the VRIO framework treats resources as singular distinct items (Black &Boar, 1994). Furthermore, with the notable exception of Ray et al.,(2004), no research has been published that explores the RBV logic in context to organizational routines.

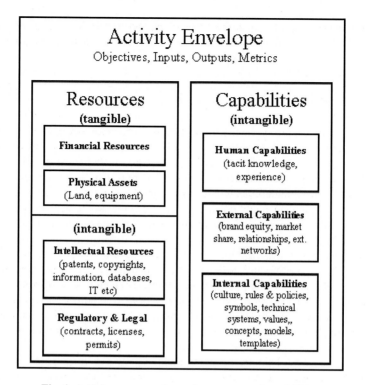

Fig. 1. Activity as an envelope of resources and capabilities

Building on (Polanyi,1958) and (Wittgenstein,1995), (Sveiby,1994,1997) defines knowledge as a capacity-to act, (which may or may not be conscious). Knowledge defined as a "capacity-to act" is dynamic, personal and distinctly different from data (discrete, unstructured symbols) and - when applied to an organizational context – it can only be actuated in routines or activities that an organization performs. Davenport and Prusak (1998) argue that contextual information, and expert insight often becomes embedded not only in documents or repositories but also in organizational routines, process, practices, and norms." (p. 5).

Figure 1 illustrates the notion of activities as collections of resources and capabilities, which have been assembled (i.e. bundled) and enabled to accomplish a predefined business objective or outcome. Thus business activities can be viewed as a bundling mechanism (or envelope) for resources and capabilities. This envelope specifies the needed resource inputs (e.g., capital, material, physical assets), the required capabilities (e.g., skills, knowledge, policies) and define the overall purpose, objectives and output (i.e., new resources and capabilities). In other words, the activity envelope defines the objective, goal, measures and the inputs (i.e. necessary resources and capabilities) to achieve a predefined output or outcome to the business.

In this view, activities are the enabler of organizational exploitation of the resources possessed by the firm, corresponding to Barney and Hesterly's (2007) notion of organizational exploitation in the VRIO framework. In order to provide a source of sustained competitive advantage, the firm must be organized to exploit the resource.

Firms that fail to exploit their resources and capabilities through efficient and effective activities are not in a position to realize the potential of these resources (Ray et al.,2004).

3   Theoretical Foundation of Strategic Outsourcing

Ideally, a firm would aim to have superior performance in as many activities as possible. In reality however, it is only possible to achieve superior performance positions in a limited number of business activities due to the resources required to maintain such a position. In certain instances, any superior performance position currently held by the firm is not sustainable and can be replicated by competitors over time.Thus it may be more prudent to focus on those activities in which the organisation holds a strong competitive position and which are critical to success in the future (McIvor, 2008b).

Increasingly, many organisations are recognising that competitive advantage can be achieved by integrating activities externally, rather than integrating them hierarchically. Companies such as Dell and Cisco Systems in hi tech industries have successfully been pursuing this strategy with their suppliers. These companies outsource much of the product design to specialist design companies as well as the majority of manufacturing, whilst maintaining control over final assembly, test and customisation of the end product to customer requirements.

This based on the believe that many of these activities create little value and differentiation for the end customer and can be more readily sourced from the supply market (Dedrick and Kraemer, 2005). A strategy of 'virtual integration' is pursued, that involves the sourcing of relevant services from the supply market and developing strong collaborative relationships with their most important suppliers. Specialist suppliers are expected to deliver costs efficiencies whilst offering higher capabilities resulting in superior performance. However, this potential for performance improvement has to be balanced against the potential for opportunism and high transaction costs in the supply market (McIvor, 2008b),

Transaction cost economics has been the dominant theoretical lens in outsourcing research (Lacity and Willcocks, 2001), with strong emphasis on asset specificity as the independent variable. More recently, a number of frameworks proposed in the literature have focused on the strategic implications of the outsourcing decision (Roy and Aubert, 2002; Insinga and Werle, 2000; Quinn, 1999; Venkatesan, 1992). Many of these outsourcing approaches have been influenced by the principles associated with the resource-based view.

Asset specificity, as defined by transaction cost economics (Williamson,1979), is closely related to the strategic importance of resources and has complementary properties in relation to competitive advantage when viewed from different theoretical perspectives (Dibbern et al., 2000). Thus, asset specificity, if it includes intangible specificities such as human capital, knowledge or culture, possesses properties which are similar to resources that contribute to competitive advantage. It can be argued that industrial economics and strategic management seek to explain similar phenomena, but through complementary theoretical lenses (Williamson, 1999).

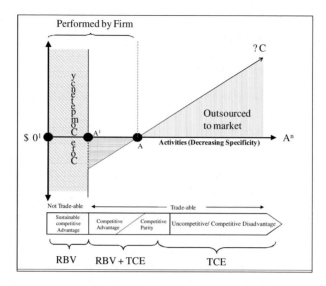

Fig. 2. Outsourcing framework for activities, using RBV and TCE Adapted from Langlois (1992) and (Dibbern et al. 2000)

Figure 2 graphs a curve ΔC as the normalized per-unit cost premium the firm must pay for the output of a particular activity if it hierarchically integrates that activity, measured relative to the per-unit cost it would incur, by obtaining the output from a market contract. Whenever this premium is negative, there is a cost advantage to internal organization. An implies a cost advantage of the market and A1 lower in-house costs of the firm, based on the TCE price mechanism. A is the point of delimitation between market and hierarchy, and A1 01 represents non-tradable distinctive competencies which must be integrated at all cost, indicating that TCE does not apply to outsourcing decision-making when competitive advantage is involved, regardless of cost economics.

The recommendations of TCE and the distinctive competencies approach of the RBV have strong similarities. In many ways, the approaches complement each other perfectly. The requirements for strategic resources – being non-imitable and non-substitutable "are fulfilled in particular if they are firm-specific" (Dierickx & Cool, 1989, p. 1505; see also Barney, 1986). Williamson (1979) points out that the idiosyncratic nature of firm specific assets precludes their tradability in open markets. Hence, there is a direct link between asset specificity from TCE and the concept of rare (thus specific) resources used in RBV logic (Dibbern, Güttler & Heinzl, 2001; Foss, Knudsen & Montgomery, 1995; Poppo & Zenger, 1998).

According to the logic of TCE, when activities utilizing specific (TCE) capabilities are outsourced, the firm's performance can be negatively affected, since the risk of opportunist behavior increases, and the contracting parties have incentives to appropriate rents by using post-contractual power or the threat of terminating the contract (Klein *et al.*, 1978).

From the RBV's point of view, outsourcing decisions depend on the extent to which a given activity permits the exploitation of different knowledge, capabilities and routines within the organization to appropriate rents. The greater the access to a set of valuable routines and processes and specific skills, the greater the likelihood of influencing competitive advantage and the lower the cost of their perpetual evolution will be (Poppo and Zenger, 1998; Ray *et al.,* 2004).

While TCE provides a very short-term, cost-based only approach, the RBV takes long-term strategic objectives into consideration. Thus the more short term operative cost aspects of TCE and long-term strategic aspects can be brought together with the more long term strategic perspectives (e.g. importance and contribution) of an activity.

In summary, TCE acknowledges that variation in firm production technologies (as a result of asset specificity or small numbers) may affect governance choice, the RBV may provide direction as to when and where such variation is likely to arise (Silverman, 2002) when making boundary decisions. While both theories look at specific or rare resources, the RBV is concerned with strategic matters while TCE has a pure cost focus. When taken together, they offer a more complete understanding of the firm's activities as a source of competitive advantage. Although the RBV and TCE are focusing on two different issues (1) the search for competitive advantage and (2) the most efficient governance structure, organisations have to deal with these two important issues when making outsourcing decisions (McIvor, 2008a)

4 Conceptual Model

In contrast to the neoclassical assumption that all factors are freely available in the market, RBV is quite ardent about the heterogeneity and immobility of firm resources. More importantly, not all firm resources hold the same potential of competitive advantage. To enjoy the full competitive potential a resource must hold four attributes: (1) it must be valuable, in the sense that it exploits opportunities and/or neutralizes threats in a firm's environment, (2) it must be rare amongst a firm's current and potential competition, (3) it must be inimitable or non-substitutable and, (4) must be exploited in the form of activities or organizational routines. The RBV logic may be viewed within the context of other RBV logical statements, which can be done in a hierarchical manner (see fig. 3). When RBV propositions are expressed in mathematical functions and logical expressions (Priem & Butler, 2001b), a better insight into the int errelations of the individual RBV propositions can be provided.

The RBV logic can be viewed as a hierarchy of competitive needs, similar of what Maslow uses. In this model the requirements for sustainable competitive advantage (SCA) are at the top of the hierarchy and competitive disadvantage (CD) at the base. Any higher order of competitive advantage (CA) in this hierarchy has the prerequisite of all lower orders being true. Competitive position progresses from CD to SCA as conditions are fulfilled and provide discrete and tenable states for competitiveness, to be applied as independent variables. Applying hierarchical relationships between the four RBV dimensions allows a new logical model to emerge, which can be logically expressed and empirically applied.

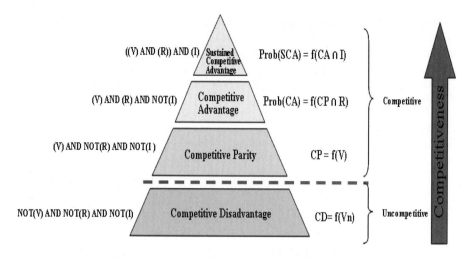

Fig. 3. Conceptual Model of Competitive Advantage

5   Competitive Disadvantage

Activities that do not hold competitive advantage are denoted as 'competitive disadvantage'. In fact, organizing to perform these activities may lead to a sustained competitive disadvantage.

$$Prob\ CD= f(Vn)$$

The probability of competitive disadvantage is a negative function of value. It can be expressed as an activity that generates no or little value to the firm. Firms performing this type of activity will be in a position of competitive disadvantage in comparison to other firms in the same industry, because value is defined in terms of relative efficiency and effectiveness. If an activity is of no value to the organization, then its effectuation or organizational exploitation constitutes a strategic disadvantage. In other words, firms that engage in activities of low or no value arguably deploy their resources ineffectively and will have a lesser competitive standing in comparison to competitors who do employ their resources in a more effectively manner (i.e., through valuable activities). Firms that engage in many such ineffective and inefficient activities would then be considered as uncompetitive.

6   Competitive Parity

Competitive Parity includes activities which hold value for the firm and are not rare.

$$Prob\ CP= f(V)$$

Competitive parity can be expressed as a valuable activity that is homogenously distributed amongst firms. If valuable activities are not rare or different from competitor's activities then it can be implied that they are homogeneously distributed amongst competing firms. In this case, such an activity constitutes a competitive parity at best.

7   Competitive Advantage

This category includes activities that support or represent the firm's products or services to its customers and may consist of significant intangible (often tacit) resources and capabilities, which are used to compete against the firm's competitors in a given industry. These activities are unique to the firm and the source of quasi rents for a given period of time, until competitors have imitated, substituted or obsoleted the product or service.

$$Prob\ (CA) = f(f(V) \cap r).$$

The probability of competitive advantage can be expressed as a function of the joint occurrence of value function and rarity of resources or capabilities. In the hierarchical view it is seen as competitive parity that is not heterogeneously distributed.

8   Sustainable Competitive Advantage

A valuable, rare and inimitable activity constitutes a sustainable competitive advantage. Imitability rests on the continuation of imperfect factor markets, the costs involved in the redesign of specific activities that will enable the firm to compete for the same product market. Conversely, if a valuable and rare activity can be imitated over time, then this activity can only be classified as a (temporary) competitive advantage.

$$Prob\ (SCA) = f(CA \cap I)\ where\ I=f(in \cap sn \cap tn).$$

The probability of Sustainable Competitive Advantage is a function of the joint occurrence a competitive advantage and non-Imitability(I), where (I) denotes the joint occurrence of non-imitability, non-substitutability and non-transferability / non-tradability.

9   Propositions

Following the logical expressions of the conceptual model of competitive advantage (Figure 3), four propositions can be derived:

P1: Activities that generate sustainable competitive advantage by comprising specific resources should not be outsourced but controlled through internal contracts.

P2: Activities that contribute to the creation of temporary competitive advantage or complementary competences, although they may require specific resources, are in some cases outsourced through closed contracts based on forms of alliance, particularly when it is very costly to develop the capabilities internally in the short term (Barney 1999).

P3: Activities that do not create competitive advantage are of comparable performance (competitive parity) when compared with similar activities of competitors in the same industry. This type of business process is frequently outsourced, providing that there are a sufficient number of suppliers who have the capability to perform them better than the firm and add value to the end consumer (Quinn 1999).

P4: Activities that provide no value to the firm represent a competitive advantage to the firm and should either not be performed at all or must be outsourced to the market.

As discussed above, those activities that hold high competitive potential should not be outsourced but controlled through hierarchical governance. Activities that contribute to the creation of complementary competences, although they may require specific resources, are in some cases outsourced through closed contracts based on forms of alliance, particularly when internal development is very costly in the short term (Barney 1999). Activities that do not form part of the distinctive competences (do not comprise of specific resources), are usually outsourced, providing that there is a sufficient amount of suppliers who perform them better than the firm and add value to the end consumer (Quinn 1999).

10 Operationalization

10.1 Independent Variables (VRI Test) (Barney and Hesterly, 2008)

The competitive position variable is determined by 3 factors or attributes: value (V), rareness (r) and imperfect Imitability (i), where inimitability is denoted by the joint occurrence of non-imitability, non-substitutability and non-transferability/non-tradability. The values of these factors stipulate four possible values (mediating variables) of competitive position (Figure 4).

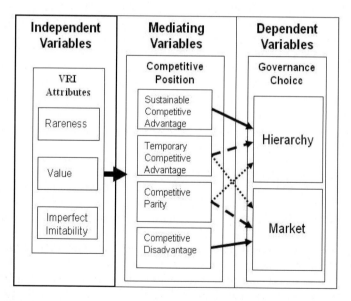

Fig. 4. Operationalized model of strategic outsourcing, applying organizational activities as the unit of analysis

Mediating Variables

These variables are logical constructs to denote the strategic importance of a given activity, which can hold 4 possible states: (1) competitive disadvantage, (2) competitive parity, (3) competitive advantage and (4) sustainable competitive advantage.

10.2 Dependent Variables

Most previous research applies aggregate dependent variables, such as 'firm success' or 'firm performance', which may be the reasons for inconclusive results of previous research (Newbert, 2007). Moreover, aggregate dependent variables may invite to an over-generalization and distraction of the key tenets of the RBV. For example, Porter (1991:108) criticises the RBV theory as being tautological, "Successful firms are successful because they have unique resources. They should nurture these resources to be successful."

Ray et al. (2004) suggest adopting business processes as the dependent variable in resource based research, since there are significant levels of performance (i.e. effectiveness and efficiency) within the portfolio of processes of a firm. A firm might excel in some activities, in others only show average performance and some activities are performed below accepted standards. In other words, firms can have competitive advantages in some business activities and competitive disadvantages in others. Thus the firms overall firm performance has a strong dependency on the implementation of its numerous business activities.

Moreover, Barney (1993) and Barney and Clarke (2007) point out that in empirical research the independent variables of the RBV are defined at one level of analysis (the level of resources), while competitive advantage, not economic rent per se, (the dependent variable) is at a different level of analysis (the level of strategies that the firm is pursuing). Put differently, the independent variable is treated at the sub firm (i.e.activity) level and the dependent variable is dealt with at the firm level. (Black & Boar, 1994) The use of sub firm level dependent variables, rather than the more common aggregate constructs such as 'competitive advantage' or 'firm performance' (see Newbert, 2007), is consistent with recent calls to identify other, less aggregated measures to appropriately test the implications of the RBV (Ray et al., 2004 p. 25).

Governance form (market vs hierarchy) can be used as the dependent variables, on the premise that activities that hold competitive advantage are performed within the firm's hierarchy, whereas uncompetitive activities have the propensity to be outsourced to the market (Lacity & Willcocks 2003).

11 Conclusion

Practitioners have to assess their firms' capabilities across a range of business areas as they are increasingly being confronted with constraints on resources. This means that they have to prioritise resource allocation in business areas where they hold competitive advantage and outsource less critical areas. The trend towards specialization in many product and service markets has opened up opportunities beyond the traditional areas of generic business activities for further outsourcing as specialist suppliers offer a wider range of capabilities in more critical business areas. In addition, many firms perceive outsourcing as a means of achieving performance improvements in many areas of the business.

The identification of the competitive value of activities and their inherent governance choices are important strategic management decisions, where only little theoretical and practical guidance is available. Previous empirical research has produced only marginal support for the RBV (Newbert, 2007). We argue that the RBV has the potential to be used for predictive analysis, such as in outsourcing decisions.

In this article we have introduced new approaches and suggestions on how some of the key concerns of the RBV can be mitigated, by using activities as a construct for combining or bundling of resources. This new construct addresses several shortfalls that currently impede the operationalization of the RBV and subsequent empirical testing: (1) identification of unobservable resources and capabilities; (2) disaggregation of firm-level dependent variables (i.e. firm performance); (3) appropriate treatment of the 4th VRIO condition, organizational exploitation, and (4) predictive use of the RBV logic for managerial decision making.

While the exact set of resource factors, competencies and distinctive competencies varies from firm to firm and over time, this conceptional model gives practitioners a starting point to more efficiently evaluate, develop, change and use their activities. The practical implication for practitioners is the mitigation of (1) the problem of inadvertently destroying a strategic resource by divestiture or abandonment, (2) the problem of making incorrect strategic decisions based on assessments that do not include firm specific resources, and (3) the problem of not understanding the relationships among resources and their importance to their utilization. If the promise of activities as a resource bundling construct holds upon confirmation by field research, then this construct will represent a new approach for operationalizing the RBV.

References

Barney, J.B.: Organizational Culture: Can It Be a Source of Sustained Competitive Advantage. Academy of Management Review 11(3), 656–665 (1986)

Barney, J.B.: Firm Resources and Sustained Competitive Advantage. Journal of Management 17(1), 99–120 (1991)

Barney, J.B., William, H.: Organizational economics: understanding the relationship between organizations and economic analysis. Sage, London (1999)

Barney, J.B.: Resource-based theories of competitive advantage: a ten-year retrospective on the resourcebased view. Journal of Management 27, 643–650 (2001)

Barney, J.B., Hesterly, W.: Strategic Management and Competitive Advantage: Concepts and Cases. Pearson Prentice Hall, Upper Saddle River (2008)

Barney, J.B., Clark, D.N.: Creating and Sustaining Competitive Advantage. Oxford University Press, New York (2007)

Bingham, C.B., Eisenhardt, K.M.: Unveiling the creation and content of strategic processes: How and what firms learn from heterogeneous experience. In: Proceedings of the Academy of Management (2006)

Black, J.A., Boal, K.B.: Strategic resources: Traits, configurations and paths to sustainable competitive advantage. Strategic Management Journal 13, 475–481 (1994)

Collis, D.J.: Research Note: How Valuable Are Organizational Capabilities? Strategic Management Journal 15, 143–152 (Winter 1994)

Dedrick, J.D., Kraemer, K.L.: The Impacts of IT on Firm and IndustryStucture: The Personal Computer Industry. California Management Review 47(3), 123–142 (Spring 2005)

Dibbern, J., Guttler, W., Heinzl, A.: Die Theorie der Unternehmung als Erklaerungsansatz fur das selektierte Outsourcing der Informationsarbeit. Zeitschrift fuer Betriebswirtschaft 71(6) (2000)

Dibbern, J., Goles, T., Hirschheim, R., Jayatilaka, B.: Informations System Outsourcing: A Survey and Analysis of the Literature. The Database for Advances in Information Systems 35(4), 96 (2004)

Dierickx, I., Cool, K.: Asset Stock Accumulation and Sustainability of Competitive Advantage. Management Science 35(12), 1504–1511 (1989)

Foss, N.J., Knudsen, C.A., Montgomery, C.A.: An Exploration of Common Ground: Integrating Evolutionary and Strategic Theories of the Firm. In: Montgomery, C.A. (ed.) Resource-based and evolutionary theories of the firm, pp. 1–17. Kluwer, Dordrecht (1995)

Galbreath, J.: Which resources matter the most to firm success? An exploratory study of resource-based theory. Technovation 25, 979–987 (2005)

Ghemawat, P.: Competition and Business Strategy in Historical Perspective. Business History Review 76, 37–74 (Spring 2002)

Godfrey, P.C., Hill, C.W.: The problem of unobservables in strategic management research. Strategic Management Journal 16, 519–533 (1995)

Hoopes, D.G., Madsen, T.L., Walker, G.: Why is there a resource-based view? Toward a theory of competitive heterogeneity. Strategic Management Journal 24, 889–902 (2003)

Insinga, R.C., Werle, M.L.: Linking outsourcing to business strategy. Academy of Management Executive 14(4), 58–70 (2000)

Klein, B., Crawford, R.G., Alchian, A.A.: Vertical Integration, Appropriable Rents, and the Competitive Contracting Process. The Journal of Law and Economics 21(2), 297–326 (1978)

Lacity, M., Willcocks, L.: Global Information Technology Outsourcing: in search of business advantage. John Wiley & Sons, Inc., New York (2001)

Lacity, M.C., Willcocks, L.P.: Sourcing Reflections - Lessons for Customers and Suppliers. Wirtschaftsinformatik 45(2), 115–125 (2003)

Langlois, R.: Transaction-cost Economics in Real Time. Industrial and Corporate Change 1(1), 99–127 (1992)

McIvor, R.: How the transaction cost and resource-based theories of the firm inform outsourcing evaluation. Journal of Operations Management, Article (in Press, 2008a)

McIvor, R.: What is the right outsourcing strategy for your process? European Management Journal 26, 24–34 (2008b)

Meyer, A.D.: What is strategy's distinctive competence? Journal of Management 17, 821–833 (1991)

Nelson, R.R., Winter, S.G.: An Evolutionary Theory of Economic Change. Harvard University Press, Cambridge (1982)

Newbert, S.L.: Empirical research on the resource-based view of the firm: An assessment and suggestions for future research. Strategic Management Journal 28, 121–146 (2007)

Poppo, L., Zenger, T.: Testing Alternative Theories of the Firm: Transaction Cost,Knowledge-Based, and Measurement Explanations for Make-Or-Buy Decisions in Information Services. Strategic Management Journal 19, 853–877 (1998)

Priem, R.L., Butler, J.E.: Is the resource-based 'view' a useful perspective for strategic management research? Academy of Management Review 26(1), 22–40 (2001a)

Priem, R.L., Butler, J.E.: Tautology in the resource-based view and the implications of externally determined resource value: Further comments. Academy of Management Review 26(1), 57–65 (2001b)

Porter, M.E.: Competitive Strategy: Techniques for Analyzing Industries and Competitors. Free Press, New York (1980)

Porter, M.: Towards a dynamic theory of strategy. Strategic Management Journal 12(1), 95–117 (1991)

Powell, T.: Competitive advantage: logical and philosophical considerations for Management Studies. Strategic Management Journal 22(9), 875–888 (2001)

Quinn, J.B.: Outsourcing Innovation: The New Engine of Growth. Sloan Management Review, 13–28 (Summer 1999)

Ray, G., Barney, J., Muhana, F.: Capabilities, business processes, and competitive advantage: chosing the dependent variable in empirical tests of the resource based view. Strategic Management Journal 25, 23–37 (2004)

Rouse, M., Daellenbach, U.: More thinking on research methods for the resource-based perspective. Strategic Management Journal 23(10), 963–967 (2002)

Roy, V., Aubert, B.A.: A resource-based analysis of IT sourcing. SIGMIS Database 33(2), 29–40 (2002)

Rumelt, R.: Toward a strategic theory of the firm. Competitive Strategic Management. Competitive Strategic Management. Prentice-Hall, Englewood Cliffs (1984)

Silverman, B.S.: Technological Resources and the Logic of Corporate Diversification, Rotledge, London (2002)

Quinn, J.B.: Strategic Outsourcing: Leveraging Knowledge Capabilities. Sloan Management Review 40(4), 9–21 (1999)

Wernerfelt, B.: A resource-based theory of the firm. Strategic Management Journal 5(2), 171–180 (1984)

Williamson, O.E.: Transaction-Cost Economics: The Governance of Contractual Relations. The Journal of Law and Economics 22(2), 233 (1979)

Williamson, O.E.: The Economics of Organizations: The Transaction cost Approach. American Journal of Sociology 87(3), 548–577 (1981)

Williamson, O.E.: Strategy Research: Governance and Competency perspectives. Strategic Management Journal 20, 1087–1108 (1999)

Zander, U., Kogut, B.: Knowledge and the speed of the transfer and imitation of organizational capabilities: An empirical test. Organization Science 6, 76–92 (1995)

An Empirical Investigation on IT Training Sources

Pedro Soto-Acosta

Department of Management and Finance, University of Murcia, Spain
psoto@um.es

Abstract. This paper analyses the presence of IT training sources used by firms and examines the influence on IT business value. Here, IT training is studied according to three IT training sources: in-house IT training, outside IT training, and self IT training by employees. In addition, differences in IT training sources are analysed according to two contingency factors: business size and business industry. Based on a simple of around 1000 Spanish firms, results show a positive relationship between IT training sources (outside and self IT training) and IT business value and confirm that IT training sources are positively related to business size and differ moderately by business industry.

1 Introduction

The contribution of information technologies (ITs) to economies has been considered fundamental for the development of productivity and knowledge-intensive products and services. Jobs demanding IT skills from employees have increased exponentially all over the world. For example, it is estimated that today there are 4.2 million IT practitioners within the European Union (EU) and that approximately 180 million people are using ITs at work (CEPIS, 2007). At the same time, new hardware, software and communications products are constantly being launched and this trend seems that will continue in the future. This rapid growth faces a barrier, however; namely the capability of the labour force to understand and use IT applications. In this sense, IT investments often are underused or not appropriately used mainly because employees do not posses sufficient IT skills to use them. This fact may cause IT to become obsolete before it pays off. Most IT experts recognize that IT training is critical to achieve productive use of the technology (Yi and Davis, 2001). This has also been confirmed by research. IT training has been identified as a key factor for the success of IT applications (McLean et al., 1993; Nelson and Cheney, 1987). Sircar et al. (2000) found a positive relationship between IT training and firm performance. Furthermore, investigations have shown a positive significant correlation between IT skills and efficient use of IT resources (Nelson and Cheney, 1987; Lee et al., 1995) and other studies' findings (e.g. Mata et al, 1995; Ravichandran and Lertwongsatien, 2005) confirmed that IT skills may be source of competitive advantage. Thus, IT training is an important link to productive IT use, which in turn may affect IT value. Nonetheless, there is a question as to how IT training has to be conducted to obtain desired outcomes (higher levels of IT value).

M.D. Lytras et al. (Eds.): WSKS 2008, CCIS 19, pp. 741–749, 2008.

The training process can be divided into three phases (Compeau et al., 1995): (1) the initiation phase; (2) the choice of training sources and formal training phase; and (3) the post-training phase. This research focuses on the second phase, the choice of training IT sources, and presents three main contributions. First, it provides knowledge about the IT training sources used by firms. Second, the effect of IT training sources on IT business value is assessed. Finally, the presence of these training sources is analysed according to business size and business industry. The paper consists of seven sections and is structured as follows: The next section reviews the relevant literature. Hypotheses are specified in section 3. Following that, the methodology used is discussed. Then, data analysis and results are examined. Finally, the paper ends with a discussion of research findings.

2 Literature Review

The literature on training suggests that training provide multiple benefits to firms. Training employees facilitates the updating of skills, leads to increased employee satisfaction (Acton and Golden, 2003), increased employee commitment to the organization (Bushardt et al., 1994), and strengthens the organization's competitiveness (Burden and Proctor, 2000). Although company commitment to training may lead to those potential benefits, there are many different categories and types of training (Huang, 2001; Mathews et al., 2001) and training delivery mechanisms (Acton and Golden, 2003). With regard to IT training, Benamati and Lederer (2001) found that education and training was the most frequently applied coping mechanism to handle changing IT, though managers might question whether they use it sufficiently. Also, IT skills have been found to be a source of sustained competitive advantage. Mata et al (1995) found that out of four IT attributes –capital requirements, proprietary technology, technical skills, and managerial IT skills- only IT managerial skills are likely to be a source of competitive advantage. Ravichandran and Lertwongsatien (2005) found that intangible IT resources such as IT skills are critical determinants of how IT is deployed in the organization, which in turn can affect performance. In this sense, Sircar et al (2000) found that IT training is positively correlated with a wide range of firm performance variables –sales, assets, equity, market share, and shares-, even more so than IT capital. IT training can be provided in a number of forms and by a variety of sources. With regard to Compeau et al.'s (1995) three phases of training, this paper focuses on the second phase, the choice of training sources. Thus this research complements other studies analyzing the initiation phase (e.g. Nelson et al., 1995), the formal training (e.g. Yi and Davis, 2001), and the post-training phase (e.g. Kay and Thomas, 1995).

The measurement of IT business value has been measured, fundamentally, by subjective measures (e.g. Soto-Acosta and Meroño-Cerdan, 2008; Tallon et al., 2000) or by using financial measures (e.g. Meroño-Cerdan and Soto-Acosta, 2007; Zhu and Kraemer, 2002). However, IT investments may provide benefits after a certain period but increase operating costs in the short term. In this sense, researchers (e.g. Soto-Acosta and Meroño-Cerdan, 2008) argue that the business process should be the primary level of analysis. This research uses for measuring IT business value the effectiveness of upstream and internal online activities.

3   Development of Hypotheses

Business size has been consistently supported as an important organizational factor for technology adoption (Damanpour, 1992). For instance, Zhu et al. (2003) measured business size by the number of employees and demonstrated that larger size firms are more likely to adopt e-business. With regard to IT training, Westhead and Storey (1997) argued that employees in small and medium-size enterprises are much likely to receive training than their counterparts in larger firms, offering two explanations: ignorance and market-forces. The former considers that small businesses are not aware of the benefits of training and consequently provide less for their employees. The latter suggest that small businesses anticipate that the costs associated with training may exceed the benefits to be derived from it. Therefore, as larger businesses usually allocate greater financial, technological and personnel resources to IT training (Soto-Acosta, 2008), larger firms might be expected to have more IT training sources.

Hypothesis 1: The presence of IT training sources is positively related to business size

H1a: The presence of in-house IT training is positively related to business size.
H1b: The presence of outside IT training is positively related to business size.
H1c: The presence of self IT training is positively related to business size.

The ability to analyze separate industries is extremely important because of their vastly different characteristics, even though some relationships may be true across a broad spectrum of firms. In this sense, the industry in which a business operates has been found to influence the business' information processing requirements (Yap, 1990). Thus, firms belonging to the service industries, which rely on the processing of information, depend heavily on information systems (Premkumar & King, 1994). In contrast, retail industries, which rely on the transfer of goods, may have a greater dependence on point-of-sale systems, whereas manufacturing industries depend more on specific information systems related to production such as ERP and CAD/CAM systems. These arguments suggest that firms from different industries may require distinct IT training sources.

Hypothesis 2: The presence of IT training sources differs by business industry

H2a: The presence of in-house IT training differs by business industry.
H2b: The presence of outside IT training differs by business industry.
H2c: The presence of self IT training differs by business industry.

Investing in IT is not a necessary nor sufficient condition for improving firm performance, since IT investments might be misused (Tallon et al., 2000). In this sense, IT assets cannot improve organizational performance if they are not used appropriately. However, when used appropriately IT is expected to create intermediary effects, such as IT being embedded in products and services, streamlined business processes, and improved decisions, which can be expected to have an influence on the performance of the firm (Ravichandran and Lertwongsatien, 2005). Ravichandran and Lertwongsatien (2005) found that intangible IT resources such as IT skills are critical determinants of how IT is deployed in the organization, which in turn can affect performance. Similarly, Mata et al. (1995) suggested that IT may be a source of sustained competitive advantage and found that IT managerial skills are likely to be a source of competitive advantage. Moreover, Sircar et al. (2000) found that IT training expenditures are significantly and positively correlated with firm performance. Thus, the third hypothesis posits a positive relationship between IT training sources and IT value.

Hypothesis 3: There is a positive relationship between IT training sources and IT business value

H3a: There is a positive relationship between in-house IT training and IT business value.

H3b: There is a positive relationship between outside IT training and IT business value.

H3c: There is a positive relationship between self IT training and IT business value.

4 Methodology

The data source for the present study is the e-business W@tch survey 2003, an initiative launched by the European Commission for monitoring the adoption of IT and e-business activity. Telephone interviews with decision-makers in enterprises were conducted in March and November 2003. The decision-maker targeted by the survey was the person responsible for IT, typically the IT manager.

The population considered in this study was the set of all firms which are active at the national territory of Spain and which have their primary business activity in one of ten sectors considered. The sample drawn was a random sample of companies from the respective sector population with the objective of fulfilling strata with respect to business size (10% of large companies, 30% of medium sized enterprises and 25% of small enterprises). The number of firms totalled 1,010.

This study used several variables for measuring IT training sources, business size, business industry and IT business value. Among several possible measures of firm size, number of employees was selected as a firm size indicator following the tradition of the IT literature (e.g. Brynjolfsson et al., 1994). Business industry identified whether the business was operating at the manufacturing, services or commercial industry and was coded as a dummy variable. By using a dichotomous scale, respondents assessed the use of three IT training sources: in-house, outside, and self IT training. For measuring IT business value, two constructs representing upstream and internal online activities were used. An exploratory factor analysis (EFA), Cronbach's alpha calculation and confirmatory factor analysis (CFA) were carried out to improve constructs reliability and validity.

5 Analyses and Results

With regard to the presence of IT training sources, 66.9% out of all analyzed firms (676) was employing at least one type of IT training source. The use of self IT training by employees was the most frequently found form of IT training, with 51.8% of the total number of firms having it. The second and third IT training sources in importance were outside and in-house IT training, respectively. Less than 30% of all analyzed companies presented in-house IT training and 44.3% were using outside IT training.

To test whether the use of IT training sources is influenced by business size, the latter was introduced as a four-level categorical variable, coding whether the business pertained to group 1 (between 1 and 9 employees), group 2 (between 10 and 49), group 3 (between 50 and 249) or group 4 (more than 250 employess).

As presented in table 1, statistical differences (between the four size groups) at the 1% level were encountered for all the IT training sources (in-house, outside, self IT training by employees). Therefore, hypotheses H1a, H1b and H1c were supported.

Table 1. IT training sources and business size

IT training source	Group 1 (1 ≤ E < 10)		Group 2 (10 ≤ E < 50)		Group 3 (50 ≤ E < 250)		Group 4 (E ≥ 250)		Chi-squared test	
	N	%	N	%	N	%	N	%	X^2	p
In-house IT training	74	19.2	69	26.5	90	33.5	35	40.2	25.3	0.000
Outside IT training	118	30.8	110	42.1	155	57.4	61	69.3	69.8	0.000
Self IT training	169	44.1	107	41.3	176	66.2	62	73.8	58.7	0.000

Note: E= employees.

The second hypothesis postulated that IT training sources differ by business industry. Business industry was coded as a three-level categorical variable that represented whether the business belonged to the manufacturing, service or commercial industry. Results (see table 2) showed that IT training sources were influenced by business industry for in-house (p= 0,000) and self IT training by employees (p= 0.000), while for outside training differences were not found (p= 0.060). Hypotheses H2a and H2c found support, whereas H2b was not supported.

Table 2. IT training sources and business industry

IT training source	Manufacturing industry		Commercial industry		Service industry		Chi-squared test	
	N	%	N	%	N	%	X^2	p
In-house IT training	85	21.5	10	19.3	143	35.9	28.57	0.000
Outside IT training	180	45.2	77	37.2	187	47.1	5.636	0.060
Self IT training	181	46.4	96	46.6	514	51.8	17.04	0.000

The third hypothesis suggested a positive relationship between IT training sources and IT business value. The statistical technique used to test this hypothesis was the hierarchical multiple regression analysis.

To assess the business value of IT training sources, two constructs representing the value of upstream and internal online activities were used. Business industry and business size were introduced as control variables in order to avoid unexpected effects on IT business value. The former identified whether the business was operating at the manufacturing, services or commercial industry and was coded as a dummy variable. The latter was measured as the total number of employees and was coded as a continuous variable.

The analysis was performed in 2 steps. The dependent variables were initially regressed on the control variables in step 1. Then, in step 2 the three IT training sources were added. Regression results are summarized in tables 2 Results in model 1 confirmed that the control variables employed do not explain the dependent variables. Model 2 showed that the direct effect of IT training sources upon IT business value was significant as the increment in the squared multiple correlation coefficient (R2) was statistically significant. The effect for outside IT training and self IT training by employees upon IT business value was positive and statistically significant (support for hypotheses H3b and H3c was found), while for in-house IT training the relationship was not significant (support for hypothesis H3a was not provided).

Table 3. Training sources and IT business value

	upstream IT value		internal IT value	
	MODEL 1	MODEL 2	MODEL 1	MODEL 2
Manufacturing industry	-0.127	-0.099	-0.131[*]	-0.106
Commercial industry	0.017	-0.044	0.015	0.057
Number of employees	0.066	0.045	0.156[**]	0.107
In-house IT training		-0.029		0.043
Outside IT training		0.208[**]		0.214[**]
Self IT training		0.137[*]		0.147[*]
F-value	1.663	3.72[**]	3.74[*]	7.84[**]
Adjusted R^2	0.022	0.091	0.038	0.124
Δ in R^2		0.069[**]		0.105[**]

Significance levels: [*] $0.01 < p \leq 0.05$; [**] $p \leq 0.01$.

6 Discussion and Conclusions

The results indicate that IT training is widespread among Spanish firms, since 66.9% out of all analyzed companies was employing at least one type of IT training source. The most frequently-found training source was self IT training by employees. Specifically, 51.8% of the sample was using self IT training. Also, this type of training was found in almost 80% of firms that have at least one form of training. These results confirm that firms make extensive use of IT training and support previous research studies, suggesting the importance of IT skills and training. For instance, Benamati and Lederer (2001) found that education and training was the most frequently applied coping mechanism to handle changing IT. Mata et al (1995) found that out of four IT attributes –capital requirements, proprietary technology, technical skills, and managerial IT skills- only IT managerial skills are likely to be a source of competitive advantage.

The results showed, as hypothesized, that the presence of IT training sources is positively related to business size. This finding is not surprising, since larger businesses usually allocate greater financial, technological and personnel resources to the development and implementation of ITs (Soto-Acosta, 2008). This result confirms Westhead and Storey's (1997) argument, which suggested that employees in small and medium-size enterprises are much likely to receive training than their counterparts in larger firms, because management is not aware of the benefits of training and considers that the costs associated with training may exceed the benefits to be derived from it. In addition, this finding supports other recent research that analyzed ITs adoption according to business size. For instance, Zhu et al., (2003) measured business size by the number of employees and demonstrated that larger size firms are more likely to adopt e-business. Similarly, Teo and Pian (2004) found evidence of a positive link between web site adoption an firm performance. Furthermore, results demonstrate that the presence of IT training sources differs by business industry. The differences appeared for in-house and self IT training, where service firms presented higher levels of adoption, while for in-house IT training differences were not found. This finding supports existing information systems literature. For instance, Goode and Stevens (2000) found business industry significant in the adoption of Internet connection, showing service industries to be the largest adopters, followed by retailers and then manufacturers.

Finally, the empirical results showed a positive relationship between IT training sources (outside and self IT training) and IT business value. The lack of relationship between in-house training and IT business value lead us to believe that this may be the reason why firms are using less this type of training. This findings confirm previous studies that found a positive relationships between IT skills/training and business value (Benamati and Lederer, 2001; Mata et al, 1995; Ravichandran and Lertwongsatien, 2005; Sircar et al., 2000) and suggest that firms may obtain better results if the use outside IT training or self IT training instead of in-house IT training.

This study presents some obvious limitations which can be addressed in future research. First, the sample used was from Spain. It may be possible that the findings could be extrapolated to other countries, since economic and technological development in Spain is similar to other OECD Member countries. However, in future research, a sampling frame that combines firms from different countries could be used in order to provide a more international perspective on the subject. Second, the IT business value measures are subjective in the sense that they were based on Likert-scale responses provided by managers. Thus, it could also be interesting to include objective performance data for measuring IT business value. Third, the key informant method was used for data collection. This method, while having its advantages, also suffers from the limitation that the data reflects the opinions of one person. Future studies could consider research designs that allow data collection from multiple respondents within an organization.

References

Acton, T., Golden, W.: Training the knowledge worker: a descriptive study of training practices in Irish software companies. Journal of European Industrial training 27(2-4), 137–146 (2003)

Benamati, J., Lederer, A.L.: Rapid information technology change, coping mechanisms, and the emerging technologies group. Journal of Management Information Systems 17(4), 183–202 (2001)

Brynjolfsson, E., Malone, T.W., Gurbaxani, V., Kambil, A.: Does information technology lead to smaller firms? Management Science 40(12), 1628–1644 (1994)

Burden, R., Proctor, T.: Creating a sustainable competitive advantage through training. Team Performance Management 6(5-6), 90–97 (2000)

Bushardt, S.C., Fretwell, C., Cumbest, P.B.: Continuous improvement through employee training: a case example from the financial services industry. The learning organization: An International Journal 1(1), 11–16 (1994)

CEPIS. Thinking ahead on e-skills for the ICT industry in Europe (2007)

Compeau, D., Olfman, L., Sein, M., Webster, J.: End-user training and learning. Communications of the ACM 38(7), 24–26 (1995)

Damanpour, F.: Organization size and innovation. Organization Studies 13(3), 375–402 (2002)

Goode, S., Stevens, K.: An analysis of the business characteristics of adopter and non-adopters of world wide web technology. Information technology and Management 1(2), 129–154 (2000)

Huang, T.C.: The relation of training practices and organizational performance in small and medium size enterprises. Education and Training 43(8-9), 437–444 (2001)

Kay, J., Thomas, R.C.: Studying long-term system use. Communications of the ACM 38(7), 61–69 (1995)

Lee, S.M., Kim, Y.R., Lee, J.: An empirical study of the relationships among end-user information systems acceptance, training, and effectiveness. Journal of Management Information Systems 12(2), 189–202 (1995)

Mata, F.J., Fuerst, W.L., Barney, J.B.: Information technology and sustained competitive advantage: a resource-based analysis. MIS Quarterly 19(4), 487–505 (1995)

Mathews, B.P., Ueno, A., Periera, Z.L., Silva, G., Kekal, T., Repka, M.: Quality training; findings from a European survey. The TQM Magazine 13(1), 61–71 (2001)

McLean, E.R., Kappelman, L.A., Thompson, J.P.: Converging end-user and corporate computing. Communications of the ACM 36(12), 79–92 (1993)

Meroño-Cerdan, A., Soto-Acosta, P.: External web content and its influence on organizational performance. European Journal of Information Systems 16(1), 66–80 (2007)

Nelson, R.R., Whitener, E.M., Philcox, H.H.: The assessment of end-user training needs. Communications of the ACM 38(7), 27–39 (1995)

Premkumar, G., King, W.R.: Organizational characteristics and information systems planning: an empirical study. Information Systems Research 1(3), 75–109 (1994)

Ravichandran, T., Lertwongsatien, C.: Effect of Information Systems Resources and Capabilities on Firm Performance: A Resource-Based Perspective. Journal of Management Information Systems 21(4), 237–276 (2005)

Sircar, S., Turnbow, J.L., Bordoloi, B.: A framework for assessing the relationship between information technology investments and firm performance. Journal of Management Information Systems 16(4), 69–97 (2000)

Soto-Acosta, P.: The e-Business performance measurement in SMEs. International Journal of Enterprise Network Management 2(3), 268–279 (2008)

Soto-Acosta, P., Meroño-Cerdan, A.: Analyzing e-Business value creation from a resource-based perspective. International Journal of Information Management 28(1), 49–60 (2008)

Tallon, P., Kraemer, K., Gurbaxani, V.: Executives' perceptions of the business value of information technology: a process-oriented approach. Journal of Management Information Systems 16(4), 137–165 (2000)

Teo, T.S.H., Pian, Y.: A model for Web adoption. Information & Management 41(4), 457–468 (2004)

Westhead, P., Storey, D.: Training provision and the development of small and medium-sized enterprises. DfEE Research Report No. 26, DfEE/HMSO, London (1997)

Yap, C.S.: Distinguishing characteristics of organizations using computers. Information & Management 18(2), 97–107 (1990)

Yi, M.Y., Davis, F.D.: Improving computer training effectiveness for decision technologies: behaviour modeling and retention enhancement. Decision Sciences 32(3), 521–544 (2001)

Zhu, K., Kraemer, K.L.: E-commerce metrics for net-enhanced organizations: assessing the value of e-commerce to firm performance in the manufacturing sector. Information Systems Research 13(3), 275–295 (2002)

Zhu, K., Kraemer, K., Xu, S.: Electronic business adoption by European firms: a cross-country assessment of the facilitators and inhibitors. European Journal of Information Systems 12(4), 251–268 (2003)

Author Index

Printing: Mercedes-Druck, Berlin
Binding: Stein+Lehmann, Berlin